P9-DUQ-036

LOOKING INTO

ABNORMAL PSYCHOLOGY

Contemporary Readings

ABNORMAL AND ABNORMAL CHILD PSYCHOLOGY

Barlow/Durand: *Abnormal Psychology: An Integrative Approach, Second Edition*

Brown/Barlow: *Casebook in Abnormal Psychology*

Chute/Bliss: *Exploring Psychological Disorders: A CD ROM for Windows/Macintosh*

Durand/Barlow: *Abnormal Psychology: An Introduction*

Kearney: *Casebook in Child Behavior Disorders*

Lilienfeld: *Seeing Both Sides: Classic Controversies in Abnormal Psychology*

Mash/Wolfe: *Abnormal Child Psychology*

RELATED TITLES

Brannon/Feist: *Health Psychology, Third Edition*

Castillo: *Culture and Mental Illness*

Castillo: *Meanings of Madness: Readings in Culture and Mental Illness*

Phares/Trull: *Clinical Psychology, Fifth Edition*

Spiegler/Guevremont: *Contemporary Behavior Therapy, Third Edition*

Watson/Tharp: *Self-Directed Behavior*

Wrightsman/Nietzel/Fortune: *Psychology and the Legal System, Fourth Edition*

LOOKING INTO

ABNORMAL PSYCHOLOGY

Contemporary Readings

SCOTT O. LILIENFELD, PH.D.

Brooks/Cole Publishing Company

I⬤T⬤P® *An International Thomson Publishing Company*

Pacific Grove ◆ Albany ◆ Belmont ◆ Bonn ◆ Boston ◆ Cincinnati ◆ Detroit ◆ Johannesburg ◆ London
Madrid ◆ Melbourne ◆ Mexico City ◆ New York ◆ Paris ◆ Singapore ◆ Tokyo ◆ Toronto ◆ Washington

Sponsoring Editor: *Marianne Taflinger*
Marketing Team: *Lauren Harp, Christine Davis, Alicia Barelli*
Editorial Assistant: *Scott Brearton*
Production Editor: *Karen Ralling*
Manuscript Editor: *Lorraine Anderson*
Permissions Editor: *May Clark/Cathleen Collins Morrison*
Design Editor: *Roy R. Neuhaus*

Interior Design: *Scratchgravel Publishing Services*
Cover Illustration: *M. C. Escher's "Hand with Reflecting Sphere"*
 © 1998 Cordon Art B. V. - Baarn - Holland. All rights reserved.
Cover Designer: *Carolyn Deacy*
Typesetting: *Scratchgravel Publishing Services*
Cover Printing: *Patterson Printing*
Printing and Binding: *Patterson Printing*

COPYRIGHT © 1998 by Brooks/Cole Publishing Company
A division of International Thomson Publishing Inc.
I(T)P ITP is a registered trademark used herein under license.

For more information, contact:

BROOKS/COLE PUBLISHING COMPANY
511 Forest Lodge Road
Pacific Grove, CA 93950
USA

International Thomson Publishing Europe
Berkshire House 168-173
High Holborn
London WC1V 7AA
England

Thomas Nelson Australia
102 Dodds Street
South Melbourne, 3205
Victoria, Australia

Nelson Canada
1120 Birchmount Road
Scarborough, Ontario
Canada M1K 5G4

International Thomson Editores
Seneca 53
Col. Polanco
11560 México, D. F., México

International Thomson Publishing GmbH
Königswinterer Strasse 418
53227 Bonn
Germany

International Thomson Publishing Asia
60 Albert Street
#15-01 Albert Complex
Singapore 189969

International Thomson Publishing Japan
Hirakawacho Kyowa Building, 3F
2-2-1 Hirakawacho
Chiyoda-ku, Tokyo 102
Japan

All rights reserved. No part of this work may be reproduced, stored in a retrieval system, or
transcribed, in any form or by any means—electronic, mechanical, photocopying, recording,
or otherwise—without the prior written permission of the publisher, Brooks/Cole Publishing
Company, Pacific Grove, California 93950.

Printed in the United States of America

10 9 8 7 6 5 4 3 2 1

Library of Congress Cataloging-in-Publication Data
Lilienfeld, Scott O.
    Looking into abnormal psychology: contemporary readings / Scott
O. Lilienfeld.
        p.   cm.
    Includes bibliographical references and index.
    ISBN 0-534-35416-5
    1. Psychology, Pathological.   I. Title
RC454.L53   1998
616.89—DC21   97-53041
                                CIP

THIS BOOK IS PRINTED ON
ACID-FREE RECYCLED PAPER

for Lori

ABOUT THE AUTHOR

Scott O. Lilienfeld received his B.A. from Cornell University in 1982 and his Ph.D. in clinical psychology from the University of Minnesota in 1990. He completed his clinical internship at Western Psychiatric Institute and Clinic in Pittsburgh from 1986 to 1987. He was a faculty member in the Department of Psychology at the State University of New York, University at Albany, from 1990 to 1994 and is currently an assistant professor in the Department of Psychology at Emory University in Atlanta, Georgia.

Dr. Lilienfeld has authored or co-authored approximately 50 journal articles and book chapters on such issues as personality disorders, psychiatric classification and diagnosis, and anxiety disorders. He is the recipient of the David Shakow Early Career Award for Contributions to Clinical Psychology from the American Psychological Association. His principal research interests concern the assessment and causation of psychopathic personality and risk factors for antisocial behavior in childhood and adulthood. He currently lives in Atlanta with his wife.

Contents

PART II
◆

Other Major Mental Disorders: Schizophrenia, Eating Disorders, Somatoform Disorders, and Childhood Disorders   49

PART III
◆

Personality Disorders, Criminality, and Substance Abuse Disorders   105

PART IV
◆
Controversial Diagnoses: Gender-Bound and Culture-Bound Syndromes

PART V
◆
Psychotherapies: Novel or Controversial Psychological Interventions

PART VI

◆

Somatic Therapies

Preface

Abnormal psychology is an immensely stimulating and rapidly changing discipline. Much of what makes this field so exciting is its dynamic and almost continuously evolving character. For those of us fortunate enough to teach abnormal psychology at the undergraduate level, one of our principal challenges is to convey this sense of intellectual vibrancy to our students. Yet students often emerge from abnormal psychology courses with scant appreciation of the active progress and lively debate that characterize modern psychopathology research at its best. Few books of readings in abnormal psychology consist of articles describing contemporary developments and controversies in psychopathology; moreover, those books that do often fail to capture the sense of excitement that many of us remember feeling as undergraduates during our first exposures to abnormal psychology.

The goal of this book of readings is twofold. First, I intend to introduce students to a broad sampling of current topics and controversies in abnormal psychology. In this way, I hope to provide students with a glimpse of some of the complex questions with which contemporary researchers in psychopathology are grappling. All of the selections in this text are recent—the publication dates of the articles range from 1991 to 1996—and deal with topics of current interest to investigators exploring the diagnosis, etiology, and treatment of mental disorders.

Second, I hope to excite students by exposing them to interesting and challenging issues in an accessible and user-friendly fashion. Almost all of the articles in this text are drawn from popular or semipopular sources, such as *Scientific American, The Sciences, New Scientist, Psychology Today, Discover,* and *Skeptical Inquirer.* Although it is important for undergraduates to acquire firsthand experience with professional journal articles, many of these articles are written in the arid, telegraphic prose that we academics have blithely become accustomed to. As a consequence, undergraduates sometimes obtain the erroneous impression that the discipline of abnormal psychology is as dry and stale as the preferred argot of its journals. Thus, I have attempted to select articles that are both engaging and challenging. Moreover, articles from nonacademic sources have the advantage of presuming considerably less background knowledge than most professional journal articles, many of which are difficult for beginning students to comprehend without extensive preparation.

This book is suitable as a supplementary text for undergraduate abnormal psychology or clinical psychology courses. Instructors who teach advanced or honors courses in abnormal psychology should also find this book to be a useful addition to their classes. In addition, this book is appropriate as a supplement for introductory psychology courses in which abnormal psychology is accorded substantial emphasis. Because a number of articles in the book focus on controversial issues—such as the research on the genetic basis of violence and aggression, the validity of the multiple personality disorder diagnosis, the use of antidepressant medications for "personality enhancement," and the efficacy of electroconvulsive therapy—instructors may want to use this text as a vehicle for stimulating in-class debate and discussion.

This book is subdivided into six major sections: (I) Mood and Anxiety Disorders, (II) Other Major Mental Disorders: Schizophrenia, Eating Disorders, Somatoform Disorders, and Childhood Disorders, (III) Personality Disorders, Criminality, and Substance Abuse Disorders, (IV) Controversial Diagnoses: Gender-Bound and Culture-Bound Syndromes, (V) Psychotherapies: Novel or Controversial Psychological Interventions, and (VI) Somatic Therapies. Each of these six sections is preceded by an introduction summarizing each selection, a set of discussion questions to accompany each article, and a list of suggestions for further reading.

This book could not have been written without the help of a number of exceptionally competent and dedicated individuals. First, I wish to thank my psychology editor at Brooks/Cole, Marianne Taflinger, who conceived of the central idea for this book and offered extremely helpful advice and encouragement throughout all phases of the project. Second, I wish to thank the following reviewers, who provided helpful recommendations and comments regarding the choice of topics and articles: Kerm Almos, Capital University; Hal Arkowitz, University of Arizona; Juris G. Draguns, Pennsylvania State University; and Michael W. Vasey, Ohio State University. Third, I thank Anne and Greg Draus at Scratchgravel Publishing Services for their diligence, hard work, and creativity. Fourth and finally, I wish to thank the authors of the 40 articles that comprise this text. Their exceptional talent and creativity have made this volume possible.

Scott O. Lilienfeld

LOOKING INTO

ABNORMAL PSYCHOLOGY

Contemporary Readings

PART I

Mood and Anxiety Disorders

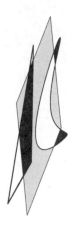

Of all forms of psychological distress, emotional disturbances are perhaps the most ubiquitous. Virtually all of us are intimately familiar with depression and anxiety, and surprising numbers of us struggle with mild feelings of sadness and tension on an almost daily basis. Moreover, many psychologists have argued that depression and anxiety are fundamentally adaptive reactions to specific stressors, namely loss in the case of depression and threat in the case of anxiety. Why, then, are mood and anxiety disorders regarded as psychopathological?

Depression, anxiety, and similar emotional reactions are generally considered abnormal only when they are disproportionate to objective life circumstances. Anxiety, for example, probably evolved as an alarm signal to warn organisms of potential danger in their environments. But some people tend to feel anxiety even when no threat is present. Such individuals, who can be thought of as experiencing "false alarms," suffer from anxiety disorders. Persons with panic disorder, for instance, experience sudden surges of extreme terror even in perfectly safe environments. It is this mismatch between the severity of individuals' emotional reactions and of objective stressors that makes panic disorder psychopathological. A similar analysis may also be applicable to depression and related emotional disorders, which can be viewed as basically normal reactions expressed in situations that do not warrant them.

In the first selection in this book, Randolph Nesse provides an intriguing and provocative perspective on a rarely asked question in psychopathology: "Why?" Traditionally, researchers in abnormal psychology have emphasized "how" questions: How do people become ill? How do genetic and environmental influences combine to produce psychopathology? How do mental disorders change in their expression over the course of development? But Nesse's article, which addresses the fascinating question of *why* we experience negative emotions, suggests that depression and anxiety serve crucial psychological functions that have been shaped by natural selection. For Nesse, depression and anxiety are best thought of as invaluable defenses against environmental stressors, rather than as useless defects that can safely be eliminated by medication. Nesse's arguments challenge us to

think in new ways about the potential evolutionary functions of unpleasant emotions and bear interesting implications for their prevention and treatment. As you read the other articles in this book, you may want to ask yourself whether Nesse's evolutionary analysis can be applied to psychopathological conditions other than mood and anxiety disorders.

In the second article, Kay Jamison provides a related, although slightly different, perspective on the potentially adaptive characteristics of certain emotional disorders, specifically manic-depression and related mood disturbances. Individuals with manic-depression or, as it is known in DSM-IV, bipolar disorder typically experience episodes of severe depression in conjunction with episodes of mania, a mood disturbance characterized by extreme elation, increased energy, grandiosity, decreased need for sleep, and a propensity toward impulsive and sometimes dangerous behaviors. Jamison reviews recent evidence suggesting that individuals with bipolar disorder exhibit substantially higher rates of creativity and artistic accomplishment than other individuals. A disproportionate number of exceptionally creative writers, musicians, and painters, Jamison notes, appear to suffer from the dramatic mood swings typical of both bipolar disorder and cyclothymia, a milder variant of bipolar disorder characterized by extreme moodiness that does not reach the extremes of either clinical depression or mania. Moreover, heightened creativity appears to be evident even among the healthy relatives of individuals with bipolar disorder. Jamison, a psychiatrist who has herself struggled with bipolar disorder for many years, offers several intriguing conjectures regarding the cognitive and affective features of bipolar disorder that may facilitate originality and inventiveness.

Bonnie Strickland next reviews research on the controversial topic of gender differences in depression. Strickland begins by pointing out that the rate of depression in the general population is approximately twice as high among women as men. The reasons for this pronounced gender difference, however, are still hotly debated. Among the explanations outlined by Strickland are neurochemical and hormonal influences, gender-role socialization, cognitive factors, discrimination, and physical and sexual abuse. Nevertheless, the old caveat that "correlation does not necessarily imply causation" applies here. Many of these factors are statistically associated with an increased risk of depression among women, but whether they are causally related to depression remains largely or entirely unknown. Moreover, you should bear in mind that the causes of most or all forms of psychopathology are almost certainly multiply determined. Consequently, a number of the potential causal factors cited by Strickland may combine or interact in complex ways to contribute to the increased prevalence of depression among women.

In the next article, Leslie Hawkins provides an overview of contemporary research on seasonal affective disorder (SAD), a mood disorder that has received increased attention in the last decade. Unlike most individuals with mood disorders, individuals with SAD tend to exhibit a clear-cut seasonal pattern of emotional changes. Most commonly, their depressive episodes occur predominantly or exclusively in the winter months. Hawkins reviews evidence implicating insufficient light exposure as a prime suspect in the etiology of SAD and discusses a number of physiological models (for example, the melatonin hypothesis) that have been posited to account for the behavioral and biological features of SAD. As Hawkins points out, light therapy (phototherapy) has been found to alleviate the symptoms of SAD, although this treatment's mechanism of action remains largely or entirely unknown. One note of caution for the reader: some sections of Hawkins's article may be a bit difficult for those of you without a background in physiological psychology. Nevertheless, his central points are understandable even without a complete grasp of his neuroanatomical arguments.

Some friends, relatives, and significant others of individuals with mood disorders have an unfortunate tendency to regard these individuals' episodes of depression as passing phases that are best ignored. This tendency is not only naive but potentially deadly: approximately 15 percent of individuals with depression will eventually commit suicide. This staggeringly high figure indicates why the prevention of suicide represents one of the greatest priorities of mental health professionals. Yet our capacity to predict suicide is notoriously poor, largely because almost all known predictors of future suicide are highly nonspecific and result in numerous false-positive errors (errors in which nonsuicidal individuals are incorrectly classified as suicidal). In an article in *Time* magazine, Christine Gorman reviews recent efforts by biological psychiatrists to identify neurochemical markers that are relatively specific to suicide. Gorman notes that many suicide victims have been found to possess low levels of the neurotransmitter serotonin, particularly in the brain's frontal regions. Moreover, serotonin levels appear to be state-dependent and to exhibit decreases prior to suicide attempts, suggesting that a laboratory test might ultimately be capable of detecting when individuals predisposed to suicide are at

greatest risk. It is important to remember, however, that like many statistical relations in abnormal psychology, the association between suicide and serotonin is asymmetrical. Many individuals who attempt or commit suicide have low serotonin, but very few individuals who have low serotonin will attempt or commit suicide. This dramatic asymmetry reminds us that there may be practical limits to our ability to predict suicide, even from relatively specific biological markers.

The next four articles explore the characteristics and causes of anxiety disorders. In the first of these selections, Helen Saul describes recent research on the etiology and treatment of phobias, which are irrational and persistent fears of objects, places, or situations. She reviews the work of Marks and Nesse, who adopt an evolutionary perspective on phobias, as well as that of Salkovskis and others, who contend that cognitive factors—such as irrational beliefs that a racing heart often portends an imminent heart attack—are central to the genesis of anxiety disorders, particularly panic disorder. Panic disorder, which will be examined in greater detail in the next article, is a condition characterized by sudden surges of extreme anxiety that often arise out of the blue. Saul also discusses research by Weissman and others on the genetic and physiological bases of panic disorder, as well as research on behavioral and psychopharmacological treatments for phobias and panic disorder. Before reading Saul's article, you should be aware that she is not always careful to distinguish specific phobia from agoraphobia. In the former condition, the individual is almost always afraid of a specific object or situation (such as dogs or heights), whereas in the latter condition, the individual is almost always afraid of having a panic attack in certain situations (for example, supermarkets or heavy traffic). Researchers now generally agree that virtually all cases of agoraphobia stem from the fear of panic attacks. You should bear the distinction between specific phobia and agoraphobia in mind while reading Saul's article.

Martin Antony, Timothy Brown, and David Barlow provide further information regarding current research and theorizing on panic disorder. After delineating the symptoms of, and diagnostic criteria for, panic disorder, the authors review biological and cognitive-behavioral models of this condition. According to Klein and biologically oriented researchers, panic disorder can be thought of as a discrete neurobiological dysfunction originating in the noradrenergic system. In contrast, Clark and other cognitive-behavioral theorists maintain that panic disorder arises from the catastrophic misinterpretation of unexpected or unusual physiological sensations. Antony, Brown, and Barlow outline an integrated model of panic disorder that draws on elements of both biological and cognitive-behavioral approaches, and discuss the implications of recent research on panic disorder for models of its etiology.

Katy Butler next describes current work on the biological underpinnings of posttraumatic stress disorder (PTSD), a condition that results from exposure to an extremely stressful and often life-threatening event. PTSD patients experience a relatively consistent constellation of symptoms, including repeated and intrusive imagery of the traumatic event, avoidance of memories of the event, irritability, an exaggerated startle reaction to unexpected stimuli, and a psychological "numbing" or sense of emotional detachment from others. Although PTSD is clearly triggered by environmental stimuli, Butler reviews recent research indicating that this disorder is associated with a number of profound physiological changes. For example, the results of several investigations suggest that severe psychological trauma can produce damage to the hippocampus, a brain structure intimately involved in memory processing. Moreover, PTSD patients exposed to reenactments of the traumatic events they experienced have been found to exhibit marked biochemical reactions, including increases in endorphin release. Butler's article reminds us of the perils of mind-body dualism. The mind, after all, is just the brain in action. As a consequence, psychological factors can affect the biology of the organism, and vice versa.

In the final article in this section, Edward Dolnick provides an excellent description of the phenomenology of obsessive-compulsive disorder (OCD), a puzzling disorder characterized by obsessions, compulsions, or both. Obsessions are repetitive and intrusive cognitions, feelings, and impulses, such as thoughts that one has left the oven on even though one remembers turning it off, that the individual typically perceives as senseless. Compulsions are ritualized behaviors, such as checking, counting, and washing, that are performed to neutralize the anxiety generated by the obsessions. Until fairly recently, the prevalence of OCD appears to have been underestimated, probably because individuals with this disorder are often embarrassed by their symptoms and are reluctant to seek treatment. Dolnick briefly discusses contemporary treatment approaches to OCD, including both biological and psychological interventions. He points out that the two most effective treatments for OCD are selective serotonin reuptake inhibitors, such as Prozac (see Readings 37 and 38), and behavior therapy, which involves exposing individuals to stimuli intended to trigger their obsessions and preventing them from performing their desired compulsions. Thus, an OCD patient with a fear of contamination might be asked to rub her hands in dirt for several hours while not washing or cleaning them. As Dolnick notes, insight-oriented psychotherapy (such as psychoanalysis), although still sometimes used for OCD, appears to have few or no beneficial effects.

DISCUSSION QUESTIONS

READING 1. R. M. Nesse, "What Good Is Feeling Bad? The Evolutionary Benefits of Psychic Pain"

1. Nesse argues that some medical conditions (for example, paralysis and seizures) are defects, whereas others (such as vomiting and diarrhea) are defenses. Which psychological disorders might best be viewed as defects? Which might best be viewed as defenses?

2. Nesse suggests that depression and anxiety are basically adaptive emotions, although he acknowledges that they sometimes become pathological. What criteria could be used to distinguish pathological depression and anxiety from normal depression and anxiety?

3. Nesse proposes several possible adaptive functions of depression, including the regulation of resource allocation. Can you think of others?

4. What implications might Nesse's evolutionary analysis have for the treatment of depression and anxiety disorders by means of psychotherapy? Might there be emotional conditions for which psychotherapy could actually be counterproductive and, if so, what might they be?

READING 2. K. R. Jamison, "Manic-Depressive Illness and Creativity"

1. Jamison points out that not all individuals with bipolar disorder exhibit high levels of creativity. What factors might distinguish individuals with bipolar disorder who are creative from those who are not?

2. In addition to bipolar disorder and cyclothymia, what other psychological disorders might be associated with heightened creativity? How might the creative productions of individuals with bipolar disorder and cyclothymia differ from those of individuals with other psychological disorders?

3. Might at least some degree of moodiness be necessary for creative accomplishment? Or can individuals with stable moods also be creative? Explain.

4. Jamison notes that bipolar disorder is associated with a dramatically increased risk of suicide. Because bipolar disorder is associated with a reduced average life span, researchers who adopt an evolutionary approach to psychopathology have long wondered why the genes predisposing to bipolar disorder have persisted in the population. How might some of the data reported by Jamison bear on this question?

READING 3. B. R. Strickland, "Women and Depression"

1. One potential causal factor not discussed by Strickland is a genetic influence on certain personality traits that may themselves be associated with an increased risk of depression. What personality traits might contribute to higher rates of depression in women than men?

2. Strickland cites the research of Nolen-Hoeksema, who argues that gender differences in depression may be partly attributable to the greater propensity of women than men to ruminate over negative events. What factors might account for this heightened propensity?

3. Strickland notes that "even controlling for income, research suggests that job loss and 'money problems' are strongly associated with high levels of depressive symptoms" (pp. 18–19). Does this finding imply that job loss and money problems are causally related to depression? Why or why not?

4. Some recent research suggests that gender differences in depression may be considerably less pronounced in Jewish populations. What might this finding imply about cultural influences on depression?

5. Evidence not discussed by Strickland suggests that there also are few or no gender differences in depression among the Amish. Interestingly, the Amish have extremely low rates of alcohol use. Some researchers have therefore suggested that Amish men who would otherwise drink heavily instead develop depression, and that alcoholism in men may be an alternative expression of the same underlying disorder that gives rise to depression in women. Do you find this hypothesis plausible? What research would be needed to test it?

READING 4. L. Hawkins, "Seasonal Affective Disorders: The Effects of Light on Human Behaviour"

1. As Hawkins notes, more northern (for instance, Scandinavian) countries tend not only to receive less light, but also to be colder. As a researcher, how might you determine whether SAD is a result of insufficient light exposure or excessive exposure to cold temperatures?

2. Individuals who receive phototherapy for SAD know that they are receiving treatment and are thus potentially susceptible to the placebo effect (that is, improvement resulting from the mere expectation of improvement). If you were conducting a study to examine the efficacy of phototherapy, how would you attempt to control for the placebo effect?

3. Hawkins discusses some differences between "larks" and "owls"—that is, early risers and late risers, respectively. How stable do you think the lark-owl distinction is within individuals? Can a lark easily become an owl, or vice versa, depending on changes in work schedule?

4. Hawkins reports that as many as 60 percent of individuals exhibit seasonal alterations in mood or sleep. Is the distinction between mild seasonal mood variation and SAD one of degree or of kind? Explain.

READING 5. C. Gorman, "Suicide Check: Advances in Biopsychiatry May Lead to Lab Tests for Self-Destructive Behavior and Other Mental Disorders"

1. Do the findings reported by Gorman indicate that low serotonin is a *cause* of suicidal behavior? Why or why not?

2. Although individuals with low serotonin appear to be at heightened risk for suicide, many individuals with low serotonin never commit or attempt suicide. What variables might combine or interact with serotonin levels to predict suicidal behavior?

3. Imagine that one day psychologists and psychiatrists were able to develop a battery of neurochemical tests to predict suicide with perfect or near-perfect accuracy. Would this imply that suicide prevention efforts should focus on drug treatments rather than psychotherapy? Explain your reasoning.

4. Imagine that a depressed patient enrolled in a research study is found to have extremely low levels of serotonin metabolites during a spinal tap. What, if anything, should this individual be told about his or her suicide risk?

READING 6. H. Saul, "Phobias: Is There a Way Out?"

1. Saul discusses the theorizing of Marks and Nesse, who contend that phobias are normal anxiety responses expressed in situations that do not warrant them. Does this reasoning imply that phobias are not mental disorders? Defend your reasoning.

2. Is it conceivable that phobias may one day be treated entirely by means of self-help guides that carefully explain the steps involved in behavioral interventions? Or might certain elements of behavioral treatment for phobias require the presence of a therapist? If so, what are they?

3. Saul refers to the work of Levinson, who argues that inner ear dysfunctions are involved in the etiology of 90 percent of phobias and panic attacks. How plausible do you find Levinson's assertions? Does the finding that benzodiazepines (minor tranquilizers) and antidepressants are effective in the treatment of these conditions provide persuasive evidence for Levinson's claims?

READING 7. M. M. Antony, T. A. Brown, & D. H. Barlow, "Current Perspectives on Panic and Panic Disorder"

1. Is the finding that panic disorder is somewhat heritable inconsistent with cognitive-behavioral models of panic? Why or why not?

2. Clark and several other cognitive-behavioral theorists argue that panic attacks occur when individuals misinterpret innocuous bodily sensations (such as rapid heartbeat) as portending disastrous outcomes (for example, a heart attack). What factors might render certain individuals especially susceptible to such misinterpretations?

3. As Antony, Brown, and Barlow note, Clark argues that the cognitions that lead to panic attacks can sometimes occur unconsciously. Is this assertion unfalsifiable and therefore nonscientific? If not, how could it be tested?

4. One area of controversy in this literature revolves around the question of whether panic anxiety differs qualitatively (that is, in kind) or quantitatively (that is, in degree) from

normal anxiety. What research designs might help to shed light on this question?

READING 8. K. Butler, "Researching PTSD: The Biology of Fear"

1. Not all individuals exposed to an extremely traumatic event develop PTSD. What psychological and biological variables might help to explain why some individuals do *not* develop PTSD following a stressor?

2. Do you agree with Butler that the finding that underproduction of cortisol can produce memory loss "challenges the Freudian speculation of a mental mechanism causing repression?" (p. 40). Why or why not?

3. What implications, if any, does the finding that severe trauma can damage the hippocampus hold for the treatment of PTSD by means of either psychotherapy or medication?

4. Butler cites neuroscientist Robert Sapolsky as suggesting that the changes in a human brain following a stressor may be partly or entirely reversible. If Sapolksy is correct, how would you use this information to design a study of the effects of treatment on PTSD?

READING 9. E. Dolnick, "Obsessed"

1. As is evident from Dolnick's article, many of the behaviors of OCD patients resemble the superstitious behaviors of normal individuals. In what ways are compulsions similar to superstitious behaviors? Are there ways in which they are different? What processes might give rise to superstitions, and might some of these same processes be involved in the genesis of compulsions?

2. How might a behaviorist, who believes that principles of reinforcement govern most or all human behaviors, attempt to explain the etiology of OCD?

3. As Dolnick notes, antidepressants (such as Prozac) have been found to be effective for many individuals with OCD. Does this finding imply that OCD and depression are related conditions? Why or why not?

SUGGESTIONS FOR FURTHER READING

Barlow, D. H. (1988). *Anxiety and its disorders: The nature and treatment of anxiety and panic.* New York: Guilford Press.

Cohen, D. B. (1994). *Out of the blue: Depression and human nature.* New York: W. W. Norton.

Goodwin, F. K., & Jamison, K. R. (1990). *Manic depressive illness.* New York: Oxford University Press.

Jamison, K. R. (1993). *Touched with fire: Manic depressive illness and the artistic temperament.* New York: Free Press.

Maser, J., & Cloninger, C. R. (1990). *Comorbidity of mood and anxiety disorders.* Washington, DC: American Psychiatric Press.

McNally, R. J. (1994). *Panic disorder: A critical analysis.* New York: Guilford Press.

Nesse, R. M. (1987). An evolutionary perspective on panic disorder and agoraphobia. *Ethology and Sociobiology, 8,* 73S–83S.

Nesse, R. M., & Williams, G. C. (1994). *Why we get sick: The new science of Darwinian medicine.* New York: Times Books. (See especially Chapter 14, "Are mental disorders diseases?")

Paykel, E. S. (1992). *Handbook of affective disorders* (2nd ed.). New York: Guilford Press.

Rapoport, J. L. (1989). *The boy who couldn't stop washing: The experience and treatment of obsessive-compulsive disorder.* New York: Penguin Books.

WHAT GOOD IS FEELING BAD?

The Evolutionary Benefits of Psychic Pain

by RANDOLPH M. NESSE

MOST PEOPLE come to me for the treatment of anxiety, but recently a new patient came in with only a simple request. "All I really need is a refill," she said, handing me a nearly empty bottle of an antidepressant medication. She had just moved from another city, and for the previous year she had been taking fluoxetine for weight loss, one of the side effects of the drug. "I lost a few pounds," she said, "but I want to keep taking it mainly because it makes me feel better." She denied feeling unusually depressed before, but she insisted that the drug made her more confident and energetic. "I used to be uncomfortable with strangers at parties, but now I can go up to anyone and say anything I want to," she said. "I don't feel nervous or worried about what people think of me. Also, I am more decisive, and people say I am more attractive. I'm usually even eager to get out of bed in the morning. Everything is just—well, better. I hardly ever feel bad anymore."

A routine psychiatric examination uncovered no history of clinical depression. In fact, even before taking fluoxetine she had had relatively few days of feeling down. She reported no family history of mood disorders, no unusual personal or family conflicts. She had sometimes felt uncomfortable in social situations, but she had not avoided giving speeches or going to parties. She denied abusing drugs or alcohol. As far as I could determine, she was a normal person whose normal feelings of distress were blocked by the drug.

Fluoxetine, commonly known as Prozac, has been on the market for slightly more than a year. In that short time it has become the most prescribed antidepressant, because it does not cause dependency and its side effects are, for most patients, few and mild. My patient had only minor insomnia and occasional nausea—and she lost those few pounds. For others, some 15 percent of patients, the side effects are intolerable, and in a few extreme cases patients reportedly became suicidal or began behaving uncontrollably after starting treatment with the drug; studies have not verified the extreme reactions in large, controlled samples of people who use the drug.

Whatever may eventually be discovered about fluoxetine, it is clear that psychopharmacology is entering a new era. In the old days—three or four years ago—all antidepressants had side effects so annoying that normal people would not take them. Fluoxetine is one of the first effective agents with only minor side effects in a class of drugs the psychiatrist Peter D. Kramer of Brown University has called mood brighteners. Several more will be introduced within the next few years, some from whole new classes of drugs that promise even more specific actions than fluoxetine with still fewer side effects.

"So what do you think, doctor?" my patient asked. "All I really want is another prescription—unless there's some danger. Do you think it's safe for me to keep taking this?" I wrestled with the question. If the drug makes her feel better, why not give it to her? Maybe it is relieving a subclinical depression. Then again, it might have unknown side effects, despite its approval by the Food and Drug Administration and a year of clinical experience. But a separate possibility gave me pause: Are bad feelings somehow useful? If they are, is blocking them wise?

Consider pain and anxiety. Much as people want to avoid those feelings, each is essential in a dangerous world. Pain motivates people to avoid actions that might cause injury or death. Anxiety induces changes that make it easier to protect oneself from physical or social threats. The capacity for such feelings must have conferred an advantage in the course of human evolution. Do other bad feelings, such as jealousy and sadness, also serve worthwhile, possibly crucial purposes? If emotions did indeed come about through natural selection—whereby nature selects characteristics if they help organisms survive longer or reproduce more—then bad, as well as good, feelings are probably useful. And though specific experiences or environmental influences may modulate feelings differently in each individual, the basic capacity for the various emotions must somehow have assisted human survival. The task of understanding the evolutionary

---

This article is reprinted by permission of *The Sciences* and is from the November/December 1991 issue, pp. 30–37. Individual subscriptions are $21 per year in the U.S. Write to: The Sciences, 2 East 63rd Street, New York, NY 10021.

functions of emotions is a scientific frontier, one that urgently needs exploration, especially if psychotropic drugs are to be used wisely.

ONE DAY in the sixth grade, when I was on the playground, a friend pointed out a boy who could not feel pain. This bit of information was not a mere curiosity but a valuable warning: if the boy wanted to give someone a good drubbing, he would be undeterred by counterpunches, no matter how solidly planted. Getting up my nerve, I asked the fellow about his unusual condition. Obviously embarrassed, he said he had no concept of pain, just as someone who is color-blind cannot fathom color. Yet he seemed to feel guilt and social rejection like everyone else. Later it came to light that his mother had to check over his entire body inch by inch every night to make sure he had not been injured. My playground group made fun of him for that, but always behind his back.

Today he is almost certainly dead. People who cannot feel pain are extremely rare and usually die in early adulthood. Their joints fail from excess strain, caused in part by the lack of the normal discomfort that makes most people shift position from time to time. The effects of multiple injuries accumulate rapidly, infections and appendicitis go unnoticed, and death from one cause or another comes prematurely. The disease syringomyelia also illustrates the utility of pain. A degeneration of the center of the spinal cord, the condition selectively eliminates pain in various parts of the body, especially the hands. Smokers with syringomyelia repeatedly let cigarettes burn down to nubbins, unaware that their fingers are being charred.

Physical pain is essential to the body's defense against future, as well as immediate, tissue injury. Years ago, a hook impaled my brother's ear while he was fishing. The acute pain moved him to extract the hook immediately (even though the fish had just started biting). And the memory of the pain arouses enough anxiety to ensure that, while fishing, he always wears a hat.

Why is pain painful? If a person simply noticed when tissue was being damaged, would the same purpose not be served? Why must suffering be involved? Surprisingly enough, there is an answer. Pain must be aversive in order to arouse the motivating mechanisms of the mind. Those mechanisms ensure that eliminating the source of pain gets the highest priority in the body's regulation of behavior, for rarely is anything more important to an individual's Darwinian fitness than stopping tissue damage. Patients with chronic pain, who are at the opposite end of the pain-arousal spectrum from my school-yard mate, know only too well the near futility of trying to ignore pain. Its urgent call for attention is crucial to its evolutionary function.

TO GAIN A broader perspective on the defensive systems of the body, consider some of the other, more elaborate mechanisms that have evolved. Many of them are triggered by disease; they include nausea, vomiting, cough, diarrhea, fever, fatigue and anxiety. Each is called forth when specialized detectors in the body warn of a threat. Nausea, vomiting and diarrhea eliminate toxins detected in the gastrointestinal tract, and coughing expels harmful matter in the respiratory tract. Fever counters infection, and fatigue prevents damage from overexertion. Anxiety protects the organism from a wide range of dangers.

Such defenses are analogous to the low-oil pressure light on an automobile dashboard. In that case it is clear the glowing light itself is not the problem; instead, the light is a protective response to the problem of low oil pressure. The dashboard indicator is one component of a system carefully designed to warn of dangerous conditions: an oil-pressure sensor set to respond at an appropriate threshold, wires for transmitting the signal, and a light bulb, positioned for visibility on the dash. If the driver has sense enough to stop, the defense system works. If instead the driver responds, say, by cutting the wire to the light, the engine is likely to be irreparably damaged.

It is important to note, however, that not all manifestations of disease are defenses; many are a result of a defect in the body's machinery. Paralysis, seizures, tumors and jaundice, for example, serve no function; they merely reflect a breakdown in the workings of the body. They are analogous to a clank in the transmission, a plume of steam from an overheated radiator or the silence one gets when turning the ignition key of a car with a dead battery.

The distinction between defenses and defects calls attention to the usefulness of defenses—and the dangers of blocking them. Physicians well know that suppressing a cough can turn a routine pneumonia into a life-threatening illness. It is also true—though not so commonly known—that blocking diarrhea can aggravate certain infections and increase complications. And forcing a fever down can prolong an illness. Even low iron levels in the blood, which often accompany chronic infections, counteract bacteria by depriving them of a crucial mineral. Physicians unaware of that defensive role may unwittingly aid a pathogen by prescribing iron supplements.

Defects, in contrast, are useless. Physicians need have no trepidation about trying to stop seizures, paralysis or jaundice. Furthermore, defects in themselves are not painful, except when they disrupt normal function. Most tumors come to medical attention only after they form noticeable lumps or when they interfere with a bodily function. Kidney failure can be quite advanced before a person notices anything wrong. And a person may be alerted to a weak leg muscle only by scuffs on the toe of one shoe. The capacity for pain is present only where, in an evolutionary sense, it has been able to help. As the evolutionist George C. Williams of the State University of New York at Stony Brook pointed out in his 1966 book *Adaptation and Natural Selection*, damage to the heart or the brain was so often fatal in the natural environment that the capacity for pain or even repair in those tissues would have been irrelevant to survival.

Thus the presence of bad feelings is most reliably associated with defenses, not defects. Nausea, diarrhea, cough, fatigue and anxiety all are distressing; they must be to carry out their protective functions. Indeed, one can argue that all bad feelings are components of defenses. Natural selection has molded each kind of bad feeling to help protect against a specific threat. A person who does not experience nausea as aversive is liable to eat the same toxic food again and again; a person who does not get fatigued will suffer damage to muscles and joints.

EMOTIONAL SUFFERING can be just as useful as physical discomfort. Emotions adjust a person's response to the task at hand. In that sense they are similar to computer programs, which adjust the setup of the computer to carry out a certain kind of task. The program may change what appears on the screen, the functions of certain keys, how memory is allocated, or the way information is processed. Like computers, living organisms are faced with a variety of challenges. The behavioral, physiological and cognitive responses that help a person elude a tiger are different from those that help woo a lover or attack a competitor. Thus fear, love and anger are highly distinct psychological subroutines gradually shaped by natural selection to improve the person's ability to cope with each challenge.

All emotions can help in certain situations but hinder in others. Anxiety is welcome when it aids escape from a pack of wild dogs, but it can become a clumsy intruder at delicate moments in courtship. Conversely, though romantic fantasizing may enhance courtship, it can fatally distract a person fleeing wild dogs. Emotions are excellent examples of the "Darwinian algorithms" described by Leda Cosmides and John Tooby, psychologists at the University of California at Santa Barbara, in the 1987 book *The Latest on the Best: Essays on Evolution and Optimality*:

When a tiger bounds toward you, what should your response be? Should you file your toenails? Do a cartwheel? Sing a song? Is this the moment to run an uncountable number of randomly generated response possibilities through the decision rule? . . . How could you compute which possibility would result in more grandchildren? The alternative: Darwinian algorithms specialized for predator avoidance, that err on the side of false positives in predator detection, and, upon detecting a potential predator, constrain your responses to flight, fight or hiding.

Why are emotions always positive or negative, never neutral? As the biologists Randy and Nancy Thornhill of the University of New Mexico have pointed out, circumstances that pose neither opportunity nor threat arouse no emotion. Why should they if they are unrelated to Darwinian fitness? A falling leaf rarely stirs any feeling, unless perhaps it is seen as a symbol of mortality. A tree leaning precariously over one's bedroom, however, arouses anxious apprehension that is quite unpleasant. If anxiety were pleasant, would people not seek out bedrooms under large, dead, leaning trees, instead of avoiding them?

There are more negative emotions than positive ones—twice as many, by one count. The imbalance arises because people encounter only a few kinds of opportunity, and so—in the Darwinian sense, again—they need only a small number of positive emotions. Happiness, excitement, joy and desire motivate people to take full advantage of each opportunity. Threats, however, come in many forms—predators, poisonous small animals, disease, exposure, starvation, exclusion from a group, loss of allies, loss of stored food, loss of territory, loss of a mate and on and on. Consequently, many distinct patterns of response have been developed to contend with those threats.

OF ALL THE NEGATIVE emotions, anxiety is the most obviously useful. Although there are many kinds of anxiety, the well-known fight-or-flight response, first described by the American psychologist Walter B. Cannon in 1915, best exemplifies the value of anxiety. In the dangerous environment of early humans the response was highly beneficial for the frequent occasions when life was in danger. The strong, rapid heartbeat that accompanies panic anxiety brings extra nutrition and oxygen to muscles and speeds the removal of wastes. Muscle tension prepares for flight or physical defense. Shortness of breath induces rapid breathing, hyperoxygenating the blood. Sweating cools the body in anticipation of flight. Greater production of blood glucose also helps bring more nutrition to the muscles. Secretion of adrenaline into the blood makes it clot faster, should injury occur. Blood circulation shifts from the digestive system to the muscles, leaving a cold, empty feeling in the pit of the stomach and a tense readiness in the muscles.

Accompanying all those physiological changes are psychological and behavioral ones. A person having a panic attack puts aside concerns about paying debts and fantasies about having sex to focus all mental energy on assessing the danger and determining the best means of escape. Often, even before finding out what the danger is, the person makes behavioral adjustments, standing ready to take headlong flight at the slightest provocation.

Social dangers pose equally severe threats. Many of my patients tell me they are too sensitive to social pressures; they are deathly afraid of being left out of a group, and they feel they must always please people. Typically, they have tried hard, sometimes with the help of a therapist, to overcome those "insecurities." They often think they should have high self-esteem regardless of social opinion. But imagine what would happen to a relentlessly self-confident person in the natural environment. Such a person would have no qualms about challenging the leader or doing other things that would cause exclusion from the group. Then the outcast might well walk off confidently onto the savanna, a response that would almost certainly end in death.

The political scientist Robert Axelrod of the University of Michigan has described some of the many ways individual human relationships depend on the exchange of favors and the adherence to certain rules. Within any network of social obligations one has many chances to violate the rules to gain a short-term advantage over one's fellows. In my view, it is the conscience that advocates following the rules and accepting the short-term costs of rule compliance for a chance at greater long-term benefits. But primitive unconscious drives lobby for violating the rules to exploit the immediate opportunity. People usually forgo ephemeral gains to avoid risking the relationship, thanks in large part to anxiety that arises out of guilt or fear of punishment. According to one of the more widely accepted findings of psychoanalysis, anxiety is aroused by socially unacceptable unconscious wishes. It thus inhibits actions that would give immediate pleasure but cause the loss of long-term rewards. Anxiety, even the vague kind that seems to have no specific source, is often useful.

Of course there are circumstances in which anxiety is excessive and serves no purpose. Although the capacity for the state came about through natural selection, environmental variables—early childhood experiences, for instance—and genetic differences affect the individual's susceptibility to anxiety. Those influences are widely recognized. But psychiatry has yet to fully acknowledge the value and evolutionary origins of anxiety and other bad feelings, though the psychiatrists Isaac M. Marks of the

University of London and Brant Wenegrat of Stanford University have begun leading the field in that direction.

ANOTHER EMOTION that often seems useless and damaging is jealousy. In a cross-cultural study of sexual jealousy the psychologists Martin Daly and Margo Wilson of McMaster University found such jealousy present in every culture they investigated. Moreover, it was consistently more intense for males than females. Male sexual jealousy is simpler than anxiety in that it defends against a fairly circumscribed threat—sexual infidelity; hence it need not arise in a variety of forms. In another sense, though, it is more complex, because it is a swirl of diverse, conflicting emotions—anger, loneliness, sadness and unworthiness, among others. For all the research on it, jealousy is still widely misunderstood.

Several years ago a patient came to me because he felt he was excessively jealous. "I am constantly jealous of my wife," he told me. "I even follow her to find out what she is doing. I know it is wrecking the relationship, but I can't help it." When I asked him whether he had any reason to be jealous, he said, "Well, she goes out a few nights a week with another man, but she says they are just friends, and that she will leave me unless I can be less jealous and give her more freedom."

He felt jealousy was abnormal and had never considered that it might be valuable. As the anthropologist Donald Symons of the University of California at Santa Barbara has pointed out, in the course of human evolution a man who did not experience jealousy would risk his wife's becoming impregnated by other men and thus having fewer children of his own. Without jealously guarding his mate, he could never be certain about who was the father of her babies. He would then run the further risk of investing effort in the parenting of other men's children, diverting effort from his own. In present times, as women achieve more power, male jealousy is becoming less beneficial to fitness, since fewer women will tolerate an intensely jealous spouse. Furthermore, there is no doubt that jealousy in the extreme has provoked men to behave destructively and abuse their mates. Nevertheless, in the long run and on average, the moderately jealous man has had more children. Jealousy in women has different cues and other motivations, which would require a separate, lengthy discussion; suffice it to say, it is directed primarily toward ensuring survival of her offspring by keeping a male provider from deserting her for another woman.

ELUCIDATING the evolutionary origin of sadness poses a special challenge. It is easy to see how happiness can be beneficial; it motivates people to seek out and meet new people, attempt difficult tasks and persist in the face of adversity. But sadness is another story. Not only does it seem maladaptive; it also is increasingly viewed as a socially unacceptable result of wrong thinking or of bad genes. When I lecture on the utility of emotions, the question invariably arises: What benefit could sadness possibly confer?

The hypothesis I favor is that mood regulates the allocation of resources. High mood allocates energy, time and social resources to the enterprises most likely to pay off. Low mood withdraws investments from wasted enterprises. According to the principles of resource allocation developed by workers in behavioral ecology, every animal must decide at every moment what to do next—sleep, forage, find a mate, dig a den. All those activities are important, but each must be done at the right time and in proper proportion. Even a single activity such as foraging requires complex decisions about which foods to pursue and how to divide the effort among the accessible patches of land. Any animal, whether wolf or wasp, that pursues less than optimal prey or does not choose the best time to pursue it will lose out in the long run.

People also must make decisions about where, when and how to invest their resources. Shall I write a paper, paint the living room, read a book or clean the basement? At every moment people are deciding. Life's important decisions are usually questions about whether to maintain the status quo or to change patterns of resource allocation.

Making changes is not easy. The life circumstances people fashion for themselves generally require substantial investments in education, physical skills, social skills, relationships and reputation. Changing long-term strategies—gaining, leaving or changing a mate; switching careers; setting new life goals—is risky business. It requires, at the least, giving up on major life investments and starting anew, usually at a lower level, in some new arena. Such a change also usually entails a period of uncertainty, as one experiments with new possibilities. Because of the risks, it is wise not to undertake such changes lightly; it is often better to persist in an enterprise that is, for the moment, not paying off. A mechanism that induces people to stay with their current life strategies despite fallow periods might be quite useful.

Evidence of such a mechanism appears in recent research showing that most people are consistently overly optimistic. Shelley Taylor, a psychologist at the University of California at Los Angeles, has reviewed extensive work showing that, on average, normal people believe that they are more highly skilled than they really are and that they have more control over their environment than they actually do. Furthermore, other work shows that people generally think fewer bad things will happen to themselves than to others. Many depressives, in contrast, seem to be brutally accurate in their assessments of themselves—not pessimistic, merely accurate. Normally, people see the world through rose-colored glasses. That optimism is just what is needed to get people to persist in temporarily unprofitable enterprises and to stay with good relationships that are not going well at the moment.

When efforts fail repeatedly, however, the rose tint fades, and people become harshly realistic about the future and their friends, abilities and problems. When things are bad enough long enough, illusions must be abandoned to make major changes possible. If a farmer plants a field three years in a row and it washes out every year, it is time to stop. If a man is turned down by every beautiful woman he asks for a date, it is time he consider other types. If a person is repeatedly passed over for a promotion, it may be time to change goals or look for another position. As the Swedish psychiatrist Emmy Gut has pointed out, depression often arises when a primary life strategy is failing and no alternatives seem available. She argues that the withdrawal and rumination characteristic of depression help motivate a deep reassessment of life goals and strategies.

The loss of a relationship through death or separation brings on a special form of sadness: grief. Although it can motivate people to prevent such losses, grief is an unusually harsh teacher. An adequate explanation of its function does not yet exist; the links between behavior and psychodynamics must first be more clearly defined and the complexities of attachment taken into account.

ANOTHER SCHOOL OF THOUGHT argues that mood helps people adapt to their social position. In the 1960s the English psychiatrist John Price proposed that primates exhibit low-mood characteristics when their continued membership in a group demands that they submit to others. The idea has been supported in experiments by the psychiatrists Michael T. McGuire and Michael J. Raleigh of the University of California at Los Angeles, who showed that the dominant males in the social hierarchy of vervet monkeys have high levels of blood serotonin, a chemical that acts as a messenger between neurons in the brain. When the dominant male is removed from the colony, however, and can no longer rule the others, his serotonin level plummets. He stops eating, huddles and appears to be deeply depressed. Intriguingly, many antidepressants, including Prozac, work by increasing serotonin in the brain. In another experiment the UCLA investigators removed the dominant monkey from each of twelve groups, and gave one of the two remaining males in each group a drug that increases serotonin. In each case the drugged monkey became dominant. The next experiment, it seems to me, is to give the drug to a submissive male while the dominant male remains in the group: I suspect the normally submissive monkey, spurred by raised serotonin levels, would foolishly challenge the leader and get beaten back into his usual place in the hierarchy. One can only wonder whether widespread use of antidepressants might similarly be tampering with the mechanisms that regulate human social hierarchies.

Several alternative explanations for sadness have been proposed. For example, perhaps it serves as a cry for help. Just like an infant's wail, sadness can elicit aid from relatives. Indeed, communication is an important function of sadness; after all, it is often marked by distinctive facial features and tears. But if the only purpose of sadness were communication, it should take place almost exclusively in public. That is evidently not the case; people often feel saddest when they are home alone at night. Some investigators think sadness may aid creativity by somehow giving people access to unconscious thoughts and feelings, but few conclusions can yet be drawn because of a lack of data and uncertainty about how creativity influences fitness. To get to the heart of sadness, the next step is to find people without the capacity for mood and to look for any disadvantages they share. If the resource-allocation hypothesis is correct, for instance, such people ought to waste substantial effort in useless enterprises and yet be unable to take full advantage of brief windows of opportunity.

AN UNDERSTANDING of the functions of negative feelings would give psychiatry the tools it needs to treat patients more effectively. Currently the field often tacitly assumes that bad feelings are caused by some defect in the brain, and many investigators are preoccupied with finding the neurochemical mechanisms that mediate anxiety and depression. People do inherit susceptibilities to depression and anxiety. In some cases, the susceptibilities certainly come from brain defects. Such conditions are true diseases arising from faulty regulation and are comparable to an excessive immune response. But if sadness is useful, a tendency to depression might better be compared with a propensity to vomit readily or to get high fevers than with diseases such as epilepsy or tuberculosis. Some people may simply have their baseline level of mood set too low, a condition called dysthymia. For others the gain of the system is excessive, causing moods to fluctuate wildly in response to ordinary events. In the clinic that condition is described as cyclothymia or, if it is severe, manic-depressive disorder.

Rather than assuming that negative feelings are symptoms of a physical abnormality or a dysfunctional personality, family or society, the therapist can consider the possibility that some suffering is part of a vital mechanism shaped by natural selection to help people survive in their environment. For many of my patients it is a wonderful revelation to realize that there are benefits to the capacities for various kinds of unhappiness—that there is some sense to their suffering. The new perspective allows them to quit blaming themselves and others and to concentrate instead on making their lives better.

If the mechanisms that regulate the emotions are products of evolution, it might seem to follow that interfering with them will usually be unwise. After all, natural selection has had millions of years to shape the mechanisms, and so by now their thresholds should be set to near-optimum levels. But everyday medical practice contradicts that conclusion. People routinely take aspirin for pain and fever with few untoward consequences; antinausea and antidiarrhea medications relieve much suffering with only occasional complications; ten million Americans each year take anxiety medications, yet there is no epidemic of risky behavior. Nature may seem overly protective, in part because the earliest human environments presented many more dangers than modern industrial society does. People today face few tigers in the street. The readiness to panic may have been a great boon at the oasis, but it is a bane at the grocery store. Exclusion from a social group may have been fatal back then, but today it is not.

A changed environment may not be the only reason defenses seem overresponsive. Be it vomiting, fever or a panic attack, a defense is usually cheap in terms of calories lost and time taken from other activities. But if the defense is not expressed when it is needed, the cost can be enormous. The absorption of bacterial toxins into the stomach, a mauling by a tiger or rejection by a mate can exact huge costs. If the defense is to protect from every instance of danger, the threshold for response must be set low, so low that many false alarms will occur—thus the illusion that the defenses are overresponsive. Patients with agoraphobia, a fear of open places, say they feel silly avoiding a place where they once had a panic attack. But if they are asked what the best response would be if years ago they had been attacked by a tiger at that spot, most quickly realize that a hundred false alarms would be worth a single escape from an attack.

EMOTIONS ARE SET to maximize Darwinian fitness, not happiness. In that dismal conclusion is a kernel of optimism. If much suffering is unnecessary, there should be many occasions on which it can be safely blocked—throughout much of the lives of chronic depressives, for instance. Given the growing power of drugs to influence feelings, top priority should go to gathering the knowledge needed to distinguish the safe occasions from others, in which bad feelings are vital. If we continue to let only side effects or dependency dictate the use of psychotropic drugs, people will take new agents to change their feelings at will, with little idea of the purposes those feelings serve. It is time to make a vigorous study of the evolutionary functions of emotions.

Until that takes place, psychiatry is increasingly going to find itself in a quandary. Indeed, with little knowledge about when bad feelings are useful, I felt quite lost with my new patient, trying to decide whether to refill her prescription. I finally agreed to let her have a few more pills, but I also asked to see her again to explore her life in more detail. And I vowed to do whatever possible to further the understanding of the evolutionary functions of emotions. ●

RANDOLPH M. NESSE is an associate professor of psychiatry at the University of Michigan in Ann Arbor, where he directs the adult ambulatory care division and the evolutionary psychiatry project. He is also associate director of the anxiety disorder program there.

Manic-Depressive Illness and Creativity

Does some fine madness plague great artists?
Several studies now show that creativity
and mood disorders are linked

by Kay Redfield Jamison

The Author

KAY REDFIELD JAMISON is professor of psychiatry at the Johns Hopkins University School of Medicine. She wrote *Touched with Fire: Manic-Depressive Illness and the Artistic Temperament* and co-authored the medical text *Manic-Depressive Illness.* Jamison is a member of the National Advisory Council for Human Genome Research and clinical director of the Dana Consortium on the Genetic Basis of Manic-Depressive Illness. She has also written and produced a series of public television specials about manic-depressive illness and the arts.

en have called me mad," wrote Edgar Allan Poe, "but the question is not yet settled, whether madness is or is not the loftiest intelligence— whether much that is glorious—whether all that is profound—does not spring from disease of thought—from moods of mind exalted at the expense of the general intellect."

Many people have long shared Poe's suspicion that genius and insanity are entwined. Indeed, history holds countless examples of "that fine madness." Scores of influential 18th- and 19th-century poets, notably William Blake, Lord Byron and Alfred, Lord Tennyson, wrote about the extreme mood swings they endured. Modern American poets John Berryman, Randall Jarrell, Robert Lowell, Sylvia Plath, Theodore Roethke, Delmore Schwartz and Anne Sexton were all hospitalized for either mania or depression during their lives. And many painters and composers, among them Vincent van Gogh, Georgia O'Keeffe, Charles Mingus and Robert Schumann, have been similarly afflicted.

Judging by current diagnostic criteria, it seems that most of these artists—and many others besides—suffered from one of the major mood disorders, namely, manic-depressive illness or major depression. Both are fairly common, very treatable and yet frequently lethal diseases. Major depression induces intense melancholic spells, whereas manic-depression,

a strongly genetic disease, pitches patients repeatedly from depressed to hyperactive and euphoric, or intensely irritable, states. In its milder form, termed cyclothymia, manic depression causes pronounced but not totally debilitating changes in mood, behavior, sleep, thought patterns and energy levels. Advanced cases are marked by dramatic, cyclic shifts.

Could such disruptive diseases convey certain creative advantages? Many people find that proposition counterintuitive. Most manic-depressives do not possess extraordinary imagination, and most accomplished artists do not suffer from recurring mood swings. To assume, then, that such diseases usually promote artistic talent wrongly reinforces simplistic notions of the "mad genius." Worse yet, such a generalization trivializes a very serious medical condition and, to some degree, discredits individuality in the arts as well. It would be wrong to label anyone who is unusually accomplished, energetic, intense, moody or

eccentric as manic-depressive. All the same, recent studies indicate that a high number of established artists—far more than could be expected by chance— meet the diagnostic criteria for manic-depression or major depression given in the fourth edition of the *Diagnostic and Statistical Manual of Mental Disorders* (*DSM-IV*). In fact, it seems that these diseases can sometimes enhance or otherwise contribute to creativity in some people.

By virtue of their prevalence alone, it is clear that mood disorders do not necessarily breed genius. Indeed, 1 percent of the general population suffer from manic-depression, also called bipolar disorder, and 5 percent from a major depression, or unipolar disorder, during their lifetime. Depression affects twice as many women as men and most often, but not always, strikes later in life. Bipolar disorder afflicts equal numbers of women and men, and more than a third of all cases surface before age 20. Some 60 to 80 percent of all adoles-

The Tainted Blood of the Tennysons

Alfred, Lord Tennyson (*right*), who experienced recurrent, debilitating depressions and probable hypomanic spells, often expressed fear that he might inherit the madness, or "taint of blood," in his family. His father, grandfather, two of his great-grandfathers as well as five of his seven brothers suffered from insanity, melancholia, uncontrollable rage or what is today known as manic-depressive illness. His brother Edward was confined to an asylum for nearly 60 years before he died from manic exhaustion. Lionel Tennyson, one of Alfred's two sons, displayed a mercurial temperament, as did one of his three grandsons.

Modern medicine has confirmed that manic-depression and creativity tend to run in certain families. Studies of twins provide strong evidence for the heritability of manic-depressive illness. If an identical twin has manic-depressive illness, the other twin typically has a 70 to 100 percent chance of also having the disease; if the other twin is fraternal, the chances are considerably lower (approximately 20 percent). A review of pairs of identical twins reared apart from birth—in which at least one had been diagnosed as manic-depressive—found that in two thirds or more of the sets, the illness was present in both twins.   —*K. R. J.*

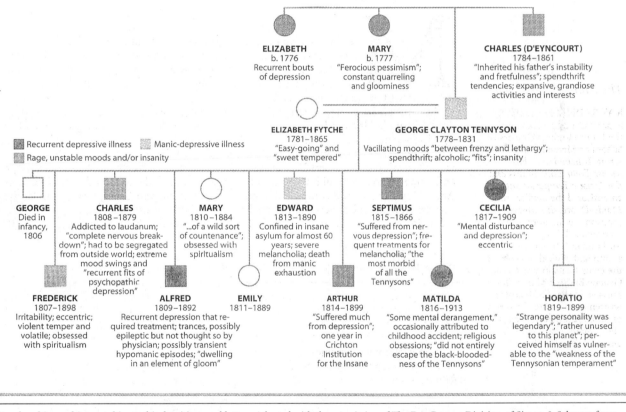

Based on biographies, autobiographical writings and letters. Adapted with the permission of The Free Press, a Division of Simon & Schuster from *Touched with Fire: Manic-Depressive Illness and Artistic Temperament* by Kay Redfield Jamison. Copyright © 1993 by Kay Redfield Jamison.

cents and adults who commit suicide have a history of bipolar or unipolar illness. Before the late 1970s, when the drug lithium first became widely available, one person in five with manic-depression committed suicide.

Major depression in both unipolar and bipolar disorders manifests itself through apathy, lethargy, hopelessness, sleep disturbances, slowed physical movements and thinking, impaired memory and concentration, and a loss of pleasure in typically enjoyable events. The diagnostic criteria also include suicidal thinking, self-blame and inappropriate guilt. To distinguish clinical depression from normal periods of unhappiness, the common guidelines further require that these symptoms persist for a minimum of two to four weeks and also that they significantly interfere with a person's everyday functioning.

Mood Elevation

During episodes of mania or hypomania (mild mania), bipolar patients experience symptoms that are in many ways the opposite of those associated with depression. Their mood and self-esteem are elevated. They sleep less and have abundant energy; their productivity increases. Manics frequently become paranoid and irritable. Moreover, their speech is often rapid, excitable and intrusive, and their thoughts move quickly and fluidly from one topic to another. They usually hold tremendous conviction about the correctness and importance of their own ideas as well. This grandiosity can contribute to poor judgment and impulsive behavior.

Hypomanics and manics generally have chaotic personal and professional relationships. They may spend large sums of money, drive recklessly or pursue questionable business ventures or sexual liaisons. In some cases, manics suffer from violent agitation and delusional thoughts as well as visual and auditory hallucinations.

Rates of Mood Disorders

For years, scientists have documented some kind of connection between mania, depression and creative output. In the late 19th and early 20th centuries, researchers turned to accounts of mood disorders written by prominent artists, their physicians and friends. Although largely anecdotal, this work strongly suggested that renowned writers, artists and composers—and their first-degree relatives—were far more likely to experience mood disorders and to commit suicide than was the general population. During the past 20 years, more systematic studies of artistic populations have confirmed these findings [*see illustration below*]. Diagnostic and psychological analyses of living writers and artists can give quite meaningful estimates of the rates and types of psychopathology they experience.

In the 1970s Nancy C. Andreasen of the University of Iowa completed the first of these rigorous studies, which made use of structured interviews, matched control groups and strict diagnostic criteria. She examined 30 creative writers and found an extraordinarily high occurrence of mood disorders and alcoholism among them. Eighty percent had experienced at least one episode of major depression, hypomania or mania; 43 percent reported a history of hypomania or mania. Also, the relatives of these writers, compared with the relatives of the control subjects, generally performed more creative work and more often had a mood disorder.

A few years later, while on sabbatical in England from the University of California at Los Angeles, I began a study of 47 distinguished British writers and visual artists. To select the group as best I could for creativity, I purposefully chose painters and sculptors who were Royal Academicians or Associates of the Royal Academy. All the playwrights had won the New York Drama Critics Award or the Evening Standard Drama (London Critics) Award, or both. Half of the poets were already represented in the *Oxford Book of Twentieth Century English Verse*. I found that 38 percent of these artists and writers had in fact been previously treated for a mood disorder; three fourths of those treated had required medication or hospitalization, or both. And half of the poets—the largest fraction from any one group—had needed such extensive care.

Hagop S. Akiskal of the University of California at San Diego, also affiliated with the University of Tennessee at Memphis, and his wife, Kareen Akiskal, subsequently interviewed 20 award-winning European writers, poets, painters and sculptors. Some two thirds of their subjects exhibited recurrent cyclothymic or hypomanic tendencies, and half had at one time suffered from a major depression. In collaboration with David H. Evans of the University of Memphis, the Akiskals noted the same trends among living blues musicians. More recently Stuart A. Montgomery and his wife, Deirdre B. Montgomery, of St. Mary's Hospital in London examined 50 modern British poets. One fourth met current diagnostic criteria for depression or manic-depression; suicide was six times more frequent in this community than in the general population.

Ruth L. Richards and her colleagues at Harvard University set up a system for assessing the degree of original thinking required to perform certain creative tasks. Then, rather than screening for mood disorders among those already deemed highly inventive, they attempted to rate creativity in a sample of manic-depressive patients. Based on their scale, they found that compared with individuals having no personal or family history of psychiatric disorders, manic-depressive and cyclothymic patients (as well as their unaffected relatives) showed greater creativity.

Biographical studies of earlier generations of artists and writers also show consistently high rates of suicide, depression and manic-depression—up to 18 times the rate of suicide seen in the general population, eight to 10 times that of depression and 10 to 20 times that of manic-depressive illness and its milder variants. Joseph J. Schildkraut and his co-workers at Harvard concluded that approximately half of the 15 20th-cen-

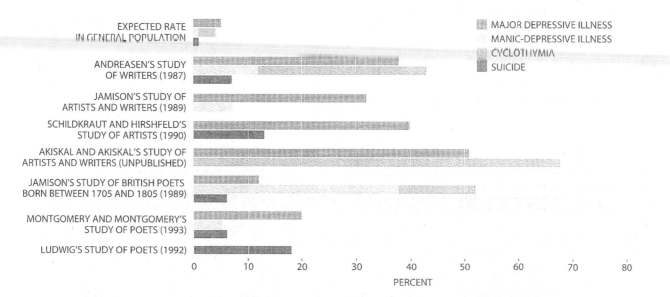

INCREASED RATES OF SUICIDE, depression and manic-depression among artists have been established by many separate studies. These investigations show that artists experience up to 18 times the rate of suicide seen in the general population, eight to 10 times the rate of depression and 10 to 20 times the rate of manic-depression and its milder form, cyclothymia.

tury abstract-expressionist artists they studied suffered from depressive or manic-depressive illness; the suicide rate in this group was at least 13 times the current U.S. national rate.

In 1992 Arnold M. Ludwig of the University of Kentucky published an extensive biographical survey of 1,005 famous 20th-century artists, writers and other professionals, some of whom had been in treatment for a mood disorder. He discovered that the artists and writers experienced two to three times the rate of psychosis, suicide attempts, mood disorders and substance abuse that comparably successful people in business, science and public life did. The poets in this sample had most often been manic or psychotic and hospitalized; they also proved to be some 18 times more likely to commit suicide than is the general public. In a comprehensive biographical study of 36 major British poets born between 1705 and 1805, I found similarly elevated rates of psychosis and severe psychopathology. These poets were 30 times more likely to have had manic-depressive illness than were their contemporaries, at least 20 times more likely to have been committed to an asylum and some five times more likely to have taken their own life.

These corroborative studies have confirmed that highly creative individuals experience major mood disorders more often than do other groups in the general population. But what does this mean for their work? How does a psychiatric illness contribute to creative achievement? First, the common features of hypomania seem highly conducive to original thinking; the diagnostic criteria for this phase of the disorder include "sharpened and unusually creative thinking and increased productivity." And accumulating evidence suggests that the cognitive styles associated with hypomania (expansive thought and grandiose moods) can lead to increased fluency and frequency of thoughts.

Mania and Creativity

Studying the speech of hypomanic patients has revealed that they tend to rhyme and use other sound associations, such as alliteration, far more often than do unaffected individuals. They also use idiosyncratic words nearly three times as often as do control subjects. Moreover, in specific drills, they can list synonyms or form other word associations much more rapidly than is considered normal. It seems, then, that both the quantity and quality of thoughts build during hypomania. This speed increase may range from a very mild quickening to complete psychotic incoherence. It is not yet clear what causes this qualitative change in mental processing. Nevertheless, this altered cognitive state may well facilitate the formation of unique ideas and associations.

People with manic-depressive illness and those who are creatively accomplished share certain noncognitive features: the ability to function well on a few hours of sleep, the focus needed to work intensively, bold and restless attitudes, and an ability to experience a profound depth and variety of emotions. The less dramatic daily aspects of manic-depression might also provide creative advantage to some individuals. The manic-depressive temperament is, in a biological sense, an alert, sensitive system that reacts strongly and swiftly. It responds to the world with a wide range of emotional, perceptual, intellectual, behavioral and energy changes. In a sense, depression is a view of the world through a dark glass, and mania is that seen through a kaleidoscope—often brilliant but fractured.

Where depression questions, ruminates and hesitates, mania answers with vigor and certainty. The constant transitions in and out of constricted and then expansive thoughts, subdued and then violent responses, grim and then ebullient moods, withdrawn and then outgoing stances, cold and then fiery states—and the rapidity and fluidity of moves through such contrasting experiences—can be painful and confusing. Ideally, though, such chaos in those able to

Figure — Robert Schumann's musical works, charted by year and opus number (each three-digit entry is an opus/work number, stacked by year of composition):

```
                                                                            146
                                                                            145
                                                                            141
                                                                            138
                                                                            137
                                                                            108
                                                                            106
                                                                            102
                                                                            101
                                                                            098
                                                                            095
                                                                            094
                                142                                         093 136
                                127                                         092 128
                                077                                         091 121
                                057                                         086 119
                                053                                         085 144 117
                                051                                         082 130 113
                                049                                         079 129 112         143
                                048                                         078 125 111         134
                                045                                         076 097 110         133
                                043                                         075 096 109 148 132
                                042                                         074 090 107 147 131
                                040                                         073 089 105 140 126
                                039                                         070 088 104 139 123
                                036                                         069 087 103 135 118
                                035                                         067 083 100 122 114
                                034
                                033
                                031
                                030 120
                        032     029 064
                124             021 028 027 054             072             084 115
                004         022 017 018 023 026 052 047     060             080 081
                003 010     011 014 012 016 020 025 038 044 050     056 061 063 068
      007 001 008 002 005 099 009 013 006 015 019 024 037 041 046     055 059 062 066
      1829 '30 '31 '32 '33 '34 '35 '36 '37 '38 '39 '40 '41 '42 '43 '44 '45 '46 '47 '48 '49 '50 '51 '52 '53 '54 '55 1856
```

Chart annotations:

- SUICIDE ATTEMPT (1833)
- HYPOMANIC THROUGHOUT 1840
- SEVERE DEPRESSION THROUGHOUT 1844
- HYPOMANIC THROUGHOUT 1849
- SUICIDE ATTEMPT (1854)
- DIED IN ASYLUM (SELF-STARVATION) (1856)

ROBERT SCHUMANN'S MUSICAL WORKS, charted by year and opus number (*above*), show a striking relation between his mood states and his productivity. He composed the most when hypomanic and the least when depressed. Both of Schumann's parents were clinically depressed, and two other first-degree relatives committed suicide. Schumann himself attempted suicide twice and died in an insane asylum. One of his sons spent more than 30 years in a mental institution.

Adapted from "Contributions to a Pathography of the Musicians: Robert Schumann," by Eliot Slater and Alfred Meyer, 1959, *Confinia Psychiatrica*, S. Karger AG. Reproduced with permission of S. Karger, AG, Basel, Switzerland.

The Case of Vincent van Gogh

Many clinicians have reviewed the medical and psychiatric problems of the painter Vincent van Gogh posthumously, diagnosing him with a range of disorders, including epilepsy, schizophrenia, digitalis and absinthe poisoning, manic-depressive psychosis, acute intermittent porphyria and Ménière's disease.

Richard Jed Wyatt of the National Institute of Mental Health and I have argued in detail that van Gogh's symptoms, the natural course of his illness and his family psychiatric history strongly indicate manic-depressive illness. The extent of the artist's purported use of absinthe and convulsive behavior remains unclear; in any event, his psychiatric symptoms long predate any possible history of seizures. It is possible that he suffered from both an epileptic disorder and manic-depressive illness.   —K. R. J.

transcend it or shape it to their will can provide a familiarity with transitions that is probably useful in artistic endeavors. This vantage readily accepts ambiguities and the counteracting forces in nature.

Extreme changes in mood exaggerate the normal tendency to have conflicting selves; the undulating, rhythmic and transitional moods and cognitive changes so characteristic of manic-depressive illness can blend or harness seemingly contradictory moods, observations and perceptions. Ultimately, these fluxes and yokings may reflect truth in humanity and nature more accurately than could a more fixed viewpoint. The "consistent attitude toward life" may not, as Byron scholar Jerome J. McGann of the University of Virginia points out, be as insightful as an ability to live with, and portray, constant change.

The ethical and societal implications of the association between mood disorders and creativity are important but poorly understood. Some treatment strategies pay insufficient heed to the benefits manic-depressive illness can bestow on some individuals. Certainly most manic-depressives seek relief from the disease, and lithium and anticonvulsant drugs are very effective therapies for manias and depressions. Nevertheless, these drugs can dampen a person's general intellect and limit his or her emotional and perceptual range. For this reason, many manic-depressive patients stop taking these medications.

Left untreated, however, manic-de-

pressive illness often worsens over time— and no one is creative when severely depressed, psychotic or dead. The attacks of both mania and depression tend to grow more frequent and more severe. Without regular treatment the disease eventually becomes less responsive to medication. In addition, bipolar and unipolar patients frequently abuse mood-altering substances, such as alcohol and illicit drugs, which can cause secondary medical and emotional burdens for manic-depressive and depressed patients.

The Goal of Treatment

The real task of imaginative, compassionate and effective treatment, therefore, is to give patients more meaningful choices than they are now afforded. Useful intervention must control the extremes of depression and psychosis without sacrificing crucial human emotions and experiences. Given time and increasingly sophisticated research, psychiatrists will likely gain a better understanding of the complex biological basis for mood disorders. Eventually, the development of new drugs should make it possible to treat manic-depressive individuals so that those aspects of temperament and cognition that are essential to the creative process remain intact.

The development of more specific and less problematic therapies should be swift once scientists find the gene, or genes, responsible for the disease. Prenatal tests and other diagnostic measures may then become available; these possi-

bilities raise a host of complicated ethical issues. It would be irresponsible to romanticize such a painful, destructive and all too often deadly disease. Hence, 3 to 5 percent of the Human Genome Project's total budget (which is conservatively estimated at $3 billion) has been set aside for studies of the social, ethical and legal implications of genetic research. It is hoped that these investigations will examine the troubling issues surrounding manic-depression and major depression at length. To help those who have manic-depressive illness, or who are at risk for it, must be a major public health priority.   [SA]

Further Reading

TENNYSON: THE UNQUIET HEART. R. B. Martin. Oxford University Press, 1980.

CREATIVITY AND MENTAL ILLNESS: PREVALENCE RATES IN WRITERS AND THEIR FIRST-DEGREE RELATIVES. Nancy C. Andreasen in American Journal of Psychiatry, Vol. 144, No. 10, pages 1288-1292; October 1987.

MANIC DEPRESSIVE ILLNESS. Frederick K. Goodwin and Kay R. Jamison. Oxford University Press, 1990.

CREATIVE ACHIEVEMENT AND PSYCHOPATHOLOGY: COMPARISON AMONG PROFESSIONS. Arnold M. Ludwig in American Journal of Psychiatry, Vol. 46, No. 3, pages 330–356; July 1992.

TOUCHED WITH FIRE: MANIC-DEPRESSIVE ILLNESS AND THE ARTISTIC TEMPERAMENT. Kay R. Jamison. Free Press/Macmillan, 1993.

Women and Depression

Bonnie R. Strickland

During this year, some 10 million Americans will be clinically depressed and could be diagnosed with an affective disorder. The experience of depression is the most common complaint of people seeking mental health care and the third leading reason individuals see physicians. The emotional toll of the affective disorders in terms of human suffering is incalculable. In addition to the despair and loss of pleasure suffered by depressed individuals (and their families), two thirds of the 30,000 reported suicides in this country each year may be linked to clinical depression. The economic expense to American society in lost productivity and health care is staggering. Annual costs for "mental illness" exceeded $129 billion in 1988. Depression and the affective disorders are recurrent and constitute a major public and mental health problem. Still, they are often unrecognized, undiagnosed, and untreated.

The predominant affective disorders are major depressive disorder, affecting some 3% of our adult population; dysthymia, affecting another 3%; and bipolar disorder (manic-depression), which affects about 1% of our citizens. Depression also often accompanies physical illness and may be a response to high-stress and disruptive life events. No sex differences are found for bi-

Bonnie R. Strickland, a former president of the American Psychological Association, is Professor of Psychology at the University of Massachusetts at Amherst. Address correspondence to Bonnie R. Strickland, Department of Psychology, University of Massachusetts, Amherst, MA 01003.

polar disorder, but females make up about two thirds of those individuals who suffer major depression and dysthymia. Around the world, whether rich or poor, black or white, of high or low socioeconomic status, women are, on the average, twice as likely to be depressed as men.[1] One of four women and one of eight men will be clinically depressed at some time in their lives. The reasons for this discrepancy are complex and poorly understood, but likely arise from an interaction of biological, cultural, and psychological factors that may be different for males and females.[2]

BIOLOGICAL PERSPECTIVES

Research suggests that the affective state of depression, such as feelings of sadness, results from both biogenic and psychosocial factors. Arousal and reactions to stress are a function of physiological responses and one's cognitive appraisal of the events that lead to such arousal. Neurotransmitter substances, such as norepinephrine, dopamine, and serotonin, cross excitatory and inhibitory neuronal synapses and are taken up by specific receptors. A dysfunction in transmission across the synapses, whether a function of the transmitter substances, the mechanisms of synaptic activity, or the uptake or reuptake of the neurotransmitters, may lead to mood dysregulation.

Gender differences in neurophysiological functioning could account for some of the reasons that women are more likely to be depressed than men. Yet little research is available on neurochemical differences. We

do know that reproductive-related events, such as menstruation, pregnancy, childbirth, and menopause, are linked to the reproductive hormones and may influence mood. Seasonal affective disorder, perhaps associated with light change and biological cycling, is also particularly pronounced for women. Those precise interactions of reproductive cycling and depression are difficult to assess, however, in view of our limited knowledge of the basic mechanisms of the reproductive hormones. Moreover, social and cultural influences may bias women's cognitive and affective descriptions of their reproductive experiences and sexual functioning.

Most women, especially in their late 20s and early 30s, report mild to minimal mood changes premenstrually, with about 5% reporting serious and severe symptoms. Typical premenstrual and menstrual symptoms are similar to those of clinical depression but are generally more mild. They include depressed mood, irritability, hostility, anxiety, and changes in sleep, eating habits, and energy.[3]

The use of oral contraceptives may also lead to depressive symptoms for some women. Pregnancy, in contrast, is associated with a low incidence of psychiatric disorders. Following childbirth, some 50% to 80% of women report mild depressive symptoms; as many as 10% experience severe postpartum depression. Depressive symptoms are also reported by women who wish to conceive and fail or cannot carry a fetus to term. The incidence of infertility appears to be increasing among young women and is a major life crisis similar to other high-stress events.[4] Many women who find themselves infertile report this to be the most upsetting experience of their lives.

A prevalent myth in regard to reproductive cycling and depression is that menopausal women are ill-tempered and depressed. Women

From *Current Directions in Psychological Science, 1,* pp. 132–135. Copyright © 1992 American Psychological Society. Reprinted with the permission of Cambridge University Press.

experiencing early, surgically induced menopause may report depression, but depression does not seem to occur as a function of natural changes from pre- to postmenopause. About 15% of menopausal women report themselves to be depressed, a rate almost identical to that of women at the same ages who are not menopausal.[5]

Depression and a sense of guilt and loss have also been assumed to be related to abortion. These feelings may occur for some women, but are typically mild and transitory. By far, the feeling most reported by women who choose to terminate their pregnancies is relief. Those factors implicated in increased risk of depression after abortion, such as lack of support for the decision and self-blame, seem similar to factors reported in research on other stressful life events.[6]

The arena of hormones and behavior is further complicated by the ways in which the reproductive hormones may be related to fat placement and weight gain. The role of adipose (fat) tissue in the storage of cholesterol and the uptake of the stress catecholamines needs continued research as a physiological mechanism involved in the regulation of mood and eating disorders.

Research on the occurrence of depression in relation to reproductive hormones and cycling is intriguing but limited. Generally, the empirical evidence that hormonal changes directly contribute to depression is weak.

PSYCHOLOGICAL AND CULTURAL PERSPECTIVES

Psychological research on gender differences and depression is relatively recent. Findings suggest that socialization patterns for males and females reinforce certain stereotypes of appropriate sex role behavior. Males are encouraged toward inde-

pendence and mastery behavior; females are expected to present themselves as attractive, sensitive to other people, and passive in relationships. Because depression is identified as lack of activity and energy, it is not surprising to find that women may be more depressed than men. (Note that men are overrepresented in those psychiatric disorders that involve active, and sometimes impulsive, behavior, namely, conduct disorders and substance abuse.)

The cognitive revolution in psychology has framed much of the current research on depression. Findings from clinical practice mesh with theoretical notions of the role of cognition and motivation in emotion. Certain cognitive styles (e.g., constructive thinking, emotional self-focus, learned helplessness or learned optimism, mindfulness, perceived control) and various self-evaluative or self-esteem variables appear to be related to health and depression.[7] Yet few of these constructs have been related systematically to gender, although one might expect differences in view of the assumed differential social cognitions of men and women. For example, *irrational thinking* is assumed to be related to depression; therapeutic interventions involve changing or reframing distorted thoughts. Yet many women live in aversive situations that they may be perceiving accurately. As with other oppressed groups, these women's perceptions may be realistic in view of the social conditions in which they live. Thus, therapeutic change for these women may demand behavioral action to escape or improve stressful life conditions as well as changing cognitions.

Within a diathesis-stress model, Abramson, Metalsky, and Alloy[8] have developed a theory of *hopelessness depression* in which a proximal sufficient cause of depressive symptoms is an expectation that one cannot change highly aversive life situations and desired and valued

outcomes will not be available. Hammen and her colleagues[9] also have suggested that specific depressive self-schemas lead to vulnerability to depression and that self-schemas may be generally different for men and women depending on their life situations. If a woman finds value in social relationships, for example, an interpersonal loss may be particularly distressful. Lowered self-esteem may also be a function of specific, self-focused disappointments rather than generalized unhappiness. Nolen-Hoeksema[1] also found women engage in more ruminative, brooding responses to negative events than do men, perhaps leading to more severe depression for a longer duration of time than for men.

Thus, social influences such as cultural expectations about women's roles appear to be major factors in the excess of depression for women as opposed to men. In our contemporary American society, stress is ubiquitous in our lives, but women may be disproportionately affected because of the generally lower power, respect, and esteem that accrue to women. Women and girls experience more discrimination, poverty, sexual harassment, and abuse than men and boys. Women also experience more stress in marriages and interpersonal relationships and are more likely than men to be the caretakers of children and the frail elderly. They often feel responsible when intimates are emotionally needy or psychologically distressed, thus living with prolonged, unremitting stress that can lead to both physical and emotional difficulties expressed as depression.

Individuals and family members with economic difficulties are often depressed, and three quarters of the people living in poverty in this country are women and children. A single mother, with unpredictable or limited economic support, is at particularly high risk for depression. Even controlling for income, research suggests that job loss and "money problems" are strongly associated with high levels of depressive symptoms. Women still have a difficult time entering the workplace, escaping sexual harassment, and advancing to positions of status and appropriate economic reward.

Sexual and physical violence against women are epidemic in this country, and women with a history of abuse are significantly more likely to be depressed than women with no such victimization. More than 90% of adult rape victims are women, and 80% of child sexual abuse involves girls. Almost two thirds of adult women recall at least one experience of sexual abuse or assault before age 18, and one third of adult women will be raped, sexually assaulted, or both. One of three married women is battered or abused during her marriage, as is one of four females in dating relationships. Moreover, regardless of whether women have personally experienced violence or abuse, they are likely to learn from friends, family, and the media that women's safety cannot be guaranteed in many situations. The burden of vigilance to ensure one's security is quite different for women than men and may be a continued source of stress resulting in depression for women.[10]

TREATMENT

The effective treatment of the affective disorders is one of the welcomed success stories of modern advances in mental health. Some 80% of individuals who are depressed and find appropriate mental health care recover in a period of a few weeks to a few months. However, depression is still often unrecognized and misdiagnosed, so that only about one in four depressed individuals will be properly treated.

The various psychotropic medications in use since the early 1950s have been one of the leading reasons for improved treatments for the affective disorders. Lithium and some of the antiseizure medications seem to be particularly useful for bipolar disorders. Psychopharmacological medications have also been effective in the treatment of major depressive disorder and dysthymia. Drugs of choice have included tricyclic antidepressants and the monamine oxidase inhibitors. Fluoxetine (Prozac) is now the drug most likely to be prescribed for depression because its effects are comparable to those of the older tricyclic antidepressants, but there are fewer unpleasant side effects. Estimates suggest that 60% of depressed individuals will respond to appropriate medication. Yet, although two thirds of antidepressant prescriptions are written for women, almost no research is available to ascertain differential responses for females versus males; little, if anything, is known about the interactions of antidepressant medications and the reproductive hormones.

Various brief cognitive-behavioral psychotherapies, especially those that focus on action and mastery behaviors, have also proven effective in treating depression. One example is feminist therapy, which addresses social and cultural aspects of depression as well as individual experiences and responses.

Psychopharmacology and psychotherapy, alone or in combination, are usually superior to placebo in the treatment of clinical depression. Cognitive therapy seems better than both other psychotherapies and pharmacology for mild and moderate depression, but appropriate antidepressant medications may be needed for the severe biological depressions and disruptive somatic symptoms. In the largest study completed to date comparing imipramine, cognitive-behavioral therapy, and brief interpersonal therapy, 57% to 69% of patients who completed 16 weeks of treatment were symp-

tom free. Results were remarkably similar across the therapies except that drug treatment seemed to relieve symptoms earliest. No sex differences were noted.[11]

Little systematic information is available as to whether men and women respond differently to various psychosocial treatments. A meta-analysis of a decade of short-term psychodynamic psychotherapy studies did find behavioral treatments for depression to be twice as effective as short-term psychodynamic psychotherapy when treatment ends and at 1-year follow-up, although this finding was reduced for samples of female patients.[12]

Preventive efforts would also be expected to influence the occurrence of depression among women. Young people are significantly more likely to be depressed than older cohorts. Girls, in particular, have diminished self-esteem and become more depressed as they move into adolescence. Changing the social conditions that limit opportunities for girls and women or devalue women's contributions should lead to enhanced well-being and less depression. Increased support for women who are disadvantaged in this society, especially special populations such as single mothers in poverty, would improve not only their well-being but also that of their children.

CONCLUSIONS

Despite the continued difficulties of definition and delineation of the affective disorders, empirical evidence from biological, psychological, and sociological perspectives suggests that the complex etiology and treatment of the depressions are steadily beginning to be understood. Despite the fact that women are twice as likely to be depressed as men, however, little research has focused on gender differences in depression. Reproductive cycling appears to be related to depression for some women. Social roles and life experiences also influence depression and the duration of dysphoric affect. Women and men may use different cognitive strategies and coping responses to negative events and thus may be differentially dysphoric or depressed. Although both psychosocial and pharmacological treatments for depression lead to the remediation of symptoms, few data are available on the issue of whether men and women respond differently to psychotherapy or antidepressant medication. Systematic basic and applied research on gender and depression must continue and be expanded if we are to understand the affective disorders and answer the age-old question as to why women are more often depressed than men.

Acknowledgments—The author is particularly indebted to Margaret Broenniman for her help in the literature review and in editing the manuscript.

Notes

1. S. Nolen-Hoeksema, *Sex Differences in Depression* (Stanford University Press, Stanford, CA, 1990).

2. E. McGrath, G.P. Keita, B.R. Strickland, and N.F. Russo, *Women and Depression: Risk Factors and Treatment Issues*, report of the American Psychological Association Task Force (American Psychological Association, Washington, DC, 1990).

3. J.A. Hamilton, B.L. Parry, and S.L. Blumenthal, The menstrual cycle in context: I. Affective syndromes associated with reproductive hormonal changes, *Journal of Clinical Psychiatry, 49*, 474–480 (1988).

4. A.L. Stanton and C.A. Dunkel-Schetter, Psychological adjustment to infertility: An overview of conceptual approaches, in *Infertility: Perspectives From Stress and Coping Research*, A.L. Stanton and C.A. Dunkel-Schetter, Eds. (Plenum Press, New York, 1991).

5. J.B. McKinlay, S.M. McKinlay, and D.J. Brambilla, The relative contributions of endocrine changes and social circumstances to depression in mid-aged women, *Journal of Health and Social Behavior, 28*, 345–363 (1987).

6. N.E. Adler, H.P. David, B.N. Major, S. Roth, N.F. Russo, and G.E. Wyatt, Psychological responses after abortion, *Science, 248*, 41–44 (1990).

7. B.R. Strickland, Internal-external control expectancies: From contingency to creativity, *American Psychologist, 44*, 4–7 (1989).

8. L.Y. Abramson, G.I. Metalsky, and A.B. Alloy, Hopelessness depression: A theory-based subtype of depression, *Psychological Review, 96*, 358–372 (1989).

9. C. Hammen, T. Marks, A. Mayol, and R. deMayo, Depressive self-schemas, life stress, and vulnerability to depression, *Journal of Abnormal Psychology, 94*, 308–319 (1985).

10. M.L. Leidig, The continuum of violence against women: Psychological and physical implications, *American Journal of College Health, 40*, 149–155 (1992).

11. I. Elkin, T. Shea, J.T. Watkins, S.D. Imber, S.M. Stosky, J.F. Collins, D.R. Glass, P. Pilkonis, W.R. Leber, J.P. Docherty, S.J. Fiester, and M.B. Perloff, National Institute of Mental Health Treatment of Depression Collaborative Research Program: General effectiveness of treatments, *Archives of General Psychiatry, 46*, 971–982 (1989).

12. M. Svartberg and T.C. Stiles, Comparative effects of short-term psychodynamic psychotherapy: A meta-analysis, *Journal of Consulting and Clinical Psychology, 59*, 704–714 (1991).

Seasonal affective disorders: the effects of light on human behaviour

Leslie Hawkins

It has long been recognized that human moods are affected by seasonal changes: Hippocrates observed that 'of constitutions some are well or ill adapted to summer, others are well or ill adapted to winter'. It is only comparatively recently, however, that seasonal affective disorders (SAD) have been the subject of serious research. This indicates that mental depression – severe in a small minority of cases – may be related to low exposure to light in the winter months. In many cases phototherapy – which may influence melatonin production – brings relief.

Living systems on this planet depend on light, either directly or indirectly, for their energy source. Green plants convert light energy into carbohydrates, which are then used by animals as a food energy source. The fact that photosynthesis is dependent on light is well known, but it is not so well appreciated that animals too have evolved a variety of mechanisms for directly utilising the sun's light. Light is, of course, only a small band within the total electromagnetic radiation spectrum emitted by the sun. Radiation with a frequency of around 10^{15} Hz – that is, a wavelength of between 420 and 700 nm – causes the retina of the human eye to be stimulated, and this in turn is translated by the brain into a visual picture of our surroundings. Other animals utilise a slightly wider range of wavelengths, extended particularly into the infra-red region (wavelengths above 700 nm), which allows them to see when to us it appears dark. This rather narrow band of electromagnetic frequencies is therefore called visible light. It provides us with what, until recently, has been thought of as the main function of light, namely to provide us with the sense of vision.

The two main non-visual reactions to light that have been understood for a long while is the synthesis in the skin of Vitamin D – a vitamin essential for the proper metabolism of calcium – and skin tanning. Tanning, which results from the effect of light stimulating the production of a dark pigment, melanin, in the skin, is thought to be a protective mechanism

Leslie Hawkins, BSc., Ph.D., CBiol., MIBiol., MIOSH.

Is Senior Lecturer in Applied Physiology and Head of the Robens Institute Occupational Health and Safety Service at the University of Surrey. His research interests concern the effects of indoor environments on health with special interest in indoor air quality, lighting and non-ionising electromagnetic radiation.

against the damaging effect of ultraviolet radiation (wavelengths between 290 and 380 nm) from the sun.

Within the last decade we have come to understand a further, perhaps far reaching, effect of light on physiological control mechanisms – that of control of circadian rhythmicity [1].

Circadian rhythms

Virtually all physiological systems exhibit periodicity in their activity (figure 1). For example body temperature peaks at about 9 o'clock in the evening and reaches a low value at 4 o'clock in the morning. The difference between the high value and low value is about 1°F (0.6°C). Hormone levels in the blood show similar characteristic rhythms. The adrenal gland produces a peak output of the hormone cortisol at 9 a.m. and this falls progressively throughout the day to a low value at 1 a.m. Mental activity, measured by various performance tasks, shows a rising level of performance throughout the morning to reach a peak around noon. Studies of mental performance have revealed two personality types – larks and owls. Larks rise early in the morning, reach a peak of mental alertness early (before noon), and then decline more rapidly so that they normally go to bed early. Owls, by contrast, rise later, take longer to reach a peak level of performance, and remain more alert in the evening, usually going to bed late. Both types show a characteristic 'post-lunch' dip in performance, although this appears to be unrelated to eating at lunch-time [2, 3].

These are given as examples to illustrate circadian rhythmicity; there are as many rhythms as there are physiological or psychological functions. The interesting thing is that each rhythm has a characteristic time to peak and dip, but different body functions peak and dip at different times of the day (figure 2). The closely co-ordinated set of individual rhythms is referred to as 'internal synchronisation'. The mechanisms that produce periodicity in physiological and

mental function and control their synchronisation have puzzled biologists for a long time. It is known from early experiments that the light–dark period of a normal day and night is an environmental cue which somehow phases the body's rhythms with the 24 hour period of the Earth's rotation. M. C. Lobban found that Indians and Eskimos from polar regions, where the alternation of light and dark is reduced, had lower amplitude rhythms (i.e. flatter rhythms) and had evidence of internal desynchronisation [4]. D. T. Krieger and F. Rizzo found similar evidence in partially sighted and blind people [5]. Other experiments concerning people kept in isolation from the natural day–night period have shown that rhythms 'free-run' – that is, they are no longer phased to a 24 hour period. Under such conditions most people free-run to a period greater than 24 hours – up to 27 hours in some cases. Additionally, each rhythm free-runs at a slightly different rate, which results in desynchronisation [6].

Such experiments have led to a number of important conclusions about circadian rhythm control.

(1) Each physiological function has its own 'internal clock'. These so called 'endogenous' rhythms can free-run if the body is removed from external cues to the period of the Earth's rotation.

(2) The most important environment cue is the periodicity of light and dark – this is termed an exogenous rhythm. There are, however, probably other cues which we have learned to use to entrain body rhythms. These include simply a knowledge of time of day, social factors, and regularity of feeding.

(3) The alternation of light and dark produces an enhanced amplitude of rhythms and acts as an external cue to synchronise the individual rhythm. This synchronisation is lost if all external cues are missing, and is greatly diminished if the light–dark cue is removed

Reprinted with permission from *Endeavour, New Series, 16*(3), pp. 122–127, 1992, Elsevier Science Ltd, Oxford, England.

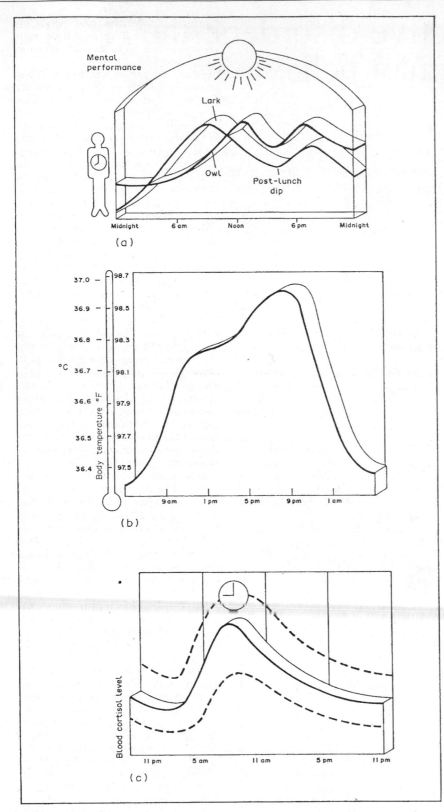

Figure 1 Some examples of circadian rhythms. (a) Rhythm of mental performance comparing larks and owls. (b) The body temperature rhythms. (c) The rhythm of blood cortisol (dotted lines are normal range).

but other cues, such as social factors, remain.

Rhythms of the type we are describing, that occur with a periodicity of about one day are termed circadian. There are, however, others which are also important to many animal species. The monthly menstrual cycle in the human female is an obvious example of a biological rhythm, but we can also recognise circa-annual rhythms (seasonal rhythms) which control breeding patterns and hibernation. Although we tend to think that man is unaffected by seasonal changes, as we learn more we may find that we, too, are influenced by the changing seasons. One such possibility, in relation to depressive illness, will be discussed later. The control of circa-annual rhythms is more complex because not only does the period of light and dark vary (according to latitude) but the seasonal variation in climate, particularly temperature, also has a strong influence [3].

The pineal gland and melatonin

In fish, amphibians, and reptiles, the pineal gland is situated near the skull and contains photoreceptors that respond directly to light entering through the skull bone. In these animals the pineal is sometimes referred to as the 'third eye'. In man, however, the pineal is situated deep in the brain and contains no active photoreceptors (figure 3). The human pineal receives information on light and dark from the rods and cones in the retina of the eye. It does so through a tortuous nervous pathway that originates in nerve fibres leaving the optic tracts near the optic chiasma. These fibres enter the hypothalamus to constitute what are often called 'retinohypothalamic' pathways. It is suspected that some control of body rhythms is exerted directly through the influence of the retinohypothalamic pathways on hypothalamic functions, because the hypothalamus directly controls a number of physiological functions and indirectly, via the pituitary gland, influences virtually the whole of the endocrine system.

However, this aside, the fibres entering the hypothalamus end up on a group of cells within it called the suprachiasmatic nucleus, and from there relay on to the reticular formation in the midbrain. Reticulo-spinal fibres pass from here down the spinal cord to terminate on a ganglion in the neck, the superior cervical ganglion. This ganglion produces a post-ganglionic (sympathetic) nerve that runs back up the neck to re-enter the cranium and to terminate eventually on the pineal gland. The nerves synapse via beta adrenergic receptors in the pineal gland, which then influence the activity of *N*-acetyl transferase, an enzyme regulating the synthesis of melatonin (figure 4). For a detailed descrip-

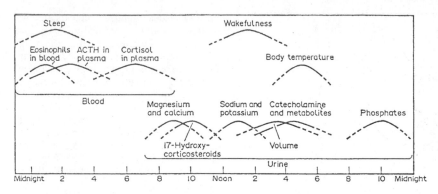

Figure 2   Different body rhythms peak at different times of the day. These are normally closely synchronised by phasing them to external cues, in particular the light–dark cycle. If the light–dark period changes the rhythms re-adjust at different rates producing a state of 'internal desynchronisation' (jet lag for example).

tion of the biochemistry of indole metabolism in the pineal, the reader is referred to D. C. Klein *et al.* [7].

The effect of light stimulating the retina is, therefore, to bring about suppression of a number of critical steps in the conversion of serotonin to melatonin. Plasma melatonin levels therefore fall rapidly on exposure of the eyes to light and increase again almost immediately the subject is in the dark. This phenomenon was first reported by A. J. Lewy in 1980, who also showed that normal indoor artificial light levels (500 lux) had a relatively insignificant effect, whilst 2500 lux was necessary to produce a characteristic suppression (figure 5) [8].

Seasonal affective disorder (SAD)

Affective disorders are broadly defined as states of abnormal mood. Normally the term is limited to the major syndromes of depression and mania although some psychiatrists include anxiety states in so far as they are related to depression [9].

During the past decade there has been increasing interest in affective disorders that show a seasonal variation. Perhaps as many as 60 per cent of the population show seasonal changes in sleep or mood but only about 5 per cent have severe seasonal depression that might require treatment. While the majority of those with a seasonal affective disorder have a winter depression, a small number have a summer depression; a few have depressive episodes in both the summer and winter [9]. The observation that there are seasonal patterns to illness, including depressive illness, has a long historical record. Hippocrates (*ca* 430 B.C.) taught that the seasons of the year were important in determining disease. 'It is chiefly the changes in the seasons which produce diseases, and in the seasons the great changes from cold or heat' [10]. Hippocrates also observed that 'of constitutions some are well or ill adapted to summer, others are well or ill adapted to winter' [10]. As well as recognizing a general relationship between seasons and disease. Hippocrates and a later Greek physician Aretaeus (*ca* 150–200) specifically noted a relationship between depression and the onset of autumn and winter [11].

The modern interest in seasonal depressive illness probably started with the work of P. Pinel [12]. He wrote that 'Maniacal paroxysms . . . generally begin immediately after the summer solstice'.

Most of the early physicians including Pinel, and later his student J. E. D Esquirol, considered that temperature was the cause of the depression. Esquirol wrote that 'heat like cold, acts upon the insane with this difference, that the continuance of warmth augments the excitement, whilst cold prolongs the depression' [13] [14].

However, the idea that light and dark may influence mood was certainly noted by the ancient physicians who, indeed, likened depression to a kind of internal darkness. Amazingly, light therapy to treat depression may have been used in the second century. Aretaeus wrote that 'lethargics are to be laid in the light and exposed to the rays of the sun (for the disease is gloom)' [15]. The first modern scientific description of phototherapy was by H. Marx. He reported successful treatment by exposure to artificial light, of soldiers in Northern Scandinavia who suffered recurrent winter depression. He also speculated (in part correctly, as we now know) that the therapeutic effects were mediated by retino-hypophyseal (via retina-hypothalamic) pathways [16]. (These are tracts to the pituitary gland running via the hypothalamus.)

The more recent upsurge in interest in

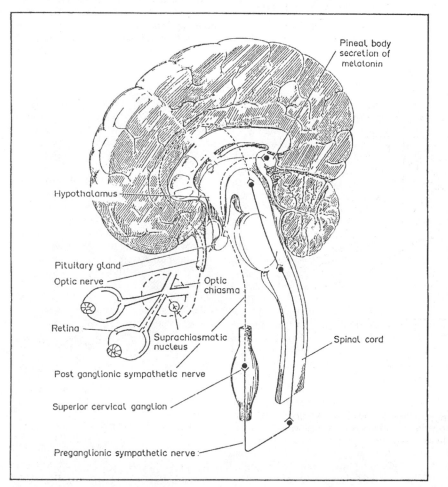

Figure 3   The anatomy of the non-visual pathways and the pineal gland.

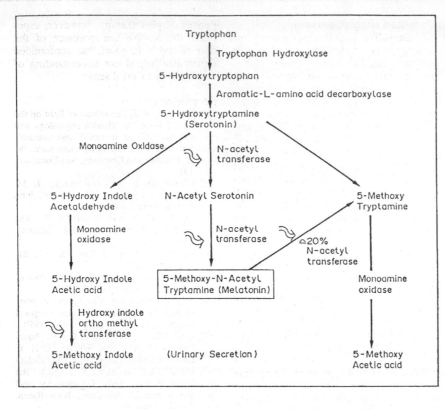

Figure 4   The formation of melatonin and associated indoles from tryptophan in the human pineal. ⤳ indicates the steps that are suppressed by light stimulation of the retinohypothalamic pathways which in turn stimulates adrenergic receptors in the pineal.

SAD began in 1982 when Lewy and his co-workers reported a case of winter depression which remitted when they used strong artificial light to lengthen the hours of daylight [17]. These same authors had recently shown that artificial light could suppress melatonin synthesis and they therefore concluded that the anti-depressive effect of phototherapy was due to an increased period of day time melatonin suppression, similar to that normally experienced in the spring or summer. Since then, a large number of scientific papers have described individual cases or the results of controlled clinical trials, and concluded overwhelmingly that bright light is a rapid and effective treatment of winter depression. The literature up to 1988 has been reviewed by N. E. Rosenthal [18] and by E. Garfield [19]. What are the treatment criteria and how does phototherapy work? A number of treatment variables could influence the effectiveness of phototherapy and these have been investigated in the past few years in some detail. The variables are intensity of light, spectral quality of the light; the duration of exposure; and time of day of exposure. Consistent with the observations that melatonin suppression requires at least 2000 lux of light intensity, Rosenthal found that light of this intensity was significantly better at alleviating symptoms than light of 300 lux (which approxi-

mates to normal indoor artificial light levels) [20]. A number of subsequent studies have replicated this finding [e.g. 21, 22].

M. Terman has reported that 10 000 lux is more effective than 2500 lux even if used for only 30 minutes per day [23]. It is quite clear, therefore, that treatment is effective only if bright light is used, and it would seem that above 2500 lux higher intensities can be traded against length of exposure. At 2000 lux most authors have reported that 4 hours exposure is superior to 2 hours or less [e.g. 24, 25]. The spectral quality of the light has received rather less attention. R. Wurtman found that in rats the most effective frequency for melatonin suppression was at 520 nm, in the green part of the visible spectrum [1]. Other workers have found that (in the hamster) blue light is most effective [26]. This finding led to an interest in developing and applying full-spectrum lighting in phototherapy. Full spectrum lighting uses fluorescent tubes that emit light that is much closer to the spectral quality of natural sunlight than to the normal fluorescent or tungsten lighting. Full spectrum tubes emit light with more ultraviolet, blue, and green light, and less yellow, orange and red. Although most phototherapy treatments employ full-spectrum lighting there is no experimental evidence that this has any greater anti-depressive effect than nor-

mal fluorescent lighting. Time of day of exposure would theoretically be an important consideration. If the effect of phototherapy is to suppress melatonin levels then early morning treatment should be more effective in ensuring a switch over from night-time secretion to day-time suppression.

Indeed, many authors have concluded that morning treatment is most effective [e.g. 27, 28], although some have shown that evening treatment is best [e.g. 29, 30], or that time of day makes no difference [e.g. 31].

In summary, therefore, bright light exposure during the daytime has been found to be an effective treatment for SAD. At least 2500 lux for 4 hours is required, although a higher intensity for lesser periods seems to be as effective and is more practical to administer. Morning exposure is most effective for the majority of sufferers, although time of day seems not to be very critical. There is no evidence that full-spectrum lighting is any more effective than ordinary fluorescent lighting, although this has not been adequately studied.

The mechanisms by which bright light treatment may be effective remain speculative, but are worthy of some discussion. There are a number of possibilities, which can be summarised as: (1) the melatonin hypothesis; (2) the circadian rhythm phase shift hypothesis; and (3) the circadian rhythm amplitude hypothesis.

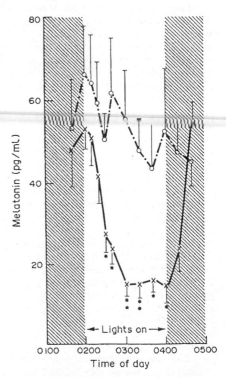

Figure 5   The suppression of melatonin production by light. Light intensity of 2500 lux (x) produces a marked suppression whilst light at ordinary indoor levels (o = 500 lux) is almost ineffective. (From: Lewy 1980, Ref. [8].)

The melatonin hypothesis

The melatonin hypothesis, which inspired the modern interest in SAD, is not in fact supported very strongly by the current evidence. This hypothesis proposed that the shortening day length (photoperiod) during the autumn triggers winter depression by extending the period of night-time melatonin secretion. During the winter months there is a delay in the morning drop in melatonin levels, caused presumably by the low levels of morning light [32]. This lengthening of the nocturnal peak of melatonin will occur in the Northern and Southern hemispheres, but should not occur nearer the equator. There is some evidence that winter depression increases in prevalence and severity with increasing latitude, which would support this hypothesis. There are however a number of pieces of evidence that argue against the melatonin hypothesis. C. Thompson and co-workers have recently found that patients with SAD show an abnormal seasonal variation in sensitivity to light [33]. They appear to be supersensitive in the winter, showing a suppression of melatonin at lower light levels (as had previously been found in patients with manic depression [34]), and subsensitive to light during the summer. This should allow patients with SAD to switch off melatonin secretion more easily in the low light levels of a winter morning, although this appears not to occur.

One argument that would support the hypothesis is that bright light phototherapy administered in the early morning is usually a more effective treatment. The benefit could therefore derive from the switching off of melatonin synthesis at the appropriate time of day and hence shortening of nocturnal peak. However, while light therapy given in the morning and the evening will extend the daytime photoperiod, there is ample evidence that the same dose of light given during the middle of the day, which does not extend the photoperiod, is also effective in many patients [35].

Other arguments against the melatonin hypothesis are that administering melatonin to patients who have had their melatonin lowered by phototherapy does not reverse the benefit of light exposure [36]. Atenolol, a β-adrenergic antagonist, blocks the β receptors in the pineal and causes, like bright light, melatonin suppression. If the melatonin hypothesis is correct therefore, atenolol should be as effective as light in reversing winter depression, although this has been shown not to be the case [37].

While much attention has been paid to melatonin, it must be remembered that it is closely related to serotonin metabolism (figure 4) and serotonin is a powerful neurotransmitter known to be implicated in depression. The role of serotonin in SAD has barely been investigated [38].

Circadian rhythm phasing

An alternative hypothesis that is now gaining more credibility is one which proposes that the shorter winter photoperiod shifts the circadian rhythm phasing. According to this hypothesis, depression occurs when the body's rhythms are phase-delayed relative to sleep because of the delay in the appearance of morning light. If this is the case, then the timing of the melatonin rhythm and other body rhythms, becomes more important than their amplitude. Phase delayed melatonin rhythms occur in normal subjects in dark winter conditions; the suggestion is that patients with SAD are more readily phase delayed that others [39]. The benefits of morning phototherapy are to advance the onset of night-time melatonin production and to correct the phase delay. This explains the effectiveness of morning therapy, but the apparent benefit of exposure to light at other times of the day, especially the evening which would further delay the rhythm, argues against the hypothesis. Thompson has suggested that when the melatonin rhythm begins to delay, the suprachiasmatic nucleus increases the individual's light sensitivity in order to compensate. This increased light sensitivity in SAD patients was commented on earlier [34]. Depression, it is suggested, occurs when the increased sensitivity still fails to restore the appropriate phase relationship [33].

Circadian rhythm amplitude

Finally, the circadian rhythm amplitude hypothesis suggests that the low levels of winter light flatten circadian rhythms (reduce their amplitude). Consistent with this hypothesis is the observation that in depression (of all types) there are abnormally low circadian rhythm amplitudes [13], and in winter depression they are especially so [31]. Phototherapy has the effect not only of phase shifting the rhythms (dependent on the timing of the exposure) but also of increasing the amplitude. The amplitude hypothesis is a relatively simple explanation, but has not yet been tested experimentally.

Whatever the explanation, there is no doubt that humans are affected by a circa-annual rhythm of mood. For most of us this is no more than a reduction in mood during the dark days of winter, but for about 5 per cent of the population this can manifest as a disabling and deep depression lasting for three or four months of the year. The explanation for this will be somewhere in our understanding of chronobiology. The relationships of the retina, the hypothalamus, the suprachiasmatic nucleus, the pineal gland and its hormones, especially melatonin, are clearly involved in an intriguingly complex fashion. Fortunately, we know that phototherapy treatment for most sufferers is a relatively simple and effective means of remission. The experiences of phototherapy, however, especially the relative unimportance of the time of day it is given, has confounded rather than helped our understanding of the aetiology of the disease.

References

[1] Wurtman, R. J. The effects of light on the human body. In: 'Human physiology and the environment in health and disease'. Readings from Scientific American. W. H. Freeman and Company, San Francisco, 1976.

[2] Minors, D. S. and Waterhouse, J. M. 'Circadian rhythms and the human', John Wright, Bristol, 1981.

[3] Ayensu, E. S. and Whitfield, P. 'The rhythms of life', Marshall Editions, London, 1982.

[4] Lobban, M. C. Q. J. Exp. Physiol., 52, 401–410, 1967.

[5] Krieger, D. T. and Rizzo, F. Neuroendocrinology, 8, 165–179, 1971.

[6] Wever, R. 'The circadian system of man. Results of experiments under temporal isolation', Springer-Verlag, Berlin, 1979.

[7] Klein, D. C., Auerbach, D. A., Namboodiri, M. A. A. and Wheler, G. H. T. Indole Metabolism in The Mammalian Pineal Gland. In: Reiter, R. J. (ed.), 'The Pineal Gland, Vol. 1, Anatomy and Biochemistry', CRC Press, Boca Raton, Florida, 1981.

[8] Lewy, A. J., Wehr, T. A. and Golodwin, F. K. et al. Science, 210, 1267–1269, 1980.

[9] Thompson, C. and Silverstone, T. 'Seasonal Affective Disorder', CNS, London, 1989.

[10] Hippocrates: Aphorisms. In: 'Hippocrates IV', trans. Jones, W. H. S., Harvard University Press, Cambridge. 1959.

[11] Lewis, A. J. Ment. Sci., 80, 1–42, 1934.

[12] Pinel, P. 'A treatise on insanity', trans. Davis, D. D., Cadell and Davis, London, 1806. Cited by Wehr and Rosenthal, 1989 [Ref. 10].

[13] Wehr, T. A. and Rosenthal, N. E. Am. J. Psychiatry, 146, 829–839, 1989.

[14] Esquirol, J. E. D. 'Mental maladies: Treatise on insanity', trans. Hunt, E. K. Lead and Blanchard, Philadelphia, 1845. Cited by Wehr and Rosenthal, 1989 [Ref. 13.]

[15] On the therapeutics of acute diseases. In the extant works of Aretaeus the Cappadocian. Ed. and trans. Adams, F. The Sydenham Society, London, 1856.

[16] Marx, H. Klin Wochenschr, 24/24, 18–21, 1946.

[17] Lewy, A. J., Kern, H. A., Rosenthal, N. E. and Wehr, T. A. Am. J. Psychiatry, 139, 1496–1498, 1982.

[18] Rosenthal, N. E., Sack, D. A., Skwerer, R. G. et al. J. Biol. Rhythms, 3, 101–120, 1988.

[19] Garfield, E. Current Contents Life Sciences, 31, 3–9. 1988.

[20] Rosenthal, N. E., Sack, D. A., and Carpenter, C. J. et al. Am. J. Psychiatry, 142, 163–170, 1985.

[21] Wirz-Justice, A., Buchelli, C. and Graw, P. et al, Acta Psychiatr. Scand., 74, 193–304, 1986.

[22] Isaacs. G., Stainer, D. S. and Sensky, T. E. et al. J. Affective Disord., 14, 13–19, 1988.

[23] Terman, M. J. Biol. Rhythms, 3, 155–172, 1988.

[24] Wirz-Justice, A., Schmid, A. C. and Graw, P. *et al. Experientia*, **43**, 574–576, 1987.

[25] Terman, M., Terman, J. S. and Quitkin, F. M. *et al., Neuropsychopharmacology*, **2**, 1–22, 1989.

[26] Reiter, R. J. In: Wurtman R., Baum, M. J. and Potts, J. T. (eds), The Medical and Biological Effects of Light. *Ann. N.Y. Acad. Sci.*, **453**, 215–230, 1985.

[27] Lewy, A. J., Sack, R. L. and Miller, L. S. *et al. Science*, **235**, 352–354, 1987.

[28] Terman, M., Quitkin, F. M. and Terman, J. S. *et al. Psychopharmacol. Bull.*, **23**, 354–357, 1987.

[29] James, S. P., Wehr, T. A. and Sack, D. A. *et al., Brit. J. Psychiatry*, **147**, 424–428, 1985.

[30] Hellekson, C. J., Kline, J. A. and Rosenthal, N. E. *Am. J. Psychiatry*, **143**, 1035–1037, 1986.

[31] Skewerer, R. G., Jacobsen, F. M. and Duncan, C. C. *et al. J. Biol. Rhythms*, **3**, 135–154, 1988.

[32] Kripke, D. F. In: Wurtman, R., Baum, M. J. and Potts, J. T. (eds), The Medical and Biological Effects of Light, *Ann. N.Y. Acad. Sci.*, **453**, 270–281, 1985.

[33] Thompson, C., Stinson, D. and Smith, A. *Lancet*, **ii**, 703–706, 1990.

[34] Lewy, A. J., Wehr, T. A. and Goodwin, F. K. *et al. Lancet*, **i**, 383–384, 1981.

[35] Wehr, T. A., Jacobson, F. M. and Sack, D. A. *et al. Arch. Gen. Psychiatry*, **43**, 870–875, 1986.

[36] Rosenthal, N. E., Jack, D. A. and Jacobsen, F. M. *et al. J. Neurol. Transm.* (suppl.), **21**, 257–267, 1986.

[37] Rosenthal, N. E., Jacobsen, F. M and Sack, D. A. *et al. Am. J. Psychiatry*, **145**, 52–56, 1988.

[38] O'Rourke, D. A., Wurtman, J. J. and Brezinski, A. *et al. Psychopharm. Bull.*, **23**, 358–359, 1989.

[39] Arendt, J., Broadway, J. and Folkard, S. *et al.* In: Thompson, C. and Silverstone, T. (eds), 'Seasonal Affective Disorder', pp. 133–144, CNS, London, 1989.

▓ BEHAVIOR

SUICIDE CHECK

Advances in biopsychiatry may lead to lab tests for self-destructive behavior and other mental disorders

By CHRISTINE GORMAN

IT IS A CRISIS THAT FEW IN THE EMERgency room are equipped to handle. Concerned friends have just arrived with a frightened man in his 20s. He is not bleeding. Nothing's broken. Yet he cannot stop crying, and his companions are worried that he might kill himself. Is he just having a bad night, or is he likely to do himself harm? When it comes to determining an individual's desire to commit suicide, physicians rely heavily on experience and intuition. There has never been a laboratory test that doctors could order that would help them measure the risk more precisely.

That predicament seems likely to change in the next few years, as scientists learn more about the biochemistry of behavior. Some of the latest research—parts of which were presented at last week's meeting of the Society for Neuroscience in Miami—suggests that measuring the levels of certain chemicals in the brain can identify those people with a biological predisposition to self-destruction. "More than 95% of the people who commit suicide show these changes in the brain [at autopsy]," says Dr. John Mann of the Columbia University College of Physicians and Surgeons in New York City. "But the biochemical abnormality is there even in those who attempt to kill themselves. And

it is most pronounced in those who make the most dangerous attempts."

A lab test for suicide—the eighth leading cause of death in the U.S.—sounds incredible. Yet it is only one of the promising developments being pursued in the hot new field of biological psychiatry. What was once the purview of priests and analysts, who try to probe the mind by listening and observing, is now a frontier for neuroscientists, who use blood tests, brain scans and spinal taps. Psychiatrists at some research centers are already using these tools to distinguish among types of depression and schizophrenia, and predict with some degree of certainty the best course of treatment for their patients.

There have been setbacks. Despite compelling evidence that manic depression, a mental illness characterized by extreme mood swings, runs in families, no one has isolated the genes responsible for the disorder. Several candidates have been identified, only to be discarded. But while the geneticists have hit a snag, the brain chemists are moving faster than anyone thought possible, and have produced an impressive array of practical results.

From *Time, 144,* pp. 65–66, November 28, 1994. Copyright © 1994 Time Inc. Reprinted by permission.

Nowhere is this bonanza more apparent than with the research into the brain chemical called serotonin. One of the many signaling chemicals used by nerve cells to communicate with one another, serotonin is intricately linked to those parts of the brain that affect mood and impulse control. Nerve cells manufacture, release and absorb serotonin in quick bursts that ripple throughout the cerebrum. Although no one understands quite why, low levels of the chemical are associated with clinical depression. As a result, serotonin has become the target for a whole new genre of antidepressant drugs—the most popular of which is Prozac—that keep it active in the brain longer than usual.

Not everyone who is depressed attempts suicide; nor does a low serotonin level automatically doom a person to self-destruction. According to Mann and his colleagues at Columbia and the New York State Psychiatric Institute, changes must occur in specific regions of the brain to create that danger. Their research, presented at last week's Neuroscience meeting, focuses on a section of white matter—the orbital cortex—that sits just above the eyes and modulates impulse control. In autopsies of 20 suicide victims, Mann's group found that in almost every case, not enough serotonin had reached that key portion of the brain. The neurological failsafes that normally prevent people from hurting themselves seem to have been disabled. "Having the biochemical deficiency alone is not enough to make you commit suicide," Mann says. "Stress alone is not enough. But if you have the pre-existing condition and you pile on a major depression or a substance-abuse problem, then the chances go up."

Other research on people who have survived suicide attempts suggests that some of the biochemical changes are temporary and may peak in the weeks prior to the act. If that finding holds up, it could lead to a lab test that would identify those who are most immediately vulnerable. Studies show that half of all people who commit suicide visit their doctor in the month prior to their death. Most of the time the physician finds nothing medically wrong with them and sends them home. Doctors may someday be able to give these people a blood test that measures their body's ability to manufacture serotonin. Those whose capacity is impaired would be considered at greatest risk of hurting themselves.

The swift pace of biopsychiatric research has led to new tests for other mental illnesses. Leslie Prichep and her colleagues at the New York University Medical Center in Manhattan have retooled the electroencephalogram, or EEG,

which measures the electrical activity of the brain, to identify various subtypes of schizophrenia, depression and other disorders. Their goal is to eliminate some of the trial and error that psychiatrists typically have to go through when prescribing pills for their patients. They have already seen results with obsessive-compulsive disorder, or OCD, a condition in which people continuously repeat the same sequence of thoughts or behaviors. By performing sophisticated computer analyses of patients' EEG readings, they have been able to describe distinct patterns that distinguish those who are more likely to respond to drugs from those who are not.

The rush to embrace biological explanations of human behavior is not without its critics. "We have some links, but they don't prove cause and effect," says Dr. Donald Mender, author of The Myth of Neuropsychiatry. It's the same statistical quandary that basketball coaches face all the time. Nearly all great male hoopsters tower over 6 ft. 5 in. But that does not mean that all tall men are great basketball players. Says Mender: "The danger lies in seeing people as if they were machines."

There is also a risk that research results could be abused. If suicide is linked to low serotonin levels, does that mean that violence against others can also be tied to depleted stores of the brain chemical? Scientists who are looking into that possibility are worried that their work could be used to label troubled children as incorrigible and excuse the lack of services designed to help them. "It's almost impossible to discuss scientifically," says Dr. Frederick Goodwin, former director of the National Institute of Mental Health. "People always overinterpret the science in this area."

Despite these concerns, the push to discover the biological markers of behavior shows no signs of abating. No lab test will ever solve the suicide crisis. But by raising the question—and by giving doctors another way to verify their suspicions—it could save lives. —**With reporting by Dick Thompson/ Washington**

Did Prozac Make Him Do It?

ON THE MORNING OF SEPT. 14, 1989, JOSEPH WESBECKER—AN OUT-OF-work pressman—walked into the printing plant of his former employer, the Standard Gravure company of Louisville, Kentucky, and began blasting away with an AK-47. When the shooting was over, 12 people were wounded and nine dead—including Wesbecker, from a self-inflicted pistol shot.

What makes this tragedy different from other mass shootings is that for a month before the incident, Wesbecker, who suffered from depression, had been taking Prozac. In a case being heard by a Louisville jury, survivors and the families of the victims are trying to prove that Prozac—the most widely prescribed antidepressant—triggered the rampage, and they are seeking damages from Prozac's manufacturer, Eli Lilly.

> **Joseph Wesbecker shot 20, then killed himself.**

Prozac is the most popular of a new class of drugs that treat depression by increasing levels of the brain chemical serotonin. Doctors have known for some time that raising serotonin levels can positively affect a patient's mood, but they can't always be sure that the drug will have the desired effect.

In this case, the plaintiffs are trying to show that Lilly knew that some patients became suicidal or agitated during clinical trials. Lilly lawyers will argue that Wesbecker's was not a sudden, Prozac-induced rage but rather a carefully plotted attack, and that the plaintiffs' claim lacks scientific merit.

Psychiatrists are keeping a close eye on the Louisville case, the first of 160 civil suits against Lilly to make it to trial. After the shooting, the Citizens Commission on Human Rights, a group founded by the Church of Scientology, tried to capitalize on the Louisville incident as part of an all-out campaign to discredit Prozac and psychiatry.

It hasn't worked. In 1991 the FDA denied a CCHR petition to take Prozac off the market, and an FDA panel found "no credible evidence" of a link between the drug and violent behavior. In 56 criminal cases, defendants who tried the Prozac-made-me-do-it defense have been equally unsuccessful. But a verdict against Prozac might, unfortunately, scare patients off the best available medicine, says Louisville psychiatrist Dr. David Moore. "The courtroom is no place for finding scientific truth." —**By Lawrence Mondi. Reported by Gideon Gil/Louisville**

Phobias: Is There a Way Out?

New insights into anxiety are bringing fresh hope to the millions of people whose lives are blighted by phobias

Helen Saul

WHEN Sylvia Hadley goes out to finish her Christmas shopping she will put on her shoes and coat and walk out the door with one of her relatives. But preparing for the festive season was not always this simple. For many years she had agoraphobia, and even the thought of going shopping could send her into a panic. She would tidy up at home, lock the doors and windows, put on her hat and coat, then take them off again, do some more tidying, check the doors and windows and try again. This routine could go on for hours before she finally plucked up the courage to dash outside, scurry down to the shops and then rush back home.

Christmas can be a particularly difficult time for people with phobias. Like Hadley, agoraphobics find that large crowds make public places such as shopping malls more worrying than usual, while social phobics may freeze at the thought of parties. Claustrophobics worry about squeezing onto exceptionally busy trains and buses, and microphobics, afraid of passing on germs, may dread having to entertain friends and family.

People uncomfortable in open spaces, and those worried by social gatherings are deemed to have "complex" phobias in that many complicated factors contribute to their development. The complex phobias are surprisingly common and they can be devastating. Agoraphobia, for example, affects one person in twenty at some stage in their lives and can confine sufferers to their homes for years. This kind of reaction can seriously damage marriages, work prospects and social lives.

But not all phobias wreak so much damage. People with simple or specific phobias, often to completely harmless objects such as velvet or cotton wool, tend not to be as generally anxious or demoralised as the person with agoraphobia. But specific phobias are even more common: studies suggest that between 8 and 40 per cent of the population have a severe dislike of something.

Until recently, people with both kinds of phobia attracted little public sympathy. And according to Isaac Marks, a psychiatrist, at the Institute of Psychiatry in London, and an authority on fear and anxiety, phobias are still not taken seriously enough. "People with phobias are often told to pull themselves together. They are ashamed of their phobias and try to hide them," he says. Fortunately, the tide is turning as awareness increases and people begin to take the treatment of phobias more seriously. New ways of thinking about phobias are producing cheap treatments that work fast.

Recent research shows a single session of psychotherapy can be just as good as a course lasting weeks or months. Sometimes even leaving the patient to read a book or follow a computer program unsupervised gives similar success rates. Some researchers back physiological models to explain some phobias and believe that drugs can help the phobic overcome their fears, while others think that finding the genetic basis is the way forward. There are also those who think that hormone levels and exposure to

> 'People with phobias are often told to pull themselves together. They are ashamed of their phobias and try to hide them'

artificial light may explain certain phobic disorders. One of the key pieces of work driving this new research and the search for treatments comes from Marks and Randolph Nesse, psychiatrist at the University of Michigan, Ann Arbor. They collaborated on an unpublished paper that suggests anxiety is a normal defence mechanism, comparable to the immune system. Anxiety acts against macro threats in the way the immune system acts against pathogens, they say.

Normal reaction?

Both systems involve carefully regulated physiological changes, and any disruption will prompt an exaggerated response. Phobias can therefore be understood as an excessive expression of a normal response to anxiety. Marks and Nesse say the anxiety system developed as a result of natural selection and different responses originated as a defence to a particular threat. People who are afraid of heights, for example, may "freeze" when they are confronted by a sudden drop, thereby reducing the chances of a fall. Fear of blood or injury, unlike other phobias, makes blood pressure drop and can make people faint. This could cut down on blood loss and the lack of movement may deter predators from further attacks.

Nesse and Marks argue that fear increases Darwinian fitness in times of danger and they believe there is a normal distribution of anxiety in the population with phobics at the far end of that normal spectrum. The theory applies to both complex and specific phobias. Marks believes the explanation also has a direct bearing on the treatment of all kinds of anxiety. "Some psychiatrists, more in the States than here, splash anti-anxiety drugs around for any anxiety. We feel that one wants to consider whether the anxiety is normal or not. If it's normal, we wouldn't want to treat it. Drug treatment can be harmful in preventing people facing up to and dealing with particular problems."

One limitation of this theory is that while it attempts to explain why humans evolved as a species with the capacity for anxiety, it doesn't address the question of why only some people have an excessive response. Or why there are twice as many female as male agora-phobics, while social phobia is more common in men. These questions are being considered by research into genetics, biochemistry and conditioning.

The classic theory to explain specific phobias is one of Pavlovian conditioning to an unpleasant stimulus. In a highly unethical experiment on "Little Albert" in the 1920s, a small boy was given a fluffy toy rabbit to play with. Then someone crept up and hit a gong behind him. Not surprisingly, the little boy associated the rabbit with the shock he received and refused to play with the toy again.

More sophisticated experiments by Sue Mineka, professor of psychology at Northwestern University, Evanston, Illinois demonstrated that monkeys reared in the laboratory could be conditioned to fear snakes by looking at a split video screen showing a scared adult monkey on one side and a snake on the other. The same approach failed to induce a fear of leaves or flowers, thus backing up the evolution theory because a snake is a very real threat for a monkey.

In another of her experiments she showed that it may be possible to "inoculate" monkeys against developing phobias

From *New Scientist*, 140, pp. 23–25, December 18, 1993. Reprinted with permission of IPC Magazines Ltd.

A simple explanation for complex phobias

SIMPLE, or specific, phobias are an intense dread of specific objects or situations. They include phobias about animals, which almost invariably start between the ages of three and eight, and may continue for many years. Other specific phobias may start in early adulthood. People feel anxious at the thought of certain situations and avoid these situations where possible. Specific phobias are more common in women than men.

Examples include:

Arachnophobia—
fear of spiders

Trypanphobia—
fear of blood or needle injury

Cynophobia—
fear of dogs

Aerophobia—
fear of draughts or of flying

Triskaidekaphobia—
fear of the number 13

COMPLEX phobias start later in life, agoraphobia typically starts between the ages of 18 and 28 and social phobia between 11 and 16. They tend to cause people far more distress and disability than simple phobias. Agoraphobia is more common in women, social phobia is more common in men. The psychological disturbance is complex and long lasting. An adult who has been suffering from for a year tends to change little over the next five years, but many social phobias improve gradually with time.

Examples:

Agoraphobia—
fear of open spaces and public places

Social phobia—
fear of a situation in which the person might be watched by other people, such as restaurants, dinner parties, public transport

by first introducing them to snakes next to a picture of a contented adult monkey. This sort of research led to the long-standing principle behind many treatments: that gradual and increasing exposure to the feared object will desensitise or habituate the person to it and their fear will subside.

Conventional programmes which used this approach often took place over weeks or months. Newer research suggests good results can be obtained much more quickly. A controversial project at London Zoo, "The Friendly Spider Programme", claims consistently to cure 36 people out of groups of 40, of their fear of spiders in a single afternoon. The groups listen to talks on phobias and spiders. This is followed by a group session of hypnosis lasting about half an hour, and the climax is a trip to the Spider House.

Elsewhere studies on the value of single session intervention are also showing encouraging results. Lars-Göran Öst from the University of Uppsala in Sweden and Paul Salkovskis, a psychologist at the University of Oxford's Warneford Hospital, found that after a single session of up to three hours with a therapist, 71 per cent of people with arachnophobia showed significant improvement. This improvement was still apparent a year later. In sessions with the therapist, patients had increasing contact with a spider until they could allow it to crawl on their back or in their hair with little anxiety.

Öst and Salkovskis's research showed that only 6 per cent of people left to follow a self-treatment plan achieved similar levels of success. But in another study, Marks found self-help as successful as therapist intervention. Phobic patients were randomly allocated either to treatment with a therapist, or given a copy of a book, which contains a step-by-step self-help guide. The third group sat at a computer and worked through their fears with the help of some special software. This was designed to identify the user's fear by prompting them to describe their anxiety through answering a number of questions. From this information the software suggests tasks centred around the feared object or environment to be completed before the next session.

To Marks's surprise, the success rates among patients in the three groups was almost identical. But he warns that it is not clear whether the success rates would be as good if either the book or computer were used without the initial psychiatric assessment. "We'd like to know whether it would work if people came in off the street and just sat at the computer." He

also points out that very little is known about how behaviourial therapy works.

Salkovskis, however, believes that he does have an answer and that faults in the cognitive process are to blame for panic disorders and phobias. He cites the example of shoppers in the supermarket. Most are thinking about what to buy and which queue to stand in and are unaware of a temporarily increased heart rate or slight breathlessness. Phobic patients tend to focus their attention internally, are more aware of bodily sensations and are more likely to misinterpret those sensations as catastrophic.

Vicious circle

If these people believe a racing heart or breathlessness means they are about to have a heart attack or suffocate, they are naturally anxious. The anxiety fuels the heart rate and a vicious circle sets in which can end in a full-scale panic attack.

An interesting feature, Salkovskis says, is why, after repeated incidents that fail to result in a heart attack, sufferers cling onto their misinterpretation. He believes techniques used by patients to protect themselves, such as sitting down or going outside for air, merely serve to bolster faulty perceptions. "Instead of thinking 'I didn't faint', they think 'I was just a fraction of an inch off fainting'. The episode becomes an example of a time they nearly passed out, and it reinforces their belief."

Salkovskis showed that all-verbal sessions that counter these beliefs have a big impact on panic attacks. He worked on a trial comparing four different treatments. The first group of patients received cognitive therapy based around a series of discussion sessions designed to convince the patient that they are not going to have a heart attack, the second group remained on the waiting list and received no treatment, the third group took the antidepressant drug imipramine, and the fourth group learnt applied relaxation, a specially modified form of relaxation for use during a panic attack. Following normal practice, he prescribed weekly psychotherapy sessions over 12 weeks, and drugs for much longer. All three active treatment groups showed more improvements than the control but, both in the long and short term, cognitive therapy was the most effective form of treatment, he says. At the end of treatment, people who were still misinterpreting bodily sensations were more likely to have relapsed a year later.

Some researchers, such as Myrna Weissman, professor of epidemiology in psychiatry at Columbia University, New

York are looking for a genetic explanation of these reactions. Weissman says agoraphobia and panic are "highly familial". Many large-scale studies in the US show that around two per cent of the population have experienced panic attacks at some point in their lives. Other researchers estimated that people with first-degree relatives such as mothers, brothers and sisters, who have experienced a panic attack are up to ten times more likely to have an attack than someone picked at random. And this correlation is even more noticeable with identical twins.

Weissman says she "couldn't begin to speculate" on the mechanism by which genes could increase vulnerability. She says panic disorder, like diabetes and heart disease, is considered a complex gene disorder in which several genes act together to contribute only a portion of the individual's susceptibility. But because it is transmitted from one generation to the next with reasonably high lifetime risks among first-degree relatives, the disorder can be studied by looking for similar segments in the chromosomes, she says. Finding the responsible gene or genes will be only one step to uncovering the full story of the psychopathology.

Other researchers are looking for a physiological explanation of phobias. David Nutt at the University of Bristol, for example, reviewed the neurochemical model in *The British Journal of Psychiatry* last year. In the 1960s, researchers showed that an intravenous infusion of sodium lactate produces panic in susceptible individuals, but not in normal subjects. No one knows how it works, but a possible explanation is that sodium lactate is broken down to carbon dioxide in the blood stream. The carbon dioxide permeates the central nervous system and stimulates chemoreceptors in the brain to increase the respiratory rate and promotes a panic response. A more recent suggestion is that lactate simply increases the uptake of serotonin by neurones in the brain, which reduces the neurotransmitter's calming effect.

Nutt says people who suffer from panic attacks may have a system that overreacts to threats. It was shown in the 1940s that anxious patients produce more lactate during exercise than less anxious people in the same situation. More recently, a report in *The Journal of Affective Disorders* (1990, vol 19, p 229) suggested panic patients have an abnormal response even

to the physiological challenge of standing up. Features of their cardiovascular system, such as heart rate, also show more variability than normal. Nutt says this points to a problem in the regulation of their autonomic response—and a biological cause of panic.

He believes drug treatment should be used first for all types of anxiety. "We're getting more and more appreciation of how effective drug treatments are. They're cost-effective and easy to use. Patients have a slightly higher relapse rate than with other forms of therapy, but two-thirds do well on drug treatment alone." In particular Nutt cites the

'Phobic patients tend to focus their attention internally, are more aware of bodily sensations and are more likely to misinterpret those sensations as catastrophic'

antidepressant used by Salkovskis in his trial, imipramine, which blocks the effect of lactate, and to newer serotonin reuptake inhibitors as successful treatments for the anxiety brought on by phobias.

Pregnant pause

Neither conditioning, genetics nor biology explain all features of phobias and many questions remain. One former agoraphobic, Mary Dwarka, set out to find why agoraphobia is so common among women by questioning a group of 175 women, paying particular attention to gynaecological events. Interestingly she found that of 55 women who became pregnant, almost half said they were free from symptoms while pregnant.

Nutt says the finding is one more argument in favour of the involvement of neurotransmitters in phobias. Pregnancy increases the levels of some steroids, in particular progesterone, the metabolites of which effect the brain, he says.

Even the role of artificial lighting in agoraphobia is being explored. Biochemist John Smith from the University of Bradford is working with Arnold Wilkins, an applied psychologist at the Medical Research Council in Cambridge. They believe that low frequency fluorescent

lighting in offices could cause stress in some patients and trigger biochemical changes in the brain that could lead to agoraphobia.

Wilkins is identifying patients with agoraphobia and subjecting them to various frequencies of fluorescent lighting. Smith then measures changes in the cortisol level, which is an indicator of stress. The work is in the very early stages, but is "encouraging" so far, says Smith.

Still more controversial work centres on possible physical causes of the problem. Harold Levinson, former associate professor of psychiatry at New York University Medical Center, says physical problems such as a defect in the inner ear are involved in nine out of ten phobias and panic attacks. The inner ear is normally responsible for balance. Levinson says all the drugs that have been helpful to phobics, such as the benzodiazepines and antidepressants, also reduce motion sickness, which suggests they work on the inner ear system controlling balance.

He says there is a strong link between dyslexia and phobias: people with one are more prone to the other. The underlying explanation, he says is a defect in the inner ear. "People with agoraphobia can't stand crowds. It isn't that they are afraid of people, but where there is a lot of activity and noise, they get sensory overload and feel dizzy," he says.

Current research into phobias is raising many questions. But it is also providing some comfort for phobics. Extrapolation from the evolutionary theory suggests there may be people who are equally disadvantaged because they have too little anxiety. Nesse says the anxiety that drives us to work for exams or stops us arguing with the boss can be helpful. "It would be interesting to look at a group of secondary school children, identify those with the least anxiety and follow them up to see what kind of trouble they got into."

Further, anxiety may make people more desirable as friends. Many highly anxious people try desperately hard to please. As Nesse points out: "Social phobics may be very attentive to the needs of others. They are very often very attractive people." So there is a good chance that some of the more fun people you meet at parties during the festive season find such events a frightening experience. □

Helen Saul *is a freelance writer specialising in medical and health issues.*

Current Perspectives on Panic and Panic Disorder

Martin M. Antony, Timothy A. Brown, and David H. Barlow

The emotions of panic, fear, and anxiety are familiar to anyone who has been faced with some threat or danger. However, for some people, rushes of intense fear (i.e., panic attacks) can occur out of the blue, without any obvious trigger, particularly following periods of stress. Furthermore, in a subset of these people, spontaneous panic attacks occur frequently and independently of stressful life events.

A diagnosis of panic disorder (PD) is given to individuals who experience panic attacks frequently (i.e., more than four times per month) or who worry excessively about the occurrence of these attacks. Typical panic symptoms include physical sensations such as breathlessness, dizziness, palpitations, trembling, nausea, and sweating and cognitive symptoms such as fears of dying, going crazy, and doing something uncontrolled.

As a result, many PD patients develop agoraphobia, a fear of situations in which escape—should a panic attack occur—might be difficult or embarrassing. Agoraphobics tend to avoid crowds, driving, public transportation, large stores, enclosed places, traveling, being home alone, and, in extreme cases, leaving the house. To illustrate the impact of PD on a patient's life, consider the following case history:

Sally experienced her first panic attack out of the blue 3 weeks after completing her senior year in college. She had just finished a job interview and was meeting some friends for dinner. In the restaurant, she began to feel dizzy. Within a few seconds, her heart was pounding, and she was feeling breathless, as though she might pass out. Her friends noticed that she did not look well and offered to drive her home. Sally suggested they stop at the hospital emergency room instead. Although she felt better by the time they arrived at the hospital, and tests indicated nothing wrong, Sally experienced a similar episode a week later while at a movie.

Sally began to wonder if she had some heart problem not detected by the hospital staff. She found herself scanning her body for unusual sensations. She also felt uneasy about going back to the same restaurant and movie theater where the attacks occurred.

Her attacks became more and more frequent. Before long, she was having several attacks per week. In addition, she constantly worried about having attacks. She began to avoid exercise and other activities that produced physical sensations. She also noticed the attacks were worse when she was alone. She began to avoid driving, shopping in large stores, and eating in all restaurants. Some weeks she avoided leaving the house completely. Sally stopped looking for work, fearing that she would be unable to stay at her job in the event of a panic attack.

Research focused on PD and its treatment has increased dramatically in the past 10 years for several reasons. First, recent epidemiological studies estimate that PD occurs in almost 2 out of 100 people. Second, PD can lead to marked impairment in social and occupational functioning, and suicidal ideation and suicide attempts may be more prevalent than in other psychiatric disorders, including major depression. Finally, agoraphobia is an enormous burden on the health care system. Figures from 1988 estimate the average medical costs (e.g., for tests, medications, hospitalizations) per patient in the first 9 years after PD onset to be over $10,000. With the rapidly increasing costs of health care in the United States, these figures will continue to rise.

HISTORICAL BACKGROUND

Historically, panic attacks and agoraphobia have been described and explained within a psychoanalytic framework. For example, the 1968 edition of the American Psychiatric Association's *Diagnostic and Statistical Manual of Mental Disorders* (DSM-II)[1] included diagnoses such as *anxiety neurosis* and *phobic neurosis* to describe people who now would receive diagnoses of PD with or without agoraphobia.

The 1980 edition of DSM, DSM-III,[2] was intended to provide an "atheoretical" description of psychiatric disorders. To this end, terms reflecting psychoanalytic theory, such as *neurosis*, were no longer emphasized in the text. DSM-III included a PD category to describe the experience of frequent, spontaneous panic attacks. Although a relationship between panic attacks and agoraphobic avoidance was recognized, agoraphobia was viewed as primary when the two occurred together. In other words, DSM-III implied that panic attacks were a manifestation of agoraphobia.

In 1987, with the publication of DSM-III-R,[3] the relationship between panic and agoraphobia was

Martin M. Antony is a doctoral candidate at SUNY-Albany. **Timothy A. Brown** is Associate Director of the Phobia and Anxiety Disorders Clinic. **David H. Barlow** is Distinguished Professor of Psychology at SUNY-Albany and Director of the Phobia and Anxiety Disorders Clinic. Address correspondence to David H. Barlow, Center for Stress and Anxiety Disorders, University at Albany, State University of New York, 1535 Western Ave., Albany, NY 12203.

From *Current Directions in Psychological Science*, 1, pp. 79–82. Copyright ©1992 American Psychological Society. Reprinted with permission of Cambridge University Press.

reversed, such that PD was given priority. This change was consistent with recent research demonstrating that agoraphobic avoidance tends to develop in response to unexpected (spontaneous) panic attacks.[4] In DSM-III-R, a person who meets the criteria for PD is assigned a diagnosis of PD with or without agoraphobia, as opposed to agoraphobia with or without panic attacks, as was the case in DSM-III.

CURRENT ETIOLOGICAL MODELS

Current research on panic and PD is dominated by two broad schools within psychology: biological and cognitive-behavioral. Although numerous theories of panic have been proposed recently, most of them have their basis in early statements of either Klein's biological model of panic[5] or Goldstein and Chambless's cognitive-behavioral *fear-of-fear* model.[6]

Biological Models

The biological approach dates back to the 1960s, when Klein observed that the tricyclic antidepressant imipramine effectively blocked panic attacks but not the anticipatory anxiety accompanying panic. Klein and colleagues[7] concluded that panic and anxiety are qualitatively distinct.

Furthermore, in Klein's model, panic attacks are viewed as surges of autonomic arousal, possibly originating in a dysfunctional noradrenergic neurotransmitter system. Although people often misinterpret these surges as dangerous, the model considers such misinterpretations independent of the surges themselves. In contrast to panic, anticipatory anxiety and agoraphobic avoidance are presumed to be mediated by psychological processes such as fearful interpretations of the panic sensations and attempts to avoid situations where panic attacks might be especially uncomfortable.

Since Klein's model was first articulated, several other biological models have been proposed, hypothesizing specific dysfunctions in noradrenergic activity and in other transmitter systems. In addition, theorists have suggested specific brain regions that might be relevant to panic. Evidence often presented in favor of biological models of panic includes studies showing that (a) PD is somewhat heritable, (b) PD patients respond fearfully to biological challenges that directly or indirectly affect noradrenergic activity (e.g., carbon dioxide inhalation, sodium lactate infusion), (c) patterns of cerebral blood flow are different in PD patients and non-anxious subjects, (d) noradrenergic metabolites differ between PD patients and non-anxious subjects, and (e) noradrenergic reuptake blockers such as imipramine are effective for treating PD.

Cognitive-Behavioral Models

Goldstein and Chambless developed the fear-of-fear model to account for panic, agoraphobic avoidance, and their relationship. In this model, the focus of agoraphobic fear is not the external situation avoided by the agoraphobic, but rather the physical sensations and possible consequences of panic. The initial panic attack occurs following a period of stress. A subset of people interpret the initial attack as the beginning of an impending disaster and develop a fear of panic sensations (e.g., racing heart, dizziness) via classical conditioning, just as a single pairing of nausea with a particular food can lead to a conditioned taste aversion upon subsequent exposure to that food. Thus, panic attacks are viewed as conditioned responses to somatic sensations: The patient learns to respond fearfully to certain physical sensations (e.g., heart rate fluctuations) that might not even be noticed, let alone feared, by a non-anxious person.

Findings often cited in favor of cognitive-behavioral models of panic include research showing that PD patients evidence heightened anxiety focused on panic sensations, information processing biases for attending to threat-related cues, and heightened awareness of certain physical sensations such as heart beats. Moreover, research demonstrating the efficacy of cognitive-behavioral treatment (e.g., exposure to feared cues, cognitive therapy) for PD and agoraphobia has been offered in support of cognitive-behavioral models of panic.

Since Goldstein and Chambless first published their model of panic, numerous cognitive-behavioral models of panic have been developed. Although each views panic as a fearful response to certain somatic symptoms, the models differ on several subtle points. For example, some theorists (e.g., Clark[8]) emphasize the cognitive aspects of panic, such as catastrophic misinterpretations leading to the panic response.

Like Goldstein and Chambless, Clark believes that panic attacks are fearful responses to physical sensations. However, according to Clark, classical conditioning alone cannot account for panic. If the emotion of fear were, in fact, classically conditioned to occur following the perception of relevant sensations, one might expect a panic attack to occur each time these sensations are experienced. In fact, PD patients do not panic every time the sensations occur. For example, many patients do not fear the sensations when they are exercising. According to Clark, panic attacks occur only when people catastrophically misinterpret the sensations. This process is most likely to occur when there is no obvious, benign cause for the sensations. For example, a racing heart in the absence of obvious triggers might be interpreted as an impending heart attack. Such a catastrophic misinterpretation would lead to apprehension, fear, and exacerbation of symptoms, culminating in a panic attack.

Clark emphasizes that cognitions need not be conscious to affect behavior. Rather, the process of misinterpreting sensations may be quick, automatic, and outside awareness, leading to panic attacks that appear spontaneous.

Clark, like many theorists, suggests that panic and generalized anxiety are qualitatively similar, differing only in intensity. This view is not common to all current cognitive-behavioral models of panic, however. Other theorists, including the present authors, argue that the experience of panic is distinct from generalized anxiety.

An Integrated Model of Panic

Recently, Barlow[9] has attempted to integrate several theoretical approaches into a unified theory of panic. Because panic and anxiety are essentially emotional phenomena, this model incorporates the work of emotion theorists such as Lang and Izard, who distinguish, in different ways, between the experiences of fear and anxiety.

In this model, fear is a tightly organized, cohesive emotion, stored in memory and accessed under certain conditions, including imminent threat. Designed to deal with immediate danger, fear is therefore accompanied by an intense desire to escape the situation. In contrast, anxiety (i.e., anxious apprehension) is viewed as a loosely structured, cognitive-affective network stored in memory, with the purpose of "preparing" the individual to deal with the possibility of future threat. Anxiety involves a tendency toward vigilance and "freezing" and is characterized by high levels of negative affect, a sense that negative events are unpredictable and uncontrollable, and a rapidly shifting focus of attention.

Unlike Klein, Barlow equates panic with the emotion of fear. In his model, the initial panic attack occurs in vulnerable individuals, following a period of stress. This attack is called a *false alarm* because it typically occurs in the absence of real threat. Biological factors, including a possible genetic predisposition expressed in part as an easily aroused sympathetic nervous system, are believed to make some people more vulnerable than others to the experience of panic attacks in response to stress.

Many people who experience an occasional panic attack attribute the symptoms to some external or benign cause. However, a subset of infrequent panickers may have a psychological vulnerability to develop PD. This psychological vulnerability consists of a learned tendency to view events, in general, and emotions, in particular, as unpredictable and uncontrollable. In vulnerable individuals, unexpected panic attacks may lead to heightened arousal, shifts in attention, and anxious apprehension over having additional attacks. The process of anxious apprehension itself may lead to additional panic attacks (or *learned alarms*) as internal cues become associated with the original false alarm. Agoraphobic avoidance develops in an attempt to avoid experiencing panic in particular situations.

A potential advantage of this model over earlier conceptualizations is the explicit attempt to define relevant terms such as panic and anxiety. In addition, this model encompasses both biological and cognitive-behavioral contributions.

THE RELATIONSHIP BETWEEN RESEARCH FINDINGS AND PD ETIOLOGY

Unfortunately, the main arguments and research findings used to support cognitive-behavioral and biological models of panic can be explained within either framework and, therefore, provide little insight into the origins of PD.

For example, proponents of the cognitive-behavioral perspective might argue that drugs simply decrease physiological arousal or fluctuating sensations, thereby reducing the intensity of panic triggers (i.e., feared sensations) and resulting in fewer panic attacks in reaction to these sensations. Furthermore, changes in cerebral blood flow and noradrenergic metabolites may be viewed as manifestations of anxiety and perhaps panic, and, by themselves, provide little information regarding the etiology of panic. Finally, psychological theorists have suggested that biological challenges trigger panic in PD patients by eliciting relevant cues. Non-anxious people do not fear these cues and therefore do not panic during these challenges. Interestingly, recent evidence suggests that increasing a PD patient's perceived sense of control over the flow of carbon dioxide can greatly decrease his or her tendency to panic during carbon dioxide inhalation, suggesting that psychological factors are important.[10]

Likewise, evidence favoring cognitive-behavioral approaches is typically unconvincing to strict biological theorists. For example, studies demonstrating heightened fear of panic sensations, attentional biases, and heightened awareness of physical sensations are often viewed as irrelevant to the etiology of panic. Rather, many biological theorists maintain that these phenomena may represent psychological reactions to having several biologically triggered spontaneous attacks. In addition, the efficacy of psychological treatments does not rule out a biological etiology. In fact, many psychologically treated and drug-treated patients still report occasional muffled autonomic surges, although the surges may no longer arouse fear.

Clearly, psychological and biological processes are both involved in PD, but it is difficult to know how these variables relate to the etiology of panic. Experimental paradigms that manipulate the occurrence of panic in the laboratory provide only limited information about the nature of PD because they tell us little about the processes involved in naturally occurring panics. As with any psychological disorder, questions regarding the etiology of PD are best answered by longitudinal studies of panic in the natural environment. Studying people at risk for developing PD (e.g., children of PD patients, infrequent panickers) might explicate causal factors. For example, do catastrophic misinterpretations or information processing biases exist before the development of PD?

Numerous questions remain to be answered. For example, what is the relationship between panic attacks and generalized anxiety? In addition, systematic study and comparison of nonclinical panic (i.e., occasional panic attacks that do not develop into PD), nonfearful panic (i.e., autonomic surges that are not accompanied by fearful cognitions), and panic in PD patients will provide insight into the nature and etiology of PD.

Finally, unidimensional models of panic, such as those derived exclusively within a biological or cognitive-behavioral framework, are viewed increasingly as being inadequate. Instead, researchers have begun to recognize the utility of conceptualizations that integrate emerging concepts from a variety of theoretical frameworks.[9] A better alternative than the question "Is panic caused by biological factors, cognitive factors, or classical conditioning?" might be "How do these factors interact to produce PD?" Furthermore, despite the questions that remain unanswered, biological and cognitive-behavioral models have led to specific, theory-driven treatments that are successful in the majority of PD patients, who previously were among the most difficult patients to treat. Large clinical trials are currently under way, testing the separate and combined effects of cognitive-behavioral and drug treatments.

Notes

1. American Psychiatric Association, *Diagnostic and Statistical Manual of Mental Disorders*, 2nd ed. (Author, Washington, DC, 1968).

2. American Psychiatric Association, *Diagnostic and Statistical Manual of Mental Disorders*, 3rd ed. (Author, Washington, DC, 1980).

3. American Psychiatric Association, *Diagnostic and Statistical Manual of Mental Disorders*, 3rd ed., rev. (Author, Washington, DC, 1987).

4. M.G. Craske and D.H. Barlow, A review of the relationship between panic and avoidance, *Clinical Psychology Review*, 8, 667–685 (1988).

5. D.F. Klein, Anxiety reconceptualized, in *Anxiety: New Research and Changing Concepts*, D.F. Klein and J. Rabkin, Eds. (Raven Press, New York, 1981).

6. A.J. Goldstein and D.L. Chambless, A reanalysis of agoraphobia, *Behavior Therapy*, 9, 47–59 (1978).

7. D.F. Klein and J.M. Gorman, A model of panic and agoraphobic development, *Acta Psychiatrica Scandinavica*, 76, 87–95 (1987).

8. D.M. Clark, A cognitive model of panic attacks, in *Panic: Psychological Perspectives*, S. Rachman and J.D. Maser, Eds. (Erlbaum, Hillsdale, NJ, 1988).

9. D.H. Barlow, *Anxiety and Its Disorders: The Nature and Treatment of Anxiety and Panic* (Guilford Press, New York, 1988).

10. W.C. Sanderson, R.M. Rapee, and D.H. Barlow, The influence of an illusion of control on panic attacks induced via inhalation of 5.5% carbon dioxide-enriched air, *Archives of General Psychiatry*, 46, 157–162 (1989).

Recommended Reading

Barlow, D.H. (1988). *Anxiety and Its Disorders: The Nature and Treatment of Anxiety and Panic* (Guilford Press, New York).

Rachman, S.J., and Maser, J.D. (Eds.). (1988). *Panic: Psychological Perspectives* (Erlbaum, Hillsdale, NJ).

RESEARCHING
PTSD
■■■■■

THE BIOLOGY OF FEAR

*Some new
research offers
startling
insights into
the nature
of PTSD*

NOT LONG AGO, MOST THERAPISTS WHO HEARD A STORY like Albert Grow's would have thought about what his experience in Vietnam did to his relationship with his family, his community and his sense of self. Few would have given much thought to what it did to his biochemistry. That is about to change.

Grow, a policeman in Salem, New Hampshire, came back from Vietnam nearly 30 years ago on a "freezer flight"—a transport plane piled with body bags. At the Boston airport, a woman called him trash and spit in his face. Not long afterward, he punched out two coworkers in a photo lab because they wore black arm bands to honor the Vietnamese dead. After a brief stay on a psychiatric ward, he burned his Marine uniform in his parents' backyard. He avoided war movies. He didn't go to his sister's wedding.

Grow moved to New Hampshire and for decades lived an ordinary life: he finished college, became a

BY KATY BUTLER

This article first appeared in the July/August 1996, *Family Therapy Networker, 20,* pp. 39–45, and is copied here with permission.

husband and a father and coached Little League. Then, during the Gulf War, he watched American missiles explode on television and thought about his 14-year-old son. "I remember saying, You're not going to do it to him. Not him," he says. "It was like somebody took the switch I had turned off and turned it back on."

He began to see the faces of dead young men he had long succeeded in forgetting. He would drive fast for miles, going nowhere, or rent a motel room and sit in the dark for days to keep his anger away from his wife and son. He was put on anti-depressants and anti-anxiety drugs. "I smell something and I'm back in the jungle. I have nightmares and wake up in a pool of perspiration," he says. "I'm very jumpy, almost like I'm on alert."

"I want to learn some new coping skills," says Grow, who is currently an inpatient at the Department of Veterans Affairs medical center at West Haven, Connecticut, a leading site for federal research on the emerging neuroscience of Post-Traumatic Stress Disorder (PTSD). "I can feel anger and rage like *that,* but where's the good stuff? I love my son, but I have a very hard time saying it. I love my wife, but I isolate. I'm tired of the sleepless nights, the dreams. I wish they could do lobotomies and get rid of it."

It is a story that a psychologist trained in talk therapy, not neurobiology, might find comfortingly familiar at first. A good clinician might note Grow's abandonment by his culture after living through a year of horrors; his love for his son; his profound rage against the illusions propagated about war. In the 1970s and 1980s, when men like him began pouring into vets' centers, it was thought that rap groups, talk therapy and alcohol counseling would ultimately resolve things. But talk therapy has not done the trick, neither for veterans nor for many survivors of torture, severe childhood abuse and other trauma.

Now, research psychiatrists at the West Haven VA, Yale, Harvard, UCLA and Dartmouth are documenting what many clinicians have come, over time, to suspect: PTSD is not only an emotional response to troubling events, it is the expression of a persistent disregulation of body and brain chemistry. The research so far suggests that moments of overwhelming terror can alter brain chemistry for decades, and may kill brain cells crucial to memory.

Whether this process can be reversed is not yet known. It is clear, however, that therapists who want to treat PTSD effectively are about to venture into an unfamiliar landscape. Here, all of the signposts are in a foreign language. The metaphors have changed. Talk of fear, rage, family process and dissociation has been replaced by "den-dritic atrophy," "neuronal death" and "glucocorticoids." For therapists whose last exposure to physiology or neurochemistry was a ninth-grade frog autopsy, the new territory may be unnerving. It requires an understanding of systems theory more complex and subtle than anything most family therapists bargained for. But hidden in this uncharted landscape may be ways of alleviating a form of suffering that has only recently come to light.

POST-TRAUMATIC STRESS DISORDER can mean anything from a nightmarish few months to a lifetime of misery. About 5 to 10 percent of us can expect to suffer PTSD symptoms at some point in our lives: 46 percent of women and 65 percent of men who have been raped suffer acute PTSD, as do 21 percent of women and 2 percent of men who are physically attacked. Studies suggest that chronic PTSD—a condition lasting more than 6 months—affects 15 percent of Vietnam combat veterans and 50 percent of Cambodian refugee youth who witnessed genocide.

People with PTSD complain of almost unbearable states of physiological arousal: a hypersensitive emotional trip-wire, an exaggerated startle response and profound distortions of memory. In paradoxical, oscillating fashion, sleeplessness and hypervigilance alternate with numbness and withdrawal; amnesia coexists with flashbacks. These wildly swinging inner states make people

Research so far suggests that moments of overwhelming terror can alter brain chemistry for decades, and may kill brain cells crucial to memory.

feel helpless—they fear they're going crazy and sense that they're not the same person they used to be. This, in turn, can set off a cascade of negative effects, disrupting relationships and driving people to self-medicate with alcohol or drugs.

Six weeks after being raped in Des Moines, Iowa, Nancy Ziegenmayer was so afraid at night that her husband had to escort her from the bedroom to the bathroom. In California, a computer-graphics artist injured while driving on a rain-swept freeway jumped at unexpected noises for months afterward, raged at her husband over trivial things and was too frightened to ride her bike. A New Haven woman who had never told anyone about being raped at 12 by her father appeared at a psychiatric emergency room at the age of 18, overwhelmed by panic attacks. At the first snowfall of the year, a retired Chicago policeman who survived the merciless winter slaughter in Belgium during the Battle of the Bulge becomes unusually quiet and withdrawn; he once told his daughter that he sees blood on the snow.

For more than 100 years, doctors and therapists have wondered whether such symptoms were neurophysiological, emotional or merely a sign of borderline personality disorder or weak character. In the 1860s, doctors described frequent coronary troubles in Civil War veterans as "soldier's heart." Victims of World War I "shell-shock" were thought to be suffering from the physical impact of repeated bombardments. During World War II, "traumatic neurosis" and "battle fatigue" were sometimes explained in symbolic or psychoanalytic terms, as the expression of a conflict between the id's drive to

one-time experience, like being trapped in a hurricane or almost dying in an auto accident," he told *The New York Times*. "All uncontrollable stress can have the same biological impact." Boris Pasternak put it another way in *Doctor Zhivago*: "Our nervous system isn't just a fiction," he wrote. "It's a part of our physical body, and our soul exists in space and is inside us, like the teeth in our mouth. It can't be forever violated with impunity."

pending on the dose. Anyone who has felt the senses quicken and the mind clear in the face of danger knows the benefits of the "adrenaline rush." Raised levels of epinephrine and norepinephrine (the two primary fight-or-flight hormones, also known as adrenaline and noradrenaline) increase the brain's alertness, enhance memory and quicken the heartbeat. People can do extraordinary things, like lift a car that is crushing a loved one or push a baby carriage out

For decades, clinicians have speculated about what was going on inside their clients' brains and nervous systems. But they were Kremlin-watchers, working with hints and hunches, trying to map the contents of a black box they could not open. Now the box is opening.

survive and the superego's sense of patriotic obligation.

The syndrome got a new name after Vietnam, and entered the DSM lexicon in 1980 as Post-Traumatic Stress Disorder. Naming it was one thing, but understanding its mechanics—much less, treating it effectively—was something else again.

For decades, clinicians have listened and speculated about what was going on inside their clients' brains and nervous systems. But they were Kremlinwatchers, trying to map the contents of a black box they could not open. Now the box is opening, thanks to new findings from endocrinology, animal behavior, neurochemistry and computerized brain-imaging devices like Magnetic Resonance Imaging (MRI) and Positron Emission Tomography (PET). It is clear that PTSD is more than a symbolic and existential crisis of meaning and human betrayal.

"Victims of devastating trauma may never be the same, biologically," says Dennis Charney, head of the clinical neuroscience division of the National Center for PTSD at the West Haven VA "It does not matter if it was the incessant terror of combat, torture or repeated abuse in childhood, or a

THE BIOLOGICAL PART OF THE PTSD story is summarized in a dauntingly technical 1995 book called *Neurobiological and Clinical Consequences of Stress* (Lippincott-Raven), written mostly by research psychiatrists funded by the Veterans Administration and the congressionally mandated National Center for PTSD. Their informed speculation is that the body responds to extreme stress by releasing a cascade of cortisol, adrenaline and other hormones that can damage brain cells, impair memory and set in motion a long-lasting and worsening disregulation of the body's complex biochemistry. "The system gets overtaxed and starts flailing," says Harvard trauma researcher Bessel van der Kolk, coauthor of the forthcoming *Traumatic Stress* (Guilford Press). "It's a breakdown of the normal stress response."

Disregulation of the Flight-or-Fight Response

The neurochemical response to extreme stress illustrates the saying that you can have too much of a good thing. Just as a single Martini can stimulate singing and laughter, while a fifth of Jack Daniels brings on depression, brain chemicals can help or harm, de-

of the path of a speeding train.

When stress becomes overwhelming, too much epinephrine and norepinephrine induce confusion and impair learning and memory. At a fatal car crash, one person may display self-possession, while another may "run around like a chicken with its head cut off," or appear "scared out of his wits." At high enough levels in maze-running laboratory rats, the fight-or-flight hormones induce amnesia.

The negative effects of too much epinephrine and norepinephrine are both immediate and delayed. Although the underlying brain chemistry is not understood, repeated adrenaline rushes seem to progressively sensitize brain chemistry, provoking ever-greater floods of adrenaline at lower thresholds. Laboratory animals who have been previously shocked release even more norepinephrine when shocked again. The same increasing vulnerability probably occurs in humans, as the old proverb, "once bitten, twice shy," suggests: a 1993 West Haven study of 66 veterans found that those with childhood histories of physical or sexual abuse were significantly more likely to develop PTSD after combat in Vietnam.

Emotional reactivity is a hallmark of PTSD. Years after trauma, its sufferers startle at the slightest surprise and remain easily frazzled. The fight-or-flight response is disregulated; the nervous system is always on alert. A 1987 study of the urine of PTSD veterans found chronically elevated levels of epinephrine and norepinephrine. Heightened norepinephrine levels were also reported recently by National Institutes of Health researcher Frank Putnam in an ongoing longitudinal study of 80 sexually abused girls aged 7 to 14.

The hyperactive fight-or-flight response can also be activated by specific reminders of trauma: a tape of machine-gun fire, for instance, will provoke sweating, heart-pounding and rising blood pressure in combat veterans with PTSD, but not in matched controls. This mildly disturbing event, it seems, is "read" by the PTSD-affected brain and nervous system as life-threatening, even when the rational mind knows otherwise. Sometimes, one cannot talk oneself out of fear.

doing these studies not quite 10 years ago, some people thought symptoms like flashbacks were completely the products of mentation—that they were just psychological phenomena, and didn't have any basis in the physiology of the brain," says Yale professor and West Haven VA research psychiatrist John Krystal. "Now, it's obvious that's not so."

The experiment suggests a link between flashbacks and high brain levels of norepinephrine, because yohimbine temporarily disables alpha-2 receptors—brain-cell structures that act as tiny governors, slowing and calibrating the release of epinephrine to the brain. Other research has shown that PTSD patients, for reasons not yet understood, have 40 percent fewer of these alpha-2 receptors than normal controls.

The research suggests that the brain chemistry of traumatized people may have changed, so that arousing events—even those dissimilar from the original trauma—can provoke flashbacks. The

Damage to Brain Structure

The most disturbing recent neuroscience suggests that trauma may do long-lasting damage to the hippocampus, a seahorse-shaped structure deep in the brain. Much about the hippocampus remains mysterious, but it is crucial to short-term memory and may play a role in the sorting and storing of long-term memories, a process that takes about a month. (H.M., a famous patient whose hippocampus was removed in the 1950s to mitigate his epilepsy, could remember his past prior to his surgery, but accumulated no additional memories, forgetting new faces or names after a few minutes.)

Three 1995 studies found significant reductions in the size of the hippocampus in traumatized people, compared to nontraumatized controls. The studies used Magnetic Resonance Imaging, (MRI), a relatively new diagnostic device that produces precise, three-dimensional blueprints of the ar-

The body responds to extreme stress by releasing a cascade of cortisol, adrenaline and other hormones that can damage brain cells, impair memory and set in motion a long-lasting and worsening disregulation of the body's complex biochemistry.

Floods of epinephrine and norepinephrine not only increase and accompany emotional and neurobiological arousal, they also can trigger the seizure-like cinematic relivings of trauma known as flashbacks in previously traumatized people. In 1990, researchers at West Haven VA injected 15 veterans suffering from PTSD with yohimbine, a psychoactive drug from the bark of a South American tree that stimulates secretions of norepinephrine. Nontraumatized people usually feel a little heart-pounding under the influence of yohimbine; but nine of the vets suffered panic attacks and six had fullblown flashbacks. One veteran given the drug told researchers he could see a helicopter go down in a bright flash and a trail of smoke. "When we started

result is a vicious circle: arousing the fight-or-flight response can trigger flashbacks, and flashbacks can further intensify the fight-or-flight response.

Other hormonal systems—especially those involving cortisol and brain opiates—continue to function abnormally years after trauma. A 1992 study by Roger Pitman, van der Kolk and others found that veterans with PTSD who watched a 15-minute video of combat scenes from *Platoon* registered a 30-percent drop in pain sensitivity; their brains released natural opiates with the pain-killing equivalent of eight milligrams of morphine. This over-activation of a natural anesthetic response, in the face of something rationally known not to be dangerous, may partly explain the numbness reported by some people with PTSD.

chitecture of the brain. At the West Haven VA, J. Douglas Bremner and Dennis Charney found a 13-percent reduction in left hippocampal volume in 12 male and 5 female survivors of severe childhood abuse with PTSD, compared with carefully matched controls. Their similar study of 26 veterans with PTSD found an 8-percent decrease in right hippocampal volume compared with matched controls. Meanwhile, Murray Stein of the University of California at San Diego measured hippocampal volume in 43 women recruited at a women's health clinic; the 22 with histories of prolonged childhood sexual abuse had hippocampi 5 percent smaller than the 21 nonabused women. Those with the smallest hippocampi, Stein says, displayed the most symptoms of PTSD and dissociation—the tendency to "space out," feel detached from one's body and have unpredictable lapses in memory.

Nobody knows exactly how trauma damages the hippocampus, or whether people with small hippocampi are simply more prone to develop PTSD. But if damage is done, the prime biochemical suspect is cortisol (also known as hydrocortisone), a hormone secreted by the adrenal glands just above the kidneys, which circulates at high levels in the bloodstream and brain for hours and sometimes days after extreme stress. Moderate levels of cortisol help the body to release glucose into the bloodstream and reduce inflammation. In animals, moderate to high levels of

from dissociation—a failure to integrate fragments of memory into a coherent personal history or sense of self.

Raised cortisol levels were also found in the sexually abused girls first studied by Putnam in 1988, but the levels are declining over time. Studies of Vietnam veterans and of women who reported a previous experience of rape when reporting to an emergency room after a sexual assault found unusually low levels of cortisol. This research suggests that the body may over-reduce cortisol levels after prolonged stress. Paradoxically, low cortisol levels are associated with brain-cell death in an innermost section of the hippocampus called the dentate gyrus, a region thought to contribute to the creation

and in subsequent weeks, things go back to normal. Parsimony would suggest that if this [hipppocampal damage] happens in humans—which we don't know for sure yet—the same thing probably occurs."

Changes in Memory

Clinicians often informally note memory lapses, amnesia and fragmentary memories in Vietnam veterans and adults severely abused as children. In the ideological war over recovered memory, these reports are sometimes dismissed as therapeutic folklore. But the latest research suggests that trauma affects even short-term memory of simple facts. In 1993, Bremner ran a battery of neuropsychological tests with 47 sexual abuse survivors and combat veterans with PTSD and found significant deficits in verbal recall and other forms of short-term memory, compared with matched, nontraumatized controls.

"The assumption is that people who have been exposed to extreme stress have normal memory," says Bremner. "But the evidence is that they don't. Some of them can't remember the grocery list. Their memory deficits can be as extreme as those in people who have severe epilepsy and have had parts of their hippocampus removed."

Another study, published in May in *The Archives of General Psychiatry*, suggests that some memories of trauma are very different from "ordinary forgetting and remembering." Harvard research psychiatrists Scott Rauch, Roger Pitman and Bessel van der Kolk stimulated flashbacks in eight combat veterans and sexual abuse survivors with PTSD by playing a tape of their most horrific memory. Then they recorded brain activity using Positron Emission Tomography (PET). The PET scan traced the brain's metabolism of radioactively tagged oxygen to create a living show, a moving picture of activity in the brain. The researchers found that during flashbacks, areas of the brain's cortex involved in sensory memory were relatively active, while Broca's area—known to play a role in the verbal articulation of experience—was relatively quiescent. When the subjects were asked to recall something mundane, like making a bed, the opposite pattern pertained: Broca's area was more active and the visual areas relatively quiet. The PET scans suggest, says van der Kolk, that trauma survivors remember their past horrors in a state of "speechless terror." When they don't describe them to therapists, they may

It challenges both the Freudian speculation of a mental mechanism called repression and the assertion that traumatic amnesia is nothing more than ordinary forgetting.

cortisol are toxic to some brain cells in the hippocampus: autopsies of monkeys who died from the stress of prolonged laboratory overcrowding revealed high cortisol levels and hippocampal shrinkage. Animal researchers have found a link between high cortisol levels over a period of weeks and the withering of dendrites—the feathery branches that allow brain cells to form communication pathways and associational networks with hundreds of thousands of their neighbors. If cortisol levels stay high for months, it can cause irreversible brain-cell death. This suggests that a single, horrific car wreck may do less damage than a decade of child abuse or a year in Vietnam. A loss of neurons and dendrites could explain, Bremner speculates, why many trauma survivors suffer

and recall of long-term memories. This suggests that biochemically induced physical damage, not psychological defenses, may explain some memory loss in trauma survivors; it challenges both the Freudian speculation of a mental mechanism called repression and the assertion that traumatic amnesia is nothing more than ordinary forgetting.

Even though the sexual abuse survivors and PTSD veterans studied showed unusually small hippocampi decades after trauma, research suggests that the brain can bounce back from short-term stress. "Dendritic atrophy in rats is totally reversible," says Stanford University animal neuroscience researcher Robert Sapolsky, author of *Why Zebras Don't Get Ulcers*. "Stop the stress and the dendrites grow back,

not merely be shy, shameful or with-holding: their brains may literally be unable to put their shocking experiences into words.

Researchers have also chemically induced the state of "dissociation"—the tendency of some traumatized people to space out, suffer memory lapses and experience distortions in body image, including the sensation of being out of their bodies. In 1994, Yale/West Haven VA researchers injected normal volunteers with ketamine hydrochloride, a psychoactive drug that selectively disables a brain-cell receptor concentrated in the hippocampus. The volunteers experienced a wide range of dissociative symptoms, including having out-of-body experiences, feeling that their arms were like toothpicks and sensing gaps in time or having time stand still.

THESE EXPERIMENTS HAVE PROduced little more than hints: what is now known about the brain is dauntingly reminiscent of a 16th-century European conception of Africa: boats have landed and a few search parties have returned with stories of fertile river valleys and mysterious, unclimbed peaks, but few coordinates have been precisely plotted. Only since the mid-1980s have the PET scan and the MRI allowed researchers to peer directly into the brain's glimmering, wet-wired sponge of neurochemicals and electromagnetic fields and get a glimpse of its 100 billion branching neurons at work. Researchers have measured the hippocampus, but have only the sketchiest idea of what it does. Far more is unknown than is known.

If the clinical neuroscience of traumatic damage is in its infancy, the neuroscience of psychological healing is still in the womb. Researchers have shown that the smell of jasmine can subtly alter brain function, as can the tug of a baby's mouth on a mother's nipple. Holding hands lowers cortisol levels in both apes and humans. While undergoing cardiac catheterization, those who talked to their doctors about their fears had lower cortisol levels than those who toughed it out.

Therapy can alter PET scans as well: the February 1996 issue of *The Archives of General Psychiatry* shows "before" and "after" PET scans of nine patients with obsessive-compulsive disorder, treated successfully with cognitive-behavioral techniques, which are like a science-fiction version of a *Glamour* magazine makeover.

In the meantime, neuroscience offers only the vaguest hints to therapists struggling with emotionally volatile, impulsive and chronically terrified or rageful people with PTSD. Years of sleeplessness, flashbacks and intrusive thoughts have taken their toll on marriages, jobs and self-image, and this negative outer cascade needs repair as much as—or more than—the inner neurophysiological cascade. Successful therapy remains a carefully timed and

Clinicians are far more hopeful when treating people in the first six months after a trauma. For reasons not yet fully understood, chronic PTSD often seems intractable. Treating it is a process of incremental victories. The first step, as the new neuroscience research strongly suggests, is not to dig into the trauma but to restabilize clients neurobiologically, using such simple techniques as stress reduction, meditation, hard exercise, regular meals and a decent sleep-

> ## Successful therapy remains a carefully timed and finely sewn patchwork of interventions at the biological, individual, family and social levels.

finely sewn patchwork of interventions at the biological, individual, family and social levels. What works, and what doesn't, is still less informed by PET scans than by clinical observation, guesswork and common sense.

Different stages of PTSD call for different responses. Immediately after a trauma, reassuring therapy—or perhaps even massage—may be critical to help lower cortisol levels the way hand-holding can. Later, sufferers and their families can be taught that flashbacks and other alarming symptoms are natural responses to extreme stress. David Foy, a cognitive-behavioral psychologist at Pepperdine University, says early therapy can challenge beliefs that tragedy could have been avoided or that the victim was to blame. "If people don't label themselves as abnormal, some will naturally recover if they give themselves six weeks to settle down again biologically," he says. This is the rationale behind "critical incident debriefing," now routine for disaster workers, police officers and children affected by schoolyard shootings and other sudden tragedies.

ing schedule. No medication is a magic bullet, but many therapists report good results with Prozac.

"I can't imagine working without it," says Bessel van der Kolk. "The very first patient I tried it with, in the late '80s, was a very bulimic incest victim. After four days, she came in and said, 'Food is food. When I am hungry, I eat, and when I'm not, I do other things.' Such medications can aid therapy by helping clients tolerate the negative emotions that talking about trauma can arouse."

Meditation can also help people tolerate and contain unpleasant emotional states, rather than impulsively express them or try to avoid them. At the stress-reduction clinic at the University of Massachusetts Medical Center in Worcester, Massachusetts, mindfulness meditation is taught to about 900 people a year, about 10 percent of whom suffer from PTSD due to combat, child sexual abuse or repeated car accidents. "We see a real change in the response pattern, and that manifests physiologically, but it's all anecdotal," says Ferris Urbanowsky, director of training. "We had a vet here recently who, if his wife tried to wake him from a nap and touched him, would go for her throat. After he began meditating, he found over time that the same reaction just did not occur anymore." Other victims report success with yoga, t'ai chi, massage and body work and other forms of moving meditation.

Meditation is no magic bullet: Vietnam veteran Claude Thomas, now an ordained Zen Buddhist monk, is still

exposure works when paired with some form of new learning, such as an understanding that one was not to blame for the tragedy or that the world is not always as dangerous as it was then. Many veterans, however, find exposure therapy so aversive that they drop out of treatment.

Neuroscience has no answers to such quandaries so far. Therapists trying to familiarize themselves with the new paradigm without throwing out the intuitive

the complexity of the interplay of hormonal systems involved, its unlikely that a single magic bullet—biochemical or psychosocial—will ever eliminate PTSD. In the meantime, PTSD treatment will remain an extreme example of a universal human struggle: to master social, familial, biological and practical givens while recognizing that the neurobiological inner cascade and the outer social cascade continually inform and impinge upon each other. Perhaps the new neu-

Given the complexity of the interplay of hormonal systems involved, it's unlikely that a single magic bullet—biochemical or psychosocial—will ever eliminate PTSD.

plagued by sleeplessness and flashbacks, despite years of meditation. "They haven't gone away, but my relationship to them has changed," says Thomas. "They don't control my life in the same way. Being able to breathe, to slow down, buys me some time. I invite myself to just hold these feelings, to just sit with them, and when they start to come, I recognize them much sooner."

One of the most vexing unanswered questions is how much—if any—reliving of trauma is necessary for healing. Too hasty and too vigorous digging can have disastrous results: one study found that alcoholic veterans who had achieved sobriety were more likely than controls to return to heavy drinking if they underwent exposure therapy, which requires repeatedly remembering traumatic memories. Incest clients have been known to arrive at sessions, pour out accounts of horrific childhood molestation and then go home to drink, attempt suicide or mutilate themselves. Yet, some level of emotional arousal may be required for healing. The favored behavioral treatments for veterans with PTSD—exposure, flooding and systematic desensitization—all require remembering traumatic events repeatedly until the conditioned response to them is extinguished. The handful of outcome studies of PTSD therapy suggests that

wisdom of the old will find themselves caught between vocabularies and metaphors. The bridge between the symbolic and the neurological worlds is only half-built. Many of the psychiatrists conducting the leading-edge neuroscience research are also clinicians, and even for them the language of neurology goes only so far.

When asked about the clinical implications of their work, talk of hippocampal volume and glucocorticoid levels and biological substrates falls away, and the terminology of the clinical world returns. Neuroscientists with psychodynamic training speak with great conviction about the healing value of putting experience into a personal narrative. Cognitive-behavioral psychologists talk with equal conviction about the virtues of exposure and correcting misapprehensions. They fall back on what they knew before the black box of the brain began to open; sometimes, they seem a little like Wile E. Coyote suddenly realizing that he has walked off a cliff and is sauntering along in midair.

But perhaps that's inevitable. People live in many worlds and use many languages to describe their places in them. PTSD, like everything else in life, is multifactorial, and will demand multiple interventions even after the biological part of the story is fully told. Given

roscience will encourage PTSD sufferers to treat themselves with more compassion, to understand how much lies outside conscious mental control and to develop an observer self that may help them take a breath before they fly off the handle.

Although the neuroscience of PTSD is daunting and somewhat depressing, it will plot directions for future research and clinical work. At the very least, it maps out two challenges for working psychotherapists. The first is to give more weight to the body's physiology and to have an open mind about the contributions of a new, more sophisticated version of biological psychiatry. The second is to continue to explore the pure power of human contact to heal disregulated brain chemistry.

"We already know to what degree matter can alter mind," is the way van der Kolk puts it. "The great challenge now is to use psychological tools to re-regulate people's biological systems—to show to what degree mind can alter matter." ■

Networker *consulting editor Katy Butler, a former reporter for the* San Francisco Chronicle, *has contributed to* The Los Angeles Times, The New Yorker, The New York Times Book Review *and* The Washington Post. *Address: c/o Family Therapy Networker, 7705 13th Street N.W., Washington, DC 20012.*

Obsessed

BY EDWARD DOLNICK

WHEN OUR LIVES go wrong, we search for explanations. But lives can skid off track without warning and without reason. For Joshua Brown, and for his parents and his brother, life began to change in June 1991.

Josh was 13 then, a friendly, good-looking boy who had just finished seventh grade. In June his family moved from St. Louis to the suburbs of Washington, D.C., and settled into a handsome house in a tree-lined neighborhood. The transition, especially Josh's move from a small school to a big, crowded, and anonymous one, wasn't easy.

Short and thin but a good athlete, Josh began devoting more and more time to sports. He played soccer, wrestled, and carried out a self-imposed calisthenics regimen. "We just attributed it to the fact that he hadn't made friends yet," says his mother, Tina. "He was filling his time with things that ordinarily would have been fine, but then they began to take on a singular kind of focus."

By February, Josh had become fanatical about exercise. For hours at a time, long after his muscles had given out, he would force himself to do push-ups and sit-ups. "He'd be screaming in agony," Tina says, "but he couldn't stop exercising. One time a neighbor came over and asked if someone had fallen down the stairs, because she heard someone screaming."

Josh's compulsions grew worse. In the bad stretches, it was a welcome break if he didn't wake up once or twice in the night to exercise. At one point, in an attempt to impose order on the chaos that their lives had become, Tina compiled a list of Josh's symptoms. It covered half a page, each entry seemingly unrelated to the others. "Check-ing doors" and "unable to shower without compulsively washing one foot," it read, and "fear of someone behind him" and "repeating sentence or words while trying to override intrusive thoughts."

By the start of the next school year, matters had spiraled out of control. On the first day of his freshman year in high school, Josh sat in Spanish class, eyes squeezed closed, picking his pencil up from his desk and then placing it back down, picking it up and placing it down, over and over. For 15 minutes, his classmates and teacher tried,

TRAPPED IN A WEB OF SENSELESS RITUALS, THEY SCRUB THEIR HANDS RAW AND CHECK REPEATEDLY TO SEE IF THE DOOR IS LOCKED. NOW, FOR THESE COMPULSIVE MILLIONS, THERE'S HOPE OF RELEASE.

From *Health*, 8, pp. 78–84, September 1994. Reprinted with permission from *Health*, ©1994.

BEFORE i CAN TURN ON THE TV, I HAVE to wash my HANDS. Then i Look IN BACK OF THE TV FOUR TIMES. washing my HANDS IN BETWEEN. FINALLy I TURN the TV ON.

unsuccessfully, to divert him. "People were touching me and asking if I was okay," Josh says now. "My teacher thought I was having a seizure." In his next class, Josh was unable to sit down. He would settle on his chair for a moment and then stand up, sit down and stand up, sit down and stand up.

Josh seemed unable to explain what was happening to him, as baffled by his own behavior as any outsider. "It must have looked really stupid," he says sheepishly, "a kid with his eyes closed, cringing, standing up and sitting down." It was as if he was in thrall to a capricious demon, trapped in a malevolent version of Simon Says.

Josh was certain that if he tried to resist these urges some horrible fate—he could never specify exactly what it might be—was sure to follow. "I would wipe his forehead with a cold washcloth and sit with him for hours, telling him I'd help him through it and that he was safe," Tina says. "He sounded so frightened, as if he had some horribly scary monster-movie creature in his mind that said,"—Tina's voice rises in pitch, ghost story–style—"'If you don't do this right, I'm going to get you.'"

The Browns had taken Josh in for scores of tests, both psychological and physical, and visited doctors of every stripe. The burden of doctors' appointments would eventually grow so overwhelming that Tina would have to quit her job. The breakthrough came at the National Institutes of Health, by fortunate coincidence only a mile or two from the Browns' home. Josh was told he had obsessive-compulsive disorder. Neither he nor his parents had ever heard the phrase.

OBSESSIVE-COMPULSIVE DISORDER is a bizarre disease but a surprisingly common one. It is about twice as prevalent as Alzheimer's disease, affecting one to 2 percent of the population, perhaps 4 million or so Americans. It occurs equally often in men and women and can strike at any age, though somewhere around 18 or 20 is most common. Josh was young, but the medical literature is dotted with cases that began as early as age two or three. The cause is rarely known, nor is the trigger for individual episodes. One leading psychiatric authority can do no better than to liken the disease to "a kind of hiccup in the brain."

With the onset of the disorder, people whose lives were utterly ordinary suddenly find themselves tormented by unwelcome thoughts and compelled to carry out meaningless rituals. The paradox is that they recognize their rituals are pointless and "crazy," yet they remain powerless to resist. Victims of obsessive-compulsive disorder are perfectly sane people who find themselves marooned on islands of madness.

Across cultures and across centuries, patients tell eerily similar stories. Judith Rapoport, a psychiatrist at the National Institute of Mental Health and the author of *The Boy Who Couldn't Stop Washing*, the best account of obsessive-compulsive disorder, reports that 85 percent of her patients have a frenzied fear of contamination. They wash themselves as many as three hours a day, scrubbing their skin red and raw.

The strength of the disease's hold is hard to imagine. One woman with an obsessive fear of germs saw cockroaches in the supermarket one day and for the next *14 years* washed her groceries before she put them away. Eventually she began washing books, paint cans, mail, newspapers, toys, tools, pictures, and everything else she brought into the house.

Entire families can be held hostage to one member's obsessions. Another woman with a pathological fear of germs spent up to 16 hours a day cleaning her house. Her husband and son were allowed indoors, but relatives and family friends were banned, to make sure they didn't carry in germs. In time, the husband was allowed upstairs to his bedroom only if he had showered downstairs, and he was forbidden to go into his second-floor study at all.

For the Browns, no outing, no matter how minor, was ever routine. On a Fourth of July trip to the beach, for example, Josh was playing in the waves, but suddenly the game changed character and he began swimming compulsively, straight out to sea. Josh's brother and his father, not much of a swimmer, had to race after him and drag him back to shore against his will. Josh fought so hard and screamed so loudly on this occasion that his father decided to carry a doctor's letter at all times, explaining that Josh was his son and that he was not abducting or abusing him.

Like Josh, most obsessive-compulsive people can recite a long and constantly evolving lineup of symptoms. Obsessions are terrifying and intrusive thoughts; compulsions are ritual acts, like Josh's pencil dropping. Counting is one compulsion that turns up time and again. People count their steps, their words, or almost anything else, embracing "good" numbers with relief and shrinking from "bad" ones in fear. For a while, Josh counted things in threes. One ritual involved the clock on the microwave oven. He had to see the digits at exactly the moment they turned and at the same instant had to visualize three particular images in his mind. If it didn't feel "right," he felt compelled to do it again. One of Rapoport's patients felt she had to color in the round part of every *o* and *p* and *a* and *q* and *e* and *d* and *g* and *b* she encountered, and to count to 50 between every word she read or wrote.

Such obsessions can consume a life. One woman explained to her therapist the elaborate ritual she developed to turn on her television: "Before I start to turn it on, I have to wash and dry my hands. Then I go and touch the corner curtain followed by touching the side of the TV two times. Then I have to go back and wash my hands. When I am finished with that I will look behind the lamp two times, go back and wash my hands, come back, move the lamp to the left and look behind it, move the lamp two times to the right and look behind it, go back, wash my hands, and then look in back of the TV on the left four times, washing my hands in between each one. Then I look in back of the TV on the right eight times, wash my hands, and put the TV on channel six. Then I turn the knob from channel six to seven, four times, and from channel six to channel eight, four times. Then finally I turn it on."

Confronted with such rituals, therapists sound like bewildered anthropologists trying to grasp unfamiliar religious rites. Judith Rapoport still recalls her amazement at seeing her first obsessive-compulsive patient, a 60-year-old solid citizen, who, out of nowhere, developed a compulsion to pick up small pieces of trash on the street. "His house grew crowded with bags full of it, which were stored in the halls and piled on the furniture." Eventually the man spent so much of his day collecting scraps that he was unable to make it to work.

Howard Hughes, too, suffered from obsessions and compulsions. Rather than seek help, he hired aides to indulge him. "Before handing Hughes a spoon, his attendants had to wrap the handle in tissue paper and seal it with cellophane tape," according

Are You Obsessive-Compulsive?

W E TEASE A "compulsive" friend who keeps her CDs in alphabetical order or arranges her closets with military precision. We all know people "obsessed" with cooking or sports or gardening. Many people knock on wood for luck or step over a sidewalk crack to avoid breaking their mother's back or can't resist the urge to straighten every crooked picture on the wall. Such everyday habits and superstitions are *not* signs of obsessive-compulsive disorder—unless you become, well, compulsive about them.

Most cases of obsessive-compulsive disorder come on fairly suddenly and are impossible to ignore. People with milder forms of the disorder, however, may carry on normal lives after having devoted a number of hours each day to what Freud called their "secret doings" in the privacy of their homes. One study found that 37 percent of the patients who visited a dermatology clinic with nonspecific dermatitis were obsessive-compulsives who had brought on the condition by overzealous washing. Yet none had sought treatment for the disorder. Even without treatment, about 40 percent of patients are symptom-free or in fairly good shape at any given time.

The following is a list of the most common symptoms of the disease. The American Psychiatric Association says that garden variety obsessions and compulsions cross over to a disorder only when they become severe enough to cause excessive anxiety, take up more than one hour of your time each day, or significantly alter your routine.

Constant checking and rechecking of whether appliances have been turned off or doors locked

An overwhelming concern for order and tidiness

Fear of contagion, leading to excessive washing

Repetition of numbers, tunes, words, or sounds

Fear of violent or aggressive actions toward oneself or others

Intrusive sexual, offensive, or blasphemous thoughts

The division of behavioral medicine at the St. Louis University Health Sciences Center can send you a free educational tape on obsessive-compulsive disorder. Call 314/768-1550.

to one medical text. "A second piece of tissue was wrapped around the first protective wrapping. . . . On receiving the protected spoon, Hughes would use it only with the handle covered. When he finished with it, the tissue was discarded into a specially provided receptacle." In the end, Hughes's compulsions grew so numerous and so complex that they left him no time or freedom to care for himself.

Perhaps the strangest feature of this strange disease is that its victims refuse to believe their senses. The French call obsessive-compulsive disorder *folie de doute*, the doubting disease. Patients' doubts recall the skeptical views of the philosopher David Hume, who asked how we can be sure that the universe doesn't change utterly everytime we turn our backs. For most of us, this is merely an academic riddle. For obsessive-compulsive people, Hume's query is literally of compelling interest. They cannot stop checking to see if the stove is off, the doors are locked, the windows are shut, no matter that they have checked ten or a hundred times already. Many patients say that, if not for fear of losing their job or their family, they would continue checking all day long.

With hindsight, Tina Brown now recalls that even before the move from St. Louis, on nights when his father was out of town, Josh would check and recheck that the house was locked. "He might check for fifteen minutes," Tina says. "It seemed odd, but Jim was traveling a lot, and I attributed it to Josh's need to reassure himself when his father was gone."

"I check *everything*," says Eric Stein, a graduate student in chemistry and an obsessive-compulsive since he was 17. "We have four cats, and when my wife washes the clothes, I say, 'Don't turn it on yet. Did you make sure there are no cats in there?' I push all the clothes aside to make sure there aren't any cats in the washing machine. When I open the refrigerator door, I open it, close it, open it, close it, two or three times, to make sure there are no cats in the refrigerator. I check the dishwasher two or three times to make sure there are no cats in *there,* and they would never climb in there. Even though I open it up and look in and see no cats, I still think there might be a cat in there. Same with the oven."

Often the checking is more poignant. Stein's wife, Kris, describes his constant need for reassurance. "He'll ask, 'I'm not a bad person, am I?' 'I'm not bad, am I?' 'I wouldn't hurt anybody, would I?' over and over, like a broken record," she says. "One or two reassurances don't work. You get to the point where you're sick of saying, 'You're okay,' 'You're not bad.' It gets to be," Kris says, her voice growing harsh, "'Don't ask me again!'"

Stein's need for reassurance is understandable. Like others plagued with obsessions, this earnest man is tormented by violent thoughts that come to him unbidden. As mundane an item as the autoclave in the chemistry lab, a kind of pressure cooker, can conjure up terrors. "I would have thoughts that popped into my head of putting my daughter—I love my daughter very much—of putting her into the autoclave and watching her scream and suffer," Stein says quietly, "and I couldn't get that thought out of my head."

WHAT COULD BE MORE NATURAL than to assume that a person who spends two hours stuck in a doorway, unable to cross the threshold, is afraid of something on the other side? How can we hear of someone washing her hands hour after hour and not think of Lady Macbeth trying to cleanse her guilty conscience? For decades, psychoanalysts took for granted that obsessive-compulsive disorder had psychological causes, that it grew out of a person's fears and guilty wishes and shameful secrets. They saw their patients' case histories as larded with symbols, like short stories by a heavy-handed author, and they approached the disease as

"WHEN I OPEN THE REFRIGERATOR, I OPEN IT, CLOSE IT, OPEN IT, CLOSE IT, TWO OR THREE TIMES, TO MAKE SURE THERE ARE NO CATS IN THERE."

literary critics rather than as scientists.

Today doctors see things differently. The common belief that people with the disorder must have been raised by overly rigid parents has not been borne out by the research. A recent study at the St. Louis University School of Medicine, for instance, found that people with obsessions and compulsions were *less* likely than other patients to report that their fathers were demanding. Other studies of people with obsessions and compulsions turn up run-of-the-mill biographies, with no more than the usual quota of misery. Once the illness is in place, Rapoport concedes, fear and stress may make its symptoms worse, but she contends that psychological factors are probably not the *source* of the disorder. Rapoport says she can recall only "one case out of thousands"—a victim of a gang rape who became obsessed with showering—where she believes that a specific trauma may have precipitated the disease.

Josh's case provides compelling evidence that biology, not psychology, is to blame. When Josh's panicky parents brought him to the National Institutes of Health, doctors told them that his obsessions and compulsions might have been triggered by a raging strep infection, which hadn't produced the usual sore throat symptoms. It seems that in rare cases, when certain people get strep infections, their immune systems churn out antibodies that target brain cells as well as the strep itself. The vulnerable cells are in the basal ganglia, the region of the brain that has been shown to be abnormal in people with the disorder. Researchers think that overactivity in this part of the brain leads to the repetitive behavior characteristic of obsessive-compulsives. An MRI scan of Josh's brain confirmed the ominous finding. Structures within the basal ganglia were swollen and damaged. In essence, Josh's body had assaulted his brain; there was no way of telling how long the attack had been going on or if there had been similar attacks in the past.

Other case histories provide further, and equally bizarre, proof that obsessive-compulsive behavior is biological. It can sometimes arise, full-blown and seemingly out of nowhere, as a result of blows to the head or

epileptic seizures or strokes. And it can go away just as accidentally. In 1988, for example, a 22-year-old man shot himself in the head because his compulsions had made his life unbearable. He lived. And his obsessions and compulsions vanished.

WHAT, SHORT OF A BULLET to the head, helps? Not psychotherapy. According to one authoritative textbook, there is not a single case report in the modern psychiatric literature where psychoanalysis cured a patient with obsessions and compulsions.

Medication, on the other hand, can transform lives. Anafranil (clomipramine), Prozac (fluoxetine), and several other antidepressants can sometimes cut down on obsessions and compulsions that have endured for years, and can do so in a matter of weeks. Between 50 and 80 percent of obsessive-compulsive patients, depending on the study, respond well to medication. But only a few people are freed from all their symptoms. For a typical patient, symptoms decline 30 to 70 percent.

The successful drugs share a chemical property: They all affect the brain's metabolism of serotonin, a chemical messenger that helps regulate sleep, mood, aggression, and repetitive behavior. Antidepressants that don't affect serotonin don't seem to cut down on obsessions and compulsions. Experiments with dogs confirm that observation. Some dogs lick their paws so compulsively that they lose their fur and make their skin bleed. The same antidepressants that work in obsessive-compulsive people help these dogs, too, and ones that don't work in people are also ineffective in dogs.

But since drugs that affect serotonin don't *always* work, that means serotonin can't be the whole story. Besides, no one has yet found any differences between the serotonin levels in healthy and obsessive people. And all the effective antidepressants change the brain's serotonin levels almost at once. So why does it take at least two weeks for symptoms to start to disappear?

In Josh's case, the question was more immediate. Why weren't these miracle drugs working? Josh had been on

Other case histories provide further, and equally bizarre, proof that obsessive-compulsive behavior is biological. It can sometimes arise, full-blown and seemingly out of nowhere, as a result of blows to the head or epileptic seizures or strokes.

medication since shortly after he was diagnosed in May 1992. It didn't help. A few months later, with the illness ruining his life, the doctors at NIH tried a new and drastic tack. "That was when it all peaked," Tina Brown says. "He couldn't get into bed at night without doing two hours of gymnastics, he couldn't talk without repeating his words over and over, he couldn't eat a bowl of cereal because he had to put his spoon in just the right way. We just thought he was"—she searches for a word—"going."

The NIH doctors opted for an experimental treatment. They would take all the blood from Josh's body and clean it, straining out the antibodies that were attacking his brain. Six times in the next two weeks, for about two and a half hours each time, doctors put a needle connected to a tube into Josh's forearm, drew his blood out and cleaned it in a centrifuge, then returned it to his

Josh wrote his doctor a love letter thanking her. "It was one of those letters you save in your wallet."

body through a needle in the other arm. Josh lay in bed at the center of a network of tubes reading Stephen King novels.

"They did brain scans, and there was a decrease in the swelling after just two treatments," Tina says. "It was amazing to see. Josh started smiling again, the muscles in his face relaxed. It was unbelievable."

After six blood cleanings, Josh's obsessions and compulsions were far weaker, though not entirely gone. Then came three weeks of intensive behavior therapy. The treatment is grueling, because it requires that patients confront their demons, trying to pry themselves free from rituals that have their claws in deep. But it has a good record. Between 60 and 90 percent of patients benefit from behavior therapy.

The strategy is simple enough. "Let's say somebody spends two hours a day washing his hands," says Daniel Trigoboff, a Buffalo, New York, psychologist. "I might begin by asking him to refrain from washing for ten seconds, so it's only one hour, fifty-nine minutes, and fifty seconds. Most people don't believe they can manage even that change.

"The next week I might say, 'You did ten seconds. How about trying a minute?' And we'd also deal with what happens if they fail, what to do about panic, and so on. Eventually people begin to get the idea that symptoms are controllable. It's not the kind of thing where you have to cut down ten seconds a week for four years. It's ten seconds, a minute, five minutes, and then all of sudden, in the fourth week, they might cut out an hour."

"Josh had this bizarre 'homework,'" Tina says, grinning. "Every night he had to go around the house kicking the woodwork, because he'd gotten so he couldn't go up the stairs, because he was worried about scuffing them with his shoes." Tina shakes her head in weary amazement. "It sounds crazy, but you become a believer in anything when it works."

And behavior therapy worked perfectly for Josh. "After three weeks," Tina says, "he was completely in control again. There were no symptoms, nothing. We felt that we had come through the tornado and somehow we'd been among the lucky ones. It had been enormously scary, but we'd been lucky and we'd gotten through it. Josh wrote his doctor a love letter thanking her for saving his life." It was, the doctor says, "one of those letters you save in your wallet."

BUT THIS IS A DISEASE that can eat away at its victims' sense of security. They can never be sure where they stand, for obsessive-compulsive disorder follows a waxing and waning course in which symptoms often appear and disappear and mutate. And no one knows which patients will benefit from which treatments. Anafranil, for example, is no help to about one-third of those who try it. How to tell the lucky from the damned? Eventually, with drugs or behavior therapy or both, 80 percent of patients will improve significantly.

Josh Brown seemed to be a success story, too, but things went awry again. After he had his blood "cleaned" in September 1992, life seemed good. Josh, who was on the antibiotic amoxicillin to stave off another strep attack, seemed safe.

"That held until January," his mother says, "and then he started hopping up and down and doing jumping jacks, and he couldn't stop. It just came out of the blue, and on his birthday, January 24, it really peaked again. I thought, 'Oh God, why? He's been taking amoxicillin religiously!'"

It turned out Josh did have another bacterial infection, this time a different strain unaffected by the medicine he was taking. Through the spring, he grew worse. Making matters scarier still, somewhere along the way he developed anorexia. Many obsessive-compulsive people develop eating disorders. Anorexics seem to be obsessives with a specialty in food and body image.

In combination, the two illnesses were terrifying. "At that point, Josh couldn't stop running," Tina recalls, "and if he didn't do it right, he'd have to go back and do it again. He might do hills ten times and so the runs became excruciating, and at the same time he was also cutting back on his nutrition, so he was just exhausted."

Josh's doctors were eager to find a solution other than another experimental blood cleaning. "But once you've seen your child a slave to this disease, you beg for something that you've seen help him before," she says. Eventually the doctors decided that another blood cleaning *was* the best bet. "We were so excited we were practically dancing," Tina says.

All for naught. Josh's condition barely improved.

That was in June 1993. A year later, a new combination of medicines seems to be working. Josh has gained weight and his compulsions have stopped completely. He has begun to laugh and joke again. Last March, he started at a new school. (An admissions essay for one school began: "I have had an unusual twist to my childhood in the last two years.")

"We hit bottom," Josh's father says, "and we're on the way back up." But it will be a long time before any of the Browns let down their guard. Like farmers on flood-prone land, they watch and wait, at the mercy of fickle and powerful forces beyond their control.   H

Edward Dolnick is a contributing editor.

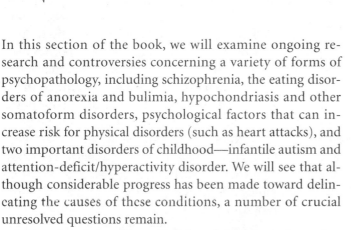

PART II

Other Major Mental Disorders: Schizophrenia, Eating Disorders, Somatoform Disorders, and Childhood Disorders

In this section of the book, we will examine ongoing research and controversies concerning a variety of forms of psychopathology, including schizophrenia, the eating disorders of anorexia and bulimia, hypochondriasis and other somatoform disorders, psychological factors that can increase risk for physical disorders (such as heart attacks), and two important disorders of childhood—infantile autism and attention-deficit/hyperactivity disorder. We will see that although considerable progress has been made toward delineating the causes of these conditions, a number of crucial unresolved questions remain.

Schizophrenia is a severe disorder of thought and emotion that afflicts approximately 1 in 100 individuals. Individuals with schizophrenia (which should not be confused with multiple personality disorder; see Reading 25) tend to display a myriad of puzzling symptoms, including disordered thinking, emotions that are either greatly attenuated in intensity or grossly inappropriate to the objective situation, and marked social withdrawal. In addition, schizophrenics frequently suffer from *delusions* (false beliefs that are not susceptible to corrective feedback) and *hallucinations* (false sensory experiences).

In the first of three articles on schizophrenia, Phyllida Brown provides a useful overview of the clinical picture of schizophrenia and of recent research on its biological underpinnings. Brown points to a number of promising leads concerning the physiological substrate of schizophrenia, including reports of linkage to specific genetic markers and studies of dopaminergic abnormalities. She places particular emphasis on research using both structural (for example, magnetic resonance imaging) and functional (for instance, positron emission tomography) brain imaging techniques. The former enable investigators to examine morphological abnormalities in brain structure, whereas the latter enable investigators to examine abnormalities in the ongoing activity of various brain regions. Brown discusses findings suggesting that schizophrenics tend to possess abnormally large cerebral ventricles and abnormally small hippocampi, as well as show reduced activity in the prefrontal cortex while performing tasks that normally activate this brain area. As Brown notes, however, the precise relevance of these discov-eries to the symptoms of schizophrenia remains a matter of considerable debate. Moreover, the means by which environmental factors trigger the underlying biological predisposition to schizophrenia remain unknown.

Tony Dajer next describes the preliminary results of a remarkable twin study of schizophrenia jointly coordinated by E. Fuller Torrey and Irving Gottesman. Torrey and Gottesman, who are both research collaborators and friendly adversaries in their search for the causes of schizophrenia, have made good use of a rare but extremely informative natural experiment. Because only about 50 percent of the identical or monozygotic (MZ) co-twins of schizophrenics are themselves schizophrenic, Torrey and Gottesman identified a sample of MZ twin pairs who are *discordant* for schizophrenia. Discordant pairs are those in which only one twin has the disorder. The power of the discordant MZ twin paradigm stems from the fact that because MZ twins are genetically identical, any differences between them are necessarily environmental. Consequently, researchers can examine MZ twin pairs discordant for schizophrenia in an effort to identify environmental factors that accounted for this discordance. Somewhat paradoxically, then, a research design traditionally used to study genetic influences—namely, the twin study—provides an ideal vehicle for pinpointing environmental influences. As Dajer notes, Torrey hypothesizes that prenatal viral exposure is the crucial environmental ingredient in the genesis of schizophrenia. Moreover, Torrey believes that genetic influences are of only subsidiary importance in schizophrenia, and that viruses will ultimately be found to account for most of the physiological abnormalities observed in this disorder. Dajer goes on to describe research findings consistent with Torrey's bold, and still highly controversial, conjecture. Gottesman, however, remains unconvinced. He suspects that genes are the principal players in the etiology of schizophrenia and that the primary environmental variables relevant to this disorder are nonviral.

Dan Hurley next describes some of the vexing legal and societal implications raised by homeless individuals with schizophrenia, especially those with histories of dangerous behavior. Using the tragic case of Mark Sallee, a schizophrenic who committed murder shortly after his release from psychiatric care, as a backdrop for his discussion, Hurley observes that the large-scale program of deinstitutionalization in the United States during the 1960s had several unintended consequences. In particular, this program left many individuals with schizophrenia, some with violent propensities, largely or entirely to their own devices. Because most antipsychotic drugs have unpleasant side effects, and because many individuals with schizophrenia do not perceive themselves as mentally ill, large numbers of these individuals promptly discontinued their medications upon release from psychiatric hospitals. As a consequence, the plight of the homeless mentally ill, many of whom suffer from schizophrenia and related psychotic disorders, represents one of the most troublesome dilemmas for American society at the turn of the 21st century. As you read Hurley's article, you may want to ask yourself where the rights of individuals with schizophrenia, some but not most of whom are at heightened risk for violence, end and the rights of society to be protected from potentially dangerous individuals begin.

The next two articles address the issue of eating disorders, with particular emphasis on anorexia nervosa. Anorexia nervosa, better known simply as anorexia, is characterized by dramatic weight loss coupled with profound body image distortion. Individuals with anorexia, who are predominantly female, see themselves as overweight even after losing massive, and in some cases life-threatening, amounts of weight. In addition, they are "weight phobic"—that is, intensely afraid of gaining weight. But what are the causes of this puzzling condition?

Hara Marano summarizes the research of Sarah Leibowitz, an investigator at Rockefeller University, whose work on the biochemistry of appetite may provide at least a partial answer to this question. Leibowitz has found that two neurochemicals—neuropeptide Y (NPY) and galanin—play crucial roles in appetite regulation. NPY, she claims, is responsible for carbohydrate craving, whereas galanin is responsible for fat craving. Moreover, these two substances differ in their patterns of activity over both the course of a day and the course of development. Leibowitz contends that NPY and galanin hold the key to the mystery of eating disorders, and that normal physiological mechanisms switched on at puberty interact with certain personality traits (such as perfectionism and need for control) to produce anorexia and related conditions.

In a brief article from *Newsweek* magazine, Jean Seligmann explores a disturbing and relatively recent trend—an increase in the reported rates of eating disorders, including anorexia, among American males. As Seligmann points out, it is not clear whether this trend represents a genuine increase in prevalence, an increase in the reporting of disorders that have been present all along, or both. But the research reported by Seligmann calls into question the longstanding assumption that eating disorders are almost exclusively disorders of women. Whether the underlying causes of these disorders differ for men and women remains an important question for future research.

In the next two articles, we examine two types of somatoform disorders, conditions characterized by symptoms that superficially suggest the presence of a physical ailment. In all cases of somatoform disorders, however, medical testing repeatedly fails to reveal any evidence for this underlying physical ailment. Benedict Carey first describes the enigmatic disorder of hypochondriasis, a condition in which affected individuals misinterpret innocuous physical symptoms as indicative of a dreaded disease, such as cancer, AIDS, or multiple sclerosis. The cardinal feature of hypochondriasis is "disease conviction," an unshakable belief that one is seriously ill despite overwhelming evidence to the contrary. Unlike most of us, who become preoccupied with our physical health from time to time, individuals with hypochondriasis typically express disappointment, rather than relief, when medical tests reveal no signs of an underlying disease. As Carey notes, cognitive-behavioral approaches, which involve questioning and challenging deep-seated assumptions and interpretations, appear to hold some promise in the treatment of hypochondriasis. Nevertheless, both the causes and treatment of hypochondriasis have received relatively little attention from research psychologists, in part because individuals with this disorder typically come to the attention of medical, rather than mental health, professionals.

A somatoform disorder that has received even less attention from psychologists is body dysmorphic disorder (BDD), known in the older literature as dysmorphophobia. Bruce Bower provides a brief overview of current research on the correlates and treatment of this largely neglected condition, which is characterized by a marked preoccupation with an imagined or extremely minor defect in appearance (for instance, a small facial mole or a slightly misshapen nose). Not surprisingly, many of these individuals seek cosmetic surgery to correct their supposed physical imperfections. In some cases, Bower observes, BDD can become delusional in intensity. BDD covaries with a number of other psychological disorders, including obsessive-compulsive disorder (see Reading 9) and social phobia, an extreme and persistent fear of scrutiny from others. In addition, like obsessive-compulsive disorder, BDD may respond positively to treatment with selective serotonin reuptake inhibitors (such as Prozac), as well as to behavioral treatments designed to expose individuals to their imagined physical anomalies. The relation of BDD to OCD and other anxiety disorders, however, requires further investigation.

It is becoming increasingly accepted among psychological researchers that personality variables can predispose individuals to certain physical conditions. Perhaps the best known of these variables is the Type A behavior pattern, which has been reported in many (but not all) studies to be associated with an increased risk of coronary heart disease. This pattern, which was first identified by the cardiologists Rosenman and Friedman, is associated with extreme time urgency, competitiveness, and hostility. As Edward Dolnick explains, however, most investigators now believe that Rosenman and Friedman's initial conceptualization of the Type A construct was overly broad. Instead, there is an emerging consensus that hostility is the only component of this pattern that is directly linked to subsequent heart disease. Some researchers, including Aron Siegman, further argue that only the overt expression of hostility, rather than subjective anger, is the principal culprit in coronary heart disease. Siegman's hypothesis is highly controversial, largely because it implies that the conscious suppression of anger may actually improve physical health. As Dolnick notes, this suggestion runs directly counter to psychoanalytic theorizing, which posits that catharsis—the release of pent-up emotions and impulses—is beneficial for both psychological and physical well-being.

The final two articles in this section deal with two disorders that have their origins in childhood or infancy. Uta Frith provides a glimpse into the bizarre and mysterious disorder of infantile autism, a condition marked by profound deficits in communication, social interaction, and imagination. Autistic individuals, Frith notes, exhibit severe deficits in language, experience difficulty forming close emotional bonds to others, and display profoundly restricted patterns of interests and activities. Since the formal discovery of autism by Leo Kanner in 1943, psychologists have wondered whether the strange pattern of abnormalities observed in this condition can be explained in terms of a single underlying dysfunction. Frith believes that it can. Specifically, she maintains that the features of autism derive from a specific neurological defect that in turn results in the absence of a "theory of mind." A theory of mind, according to Frith, involves the capacity to understand others' mental states—to theorize, so to speak, about what others are thinking and feeling. Such a theory permits us to empathize with, and anticipate the emotions and reactions of, other individuals. But a theory of mind has a darker side as well: it permits us to deceive others. Such capacities, Frith notes, are glaringly absent in the autistic individual, who can be thought of as "mindblind." The primary challenge for Frith and future researchers will be to demonstrate that the inability to comprehend others' mental states can account for all the major clinical features of autism.

Time magazine reporter Claudia Wallis concludes this section with a discussion of the controversial and, according to many critics loosely applied, diagnosis of attention-deficit/hyperactivity disorder (ADHD). Known simply as hyperactivity in the older psychological literature, ADHD is characterized by problems with inattention, impulsivity, and motoric overactivity that begin in childhood. As Wallis points out, ADHD is typically treated with either stimulant drugs (such as Ritalin), behavioral therapy designed to reinforce appropriate behavior, or both. Wallis describes some of the recent research on this condition, including findings that ADHD is associated with an increased risk for later antisocial behavior and substance abuse, is influenced by genetic factors, and is characterized by reduced blood flow in the prefrontal cortex. Despite a large body of literature on ADHD, however, its diagnosis and treatment remain controversial. Wallis's article raises at least two unsettling questions. Is the diagnosis of ADHD being applied by psychologists and psychiatrists to such a broad range of "normal" problems as to render it virtually meaningless from a practical perspective? And are large numbers of American children being medicated for mild and transient difficulties that are best handled by behavioral management—or perhaps just a helping of old-fashioned discipline?

DISCUSSION QUESTIONS

READING 10. P. Brown, "Understanding the Inner Voices"

1. Brown describes a number of intriguing findings concerning the physiology of schizophrenia, including enlarged cerebral ventricles and reduced prefrontal activity. How might one determine whether these abnormalities are a cause or a consequence of schizophrenia?

2. Brown discusses the work of Goldman-Rakic, who has used animal models in an effort to better understand the cognitive and behavioral symptoms of schizophrenia. How generalizable are animal models to human schizophrenia? What are their potential advantages and disadvantages?

3. Positron emission tomography (PET) scan studies have provided important insights into potential neurophysiological abnormalities in schizophrenia. But might PET scan studies have certain limitations for elucidating the etiology of schizophrenia? If so, what might they be?

4. As pointed out by Brown, some investigators have suggested that schizophrenia results from a failure to filter out irrelevant or extraneous stimuli. Do you believe that this hypothesis can account for all of the major clinical symptoms of schizophrenia? Why or why not?

READING 11. T. P. Dajer, "Divided Selves"

1. The study of MZ twins who are discordant for schizophrenia provides an extremely powerful vehicle for investigating possible environmental influences on this disorder. If you were conducting such a study, what potential environmental influences on schizophrenia would you examine and why?

2. How might a proponent of the viral hypothesis of schizophrenia, such as Torrey, explain the well-documented find-

ing that the concordance rate of schizophrenia is higher among MZ than dizygotic (DZ) twins? How might Torrey explain the results of adoption studies of schizophrenia, which show that offspring adopted away from biological parents with schizophrenia are at heightened risk for schizophrenia compared with offspring adopted away from non-schizophrenic biological parents?

3. A number of researchers have speculated that schizophrenia is not one disorder, but rather a collection of etiologically different disorders characterized by superficially similar symptoms. Is it therefore possible that both Torrey and Gottesman could be correct? How would you investigate the possibility that certain subtypes of schizophrenia are primarily viral in origin whereas others are primarily genetic in origin?

READING 12.   D. Hurley, "Imminent Danger"

1. Do you believe that individuals should be hospitalized against their will only if they are an imminent danger to themselves or others or are incapable of caring for themselves? Do you think that all severely psychotic individuals should be institutionalized against their will? Explain your reasoning.

2. Although Hurley asserts that mentally ill individuals are at no greater risk for violence than other individuals, recent research by John Monahan at the University of Virginia suggests that certain mentally ill individuals—especially those with delusions and hallucinations—may in fact be at somewhat heightened risk for dangerous behavior. What implications, if any, should Monahan's work have for involuntary commitment laws and other social policies directed toward the mentally ill?

3. It is well known among psychologists that future violence is extremely difficult to predict, largely because the vast majority of individuals who appear to be dangerous will in fact never engage in a violent act. If you were interviewing a mentally ill individual to ascertain his or her risk for imminent violence, what variables would you assess?

READING 13.   H. E. Marano, "Chemistry and Craving"

1. As described by Marano, Leibowitz's neurobiological model of appetite seems most clearly applicable to anorexia. How might Leibowitz's model be extended to bulimia, a condition typically associated by alternating episodes of binging and purging food?

2. Leibowitz argues that the body image distortion of the anorexic is a consequence, rather than a cause, of the disorder. Do you find this hypothesis plausible? How might you attempt to test it systematically?

3. Design a study to test Leibowitz's hypothesis that dieting increases the likelihood of anorexia and other eating disorders.

READING 14.   J. Seligmann, P. Rogers, & P. Annin, "The Pressure to Lose: Anorexia and Other Eating Disorders Are Gnawing Away at Young Men"

1. How would you attempt to determine whether the apparent increase in eating disorders among men represents a true rise in prevalence or a rise in the reporting of disorders that have been present all along?

2. What factors might cause males to want to lose massive amounts of weight? Are some of the variables that contribute to anorexia in females different from those that contribute to anorexia in males? If so, what might they be?

READING 15.   B. Carey, "The Mind of a Hypochondriac"

1. Some of the cognitive and behavioral characteristics of hypochondriasis appear similar to those of panic disorder (see Reading 7). In what ways are hypochondriasis and panic disorder similar, and in what ways are they different? How would you investigate the hypothesis that hypochondriasis and panic disorder stem from the same underlying mechanisms?

2. What types of personality characteristics might predispose individuals to hypochondriasis? What life experiences might interact with these personality traits to produce hypochondriasis?

3. How would a behaviorally oriented psychologist attempt to treat hypochondriasis?

READING 16.   B. Bower, "Deceptive Appearances: Imagined Physical Defects Take an Ugly Personal Toll"

1. As Bower points out, BDD sometimes reaches delusional proportions. Why, then, is BDD classified as a somatoform disorder rather than a psychotic disorder?

2. Might some or most cases of BDD represent atypical manifestations of obsessive-compulsive disorder? How would you attempt to test this possibility?

3. Should plastic surgeons refuse to perform operations on patients with BDD? Are there some cases in which such surgery could actually be psychologically harmful? If so, what might they be?

READING 17.   E. Dolnick, "Hotheads and Heart Attacks"

1. Do studies showing a longitudinal association between the Type H personality and later heart disease demonstrate a *causal* link between these two variables? Explain your reasoning.

2. It has been found that individuals who are hostile also tend to be more likely than other individuals to feel anxious and mistrustful of others. If you were designing a study, how would you attempt to rule out the hypothesis that anxiety and/or mistrust, rather than the Type H personality *per se*, is responsible for an increased risk of coronary heart disease?

3. Design a study to test Siegman's hypothesis that the conscious suppression of anger may actually reduce risk for subsequent heart attacks.

4. Are there certain individuals for whom the conscious suppression of anger might be beneficial, but others for whom it might be harmful? If so, what characteristics might differentiate these two groups of individuals?

READING 18. U. Frith, "Autism"

1. Do you believe that the absence of a "theory of mind" (that is, the inability to understand the minds of others) can account for all of the clinical features of autism? Are there symptoms of autism that seem difficult to explain by means of Frith's model? If so, what are they?

2. Most researchers believe that with the possible exception of a few extremely intelligent species (such as chimpanzees, orangutans, and dolphins), very few animals possess a theory of mind. Dogs and cats, for example, appear incapable of understanding another organism's state of mind. Would this imply that dogs, cats, and most other animals can be regarded as "autistic"? Or are there important ways in which such animals differ from autistic individuals?

3. When an autistic individual is watching a film, what types of interpersonal interactions is he or she unable to comprehend? What types of interpersonal interactions is he or she able to comprehend?

4. What research findings, if any, could *in principle* falsify Frith's model of autism?

READING 19. C. Wallis, "Life in Overdrive"

1. As noted by Wallis, many critics have charged that the ADHD diagnosis is often applied by clinicians to "normal-range" problems with inattention, impulsivity, and hyperactivity. How would you attempt to investigate this assertion systematically?

2. Wallis asks rhetorically, "How do you draw the line between a spontaneous, high-energy person who is feeling overwhelmed by the details of life and someone with a neurological disorder? Where is the boundary between personality and pathology?" (p. 102). If you were a researcher in this area, how would you seek to answer Wallis's questions? And how might you determine whether there even *is* a clear boundary between "normal" inattention, impulsiveness, and activity, on the one hand, and ADHD, on the other?

3. As Wallis points out, studies have shown that even normal individuals exhibit marked improvement in their attentional functioning after taking Ritalin and other stimulants. Does this finding call into question the validity of the ADHD diagnosis? Why or why not?

4. Wallis briefly discusses the evolutionary theorizing of Thom Hartmann, who suggests that many of the characteristics associated with ADHD, such as heightened vigilance and quick decision making, were adaptive in past hunting societies and have therefore been retained in the population by natural selection. Do you find Hartmann's explanation plausible? Is it testable by means of extant data? If so, how?

SUGGESTIONS FOR FURTHER READING

Baron-Cohen, S. (1995). *Mind-blindness: An essay on autism and theory of mind.* Cambridge, MA: MIT Press.

Barsky, A. J., & Klerman, G. L. (1983). Hypochondriasis, bodily complaints, and somatic styles. *American Journal of Psychiatry, 140,* 273–283.

Frith, U. (1989). *Autism: Explaining the enigma.* Oxford: Blackwell.

Gottesman, I. I. (1991). *Schizophrenia genesis: The origins of madness.* New York: W. H. Freeman.

Gottesman, I. I., & Shields, J. (1982). *Schizophrenia: The epigenetic puzzle.* Cambridge, England: Cambridge University Press.

Hinshaw, S. P. (1994). *Attention deficits and hyperactivity in children.* Thousand Oaks, CA: Sage Publications.

Kirmayer, L. J., Robbins, J. M., & Paris, J. (1994). Somatoform disorders: Personality and the social matrix of distress. *Journal of Abnormal Psychology, 103,* 125–136.

Williams, R. B. (1989). *The trusting heart: Great news about Type A behavior.* New York: Times Books.

TIMOTHY is trying to explain what it feels like to have a near-constant stream of spoken thoughts intruding into his mind from outside. He holds the remote-control handset in front of the TV. "Suppose I want to watch 2. Well, the thoughts in my head will say, 'Why don't you press 3? We want to watch 3'."

That's just the trivial, everyday irritation of an illness that has profoundly affected Timothy's whole life. In fact, he has lost almost everything. He has not seen his son for eight years. His marriage broke down more than a decade ago and he hasn't had a relationship since. He has given up his business and his flat. For someone whose life has been torn apart by disease, he does not seem bitter.

Schizophrenia is still one of the most controversial areas in both psychology and neuroscience. Do the answers lie in imaging techniques and genetics? Phyllida Brown investigates

biological disorder of the brain, not some mysterious demon. Increasingly, the evidence points to abnormalities that arise very early in life, probably before birth, which disrupt the normal development of the brain. The challenge facing scientists is not only to uncover the precise nature of those abnormalities and devise methods of treating them, but also to show how they relate to the disturbances of mind suffered by schizophrenics. The task will keep researchers busy for years, but if they succeed the benefits of their work will bring them up against some of the biggest questions in neuroscience—the neural roots of personality, language and perhaps even consciousness itself.

First, a rapid tour of what little we

UNDERSTANDING THE INNER VOICES

But then perhaps he is just being polite.

Timothy (not his real name) has schizophrenia. Half a million others in Britain, and 2 million in the US, will suffer from the disease at some time in their lives, making it one of the commonest health problems in industrialised societies. For each sufferer, a string of relatives will also be affected. One estimate suggests that schizophrenia costs Britain about £2·7 billion a year, or 2 per cent of GNP.

Bizarre symptoms

Yet our knowledge of the roots of the disease and our ability to treat it remain primitive. Almost a century after the syndrome was first labelled, psychiatrists must still rely on signs and symptoms alone to diagnose schizophrenia. Drugs have improved, but their effect is mostly to dampen down the most bizarre symptoms, leaving equally disabling aspects of the disease untouched.

Meanwhile, public ignorance about schizophrenia seems as great as ever. While a scattering of violent attacks has led the media to stereotype schizophrenics as a threat to society, the truth is that

overall, they are no more likely to be violent than anyone else. The only person a schizophrenic is likely to harm is himself or herself; one study found that almost a third of schizophrenics had tried to commit suicide at some time.

All this might sound bleak, but research into schizophrenia is slowly beginning to gather momentum. Imaging techniques are helping to identify physical abnormalities in schizophrenics' brains, and now scientists are trying to link these abnormalities with specific symptoms of the disease. Geneticists are searching for the "schizophrenia gene" or genes (see "Elusive genes"), applying the techniques that have been successful in pinpointing the genes behind disorders such as cystic fibrosis. Molecular biologists are analysing differences identified in the architecture of nerve cells in the brains of schizophrenics and abnormalities in receptor molecules on the surfaces of these cells. And a few researchers even claim to be making progress in understanding the disease through experiments on animals.

The main message from all these separate strands is clear; schizophrenia is a

already know. Schizophrenics do not, as popular myth holds, have split personalities. Rather, the disease causes a wider fragmentation of their intellect and social selves, attacking the very qualities that make us human. Schizophrenics often have difficulty communicating in language or facial expression and are unable to put themselves in someone else's shoes, or to judge others' intentions towards them. There are clear physical and structural differences in schizophrenics' brains. For example, studies using computerised tomography (CT) scans have shown that the lateral ventricles tend to be significantly bigger than in healthy brains. And a form of magnetic resonance imaging has revealed that schizophrenic brains often have a smaller volume of tissue in the left temporal lobe than normal brains. But the links between such abnormalities and symptoms are still unclear.

Ferrying impulses

In chemistry as well as structure, the schizophrenic brain differs from the normal brain. For example, there are complex differences which have yet to be fully understood in the way it handles

From *New Scientist*, 143, pp. 26–31, July 9, 1994. Reprinted with permission of IPC Magazines Ltd.

Healthy brains tend to generate a random sequence, such as 'red, red, black, red, black, red'. Schizophrenics are more likely to come up with a stereotyped response, such as 'red, black, red, black, red, black'.

dopamine, a neurotransmitter, that ferries impulses between nerve cells (see "The dopamine link").

Increasingly, scientists believe that schizophrenia may be a syndrome caused by more than one underlying disease. If the different diseases could be singled out, scientists argue, then the search for genes and other causative factors might be much easier.

In psychiatrists' jargon, schizophrenics' symptoms are divided into so-called "positive" and "negative" categories. Positive symptoms include hearing voices or others discussing you in the third person, paranoia and thinking that thoughts are coming into your head from elsewhere.

Frightening as these experiences must be, it is the so-called negative symptoms that may be more disabling in the long term. People with schizophrenia tend to be extremely poor communicators. Many lack the ability to make small talk and if you ask questions you will tend to get one-word answers. Critically, they also seem to have difficulties with what psychologists call working memory—the ability to keep information in mind long enough to use it for a specific task. For example, our brains use working memory to speak in sentences, holding the beginning of a sentence in mind until we finish it. And schizophrenics tend to lack the will to initiate actions, relying instead on external stimuli to do so.

So far, such knowledge has grown slowly, but now the pace is accelerating. One fashionable area involves the use of scanning techniques such as PET (positron emission tomography), which measures the flow of blood in the brain and allows scientists to identify which bits of the brain "light up" as people perform psychological tests. Its enthusiasts hope

So far, no one has found any specific abnormalities common to all schizophrenics, but they have found that particular symptoms go hand in hand with particular abnormalities.

to reduce schizophrenia to specific cognitive processes mapped to particular networks of neurons in the brain.

One such team, led by Chris Frith and others funded by the Medical Research Council at the Hammersmith Hospital in London, is comparing normal and schizophrenic brains as they tackle specific psychological tests. With PET, you can—in theory—watch how these tests affect the brain. But, warns Frith, it is vital to study normal brains first and, because of the broad range of symptoms that are lumped together as schizophrenia, essential also to study subgroups of patients who all have the same symptoms, such as intruding thoughts, rather than patients with varying symptoms who have all been diagnosed as schizophrenic. So far, no one has found any specific abnormalities common to all schizophrenics, but they have found that particular symptoms go hand in hand with particular abnormalities.

Cognitive tests are a way of modelling a thought process. Take, for example, the observation that schizophrenics suffer from lack of will. In cognitive terms, says Frith, this can be modelled by asking a person to guess what colour the next card in a pack will be. The point is not to guess correctly, but to be able to initiate thoughts about the colours. Healthy brains tend to generate a random sequence, such as "red, red, black, red, black, red". Schizophrenics are more likely to come up with a stereotyped response, such as "red, black, red, black, red, black"; or "red, red, red, red, red, red".

So far, studies by Frith's group and others in Sweden and the US consistently find reduced brain activity in the prefrontal cortex in schizophrenics with negative symptoms. Occupying almost a third of the entire cortex, this cortex has evolved in humans to greater complexity and size than in any other organism. The PET results also reveal abnormalities in other brain structures, including the hippocampus, which is con-

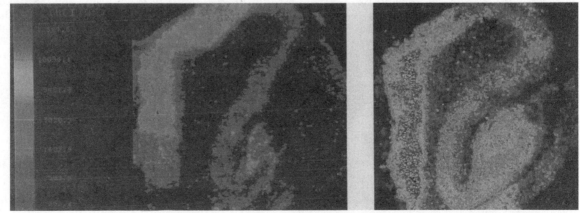

Imaging studies show reduced levels of a receptor for glutamate in the brain of a schizophrenic (left). The structure here is the hippocampus, involved in learning and memory. The right image is of a normal hippocampus

cerned particularly with learning and memory. Most researchers believe there is no single brain structure at fault.

In a separate study, Philip McGuire at the Institute of Psychiatry in London and colleagues scanned schizophrenics with positive symptoms while they were "hearing voices". Using the technique of single-photon emission tomography (SPET), the team found that during these episodes of voice-hearing, the blood flow was greater than normal to the part of the brain known as Broca's area, which has long been linked with articulated language. The same people were scanned again under identical conditions some weeks later when their voices had stopped; this time, there was no significant increase in the flow of blood to Broca's area.

Language flow

Daniel Weinberger at the National Institute of Mental Health (NIMH) in Washington DC has studied identical twins where one is schizophrenic. This approach has the advantage that the twins act as each other's controls, differences in the brain of the affected twin are far more likely to be due to the disease itself than to other factors. Weinberger's findings add to the evidence that the prefrontal area functions abnormally in schizophrenia. They also show that in affected twins the hippocampus is smaller and becomes overactive during tasks that require working memory. Indeed, the less active the prefrontal cortex in the affected twin, the smaller the hippocampus. This strengthens the idea that schizophrenia involves faults in different areas of the brain rather than one single region.

Studies like these are still in their

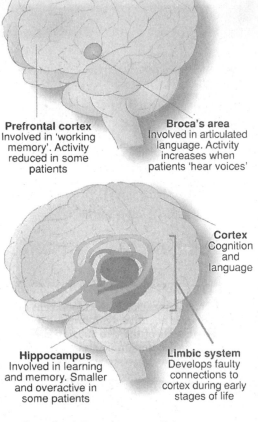

Prefrontal cortex
Involved in 'working memory'. Activity reduced in some patients

Broca's area
Involved in articulated language. Activity increases when patients 'hear voices'

Cortex
Cognition and language

Hippocampus
Involved in learning and memory. Smaller and overactive in some patients

Limbic system
Develops faulty connections to cortex during early stages of life

Some of the abnormalities seen in schizophrenic brains

infancy, and there are pitfalls, warn the researchers. For example, if patients are being scanned while they attempt some task that they find difficult (such as guess the colour of the next card), isn't it to be expected that the pattern of brain activity will differ from the pattern in people who find the task easy? Can that difference necessarily be attributed to schizophrenia? How do you account for the effects of drug treatments? And, with the exception of twin studies, how do you ensure you

have a proper control group?

The research also makes unusual demands on their participants. Timothy has been involved in several studies with the Institute of Psychiatry that have required him to spend long periods of time in the scanner. "When they did one scan, the thoughts were really bad that day," he says. But he thinks the research is worthwhile. "So it sounds masochistic, but in a way I was pleased," he says.

There are more fundamental concerns, too. Some scientists, such as Robert Knight at the University of California, Davis, think that the rush to use PET may be naive unless researchers make careful use of the results. There is a risk, says Knight, that the approach could degenerate into a kind of latter-day phrenology. PET can tell you that specific areas of the brain have been activated, he says, but not how they are interacting. Moreover, broad brush neuroanatomical insights of the kind produced by PET may in the end reveal little about the detailed molecular or cellular basis of conditions such as schizophrenia.

Another, more extreme, attempt to reduce schizophrenia to its component parts uses animals. The idea here is to take the mental abilities that are believed to break down in the disease, look for their counterparts in animals and locate the neuronal networks that are activated when the animals display these abilities. The high priestess of this approach is Patricia Goldman-Rakic at Yale University, who is studying working memory in monkeys. You might reasonably ask how an animal without language skills can tell you anything about schizophrenics, but Goldman-Rakic is adamant: "There is a lot of reason to believe that

Elusive genes

IN THE past gene hunters have claimed to find evidence for a "schizophrenia susceptibility gene" on chromosomes 5, 11, 22 and the X chromosome. Some of these claims have fallen flat, others remain unsubstantiated, and few teams expect to find such a gene tomorrow. Nevertheless, scientists are confident that schizophrenia has a large inherited component, partly because in

studies where both twins suffer from the disease, a higher proportion are identical than nonidentical.

In the 1990s, scientists are using molecular methods to speed up the hunt for schizophrenia genes. Some, such as Peter McGuffin and Mike Owen at the University of Wales College of Medicine in Cardiff, are using the techniques known as positional cloning to search through the DNA of individuals from at least 200 pairs of sib-

lings affected by schizophrenia in the hope of locating genes linked with the disorder.

The Cardiff team and others in the US are also planning another approach. There is some evidence, still controversial, that schizophrenia develops at earlier and earlier ages in successive generations of families heavily affected by the disease. This pattern has parallels with certain other conditions such as fragile X syndrome and Huntington's disease, which

are known to be caused by defective genes made up of DNA "stutters"—repeated sequences of triplets of base pairs of varying length. The longer the repeat, the more severe the syndrome and the earlier the disease starts. If schizophrenia has a similar genetic basis, some scientists believe that hunting for trinucleotide repeats in the genomes of affected family members may help them to close in on their quarry.

the breakdown of working memory function is the essence of thought disorder."

Her model of working memory in monkeys focuses on the animals' ability to hold a visual image in mind. Goldman-Rakic says the team has identified subsets of neurons in the prefrontal cortex that are "programmed" specifically to hold visual images in working memory. Different subsets of neurons are dedicated to handling different types of information, she says.

The researchers believe they have more support for their theory from observations of people with localised brain damage in the prefrontal cortex—caused, for example, by a tumour or a stroke. Often, such people suffer specific symptoms, such as apathy and social withdrawal, similar to certain aspects of schizophrenia. "There is a profound similarity in the symptoms exhibited by schizophrenics and patients with prefrontal lobe damage," says Goldman-Rakic.

In her latest study, she asked a group of people with prefrontal brain damage and a group of schizophrenics to perform a modified version of the monkeys' working-memory task. Both groups' performance on the test was impaired, she says, compared with healthy volunteers and people with damage in other regions of the brain.

Fatty substances

Goldman-Rakic and others, such as Weinberger at the NIMH and Jay Pettegrew at the University of Pittsburgh, are now taking the next step to try to identify the biochemical changes that make networks of neurons malfunction in schizophrenia. No one has made a breakthrough yet, but several teams have detected imbalances in constituents of the fatty substances called phospholipids that make up the cell membranes of neurons. Alterations in the membrane could affect the communication between cells and disrupt the performance of specific receptors for neurotransmitters such as dopamine or acetylcholine. For example, researchers in Scotland have found abnormalities in two

> **"There is a profound similarity in the symptoms exhibited by schizophrenics and patients with prefrontal lobe damage."**

long-chain fatty acids in the blood cells of people with negative symptoms. Breakdown products of the two substances are involved in the dopamine system.

While the reductionist approach of these studies may produce intriguing results, not everyone is satisfied. Most scientists seek a more complete theory to explain schizophrenia. Frith, for example, contends that the essential problem is a breakdown in the brain's ability to monitor the information it handles. This would tend to make the brain "think" that internal events were externally driven, he says—for example, voices or thoughts that are generated within the mind but perceived as someone else's.

Flailing room

There are parallels for this monitoring system: for example, when your eyes scan around a room, the room appears to stay still. By contrast, if you gently move your eyeball from side to side by mechanically shifting it with a fingertip, the room starts to flail about alarmingly. More than a century ago, scientists concluded from this observation that the brain must be monitoring visual information and correcting it to make sense.

Frith's theory finds some indirect support from work by Robert Knight in California. A healthy brain, says Knight, constantly filters out irrelevant stimuli—the sound of air conditioning in an office, for example—but will react sharply to new information—such as the sound of a fire alarm. By measuring the electrical activity of the brain in response to specific stimuli, Knight has shown that stroke patients' with damaged prefrontal brains are both less efficient at screening out irrelevant information, and less likely to enhance new stimuli, than healthy brains.

No one is yet saying that Knight's findings in stroke patients can explain the intruders in schizophrenics' heads, but his theory of damaged filtering finds striking similarities with the way schizophrenics describe their symptoms. "Everything was very loud," said one in interviews with Fiona Macmillan, a researcher who collected the experiences of many schizophrenics during the 1980s. "I could hear the ash cracking off the end of

---

The dopamine link

THE STRONGEST evidence to support the involvement of dopamine in schizophrenia is that drugs which block certain dopamine receptors in the basal ganglia reduce the symptoms of the disease, while other drugs that stimulate the dopamine system, such as amphetamines, can produce schizophrenia-like symptoms even in healthy people. These observations led scientists to predict that the dopamine system was somehow "turned up" in schizophrenia: either there was too much dopamine in the schizophrenic brain, or there were too many receptors.

It seems that neither explanation is right. The disturbance of the dopamine system must be secondary to some other molecular effect, scientists believe, such as imbalances in components of cell membranes.

Lyn Pilowsky and her colleagues at the Institute of Psychiatry in London and at the Institute of Nuclear Medicine have used single-photon emission tomography (SPET) to track a radiolabelled mimic of dopamine in the brains of schizophrenics and to watch the activity of drugs that are believed to block its receptors. There are five known types of dopamine receptor, dubbed D1 to D5, and probably many more waiting to be discovered. The team has found no overall dif-

Dopamine pathway

Some schizophrenics have abnormalities that affect the way their brain uses dopamine

Basal ganglia

ferences from normal brains, but has detected subtle abnormalities in D2 receptors in the basal ganglia, including an apparent increase in the density of receptors. This higher binding capacity seems to be more pronounced in men than women and seems to be restricted to the left hemisphere.

Schizophrenia, maybe, is the evolutionary price we pay for the human

brain's highly developed capacity for language and social activity . . .

the genes responsible must carry other advantages that help to conserve them

the cigarette and hitting the floor.

Attempts like these to devise an overall theory of the malfunctions that add up to schizophrenia may help scientists to frame the right research questions. But they cannot help to solve the mystery of what causes the disease, and on this matter the jury is still out. After years of supposing that the abnormalities in the brain arose at the time of the onset of disease—usually early adulthood—neurobiologists are now suggesting something very different.

Weinberger argues instead that the disorder begins early in the development of the brain, probably before the end of the second trimester of pregnancy. Either because of a genetic defect or an environmental insult such as a viral infection, the migration of neurons to their correct places in the forming brain may be disrupted, he argues. As a result, the cortex of the brain develops faultily and there are abnormal connections between the cortex and the limbic system, the group of structures including the hippocampus and the hypothalamus that are thought to be concerned with emotion and motivation.

The latest evidence for this idea comes from the Institute of Psychiatry in London, where Robert Kerwin and his colleagues have made postmortem studies of the brains of people with schizophrenia. They have found abnormalities and reductions in the numbers of some types of glutamate receptor, particularly in the regions of the temporal lobe that are physically abnormal. It is already known that certain types of glutamate receptor are involved in the development and migration of embryo neurons.

But if the seeds of schizophrenia are sown before birth, why does the disease only become noticeable a couple of decades later? One idea is that, once damaged brain architecture sets the scene, certain features of normal adult brain development trigger the disease, and this is where dopamine and environ-

mental factors may come into play, says Weinberger. The basic idea is not new but has been given fresh impetus from experiments with rats. Based on the results, Weinberger claims that faulty development of the connections between the limbic system and the prefrontal cortex may lead to symptoms in young adulthood that are triggered by environmental stress.

Some researchers are bent on finding a deeper explanation for the causes and orgins of schizophrenia. One of the most controversial ideas comes from Tim Crow at the Clinical Research Centre at Northwick Park Hospital in Harrow, north London. Schizophrenia, he argues, is the evolutionary price we pay for the human

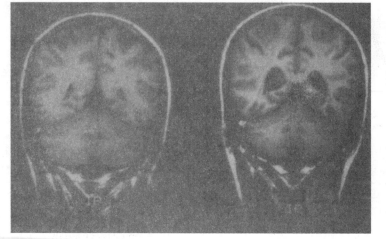

Disease anatomy. these MRI scans of identical twins, one with schizophrenia, reveal enlarged cerebral ventricles in the affected twin (right)

brain's highly developed capacity for language and social activity.

Crow's starting point is the surprisingly uniform incidence of schizophrenia worldwide, between 0·7 and 1·4 per cent in all societies studied to date, when the disease is narrowly defined. Crow argues that this suggests a genetic disease independent of environmental triggers such as viruses. He also points out that the disease remains common even though schizophrenics are less likely to have children than the general population. So, he argues, the gene responsible must

carry other advantages that help to conserve it in the gene pool.

Crow and others claim to have evidence—disputed in some circles—that schizophrenics' brains are less likely than normal brains to show specialisation of one side of the brain. Hemispheric specialisation—or "asymmetry"—is a normal characteristic in humans which varies from person to person. Numerous teams have also found that the structural and functional abnormalities in the brains of schizophrenics tend to be concentrated in the left hemisphere, which deals with language in right-handed people. Crow argues that a diversity in the population of different degrees of asymmetry is associated with normal variation in personality and intelligence. If we suppose there is a gene or genes governing asymmetry, then in Crow's theory, schizophrenia—and other forms of psychosis such as manic depression—are the extreme and disadvantageous ends of the range, resulting from particular forms of the gene or genes.

For people with schizophrenia like Timothy, no theory is much comfort unless it can hasten the development of better drug treatments and therapies. Nevertheless, he continues to participate in research because he knows that schizophrenia runs in families—his own included—and he wants to see progress for the next generation. By the time children born into schizophrenic families today reach adulthood, there may be some hope, says Goldman-Rakic. "In 20 years there won't necessarily be a cure," she says. "But I think we will maybe understand better the genes that are involved, and the changes in receptors." She foresees a more sophisticated armoury of drugs for the disease, which will not merely suppress the positive symptoms but also maintain normal cognitive processes, such as working memory. "None of this is saying that we will be able to make schizophrenics normal," she says, but it might make their lives more tolerable. □

FULLER TORREY HAS ONE GOAL IN LIFE: to prove Irving Gottesman wrong. Gottesman, for his part, is just as determined to nail Torrey. And either would be delighted to see the other win. ▪ Torrey, 55, senior psychiatrist at St. Elizabeths Hospital in Washington, D.C., is a world expert on the viral theory of schizophrenia. Gottesman, 61, Commonwealth Professor of Psychology at the University of Virginia, is one of the best gene sleuths around. The question at hand: whether the baffling illness of

By Tony Dajer

PHOTOGRAPHS BY
Max Aguilera-Hellweg

Discordant twins:
Marjorie Murphy (far right)
has schizophrenia;
her sister, Sharon, is well.

divided
selves

To get to the bottom of schizophrenia, two scientific rivals are seeking help from some unusual twins— twins who are identical in all respects but one.

schizophrenia springs primarily from an infection or is caused by defective genes. To settle the issue, the friendly arch-rivals have embarked on an unusual venture designed to leave one of them in the dust. "Irving," says Torrey, "is a lively and honest researcher with whom I can disagree with pleasure." ▪ The whole enterprise hinges on a medical quirk. Schizophrenia is a common disease, affecting over a million people in this country alone. Given such large numbers it's possible to find occasional cases of people with schizophrenia who have an identical twin, a sibling who shares their exact genetic heritage. About half the

From *Discover, 13,* pp. 38–69, September 1992. Tony Dajer/© 1992 The Walt Disney Co. Reprinted with permission of Discover Magazine.

time the twin is also schizophrenic, but the rest of the time the twin is normal (though some display borderline schizophrenic traits that label them as slightly eccentric). These "discordant" twin pairs—one ill, one well—constitute a potentially powerful means to tease out schizophrenia's secrets.

Despite the mental devastation it creates, schizophrenia leaves maddeningly few traces. You can't point to a definite cause like a virus or a bacterium or a defective gene, as you can with many other brain diseases. Nor can you see glaring damage like holes or scars when you autopsy a schizophrenic's brain. And although researchers have tried scanning the brains of hundreds of schizophrenics and healthy volunteers, they've been unsure if the dif-

striking dissociation of reason and emotion that makes patients laugh during funerals or imbue a mundane object or gesture with some spectacularly inappropriate significance. Schizophrenics, who are typically diagnosed when they are adolescents or young adults, become prey to fantastic hallucinations and hear voices conversing in their head. They may develop paranoid or grandiose delusions—a fear that the CIA can control or read their thoughts, for example, or the conviction that their destiny is to fulfill some exalted messianic mission. Yet they can also become intensely withdrawn, apparently unfeeling, or overcome by an apathetic stupor. So profoundly does schizophrenia unhinge the mind that many victims never make their way back to reality.

medical world with his discovery that so-called slow viruses could linger in the brain for 20 years or more before causing symptoms. The classic disease of this kind was kuru, which started as clumsiness and ended as mind-obliterating dementia and which afflicted only tribesmen in the New Guinea highlands who ate the brains of the deceased during their funeral rituals. To contract kuru, Gajdusek found, you had to consume the brain of someone already infected. Gajdusek (who won the 1976 Nobel Prize for medicine) proved his point by injecting infected brain tissue into chimpanzees: not only did they get the disease, but their damaged brains developed the same peculiar Swiss-cheese appearance as those of human kuru victims. "When

"The first thing Gajdusek did was blast me: You psychiatrists have gotten so hung up on Freud, you've forgotten how to be scientists."

ferences they saw were due to schizophrenia or to individual brain variation.

That's why twins are so inordinately useful for this kind of study. If you could compare a schizophrenic with his or her genetically identical yet normal twin, any differences would very likely be due to the disease process. It would be like superimposing, in the same person, the cardboard cutout for disease on the one for health. If you found discrepancies between the two, you could conclude that that's where schizophrenia probably lurks and search for its cause.

That, in short, was Torrey's reasoning. So in 1986, after seeking out Gottesman's involvement as a "respected counterpoint to my own bias," he assembled a sample of willing twins and a network of psychologists, geneticists, virologists, biochemists, statisticians, and brain scanners to launch an unprecedented assault on the roots of madness.

The first descriptions of what a modern psychiatrist would call schizophrenia were written in 1809, but it wasn't until a century later that Eugen Bleuler, a Swiss psychiatrist, gave the disease a name. Schizophrenia literally means "split mind," but popular myth notwithstanding, it has nothing to do with multiple personalities. Bleuler was referring to an odd ungluing of the mind, to the kind of

Torrey vividly remembers his first encounter with the illness. He was 19 and a premed student at the time. "It was the summer before Rhoda, my seventeen-year-old sister, was supposed to start college," he recounts. "She began having delusions that the British redcoats were attacking America. My mother told me she would discuss the Revolutionary War at dinner, the kind of stuff you learn in history class. At first my mother thought Rhoda was kidding. But then one day she found her lying on the front lawn talking to imaginary voices about the British attacks. When I got home from college, my sister looked physically, neurologically sick to me. In just weeks she'd gone from normalcy—the sister I'd grown up with—to full-blown psychosis."

BY THE END of medical school Torrey had decided to specialize in psychiatry. After completing his residency at Stanford Medical School and doing a stint at the National Institute of Mental Health, he was put in charge of a ward at St. Elizabeths. There the young psychiatrist quickly found himself immersed in the mystery of his patients' insanity.

A major influence on him at the time was the physician and virologist Carleton Gajdusek. In 1972 Gajdusek jolted the

New Guinea highlanders stopped eating brains," Torrey says, "they stopped getting kuru."

As a psychiatrist, though, Torrey was swimming against the tide of his profession by even considering biological explanations for mental illness. The rise of psychoanalysis at the turn of the century—and a paucity of biological findings—had given psychological explanations like upbringing and bad parenting a stranglehold on the debate over the causes of schizophrenia.

"When I met Gajdusek," he recalls, "the first thing he did was blast me: You psychiatrists have gotten so hung up on Freud, you've forgotten how to be scientists! And he was right; we had stopped treating schizophrenia like a physical, measurable disease." Goaded by Gajdusek, Torrey began acting like a microbiologist. He asked permission from patients to perform spinal taps and analyze their cerebrospinal fluid, the fluid that bathes

MRI scans show that ventricles at the brain's core are larger in a schizophrenic (center right) than in his normal twin (top left).

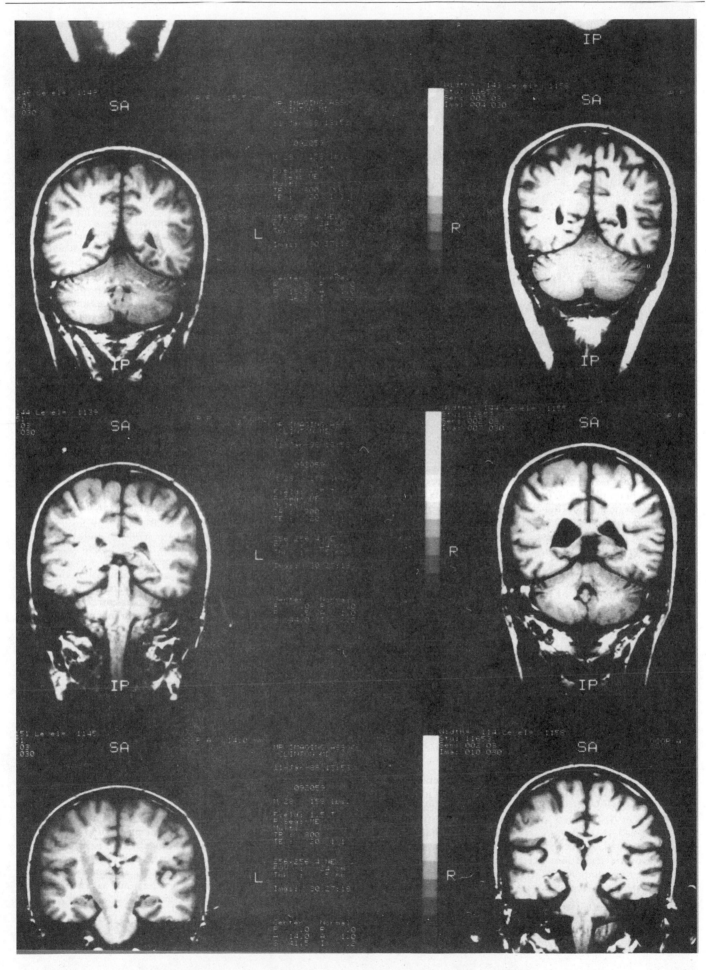

But while studies like these showed that schizophrenia had to have a genetic component, they left a thorny question in their wake: If schizophrenia were due only to genes, why didn't 100 percent of the identical twins—not the observed 50 percent—share the disease?

the brain and spinal cord, to look for the footprints of viral infection. He didn't find much, but back then, no one did. (Gajdusek tried injecting chimps with brain tissue taken from autopsied schizophrenics, but the experiment failed to work.) "When I look back," says Torrey, "I shudder to think how primitive our methods were. In the 1970s viral research was barely in its infancy."

In the meantime, however, the advocates of a biological explanation were getting reinforcements from a very different quarter. Although it was known that schizophrenia can run in families, the blame had usually been ascribed to nurture (the home environment) rather than to nature (the patients' genes). But in the late 1960s and early 1970s studies began to show that genes far outweighed upbringing as a risk factor for schizophre-

nia. Children of schizophrenics adopted by normal families, for example, had the same risk of developing the illness as children raised by schizophrenic parents. What's more, an identical twin of a schizophrenic was four times as likely to develop the illness as a nonidentical twin.

One of the young researchers who was helping kick the door open for biology was Gottesman. In 1971 he had joined a pioneering team of Danish geneticists that was studying the children of identical twins who were discordant (one ill, one well) for schizophrenia. After following the families for 18 years, Gottesman confirmed the startling finding that the risk of schizophrenia in the children of either twin was exactly the same: 17 percent. That meant that even if "schizogenes" were not activated in one generation, they could be passed on to

the next and then make mischief.

But while studies like these showed that schizophrenia had to have a genetic component, they left a thorny question in their wake: If schizophrenia were due only to genes, why didn't 100 percent of the identical twins—not the observed 50 percent—share the disease? "The most likely explanation," ventures Gottesman, "is that the right combination of genes—probably four or five—plus some as yet undefined environmental stressors must be thrown together to trigger schizophrenia. But before we can figure out what activates the genes in the twins who become ill, we must first find the genes themselves. The trick now is to hunt those genes down to their chromosomes and map them"—a trick that he hopes some of Torrey's twins will help him pull off.

While Gottesman was making a name for himself studying Danish twins, Torrey continued to collect schizophrenics' cerebrospinal fluid and blood in pursuit of a "schizovirus." It was a monumental wild-goose chase, but a number of clues sustained him in his belief.

For example, viral infections of the temporal lobes—notably herpes simplex type I, the common cold-sore virus—can produce hallucinations and bizarre behavior bearing an uncanny resemblance to schizophrenia. In fact, physicians often mistake the one for the other. Moreover, unlike any other mental illness, schizophrenia is more common among those born in winter, when viral infections abound. In a Scandinavian study of children with a strong family history of schizophrenia, an increase of 70 percent in the rate of schizophrenia was found among those whose mothers had contracted influenza during the second trimester of pregnancy.

Yet despite such circumstantial evidence, Torrey's cerebrospinal-fluid and blood analyses failed to turn up solid viral suspects. And even if his schizovirus existed, those tests couldn't tell him where in the brain it might be doing its work. To identify the virus he would have to locate its base of operations.

". . . the right combination of genes . . . plus some as yet undefined environmental stressors must be thrown together to trigger schizophrenia."

A possible approach turned up in the 1980s with the introduction of a brain-scanning technique called magnetic resonance imaging (MRI). Compared with existing technologies such as CT scans, the new tool produced dazzling brain pictures with an astonishing amount of anatomical detail. Even so, it wasn't initially all that helpful for schizophrenia. It found variations in schizophrenics' brains—but they were subtle and not peculiar enough to schizophrenia to distinguish it from other brain diseases or even from normal variation. Studies showed, for example, that the ventricles, a pair of fluid-filled structures that curl around the brain's inner pith like ram's horns, were often unusually large in schizophrenics. But enlarged ventricles were also seen in Alzheimer's and Parkinson's patients, and even in normal old people.

By 1986 it was clear to Torrey that only identical twins who were discordant for schizophrenia could show up the small discrepancies he needed to flush out his prey. Through the National Alliance for the Mentally Ill, he gathered twins that fit the bill. So far he has found 30 pairs of clearly discordant twins—and, for comparison, 30 more pairs who are either both schizophrenic, both normal, or somewhere in between (one schizophrenic twin and one ostensibly normal twin with schizophrenic tendencies).

The studies haven't been easy to do, however. MRI scans are obtained by submitting the brain to strong magnetic fields and then measuring the signals from the different tissues inside it. Taking these images requires patients to lie without moving a muscle inside a dark, clanking, tubelike chamber, a process that terrifies even normal patients who have a touch of claustrophobia. For patients whose grip on reality is already fragile, the procedure required immense courage. With one schizophrenic twin, Torrey recalls, "I had to promise to buy her a skirt and blouse if she went through the whole thing. I held her hand the whole time. She was very brave." Altogether, 15 pairs of discordant twins were examined for Torrey's initial MRI study.

The results, published in March 1990 in the New England Journal of Medicine, caused quite a stir. Like earlier MRI studies, this one showed that the schizophrenic twins had enlarged ventricles, but it also revealed a striking change in a crucial brain structure called the hippocampus. The hippocampus (the name derives from the Greek for "sea horse," which it's said to resemble) clings to the inner surface of the temporal lobes, which are behind the temples, on either side of the brain. The hippocampus is apparently where input from the senses is hammered into new memories and where the components of old memories are reassembled for recall. And lo and behold, in Torrey's schizophrenics, the hippocampus, especially the left half of the hippocampus, was noticeably smaller than in the normal twins. Indeed, his scanning team thinks that the ventricles may become enlarged in schizophrenics because of a loss of surrounding tissue, including shrinkage of the hippocampus.

That evidence seemed to tie in nicely with autopsy studies begun in the mid-1980s that showed signs of cell loss and disarray in the left hippocampus and its anatomic neighbors in the limbic system. The limbic system controls our emotional response—another function thrown out of whack by schizophrenia. And it fit with another finding: that schizophrenics did poorly on certain memory tests, suggesting that impaired memory was perhaps a component of schizophrenia.

Classically, schizophrenia was considered a disease of the frontal lobes, the seat of abstract, higher thought. (This idea had unfortunate repercussions: in the 1940s, it served as the rationale for the frontal lobotomies that were performed on thousands of schizophrenics.) But the left hippocampus, linchpin of memory, is part of the left temporal lobe. Could schizophrenia be a problem of the left temporal lobe instead?

ANOTHER NEWER school of thought implicated the entire left side of the brain—the hemisphere that generates language and thus defines the interpretation of words and symbols. One thing that makes the world so terrifying for schizophrenics is the destruction of those defining limits. Thus a misplaced coffee cup can become imbued with peculiar meaning; a stranger's gesture can signal the arrival of the redcoats or the CIA. The result is a paralyzing paranoia.

Torrey, for his part, suspected that the temporal lobe was to blame. But for him the hallmark of schizophrenia is hearing voices. "No other symptom," he argues, "is as specific to schizophrenia: 75 percent of all patients hear voices—voices that command you to kill yourself, voices from outer space, two voices carrying on

In Torrey's schizophrenics, the hippocampus, especially the left half of the hippocampus, was noticeably smaller than in the normal twins. . . . Could schizophrenia be a problem of the left temporal lobe instead?

a conversation, even the voice of God. To us scientists, they seem to be saying, Pay attention, there may be a big clue here."

The temporal lobe, it turns out, is home not only to the hippocampus and other limbic structures but to the nerve fibers that carry input from the ears. If an infection caused the limbic-system damage seen in the autopsy studies, Torrey argues, then maybe it could damage these fibers as well, and one might hear voices. "Autopsies showing cell disarray in these areas," he says, "appear to fit with what we've found on our MRIs."

Still, good as the MRIs have been at locating abnormalities in the brain, they could say nothing about when the damage occurred. That's the question Stefan Bracha, a psychiatrist at the University of Arkansas Medical School in Little Rock, set out to answer. One of schizophrenia's peculiarities is its predictable age of onset: 18 for men, 23 for women, on average. Does that mean that young adults are more susceptible than other age groups to certain viruses or genetic malfunctions? Or is schizophrenia a delayed reaction to damage that occurred years before? (Kuru, recall, took up to 20 years to manifest itself in New Guinea highlanders who had eaten infected brains.)

Pathological studies of schizophrenic brains have never shown signs of the scarring one would expect from viral infections. However, in the special case of damage caused to a fetus in its mother's womb, the brain doesn't form scar tissue. Instead it ends up with just the kind of cell disorganization described in the autopsies. At the very least, then, these autopsy findings were consistent with the idea that the damage had occurred prenatally. Adding weight to the notion was

wanted to do it," he recalls wryly. He also knew that the second trimester of pregnancy is a time of major brain-cell reorganization. If a virus hits at that particular time, it might also affect the hands, which are simultaneously undergoing finishing touches.

UNLIKELY AS IT sounds, it is possible for a virus to infect one identical twin fetus and not the other. So Bracha examined 24 pairs of Torrey's twins for the odd fingerprint whorls and stunted digits that are the "fossilized" evidence, as he puts it, of infections inside the womb. His study, published in November 1991, found that schizophrenics had four times as many abnormalities as their healthy twins, who showed Bracha what the schizophrenics' hands "should have looked like."

These divergent fingerprints suggested that the seeds of schizophrenia are indeed sown very early in life. In the same vein, Torrey has recently completed another study, which uses family interviews and school records to show that the twins start diverging before the age of five. By putting a ceiling on the time of infection, he can focus his search on agents that act in infancy or before.

Meanwhile, back in the geneticists' camp, Gottesman is aware that Torrey has stacked the deck a bit by focusing on clearly discordant twin pairs. This group most likely has a low genetic predisposition to schizophrenia, requiring a big environmental jolt to make the twins so different. But Torrey, remember, has also recruited less clear-cut pairs, where one twin is schizophrenic and the other, apparently healthy one is only mildly

display subtle physical signs like abnormal eye tracking or easy distractibility. If we're lucky, these abnormalities may lead us to DNA 'markers,' which are like visible flags inherited along with the actual disease genes. Then we can look for each marker to see if it turns up consistently among families of schizophrenics. If the markers and genes are truly linked—that is, are situated close by on the same stretch of DNA—we may be able to track down some of the genes we think are involved."

In practice, this approach works well for single-gene diseases such as Huntington's chorea. But when four or five genes are involved, as is thought to be the case with schizophrenia, the task explodes into mind-numbing complexity. Yet if the genes can be found, the rewards will be enormous: researchers will be able to tell very quickly what proteins they make and, eventually, what the proteins do (or fail to do) to cause schizophrenia.

WHILE Gottesman pursues the genes that make the schizophrenic brain malfunction, Torrey is beginning to look at how and where it malfunctions. The procedures he and his colleagues are using can literally see the brain in action. Cerebral blood flow studies and PET (positron emission tomography) scans offer a color-coded glimpse into the brain's workings as eerie as MRI's sharp dissection of its living anatomy. For the cerebral blood flow studies, xenon gas is inhaled into the lungs to make the patient's blood briefly radioactive; the harder the cells in a particular brain region work, the more blood flow they get and the more detectable radiation they emit. PET uses radioactive glucose or

Three-quarters of all patients hear voices—voices that command you to kill yourself, voices from outer space, even the voice of God.

the Scandinavian study suggesting that influenza infection in the second trimester of pregnancy—months four, five, and six—boosted the risk of schizophrenia.

Bracha knew that the time-tested way of looking for evidence of prenatal infection was dermatoglyphics, the study of fingerprints and finger structure. "But it was old technology, so no one else

schizoid. From Gottesman's point of view, these twins may prove the most useful of all.

"In these pairs, the healthy twin has some, but not all, of the symptoms of schizophrenia," he says. "So we assume they carry some predisposing genes for the disease, even if they're not fully turned on. Moreover, these healthy twins often

oxygen to similarly light up areas of "hot" metabolic activity in the brain.

Initially Torrey was reluctant to subject his twins to PET scans. "The scans are tough. I take all the tests the patients do, and I found this one uncomfortable. They have to lie in a ring of sensors with their head pinned by a form-fitting mask and

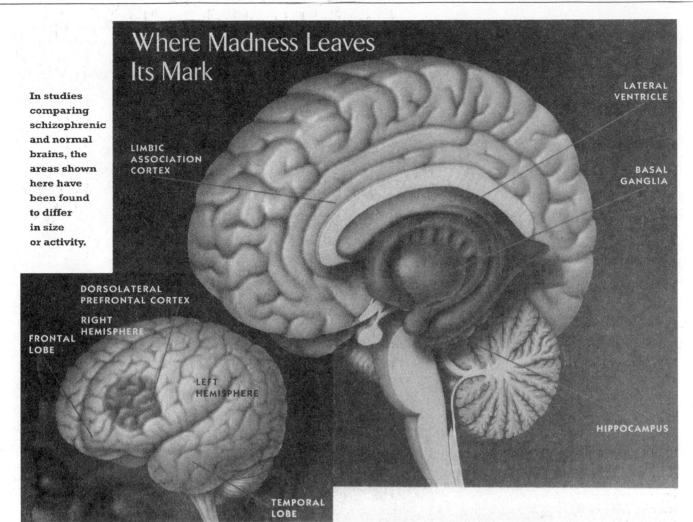

Where Madness Leaves Its Mark

In studies comparing schizophrenic and normal brains, the areas shown here have been found to differ in size or activity.

LIMBIC ASSOCIATION CORTEX

DORSOLATERAL PREFRONTAL CORTEX

RIGHT HEMISPHERE

FRONTAL LOBE

LEFT HEMISPHERE

TEMPORAL LOBE

LATERAL VENTRICLE

BASAL GANGLIA

HIPPOCAMPUS

IV lines in their arms. And besides, you're asking to read the thoughts of someone who's already paranoid about his thoughts being read." What changed his mind was a study by Susan Resnick, another of his extended network of researchers, at the University of Pennsylvania. PET scans of seven schizophrenics and their normal twins showed a consistent difference in the basal ganglia, acorn-size cell clusters lying beneath the ventricles at the brain's center. The ganglia are action integrators—if you're a catcher, they help you get the mitt between the fastball and your groin—but in seven out of seven schizophrenics (in contrast to their well twins) the basal ganglia mysteriously "lit up," even when they were resting.

Using such scans, Torrey's Washington team made another intriguing discovery. When they challenged twins to sort playing cards by suit, number, or color, they found that the schizophrenics not only did worse than the normals but also failed to activate a region—technically known as the dorsolateral prefrontal cortex, or DLPFC—within the frontal lobe. This region, says Daniel Weinberger, a psychiatrist collaborating with Torrey, is critical to performing complicated tasks and thinking well-ordered thoughts: "It's highly evolved and serves perhaps more than anything else as a hallmark of the human brain." What's more, this year, by comparing the blood-flow scans with MRI data, the team showed that poor DLPFC activation correlated with small hippocampus size. For the first time in the history of schizophrenia research, a functional deficit in one brain area was linked to an anatomical defect in another.

That seems to imply, says Torrey, that schizophrenia is not simply a disorder of particular areas in the brain, but a breakdown—most likely on the brain's left side—in the connections between them. And it so happens that the DLPFC, the hippocampus, the emotion-regulating limbic system, and the basal ganglia are all part of what's known as the brain's dopamine network. Dopamine is a neurotransmitter, and almost all the drugs for treating schizophrenia's symptoms are now known to block dopamine receptors.

In the dopamine network, too little activity in one area could lead to overactivity in another. A DLPFC that's too quiet, Weinberger speculates, "may disinhibit the limbic system and lead to the florid, inappropriate emotionality seen in many schizophrenics." In other words, if the Speaker of the House falls asleep, overemotional congressmen may soon get out of control.

Of course, that still doesn't settle the question that launched Torrey and Gottesman's original bet: Are genes or a virus the main actor in schizophrenia? Although there's evidence for both, neither researcher is ready to call it a draw. The point is, says Gottesman, to what degree is each important? Could schizophrenia occur without a viral insult? Could there even be nongenetic cases?

"We must each push our theory as far as it will go," Gottesman insists. "If we don't try our darnedest to prove the other wrong, we'll never prove anything right. Is schizophrenia nine-tenths genetic, or one-twentieth? That's what we need to find out." D

Discharged from the Army after being diagnosed as schizophrenic, Mark Daniel Sallee returned to his hometown of Okolona, Kentucky, in July of 1986, and joined the ranks of the country's homeless mentally ill. Sometimes he slept beneath a culvert that ran over one of the half-dry drainage ditches in the Louisville suburb. Other times he lived inside a makeshift lean-to in a wooded area, in the back of an abandoned school bus, inside an empty train car, or out in the middle of a field. Dirt and grease covered him so completely that a waitress at a local eatery took to calling him "black boy." He stole things from shopkeepers and spoke to no one, including his family, except to threaten them. Once he promised to kill a police officer.

On January 10, 1989, he kept his promise. The story of that event presents a highly revealing picture of how the dangerous mentally ill slip through the cracks of American society.

Leaving his lean-to that morning, he carried a loaded .22 caliber rifle and wore a one-piece insulated coverall, both of which he had bought two weeks earlier at a nearby sporting goods store. (Lisa Ludwig, the clerk who sold him the gun, is notable for being one of the only people in Sallee's voluminous court record to ever describe him as seeming sane.) By 10:30 A.M., he came across a man he had never met, Brian Madison, walking along a creek behind an apartment complex. Sallee raised his rifle and shot at him, but missed.

He was next seen less than an hour later standing on the east side of busy Smyrna Road. When a red Ford pickup truck passed close to him on the narrow shoulder, Sallee raised the rifle to his shoulder, pointed it at the truck, and fired. Again he missed. But a passing motorist saw the incident and called 911 on his car phone. He said he thought Sallee looked "upset and angry."

Dispatched to the scene was 42-year-old Officer Frank Pysher, Jr., a grandfather and 16-year veteran on the Jefferson County force. That morning Pysher had told a fellow officer about his plans to retire in a few more years. "I'm going down to my house on Rough River, fish, and watch the world go by."

At 12 minutes past noon, Officer Pysher spotted Sallee walking south along Smyrna Road where it crossed over a freeway. He probably recognized Sallee from previous encounters, as did almost all the other police in the area. He pulled over and rolled down his window to speak. Without warning, Sallee allegedly turned, raised his rifle to his shoulder and fired two shots through the windshield, striking Officer Pysher twice in the forehead. At 1:58 P.M., Pysher would be declared dead, the first county police officer to die in the line of duty in three years.

Sallee ran from the scene through the semi-rural suburbs until he came to the backyard of Barry A. Mantooth, 35. "What are you doing?" asked Mantooth when he saw Sallee running. "What is the matter?"

"Who are you talking to?" asked Sallee, and allegedly fired his shotgun for a fifth time that day, this time striking Mantooth in the forearm. Mantooth would be treated and released from the hospital that afternoon.

Imminent DANGER

By now, more than 25 police officers in helicopters, cars, and on foot were chasing Sallee. He ran another mile or so until he was cornered in a yard next to the Deeper Christian Life Center. When Officer Dale Mobley ordered Sallee to drop his rifle, Sallee replied, "Fuck you. I am not putting it down!"

After a warning shot was fired, according to Detective Dick Brewer, Sallee "continued to talk and act as if he hadn't heard the shot." Sallee waved them away with his hands and shouted something many of the officers couldn't make out, but that "sounded as if he were talking about shooting," said Brewer. When he seemed to be lifting the rifle again, the police opened fire and struck Sallee once in the chest. Seriously wounded, he was taken by ambulance to the same hospital where Officer Pysher died.

"What did I do?" he yelled as police and medics struggled to restrain him. "I haven't done anything!"

His mother, Mrs. Donna Dalton, had reason to fear otherwise. Even before she heard his name on the television news later that day, she immediately thought, "It's Mark. Oh God, it's Mark."

Her only son had been diagnosed as having paranoid schizophrenia back in 1978 when, at the age of 17, he shot and killed his stepfather, Mrs. Dalton's second husband, before her eyes. Yet despite Mrs. Dalton's repeated pleas to judges and psychiatrists over the years to help her deranged son, even after Mark had threatened to kill his sister and a police officer, he was simply allowed to wander about until he killed again. Now at last, the sick young man who everyone had done their best to ignore for 11 years had been catapulted into the top news story of the year in Louisville, with one TV news team even boasting in its commercials that it had been the first to reach the murder scene.

The story of Mark Daniel Sallee would be sad enough were it a rare instance of one dangerously psychotic person slipping through the cracks. But Sallee's case is just about business-as-usual in Kentucky and the rest of the United States in 1994. A recent story that grabbed national headlines broke on June 6, 1991, when a homeless man named Kevin McKiever fatally stabbed a 30-year-old former Rockette, Alexis Fichs Welsh, with an 11 inch butcher knife near New York City's Central Park as she walked her two cocker spaniels. Fifteen months earlier, he had spent just 30 days in jail after stabbing another woman who lived in Welsh's apartment building. His mother told reporters that McKiever had been diagnosed as suffering from "schizophrenia and manic depression" as long ago as the mid-1970s, but that he had never gotten adequate treatment. "The system has absolutely failed him," she said.

In 1963, President John F. Kennedy announced a "bold new approach" to serious mental illness. With the development of antipsychotic medications in the 1950s that were found to be at least partly effective in relieving symptoms for 90 percent of schizophrenics, Kennedy envisioned the opening of hundreds of community mental health centers, where people with schizophrenia could get day-to-day

Today, there are twice as many people with schizophrenia living on the streets and in public shelters as there are in public mental hospitals. Episodes of violence by people with untreated serious psychiatric illness are on the rise. By Dan Hurley

From *Psychology Today*, 27, pp. 54–68, June/July 1994. Reprinted with permission from Psychology Today Magazine, Copyright © 1994 (Sussex Publishers, Inc.).

help in managing their lives. "When carried out," he declared, "reliance on the cold mercy of custodial isolation will be supplanted by the open warmth of community concern and capability."

Hand in hand with the new federal policy, civil rights laws in all but a handful of states threw out all permissible reasons to institutionalize a person against his or her will, no matter how sick, save one: imminent danger. Unless a person was found to be in imminent danger of seriously harming himself or others—imminent as in the next few minutes or, in the case of malnutrition, days—that person would be free to go on living in the community.

The deinstitutionalization movement did succeed in bringing down the number of state mental hospital patients from a high of 552,150 in 1955 to 68,000 today. But despite $40 to $100 million in federal tax dollars given to community mental health centers beginning in 1965, according to a recent study by the National Alliance for the Mentally Ill (NAMI) and the Public Citizen Health Research Group, "It is clear that whatever was supposed to happen did not happen and that deinstitutionalization was a disaster."

Many schizophrenics remained out of sight and out of mind until the flophouses and single-room-occupancy hotels where they had found a last refuge began to disappear in the mid-1980s. Today, according to the NAMI-Public Citizen report, there are more than twice as many people with schizophrenia and manic–depressive psychosis living in public shelters and on streets than there are in public mental hospitals. In all, about 30 percent of the country's homeless—an estimated 150,000—are seriously mentally ill.

As a result, "It is clear that episodes of violence by individuals with untreated serious mental illnesses are on the increase," the report states. Although mentally ill people, when receiving treatment, are believed to be no more violent than average, when they are not treated "some of them will occasionally commit acts of violence," according to the report.

What spurs them on is the disease itself: paranoia may make them think they're being attacked, delusional thinking may make them believe their

An Almost-Smoking Gun

What causes the scrambling of mind that characterizes schizophrenia? At a lecture given in the spring of 1993 at Harvard Medical School, Daniel Weinberger, M.D., chief of the National Institute of Mental Health's Brain Disorder Branch, spoke of the latest findings. "We don't have a smoking gun yet," he admitted, "but we have a gun that is threatening to smoke."

Many researchers have identified differences in the brains of schizophrenics compared to non-schizophrenics. A few years ago, Dr. Torrey was one of the first to use magnetic resonance imaging to show that the fluid-filled ventricles in the brains of schizophrenics are larger than those of their non-schizophrenic twins. More recently, researchers at the University of California at Irvine found, in a post-mortem study of seven schizophrenics, that most of the neural cells that should have migrated during the second trimester of pregnancy to higher brain regions, the hippocampus and neocortex, never made it out of lower brain areas such as the white matter of the temporal and frontal lobe.

Then, in August of 1992, The New England Journal of Medicine published a major study linking a specific symptom of schizophrenia with specific changes in the brain. Harvard University researchers found that the jumbled and disordered thinking of schizophrenia was associated with brain-size reductions of up to 19 percent in regions of

Some of the most chilling rampages across the country in recent years were caused by people long known to the mental health system as dangerous schizophrenics, but who never qualified as being "imminent" dangers.

mother is really the devil, and auditory hallucinations may order them to kill. Since 1965, eight studies have found that violent acts by untreated psychiatric patients are on the rise.

Some of the most chilling rampages across the country in recent years were caused by people long known to the mental health system as dangerous schizophrenics, but who never qualified as being "imminent" dangers. In Berkeley, California, in the summer·of 1990, Mehrdad Dashti stormed a bar, killed one man, wounded seven, and took 33 hostages before police shot him dead. Documents found in his apartment showed that he had recently been diagnosed as paranoid schizophrenic. Earlier that year, Calvin Brady shot and killed a man and wounded four others in an Atlanta shopping mall the day after he was released from a mental hospital. In his pocket was found a document describing him as having "homicidal and suicidal tendencies." In October, 1985, Sylvia Seegrist opened fire in a Philadelphia shopping mall, killing three and wounding 10. She had been committed 12 times to mental hospitals, had stabbed a hospital worker, and had repeatedly made violent, bizarre threats in the mall.

Just what does a person have to do to be considered in imminent danger of harming himself or others?

"As soon as the bullet comes out of the gun, then we can arrest him," says Herbert Pardes, M.D., former director of the National Institute of Mental Health and now chairman of the Department of Psychiatry at Columbia University in New York. "In an attempt to protect the rights of the patients, we have compromised the rights of society."

Says John Bell, M.D., who recently retired as director of the emergency psychiatric unit at Humana Hospital-University Louisville, and who personally treated Sallee for several years after he killed his stepfather, "There are 15 to 30 people out there in Louisville right now about whom the mental health workers at the hospital have said, 'This guy is going to kill somebody if we release him,' yet we were powerless to do anything about it. I'm a very liberal guy, a long-term member of the ACLU. But when there are people who have already proven that they're dangerous, some of them murderers, I feel society has a right to protect itself."

According to E. Fuller Torrey, M.D., the psychiatrist who led the NAMI-Public Citizen report and who has devoted his career to researching and treating schizophrenia and advocating for better services, America's mental health system "exhibits more thought disorder than most of the patients the system is supposed to treat."

"On the question of services for the severely mentally ill," says Senator Pete Domenici (R-Arizona), "there's no question that we're doing very poorly. Very few plans distribute services in a rational way."

Like most people who develop schizophrenia, Sallee was a normal, well-behaved, seemingly happy young man up until his midteens. (The disease affects equal numbers of men and women, but tends to strike men in their teens, and women in their twenties.) His younger sister, Lisa, remembers him as "very sweet. He always helped me with my homework." His high school cross-country coach, John Sears, says, "Mark was a good kid around school. He didn't have any problems. He seemed sort of introverted, but most of the kids liked him. Kids who run cross-country are usually your better kids, and Mark was no exception."

When Mark was 16, "he withdrew," recalls his mother. "He wouldn't go to school, he wouldn't have friends, he lost interest in

> ❛It must look queer to people when I laugh about something that has nothing to do with what I am talking about.❜

everything. His whole personality changed."

At first, the changes seemed to be little more than what many teenagers go through. By 1976, his parents had divorced and remarried, and Mark tried moving in with his father, a truck driver, in Elizabethtown, 43 miles south of Louisville. He started skipping school there after the first couple of months, however, and eventually returned to his mother and stepfather's home in Okolona. He re-entered Moore High School, but dropped out for good on March 20, 1978. As spring turned to summer, it became glaringly obvious that Mark was suffering from more than teenage angst.

The once quiet, helpful young man was now sitting in his room for hours, refusing to talk to anyone or let anyone in. "We could hear him in his room giggling and talking to the radio as though someone was in there," says Mrs. Dalton. "I'd go in to talk to him and he'd look right through me, like I wasn't even there." When his sister Lisa asked him to turn his stereo down one day, he pushed her to the ground and choked her. He didn't let go until their other sister pulled him off.

Taken together, these are among the classic early signs of schizophrenia. Although no single symptom affects all schizophrenics, hearing voices is common, and they often have bizarre, irrational or paranoid delusions. How bizarre? Carol, a 31-year-old black woman living in Wisconsin who is now responding to medication but who spent a decade gripped by psychosis, tried to explain the thought process that made her think she was the devil.

"Something was going through my mind that everything in my past was negative," she said. "It wasn't godly things I'd done—it was all satanic. So I thought I was the devil. And I thought I was getting all these powers because I was the devil—the power to hear other people's thoughts. It was amusing at first to think I was

Treating Schizophrenia

Whatever the causes of schizophrenia may be—genetic, obstetric, viral, or environmental—the primary treatment is with any of more than a dozen types of antipsychotic medications, including Thorazine, Clozapine, and Haldol.

Studies have shown that about 70 percent of schizophrenics clearly improve on these drugs, with 20 percent improving minimally at best, and 5 percent getting worse. But over the course of a lifetime, improvements are more limited: while one-fourth do recover fully

from their first psychotic episode and never experience a relapse, and another fourth recover well enough to live and work independently, the remaining half need help in taking care of themselves the rest of their lives, especially when their illness flares up, as often happens with this notoriously cyclical disease.

But medications don't work when schizophrenics don't take them. And experts estimate that half to three-fourths of schizophrenics stop taking their medications within one year of walking out the hospital door. Most are unable to understand that they need the drug to get better; most, in fact, can never see past their delusions to realize they're sick in

the first place.

Many drugs also have a harrowing array of side effects. A schizophrenic who takes antipsychotics for years might find that his hands shake, his tongue pokes and curls out of his mouth, his emotions feel numb and flat. Or he might feel unbearably agitated. New hope has come with the recent introduction of the drug Clozaril, which can produce seemingly miraculous recoveries in about one-third of people for whom no other medication worked. And in mid-1993, the FDA approved yet another antipsychotic, risperidone, which appears to be as effective as Clozaril with fewer side effects.—D.H.

Danger

chosen and special. But in the end it was terrible. I'd say, this can't be, this isn't right. I remember telling one of my brothers and his friends I was the devil, and they just said it was all in my mind. I didn't believe them. They couldn't tell me differently." Not until she attacked her mother with a knife was she involuntarily hospitalized and started on the road to recovery.

But schizophrenics' thinking is more than delusional; the hallmark of the condition is disorganized thinking—Torrey describes the schizophrenic mind as being like a blender. It jumbles all thoughts, making it hard for them to hold a conversation or follow instructions.

Speaking in a kind of "word salad," as psychiatrists call the mixed-up language that flows from schizophrenics' disordered thinking, a sturdy-looking young man named John, also from Wisconsin, tried to tell a visitor why he likes taking the antipsychotic medication Clozapine. "It's better than antidepressants," he began, sounding reasonable enough. And then he went on, "They're made of crushed spiders. Arachnids. A voice told me to cut myself open today. I thought a vampire was behind me." As if in afterthought, he added, "I could look at a point in the floor and just crawl right into it."

Perceptions of colors, sounds, heat, smells, and pain might also be distorted. In the early 1980s, Beatrice Phillips' sister—once a svelte, meticulous fashion model and dancer who toured Europe—began wandering outside her mother's Philadelphia home in the middle of winter in jeans ripped all the way up to her crotch and shoes without soles. She stopped bathing, wore the same urine-soaked rags for months at a

the temporal lobe crucial to speech and language. The more disordered the thinking, the smaller the regions. "This is one of the first times that a relationship has been found between specific clinical symptoms of schizophrenia and brain reduction in a specific area," said Althea Wagman, Ph.D., chief of the NIMH Schizophrenia Research Branch's neuroimaging and electrophysiology research program. "This may have significant implications for how we ought to design future studies, to ask questions about the re-

"It's better than antidepressants. They're made of crushed spiders. Arachnids. A voice told me to cut myself open today. I thought a vampire was behind me."

lationship between brain dysfunction and behavioral dysfunction."

Genes almost surely play a role in these changes: a recent study in the British journal *Nature* reported the presence of repeated segments of the gene that codes for the dopamine receptor protein on the surface of brain cells. And since excess amounts of the neurotransmitter dopamine have been shown to be associated with schizophrenia, researchers believe that the genetic mutation may be the cause, by preventing brain cells from properly absorbing dopamine.

Many other studies of inheritance patterns have also suggested a genetic link. Most recently, Josef Parnas, M.D., of Copenhagen University published a study showing that 16 percent of the children of schizophrenic mothers grow up to be schizophrenic themselves—compared to just 1.9 percent of the children of non-schizophrenic mothers.

Yet genes are clearly not the only cause.

time, threw all her possessions in the garbage, and spent hours in her room with a sheet over her head.

Often schizophrenics' emotions are strikingly inappropriate to what's going on around them. "These inappropriate emotions produce one of the most dramatic aspects of the disease—the victim suddenly breaking out in cackling laughter for no apparent reason," writes Torrey. One patient told him, "It must look queer to people when I laugh about something that has nothing to do with what I am talking about, but they don't know what's going on inside and how much of it is running round in my head. You see I might be talking about something quite serious to you and other things come into my head at the same time that are funny and this makes me laugh." Eventually, though, the emotions of schizophrenics tend to flatten as the disease progresses, so much so that Torrey tells of one patient who set his house on fire and then sat down serenely to watch TV.

As serious a medical illness as schizophrenia is, thousands of psychologists, social workers, and even psychiatrists cling to the myth, popularized in the 1960s, that schizophrenia is caused by "bad mothers" or "crazy families."

Such was apparently the view of psychologist A.P. Tadajewski, Ph.D., to whom Mark's mother took him at a local child guidance clinic beginning in the summer of 1978. "He wanted to know about the relationship between Mark and us, to find a reason for the behavior," she says. "We were made to think it was our fault. I told him, 'Hey, what are we going to do? This can't go on.' And he said, 'Mark's very rebellious. He has a lot of anger.' I don't even know if this man knew what schizophrenia was."

On the night of Friday, September 1, 1978, the family had some friends over and by 10 o'clock, two of Mark's sisters were walking a neighbor home. Mark's mother and her husband, Paul Hicks, had just gone into their bedroom when Paul said, "Hey, where is my Baretta?" The gun case on the bedroom wall, he noticed, was missing one of the shotguns he used for hunting.

"I don't know," said Mark's mother.

Danger

"Mark's been home all day. Maybe he knows."

She walked across the hall and knocked on Mark's door, closed as usual. When no answer came, she opened it and found him lying in the darkness. She walked over to his bedside lamp to switch it on, but the lamp remained dark. Mark fumbled with it and knocked it onto the floor. As she stooped down to pick it up, she saw Mark rising from the bed with something in his hands. Suddenly three gunshots broke the silence. She turned to see her husband in the doorway fall with three wounds to the chest.

"I just stood there," Mark's mother recalls, her voice shaking with sobs. "I didn't know what to do. I didn't scream. I just closed my eyes and thought, `I'm dreaming this. I'll wake up in a minute.' Then I opened my eyes and Paul was just lying there."

Realizing she needed to get the Baretta, she quietly yet firmly said to her son, "Mark, give me the gun." She reached toward him, he pulled back, and then he handed it over.

After calling the police, she went back to her husband as he lay on the floor, gasping for air. By midnight, Paul was dead. Eight hours later, after hiding out all night from police and neighbors, Mark was found curled up under shrubbery next door, and arrested.

The official line from schizophrenia researchers and foundations is that schizophrenics are no more violent on average than ordinary people. And surely it would be an injustice to perpetuate the groundless fears that many people have of the seriously mentally ill. Most schizophrenics, in fact, are said to become passive, listless, nearly mute. Of those who do become violent, most become their own victims: fully one of 10 schizophrenics die at their own hands.

Even so, in a three-month investigation including interviews with over 100 people across the country and visits to homes and institutions in Wisconsin, Florida, Louisville, New York, and New Jersey, it was impossible to find a parent living at home with a schizophrenic child who wasn't afraid of him or her.

"I think the national leadership greatly underestimates the level of violence," says Barbara Rankin, forensic coordinator for the Kentucky Alliance for the Mentally Ill and a member of the forensics committee of the national alliance. "They think the violence adds to the stigma. But I don't know of one family in my support group in Lexington whose schizophrenic children don't get violent when they're delusional. I can't think of anyone who hasn't had at least very real threats—and usually worse than that. With appropriate treatment, they're no more dangerous than other people. But untreated, you never know."

Rankin's schizophrenic son, James, was in and out of mental hospitals three times in the year leading up to June of 1985. Even then, though, no law required him to continue taking his medications once he was back home, and soon he was talking about killing Rankin's second husband. On June 27, 1985, James walked out to his truck, picked up a compound bow and arrow, came into the kitchen and shot her husband through the heart. He was found "guilty but mentally ill" on charges of manslaughter, and is now serving a 10-year prison sentence.

Although only a month and a half from his 18th birthday, Mark Sallee was still technically a juvenile and not legally required to stand trial for the killing of his stepfather. A coroner's jury did find that he

---

The Search for Model Treatment

Balancing the civil rights of the severely mentally ill against society's right to safety.

Many experts have come to the conclusion that the aggressive use of so-called outpatient commitment laws may be the best answer. Already in place in a handful of states but used regularly in only a few progressive counties, outpatient commitment permits schizophrenics only about three visits to the psychiatric emergency room before they are put on long-term court-ordered medication as a condition of leaving the hospital or avoiding a jail term. The counties soon find that keeping a close eye on each patient, making sure they're followed up and taking their medication—and not standing around naked in the middle of an airport, as was a man I recently saw—is a lot less expensive than waiting for them to get so sick they must return to the hospital.

Some psychiatrists argue, however, that outpatient commitment laws are beside the point. What's really needed are good community programs that put caregivers in close, regular contact with schizophrenic patients. Such programs, which amount to the community mental health centers envisioned by President Kennedy, are seen as the missing foundation of what should be the country's response to the crisis of homeless, violent schizophrenics.

Two fundamental models have been developed:The clubhouse model was first pioneered by Fountain House in New York City. About 400 severely mentally ill people each day come to socialize with fellow patients, develop work skills, and get ongoing help in finding housing, finding a job, managing money—and taking medications.

Says Jim Schmitt, Fountain House director, "The biggest thing is not just housing. They have to have a life—something to do during the day—or life becomes oppressive."

The second model, based on the Program of Assertive Living Treatment (PACT) in Dane County, Wisconsin, has the doctors and social workers go to the schizophrenics, by making weekly, sometimes even twice-daily, house calls.

The federal Substance Abuse Mental Health Services Adminstration has put $20 million toward creating a model program in one city. In New York, meanwhile, the governor and legislature agreed late in 1993 that five of the state's all-but-empty psychiatric hospitals will be closed with the $210 million in savings dedicated to community treatment programs—an estimated 20 to 25 percent increase in the state's spending on such programs.

had killed him, but due to Mark's age and a diagnosis of schizophrenia, he spent only a few months in a private psychiatric hospital, Our Lady of Peace. His symptoms soon controlled by antipsychotic medications, he was released into his father's custody shortly after Christmas, less than four months after the shooting.

For two and a half years, Mark did fairly well. He took his medications, earned a high school diploma, enrolled at a local community college, and worked at a few jobs. Then he complained of being unhappy living with his father and moved in with his grandmother. Eventually, he stopped taking his medication.

"He was exhibiting strange behavior again," recalls his mother. "He'd be laughing at nothing, sitting with a blanket over his head and giggling." This time Mark voluntarily agreed to return to Our Lady of Peace. One day, after about a month, his mother came to visit.

"He was standing there with his bags packed," she recalls, "and they were waiting for me to sign the papers. They said he could go home. I had told the doctors I couldn't handle him, but I didn't know what else to do. So I took him home."

Sallee's mother and her three daughters lived in fear that Mark would become violent again. Although he had stopped taking his medication and was becoming increasingly menacing, his mother could get no advice from his doctors, or even any information on what treatments he had received while in the hospital. That information was confidential, they were told.

"I couldn't go anywhere," she says. I had a six-year-old and two teenage girls. I was afraid to leave them with Mark. We were sleeping all in one room with the door locked. He'd walk around the house, giggling and throwing things. Our lives just stopped. My daughters quit school, they couldn't stand it." Routinely Mark made violent threats. Once he tried to kill the family cat. And now he had taken to smoking marijuana, a common problem among many schizophrenics as their disease progresses. (There is no evidence that drug abuse can cause schizophrenia. But when schizophrenics abuse drugs, in an apparent attempt at self-medication, the drugs can make the symptoms worse.)

Finally, Mark's mother decided she had to involuntarily commit him to the state mental hospital. But at his commitment hearing, the judge ruled that none of his actions constituted an imminent danger and declared him free to go. At that point, his mother raised her hand and said, "Am I allowed to say anything?" The judge said she was. "Please, please keep him," she begged. "I know that he needs long-term help. He has never had really long-term therapy anywhere."

The judge turned to Mark and said, "Are you sick?"

"No," said Mark.

And that was that. Mark wanted to go home with his mother afterward, but she had to refuse for the safety of her family.

"Most people felt sorry for Mark," she later told a Louisville radio station, WHAS. "And I think a lot of people thought, you know, what kind of person is she? She knows her son is in this shape. Poor thing's out there digging in garbage cans to eat. Out in the cold." At that point, she broke down crying on the air. "That's the choice you have to make," she continued. "After society, the system fails, and they're pushed out by them, you keep them as long as you can, until you know it's gonna be them or the rest of your family. So you have to push them out."

After that, Mark broke off all contact with his family. Then, on May 29, 1984, he enlisted in the Army. In less than two years, however, a mental status evaluation found him to be depressed and delusional, with a bizarre thought process. At one point during his evaluation, he told the Army psychiatrists that President Carter had recently mentioned him in a speech and told "peanut jokes" about him. The psychiatrists diagnosed him as suffering from "schizophreniform disorder" and "schizotypal personality disorder." He was discharged on July 28, 1986.

Returning to Okolona, Sallee appears to have gone quickly downhill. Reports in his police file chronicle his run-ins with local residents and shopkeepers: stealing a car radio, shoplifting from a Majik Mart, throwing rocks at cars passing beneath a bridge, yelling at people who happened to walk by his lean-to, threatening a mall security officer, rummaging through garbage bins behind restaurants, walking down the highway collecting bottles and cans.

On April 24, 1987, Sallee was jailed after he rushed at a police officer who was questioning him. The officer had to hold Sallee down on the ground until other officers arrived, and Sallee was still so agitated when put into the car that, according to the police report, he damaged the police car's back seat as he was driven to the station. Yet based on only a single interview, without any check into his 10-year history of violence and psychosis, a staff psychiatrist at Central State Hospital in Louisville concluded on May 4, 1987, that Sallee "is not a danger to himself or others."

Eighteen days later, on May 22, Sallee was arrested again, this time for stealing a shopping cart. (Jailing of severely mentally ill people for seemingly minor offenses is common across the country, in an apparent attempt by police to get them off the streets on whatever technicalities they can find. As a result, there are now about 100,000 people with schizophrenia and manic–depressive psychosis in U.S. prisons

---

Other studies have shown that higher rates of schizophrenia occur in offspring whose birth was marked by obstetric complications and in those born to mothers who caught the flu during the fifth month of pregnancy.

Other environmental causes have also been suggested: a 14-year study of 49,000 young Swedish men by Glyn Lewis, M.D., of London's Institute of Psychiatry found that those who had grown up in cities were 65 percent more likely to develop schizophrenia than those who had been raised in rural areas. In perfect dose-response fashion, those reared in large towns had a risk midway between that of city reared and country reared.

Although Lewis noted that viral illnesses and head injuries are both more common in cities, it could also be the stress of urban life that contributes to the risk of developing schizophrenia. Indeed, other studies have found that in the U.S., the states with the greatest proportion of people living in cities (particularly in the Northeast) have about twice the rate of schizophrenia as those with the fewest. Worldwide, the disease appears to be far more common in westernized countries than in Third World countries. Historically, too, some researchers believe that schizophrenia has become increasingly prevalent in the past 200 years, with the rise of urbanization.

and jails—more than in public mental hospitals.) After a Winn Dixie manager had reported seeing Sallee take the cart, Officer William E. Brough found him near the corner of Preston Highway and Chateau Lane, where he was living in a ditch. Sallee told Officer Brough, "I gave you a break. If I wanted to, I could have killed you. I will kill you when I get out."

He was out again within days. For the next 20 months, he threatened anyone who dared go near him. When his own sister, Sandra, approached him on the street in late 1988 to offer him some warm clothing and money, he threw a large rock at her and told her to go away or he would kill her. The family's only recourse was to find out from police what his normal roaming area was and stay clear of it. Hearing how bad things had gotten, his father drove up from Georgia, where he had moved, to try and find his son. He found him on the side of Preston Highway. But Mark didn't even seem to recognize him.

On November 30, 1988, Mark walked into a branch of the First National Bank, set down a piece of paper with his name, address, and a number on it, and said to a clerk, "C.D." She asked if he wanted to buy a Certificate of Deposit. Mark replied, "No, cash it." Checking the bank records, she found that Mark had indeed bought a $5,000 C.D. two years earlier (probably with money he had earned from the Army). The next day, she gave him $5,478.76 in cash and change, representing the interest he had earned.

Two days after Christmas, Mark took his money and went to a nearby Herman's sporting goods store. He bought a Marlin 60 rifle, a red wooden box of .22 caliber cartridges, and some rifle-cleaning equipment. A few days later he returned and bought the blue snowmobile jumpsuit that he would be wearing when he allegedly shot and killed Officer Pysher. Of course, selling a gun to a mentally ill person is against the law in Kentucky. And of course, had the federal Brady Bill been in effect in 1988, a police check during the required five-day waiting period would have easily picked up Sallee's record of violence. Instead, it was up to the Herman's employee to satisfy herself that Sallee was mentally fit.

No one can say for certain where Mark was heading when Officer Pysher stopped him on the Smyrna Road overpass, but this much is fact: He had already walked more than two miles from his campsite and was then just one block from the house where he grew up, the same house where he shot and killed his stepfather, the house where his sister Lisa now lived with her husband and daughter. Officer Pysher might well have given up his own life to save theirs.

In the absence of effective community mental-health programs, over 100,000 friends and family members of schizophrenics have organized themselves into the National Alliance for the Mentally Ill, with chapters now located in every state.

Ultimately, the real solution to the tragedy of schizophrenia is to find a cure. "Research is progressing at an accelerated pace," says Sam Keith, M.D., former director of NIMH's schizophrenia research branch and now head of psychiatry at the University of New Mexico. Even he admits, though, that "many of our very fine treatments turn to trash when they're not administered appropriately, either due to overtreatment with a medication or undertreatment."

After being arrested for the killing of Officer Pysher, Mark Sallee spent more than a year at the Fayette County Jail, without any treatment whatsoever. On December 13, 1989, psychiatrist Robert P. Granacher, Jr., M.D., examined him in his cell and found him huddled nude, with a sheet and blanket over his head. For 11 months Mark had sat psychotically mute and motionless.

Within weeks of being ordered to begin antipsychotic medication at Kentucky Correctional Psychiatric Center, Mark improved dramatically enough to dress and clean himself, talk with guards and fellow patients, and even show interest in watching television and having a cup of coffee. Although he is not yet well enough to stand trial, if that day does come, he will be prosecuted for murder in the first degree, and could end up on death row.

This, then, is the ultimate irony of Mark Daniel Sallee's story: the only reason a Kentucky court ever forced him to take his antipsychotic medications was to make him well enough that they might one day execute him.

"It's too late for my son," says his mother. "But there's so many more out there." ∎

NOT THE SAME OLD DIET STORY

At the table, there are a variety of physiologic signals guiding what we now believe to be free will. Two brain

Chemistry & Craving

chemicals—neuropeptide Y and galanin—control the appetite for carbohydrate-rich and fat-rich foods.

some revolutions are waged with guns. Others are waged with words. But perhaps the major American revolt of the past two decades has been waged primarily with knife and fork. With butter banished, red meat in retreat, and humble grains advancing on our plates, we've toppled the old dietary regime on the grounds that you are what you eat.

Still, decisive victories in the battle of the bulge, the war on heart disease, and just plain healthy appetites elude us. And so we begin each year with solemn vows to tackle anew our waistlines and our arteries. But if a behavioral scientist in New York is right, a winning strategy can come only from a simple turn of the tables—we eat what we are.

In meticulous studies over the last 10 years, Sarah F. Leibowitz, Ph.D., of The Rockefeller University, has discovered that what we put in our mouths and when we do it is profoundly influenced by a brew of neurochemicals based in a specific part of our brain. They not only guide our selection of morsels at breakfast, lunch, and dinner—and even the need for high tea—they are probably the power behind individual differences in appetite and weight gain. They appear to determine whether we are sitting ducks for the eating disorders that now afflict 30 percent of Americans.

Unless we take into account the physiological function of these brain chemicals in dictating natural patterns of food intake and metabolism, we will never get closer than annual avowals in regulating our eating behavior, whatever our reason for doing so. The only plausible way to control body weight is by working *with* the neurochemical systems that control appetite—and re-tuning them.

Leibowitz' studies point far beyond our forks. They challenge the deeply held belief that we are strictly self-determining individuals acting, at least at the table, by unfettered choice—whim, if the moon is right. Sooner or later, in one context or another, we will have to overhaul our view of human behavior to acknowledge that there are a variety of physiological signals guiding what we now believe to be free will.

Leibowitz, however, has little taste for the philosophical soup. In classic meat-and-potatoes neuroscience, she has located the epicenter of eating behavior. It is a dense cluster of nerve cells, the neurochemicals they produce, and the receptors through which they act and are acted upon. They make up the paraventricular nucleus, deep in the brain's hypothalamus, a structure toward the base of the brain already known to control sexuality and reproduction.

A Matter of Energy

The neurons that affect eating are part of the body's elaborate mechanism for regulating energy balance, the power ensuring that we take in sufficient fuel, in the form of food, to meet internal and external energy demands to survive from day to day. This is perhaps the body's most fundamental need.

Given so crucial a need, the location of the nerve cells of appetite in the hypothalamus is no accident of nature. They are the neurons next door to those that orchestrate sexual behavior. Leibowitz has found that we have clear-cut cycles of preference for high-carbohydrate and fat-rich foods, and they are closely linked to reproductive needs—that is, the ability of humans to survive from generation to generation. After all, the power to reproduce requires that we maintain a sufficient amount of body fat. The group of cells that tangle with sex and the cells that fancy our forks are in constant communication—like the sometimes overprotective mother she is, nature is constant-

BY HARA ESTROFF MARANO

From *Psychology Today, 26,* pp. 30–74, January/February 1993. Reprinted with permission from Psychology Today Magazine, Copyright ©1993 (Sussex Publishers, Inc.).

ly seeking reassurance that we have enough body fat for the survival of the species.

There are, in truth, many other brain areas that influence appetite. But from the lower brain stem up to the thalamus, which controls sensory processes such as taste, and on up to the forebrain and the cortex, where pleasure, affect, and cognitive aspects come into play, everything converges on the hypothalamus. The hypothalamus integrates all of the information affecting appetite.

Taste preferences for fat and carbohydrate, dictated by brain chemicals, show up early in life and reflect differences in genetic makeup.

petite. Its neurochemical signals coordinate our behavior with our physiology.

Through a daunting system of chemical and neural feedback, the brain monitors the energy needs of all body systems moment to moment. And it makes very emphatic suggestions to the stomach as to what we should ingest.

On the menu are the standard nutritional war-horses: carbohydrate for immediate fuel, fat for longer-term energy reserves—it is particularly essential for reproduction—and protein for growth and muscle maintenance. Directives from the brain to the belly are issued by way of neurochemical messengers and hormones. These directives, Leibowitz finds, have their own physiological logic, their own sets of rhythms, and are highly nutrient-specific. There's one thing we now know for sure—the stomach definitely has a brain.

A Taste for Carbo

In the dietary drama unfolding in Leibowitz' ground-floor laboratory, there are two star players. One is Neuropeptide Y (NPY), a neurochemical that dictates the taste for carbohydrate. Produced by neurons in the paraventricular nucleus (PVN), it literally turns on and off our desire for carbohydrate-rich foods.

In animal studies the researcher has conducted, the amount of Neuropeptide Y produced by cells in the PVN correlates directly, positively, with carbohydrate intake. The more Neuropeptide Y we produce, the more we eat carbohydrate.

"These Cells Tell Us To Eat"

"We can see these neurons and analyze the neuropeptides in them," says Leibowitz. "We know that these cells tell us to eat carbohydrate. In studies, we either give injections of a known amount of Neuropeptide Y, or measure the amount of Neuropeptide Y that's naturally there. Then we correlate it to what the animal ate in carbohydrate." Neuropeptide Y increases both the size and duration of carbohydrate-rich meals.

If production of Neuropeptide Y turns on the taste for carbohydrate, what sets production of Neuropeptide Y spinning? Probably signals from the burning of carbohydrates as fuel are the routine appetite stimulants. But Leibowitz has found that cortisol, a hormone produced by the body during stress, has a particular propensity to turn on the taste for carbohydrate by revving up production of Neuropeptide Y. High levels of Neuropeptide Y lead to weight gain by prompting overeating of carbohydrate.

Fat's Chance

The body also has a built-in appetite system for fat, the most concentrated form of energy, and it marches to a different neurochemical drumbeat, a neuropeptide called galanin, also produced in the paraventricular nucleus of the hypothalamus. Galanin is the second star player in Leibowitz' studies.

These have shown that the amount of galanin an animal produces correlates positively with what the animal eats in fat. And that correlates with what the animal's body weight will become. The more galanin produced, the heavier the animal will become later on. To add insult to injury, galanin not only turns on the taste for fat, it affects other hormones in such a way as to ensure that fat consumed is turned into stored fat.

What turns on the taste for galanin? When the body burns stored fats as fuel, the resulting metabolic byproducts signal the paraventricular nucleus for more fat—a case of nature safeguarding our energy storage. But hormones also turn galanin production on. To be specific, the sexual hormone estrogen activates galanin.

"Estrogen just increases the production of galanin and it makes us want to eat. It makes us want to deposit fat," says Leibowitz. The influence of estrogen on our taste for fat "is important in the menstrual cycle and in the developmental cycle, when we hit puberty."

Of Time and the Nibbler

The two neurohormones of nibbling are not uniformly active throughout the day. Each has its own built-in cycle of activity.

Neuropeptide Y has its greatest effect on appetite at the start of the feeding cycle—morning, when we're just waking up. It starts up the entire feeding cycle. After overnight fasting, we have an immediate need for energy intake. Neuropeptide Y is also switched on after any environmentally imposed period of food deprivation—such as dieting.

And by stress. "If you have lots of Neuropeptide Y in the system at breakfast," says Leibowitz, "you're going to be doing lots of eating."

Necessary as a quick-energy start is to get going, man cannot live by carbohydrate alone. After carbohydrate turns on our engines, the desire for this nutrient begins a slow decline over the rest of the daily cycle.

Around lunchtime, we begin looking for a little more sustenance. An afternoon of sustained energy expenditure stretches before us; we can afford to take in the other major nutrients—fat to refill our fat cells and protein to rebuild muscle. Both of these are converted more slowly to fuel. Our interest in protein rises gradually toward midday, holds its own at lunch, and keeps a more or less steady course during the rest of the day.

A Clockwork Orange

After lunch, the taste for fat begins rising, supported by increasing sensitivity to galanin and increasing galanin production; it peaks with our heaviest meal, at the end of the daily cycle. That's when the body is looking to store energy in anticipation of overnight fasting.

Take a late-afternoon coffee—or tea—break and you're virtually programmed to dive for energy-rich pastry, as appetite, spearheaded by the drive for fat, is gaining. We might, however, be better off appeasing the chemicals of consumption with a banana, or an orange.

Leibowitz believes that circadian cycles of neurochemical activity play a major role in eating problems. A late-afternoon fat snack, for example, could prime us neurochemically to consume more fat later into the night. Galanin activity late in the day gives fat consumed at dinner a head start, as it were, on our thighs.

Silent Signals

What drives us from a carbohydrate-rich breakfast to a more nutrient-mixed lunch? The car-bohydrate we take in at breakfast has a direct impact on more widely distributed neurotransmitters such as serotonin. Active in many systems of the brain, including learning and memory, serotonin is believed to play a general role of modulator; it is essentially an inhibitor of activity.

Eating carbohydrate leads straightaway to synthesis of serotonin. Under normal conditions, rising levels of serotonin are the feedback signals to the paraventricular nucleus to shut off production of Neuropeptide Y and put a stop to the desire for carbohydrate.

Behind the Binge

Leibowitz now thinks that this serotonin signal is directly related to the bingeing behavior that is the *sine qua non* of bulimia. "Bulimics have a deficit in brain serotonin. The mechanism for stopping carbohydrate intake doesn't seem to be there."

Every meal, then, and the appetite for it, is differently regulated and presided over by a separate cocktail of neurochemicals. The neurochemically correct breakfast is a quick blast of carbohydrate right after awakening. Say, a glass of orange juice for speedy transport of sugar into the bloodstream to restore glycogen. Then a piece or two of toast, a more complex carbohydrate to deliver a more sustained supply of glucose over the morning.

For those who don't do it regularly, a breakfast of, say, eggs benedict—rich in protein and fat as well as carbohydrate—will send your neurochemicals spinning, throw off their normal rhythm of production, and affect many other neurotransmitters in the bargain. Ever wonder why you're just not sharp enough after an unusually rich breakfast?

The Big Switch

Not only are the neurochemicals of appetite active at different times over the course of a day, they are differently active over the course of development. Before puberty, Leibowitz finds, animals have no interest in eating fat. Children, too, have little appetite for fat, preferring carbohydrates for energy and protein for tissue growth. But that, like their bodies, changes.

In girls, the arrival of the first menstrual period is a milestone for appetite as well as for sexual maturation. It stimulates the first desire for fat in foods. And that, says Leibowitz, is when a great deal of confusion sets in for anorexics. (See page 34.)

Through a daunting system of chemical and neural feedback, the brain monitors the energy needs of all body systems moment to moment and makes very emphatic suggestions to the stomach as to what and how much we should eat.

"We hit puberty and that turns galanin on." The female hormone estrogen primes the neurochemical pump for galanin.

There are other sex-based differences in nutrient preference. In studies of animals, young females tend to have higher levels of Neuropeptide Y and favor carbohydrates. Their preference for carbohydrates peaks at puberty. Males favor protein to build large muscles.

When puberty strikes up the taste for fats, males are inclined to mix theirs with protein—that sizzling porterhouse steak. Women, their already high levels of

A Radical New View of Anorexia

Anorexia nervosa is regarded as an eating disorder. But Sarah Leibowitz looks on it as an appetite disorder. Where does body image come into it? After the physiology. She believes it's a case where physiology sets the stage for the psychology, and the neurochemical switching on of fat appetite is the trigger event.

"If physiology is telling you you're going to be a little bit heavy, anyone who has a problem with body weight, body shape is going to have the stage set for a problem." Leibowitz insists that anorexia is a no-holds-barred attempt to avoid fatness in those predisposed to plumpness either because of family history or metabolism. "They are," she says, "trying to avoid the inevitable."

Explaining her neurochemical model of anorexia, Leibowitz points out that anorexia typically starts at puberty—just when the brain's eating center suddenly switches on the taste for fat in foods. "You see yourself getting fat, and the culture is telling you it's wrong. Your boyfriend is telling you not to get fat. Your mother is telling you not to get fat. Then you come to this bottleneck in development. You're asking, 'Who am I?' 'Am I going to be as fat as my mother?' Psychology plays into it, but it is also a matter of just fighting a natural tendency."

Her view contradicts conventional wisdom, and regards the failure of sexual maturity that typifies anorexia as a *consequence* of the disorder, not its raison d'être. Before puberty, appetite in girls is dominated by a physiologically based preference for carbohydrate. Production of Neuropeptide Y in the supraventricular nucleus of the hypothalamus presides over this taste preference.

At puberty, rising levels of estrogen turn on production of the neurochemical galanin, which drives an everyday appetite for fat. It's part of nature's attempt to ensure a future for the species; reproduction in women requires a substantial amount of body fat. With their energy needs so intertwined, the brain center for eating behavior and the brain center for reproduction, located just next to it in the hy-

pothalamus, Neuropeptide Y joined by galanin, are set to crave high-calorie sweets—chocolate cake, say, or ice cream. It's bread-and-butter nutritional knowledge that carbohydrate makes fat palatable in the first place.

This neurochemical combo particularly sets women up for late-afternoon snacking, possibly bingeing. Late afternoon may be the time when those who skip breakfast are particularly likely to pay for it, and there in turn with exaggerated increases in their Neuropeptide Y levels leading them into late-day gorging.

Patterns of Preference

When Leibowitz allows animals to choose what they eat, they show marked individual preferences for nutrients. These nutrient preferences, in turn, create specific differences in feeding patterns. In this animals are just like people, and fall into one of three general categories.

In about 50 percent of the population, carbohydrate is the nutrient of choice. Such people naturally choose a diet in which about 60 percent of calories are derived from carbohydrate, and up to 30 percent come from fat. They are neurochemically in line with what nutritionists today are recommending as a healthy diet. High-carbohydrate animals consume smaller and more frequent meals, and they weigh significantly less, than other animals.

Some Like It Fat

A small number of people and animals are dedicated to protein. But 30 percent of us have a predilection for fat. And those who do take in 60 to 70 percent of their calories in straight fat, as opposed to the 30 percent considered appropriate to a lifestyle that's more sedentary than our

Those people chemically constituted to favor fat consume the most calories and weigh the most. And they seem to be particularly predisposed to food cravings late in the day.

ancestors'.

Not only is this not likely to sit well with arteries, but such preferences also correlate highly with body weight in animals. Those constituted to favor fat consume the most calories and weigh the most. And they seem to be particularly predisposed to food cravings late in the day.

Early Indicators

What is perhaps most intriguing in all of this to Leibowitz is that individual taste preferences first show themselves when animals are very young, notably at the time of weaning, even before their neurochemical profiles are fully elaborated. The same is true of people. "We know early in family life what we are going to become," she contends.

The New York researcher be-

pothalamus, coordinate their activities through regular neurochemical cross talk.

When the switched-on taste for fat alerts young women to the possibility of getting fat, some women swing into high gear—notably those with obsessive-compulsive personality traits. Performing a behaviorally heroic feat, they shun fat altogether. They cling instead to the prepubertal pattern of food intake—very small, frequent meals based on carbohydrate. "They're trying to keep going all day on what is normally that early-morning feeling. It takes very little food." They are literally starving.

Here's the catch. Starvation pumps up abnormally high levels of Neuropeptide Y in the brain. Neuropeptide Y confines their dietary interest to foods with carbohydrate. But the high levels of Neuropeptide Y have an effect on the sex center next door as well; they turn off production of gonadal hormones, which diminishes sexual function.

"It's important for anorexics and bulimics to know that there's this chemistry of the brain that they're fighting. Then they don't feel that they're just crazy. They're fighting nature. Of course, the approach is to alter that tendency before they become anorexic."

Not surprisingly, Leibowitz' unconventional view of the disorder leads her into a new approach to treatment. She wants to temporarily shut off production of galanin at puberty, the neurochemical that turns on the appetite for fat. "Eating disorders set in very close to the onset of menstruation. We find that estrogen increases the production of galanin, and it makes us want to eat. It makes us want to deposit fat, and it makes us want to eat fat."

She has administered to animals a substance that blocks production of the appetite stimulant for fat. It is an antagonist to galanin. "It is a newly developed experimental drug, M40. The animals just stop eating fat. It doesn't affect carbohydrate or protein intake. Now, if we can work with an individual who is getting all stressed out about having to eat fat, we can help her over the hump with the drug. Then we have a fighting chance to bring on board behavioral modification, nutrition, and education, which work more gradually to control appetite."

lieves that by sampling infants' tastes, it will be possible to predict eating and weight-control problems long before they occur. And, of course, if we choose, do something to prevent them from ever occurring.

More than Metabolism

At the time of weaning—21 days in rat pups, 1½ to 2 years in human infants—taste preferences largely reflect differences in genetic makeup. And in those animals that prefer sucrose or fat—"you put it on an infant's tongue and watch how they react to it, whether they become active or not"—their appetite is strongly predictive of how much weight they will gain later on in life. And their neurochemical make-up.

"We believe there is strong appetitive component to pre-ordained weight gain," Leibowitz says. "We think there's more to it than just metabolism. We are on the verge of linking that early taste with later eating behavior and weight gain."

The Wages of Stress

These ground-breaking studies of nutrient preferences show that inborn patterns are one way we can be set up for eating problems or weight gain we might prefer not to have. They also implicate another—stress. Stress potentially wreaks havoc with our eating patterns by altering us internally.

When we feel under stress, the body increases production of the hormone cortisol, from the adrenal gland. The purpose of this chemical messenger of alarm is to marshall forces of energy for immediate use—to prepare us, as it were, for fight or flight. It puts our whole system on alert, and makes us hyper-vigilant.

As it enters the bloodstream from the adrenal gland and circulates throughout the body, cortisol sees that carbohydrate, stored in muscles and liver as glycogen, is swiftly turned into glucose for fuel. If we are not burning up glucose, we have no energy. One reason cortisol is elevated in the

> Skipping meals upsets the natural rhythm of neurochemicals, and that's important because the body works on routines. It affects your mood, your energy, even your sex life. And it turns your next meal into a high-carbohydrate binge.

morning is because the food deprivation of overnight fasting is a kind of stress to the body, destabilizing the system.

Cortisol, however, is also critical in the regulation of the neurochemicals that control eating behavior. "It up-regulates the neuropeptides when you don't want it to," says Leibowitz. Cortisol specifically stimulates production of Neuropeptide Y, which turns on the appetite—for more carbohydrate. "Stress is very much related to turning on Neuropeptide Y," reports Leibowitz. "It doesn't appear to increase galanin."

What's particularly tricky is that the effect of stress on eating is not uniform throughout the day. A bout of stress at the right time in the morning may keep Neuropeptide Y turned on all day. "We know that some people under stress get fat and others do not overeat. It depends on when the stress is occurring. Wouldn't it be nice to get your stress at a time when you are not so vulnerable?" Now if only she knew when that was.

Why We Overeat

What she does know is that if there is no muscular activity to use up the carbohydrate stress sets us up to eat, the carbohydrate is put directly into storage as fat. But wait—there are other consequences. It is an axiom of neuro-

Chemistry & Craving

science that the same chemical messenger has different effects at different sites.

Through neurochemical cross talk in the hypothalamus, the increase in Neuropeptide Y activity affects the master switch for sexual and reproductive behavior in the cluster of cells next door. In this back-and-forth signaling between cell groups, high levels of Neuropeptide Y, hell-bent on carbohydrate intake, turn off the gonadal hormones, which are far more interested in fat. The upshot is a dampening of sexual interest and activity. This effect turns out to be critically important in anorexia.

Eating carbohydrate under stress, however, has something going for it. It chases away the stress-induced changes in neurochemistry. The hormonal alarm signals dissipate. "After we eat a carbohydrate-rich meal, the world actually seems better," explains Leibowitz. We feel less edgy. "That's why we overeat."

Dieting—Bad for the Brain

Many studies have shown that curbing body weight by food restriction—dieting—makes no sense metabolically; in fact it's counterproductive. Leibowitz finds it also makes no sense to the biochemistry of our brains, either. "All dieting does is disturb the system." she says emphatically. "It puts you in a psychological altered state. You're a different person. You respond differently."

Erratically skipping meals upsets the natural daily rhythm of neurochemicals, "that's important because the body works on routines. If you disturb the routine, you're going to be a different person at lunch than if you didn't skip breakfast." What's more, "the chemicals that regulate appetite also directly affect moods and state of mind, our physical energy, the quality of our sex lives," says Leibowitz.

Fasting—restricting, in the parlance of those who study eating behavior—is particularly counterproductive to appetite. It simply turns on the neurochemical switches. "It's got to come out somehow," says Leibowitz. It specifically drives up levels of Neuropeptide Y and cortisol. Then, when the next meal rolls around, it turns it into a high-carbohydrate binge. "Neuropeptide Y is truly the neurochemical of food deprivation." Fasting or dieting drives the body to seek more carbohydrate. Her stud-

ies show that animals that love carbohydrate have higher levels of Neuropeptide Y in the paraventricular nucleus.

The Way We Were

How, then, to lose weight? Certainly not diet pills. One reason they don't work is that they don't even aspire to cope with the array of neurochemicals setting the table for appetite. Assuming such an approach to be possible or even desirable, it would, in fact, take assorted concoctions of chemicals at different times of the day, since each meal is regulated differently.

Nevertheless, the way to control appetite and body weight, Leibowitz believes,

W e need to help people understand what they are, what their appetite is, and how to work with their body the way it is."

is by working *with* the neurochemical systems—and re-tuning them. "We need to help people understand what they are and what their appetite is, and how to work with the body the way it is. Some people are more sensitive." This may be a far gentler approach than skipping lunch, but in the long run, it may be the only workable one, the only one that can possibly do away with the preoccupation with dieting that now consumes 50 to 70 percent of all women.

However deterministic biochemistry at first appears, that is not, within broad bounds, the case with behavior. We are not wholly slaves of neurochemistry. "Neurons are plastic. They change. We can therefore educate the neurons," explains Leibowitz. "You can say that God dictated this biochemical pattern. But we are here to mold ourselves and train ourselves."

The secret to modifying neurons is to introduce a very gradual shift in their sen-

sitivity to the neurochemicals of appetite—to down-regulate them s-l-o-w-l-y.

Given the plasticity of neurons, early experience is heavily weighted in shaping the behavior of brain cells for life. Early exposure to a certain nutrient—say, a high-fat diet—will bias neurochemistry—It will up-regulate sensitivity to galanin and prompt production of greater amounts of it, aiding and abetting the appetite for fat. "Your training, your habits, all have an effect," says Leibowitz. "We don't know how much is permanent and how much is reversible. It may be like the case with fat cells in the body; if you overeat when young and get fat cells, you may not be able to get rid of them." The bottom line is, we may be remarkably adaptable but not infinitely malleable.

Taste Tests for All?

The ideal, then, is to start the neurochemicals of appetite out on the right foot, "to modulate them before an eating disorder sets in, or any disturbance in dieting. It's got to be preventative. What you eat is going to affect production of these peptides." At some point in the future, it may be possible to determine the right calorie and nutrient mix even to dampen the genetically outlined production of the appetite hormones.

Leibowitz would bypass the dismal enterprise of dieting altogether with a taste test at age two. "We're aiming for the goal of trying to characterize people at a very early age, just as we can now do with animals. We can predict adult height at two years of age. We may also want to predict adult eating behavior and weight gain."

Then, with nutrition and planning and behavioral therapy she would set out to educate the appetite. "I'm not thinking drugs, but there could be drugs. If we could do this ahead of time, we could prevent the development of eating disorders," disorders that now affect, by her calculation, 30 percent of the population.

"The question is, can we find some specific dietary situation, different foods at different times, that might help us to reduce neuropeptide activity without depriving ourselves. The whole point is, we can't deprive ourselves. But if we know that what we eat and when we eat it affect the production of neuropeptides, we can modulate what we eat and work the appetite so that we can get a new routine in."

Gastronomy may never be the same again. ■

The Pressure to Lose

Health: Anorexia and other eating disorders are gnawing away at young men

AT 5 FEET 9, ALAN BAUM HAS NEVER topped 120 pounds. But during his freshman year of college, disappointment and frustration began to eat away at what little flesh he had. Baum, now 25, dropped out of Salem College in West Virginia and went back home to Macungie, Pa., to live with his parents and save money for a better school. Depressed by the derailment of his career plans and cut off from the friends he'd made at college, he decided to try to take control of his weight. First he began skipping breakfast, then lunch, and eventually shrank his supper to a bowl of cereal. "Every time I ate, I felt like I had lost that feeling of control," he says. If he went off his diet, he'd force the food back up by vomiting. Hospitalized (for the first of 11 times) at 84 pounds, Baum has been near death more than once in the past five years, at one point dwindling to 72 pounds. "I didn't realize anything was wrong," he says. "I didn't think I looked skinny. The more weight you lose, the more your mind becomes distorted and you can't see yourself clearly." After finally facing up to his problem and entering an eating-disorders program, Baum now works—paradoxically—as a waiter in a restaurant and weighs 102 pounds. "I still feel that if I try to eat normally," he admits, "I'm just going to balloon and get fat."

Baum is a classic case of anorexia—except that he's a man. Long considered "women's diseases" that afflict primarily young white females from privileged homes, eating disorders are now gaining recognition as equal-opportunity plunderers. Well, almost equal: according to one estimate, anorexia (self-starvation), bulimia (gorging and vomiting) and B.E.D. (binge eating disorder), characterized by unhappy, uncontrollable eating *without* purging, affect some 7 million American women and 1 million men. But the disparity may be partly due to underdiagnosis. In a 1992 survey of 1982 Harvard graduates, eating disorders in women had dropped by half, but among men, they had doubled. And a study of 131 Cornell University lightweight football players, completed this spring, found that 40 percent engaged in "dysfunctional eating patterns" (mostly binging or purging), with 10 percent classified as having outright eating disorders.

Researchers don't know if there are more new cases of eating disorders in men—or simply more recognition. There are, they agree, both similarities and differences in how men and women are afflicted. In both genders, eating behavior is likely to go awry at key points of separation from home and family or reaching a new, adult stage in life: going away to college or graduate school or starting a new job appear to be triggers. So is puberty. In girls, says University of Iowa psychiatrist Dr. Arnold Andersen, who has treated more than 1,000 girls and women with eating disorders and about 120 men, the onset of anorexia in early adolescence is often partly a frightened retreat from sexuality. (Curves disappear, menstruation

> "Every time I ate, I felt like I had lost that feeling of control. . . . I didn't realize anything was wrong. I didn't think I looked skinny. The more weight you lose, the more your mind becomes distorted and you can't see yourself clearly. . . . I still feel that if I try to eat normally, I'm just going to balloon and get fat."

From *Newsweek, 123*, pp. 60–61, May 2, 1994, ©1994, Newsweek, Inc. All rights reserved. Reprinted by permission.

"I wanted to get rid of a little bit of flab around my stomach. I looked in the mirror all the time. I didn't see that I was losing weight. . . . I felt ashamed. I felt like I was partaking in a woman's disease and that it wasn't very manly."

junior-high-school football (at 210 pounds) and wrestling (at 170 pounds) in northern New Jersey. Kicked out of school at 14 for drug and alcohol abuse, Balser was sent to the Hazelden rehab center in Minnesota, where he picked up the habit of compulsive eating, purging and exercising. Between the ages of 16 and 19, he says, left pretty much on his own by divorced parents, he would alternately starve himself and binge. Intensely hungry, he craved cookies, cake and ice cream—and would often cram in huge quantities at one sitting. It took him a while to become adept at purging, but with a little practice, he could just lean over the toilet, flex his stomach muscles and throw up. "I wanted to get rid of a little bit of flab around my stomach," he says. "I looked in the mirror all the time. I didn't see that I was losing weight."

'A woman's disease': At 19, six feet tall and weighing 137 pounds, Balser was purging 40 times a day and spending $100 on food; sometimes he even stole to support his habit. "I felt ashamed," he says. "I felt like I was partaking in a woman's disease and that it wasn't very manly." Finally Balser got help at a residential treatment program in Florida. He now lives in Branford, Conn., attends college nearby, has a girlfriend— and weighs a solid 185 pounds.

stops.) In males, who tend to develop anorexia symptoms a couple of years later—in late adolescence or their early 20s—anorexia sometimes signals confusion over sexual orientation. According to Andersen, about 22 percent of male anorexics are homosexual. "Being gay is a risk [for the disease], but not a requirement," he says.

Actors and jockeys: For women, the overwhelming social and cultural pressure to be slim can produce such ferocious fear of fatness that the result is anorexia. For men, says Andersen, such pressures are a significant cause of anorexia primarily in a subset that includes models, actors, gymnasts, wrestlers and jockeys. But for many males, nonprofessional sports training can lead down the road to an eating disorder. "When the season is over, they find themselves in an addictive pattern," says Anita Sinicrope of the Pennsylvania Educational Network for Eating Disorders. Tony Muno, now 27, who grew up in a Chicago suburb, got a gymnastics scholarship to college and

found that when he began taking off weight for competition, he simply couldn't stop. "I just got obsessed with it," he says. "It started to consume my thoughts." When he reached 113 pounds (at 5 feet 10), he dropped out of school and checked himself into a hospital for three months, where he began a recovery process that took 2½ years.

Men can also develop eating disorders in connection with what behavior experts call "obligatory running" and other endurance sports. In a world of deprivation chic, pain and hunger take a back seat to miles-per-day and body-fat-percentage numbers. (In female compulsive athletes, the anorexia often precedes the exercise addiction.) "There is a certain social acceptance of [excessive] exercise," says Steven Zelicoff, a Pittsburgh-based exercise physiologist. "You would be frowned upon for being neurotic about the way you eat, but celebrated as a local legend for the way you exercise."

Chris Balser, 26, saw his weight bounce all over the scales when he went in for

Perhaps the ultimate indignity for men with eating disorders has been that for years, doctors failed to recognize the problem. Now there is growing awareness, says Andersen, that these illnesses can strike "males, matrons and minorities" as well as young white teenage girls. (They also affect some older men, driven to extreme dieting by fear of heart disease.) But men are still often reluctant to enter treatment programs where they may be the only males—and where the women sometimes resent and sneer at them. Without treatment, declares Andersen, the outlook for men and women with eating disorders can be ominous. With help, including group and family therapy, antidepressants and possibly male hormones for men, the recovery rate is 90 percent. And for someone who starts treatment now, there's the prospect of enjoying a normal Thanksgiving dinner, maybe even including a slice of pumpkin pie.

JEAN SELIGMANN *with* PATRICK ROGERS
in New York and PETER ANNIN *in Chicago*

THE
MIND
OF A

Hypochondriac

Did you ever suspect your headache was really a brain tumor?

BY BENEDICT CAREY

B ERGEN, NORWAY, could be a modern, mad-scramble metropolis if only city planners would install expressways and condos in place of all the cobblestone streets and ginger-bread houses. Or if, say, there were a little crime and poverty, maybe a few malcontents who'd fallen off the national health insurance, or even one drunk in your face. As it is, the only thing in your face is a cool breeze from the mountains and the spectacle of Bergen harbor, a port so well protected from the North Sea swell that it's as placid as a small lake, a flat lens that in the late afternoon reflects the town's every baroque detail.

This city of 200,000 samaritans is so blessedly free of everything associated with 20th century angst that it puts to rest any doubt that we humans—whether we live in Bergen, Norway, or Bergen County, New Jersey—will always find a way to invent our own. For it is here that a doctor named Ingvard Wilhelmsen founded the Psychosomatic Clinic, the first hospital-based facility devoted to the treatment of severe health anxiety, otherwise known as hypochondria.

Doctors in the United States and abroad are watching Wilhelmsen's efforts closely because, as recently as five years ago, hypochondria appeared all but untreatable. And despite revolutionary advances in medicine this century, the incidence of psychosomatic illness—real if harmless symptoms wrought by an overactive imagination—is apparently at an all-time high. Surveys of family practices across the country show that at least 20 percent of patients complaining of symptoms have no underlying medical problems. HEALTH's nationwide survey of physicians found that a third of doctors think that more than half the patients they see arrive with psychosomatic symptoms; physically, they're just fine.

Wilhelmsen's first patient, a soft-spoken engineer named Thor, is a Bergener who by all outward appearances has a rich and serene life. "The stereotype of the Norwegian is a person hiking in the mountains with a backpack, and that is me," Thor says over the clang and bang of a busy restaurant. Like many Norwegians, Thor speaks English easily, if slowly, with an accent that could be Minnesotan. "I know these mountains like the insides of my pockets. When I am there I can forget all the rest."

The rest is an embarrassment for a sturdy-looking 39-year-old who is so clearly capable and curious, who skis and fishes and sings bass in a Lutheran choir that performs Bach, Vivaldi, and black gospel music. When Thor mentions Robeson's rendition of "Ol' Man River," he waxes reverent, tender; when he mentions his medical history, he simply looks waxed, an awful quiver running through his long face and large eyes. "In 1989 I got diarrhea," he

From *Health, 10,* pp. 82–86, October 1996. Reprinted with permission from *Health,* © 1996.

begins, staring at the table for a moment, then looking back up. "But very intense."

Intense enough that Thor couldn't go more than an hour without hunching over in pain, and relentless enough that he couldn't blame it on bad venison sausages. He researched his symptoms exhaustively, and one day an awful word popped into his head: *kreft*—he must have cancer, either in his colon or his stomach. Incredulous when his doctor's tests failed to find a lump, he demanded to see a specialist—who ran the tests again, to no avail. Yet Thor's pains only worsened, until one morning he noticed blood in his stool and, a few hours later, collapsed in pain. He awoke in the hospital, his long-suffering colon again worked over by the ungentle touch of the colonoscope and ultrasound probe. "It was useless," he says. "They couldn't even tell me why there would be blood."

Desperate, Thor quit his job and drifted onto the byroads of medical healing. He experimented with a sugarless diet, advised by a homeopath, and a vegetables-only diet, suggested by another alternative practitioner. His bowels were utterly impervious. "Both me and my doctor became very uhhhh—frustrated," Thor says. "I felt like every time I saw him it was a confrontation. He was courteous, but I could tell he was tired of me complaining."

So it is with hypochondriacs. Whether the problem is a grumbly stomach or a vague sense of fatigue, after a while their complaints inspire about as much sympathy as Ivana Trump's. Yet the tough-love advice of many friends and doctors—get over it!—doesn't work for them. They come back, they want more tests, they insist on a diagnosis. Often the medical system has been obliging, diagnosing psychosomatic symptoms as "spinal irritation" throughout mid-19th century Europe and "neurasthenia" among turn-of-the-century Americans. Today, poorly defined conditions such as chronic fatigue and fibromyalgia are controversial precisely because they involve long lists of symp-

"I had people around me dying, associates and friends of friends. I kept thinking, People are dying all the time, every day—why not me?" . . . The purebred hypochondriac is more often an intelligent, sensitive, and highly suggestible person who's simply confounded by the modern-day barrage of complex, often conflicting health information

toms commonly caused by high anxiety.

In recent years, however, doctors have finally figured out where and how to treat the hypochondria itself. They've also discovered where *not* to do it: a psychiatrist's office.

"By definition, hypochondriacs believe they have some sort of physiological disease," says Wilhelmsen, a psychiatrist who is also licensed as a gastroenterologist. "So of course they want nothing to do with therapists of any kind. They're insulted, because the pain is very real for them."

Certainly Thor's pains were real, cutting into him like pins into a voodoo doll. So when he was referred to the newly opened hospital-based program last year, he practically went limp with relief. "It was very important to me that Dr. Wilhelmsen was trained in organic disease," Thor says.

Says Wilhelmsen: "They want to be seen in a hospital. So that's what I decided to do."

THE PSYCHOSOMATIC clinic is a pair of nondescript offices within the gastroenterological branch of the Deaconess Home Hospital. The rooms are sparsely furnished with a desk, a couple of chairs, and nothing resembling a therapist's couch. Wilhelmsen himself is a meditative host, a slight man with a thin, blond beard who exhibits the kind of determined patience that comes from explaining things more than twice. "The first thing to understand is that all of us have health anxiety once in a while," he says. "Maybe we are exhausted or feeling strange pains, and then we read an article about a new disease or we hear of someone who has suddenly died."

Let's say it was the mail room clerk, of stomach cancer. For the next few days everyone in the office is on edge; some check their abdomens for lumps, and the high-strung types who already have shifty stomachs are beside themselves. Like any anticipation of threat, health anxiety can cue the release of stress hormones: Heart rate and breathing speed up, digestion shuts down, blood shifts from the gut to limbs, and the colon dumps its contents. Voilà: psychosomatic cramps and diarrhea. When the anxiety subsides, says Wilhelmsen, so do the symptoms, and the episode might make a funny story later on.

Less comical is what Harvard psychiatrist Arthur Barsky calls transient hypochondriasis, a condition in which people repeat cycles of angst and relative calm. These are the sickly Aunt Helen types who seem to contract every disease that makes the cover of *Newsweek*. Anyone who's ever felt a passing but intense fear of having the AIDS virus (that one-night stand in Denver), cancer (the headaches, the lump in the throat), an ulcer (two nights of heartburn), or chronic fatigue syndrome (too tired for sex) knows this condition. And anyone who has fixated on a disease for any length of time, attributing to it any and all odd sensations—*it's the brain tumor, it must be spreading*—knows full-blown hypochondria.

In short, the difference between hypochondriacs and the rest of us neurotics is one of degree, not kind. While a visit to the doctor reassures the merely anxious and even the temporarily obsessed, for the hypochondriac it provides only the sort of short-lived comfort that a cocktail brings to an alcoholic. "The whole idea of reassurance has to be redefined for these people," says Paul Salkovskis, the University of Oxford psychiatrist who pioneered the treatment of hypochondriasis in the early 1980s. "When they hear there's nothing wrong or that a test is negative, they ask, 'Are you sure, Doc? Are you sure?'" At the peak of his paranoia, Thor visited his doctor twice a month; another of Wilhelmsen's patients, a jovial, 50-year-old businessman named Jostein Ekrem, has pestered his doctor 20 times in the past year and undergone two brain scans in search of a tumor that never appeared. "I had people around me dying, associates and friends of friends," says Ekrem. "I kept thinking, People are dying all the time, every day—why not me?"

Salkovskis compares living in such turmoil to being on a plane during a heavy storm. "You're sitting there, being knocked around, and you know the chances are like one in a billion that you'll be in a crash—but you also know this is the one. So you clutch the seat harder. The anxiety has switched off your otherwise rational system and left you focusing on the extremes."

Of course they're telling me everything's fine. They don't want me to panic!

What causes health anxiety? To be sure, it sprouts readily around deeper roots of guilt, shame, and, most of all, depression. "The depressed patient is the sad, fearful woman who comes in and says, 'There are white bumps on my tongue, Doc, and I had an affair two years ago. I must have AIDS,'" says Brian Fallon, a professor of psychiatry at Columbia University who has treated some of these patients successfully with Prozac. "Despite having had tests done, she has a conviction she's dying that's associated with the guilt she feels over past behavior."

But the purebred hypochondriac is more often an intelligent, sensitive, and highly suggestible person who's simply confounded by the modern-day barrage of complex, often conflicting health information. Coverage of health throughout Europe and North America has exploded in the past ten years, says Wilhelmsen, and so has the number of people who come to the doctor's office saying, "I just read this article. . . ." And while diagnostic tests have become more advanced, they are also more confusing.

"Once upon a time the doctor told you that you were sick or you were fine," says Salkovskis. "Now they're telling you that you have 20 times the average risk of developing colon cancer based on a genetic test. The technology is better, but the way doctors present the information only makes us worry more."

"Both Thor and Jostein are the sort of people who read self-exam articles in newspapers and magazines and think, My God, that's me!" says Wilhelmsen. "Then they proceed to examine themselves like crazy, as many hypochondriacs do." Fallon recalls a woman who, afraid she had a cancerous mass, continually kneaded her breast. "When I finally saw her she did have a mass—a blood clot from all the palpating."

This gallery of tormented souls quickly devolves into farce, with people convinced their brains are shrinking or certain their

RATE YOUR HEALTH ANXIETY

IT'S HUMAN TO WORRY. It's even normal for jumpy nerves to cause an occasional upset stomach or aggravate a sore back. But when you're prone to anxiety-related symptoms *and* to interpreting them as real medical problems, you can literally worry yourself sick. Are you sensitive to—and scared of—everyday aches and pains? Take this simple test to gauge your bodily angst.

1 Have you ever felt ill after reading in the paper about an outbreak of food poisoning?

2 Do you continually readjust the temperature controls in your car because you're always either too cold or too hot?

3 If you woke up feeling nauseated, would you stay home from work even if the discomfort went away?

4 If you noticed your hands tingling for no apparent reason, would you worry it was a sign of a medical problem?

5 Let's say your grandmother died of cancer at age 50. Would you fixate on the idea that you will die from the same disease?

6 You feel an unfamiliar pain in your chest one night. Would you go to the emergency room to have it checked out?

7 Have you ever felt disappointed when your doctor told you that your symptoms were benign and you were fine?

8 Do you take a pain reliever every time you get a headache?

9 When you develop a cough, do you assume it won't go away until your physician gives you antibiotics?

10 Are you likely to insist on having lab tests redone, even when results show no problem?

COUNT THE NUMBER OF YES ANSWERS

FOUR OR FEWER: Consider yourself lucky; your body is not particularly sensitive to aches and pains, and you react calmly to those you have.

FIVE TO SEVEN: Though you're a bit touchy about pain and perhaps eager to seek medical help, you probably aren't worrying yourself sick.

EIGHT OR MORE: Anxiety has no doubt created and exacerbated health problems for you. Talk to your doctor about how you can learn to interpret your symptoms more accurately, or about referring you to a behavioral therapist who treats health anxiety. —*Kate Lee*

penises are retracting into their pelvises, a phobia common enough among Malaysian men that it has a name, *koro*. ("Some of these guys hang weights from their genitals, for fear they'll disappear altogether," says Fallon.) Yet even the most sanguine among us will find that symptoms are easy to create. "If you keep swallowing quickly, you'll find that you can't swallow anymore," says Charles Ford, a psychiatrist at the University of Alabama, "and if you focus all your attention on that spot, it's going to start throbbing."

Once symptoms start, doctors often have no way of knowing whether the cause is anxiety or disease. Afflictions such as lupus, multiple sclerosis, and Lyme disease defy easy diagnosis, Fallon says, and doctors frequently label such frustrating con-

internal dialogue has a great impact on how we feel."

Thor's treatment began with a homework assignment. "I made a diary of each day, describing all my symptoms for two weeks." This helped him see that his anxiety preceded his plumbing problems and could, in fact, induce the sensations.

"I told Thor that the same transmitters in the brain are found in the gut, so it's very natural that anxiety causes these sensations in the stomach and colon," Wilhelmsen says. Over several hour-long sessions, about one a month, the gastroenterologist also pruned a few of Thor's misconceptions about good health.

"He said I could never be sure I'm not sick," remembers Thor, "and that if anything I'm less likely than *anyone* to have colon cancer because I've had all these negative tests. Sudden-

"People equate it with malingering, but I don't buy that. Hypochondriacs suffer."

ditions hypochondria. Meanwhile, the symptoms created by anxiety can mimic those of any ailment short of leprosy. Gastrointestinal pains are so common among hypochondriacs in part because the gut is encased in a sheaf of nerve cells, called the enteric nervous system. That system has moods delivered to its doorstep via the "brain-gut axis"—a direct pathway for neural activity and stress hormones. But stress hormones act throughout the body, in all tissues, and they can induce headaches, insomnia, chest pains, even rashes.

And some people are just highly sensitive, it turns out. In a study at Harvard, Barsky had a group of 60 hypochondriacs rate the discomfort of common ailments such as heartburn and constipation. Compared to a control group, these panicky patients grimaced with almost every breath. "They experience the normal sensations of the body much more intensely than most of us," says Barsky. Ford puts it another way: "People equate hypochondria with malingering. I just don't buy that. There's no question these people suffer."

THOR BLAMES HIS PREDICAMENT on his high school language teacher, a Nordic leviathan named Yvand. "He was very dominant, very aggressive, and if you didn't recite your assignment correctly he'd grab you by the collar and shake you," he says. "He was a real Viking." Yvand's reign of terror snuffed his student's confidence and instilled a miserable dread that, Thor believes, later curdled into constant anxiety and pain.

Wilhelmsen says he doesn't usually heed such self-analysis because it rarely helps patients progress. "It is a common belief that if you get hypochondriacs to admit that their symptoms are partly mental, then they're cured," he says. "Well, it's not true. Even when they know there's a mental component, they wonder if there's something else. The anxiety is still there."

That's why practitioners such as Wilhelmsen and Salkovskis address the agitation directly, coaching people to recognize what people, places, and thoughts trigger their morbid fantasies and how to short-circuit those associations. Called cognitive-behavioral therapy, the approach is employed to treat a variety of compulsions, from smoking to bulimia.

Wilhelmsen describes the method: "We try to find out whether the patient really misinterprets his or her bodily symptoms—whether they assume a headache is a brain tumor. We also try to identify dysfunctional 'life rules,' such as 'I have to be 100 percent certain that I am not ill,' or 'A bodily symptom is always a sign of serious disease.' The whole idea is that our

ly I wasn't worried about the colon cancer as much."

Another sign of progress turned up when Thor began feeling pain in his joints (never underestimate a hypochondriac's ability to diversify). He insisted on tests for rheumatoid arthritis. "He said he was 80 percent certain the tests would be positive," says Wilhelmsen. "I told him I was 95 percent sure they would be negative. They were negative, of course. After that, Thor actually said, 'This shows my tendency to exaggerate.'"

"I've started to think about what I'm thinking," says Thor. "When I feel anxious, I've learned to say, 'This has nothing to do with disease. You can cope with this.'"

Yet as recently as last fall, he was a corked blowfish, bloated and gaseous. The sensation came after meals, especially dinner, the pressure percolating at night until it interrupted his sleep. Burps wouldn't come as the vapor worked its way up his gullet and was trapped by a flap at the back of his mouth. With every dark hour, Thor felt more pressure, his throat tight as a drum.

"He thought," says Wilhelmsen, "he would explode."

He didn't. Says Wilhelmsen, "I showed him what the esophagus looks like and explained that there's no valve, nothing that blocks the passage—it's designed to let air come right out."

Such therapy, Wilhelmsen admits, amounts to little more than nuggets of common sense provided by someone with impeccable authority who takes every symptom seriously, as an actual physical sensation. In two trials at Oxford using 50 patients, Salkovskis demonstrated that cognitive-behavioral treatment changes the compulsive habits of nine out of ten hypochondriacs. In the past year and a half Wilhelmsen has seen 90 patients, almost all of whom regained some control of their lives and learned to resist nagging urges to see their doctors. "What it really comes down to," he says, "is teaching people what it feels like to be healthy."

To be sure, that's a day-to-day proposition for someone like Thor. Though his diarrhea subsided and his fear of cancer dissipated, something new gnaws at him. It has to do with his muscles, which have been a little sore, and his afternoons, when he's exhausted. He thinks he might have fibromyalgia.

What is fibromyalgia?

He stares blankly at the question. Then the large eyes bulge, he barks, "No one knows!" and for a moment Thor laughs with his entire body at the thought that his mother's favorite son imagines he has a disease that may not be a disease at all. **H**

Benedict Carey is a staff writer.

Deceptive Appearances
Imagined physical defects take an ugly personal toll

By BRUCE BOWER

It sounds like an episode from *The Twilight Zone*. Submitted for your approval: In communities across the country, teenagers and young adults watch their bodies undergo horrid transformations. Noses sprout revolting bumps, faces break out in red spots, breasts and genitals shrink or enlarge drastically, and mouths branch crookedly from one cheek to the other, to cite a few examples. A cruel force seems to be taking grotesque liberties with human anatomy.

Yet only those whose bodies succumb to the force can see the bizarre physical mutations. Families and friends look on in confusion and exasperation as afflicted individuals continually check their appearance in mirrors, try to hide their defects with makeup or clothing, and sink into years of social isolation and depression. Some haunt the offices of plastic surgeons, going under the knife again and again until they take on a distorted look that ironically confirms their fears of ugliness.

This scenario may resemble an eerie fantasy, but it reflects the experiences of real people. For instance, 33-year-old Ted has complained of repulsive facial freckles and acne for more than a decade. He picks his skin constantly and thinks people stare at him whenever he makes one of his rare appearances outside. Heavy drinking helps to dull his anxiety about social encounters. Ted's wife left him after tiring of his inability to talk about anything other than his perceived skin problems. Years of treatment by dermatologists and psychotherapists left Ted as miserable as ever.

Consider Helen, a woman of uncommon beauty who as a teenager became convinced that her nose was repugnantly small. After undergoing three separate cosmetic surgery procedures, she still viewed her nose as misshapen. Helen went to a psychotherapist who spent 2 years trying to convince her that her nose looked lovely, to no avail. A host of prescribed psychoactive drugs made no dent in Helen's despair.

Finally, psychoactive medications that boost the amount of the chemical messenger serotonin available to brain cells lessened the bodily preoccupations and lifted the spirits of Ted and Helen (not their real names). Katharine A. Phillips, a psychiatrist at Butler Hospital in Providence, R.I., notes that Ted responded favorably to fluoxetine (Prozac), and Helen showed considerable improvement on clomipramine (Anafranil).

Research conducted by Phillips and other investigators, described in May at the annual meeting of the American Psychiatric Association (APA) in Miami, is beginning to unravel the prevalence and nature of what clinicians refer to as body dysmorphic disorder (BDD).

"This problem strikes a chord with almost everyone living in modern cultures," contends Eric Hollander, a psychiatrist at Mount Sinai School of Medicine in New York City. "BDD patients come in all shapes and sizes, and there are nearly as many males as females."

For much of the last century, clinicians have written about people bedeviled by an unwarranted belief that their bodies have changed in weird or disgusting ways. Until the past decade, investigations of what has often been called dysmorphophobia have occurred mainly in Europe and Japan.

The official manual of psychiatric diagnoses, published by APA, included BDD for the first time in 1987. In its latest version, the manual treats BDD as one of several "somatoform disorders." These include hypochondriasis and other conditions characterized by physical symptoms not attributable to a medical illness or to another mental disorder.

BDD involves preoccupation with one or more imagined defects in appearance, resulting in marked emotional distress and severe problems at work and in social situations (SN: 2/13/93, p.108).

Some investigators now suspect that BDD stems from an as yet unspecified brain disturbance that also contributes to obsessive-compulsive disorder (OCD), social phobia (an intense fear of being seen or scrutinized by others in public situations), and perhaps major depression. Serotonin and another chemical courier, dopamine, probably play important roles in this core cerebral ailment,

> **33-year-old Ted has complained of repulsive facial freckles and acne for more than a decade. He picks his skin constantly and thinks people stare at him whenever he makes one of his rare appearances outside. . . .**
> **Years of treatment by dermatologists and psychotherapists left Ted as miserable as ever.**

From *Science News, 148,* pp. 40–41, July 15, 1995. Reprinted by permission of Science News.

the scientists theorize.

Although the details of BDD's underlying biology remain murky, the condition does seem to occur relatively frequently in combination with OCD. A national survey of 419 people treated for OCD, directed by Mount Sinai's Hollander, finds that nearly one in four suffers from BDD as well. Although no one knows how prevalent BDD is, OCD afflicts about 2.4 million people in the United States at some time in their lives.

Both disorders, marked by obsessive thoughts and compulsive acts that disrupt daily life, tend to emerge in late adolescence and to last well into adulthood. OCD provokes ritual behaviors often intended to quell fears of contamination, aggressive or sexual impulses, or doubts about previous actions (such as whether doors have been locked). BDD usually involves a preoccupation with several imagined bodily defects, often including the nose, hair, skin, and mouth. Sometimes, perceived physical abnormalities appear on a family member or close friend.

BDD stands apart from OCD in some important ways, notes Mount Sinai psychiatrist Daphne Simeon. BDD patients rarely realize that their fears are unfounded, get little relief from constant examination of themselves in mirrors, and often cannot work or otherwise function in public. In contrast, many OCD patients recognize the strangeness of their obsessive thoughts, feel better after performing rituals (such as hand washing or door checking), and function relatively well in the social world.

Simeon bases her observations on a study of 442 people diagnosed with OCD, 51 of whom also suffered from BDD.

In another investigation, Butler Hospital's Phillips and her colleagues determined that 47 of 131 BDD patients had first developed social phobia, while many others experienced intense fear of public scrutiny and exposure as a result of their perceived ugliness. In fact, Japanese and Korean researchers treat BDD as a form of social phobia, Phillips notes.

Moreover, BDD occurs in about 15 percent of people who suffer from "atypical" major depression and 5 percent of those with more common symptoms of major depression, according to Phillips. She and her associates studied 172 outpatients diagnosed with major depression, including 53 atypical cases. Symptoms unique to atypical depression include increased appetite, oversleeping, a tendency to feel cheered up temporarily in response to positive events, and extreme sensitivity to perceived rejection by others.

To top it off, preliminary studies indicate that severe personality disorders commonly accompany BDD. Patients exhibit a variety of symptoms, including social anxiety, clinging dependency on others for approval, fears of intimacy, manipulation of others in close relationships, and impulsive fighting, says Fugen A. Neziroglu of the Institute for Bio-Behavioral Therapy and Research in Great Neck, N.Y..

A study directed by Neziroglu identified widespread signs of personality disorder in 13 of 17 BDD patients undergoing a 4-week trial of cognitive-behavioral therapy. Weekly therapy sessions attempted to reduce faulty beliefs about physical appearance and expose patients to their perceived defects without allowing them to engage in compulsive reactions (such as picking their skin or checking repeatedly in the mirror).

This approach reduced BDD symptoms modestly and left personality disturbances largely intact, Neziroglu notes.

Available data cannot resolve whether BDD represents a form of obsessive-compulsive disorder or arises from severe personality disturbances, she asserts.

Whatever its origins, BDD often sparks an unyielding belief in the reality of the imagined physical defects—a certainty that qualifies as delusional, Phillips contends. For instance, her patient Helen's absolute conviction that her nose was misshapen couldn't be changed by contrary opinions or repeated plastic surgery.

In contrast, Phillips' other patient, Ted, displayed a greater sense that his skin complaints were strange and had created enormous problems in his life.

Interviews conducted by Phillips and her colleagues have uncovered strong delusions in 73 of 130 people diagnosed with BDD. Delusional patients showed more severe symptoms of the disorder and had performed more poorly in jobs and at school, Phillips reported at the APA meeting.

Serotonin-boosting drugs such as Prozac and Anafranil (the latter is often prescribed for OCD) offered significant relief to delusional BDD patients, she notes.

"This finding needs to be confirmed in controlled trials," Phillips holds. "But the data so far fly in the face of our standard treatment for delusional disorders, which is to prescribe neuroleptic [antipsychotic] medication."

Clinicians need to treat delusions as an aspect of BDD that can wax and wane, depending on the circumstances, she adds. For example, some people cite a fair amount of insight into the unreality of their bodily complaints when they are at home but become certain of their perceived ugliness when they go out in public or to a physician's office.

Some BDD patients apparently experience vivid visual illusions that bolster their certainty of the reality of physical defects, Phillips asserts. "When they get better on [serotonin-enhancing] drugs, some patients say that they see the spots on their face disappear or the unsightly body hair fall out," she remarks.

Not surprisingly, plastic surgery proves more alluring to many BDD sufferers than psychiatric help. Still, the proportion of plastic surgery patients plagued by imaginary physical defects may be far greater than now assumed, contends Mount Sinai psychologist Bonnie Aronowitz.

About 1 person in 50 who request plastic surgery exhibits BDD, according to a currently accepted estimate. But a survey directed by Aronowitz found that nearly one patient in two at an urban, hospital-based plastic surgery clinic met diagnostic criteria for BDD.

"We don't yet know if this high rate generalizes to all plastic surgery patients," Aronowitz says. "Further surveys need to be done at private and community clinics."

She and her coworkers administered questionnaires to 75 women and 16 men seeking help at Mount Sinai's plastic surgery clinic between January and May 1995. About two-thirds wanted cosmetic surgery; the rest cited medical problems that required surgical help.

Aronowitz found that 39 survey participants, or 43 percent, displayed BDD. Preoccupations with imagined defects in appearance and related BDD symptoms appeared more often in cosmetic surgery patients. However, several patients cited plastic surgery as a medical expense on Medicaid forms when they in fact sought cosmetic procedures, Aronowitz maintains.

Researchers do not yet know whether people with BDD can be screened out at plastic surgery clinics or, if that proves possible, whether plastic surgeons should refuse them surgery, referring them instead to psychiatrists.

Plastic surgeons now follow BDD research closely, Aronowitz points out. Of particular concern is the tendency of BDD sufferers to go from one physician to another and end up receiving numerous cosmetic procedures—as many as 15 in some cases—while experiencing an escalating sense of dissatisfaction with the results.

Psychiatrists also express concern over the lack of controlled treatment studies of BDD, Hollander asserts. Preliminary findings of an 8-week pilot trial, funded by the Food and Drug Administration and directed by Hollander, suggest that clomipramine provides more relief from BDD symptoms than does desipramine, an antidepressant that alters dopamine transmission.

Excessive serotonin activity in the brain may significantly influence the imagined physical defects at the heart of BDD, Hollander theorizes. A surplus of dopamine transmission may also play a role in some aspects of BDD, he adds, such as anxiety about imaginary physical defects and unwavering confidence in their reality.

"This is a real disorder that is relatively common," he argues. "We need to pay more scientific attention to it." □

hotheads
andheartattacks

Blowing your stack—or even seething silently—can put your heart at risk. So what are you supposed to do about it? Take a deep breath and read on ✳ **By Edward Dolnick**

Jaw clenched,

voice rising, short, sturdy finger jabbing furiously as if to impale her victim, Mary Brown pauses momentarily to catch her breath. "She's my grandmother, for God's sake!" she yells at the nursing home supervisor. "We're paying all this money, and nobody even checks on her? Don't you tell me you can't do it. You went into this business to take care of people. If you can't do it, get out of the business!"

The anger is real, but little else in the scene is genuine. Brown, though she seems to have forgotten it, is a volunteer in a study designed to gauge the impact of anger on the heart. Hooked up to a blood pressure cuff and heart monitors in a physiology lab at Baltimore's V.A. hospital, she is simply acting a role, though it helps that her own grandmother was once neglected by the staff at a nearby nursing home.

Brown has focused all her attention on the young man playing the role of the nursing supervisor. She has ignored the true source of her torment, a small figure standing quietly at the edge of the room. He is Aron Siegman, a soft-spoken 66-year-old psychologist with a slight paunch and a fringe of white hair.

His mild appearance to the contrary, Siegman spends his days stirring up trouble—coaxing a college student to recall a spouse's adulterous affair, for example, or repeatedly interrupting a volunteer's answer to a question he has posed about her aging father. A connoisseur of anger, he is as caught up in the nuances of his favorite subject as any wine collector. The reason is simple: A host of studies seem to show that we have become a nation of Rumplestiltskins, so much more likely to lose

From *Health, 9*, pp. 58–64, July/August 1995. Reprinted with permission from *Health*, © 1995.

our cool than we were even a few decades ago that we have pushed our bodies to the breaking point.

It's not a pretty picture. Too many of us overreact to the countless provocations of everyday life—traffic jams and surly clerks and brutish bosses—by boiling over. Heart pounding, blood pressure sky-rocketing, adrenaline surging, we are doing our-selves in prematurely, the experts say, by pushing our bodies beyond what they can take. One of the leading proponents of this new theory summarizes it with a succinctness more common on bumper stickers than in science. Current wisdom, declares Duke University stress researcher Redford Williams, is that "anger kills."

Fortunately, a simple remedy may be at hand. Siegman is now testing a theory that anger in itself isn't bad for your heart; the unhealthy consequences only kick in, he says, if you act out that anger. If he is right, the cry from the sixties to "let it all hang out" had it exactly backwards. It's perfectly okay, says the University of Maryland psychologist, to think that the nitwit who just turned left from the right lane shouldn't be let outdoors without a keep-er; what's not okay is to scream at him and pound the steering wheel.

The Mary Brown experiment, for example, has two halves. First, Siegman wants to show that ex-pressing anger sets the heart racing and blood pres-sure soaring. The lab's recording devices make that clear. Her blood pressure alone, normally 176/75, has skyrocketed to 213/98 since her tirade began. The experiment's second half involves coaxing Brown to replay the same infuriating scene, but this time without any outward displays of anger. What physiological changes do the various monitors reveal when a person feels angry but chooses not to express it? "Virtually nothing," says Siegman. "We don't get anything."

Here no news truly is good news. Heart disease is the nation's leading killer, and anger is emerging as a risk factor as important as smoking or high cho-lesterol or any of the other well-known villains. If Siegman is right that anger can be tamed, and tamed fairly simply, he's on to something big.

HE KIND OF HOSTILE personality that may put people at especially high risk for heart disease does not yet have a name. For the moment, let's call it Type H, for hostility, and to acknowledge its link to the famous Type A personality. Type A behavior is a mix of impatience, aggres-siveness, anger, and competitiveness. Mix Donald Trump with Margaret Thatcher, stir in Murphy Brown, and you have a Type A. For decades, every-one living this high-strung, fast-paced life was seen as a heart attack waiting (impatiently) to happen.

By 1981, the Type A theory had earned an official stamp of approval. An all-star panel appointed by the National Heart, Lung, and Blood Institute to evaluate the evidence had come back with a hearty endorsement.

This was major news. Medicine had long paid lip service to the idea that the mind affects the body—no one who has ever blushed could deny it—but this was more. After years in the shadows, psychology had suddenly leapt onstage. In predicting heart dis-ease, a psychological trait seemed as important as any biological measure.

But no sooner had the experts committed their enthusiasm for Type A to print than a slew of new and authoritative studies appeared. Their message: Type A's faced no higher risk of heart disease than anyone else. Two studies that looked at patients who already had heart disease came to an even more unwelcome conclusion. Type A's, it seemed, fared *better* than their laid-back counterparts.

Oops!

The Type H theory salvages something important from that wreckage. Indeed, it seems Type A theo-rists weren't entirely off the mark, after all. Type A was a package, and though most of its ingredients were irrelevant to heart disease, one component—hostility—may truly be toxic. Impatience and com-petitiveness, on the other hand, seem to have been innocents who got a bad reputation by hanging out with the wrong crowd.

Type H theory rests on some compelling findings. In one study, for example, 255 doctors who had tak-en a standard personality test while attending the University of North Carolina's medical school were tracked down 25 years later. Those whose hostility scores had been in the top half were four to five times as likely to have developed heart disease in the intervening decades as were those whose hostility scores had been in the lower half.

A similar study that looked at 118 lawyers found equally striking results. Of those lawyers who had scored in the top quarter for hostility, nearly one in five was dead by age 50. Of those in the lowest quarter, only one in 25 had died.

What's more, say the Type H proponents, such findings have a straightforward biological explana-tion. Evolution, they note, has designed the human body to respond to acutely stressful situations with a cascade of changes. In crises, your heart pumps faster and harder, arteries that carry blood to your muscles dilate so that blood flow increases still more, your platelets become stickier so that you are less likely to bleed to death if an attacker takes a bite out of you.

It's a fine system if you're running from a lion. If you start the whole process up every time the eleva-tor is late, though, everyday life will soon lay you low. As blood surges through your arteries and stress hormones pour from your adrenal glands, once-smooth artery walls begin to scar and pit. Then fatty cells clump on that pocked surface, like mineral deposits in an old water pipe. Arteries nar-row, blood flow decreases, and your body is starved of oxygen. The downward spiral eventually ends in chest pain or strokes or heart attacks.

The mechanism behind Type A, in contrast, was a good deal harder to picture. Exactly how would

A study that looked at 118 lawyers found that of those who scored in the top quarter for hostility, one in five was dead by age 50.

competitiveness, say, put the body at risk? Even in its heyday, Type A had other problems, as well. For one, it seemed to call for a personality transplant. To teach his frazzled patients mellowness, for example, one Type-A pioneer had them wait in the longest line at the bank or drive all day in the right-hand lane. It sounds brutal, the brainstorm of a malicious researcher who had grown bored with harassing rats and was looking for bigger game.

"With the original Type A," says David Krantz, a psychologist at Uniformed Services University of the Health Sciences, in Bethesda, Maryland, "people would say, 'You're telling me I can't be competitive? I shouldn't meet deadlines? How am I going to explain that to my boss?' Now the message is more manageable: 'Ambition is not the problem. Aggressiveness is not the problem. *Hostility* is the problem.'

"What your boss wants is for you to get a hell of a lot of work done," Krantz adds. "He doesn't necessarily want you to act like a son of a bitch."

The Type H theory differs from its forebear in one other important way—it specifically includes women. In theory, Type A did, too, but in practice it focused heavily on males. In part, the reason was a matter of convenience for the researchers: Most men have their heart attacks ten years earlier than women; in larger part, the reason was that when scientists thought Type A, the stereotype that came to mind was a male executive.

They might have thought of Mary Brown instead. She is a delightful woman, lively and down-to-earth and a good storyteller. It's just that, as the Pompeians said about Vesuvius, there is this one, tiny quirk. Brown is in her sixties now and works hard to keep her temper in bounds, but for as long as she can remember she has erupted at the slightest provocation. "I'm real proud if I can go two days without getting upset," she says. "I blow up. I know it's terrible, but I just do."

If someone cuts ahead of her in the supermarket line, Brown tells them off. "I'd like to see someone try to butt in front of me," she boasts. If they venture into the express line with a dozen items rather than the legal ten, Brown dresses them down and makes sure the cashier knows of their sin, too. On the freeway, preparing to exit, she sticks close to the car in front of her so that no one else can cut in. "I'm not going to let you in," she snarls at anyone trying it. "You should have moved in way back there."

Mary Brown is no tyrant. She's funny, and, once the storm has passed, she can laugh at her tirades. She has been married to the same man for 50 years. "It's incredible, some of what he's had to put up with," she says with a rueful smile. And she is close to her son and daughter.

Outsiders are more at risk. Brown cannot abide injustice, and she sees it in every driver who runs a yellow light, in every shopper with an extra can of soup. "To me," she says, "silence is acceptance. If I don't say anything, I'm agreeing with something that's wrong, and"—she hammers out the last words, like a general exhorting the troops to defend their homeland—"that cannot happen."

THE MEDICAL ESTABLISHMENT tends to wrinkle its nose in distaste at this whole subject. Many cardiologists concede that a diseased heart can be undone by such sudden stresses as winning the lottery or getting robbed at gunpoint; in ways that are not well understood, stress somehow sets the heart's ventricles to chaotic quivering. But they question whether chronic stress in general, or hostility in particular, can undo a healthy heart.

Look again, for example, at the study that showed a high number of deaths among hostile lawyers. It's tempting, critics say, to conclude that hostility gradually undermined their healthy hearts. But maybe not. Maybe heart disease strikes randomly at the hostile and the pleasant alike, and hostility serves only to speed up the dying process in those who are already vulnerable. In large measure, this is simply "show me" skepticism. Where, doubters ask, is clear-cut proof?

Part of the problem is that a theory based on hostility is harder to pin down than one based on something as easy to measure as blood pressure. Even Siegman concedes that the case for Type H is far

Men, Women, and Anger

Is a fiery display of temper as common in
a woman as it is in a man? Lately psychologists
have begun to fill in the hostility picture.

WE ALL GET ANGRY

According to a number of studies, women and men tend to get
angry equally often (about six or seven times a week), equally
intensely, and for more or less the same reasons. Tests designed
to reveal aggressive feelings, hidden anger, or hostility turned
inward haven't discovered any sex differences at all.

MEN EXPLODE, WOMEN MOSTLY SEETHE

Some angry women do shout and pound their fists, of course—
just as some men do. But in general, studies show, women and
men have very different styles when it comes to getting angry.
Women are more likely to express anger by crying, for example, or to keep their anger under wraps. "Women have cornered
the market on the seething, unspoken fury that is always threatening to explode," says Anne Campbell, a psychologist at England's Durham University. Women are also more likely to
express their anger in private. They might get angry at a boss
or coworker, but chances are they'll wait until they're alone or
with a spouse or close friend to show their anger.

IN WOMEN, AN ANGRY OUTBURST, THEN REGRET

Surveys show that anger itself means different things to
men than it does to women. Men's anger tends to be uncom-
plicated by restraint and guilt, says Campbell. It is straightfor-
wardly about winning and losing. Women are more likely
to feel embarrassed when they show anger, equating it with
a loss of control, she says. Women are also more likely than
men to believe their anger is out of proportion to the events
that caused it. "After an outburst," she says, "women tell themselves, 'Whoa! Get a grip.' Men say, 'That ought to show him.'"
According to one study, the more furious a woman gets, the
longer it takes her to get over the episode. That's not true for
men—at least not to the same degree.

The way women and men view crying is different, too.
According to Campbell and other researchers, men often see
women's crying as a sign of remorse or contrition—or as a
tactic used to win a fight. Women are more likely to view crying as a sign of frustration or rage—a way to release tension.
According to one study, 78 percent of women who cried during fights did so out of frustration.

So what does all this mean for women's risk of heart disease?
Researchers say that whether anger is expressed through
clenched teeth or raised voices, in public or in private, it appears
to wreak the same havoc on the heart. —E.D.

from airtight. "Look," he says, "it's a complicated
story. It was the same with cholesterol. That started
out, Cholesterol is bad. Then somebody found out
cholesterol levels alone didn't predict so well, and
then there was HDL and LDL, and then the ratio
between them. It's an ongoing story."

But even if Siegman and his colleagues are right
that hostility is bad for the heart, is there anything
we can do about it?

To begin with, everyone agrees that we cannot
banish anger. Even if we wanted to, we could no
more stop getting angry than we could stop getting
hungry. But who would want to? Anger has its place.
There is injustice in the world, after all, and righ-
teous indignation is an honorable emotion.

In a rare lyric moment, psychologists have dubbed
the real problem free-floating hostility. An occasional flash of temper is fine, they say; a permanent
snarl is not. Hostile people are perpetually suspicious, wary, and snappish, forever tense and on edge.
They see every sales clerk as determined to linger on
the phone for hours, every compliment as a dig in
disguise, every colleague as a rival in waiting.

That's bad for two reasons, says Timothy Smith,
a psychologist at the University of Utah in Salt Lake
City. First, hostility is harmful for all the Type H
reasons. Second, hostility feeds on itself, typically
leaving its "victims" precariously alone. That's wor-
risome because a variety of studies have shown that
people with friends and families, or even pets, fare
better than those without such support.

So what is a hostile person to do? The advice from
the experts is surprisingly straightforward: Relax,
take a deep breath, decide whether this latest injustice really merits a battle. Give in to your anger, they
say, and you become all the more angry. Resist it, by
keeping your voice down or your teeth ungritted,
and the anger seeps away.

Even if . . .
hostility is bad
for the heart, is
there anything
we can do
about it?

Are You Too Angry for Your Own Good?

THE TEST

Gauging your hostility quotient isn't as simple as measuring blood pressure or cholesterol. But the following 12 questions—supplied by Redford Williams, director of behavioral research at Duke University and the author of *Anger Kills*—could indicate whether a hostile temperament is getting the best of you.

1. Have you ever been so angry at someone that you've thrown things or slammed a door?
2. Do you tend to remember irritating incidents and get mad all over again?
3. Do little annoyances have a way of adding up during the day, leaving you frustrated and impatient?
4. Stuck in a long line at the express checkout in the grocery store, do you often count to see if anyone ahead of you has more than ten items?
5. If the person who cuts your hair trims off more than you wanted, do you fume about it for days afterward?
6. When someone cuts you off in traffic, do you flash your lights or honk your horn?
7. Over the past few years, have you dropped any close friends because they just didn't live up to your expectations?
8. Do you find yourself getting annoyed at little things your spouse does that get under your skin?
9. Do you feel your pulse climb when you get into an argument?
10. Are you often irritated by other people's incompetence?
11. If a cashier gives you the wrong change, do you assume he's probably trying to cheat you?
12. If someone doesn't show up on time, do you find yourself planning the angry words you're going to say?

To gauge your level of hostility, add up your yes responses. If you scored three or less, consider yourself one cool cucumber. A score of four to eight is a warning sign that anger may be raising your risk of heart disease. A score of nine or more puts you squarely in the hot zone for hostility, significantly increasing your risk of dying prematurely.

THE CURE

A few simple strategies can cool down even the hottest temper. First, when you feel yourself getting angry, stop long enough to ask yourself three questions: Is this really serious enough to get worked up over? Am I justified in getting angry? And is getting angry going to make any difference? If the answer to all three is yes, experts say, go ahead and get mad—it just might make you feel better. If not—if the answer to any of the questions is no—cool out. Often, just asking reasonable questions is enough to take the edge off anger. But if you're still simmering, distract yourself by picking up a magazine, turning on music, taking a walk. Or simply close your eyes and concentrate on your breathing. —*Peter Jaret*

"Anger is not just emotion, it's physiology, too," Siegman says. "Your blood pressure goes up, your voice gets loud, you clench your jaws"—he has worked himself into a mini-tirade, bellowing at the top of his voice, windmilling his arms, thrusting his chin out belligerently—"but then, if you lower your voice, speak more slowly, relax your muscles"—he has followed his own instructions and collapsed weakly into his seat, like a balloon with a slow leak—"if you do that, if you eliminate any part of the cycle, then you weaken the whole performance, and you can't sustain the feelings of anger."

Siegman's experiments seem to support this theory. In its own way, Hollywood has tested the same idea. Audiences watching an actor in a supposed rage see and hear all the familiar signs of anger—we recognize *bad* acting precisely because there is a dissonance between spoken words and body language—and actors, by their own report, feel the emotions they simulate. Similarly, studies on laughter and smiling have shown that simulated merriment offers the same benefits—increased blood flow, reduced levels of hormones that create stress, reduced pain perception—as the genuine article.

But even among those who believe that Type H's are putting themselves at risk, Siegman's strategy for taming anger is controversial. "What if your anger is unresolved?" asks Lynda Powell, a psychologist at Chicago's Rush-Presbyterian–

Give in to your anger, Siegman says, and you become all the more angry. Resist it, and the anger seeps away.

Saint Luke's Medical Center. "What if it's inside and you haven't dealt with it? Sometimes when you express it, you get it out and get beyond it. If you've just stuffed it inside, then the question is, Could that do just as much damage to your heart?"

Siegman is impatient with such objections, which he sees as smacking of an outdated Freudianism. "The psychoanalysts thought that anger was like physical energy," he complains. "They thought it couldn't be dissipated—the only choice was to express it or to repress it. But anger is not like physical energy," he says. "An angry person who chooses to divert his attention will no longer be angry. We have a lot of evidence to show that."

Siegman tries to head off the doubters by making a distinction between suppressing the outward expressions of anger, which he favors, and repressing anger itself, which he warns against. The difference, he says, is that people who repress their anger don't merely stifle it; they hide it so well that they themselves are unaware of it. The person who follows Siegman's advice walks a middle road; she neither denies her rage nor gives in to it. Instead she simply decides that the matter isn't worth the theatrical fireworks—whether expressed in pounded fists and shouting or in the seething language of gritted teeth—and calmly talks it out or lets it go. The result is that the anger neither festers nor explodes, but gradually loses its hold.

ESPITE SKEPTICS' OBJECTIONS, the hostility–heart disease connection is undeniably tantalizing. For one thing, it seems suspicious that so many studies of heart disease in the past few years have fingered hostility as a culprit. Where there's smoke, there's ire.

So if we are a long way from proof beyond a reasonable doubt, we may still have enough evidence to justify a small bet.

What seems called for, in fact, is a mundane version of Pascal's wager. The French philosopher opted to believe in God, on the grounds that he had everything to gain if he was right and nothing to lose by being wrong.

When it comes to hostility, there doesn't seem to be much downside in taking the experts' advice to ease up a bit. This is unusual. With most medical advice—quit eating chocolate cake, say—the risks are considerable. Giving up cake cuts out part of life's pleasure, first of all, and the loss could be even worse. In five years, researchers might come back and say, "It turns out we had it wrong. It's really, The more cake the better. Sorry about that."

Here, the experts' advice amounts to every grandmother's list of maxims: Take a deep breath and count to ten, look on the bright side, don't say anything if you can't say anything nice, and so on. What's the risk? At best, you'll live longer and better. At worst, you'll be better company. **H**

Edward Dolnick is a contributing editor.

Autism

*Autistic individuals suffer from a biological defect.
Although they cannot be cured, much can be done
to make life more hospitable for them*

by Uta Frith

The image often invoked to describe autism is that of a beautiful child imprisoned in a glass shell. For decades, many parents have clung to this view, hoping that one day a means might be found to break the invisible barrier. Cures have been proclaimed, but not one of them has been backed by evidence. The shell remains intact. Perhaps the time has come for the whole image to be shattered. Then at last we might be able to catch a glimpse of what the minds of autistic individuals are truly like.

Psychological and physiological research has shown that autistic people are not living in rich inner worlds but instead are victims of a biological defect that makes their minds very different from those of normal individuals. Happily, however, autistic people are not beyond the reach of emotional contact.

Thus, we can make the world more hospitable for autistic individuals just as we can, say, for the blind. To do so, we need to understand what autism is like—a most challenging task. We can imagine being blind, but autism seems unfathomable. For centuries, we have known that blindness is often a peripheral defect at the sensory-motor level of the nervous system, but only recently has autism been appreciated as a central defect at the highest level of

UTA FRITH is a senior scientist in the Cognitive Development Unit of the Medical Research Council in London. Born in Germany, she took a degree in psychology in 1964 at the University of the Saarland in Saarbrücken, where she also studied the history of art. Four years later she obtained her Ph.D. in psychology at the University of London. Besides autism, her interests include reading development and dyslexia. She has edited a book in the field of reading development, *Cognitive Processes in Spelling,* and is the author of *Autism: Explaining the Enigma.*

> **. . . autistic people are not living in rich inner worlds but instead are victims of a biological defect that makes their minds very different from those of normal individuals.**

cognitive processing. Autism, like blindness, persists throughout life, and it responds to special efforts in compensatory education. It can give rise to triumphant feats of coping but can also lead to disastrous secondary consequences—anxiety, panic and depression. Much can be done to prevent problems. Understanding the nature of the handicap must be the first step in any such effort.

Autism existed long before it was described and named by Leo Kanner of the Johns Hopkins Children's Psychiatric Clinic. Kanner published his landmark paper in 1943 after he had observed 11 children who seemed to him to form a recognizable group. All had in common four traits: a preference for aloneness, an insistence on sameness, a liking for elaborate routines and some abilities that seemed remarkable compared with the deficits.

Concurrently, though quite independently, Hans Asperger of the University Pediatric Clinic in Vienna prepared his doctoral thesis on the same type of child. He also used the term "autism" to refer to the core features of the disorder. Both men borrowed the label from adult psychiatry, where it had been used to refer to the progressive loss of contact with the outside world experienced by schizophrenics. Autistic children seemed to suffer such a lack of contact with the world around them from a very early age.

Kanner's first case, Donald, has long served as a prototype for diagnosis. It had been evident early in life that the boy was different from other children. At two years of age, he could hum and sing tunes accurately from memory. Soon he learned to count to 100 and to recite both the alphabet and the 25 questions and answers of the Presbyterian catechism. Yet he had a mania for making toys and other objects spin. Instead of playing like other toddlers, he arranged beads and other things in groups of different colors or threw them on the floor, delighting in the sounds they made. Words for him had a literal, inflexible meaning.

Donald was first seen by Kanner at age five. Kanner observed that the boy paid no attention to people around him. When someone interfered with his solitary activities, he was never angry with the interfering person but impatiently removed the hand that was in his way. His mother was the only person with whom he had any significant contact, and that seemed attributable mainly to the great effort she made to share activities with him. By the time Donald was about eight years old, his conversation consisted largely of repetitive questions. His relation to people remained limited to his immediate wants and needs, and his attempts at contact stopped as soon as he was told or given what he had asked for.

> **Autism . . . persists throughout life. . . .**

From *Scientific American, 268,* pp. 108–114, June 1993. Reprinted with permission. Copyright © 1993 by Scientific American, Inc. All rights reserved.

Autistic Behavior

The traits most characteristic of autistic people are aloneness, an insistence on sameness and a liking for elaborate routines. At the same time, some autistic individuals can perform complicated tasks, provided that the activity does not require them to judge what some other person might be thinking. These traits lead to characteristic forms of behavior, a number of which are portrayed here.

Displays indifference

Indicates needs by using an adult's hand

Parrots words

Laughs and giggles inappropriately

Joins in only if an adult insists and assists

Does not play with other children

Is one-sided in interactions

Talks incessantly about one topic

Behaves in bizarre ways

Handles or spins objects

Does not make eye contact

Does not pretend in playing

Prefers sameness

Yet some do certain things well if the task does not involve social understanding.

Some of the other children Kanner described were mute, and he found that even those who spoke did not really communicate but used language in a very odd way. For example, Paul, who was five, would parrot speech verbatim. He would say "You want candy" when he meant "I want candy." He was in the habit of repeating, almost every day, "Don't throw the dog off the balcony," an utterance his mother traced to an earlier incident with a toy dog.

Twenty years after he had first seen them, Kanner reassessed the members of his original group of children. Some of them seemed to have adapted socially much better than others, although their failure to communicate and to form relationships remained, as did their pedantry and single-mindedness. Two prerequisites for better adjustment, though no guarantees of it, were the presence of speech before age five and relatively high intellectual ability.

The brightest autistic individuals had, in their teens, become uneasily aware of their peculiarities and had made conscious efforts to conform. Nevertheless, even the best adapted were rarely able to be self-reliant or to form friendships. The one circumstance that seemed to be helpful in all the cases was an extremely structured environment.

As soon as the work of the pioneers became known, every major clinic began to identify autistic children. It was found that such children, in addition to their social impairments, have substantial intellectual handicaps. Although many of them perform relatively well on certain tests, such as copying mosaic patterns with blocks, even the most able tend to do badly on test questions that can be answered only by the application of common sense.

Autism is rare. According to the strict criteria applied by Kanner, it appears in four of every 10,000 births. With the somewhat wider criteria used in current diagnostic practice, the incidence is much higher: one or two in 1,000 births, about the same as Down's syndrome. Two to four times as many boys as girls are affected.

For many years, autism was thought to be a purely psychological disorder without an organic basis. At first, no obvious neurological problems were found. The autistic children did not necessarily have low intellectual ability, and they often looked physically normal. For these reasons, psychogenic theories were proposed and taken seriously for many years. They focused on the idea that a child could become autistic because of some existentially threatening experience. A lack of maternal bonding or a disastrous experience of rejection, so the theory went, might drive an infant to withdraw into an inner world of fantasy that the outside world never penetrates.

These theories are unsupported by any empirical evidence. They are unlikely to be supported because there are many instances of extreme rejection and deprivation in childhood, none of which have resulted in autism. Unfortunately, therapies vaguely based on such notions are still putting pressure on parents to accept a burden of guilt for the supposedly avoidable and reversible breakdown of interpersonal interactions. In contrast, well-structured behavior modification programs have often helped families in the management of autistic children, especially children with severe behavior problems. Such programs do not claim to reinstate normal development.

The insupportability of the psychogenic explanation of autism led a number of workers to search for a biological cause. Their efforts implicate a defective structure in the brain, but that structure has not yet been identified. The defect is believed to affect the thinking of autistic people, making them unable to evaluate their own thoughts or to perceive clearly what might be going on in someone else's mind.

Autism appears to be closely associated with several other clinical and medical conditions. They include maternal rubella and chromosomal abnormality, as well as early injury to the brain and infantile seizures. Most impressive, perhaps, are studies showing that autism can have a genetic basis. Both identical twins are much more likely to be autistic than are both fraternal twins. Moreover, the likelihood that autism will occur twice in the same family is 50 to 100 times greater than would be expected by chance alone.

Structural abnormalities in the brains of autistic individuals have turned up in anatomic studies and brain-imaging procedures. Both epidemiological and

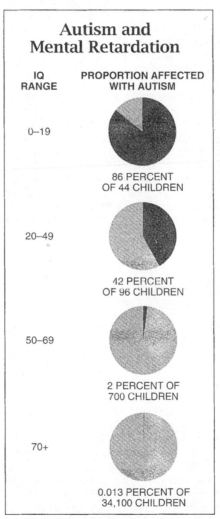

Autism and Mental Retardation

IQ RANGE	PROPORTION AFFECTED WITH AUTISM
0–19	86 PERCENT OF 44 CHILDREN
20–49	42 PERCENT OF 96 CHILDREN
50–69	2 PERCENT OF 700 CHILDREN
70+	0.013 PERCENT OF 34,100 CHILDREN

SOURCE: Lorna Wing, Medical Research Council, London

CLOSE LINK between autism and mental retardation is reflected in this chart. The percentage of children showing the social impairments typical of autism is highest at low levels of intelligence as measured by tests in which an intelligence quotient (IQ) below 70 is subnormal. For example, 86 percent of 44 children in the lowest IQ range showed the social impairments of autism. The data are drawn from a population of about 35,000 children aged under 15 years.

neuropsychological studies have demonstrated that autism is strongly correlated with mental retardation, which is itself clearly linked to physiological abnormality. This fact fits well with the idea that autism results from a distinct brain abnormality that is often part of more extensive damage. If the abnormality is pervasive, the mental retardation will be more severe, and the likelihood of damage to the critical brain system will increase. Conversely, it is possible for the critical system alone to be damaged. In such cases, autism is not accompanied by mental retardation.

Neuropsychological testing has also contributed evidence for the existence of a fairly circumscribed brain abnormality. Autistic individuals who are otherwise able show specific and extensive deficits on certain tests that involve planning, initiative and spontaneous generation of new ideas. The same deficits appear in patients who have frontal lobe lesions. Therefore, it seems plausible that whatever the defective brain structure is, the frontal lobes are implicated.

Population studies carried out by Lorna Wing and her colleagues at the Medical Research Council's Social Psychiatry Unit in London reveal that the different symptoms of autism do not occur together simply by coincidence. Three core features in particular—impairments in communication, imagination and socialization—form a distinct triad. The impairment in communication includes such diverse phenomena as muteness and delay in learning to talk, as well as problems in comprehending or using nonverbal body language. Other autistic individuals speak fluently but are overliteral in their understanding of language. The impairment in imagination appears in young autistic children as repetitive play with objects and in some autistic adults as an obsessive interest in facts. The impairment in socialization includes ineptness and inappropriate behavior in a wide range of reciprocal social interactions, such as the ability to make and keep friends. Nevertheless, many autistic individuals prefer to have company and are eager to please.

The question is why these impairments, and only these, occur together. The challenge to psychological theorists was clear: to search for a single cognitive component that would explain the deficits yet still allow for the abilities that autistic people display in certain aspects of interpersonal interactions. My colleagues at the Medical Research Council's Cognitive Development Unit in London and I think we have identified just such a component. It is a cognitive mechanism of a highly complex and abstract nature that could be described in computational terms. As a shorthand, one can refer to this component by one of its main functions, namely the ability to think about thoughts or to imagine another individual's state of mind. We propose that this component is damaged in autism. Furthermore, we suggest that this mental component is innate and has a unique brain substrate. If it were possible to pinpoint that substrate—whether it is an anatomic structure, a physiological system or a chemical pathway—one might be able to identify the biological origin of autism.

The power of this component in normal development becomes obvious very early. From the end of the first year onward, infants begin to participate in what has been called shared attention. For example, a normal child will point to something for no reason other than to share his interest in it with someone else. Autistic children do not show shared attention. Indeed, the absence of this behavior may well be one of the earliest signs of autism. When an autistic child points at an object, it is only because he wants it.

In the second year of life, a particularly dramatic manifestation of the critical component can be seen in normal children: the emergence of pretense, or the ability to engage in fantasy and pretend play. Autistic children cannot understand pretense and do not pretend when they are playing. The difference can be seen in such a typical nursery game as "feeding" a teddy bear or a doll with an empty spoon. The normal child goes through the appropriate motions of feeding and accompanies the action with appropriate slurping noises. The autistic child merely twiddles or flicks the spoon repetitively. It is precisely the absence of early and simple communicative behaviors, such as shared attention and make-believe play, that often creates the first nagging doubts in the minds of the parents about the development of their child. They rightly feel that they cannot engage the child in the emotional to-and-fro of ordinary life.

My colleague Alan M. Leslie devised a theoretical model of the cognitive mechanisms underlying the key abilities of shared attention and pretense. He postulates an innate mechanism whose function is to form and use what we might call second-order representations. The world around us consists not only of visible bodies and events, captured by first-order representations, but also of invisible minds and mental events, which require second-order representation. Both types of representation have to be kept in mind and kept separate from each other.

Second-order representations serve to make sense of otherwise contradictory or incongruous information. Suppose a normal child, Beth, sees her mother holding a banana in such a way as to be pretending that it is a telephone. Beth has in mind facts about bananas and facts about telephones—first-order representations. Nevertheless, Beth is not the least bit confused and will not start eating telephones or talking to bananas. Confusion is avoided because Beth computes from the concept of pretending (a second-order representation) that her mother is engaging simultaneously in an imaginary activity and a real one.

As Leslie describes the mental process, pretending should be understood as computing a three-term relation between an actual situation, an imaginary situation and an agent who does the pretending. The imaginary situation is then not treated as the real situation. Believing can be understood in the same way as pretending. This insight enabled us to predict that autistic children, despite an adequate mental age (above four years or so), would not be able to understand that someone can have a mistaken belief about the world.

Together with our colleague Simon Baron-Cohen, we tested this prediction by adapting an experiment originally devised by two Austrian developmental psychologists, Heinz Wimmer and Josef Perner. The test has become known as the Sally-Anne task. Sally and Anne are playing together. Sally has a marble that she puts in a basket before leaving the room. While she is out, Anne moves the marble to a box. When Sally returns, wanting to retrieve the marble, she of course looks in the basket. If this scenario is presented as, say, a puppet show to normal children who are four years of age or more, they understand that Sally will look in the basket even though they know the marble is not there. In other words, they can represent Sally's erroneous belief as well as the true state of things. Yet in our test, 16 of 20 autistic children with a mean mental age of nine failed the task—answering that Sally would look in the box—in spite of being able to answer correctly a variety of other questions relating to the facts of the episode. They could not conceptualize the possibility that Sally believed something that was not true.

Many comparable experiments have been carried out in other laboratories, which have largely confirmed our prediction: autistic children are specifically impaired in their understanding of mental states. They appear to lack the innate component underlying this ability. This component, when it works normally, has the most far-reaching consequences for higher-order conscious processes. It underpins the special feature of the human mind, the ability to reflect on itself. Thus, the triad of impairments in autism—in communication, imagination and socialization—is explained by the failure of a single cognitive mechanism. In everyday life, even very able autistic individuals find it hard to keep in mind simultaneously a reality and the fact that someone else may hold a misconception of that reality.

The automatic ability of normal people to judge mental states enables us to be, in a sense, mind readers. With sufficient experience we can form and use a theory of mind that allows us to speculate about psychological motives for our behavior and to manipulate other people's opinions, beliefs and attitudes. Autistic individuals lack the automatic ability to represent beliefs, and therefore they also lack a theory of mind. They cannot understand how behavior is caused by mental states or how beliefs and attitudes can be manipulated. Hence, they find it difficult to understand deception. The psychological undercurrents of real life as well as of literature—in short, all that gives spice to social relations—for them remain a closed book. "People talk to each other with their eyes," said one observant autistic youth. "What is it that they are saying?"

Lacking a mechanism for a theory of mind, autistic children develop quite differently from normal ones. Most children acquire more and more sophisticated social and communicative skills as they develop other cognitive abilities. For example, children learn to be aware that there are faked and genuine expressions of feeling. Similarly, they become adept at that essential aspect of human communication, reading between the lines. They learn how to produce and understand humor and irony. In sum, our ability to engage in imaginative ideas, to interpret feelings and to understand intentions beyond the literal content of speech are all accomplishments that depend ultimately on an innate cognitive mechanism. Autistic children find it difficult or impossible to achieve any of these things. We believe this is because the mechanism is faulty.

This cognitive explanation of autism is specific. As a result, it enables us to distinguish the types of situations in which the autistic person will and will not have problems. It does not preclude the existence of special assets and abilities that are independent of the innate mechanism my colleagues and I see as defective. Thus it is that autistic individuals can achieve social skills that do not involve an exchange between two minds. They can learn many useful social routines, even to the extent of sometimes camouflaging their problems. The cognitive deficit we hypothesize is also specific enough not to preclude high achievement by autistic people in such diverse activities as musical performance, artistic drawing, mathematics and memorization of facts.

It remains to be seen how best to explain the coexistence of excellent and abysmal performance by autistic people on abilities that are normally expected to go together. It is still uncertain whether there may be additional damage in emotions that prevents some autistic children from being interested in social stimuli. We have as yet little idea what to make of the single-minded, often obsessive, pursuit of certain activities. With the autistic person, it is as if a powerful integrating force—the effort to seek meaning—were missing.

The old image of the child in the glass shell is misleading in more ways than one. It is incorrect to think that inside the glass shell is a normal individual waiting to emerge, nor is it true that autism is a disorder of childhood only. The motion picture *Rain Man* came at the right time to suggest a new image to a receptive public. Here we see Raymond, a middle-aged man who is unworldly, egocentric in the extreme and all too amenable to manipulation by others. He is incapable of understanding his brother's double-dealing pursuits, transparently obvious though they are to the cinema audience. Through various experiences it becomes possible for the brother to learn from Raymond and to forge an emotional bond with him. This is not a farfetched story. We can learn a great deal about ourselves through the phenomenon of autism.

Yet the illness should not be romanticized. We must see autism as a devastating handicap without a cure. The autistic child has a mind that is unlikely to develop self-consciousness. But we can now begin to identify the particular types of social behavior and emotional responsiveness of which autistic individuals are capable. Autistic people can learn to express their needs and to anticipate the behavior of others when it is regulated by external, observable factors rather than by mental states. They can form emotional attachments to others. They often strive to please and earnestly wish to be instructed in the rules of person-to-person contact. There is no doubt that within the stark limitations a degree of satisfying sociability can be achieved.

Autistic aloneness does not have to mean loneliness. The chilling aloofness experienced by many parents is not a permanent feature of their growing autistic child. In fact, it often gives way to a preference for company. Just as it is possible to engineer the environment toward a blind person's needs or toward people with other special needs, so the environment can be adapted to an autistic person's needs.

On the other hand, one must be realistic about the degree of adaptation that can be made by the limited person. We can hope for some measure of compensation and a modest ability to cope with adversity. We cannot expect autistic individuals to grow out of the unreflecting mind they did not choose to be born with. Autistic people in turn can look for us to be more sympathetic to their plight as we better understand how their minds are different from our own.

FURTHER READING

AUTISM: EXPLAINING THE ENIGMA. Uta Frith. Blackwell Publishers, 1989.

THE COGNITIVE BASIS OF A BIOLOGICAL DISORDER: AUTISM. Uta Frith, John Morton and Alan M. Leslie in *Trends in Neurosciences*, Vol. 14, No. 10, pages 433-438; October 1991.

AUTISM AND ASPERGER SYNDROME. Edited by Uta Frith. Cambridge University Press, 1992.

UNDERSTANDING OTHER MINDS: PERSPECTIVES FROM AUTISM. Edited by Simon Baron-Cohen, Helen Tager-Flusberg and Donald J. Cohen. Oxford University Press, 1993.

LIFE IN OVERDRIVE

By CLAUDIA WALLIS

DUSTY NASH, AN ANGELIC-looking blond child of seven, awoke at 5 one recent morning in his Chicago home and proceeded to throw a fit. He wailed. He kicked. Every muscle in his 50-lb. body flew in furious motion. Finally, after about 30 minutes, Dusty pulled himself together sufficiently to head downstairs for breakfast. While his mother bustled about the kitchen, the hyperkinetic child pulled a box of Kix cereal from the cupboard and sat on a chair.

But sitting still was not in the cards this morning. After grabbing some cereal with his hands, he began kicking the box, scattering little round corn puffs across the room. Next he turned his attention to the TV set, or rather, the table supporting it. The table was covered with a checkerboard Con-Tact paper, and Dusty began peeling it off. Then he became intrigued with the spilled cereal and started stomping it to bits. At this point his mother interceded. In a firm but calm

"They just felt I was being bad—too loud, too physical, too everything." A rebellious tomboy with few friends, she saw a psychologist at age 10, "but nobody came up with a diagnosis." As a teenager she began prescribing her own medication: marijuana, Valium and, later, cocaine.

The athletic Bloomgarden managed to get into college, but she admits that she cheated her way to a diploma. "I would study and study, and I wouldn't remember a thing. I really felt it was my fault." After graduating, she did fine in physically active jobs but was flustered with administrative work. Then, four years ago, a doctor put a label on her troubles: ADHD. "It's been such a weight off my shoulders," says Bloomgarden, who takes both the stimulant Ritalin and the antidepressant Zoloft to improve her concentration. "I had 38 years of thinking I was a bad person. Now I'm rewriting the tapes of who I thought I was to who I really am."

Fifteen years ago, no one had ever heard of attention deficit hyperactivity disorder. Today it is the most common behavioral disorder in American children, the

Doctors say huge numbers of kids and adults have attention deficit disorder. Is it for real?

voice she told her son to get the stand-up dust pan and broom and clean up the mess. Dusty got out the dust pan but forgot the rest of the order. Within seconds he was dismantling the plastic dust pan, piece by piece. His next project: grabbing three rolls of toilet paper from the bathroom and unraveling them around the house.

It was only 7:30, and his mother Kyle Nash, who teaches a medical-school course on death and dying, was already feeling half dead from exhaustion. Dusty was to see his doctors that day at 4, and they had asked her not to give the boy the drug he usually takes to control his hyperactivity and attention problems, a condition known as attention deficit hyperactivity disorder (ADHD). It was going to be a very long day without help from Ritalin.

Karenne Bloomgarden remembers such days all too well. The peppy, 43-year-old entrepreneur and gym teacher was a disaster as a child growing up in New Jersey. "I did very poorly in school," she recalls. Her teachers and parents were constantly on her case for rowdy behavior.

subject of thousands of studies and symposiums and no small degree of controversy. Experts on ADHD say it afflicts as many as 3½ million American youngsters, or up to 5% of those under 18. It is two to three times as likely to be diagnosed in boys as in girls. The disorder has replaced what used to be popularly called "hyperactivity," and it includes a broader collection of symptoms. ADHD has three main hallmarks: extreme distractibility, an almost reckless impulsiveness and, in some but not all cases, a knee-jiggling, toe-tapping hyperactivity that makes sitting still all but impossible. (Without hyperactivity, the disorder is called attention deficit disorder, or ADD.)

For children with ADHD, a ticking clock or sounds and sights caught through a window can drown out a teacher's voice, although an intriguing project can absorb them for hours. Such children act before thinking; they blurt out answers in class. They enrage peers with an inability to wait their turn or play by the rules. These are the kids no one wants at a birthday party.

Ten years ago, doctors believed that the

From *Time*, 144, pp. 42–50, July 18, 1994. Copyright ©1994 Time Inc. Reprinted with permission.

symptoms of ADHD faded with maturity. Now it is one of the fastest-growing diagnostic categories for adults. One-third to two-thirds of ADHD kids continue to have symptoms as adults, says psychiatrist Paul Wender, director of the adult ADHD clinic at the University of Utah School of Medicine. Many adults respond to the diagnosis with relief—a sense that "at last my problem has a name and it's not my fault." As more people are diagnosed, the use of Ritalin (or its generic equivalent, methylphenidate), the drug of choice for ADHD, has surged: prescriptions are up more than 390% in just four years.

As the numbers have grown, ADHD awareness has become an industry, a passion, an almost messianic movement. An advocacy and support group called CHADD (Children and Adults with Attention Deficit Disorders) has exploded from its founding in 1987 to 28,000 members in 48 states. Information bulletin boards and support groups for adults have sprung up on CompuServe, Prodigy and America Online. Numerous popular books have been published on the subject. There are summer camps designed to help ADHD kids, videos and children's books with titles like *Jumpin' Johnny Get Back to Work!* and, of course, therapists, tutors and workshops offering their services to the increasingly self-aware ADHD community.

IT IS A COMMUNITY THAT VIEWS ITSELF with some pride. Popular books and lectures about ADHD often point out positive aspects of the condition. Adults see themselves as creative; their impulsiveness can be viewed as spontaneity; hyperactivity gives them enormous energy and drive; even their distractibility has the virtue of making them alert to changes in the environment. "Kids with ADHD are wild, funny, effervescent. They have a love of life. The rest of us sometimes envy them," says psychologist Russell Barkley of the University of Massachusetts Medical Center. "ADHD adults," he notes, "can be incredibly successful. Sometimes being impulsive means being decisive." Many ADHD adults gravitate into creative fields or work that provides an outlet for emotions, says Barkley. "In our clinic we saw an adult poet who couldn't write poetry when she was on Ritalin. ADHD people make good salespeople. They're lousy at desk jobs."

In an attempt to promote the positive side of ADHD, some CHADD chapters circulate lists of illustrious figures who, they contend, probably suffered from the disorder: the messy and disorganized Ben Franklin, the wildly impulsive and distractible Winston Churchill. For reasons that are less clear, these lists also include folks like Socrates, Isaac Newton, Leonardo da Vinci—almost any genius of note. (At least two doctors interviewed for this story suggested that the sometimes scattered Bill Clinton belongs on the list.)

However creative they may be, people with ADHD don't function particularly well in standard schools and typical office jobs. Increasingly, parents and lobby groups are demanding that accommodations be made. About half the kids diagnosed with ADHD receive help from special-education teachers in their schools, in some cases because they also have other learning disabilities. Where schools have failed to provide services, parents have sometimes sued. In one notable case that went to the U.S. Supreme Court last year, parents argued—successfully—that since the public school denied their child special education, the district must pay for her to attend private school. Another accommodation requested with increasing frequency: permission to take college-entrance exams without a time limit. Part of what motivates parents to fight for special services is frightening research showing that without proper care, kids with ADHD have an extremely high risk not only of failing at school but also of becoming drug abusers, alcoholics and lawbreakers.

Adults with ADHD are beginning to seek special treatment. Under the 1990 Americans with Disabilities Act, they can insist upon help in the workplace. Usually the interventions are quite modest: an office door or white-noise machine to reduce distractions, or longer deadlines on assignments. Another legal trend that concerns even ADHD advocates: the disorder is being raised as a defense in criminal cases. Psychologist Barkley says he knows of 55 such instances in the U.S., all in the past 10 years. ADHD was cited as a mitigating factor by the attorney for Michael Fay, the 19-year-old American who was charged with vandalism and caned in Singapore.

Many of those who treat ADHD see the recognition of the problem as a humane breakthrough: finally we will stop blaming

kids for behavior they cannot control. But some are worried that the disorder is being embraced with too much gusto. "A lot of people are jumping on the bandwagon," complains psychologist Mark Stein, director of a special ADHD clinic at the University of Chicago. "Parents are putting pressure on health professionals to make the diagnosis." The allure of ADHD is that it is "a label of forgiveness," says Robert Reid, an assistant professor in the department of special education at the University of Nebraska in Lincoln. "The kid's problems are not his parents' fault, not the teacher's fault, not the kid's fault. It's better to say this kid has ADHD than to say this kid drives everybody up the wall." For adults, the diagnosis may provide an excuse for personal or professional failures, observes Richard Bromfield, a psychologist at Harvard Medical School. "Some people like to say, 'The biological devil made me do it.'"

A DISORDER WITH A PAST Other than the name itself, there is nothing new about this suddenly ubiquitous disorder. The world has always had its share of obstreperous kids, and it has generally treated them as behavior problems rather than patients. Most of the world still does so: European nations like France and England report one-tenth the U.S. rate of ADHD. In Japan the disorder has barely been studied.

The medical record on ADHD is said to have begun in 1902, when British pediatrician George Still published an account of 20 children in his practice who were "passionate," defiant, spiteful and lacking "inhibitory volition." Still made the then radical suggestion that bad parenting was not to blame; instead he suspected a subtle brain injury. This theory gained greater credence in the years following the 1917-18 epidemic of viral encephalitis, when doctors observed that the infection left some children with impaired attention, memory and control over their impulses. In the 1940s and '50s, the same constellation of symptoms was called minimal brain damage and, later, minimal brain dysfunction. In 1937 a Rhode Island pediatrician reported that giving stimulants called amphetamines to children with these symptoms had the unexpected effect of calming them down. By the mid-1970s, Ritalin had become the most prescribed drug for what was eventually termed, in 1987, attention deficit hyperactivity disorder.

Many adults respond to the diagnosis with relief—a sense that "at last my problem has a name and it's not my fault."

Nobody fully understands how Ritalin and other stimulants work, nor do doctors have a very precise picture of the physiology of ADHD. Researchers generally suspect a defect in the frontal lobes of the brain, which regulate behavior. This region is rich in the neurotransmitters dopamine and norepinephrine, which are influenced by drugs like Ritalin. But the lack of a more specific explanation has led some psychologists to question whether ADHD is truly a disorder at all or merely a set of characteristics that tend to cluster together. Just because something responds to a drug doesn't mean it is a sickness.

ADHD researchers counter the skeptics by pointing to a growing body of biological clues. For instance, several studies have found that people with ADHD have decreased blood flow and lower levels of electrical activity in the frontal lobes than normal adults and children. In 1990 Dr. Alan Zametkin at the National Institute of Mental Health found that in PET scans, adults with ADD showed slightly lower rates of metabolism in areas of the brain's cortex known to be involved in the control of attention, impulses and motor activity.

Zametkin's study was hailed as the long-awaited proof of the biological basis of ADD, though Zametkin himself is quite cautious. A newer study used another tool—magnetic resonance imaging—to compare the brains of 18 ADHD boys with those of other children and found several "very subtle" but "striking" anatomical differences, says co-author Judith Rapoport, chief of the child psychiatry branch at NIMH. Says Zametkin: "I'm absolutely convinced that this disorder has a biological basis, but just what it is we cannot yet say."

WHAT RESEARCHERS DO say with great certainty is that the condition is inherited. External factors such as birth injuries and maternal alcohol or tobacco consumption may play a role in less than 10% of cases. Suspicions that a diet high in sugar might cause hyperactivity have been discounted. But the influence of genes is unmistakable. Barkley estimates that 40% of adhd kids have a parent who has the trait and 35% have a sibling with the problem; if the sibling is an identical twin, the chances rise to between 80% and 92%.

Interest in the genetics of ADHD is enormous. In Australia a vast trial involving 3,400 pairs of twins between the ages of 4 and 12 is examining the incidence of ADHD and other behavioral difficulties. At NIMH, Zametkin's group is recruiting 200 families who have at least two members with ADHD. The hope: to identify genes for the disorder. It is worth noting, though, that even if such genes are found, this may not settle the debate about ADHD. After all, it is just as likely that researchers will someday discover a gene for a hot temper, which also runs in families. But that doesn't mean that having a short fuse is a disease requiring medical intervention.

TRICKY DIAGNOSIS In the absence of any biological test, diagnosing ADHD is a rather inexact proposition. In most cases, it is a teacher who initiates the process by informing parents that their child is daydreaming in class, failing to complete assignments or driving everyone crazy with thoughtless behavior. "The problem is that the parent then goes to the family doctor, who writes a prescription for Ritalin and doesn't stop to think of the other possibilities," says child psychiatrist Larry Silver of

Is ADD truly a disorder?
Just because something responds
to a drug doesn't mean
it's a sickness.

Georgetown University Medical Center. To make a careful diagnosis, Silver argues, one must eliminate other explanations for the symptoms.

The most common cause, he points out, is anxiety. A child who is worried about a problem at home or some other matter "can look hyperactive and distractible." Depression can also cause ADHD-like behavior. "A third cause is another form of neurological dysfunction, like a learning disorder," says Silver. "The child starts doodling because he didn't understand the teacher's instructions." All this is made more complicated by the fact that some kids—and adults—with ADHD also suffer from depression and other problems. To distinguish these symptoms from ADHD, doctors usually rely on interviews with parents and teachers, behavior-ratings scales and psychological tests, which can cost from $500 to $3,000, depending on the thoroughness of the testing. Insurance coverage is spotty.

Among the most important clues doctors look for is whether the child's problems can be linked to some specific experience or time or whether they have been present almost from birth. "You don't suddenly get ADD," says Wade Horn, a child psychologist and former executive director of CHADD. Taking a careful history is therefore vital.

For kids who are hyperactive, the pattern is unmistakable, says Dr. Bruce Roseman, a pediatric neurologist with several offices in the New York City area, who has ADHD himself. "You say to the mother, 'What kind of personality did the child have as a baby? Was he active, alert? Was he colicky?' She'll say, 'He wouldn't stop—waaah, waaah, waaah!' You ask, 'When did he start to walk?' One mother said to me, 'Walk? My son didn't walk. He got his pilot's license at one year of age. His feet haven't touched the ground since.' You ask, 'Mrs. Smith, how about the terrible twos?' She'll start to cry, 'You mean the terrible twos, threes, fours, the awful fives, the horrendous sixes, the God-awful eights, the divorced nines, the I-want-to-die tens!' "

Diagnosing those with ADD without hyperactivity can be trickier. Such kids are often described as daydreamers, space cases. They are not disruptive or antsy. But, says Roseman, "they sit in front of a book and for 45 minutes, nothing happens." Many girls with ADD fit this model; they are often misunderstood or overlooked.

Christy Rade, who will be entering the ninth grade in West Des Moines, Iowa, is fairly typical. Before she was diagnosed with ADD in the third grade, Christy's teacher described her to her parents as a "dizzy blond and a space cadet." "Teachers used to get fed up with me," recalls Christy, who now takes Ritalin and gets some extra support from her teachers. "Everyone thought I was purposely not paying attention." According to her mother Julie Doy, people at Christy's school were familiar with hyperactivity but not ADD. "She didn't have behavior problems. She was the kind of kid who could fall through the cracks, and did."

Most experts say ADHD is a lifelong condition but by late adolescence many people can compensate for their impulsiveness and disorganization. They may channel hyperactivity into sports. In other cases, the symptoms still wreak havoc, says UCLA psychiatrist Walid Shekim. "Patients cannot settle on a career. They cannot keep a job. They procrastinate a lot. They are the kind of people who would tell their boss to take this job and shove it before they've found another job."

Doctors diagnose adults with methods similar to those used with children. Patients are sometimes asked to dig up old report cards for clues to their childhood behavior—an essential indicator. Many adults seek help only after one of their children is diagnosed. Such was the case with Chuck Pearson of Birmingham, Michigan, who was diagnosed three years ago, at 54. Pearson had struggled for decades in what might be the worst possible career for someone with ADD: accounting. In the first 12 years of his marriage, he was fired from 15 jobs. "I was frightened," says Zoe, his wife of 35 years. "We had two small children, a mortgage. Bill collectors were calling perpetually. We almost lost the house." Chuck admits he had trouble focusing on details, completing tasks and judging how long an assignment would take. He was so distracted behind the wheel that he lost his license for a year after getting 14 traffic tickets. Unwittingly, Pearson began medicating himself: "In my mid-30s, I would drink 30 to 40 cups of coffee a day. The caffeine helped." After he was diagnosed, the Pearsons founded the Adult Attention Deficit Foundation, a clearinghouse for information about ADD; he hopes to spare others some of his own regret: "I had a deep and abiding sadness over the life I could have given my family if I had been treated effectively."

PERSONALITY OR PATHOLOGY? While Chuck Pearson's problems were extreme, many if not all adults have trouble at times sticking with boring tasks, setting priorities and keeping their minds on what they are doing. The furious pace of society, the strain on families, the lack of community support can make anyone feel beset by ADD. "I personally think we are living in a society that is so out of control that we say, 'Give me a stimulant so I can cope.' " says Charlotte Tomaino, a clinical neuropsychologist in White Plains, New York. As word of ADHD spreads, swarms of adults are seeking the diagnosis as an explanation for their troubles. "So many really have symptoms that began in adulthood and reflected depression or other problems," says psychiatrist Silver. In their best-selling new book, *Driven to Distraction,* Edward Hallowell and John Ratey suggest that American life is "ADD-ogenic": "American society tends to create ADD-like symptoms in us all. The fast pace. The sound bite. The quick cuts. The TV remote-control clicker. It is important to keep this in mind, or you may start thinking that everybody you know has ADD."

And that is the conundrum. How do you draw the line between a spontaneous, high-energy person who is feeling overwhelmed by the details of life and someone afflicted with a neurological disorder? Where is the boundary between personality and pathology? Even an expert in the field like the University of Chicago's Mark Stein admits, "We need to find more precise ways of diagnosing it than just saying you have these symptoms." Barkley also concedes the vagueness. The traits that constitute ADHD "are personality characteristics," he agrees. But it becomes pathology, he says, when the traits are so extreme that they interfere with people's lives.

THE RISKS There is no question that ADHD can disrupt lives. Kids with the disorder frequently have few friends. Their parents may be ostracized by neighbors and relatives, who blame them for failing to control the child. "I've got criticism of my parenting skills from strangers," says the mother of a hyperactive boy in New Jersey. "When you're out in public, you're always on guard. Whenever I'd hear a child cry, I'd turn to see if it was because of Jeremy."

School can be a shattering experience for such kids. Frequently reprimanded and tuned out, they lose any sense of selfworth and fall ever further behind in their work. More than a quarter are held back a grade; about a third fail to graduate from high school. ADHD kids are also prone to accidents, says neurologist Roseman. "These are the kids I'm going to see in the emergency room this summer. They rode their bicycle right into the street and didn't look. They jumped off the deck and forgot it was high."

But the psychological injuries are often

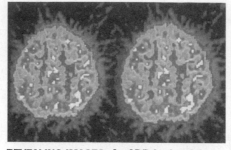

REVEALING IMAGES: An ADD brain, right, metabolizes more slowly than a normal one.

greater. By ages five to seven, says Barkley, half to two-thirds are hostile and defiant. By ages 10 to 12, they run the risk of developing what psychologists call "conduct disorder"—lying, stealing, running away from home and ultimately getting into trouble with the law. As adults, says Barkley, 25% to 30% will experience substance-abuse problems, mostly with depressants like marijuana and alcohol. One study of hyperactive boys found that 40% had been arrested at least once by age 18—and these were kids who had been treated with stimulant medication; among those who had been treated with the drug plus other measures, the rate was 20%—still very high.

It is an article of faith among ADHD researchers that the right interventions can prevent such dreadful outcomes. "If you can have an impact with these kids, you can change whether they go to jail or to Harvard Law School," says psychologist James Swanson at the University of California at Irvine, who co-authored the study of arrest histories. And yet, despite decades of research, no one is certain exactly what the optimal intervention should be.

TREATMENT The best-known therapy for ADHD remains stimulant drugs. Though Ritalin is the most popular choice, some patients do better with Dexedrine or Cylert or even certain antidepressants. About 70% of kids respond to stimulants. In the correct dosage, these uppers surprisingly "make people slow down," says Swanson. "They make you focus your at-

HAIL TO THE HYPERACTIVE HUNTER

WHY IS ATTENTION DEFICIT HYPERACTIVITY DISORDER SO COMMON? IS there an evolutionary reason why these traits are found in as many as 1 in 20 American youngsters? Such questions have prompted intriguing speculation. Harvard psychiatrist John Ratey finds no mystery in the prevalence of ADHD in the U.S. It is a nation of immigrants who, he notes, "risked it all and left their homelands." Characteristics like impulsiveness, high energy and risk taking are therefore highly represented in the U.S. gene pool. "We have more Nobel laureates and more criminals than anywhere else in the world. We have more people who absolutely push the envelope."

But why would ADHD have evolved in the first place? Perhaps, like the sickle-cell trait, which can help thwart malaria, attention deficit confers an advantage in certain circumstances. In *Attention Deficit Disorder: A Different Perception,* author Thom Hartmann has laid out a controversial but appealing theory that the characteristics known today as ADHD were vitally important in early hunting societies. They became a mixed blessing only when human societies turned agrarian, Hartmann suggests. "If you are walking in the night and see a little flash, distractibility would be a tremendous asset. Snap decision making, which we call impulsiveness, is a survival skill if you are a hunter." For a farmer, however, such traits can be disastrous. "If this is the perfect day to plant the crops, you can't suddenly decide to wander off into the woods."

Modern society, Hartmann contends, generally favors the farmer mentality, rewarding those who develop plans, meet deadlines and plod through schedules. But there's still a place for hunters, says the author, who counts himself as one: they can be found in large numbers among entrepreneurs, police detectives, emergency-room personnel, race-car drivers and, of course, those who stalk the high-stakes jungle known as Wall Street. ∎

> Snap decision making, which we call impulsiveness, is a survival skill if you are a hunter.

tention and apply more effort to whatever you're supposed to do." Ritalin kicks in within 30 minutes to an hour after being taken, but its effects last only about three hours. Most kids take a dose at breakfast and another at lunchtime to get them through a school day.

When drug therapy works, says Utah's Wender, "it is one of the most dramatic effects in psychiatry." Roseman tells how one first-grader came into his office after trying Ritalin and announced, "I know how it works." "You do?" asked the doctor. "Yes," the child replied. "It cleaned out my ears. Now I can hear the teacher." A third-grader told Roseman that Ritalin had enabled him to play basketball. "Now when I get the ball, I turn around, I go down to the end of the room, and if I look up, there's a net there. I never used to see the net, because there was too much screaming."

For adults, the results can be just as striking. "Helen," a 43-year-old mother of three in northern Virginia, began taking the drug after being diagnosed with ADD in 1983. "The very first day, I noticed a difference," she marvels. For the first time ever, "I was able to sit down and listen to what my husband had done at work. Shortly after, I was able to sit in bed and read while my husband watched TV."

Given such outcomes, doctors can be tempted to throw a little Ritalin at any problem. Some even use it as a diagnostic tool, believing—wrongly—that if the child's concentration improves with Ritalin, then he or she must have ADD. In fact, you don't have to have an attention problem to get a boost from Ritalin. By the late 1980s, overprescription became a big issue, raised in large measure by the Church of Scientology, which opposes psychiatry in general and launched a vigorous campaign against Ritalin. After a brief decline fostered by the scare, the drug is now hot once again. Swanson has heard of some classrooms where 20% to 30% of the boys are on Ritalin. "That's just ridiculous!" he says.

Ritalin use varies from state to state, town to town, depending largely on the attitude of the doctors and local schools. Ida-

The best-known therapy for ADHD remains stimulant drugs. . . . "They make you focus your attention and apply more effort to whatever you're supposed to do."

ho is the No. 1 consumer of the drug. A study of Ritalin consumption in Michigan, which ranks just behind Idaho, found that use ranged from less than 1% of boys in one county to as high as 10% in another, with no correlation to affluence.

Patients who are taking Ritalin must be closely monitored, since the drug can cause loss of appetite, insomnia and occasionally tics. Doctors often recommend "drug holidays" during school vacations. Medication is frequently combined with other treatments, including psychotherapy, special education and cognitive training, although the benefits of such expensive measures are unclear. "We really haven't known which treatment to use for which child and how to combine treatments," says Dr. Peter Jensen, chief of NIMH's Child and Adolescent Disorders Research Branch. His group has embarked on a study involving 600 children in six cities. By 1998 they hope to have learned how medication alone compares to med-

ication with psychological intervention and other approaches.

BEYOND DRUGS A rough consensus has emerged among ADHD specialists that whether or not drugs are used, it is best to teach kids—often through behavior modification—how to gain more control over their impulses and restless energy. Also recommended is training in the fine art of being organized: establishing a predictable schedule of activities, learning to use a date book, assigning a location for possessions at school and at home. This takes considerable effort on the part of teachers and parents as well as the kids themselves. Praise, most agree, is vitally important.

Within the classroom "some simple, practical things work well," says Reid. Let hyperactive kids move around. Give them stand-up desks, for instance. "I've seen kids who from the chest up were very diligently working on a math problem, but from the chest down, they're dancing like

DO YOU HAVE ATTENTION DEFICIT?

If eight or more of the following statements accurately describe your child or yourself as a child, particularly before age 7, there may be reason to suspect ADHD. A definitive diagnosis requires further examination.

1. Often fidgets or squirms in seat.

2. Has difficulty remaining seated.

3. Is easily distracted.

4. Has difficulty awaiting turn in groups.

5. Often blurts out answers to questions.

6. Has difficulty following instructions.

7. Has difficulty sustaining attention to tasks.

8. Often shifts from one

uncompleted activity to another.

9. Has difficulty playing quietly.

10. Often talks excessively.

11. Often interrupts or intrudes on others.

12. Often does not seem to listen.

13. Often loses things necessary for tasks.

14. Often engages in physically dangerous activities without considering consequences.

Source: *The ADHD Rating Scale: Normative Data, Reliability, and Validity*

Fred Astaire." To minimize distractions, ADHD kids should sit very close to the teacher and be permitted to take important tests in a quiet area. "Unfortunately," Reid observes, "not many teachers are trained in behavior management. It is a historic shortfall in American education."

In Irvine, California, James Swanson has tried to create the ideal setting for teaching kids with ADHD. The Child Development Center, an elementary school that serves 45 kids with the disorder, is a kind of experiment in progress. The emphasis is on behavior modification: throughout the day students earn points—and are relentlessly cheered on—for good behavior. High scorers are rewarded with special privileges at the end of the day, but each morning kids start afresh with another shot at the rewards. Special classes also drill in social skills: sharing, being a good sport, ignoring annoyances rather than striking out in anger. Only 35% of the kids at the center are on stimulant drugs, less than half the national rate for ADHD kids.

Elsewhere around the country, enterprising parents have struggled to find their own answers to attention deficit. Bonnie and Neil Fell of Skokie, Illinois, have three sons, all of whom have been diagnosed with ADD. They have "required more structure and consistency than other kids," says Bonnie. "We had to break down activities into clear time slots." To help their sons, who take Ritalin, the Fells have employed tutors, psychotherapists and a speech and language specialist. None of this comes cheap: they estimate their current annual ADD-related expenses at $15,000. "Our goal is to get them through school with their self-esteem intact," says Bonnie.

The efforts seem to be paying off. Dan, the eldest at 15, has become an outgoing A student, a wrestling star and a writer for the school paper. "ADD gives you energy and creativity," he says. "I've learned to cope. I've become strong." On the other hand, he is acutely aware of his disability. "What people don't realize is that I have to work harder than everyone else. I start studying for finals a month before other people do."

COPING Adults can also train themselves to compensate for ADHD. Therapists working with them typically emphasize organiza-

...whether or not drugs are used, it is best to teach kids—often through behavior modification—how to gain more control over their impulses and restless energy.

tional skills, time management, stress reduction and ways to monitor their own distractibility and stay focused.

N HER OFFICE IN WHITE PLAINS, Tomaino has a miniature Zen garden, a meditative sculpture and all sorts of other items to help tense patients relax. Since many people with ADHD also have learning disabilities, she tests each patient and then often uses computer programs to strengthen weak areas. But most important is helping people define their goals and take orderly steps to reach them. Whether working with a stockbroker or a homemaker, she says, "I teach adults basic rewards and goals. For instance, you can't go out to lunch until you've cleaned the kitchen."

Tomaino tells of one very hyperactive and articulate young man who got all the way through college without incident, thanks in good measure to a large and tolerant extended family. Then he flunked out of law school three times. Diagnosed with ADHD, the patient took stock of his goals and decided to enter the family restaurant business, where, Tomaino says, he is a raging success. "ADHD was a deficit if he want-

ed to be a lawyer, but it's an advantage in the restaurant business. He gets to go around to meet and greet."

For neurologist Roseman, the same thing is true. With 11 offices in four states, he is perpetually on the go. "I'm at rest in motion," says the doctor. "I surround myself with partners who provide the structure. My practice allows me to be creative." Roseman has accountants to do the bookkeeping. He starts his day at 6:30 with a hike and doesn't slow down until midnight. "Thank God for my ADD," he says. But, he admits, "had I listened to all the negative things that people said when I was growing up, I'd probably be digging ditches in Idaho."

LESSONS Whether ADHD is a brain disorder or simply a personality type, the degree to which it is a handicap depends not only on the severity of the traits but also on one's environment. The right school, job or home situation can make all the difference. The lessons of ADHD are truisms. All kids do not learn in the same way. Nor are all adults suitable for the same line of work.

Unfortunately, American society seems to have evolved into a one-size-fits-all system. Schools can resemble factories: put the kids on the assembly line, plug in the right components and send 'em out the door. Everyone is supposed to go to college; there is virtually no other route to success. In other times and in other places, there have been alternatives: apprenticeships, settling a new land, starting a business out of the garage, going to sea. In a conformist society, it becomes necessary to medicate some people to make them fit in.

This is not to deny that some people genuinely need Ritalin, just as others need tranquilizers or insulin. But surely an epidemic of attention deficit disorder is a warning to us all. Children need individual supervision. Many of them need more structure than the average helter-skelter household provides. They need a more consistent approach to discipline and schools that tailor teaching to their individual learning styles. Adults too could use a society that's more flexible in its expectations, more accommodating to differences. Most of all, we all need to slow down. And pay attention.   **—With reporting by Hannah Bloch/New York, Wendy Cole/Chicago and James Willwerth/Irvine**

PART III

Personality Disorders, Criminality, and Substance Abuse Disorders

In this section of the book, we will examine several different conditions, including personality disorders, criminality and the psychological disorders associated with it, and substance abuse disorders. Although these conditions differ in a number of ways, they share at least one important characteristic: they tend to produce considerable suffering not only in the afflicted individuals, but also in those around them. In addition, many personality disorders co-occur with, and increase the risk for, substance abuse disorders. For example, antisocial personality disorder (ASPD), which is characterized by a chronic history of criminal and irresponsible behavior, is associated with a heightened probability of maladaptive use of several substances, including alcohol.

Unlike the other disorders we have discussed in this book, which are coded on Axis I of the DSM-IV, personality disorders are coded on Axis II, meaning that they tend to be relatively stable over time. Whereas most Axis II disorders represent the individual's enduring personality style, most Axis I disorders (for example, major depression and panic disorder) are relatively short-lived (or at least not lifelong) conditions that are superimposed upon this personality style. Personality disorders, which are the most important Axis II conditions, are defined as syndromes in which longstanding personality traits (such as introversion, social anxiety, and impulsivity) have become inflexible and maladaptive.

Traditionally, the classification system for personality disorders, like those for other psychiatric disorders in DSM-IV, has been categorical. In a categorical scheme, abnormality is assumed to differ qualitatively (that is, in kind) from normality, and individuals are diagnosed as either belonging to a certain category or not. Recently, however, a number of researchers have argued that the most appropriate system for diagnosing and assessing personality disorders is dimensional, not categorical. In a dimensional scheme, abnormality is assumed to differ quantitatively (that is, in degree) from normality, and individuals are described along a continuum of severity. Despite the intuitive plausibility and appeal of dimensional models for personality disorder diagnosis, their assets and liabilities remain a topic of heated debate.

In a useful overview of this controversy, Bruce Bower describes a number of recent developments in research and theorizing on personality disorder dimensional models. According to Bower, one major reason for researchers' and clinicians' dissatisfaction with categorical models of personality disorders is the extensive overlap (or so-called comorbidity) of diagnoses within individuals. Many individuals simultaneously fulfill criteria for four, five, or even more personality disorders, suggesting that DSM-IV's categories have failed to "carve nature at its joints." Bower focuses on the research of Costa, McCrae, Widiger, and other investigators, who have proposed that the DSM-IV personality disorders be replaced or at least supplemented by the "Big Five," a set of five broad dimensions that have repeatedly been identified in analyses of personality measures. The Big Five—extraversion, neuroticism, agreeableness, conscientiousness, and openness to experience—have the potential to serve as a comprehensive framework within which all individuals, including those with DSM-IV personality disorders, can be described. Nevertheless, as Bower observes, adoption of the Big Five system has been hindered by theoretical disagreements concerning its applicability to DSM-IV personality disorders and by practical concerns regarding its implementation by clinicians.

The personality disorder that has received the most attention from researchers is psychopathic personality (psychopathy). Paradoxically, the diagnosis of psychopathy is technically not included in DSM-IV, although the DSM-IV diagnosis of ASPD (see first paragraph on this page) bears certain important similarities to psychopathy. Unlike ASPD, however, which is defined by antisocial and criminal *behaviors*, psychopathy is defined by a constellation of personality *traits*. In the next selection, the eminent Canadian psychologist Robert Hare, who has spent the better part of his career investigating the characteristics and causes of psychopathy, provides us with a vivid and chilling portrayal of the personality features of the psychopath. Hare describes 12 core characteristics of psychopathy, which comprise two broad categories: emotional/interpersonal features and social deviance. According to Hare, the former include guiltlessness, lack of empathy, deceitfulness, and superficial charm, whereas the latter include impulsivity, irresponsibility, craving for stimulation, and weak behavioral controls. Hare concludes with a brief discussion of what researchers have learned about the causes and treatment of psychopathy. As Hare points out, psychopaths are notoriously poor candidates for psychotherapy, in part because they do not typically perceive themselves as requiring treatment.

Although psychopathy is often associated with criminality, psychopathy is only one risk factor among many for criminal behavior. This fact underscores the point that the causes of crime are heterogeneous and complex, and involve an interplay of both genetic and environmental influences. W. Wayt Gibbs provides us with a review and discussion of recent research on the factors that appear to predispose individuals, particularly children and adolescents, to later crime. Gibbs notes that although a large number of biological correlates (for example, low serotonin, low resting heart rate, and high testosterone) and psychosocial correlates (for instance, inconsistent parental discipline, deviant peer groups, and low socieconomic status) of criminality have been pinpointed, the capacity of investigators to predict subsequent antisocial behavior remains greatly limited. Such predictions tend to yield high numbers of false positives—that is, predictions that individuals will engage in crime who do not. Moreover, as Gibbs points out, it is exceedingly difficult to determine whether the correlates of crime that have been identified are *causes* of crime. The old saw that correlation does not equal causation applies here; many of these correlates may be consequences of crime or of other variables that are themselves causally related to crime. Nevertheless, some biologically oriented researchers predict that our ability to predict future crime may dramatically improve in the near future as our understanding of the physiological underpinnings of aggressive behavior increases. As Gibbs observes, such knowledge, although potentially extremely valuable from a scientific standpoint, raises difficult and sometimes troublesome ethical questions. Should society, for example, have the right to force individuals who are at risk for crime to obtain treatment against their will?

One potential environmental risk factor for aggression that has recently received considerable attention from investigators is childhood abuse and neglect. As Craig Ferris notes in his commentary on this literature, there is ample evidence from the animal literature that early maternal deprivation or total isolation have lasting adverse effects on behavior. Monkeys separated from their mothers at birth later tend to exhibit violence when confronted with intruders; monkeys reared in complete isolation tend to later attack babies and other adults. Moreover, rodent studies demonstrate that early environmental experiences, such as gentle handling by human caretakers, can produce marked changes in neurotransmitters (such as serotonin) and receptors for hormones (such as glucocorticoids). Ferris's discussion reminds us of an extremely important point: environmental factors, such as stressful life events, can influence brain functioning.

In reading this article, however, you should be aware of one important logical error made by Ferris. Toward the end of the article, he asserts that "it is pointless to argue about nature versus nurture. Behavior is 100 percent hereditary and 100 percent environmental" (p. 127). Ferris is certainly correct that genetic and enviromental factors cannot be disentangled *within a single individual,* because genes and environment are in a state of constant interplay. But behavior-genetic investigations, such as twin and adoption studies (see, for example, Reading 11), are designed to estimate the extent to which genetic and environmental influences account for the differences in a characteristic, such as childhood aggression, *among individuals.* Thus, the question of the extent to which the differences among children in their levels of aggression are attributable to genetic versus environmental factors is perfectly reasonable from a scientific standpoint.

In the final article in this section, David Concar reviews several different lines of research on the biological origins of drug and alcohol addiction. Concar discusses the findings of Kenneth Blum and his colleagues on the A1 allele for dopamine, which has been linked by some investigators to alcoholism, addictions to other substances, and even certain "compulsive behaviors" such as gambling and binge eating. As Concar notes, Blum's hypothesis that these diverse conditions comprise an overarching "reward deficiency syndrome" is highly controversial. Concar reviews several other promising physiological findings, such as decreased body sway in response to alcohol among the relatives of alcoholics as compared with the relatives of nonalcoholics, adoption data indicating a genetic influence on at least some subtypes of alcoholism, and positron emission tomography scan results indicating marked effects of certain psychoactive substances on brain activity. Concar concludes with a discussion of recent research on the neural underpinnings of reward, with particular emphasis on the brain's dopamine systems. Concar points out that much of this research raises an intriguing possibility: that our susceptibility to certain addictions may be the price we pay for being able to experience pleasure.

DISCUSSION QUESTIONS

READING 20. B. Bower, "Piecing Together Personality: Psychological Research Presents a Challenge to Psychiatric Diagnosis"

1. Proponents of the Big Five system maintain that most or all of the 10 DSM-IV personality disorders can be described in terms of extreme scores on one or more of the dimensions of extraversion, neuroticism, agreeableness, conscientiousness, and openness to experience. As Bower notes, research by Sanderson and Clarkin, for example, suggests that patients with borderline personality disorder are character-

ized by high levels of neuroticism and low levels of conscientiousness and agreeableness. How would you characterize (a) histrionic personality disorder, (b) obsessive-compulsive personality disorder, and (c) avoidant personality disorder within the Big Five system?

2. Are the features of certain DSM-IV personality disorders difficult or impossible to accommodate fully within the Big Five system? If so, which ones?

3. What do you see as the practical advantages and disadvantages of substituting a dimensional system (such as the Big Five) for a categorical system of personality disorder diagnosis?

4. According to Bower, Auke Tellegen has proposed adding two dimensions to the Big Five, one characterized by a positive evaluation of oneself (for example, "I am great," "I am wonderful") and the other characterized by a negative evaluation of oneself (for example, "I am evil," "I am terrible"). How might Tellegen's two dimensions be useful in personality disorder diagnosis?

READING 21. R. Hare, "Predators: The Disturbing World of Psychopaths Among Us"

1. Some individuals possess high levels of the traits that Hare describes as the emotional/interpersonal features of psychopathy (such as lack of guilt, lack of empathy, and grandiosity), but very low levels of criminal behavior. Such individuals are sometimes called subclinical or successful psychopaths because they exhibit the core personality features of psychopathy but do not possess a history of repeated legal difficulties. What factors might distinguish subclinical or successful psychopaths from psychopaths who commit crimes? In what settings might subclinical or successful psychopaths be especially prevalent?

2. Psychopathy can be a difficult disorder for researchers and clinicians to assess, because the self-reports of psychopaths are notoriously untrustworthy. How would you attempt to measure the key features of psychopathy?

3. Hare notes that psychopaths have traditionally been considered extremely poor candidates for psychotherapy. Are there any treatment approaches that might have some effect on psychopaths? If so, what are they?

4. Should a diagnosis of psychopathy constitute a legitimate basis for an insanity defense? Why or why not?

READING 22. W. W. Gibbs, "Seeking the Criminal Element"

1. As Gibbs notes, predictions of crime tend to yield high false positive rates. What risk factors (other than those discussed by Gibbs) strike you as especially promising candidates as predictors of future criminality?

2. Gibbs points out that family dysfunction, separation from parents, and inconsistent parental supervision and discipline have been found to be associated with later crime. Although many researchers regard these variables as environmental causes of criminality, is there an alternative explanation? How might you determine whether these variables are causally related to crime?

3. Gibbs reviews recent analyses suggesting that certain "treatment" programs for delinquency (such as boot camp programs) may actually *increase* rates of later crime. Why might this be?

4. Do you agree with psychologist Diana Fishbein that treatment for criminals should be mandatory? Why or why not? Do you agree with her that some criminals should remain in prison indefinitely until effective treatments are found? Why or why not?

READING 23. C. F. Ferris, "The Rage of Innocents"

1. Do you agree with Ferris that it is both premature and irresponsible to attempt to solve the problem of childhood aggression by identifying which children are at greatest genetic risk for violence? Why or why not?

2. Among the social factors cited by Ferris as contributing to violence are prenatal exposure to drugs and parental criminality. Do you agree with him that these influences are necessarily social, rather than genetic, in nature? What types of studies might permit you to investigate the hypothesis that the association between these factors and aggression is environmentally rather than genetically mediated?

3. Ferris asserts that "the evidence of a genetic component to childhood aggression is thin" (p. 125). Is this claim consistent with his later statement that the effects of genetic and environmental factors are impossible to disentangle? Explain your reasoning.

4. Do the findings cited by Ferris, which show that childhood trauma can dramatically affect brain functioning and produce profound behavioral disturbances, imply that children who are neglected and abused will inevitably be at heightened risk for later adjustment problems (such as aggression)? Why or why not?

READING 24. D. Concar, "Prisoners of Pleasure?"

1. Concar observes that "a sociologist reports a high level of drug abuse in people who have recently lost their jobs" and asks, "Did they turn to drugs because of unemployment, or get fired because they're drug abusers?" (p. 128). Design a study that might help to answer Concar's question.

2. Pharmacologist Kenneth Blum has posited that alcoholism, drug addictions, gambling, Tourette's disorder, and binge eating, among other conditions, are actually part of a

larger "reward deficiency syndrome" characterized by a heightened "hunger" for pleasurable activities. Do you find Blum's hypothesis plausible? How would you attempt to test it systematically?

3. According to Concar, "In the end pleasure is a highly subjective experience, and it would be ludicrous to suppose that it could (be) boiled down to the actions of neurotransmitter pathways" (p. 131). Do you agree with this statement? Why or why not?

4. Concar notes that American troops who were addicted to heroin in Vietnam tended to show extremely low rates of heroin addiction upon returning to the United States, probably because the environmental cues that were associated with their drug use changed dramatically. How might you use this finding to generate recommendations for the treatment of drug addiction?

SUGGESTIONS FOR FURTHER READING

Blum, K., Cull, J. G., Braverman, E. R., & Comings, D. E. (1996). Reward deficiency syndrome. *American Scientist, 84,* 132–145.

Cloninger, C. R. (1987). Neurogenetic adaptive mechanisms in alcoholism. *Science, 236,* 410–416.

Costa, P., & Widiger, T. A. (Eds.) (1994). *Personality disorders and the five factor model of personality.* Washington, DC: American Psychiatric Association.

Hare, R. D. (1993). *Without conscience: The disturbing world of the psychopaths among us.* New York: Simon & Schuster.

Lykken, D. T. (1995). *The antisocial personalities.* Hillsdale, NJ: Lawrence Erlbaum Associates.

Millon, T., & Davis, R. D. (1996). *Disorders of personality: DSM-IV and beyond.* New York: John Wiley & Sons.

Schuckit, M. A. (1987). Biological vulnerability to alcoholism. *Journal of Consulting and Clinical Psychology, 55,* 301–309.

Wilson, J. Q., & Herrnstein, R. J. (1985). *Crime and human nature.* New York: Simon & Schuster.

A lice exhibited a bewildering array of problems when she entered psychotherapy. At least three separate conditions in the *Diagnostic and Statistical Manual of Mental Disorders* (DSM) — the bible of psychiatry — applied to the 24-year-old woman. Unfortunately, each diagnosis held different implications for how best to help her.

Frequent eating binges followed by induced vomiting qualified Alice for a diagnosis of bulimia. But she also heeded destructive urges to abuse a wide variety of drugs and to seek anonymous sexual encounters, felt intensely self-conscious, careened between anxiety and depression, and showed other signs of what DSM labels borderline personality disorder. And to complete the triple whammy, her extreme inhibition and timidity supported a diagnosis of avoidant personality disorder.

Faced with this morass of distress, Alice's therapist, psychologist Cynthia G. Ellis of the University of Kentucky in Lexington, took a heretical step: She abandoned DSM's guiding principles and instead evaluated her client's behavior, feelings, and motivations along five broad dimensions. This allowed the psychologist to characterize Alice as displaying a single personality disorder marked by introversion and excessive neuroticism — in Alice's case, primarily impulsive acts, emotional vulnerability, and depression.

Ellis then composed a treatment plan. First, she dealt with Alice's immediate symptoms of bulimia. Then, over the next 2½ years, therapy sessions began carefully to explore Alice's longstanding fears of emotional intimacy and their reverberations in her life.

A minority of psychotherapists would take this dimensional approach to treating Alice or anyone else whose personality somehow goes seriously awry. But an increasingly vocal group of scientists is pushing for official recognition of dimensional techniques — particularly the five-factor model employed by Ellis.

"There may never be a consensus on how to define and measure personality," asserts University of Kentucky psychologist Thomas A. Widiger. "But there's enough support for the five-factor model to indicate that it provides a useful point of departure for understanding personality disorders."

I n 1980, the DSM's authors elevated personality disorders to a status alongside so-called symptom disorders, such as depression and schizophrenia. In a single stroke, certain personality traits — enduring ways of behaving, perceiving, and thinking about oneself and others — coalesced into medical disorders that lay across a theoretical Rubicon from "normal" personalities.

Clinicians diagnose personality disorders alone or in combination with symptom disorders. However, the frequency with which personality disorders occur in the general population is unknown.

Widiger served on the task force that developed definitions of the 11 personality disorders in the current DSM and of the 10 that will be retained in the fourth edition, or DSM-IV, slated for publication by the American Psychiatric Association later this year. An appendix in DSM-IV will list two additional personality disorders deemed worthy of further study.

Although many DSM diagnoses have sparked debate, personality disorders quickly achieved the dubious distinction of arousing the most intense controversy. Psychiatrists and other mental health workers disagreed over which personality defects truly belonged in DSM, and tempers flared over proposed diagnoses that carried social and political overtones, such as the self-defeating and sadistic disorders (SN: 2/25/89, p.120).

Studies also found that clinicians often disagreed about which personality disorder to assign to a given individual. Some reports noted that people displaying severely disturbed personalities met DSM criteria for an average of four different personality disorders, a sure recipe for clinical confusion.

As psychiatrists grappled with these issues, psychologists undertook intensive studies of individual differences in personality traits for the first time in more than 20 years. This work had fallen out of favor during the 1960s and 1970s, which featured behaviorists' examinations of conditioned responses to various rewards and punishments and social psychologists' emphasis on how specific situations mold thoughts and behaviors.

Amid the current resurgence of personality research, some psychologists contend that attempts to chart unchanging traits fail to illuminate the ways in which the same personality changes from one social situation to another. Others argue that individuals construct multiple selves, a theory that questions the entire notion of stable, measurable personalities.

N evertheless, trait theories of personality — exemplified by the five-factor model — enjoy considerable prominence. Their proponents treat personality disorders as instances in which traits that are present to some degree in all people reach inflexible and harmful extremes. DSM's partitioning of personality disturbances into medical conditions ignores the underlying links between well-functioning and disrupted personalities, these researchers hold.

The five-factor model focuses on the extent to which personality traits vary across five broad dimensions: neuroticism, or proneness to various forms of psychological distress and impulsive behavior; extroversion, the tendency to seek interactions with others and feel joy and optimism; openness to experience, a measure of curiosity, receptivity to new ideas, and the ability to experience emotions; agreeableness, which indicates the extent to which someone shows both compassion and antagonism toward others; and conscientiousness, the degree of organization and stick-to-itiveness regarding personal goals.

One set of questionnaires to measure these traits comes from studies of adjectives used to describe personality. Factor analyses, which mathematically divvy up such adjectives into as few coherent groups as possible, identified five independent personality dimensions as early as 1934. In the January 1993 AMERICAN PSYCHOLOGIST, Lewis R. Goldberg, a psychologist at the University of Oregon in Eugene, describes attempts to develop ratings scales for the five factors based on factor analysis.

Perhaps the bulk of research now focuses on one particular questionnaire inspired by the five-factor model. Paul T. Costa Jr. and Robert R. McCrae, both psychologists at the National Institute on Aging's Gerontology Research Center in Baltimore, devised this instrument to elicit self-reports as well as observations by spouses, peers, and clinicians. It consists of 181 statements that describe personality attributes; those who complete the questionnaire rate their level of agreement with each statement on a scale of 0 to 4.

Costa and McCrae's questionnaire breaks down each of the five factors into a number of component parts, or facets. An overall neuroticism score, for instance,

Piecing Together Personality

Psychological research presents a challenge to psychiatric diagnosis

By BRUCE BOWER

From *Science News*, 145, pp. 152–154, March 5, 1994. Reprinted by permission of Science News.

consists of items that provide separate measures for anxiety, hostility, depression, self-consciousness, impulsiveness, and emotional vulnerability.

Studies of large groups administered this questionnaire indicate that numerous personality traits and factors proposed by other scientists — which have often created a sense of disarray in personality research — fall within the bounds of the five-factor model, Costa and McCrae argue.

On the heels of these findings comes a book in which researchers and clinicians apply the five-factor model to personality disorders. Costa and Widiger edited the volume, titled *Personality Disorders and the Five-Factor Model of Personality* (1994, American Psychological Association).

One chapter describes research supporting the view that the five-factor model accounts for both broken-down and finely tuned personalities. Directed by Lee Anna Clark, a psychologist at the University of Iowa in Iowa City, this work finds that people diagnosed with various personality disorders stretch one or more of the five basic traits to maladaptive extremes.

Clark's group administered trait questionnaires developed by Goldberg, Costa and McCrae, and her own scales derived from DSM criteria for personality disorders to groups of college students and psychiatric patients. All three inventories, particularly the one informed by DSM symptoms, accurately identified people in each population who suffered from personality disorders, Clark contends.

More specifically, in cases of borderline personality disorder, data on the five factors gleaned from Costa and McCrae's questionnaire offer valuable insight to clinicians, according to Cynthia Sanderson and John F. Clarkin, both of Cornell University Medical College in New York City. In a study of 64 women assigned this diagnosis, Sanderson and Clarkin find extremely high levels of neuroticism, as evidenced by anxiety, depression, self-consciousness, and a wide range of impulsive behaviors.

The same women also display low conscientiousness, reflected in aimlessness and a lack of clear goals, and low agreeableness, marked by cynicism, vengefulness, and constant attempts to manipulate others. Not surprisingly, psychotherapists encounter many difficulties in treating borderline personalities and need to monitor their problem traits from the start, the researchers maintain.

Widiger, Costa, and their colleagues propose five-factor profiles of each DSM personality disorder. Their profile of paranoid personality disorder, for instance, stresses excessively low agreeableness, characterized most strongly by suspiciousness and antagonism. Hostility, one facet of neuroticism, also shows

up consistently in people diagnosed with this disorder, they contend.

Agreeableness also plummets in both narcissistic and antisocial personality disorders, the researchers note. The exorbitant self-importance and arrogance typical of the former condition translate into low scores on the agreeableness facets of modesty, altruism, and empathy, they assert. The latter disorder, marked by repeated criminal, aggressive, and irresponsible acts, features low altruism

> **... people diagnosed with various personality disorders stretch one or more of the five basic traits to maladaptive extremes.**

and a copious supply of extroversion, particularly as measured by items that signal a constant need for excitement and sensory stimulation.

Five-factor descriptions of paranoid personality disorder and other diagnoses that involve odd or eccentric behavior may be improved by rewording the openness-to-experience items to address such peculiarities directly, Widiger says. Auke Tellegen, a psychologist at the University of Minnesota in Minneapolis, has completed such a revision and changed the name of the dimension from "openness-

to-experience" to "unconventionality."

Unlike its predecessor, Tellegen's unconventionality scale assesses, for instance, the tendency to read hidden and threatening meanings into others' remarks, one symptom of a paranoid personality. This scale also considers the magical thinking and perceptual illusions that often characterize schizotypal personality disorder.

Tellegen also proposes adding two new factors to the five-factor model; these tap into highly negative and positive qualities attributed to the self, such as a propensity for evil, treachery, excellence, and superiority.

A more far-reaching challenge to the five-factor model comes from research directed by C. Robert Cloninger, a psychiatrist at Washington University School of Medicine in St. Louis. In the December 1993 ARCHIVES OF GENERAL PSYCHIATRY, Cloninger and his coworkers describe the seven dimensions that they deem crucial to understanding healthy and disordered personalities.

Four dimensions account for temperament: novelty seeking, harm avoidance, reward dependence, and persistence. Individuals largely inherit their temperamental styles, which are triggered by perceptions of their surroundings, Cloninger's group theorizes. Temperament orchestrates the habitual behaviors that a person carries out unthinkingly throughout the day, they suggest.

The St. Louis scientists also devised three character dimensions: self-directedness (a measure of commitment to goals and purposes), cooperativeness, and self-transcendence (associated with deeply held spiritual beliefs and feelings of connection with nature or the universe). Character development leans heavily on a conscious sorting out of one's memories and experiences, the investigators argue. This process picks up steam during adulthood as misfortunes and death more frequently intrude on people's lives, they note.

Cloninger and his colleagues administered a true-false questionnaire consisting of 107 temperament items and 119 character items to 300 psychologically healthy adults. Volunteers ranged in age from 18 to 91. The seven personality dimensions clearly emerged in the sample, they contend. Character dimensions assumed increasing importance and complexity in older age groups.

The researchers also obtained questionnaire responses from 66 psychiatric patients who ran the gamut of DSM personality disorders. Low self-directedness and low cooperativeness emerge as core features of all personality disorders, they report. Moreover, each personality disorder displays a unique pattern of temperament and character scores, the investigators contend.

Most clinicians, and particularly psychiatrists, who deal with people suffering from personality disorders remain skeptical of the five-factor model and other dimensional measures of personality.

Theodore Millon, a psychiatrist at Harvard Medical School in Boston, considers it best to view the symptoms that make up each DSM category as a prototype, or most typical example, of that personality disorder. Individuals assigned the same diagnosis usually differ to some degree from the prototype, Millon asserts.

So, for example, a diagnosis of borderline personality disorder may apply to someone exhibiting five of the eight required symptoms listed in the current DSM. Other cases of borderline personality disorder may include more than five symptoms and may feature shifting mixes and different intensities of the various symptoms.

In this approach, the personality disorders shade into one another as they veer farther away from their prototypes. Clinicians must determine the degree to which a person's symptoms match prototypes of relevant personality disorders in order to come up with a primary diagnosis, Millon argues.

Dimensional models deal with surface characteristics that may only illuminate the few personality disorders that create moderate problems, adds John G. Gunderson, a psychiatrist at McLean Hospital in Belmont, Mass. Severe personality disorders, including borderline and antisocial disorders, occur most frequently and involve complex underlying problems that elude trait questionnaires, Gunderson asserts.

Other psychiatrists harbor more practical concerns. Although the dimensional approach holds much promise for analyzing personality disturbances, its acceptance and sophisticated use by clinicians "will require a monumental educational effort," according to Allen J. Frances of Duke University Medical Center in Durham, N.C. Frances directed work on DSM-IV.

What's more, notes five-factor proponent Thomas Widiger, many clinicians fear that discarding DSM categories for a dimensional focus on normal traits gone bad will result in denial of insurance coverage for treatment of serious personality disturbances.

Ongoing research aims to establish cutoff points at which scores on five-factor questionnaires signify major personality problems, Widiger says. Some psychologists have proposed that the American Psychological Association issue a rival DSM that takes this approach. Widiger, however, hopes that the next edition of DSM will include the five-factor model as a supplement to traditional personality disorder categories.

DSM-IV includes a statement acknowledging the existence of several dimensional models of personality but fails to recommend any of them for clinical use, Widiger says.

Michael H. Stone, a psychiatrist at Columbia University, would welcome a hybrid approach to treating personality disturbances.

"Sophisticated clinicians use both categories and dimensions all the time in thinking about their patients," Stone asserts. "But psychiatrists have largely ignored the research of personality psychologists."

In a book titled *Abnormalities of Personality* (1993, W.W. Norton), Stone lists 500 negative and 100 positive personality adjectives that he considers components of the five-factor model. He often administers to his patients questionnaires that inquire about these qualities; the results greatly assist in diagnosis and treatment planning, he says.

For the most part, though, psychiatrists prefer that personality dimensions take a backseat to DSM's personality disorders. "The general psychiatric public may not be ready for a sea change in diagnostic practice," Stone contends.

But true to form, personality disturbances continue to make waves.   □

PREDATORS

The Disturbing World of Psychopaths Among Us

Jeffrey Dahmer. Ted Bundy. Hannibal Lechter. These are the psychopaths whose stunning lack of conscience we see in the movies and in tabloids. Yet, as this report makes abundantly clear, these predators, both male *and* female, haunt our everyday lives at work, at home, and in relationships. How to find them before they find you. By Robert Hare, Ph.D.

She met him in a laundromat in London. He was open and friendly and they hit it off right away. From the start she thought he was hilarious. Of course, she'd been lonely. The weather was grim and sleety and she didn't know a soul east of the Atlantic.

"Ah, traveler's loneliness," Dan crooned sympathetically over dinner. "It's the worst."

After dessert he was embarrassed to discover he'd come without his wallet. She was more than happy to pay for dinner. At the pub, over drinks, he told her he was a translator for the United Nations. He was, for now, between assignments.

They saw each other four times that week, five the week after. It wasn't long before he had all but moved in with Elsa. It was against her nature, but she was having the time of her life.

Still, there were details, unexplained, undiscussed, that she shoved out of her mind. He never invited her to his home; she never met his friends. One night he brought over a carton filled with tape recorders—plastic-wrapped straight from the factory, unopened; a few days later they were gone. Once she came home to find three televisions stacked in the corner. "Storing them for a friend," was all her told her. When she pressed for more he merely shrugged.

Once he stayed away for three days and was lying asleep on the bed when she came in midmorning. "Where have you been?" she cried. "I've been so worried. Where were you?"

He looked sour as he woke up. "Don't ever ask me that," he snapped. "I won't have it."

"What—?"

"Where I go, what I do, who I do it with—it doesn't concern you, Elsa. Don't ask."

He was like a different person. But then he seemed to pull himself together, shook the sleep off, and reached out to her.

"I know it hurts you," he said in his old gentle way, "but think of jealousy as a flu, and wait to get over it. And you will,

From *Without Conscience: The Disturbing World of Psychopaths Among Us*, by Dr. Robert Hare. Copyright © 1993 by Robert Hare. Reprinted with permission of the author and Pocket Books, a Division of Simon & Schuster. This article also appeared in *Psychology Today, 27*, pp. 54–63, January/February 1994.

Not surprisingly, many psychopaths are criminals, but many others manage to remain out of prison, using their charm and chameleonlike coloration to cut a wide swath through society and leaving a wake of ruined lives behind them.

baby, you will." Like a mother cat licking her kitten, he groomed her back into trusting him.

One night she asked him lightly if he felt like stepping out to the corner and bringing her an ice cream. He didn't reply, and when she glanced up she found him glaring at her furiously. "Always got everything you wanted, didn't you?" he asked in a strange, snide way. "Any little thing little Elsa wanted, somebody always jumped up and ran out and bought it for her, didn't they?"

"Are you kidding? I'm not like that. What are you talking about?"

He got up from the chair and walked out. She never saw him again.

To put it simply, if we can't spot them, we are doomed to be their victims.

There is a class of individuals who have been around forever and who are found in every race, culture, society, and walk of life. Everybody has met these people, been deceived and manipulated by them, and forced to live with or repair the damage they have wrought. These often charming—but always deadly—individuals have a clinical name: *psychopaths.* Their hallmark is a stunning lack of conscience; their game is self-gratification at the other person's expense. Many spend time in prison, but many do not. All take far more than they give.

The most obvious expressions of psychopathy—but not the only ones—involve the flagrant violation of society's rules. Not surprisingly, many psychopaths are criminals, but many others manage to remain out of prison, using

their charm and chameleonlike coloration to cut a wide swathe through society and leaving a wake of ruined lives behind them.

A major part of my own quarter-century search for answers to this enigma has been a concerted effort to develop an accurate means of detecting the psychopaths among us. Measurement and categorization are of course fundamental to any scientific endeavor, but the implications of being able to identify psychopaths are as much practical as academic. To put it simply, if we can't spot them we are doomed to be their victims, both as individuals and as a society.

My role in the search for psychopaths began in the 1960s at the psychology department of the University of British Columbia. There, my growing interest in psychopathy merged with my experience working with psychopaths in prison to form what was my life work.

I assembled a team of clinicians who would identify psychopaths in the prison population by means of long, detailed interviews and close study of file information. From this eventually developed a highly reliable diagnostic tool that any clinician or researcher could use and that yielded a richly detailed profile of the personality disorder called psychopathy. We named this instrument the *Psychopathy Check list* (Multi-Health Systems; 1991). The checklist is now used worldwide and provides clinicians and researchers with a way of distinguishing with reasonable certainty true psychopaths from those who merely break the rules.

What follows is a general summary of the key traits and behaviors of a psychopath. *Do not use these symptoms to diagnose yourself or others.* A diagnosis requires explicit training and access to the formal scoring manual. If you suspect that someone you know

conforms to the profile described here, and if it is important for you to have an expert opinion, you should obtain the services of a qualified (registered) forensic psychologist or psychiatrist.

Also, be aware that people who are *not* psychopaths may have *some* of the symptoms described here. Many people are impulsive, or glib, or cold and unfeeling, but this does not mean that they are psychopaths. Psychopathy is a *syndrome*—a cluster of related symptoms.

Key Symptoms of Psychopathy
Emotional/Interpersonal:
—Glib and superficial
—Egocentric and grandiose
—Lack of remorse or guilt
—Lack of empathy
—Deceitful and manipulative
—Shallow emotions
Social Deviance:
—Impulsive
—Poor behavior controls
—Need for excitement
—Lack of responsibility
—Early behavior problems
—Adult antisocial behavior

GLIB AND SUPERFICIAL
Psychopaths are often voluble and verbally facile. They can be amusing and entertaining conversationalists, ready with a clever comeback, and are able to tell unlikely but convincing stories that cast themselves in a good light. They can be very effective in presenting themselves well and are often very likable and charming.

One of my raters described an interview she did with a prisoner: "I sat down and took out my clipboard," she said, "and the first thing this guy told me was what beautiful eyes I had. He managed to work quite a few compliments on my appearance into the interview, so by the time I wrapped things up, I was feeling unusually...well, pretty. I'm a wary person especially on the job, and can

When caught in a lie or challenged with the truth, psychopaths seldom appear perplexed or embarrassed—they simply change their stories or attempt to rework the facts so they appear to be consistent with the lie.

usually spot a phony. When I got back outside, I couldn't believe I'd fallen for a line like that."

EGOCENTRIC AND GRANDIOSE

Psychopaths have a narcissistic and grossly inflated view of their own self-worth and importance, a truly astounding egocentricity and sense of entitlement, and see themselves as the center of the universe, justified in living according to their own rules. "It's not that I don't follow the law," said one subject. "I follow my own laws. I never violate my own rules." She then proceeded to describe these rules in terms of "looking out for number one."

Psychopaths often claim to have specific goals but show little appreciation regarding the qualifications required—they have no idea of how to achieve them and little or no chance of attaining these goals, given their track record and lack of sustained interest in formal education. The psychopathic inmate might outline vague plans to become a lawyer for the poor or a property tycoon. One inmate, not particularly literate, managed to copyright the title of a book he was planning to write about himself, already counting the fortune his best-selling book would bring.

LACK OF REMORSE OR GUILT

Psychopaths show a stunning lack of concern for the effects their actions have on others, no matter how devastating these might be. They may appear completely forthright about the mat-

> **The result is a series of contradictory statements and a thoroughly confused listener.**

ter, calmly stating that they have no sense of guilt, are not sorry for the ensuing pain, and that there is no reason now to be concerned.

When asked if he had any regrets about stabbing a robbery victim who subsequently spent time in the hospital as a result of his wounds, one of our subjects replied, "Get real! He spends a few months in hospital and I rot here. If I wanted to kill him I would have slit his throat. That's the kind of guy I am; I gave him a break."

Their lack of remorse or guilt is associated with a remarkable ability to rationalize their behavior, to shrug off personal responsibility for actions that cause family, friends, and others to reel with shock and disappointment. They usually have handy excuses for their behavior, and in some cases deny that it happened at all.

LACK OF EMPATHY

Many of the characteristics displayed by psychopaths are closely associated with a profound lack of empathy and inability to construct a mental and emotional "facsimile" of another person. They seem completely unable to "get into the skin" of others, except in a purely intellectual sense.

They are completely indifferent to the rights and suffering of family and strangers alike. If they do maintain ties, it is only because they see family members as possessions. One of our subjects allowed her boyfriend to sexually molest her five-year-old daughter because "he wore me out. I wasn't ready for more sex that night." The woman found it hard to understand why the authorities took her child into care.

DECEITFUL AND MANIPULATIVE

With their powers of imagination in gear and beamed on themselves, psychopaths appear amazingly unfazed by the possibility—or even by the certainty—

of being found out. When caught in a lie or challenged with the truth, they seldom appear perplexed or embarrassed—they simply change their stories or attempt to rework the facts so they appear to be consistent with the lie. The result is a series of contradictory statements and a thoroughly confused listener.

And psychopaths seem proud of their ability to lie. When asked if she lied easily, one woman laughed and replied, "I'm the best. I think it's because I sometimes admit to something bad about myself. They think, well, if she's admitting to that she must be telling the truth about the rest."

SHALLOW EMOTIONS

Psychopaths seem to suffer a kind of emotional poverty that limits the range and depth of their feelings. At times they appear to be cold and unemotional while nevertheless being prone to dramatic, shallow, and short-lived displays of feeling. Careful observers are left with the impression they are play-acting and little is going on below the surface.

A psychopath in our research said that he didn't really understand what others meant by fear. "When I rob a bank," he said, "I notice that the teller shakes. One barfed all over the money. She must have been pretty messed up inside, but I don't know why. If someone pointed a gun at me I guess I'd be afraid, but I wouldn't throw up." When asked if he ever felt his heart pound or his stomach churn, he replied, "Of course! I'm not a robot. I really get pumped up when I have sex or when I get into a fight."

IMPULSIVE

Psychopaths are unlikely to spend much time weighing the pros and cons of a course of action or considering the possible consequences. "I did it because I felt like it," is a common response.

These impulsive acts often result from an aim that plays a central role in most of the psychopath's behavior: to achieve immediate satisfaction, pleasure, or relief.

So family members, relatives, employers, and coworkers typically find themselves standing around asking themselves what happened—jobs are quit, relationships broken off, plans changed, houses ransacked, people hurt, often for what appears as little more than a whim. As the husband of a psychopath I studied put it: "She got up and left the table, and that was the last I saw of her for two months."

POOR BEHAVIOR CONTROLS

Besides being impulsive, psychopaths are highly reactive to perceived insults or slights. Most of us have powerful inhibitory controls over our behavior; even if we would like to respond aggressively we are usually able to "keep the lid on." In psychopaths, these inhibitory controls are weak, and the slightest provocation is sufficient to overcome them.

As a result, psychopaths are short-tempered or hotheaded and tend to respond to frustration, failure, discipline, and criticism with sudden violence, threats or verbal abuse. But their outbursts, extreme as they may be, are often short-lived, and they quickly act as if nothing out of the ordinary has happened.

For example, an inmate in line for dinner was accidentally bumped by another inmate, whom he proceeded to beat senseless. The attacker then stepped back into line as if nothing had happened. Despite the fact that he faced solitary confinement as punishment for the infraction, his only comment when asked to explain himself was, "I was pissed off. He stepped into my space. I did what I had to do."

Although psychopaths have a "hair trigger," their aggressive displays are "cold"; they lack the intense arousal experienced when other individuals lose their temper.

A NEED FOR EXCITEMENT

Psychopaths have an ongoing and excessive need for excitement—they long to live in the fast lane or "on the edge," where the action is. In many cases the action involves the breaking of rules.

Many psychopaths describe "doing crime" for excitement or thrills. When asked if she ever did dangerous things just

---

A Survival Guide

Although no one is completely immune to the devious machinations of the psychopath, there are some things you can do to reduce your vulnerability.

• *Know what you are dealing with.* This sounds easy but in fact can be very difficult. All the reading in the world cannot immunize you from the devastating effects of psychopaths. Everyone, including the experts, can be taken in, conned, and left bewildered by them. A good psychopath can play a concerto on *anyone's* heart strings.

• *Try not to be influenced by "props."* It is not easy to get beyond the winning smile, the captivating body language, the fast talk of the typical psychopath, all of which blind us to his or her real intentions. Many people find it difficult to deal with the intense, "predatory stare" of the psychopath. The fixated stare is more a prelude to self-gratification and the exercise of power rather than simple interest or empathic caring.

• *Don't wear blinders.* Enter new relationships with your eyes wide open. Like the rest of us, most psychopathic con-artists and "love-thieves" initially hide their dark side by putting their "best foot forward." Cracks may soon begin to appear in the mask they wear, but once trapped in their web, it will be difficult to escape financially and emotionally unscathed.

• *Keep your guard up in high-risk situations.* Some situations are tailor-made for psychopaths: singles bars, ship cruises, foreign airports, etc. In each case, the potential victim is lonely, looking for a good time, excitement, or companionship, and there will usually be someone willing to oblige, for a hidden price.

• *Know yourself.* Psychopaths are skilled at detecting and ruthlessly exploiting your weak spots. Your best defense is to understand what these spots are, and to be extremely wary of anyone who zeroes in on them.

Unfortunately, even the most careful precautions are no guarantee that you will be safe from a determined psychopath. In such cases, all you can do is try to exert some sort of damage control. This is not easy but some suggestions may be of help:

• *Obtain professional advice.* Make sure the clinician you consult is familiar with the literature on psychopathy and has had experience in dealing with psychopaths.

• *Don't blame yourself.* Whatever the reasons for being involved with a psychopath, it is important that you not accept blame for his or her attitudes and behavior. Psychopaths play by the same rules—their rules—with everyone.

• *Be aware of who the victim is.* Psychopaths often give the impression that it is *they* who are suffering and that the victims are to blame for their misery. Don't waste your sympathy on them.

• *Recognize that you are not alone.* Most psychopaths have lots of victims. It is certain that a psychopath who is causing you grief is also causing grief to others.

• *Be careful about power struggles.* Keep in mind that psychopaths have a strong need for psychological and physical control over others. This doesn't mean that you shouldn't stand up for your rights, but it will probably be difficult to do so without risking serious emotional or physical trauma.

• *Set firm ground rules.* Although power struggles with a psychopath are risky, you may be able to set up some clear rules—both for yourself and for the psychopath—to make your life easier and begin the difficult transition from victim to a person looking out for yourself.

• *Don't expect dramatic changes.* To a large extent, the personality of psychopaths is "carved in stone." There is little likelihood that anything you do will produce fundamental, sustained changes in how they see themselves or others.

• *Cut your losses.* Most victims of psychopaths end up feeling confused and hopeless, and convinced that they are largely to blame for the problem. The more you give in the more you will be taken advantage of by the psychopath's insatiable appetite for power and control.

• *Use support groups.* By the time your suspicions have led you to seek a diagnosis, you already know that you're in for a very long and bumpy ride. Make sure you have all the emotional support you can muster. ■

for fun, one of our female psychopaths replied, "Yeah, lots of things. But what I find most exciting is walking though airports with drugs. Christ! What a high!"

The flip side of this yen for excitement is an inability to tolerate routine or monotony. Psychopaths are easily bored and are not likely to engage in activities that are dull, repetitive, or require intense concentration over long periods.

LACK OF RESPONSIBILITY

Obligations and commitments mean nothing to psychopaths. Their good intentions—"I'll never cheat on you again"—are promises written on the wind.

Horrendous credit histories, for example, reveal the lightly taken debt, the loan shrugged off, the empty pledge to contribute to a child's support. Their performance on the job is erratic, with frequent absences, misuse of company resources, violations of company policy, and general untrustworthiness. They do not honor formal or implied commitments to people, organizations, or principles.

Psychopaths are not deterred by the possibility that their actions mean hardship or risk for others. A 25-year-old inmate in our studies has received more than 20 convictions for dangerous driving, driving while impaired, leaving the scene of an accident, driving without a license, and criminal negligence causing death. When asked if he would continue to drive after his release from prison, he replied, "Why not? Sure, I drive fast, but I'm good at it. It takes two to have an accident."

EARLY BEHAVIOR PROBLEMS

Most psychopaths begin to exhibit serious behavioral problems at an early age. These might include persistent lying, cheating, theft, arson, truancy, substance abuse, vandalism, and/or precocious sexuality. Because many children exhibit some of these behaviors at one time or another—especially children raised in violent neighborhoods or in disrupted or abusive families—it is important to emphasize that the psychopath's history of such behaviors is more extensive and serious than most, even when compared with that of siblings and friends raised in similar settings.

One subject, serving time for fraud, told us that as a child he would put a noose around the neck of a cat, tie the other end of the string to the top of a pole, and bat the cat around the pole with a tennis racket. Although not all adult psychopaths exhibited this degree of cruelty when in their youth, virtually all routinely got themselves into a wide range of difficulties.

ADULT ANTISOCIAL BEHAVIOR

Psychopaths see the rules and expectations of society as inconvenient and unreasonable impediments to their own behavioral expression. They make their own rules, both as children and as adults.

Many of the antisocial acts of psychopaths lead to criminal charges and convictions. Even within the criminal population, psychopaths stand out, largely because the antisocial and illegal activities of psychopaths are *more varied and frequent* than are those of other criminals. Psychopaths tend to have no particular affinity, or "specialty," for one particular type of crime but tend to try everything.

But not all psychopaths end up in jail. Many of the things they do escape detection or prosecution, or are on "the shady side of the law." For them, antisocial behavior may consist of phony stock promotions, questionable business practices, spouse or child abuse, and so forth. Many others do things that, though not necessarily illegal, are nevertheless unethical, immoral, or harmful to others: philandering or cheating on a spouse to name a few.

ORIGINS

Thinking about psychopathy leads us very quickly to a single fundamental question: Why are some people like this?

Unfortunately, the forces that produce a psychopath are still obscure, an admission those looking for clear answers will find unsatisfying. Nevertheless, there are several rudimentary theories about the cause of psychopathy worth considering. At one end of the spectrum are theories that view psychopathy as largely the product of genetic or biological factors (nature), whereas theories at the other end posit that psychopathy results entirely from a faulty early social environment (nurture).

The position that I favor is that psychopathy emerges from a complex—and poorly understood—interplay between biological factors and social forces. It is based on evidence that genetic factors contribute to the biological bases of brain function and to basic personality structure, which in turn influence the way an individual responds to, and interacts with, life experiences and the social environment. In effect, the core elements needed for the development of psychopathy—including a profound inability to experience empathy and the complete range of emotions, including fear—are in part provided by nature and possibly by some unknown biological influences on the developing fetus and neonate. As a result, the capacity for developing internal controls and conscience and for making emotional "connections" with others is greatly reduced.

CAN ANYTHING BE DONE?

In their desperate search for solutions people trapped in a destructive and seemingly hopeless relationship with a psychopath frequently are told: Quit indulging him and send him for therapy. A basic assumption of psychotherapy is that the patient needs and wants help for distressing or painful psychological and emotional problems. Successful therapy also requires that the patient actively participate, along with the therapist, in the search for relief of his or her symptoms. In short, the patient must recognize there is a problem and must want to do something about it.

But here is the crux: Psychopaths don't feel they have psychological or emotional problems, and they see no reason to change their behavior to conform with societal standards they do not agree with.

Thus, in spite of more than a century of clinical study and decades of research, the mystery of the psychopathy still remains. Recent developments have provided us with new insights into the nature of this disturbing disorder, and its borders are becoming more defined. But compared with other major clinical disorders, little research has been devoted to psychopathy, even though it is responsible for more social distress and disruption than all other psychiatric disorders combined.

So rather than trying to pick up the pieces after the damage has been done, it would make far greater sense to increase our efforts to understand this perplexing disorder and to search for effective early interventions. The alternatives are to continue devoting massive resources to the prosecution, incarceration, and supervision of psychopaths after they have committed offenses against society, and to continue to ignore the welfare and plight of their victims. We have to learn how to socialize them, not resocialize them. And this will require serious efforts at research and early intervention. It is imperative that we continue the search for clues. ∎

Excerpted from Without Conscience: The Disturbing World of the Psychopaths Among Us *(Simon & Schuster) by Robert Hare, Ph.D. Copyright © 1993 by Robert Hare.*

Seeking the Criminal Element

by W. Wayt Gibbs, *staff writer*

I magine you are the father of an eight-year-old boy," says psychologist Adrian Raine, explaining where he believes his 17 years of research on the biological basis of crime is leading. "The ethical dilemma is this: I could say to you, 'Well, we have taken a wide variety of measurements, and we can predict with 80 percent accuracy that your son is going to become seriously violent within 20 years. We can offer you a series of biological, social and cognitive intervention programs that will greatly reduce the chance of his becoming a violent offender.' What do you do? Do you place your boy in those programs and risk stigmatizing him as a violent criminal even though there is a real possibility that he is innocent? Or do you say no to the treatment and run an 80 percent chance that your child will grow up to (a) destroy his life, (b) destroy your life, (c) destroy the lives of his brothers and sisters and, most important, (d) destroy the lives of the innocent victims who suffer at his hands?"

For now, such a choice is purely hypothetical. Scientists cannot yet predict which children will become dangerously aggressive with anything like 80 percent accuracy. But increasingly, those who study the causes of criminal and violent behavior are looking beyond broad demographic characteristics such as age, race and income level to factors in individuals' personality, history, environment and physiology that seem to put them—and society—at risk. As sociologists reap the benefits of rigorous long-term studies and neuroscientists tug at the tangled web of relations between behavior and brain chemistry, many are optimistic that science will identify markers of maleficence. "This research might not pay off for 10 years, but in 10 years it might revolutionize our criminal justice system," asserts Roger D. Masters, a political scientist at Dartmouth College.

Preventive Intervention

W ith the expected advances, we're going to be able to diagnose many people who are biologically brain-prone to violence," claims Stuart C. Yudofsky, chair of the psychiatry department at Baylor College of Medicine and editor of the *Journal of Neuropsychiatry and Clinical Neurosciences*. "I'm not worried about the downside as much as I am encouraged by the opportunity to prevent tragedies—to screen people who might have high risk and to prevent them from harming someone else." Raine, Yudofsky and others argue that in order to control violence, Americans should trade their traditional concept of justice based on guilt and punishment for a "medical model" based on prevention, diagnosis and treatment.

But many scientists and observers do worry about a downside. They are concerned that some researchers underplay the enormous complexity of individual behavior and overstate sci-

Scientists are homing in on social and biological risk factors that they believe predispose individuals to criminal behavior. The knowledge could be ripe with promise—or rife with danger.

From *Scientific American, 272*, pp. 100–107, March 1995. Reprinted with permission. Copyright © 1995 by Scientific American, Inc. All rights reserved.

entists' ability to understand and predict it. They also fear that a society desperate to reduce crime might find the temptation to make premature use of such knowledge irresistible.

Indeed, the history of science's assault on crime is blemished by instances in which incorrect conclusions were used to justify cruel and unusual punishments. In the early 1930s, when the homicide rate was even higher than it is today, eugenics was in fashion. "The eugenics movement was based on the idea that certain mental illness and criminal traits were all inherited," says Ronald L. Akers, director of the Center for Studies in Criminology and Law at the University of Florida. "It was based on bad science, but they thought it was good science at the time." By 1931, 27 states had passed laws allowing compulsory sterilization of "the feeble-minded," the insane and the habitually criminal.

Studies in the late 1960s—when crime was again high and rising—revealed that many violent criminals had an extra Y chromosome and thus an extra set of "male" genes. "It was a dark day for science in Boston when they started screening babies for it," recalls Xandra O. Breakefield, a geneticist at Massachusetts General Hospital. Subsequent studies revealed that although XYY men tend to score lower on IQ tests, they are not unusually aggressive.

Social science studies on the causes of crime have been less controversial, in part because they have focused more on populations than on individuals. But as consensus builds among criminologists on a few key facts, researchers are assembling these into prediction models that try to identify the juveniles most likely to lapse into delinquency and then into violent crime.

Perhaps their most consistent finding is that a very small number of criminals are responsible for most of the violence.

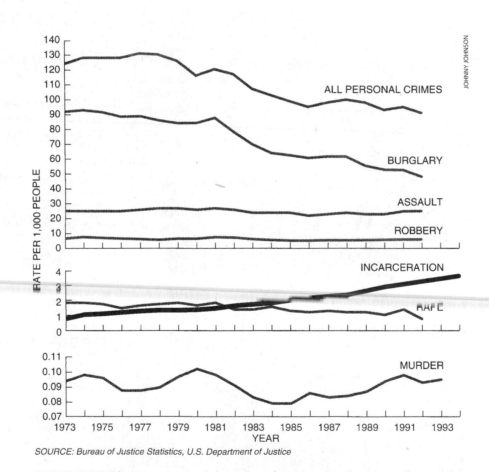

SOURCE: Bureau of Justice Statistics, U.S. Department of Justice

CRIME RATES have not responded consistently to "get tough" approaches to incarceration. Since the early 1970s the proportion of Americans behind bars has more than tripled. Property crime (including burglary, robbery and personal larceny) has dropped about 30 percent, but violent crime remains high.

Preventing just a small fraction of adolescent males from degenerating into chronic violent criminals could thus make a sizable impact on the violent crime rate, which has remained persistently high since 1973 despite a substantial decline in property crime.

One study, for example, tracked for 27 years 10,000 males born in Philadelphia in 1945; it found that just 6 percent of them committed 71 percent of the homicides, 73 percent of the rapes and 69 percent of the aggravated assaults attributed to the group.

Preventing just a small fraction of adolescent males from degenerating into chronic violent criminals could thus make a sizable impact on the violent crime rate, which has remained persistently high since 1973 despite a substantial decline in property crime. (Females accounted for only 12.5 percent of violent crime in 1992.) "For every 1 percent that we reduce violence, we save the country $1.2 billion," Raine asserts.

The problem, says Terrie E. Moffitt, a psychologist at the University of Wisconsin who is conducting long-term delinquency prediction studies, is that "a lot of adolescents participate in antisocial behavior"—87 percent, according to a survey of U.S. teens. "The vast majority desist by age 21," she says. The dangerous few "are buried within that pop- ulation of males trying out delinquency. How do you pick them out? Our hypothesis is that those who start earliest are at highest risk."

Marion S. Forgatch of the Oregon Social Learning Center tested that hypothesis on 319 boys from high-crime neighborhoods in Eugene. At the November 1994 American Society of Criminology meeting, she reported her findings: boys who had been arrested by age 14 were 17.9 times more likely to become chronic offenders than those who had not, and chronic offenders were 14.3 times more likely to commit violent offenses. "This is a good way of predicting," she says.

False Positive ID

Good is a relative term. For if one were to predict that every boy in her study who was arrested early would go on to commit violent crimes, one would be wrong more than 65 percent of the time. To statisticians, those so misidentified are known as false posi- tives. "All of these predictors have a lot of false positives—about 50 percent on average," says Akers, who recently completed a survey of delinquency prediction models. Their total accuracy is even lower, because the models also fail to identify some future criminals.

The risk factors that Akers says researchers have found to be most closely associated with delinquency are hardly surprising. Drug use tops the list, followed by family dysfunction, childhood behavior problems, deviant peers, poor school performance, inconsistent parental supervision and discipline, separation from parents, and poverty. Numerous other controlled studies have found that alcoholism, childhood abuse, low verbal IQ and witnessing violent acts are also significant risk factors. Compared with violent behavior, however, all these experiences are exceedingly common. The disparity makes it very difficult to determine which factors are causes and which merely correlates.

The difference is important, notes Mark W. Lipsey of Vanderbilt University, because "changing a risk factor if it is not causal may have no impact," and the ultimate goal of prediction is to stop violence by intervening before it begins. Unfortunately, improvements in predictive models do not necessarily translate into effective intervention strategies. Lipsey recently analyzed how well some 500 delinquency treatment programs reduced recidivism. "The conventional wisdom that nothing works is just wrong," he concludes. But he concedes that "the net effect is modest"—on average, 45 percent of program participants were rearrested, versus 50 percent of those left to their own devices. Half of that small apparent improvement, he adds, may be the result of inconsistency in the methods used to evaluate the programs.

Some strategies do work better than others, Lipsey discovered. Behavioral programs that concentrated on teaching job skills and rewarding prosocial attitudes cut rearrest rates to about 35 percent. "Scared straight" and boot camp programs, on the other hand, tended to increase recidivism slightly.

Patrick H. Tolan of the University of Illinois at Chicago has also recently published an empirical review of delinquency programs. To Lipsey's findings he adds that "family interventions have repeatedly shown efficacy for reducing antisocial behavior and appear to be among the most promising interven-

The Tangled Roots of Violence

The failure of expensive prison booms and welfare programs to beat back the historically high violent crime rates of the past 20 years has prepared fertile ground for new approaches to crime control. Encouraged by research that tentatively links a few instances of antisocial aggression with biological abnormalities, some politicians and activists are turning to science, perhaps too hastily, to identify and treat those who are likely to become dangerous.

Take the case of Everett L. "Red" Hodges, a California oilman who has spent more than $1 million to support research that implicates the trace metal manganese as a marker for violent criminal behavior. Hodges was struggling to tame a delinquent son in 1984 when he came across a *Science News* story on a study that had found high levels of lead, cadmium and copper in the head hair of violent felons.

Intrigued, Hodges offered funding to Louis A. Gottschalk, a psychiatrist at the University of California at Irvine, to conduct a

> Gottschalk did find that average levels of manganese were about 3.6 times higher in the alleged felons than in men of similar age and race at local barbershops.

controlled study to replicate the results. Analysis of hair clipped from convicted and accused felons at a prison and two county jails in southern California revealed no unusual levels of lead, cadmium or copper. But Gottschalk did find that average levels of manganese were about 3.6 times higher in the alleged felons than in men of similar age and race at local barbershops. "A new paradigm is opening in criminal justice," Hodges says, beaming. "It's a marker."

That judgment may be premature. Critics of Gottschalk's research, published in 1991 in a psychiatric (rather than a nutrition) journal, point out that average manganese levels varied from 2.2 parts per million in the prisoners to just 0.71 in one of the groups of jail inmates. Previous studies had found *lower* manganese levels in inmates than in control subjects. Skeptics also note that Gottschalk threw a wide net, measuring levels of 23 trace metals. "If you look at enough variables, you're bound to find a statistically significant association," comments Curtiss D. Hunt of

---

tions to date." According to Forgatch, two experiments in Eugene, Ore., showed that teaching parents better monitoring and more consistent, less coercive discipline techniques reduces their kids' misbehavior. "We should make parenting skills classes compulsory for high school students," argues Raine of the University of Southern California.

Unfortunately, Tolan observes, family intervention is difficult and rarely attempted. The most common kinds of programs—counseling by social workers, peer mediation and neighborhood antiviolence initiatives—are hardly ever examined to see whether they produce lasting benefits. "It usually is hard to imagine that a good idea put into action by well-meaning and enlightened people cannot help," he noted in the paper. "It may seem that any effort is better than nothing. Yet our review and several of the more long-term and sophisticated analyses suggest that both of these assumptions can be dangerously wrong. Not only have programs that have been earnestly launched been ineffective, but some of our seemingly best

ideas have led to worsening of the behavior of those subjected to the intervention."

Many researchers are thus frustrated that the Violent Crime Control and Law Enforcement Act of 1994 puts most of its $6.1 billion for crime prevention in untested and controversial programs, such as "midnight basketball" and other after-school activities. "Maybe these programs will help; maybe they won't," Tolan says. "No one has done a careful evaluation." The Crime Act does not insist that grant applicants demonstrate or even measure the effectiveness of their approach. For these and other reasons, Republicans vowed in their 1994 "Contract with America" to repeal all prevention programs in the Crime Act and to increase funding for prison construction. But that strategy ignored research. "We do know," Tolan asserts, "that locking kids up will not reduce crime and may eventually make the problem worse."

> "Not only have programs that have been earnestly launched been ineffective, but some of our seemingly best ideas have led to worsening of the behavior of those subjected to the intervention."

The failure of sociology to demonstrate conclusively effective means of controlling violent crime has made some impatient. "There is a growing recognition that we're not going to solve any problem in society using just one discipline," says Diana Fishbein, a professor of criminology at the University of Baltimore. "Sociological factors play a role. But they have not been able to explain

the Grand Forks Human Nutrition Research Center in North Dakota. "But it may be meaningless." Hunt adds that the concentration of a metal in the hair does not tell one how much is in the blood or the brain. "We know so little about manganese's role in the body that we haven't even set an RDA [recommended daily allowance] for it."

Hodges remains convinced he is on the right track. "Violence can be detected and treated," he argues. In 1987 a mugger fractured the skull of another of Hodges's sons. That year Hodges founded the Violence Research Foundation (VRF) to lobby public officials to experiment with treatment programs that use what he calls "the power of nutrition" to pacify violent criminals.

The VRF found an ally in Senator Robert Presley of California, who pushed through a bill in 1989 authorizing a study of male prisoners by Stephen Schoenthaler of California State University at Stanislaus. In the first part of the study, 402 offenders were divided randomly into three groups and given vitamin-mineral supplements equivalent to the RDA, three times the RDA or a placebo. Preliminary results

> Trace element deficiencies are just one of many frequently cited but poorly demonstrated claims that nutritional problems can cause criminal and violent behavior.

showed that rule violations among the first group dropped 38 percent during the study. Strangely, the behavior of inmates getting the higher dose did not improve significantly, whereas violations rose 20 percent among the placebo group.

Although encouraging, the equivocal results were so inconclusive that Schoenthaler decided not to publish them until he completed further studies with more controls. Hodges, however, publicized the results widely at conferences and on television talk shows, much to the scientist's annoyance.

Trace element deficiencies are just one of many frequently cited but poorly demonstrated claims that nutritional problems can cause criminal and violent behavior. A 1992 report by the Federal Bureau of Prisons stated that correctional facilities in 46 states have incorporated a wide array of dietary intervention and testing programs, even though "such programs are perceived by many physicians, scientific researchers, registered dietitians, and other health care professionals as an incorporation of food faddism into public policy." —Steven Vames and W. Wayt Gibbs

---

why one person becomes violent and another doesn't."

Some social scientists are looking to psychiatrists, neurologists and geneticists to provide answers to that question, ready or not. "Science must tell us what individuals will or will not become criminals, what individuals will or will not become victims, and what law enforcement strategies will or will not work," wrote C. Ray Jeffery, a criminologist at Florida State University, in 1994 in the *Journal of Research in Crime and Delinquency*.

Biological Factors

As medical researchers have teased out a few tantalizing links between brain chemistry, heredity, hormones, physiology and assaultive behavior, some have become emboldened. "Research in the past 10 years conclusively demonstrates that biological factors play some role in the etiology of violence. That is scientifically beyond doubt," Raine holds forth. The importance of

that role is still very much in doubt, however.

As with social risk factors, no biological abnormality has been shown to *cause* violent aggression—nor is that likely except in cases of extreme psychiatric disorder. But researchers have spotted several unusual features, too subtle even to be considered medical problems, that tend to appear in the bodies and brains of physically aggressive men. On average, for example, they have higher levels of testosterone, a sex hormone important for building muscle mass and strength, among other functions. James M. Dabbs, Jr., of Georgia State University has found in his experiments with prison inmates that men with the highest testosterone concentrations are more likely to have committed violent crimes. But Dabbs emphasizes that the link is indirect and "mediated by many social factors," such as higher rates of divorce and substance abuse.

"Low resting heart rate probably represents the best replicated biological correlate of antisocial behavior," Raine observes, pointing to 14 studies that have found that problem children and petty criminals tend to have significantly lower pulses than do well-behaved counterparts. A slower heartbeat "probably reflects fearlessness and underarousal," Raine theorizes. "If we lack

"Science must tell us what individuals will or will not become criminals, what individuals will or will not become victims, and what law enforcement strategies will or will not work."

the fear of getting hurt, it may lead to a predisposition to engage in violence." But that hypothesis fails to explain why at least 15 studies have failed to find abnormal heart rates in psychopaths.

Jerome Kagan, a Harvard University psychologist, has suggested that an inhibited "temperament" may explain why the great majority of children from high-risk homes grow up to become law-abiding citizens. One study tested pulse, pupil dilation, vocal tension and blood levels of the neurotransmitter norepinephrine and the stress-regulating hormone cortisol to distinguish inhibited from uninhibited, underaroused two-year-olds. An expert panel on "Understanding and Preventing Violence" convened by the National Research Council suggested in its 1993 report that inhibited children may be protected by their fearfulness from becoming aggressive, whereas uninhibited children may be prone to later violence. The panel concluded that "although such factors in isolation may not be expected to be strong predictors of violence, in conjunction with other early family and cognitive measures, the degree of prediction may be considerable."

Perhaps the most frequently cited biological correlate of violent behavior is a low level of serotonin, a chemical that in the body inhibits the secretion of stomach acid and stimulates smooth muscle and in the brain functions as a neurotransmitter. A large body of animal evidence links low levels of serotonin to impulsive aggression. Its role in humans is often oversimplified, however. "Serotonin has a calming effect on behavior by reducing the level of violence," Jeffery wrote in 1993 in the *Journal of Criminal Justice Education*. "Thus, by increasing the level of serotonin in the brain, we can reduce the level of violence." A front-page article in December 1993 in the *Chicago Tribune* explained that "when serotonin declines... impulsive aggression is unleashed."

Such explanations do violence to the science. In human experiments, researchers do not generally have access to the serotonin inside their subject's braincase. Instead they tap cerebrospinal fluid from the spinal column and measure the concentration of 5-hydroxyindoleacetic acid (5-HIAA), which is produced when serotonin is used up and broken down by the enzyme monoamine oxidase (MAO). Serotonin does its job by binding to any of more than a dozen different neural receptors, each of which seems to perform a distinct function. The low levels of 5-HIAA seen in violent offenders may indicate a shortage of serotonin in the brain or simply a dearth of MAO—in which case their serotonin levels may actually be high. Moreover, serotonin can rise or drop in different regions of the brain at different times, with markedly different effects.

Environment, too, plays a role: nonhuman primate studies show that serotonin often fluctuates with pecking order, dropping in animals when they are threatened and rising when they assume a dominant status. The numerous pathways through which serotonin can influence mood and behavior confound attempts to simply "reduce the level of violence" by administering serotonin boosters such as Prozac, a widely prescribed antidepressant. Nevertheless, the link between 5-HIAA and impulsive aggression has led to a concerted hunt for the genes that control the production and activity of serotonin and several other neurotransmitters. "Right now we have in our hand many of the genes that affect brain function," says David Goldman, chief of neurogenetics at the National Institute on Alcohol Abuse and Alcoholism. Although none has yet been shown to presage violence, "I believe the markers are there," he says. But he warns that "we're going to have to understand a whole lot more about the genetic, environmental and developmental origins of personality and psychiatric disease" before making use of the knowledge.

Yudofsky is less circumspect. "We are on the verge of a revolution in genetic medicine," he asserts. "The future will be to understand the genetics of aggressive disorders and to identify those who have greater tendencies to become violent."

Few researchers believe genetics alone will ever yield reliable predictors of behavior as complex and multifarious as harmful aggression. Still, the notion that biologists and sociologists might together be able to assemble a complicated model that can scientifically pick out those who pose the greatest threat of vicious attack seems to be gaining currency. Already some well-respected behavioral scientists are advocating a medical approach to crime control based on screening, diagnostic prediction and treatment. "A future generation will reconceptualize nontrivial recidivistic crime as a disorder," Raine predicted in his book, *The Psychopathology of Crime*.

Compulsory Treatment?

But the medical model of crime may be fraught with peril. When the "disease" is intolerable behavior that threatens society, will "treatment" necessarily be compulsory and indefinite? If, to reexamine Raine's hypothetical example, prediction models are judged reliable but "biological, social and cognitive intervention programs" are not,

"Right now we have in our hand many of the genes that affect brain function. . . . I believe the markers are there."

For Biological Studies, Minorities Need Not Apply

Scientists pursuing the role of biology in violent behavior have been twice shy since 1992, when shrill public criticism forced the National Institutes of Health to withdraw financial support of a conference on the ethical implications of "Genetic Factors in Crime" and compelled former health secretary Louis Sullivan to abort his proposed "Violence Initiative." Led by firebrand psychiatrist Peter Breggin, critics charged that in a society where blacks account for 12.4 percent of the population but 44.8 percent of arrests for violent crimes, such research plays into the hands of racists.

The controversy did little to dissuade scientists from their studies, which continue to grow in number. The NIH reinstated funding for the genetics conference and increased its budget for violence-related research to $58 million. Most Violence Initiative projects found support in other programs. In December 1994 the National Science Foundation began soliciting proposals for a $12-million, five-year violence research consortium.

But the political wrangling seems to have intimidated investigators from including minorities in any violence studies with a biological tinge—and from collecting medical data in multiracial studies. Designers of an 11,000-subject, eight-year study of the causes of crime in Chicago, for example, decided not to collect blood and urine samples when in 1994 Breggin organized rallies to block the project, says Felton Earls, a Harvard University professor and co-director of the study. As a result of such opposition and pressure, asserts Adrian Raine of the University of Southern California, "all the biological and genetic studies conducted to date have been done on whites. Scientifically, we can make no statements on the biological basis of violence and crime in blacks or Hispanics or Asians."

There is no reason to suspect that any genetic connection links race to antisocial behavior. But there is reason to be concerned that ostensibly objective biological studies, blindly ignoring social and cultural differences, could misguidedly reinforce racial stereotypes. Still, Earls, Raine and other researchers emphasize that biological factors, if they exist, are important only insofar as they protect individuals from—or make them vulnerable to—bad influences in their family, school and neighborhood. Research that excludes those who are most burdened by such pressures may be most expedient, but is it most useful?   —W. W. G.

---

might eight-year-old boys be judged incorrigible before they have broken any law? Calls for screening are now heard more often. "There are areas where we can begin to incorporate biological approaches," Fishbein argues. "Delinquents need to be individually assessed." Masters claims that "we now know enough about the serotonergic system so that if we see a kid doing poorly in school, we ought to look at his serotonin levels."

In his article Jeffery emphasized that "attention must focus on the 5 percent of the delinquent population who commit 50 percent of the offenses.... This effort must identify high-risk persons at an early age and place them in treatment programs before they have committed the 10 to 20 major felonies characteristic of the career criminal."

Yudofsky suggests a concrete method to do this: "You could ask parents whether they consider their infant highstrung or hyperactive. Then screen more closely by challenging the infants with provocative situations." When kids respond too aggressively, he suggests "you could do careful neurologic testing and train the family how not to goad and fight them. Teach the children nonviolent ways to reduce frustration. And when these things don't work, consider medical interventions, such as beta blockers, anticonvulsants or lithium.

"We haven't done this research, but I have no doubt that it would make an enormous impact and would be imme-diately cost-effective," Yudofsky continues. While he bemoans a lack of drugs designed specifically to treat aggression, he sees a tremendous "opportunity for the pharmaceutical industry," which he maintains is "finally getting interested."

But some worry that voluntary screening for the good of the child might lead to mandatory screening for the protection of society. "It is one thing to convict someone of an offense and compel them to do something. It is another thing to go to someone who has not done anything wrong and say, 'You look like a high risk, so you have to do this,'" Akers observes. "There is a very clear ethical difference, but that is a very thin line that people, especially politicians, might cross over."

Even compelling convicted criminals to undergo treatment raises thorny ethical issues. Today the standards for proving that an offender is so mentally ill that he poses a danger to himself or others and thus can be incarcerated indefinitely are quite high. The medical model of violent crime threatens to lower those standards substantially. Indeed, Jeffery argues that "if we are to follow the medical model, we must use neurological examinations in place of the insanity defense and the concept of guilt. Criminals must be placed in medical clinics, not prisons." Fishbein says she is "beginning to think that treatment should be mandatory. We don't ask offenders whether they want to be incarcerated or executed. They should re-main in a secure facility until they can show without a doubt that they are self-controlled." And if no effective treatments are available? "They should be held indefinitely," she says.

Moral Imperative

Unraveling the mystery of human behavior, just like untangling the human genetic code, creates a moral imperative to use that knowledge. To ignore it—to imprison without treatment those whom society defines as sick for the behavioral symptoms of their illness—is morally indefensible. But to replace a fixed term of punishment set by the conscience of a society with forced therapy based on the judgment of scientific experts is to invite even greater injustice.   SA

Further Reading

THE PSYCHOPATHOLOGY OF CRIME. Adrian Raine. Academic Press, 1993.
UNDERSTANDING AND PREVENTING VIOLENCE. Edited by A. J. Reiss, Jr., and J. A. Roth. National Academy Press, 1993.
WHAT WORKS IN REDUCING ADOLESCENT VIOLENCE. Patrick Tolan and Nancy Guerra. Available from the Center for the Study and Prevention of Violence, University of Colorado, 1994.
Crime statistics and violence prevention program information are available on the World Wide Web at http://www.ojp.usdoj.gov/bjs

THE RAGE OF INNOCENTS

Childhood trauma may string the biochemical trip wires that can set off later explosions of violence

BY CRAIG F. FERRIS

TOUGH LOVE WAS NOT ENOUGH FOR Rachel. Foster home after foster home had already given up trying to cope with her uncontrollable rages; now another one was about to do the same. When the nine-year-old started to lash out indiscriminately, flailing and kicking, her foster parents would have to pin her to the floor for an hour until she calmed down. Finally they, too, threw in the towel. They had Rachel admitted to a hospital, where a child psychiatrist translated her paroxysms of violence into the neutral vocabulary of the *Diagnostic and Statistical Manual*: attention deficit/hyperactive disorder together with conduct disorder, a blanket term covering a wide range of antisocial behavior.

The health-care workers took things a step at a time. First they took Rachel off all previous medication and put her in a quiet, nonthreatening environment, where they kept her under constant supervision. Then came three weeks of talk therapy and behavioral therapy (rewards for good behavior, time-outs for bad behavior). Her overall behavior improved markedly, but she would still explode without warning, attacking and hitting anyone within reach. The hospital staff gave Rachel a drug to manage her hyperactivity, then, when that failed to curb her aggressive behavior, another drug to stimulate her serotonin system. The combination of treatments did the trick: Rachel was quiet. She left the hospital after six weeks. Everyone who had treated her expected to see her again.

I never met Rachel. I heard about her in a case study that Joseph A. Gartner, a pediatric psychiatrist at the State Uni-versity of New York at Stony Brook, presented last fall at a three-day conference I helped organize, with the sponsorship of the New York Academy of Sciences: "Understanding Aggressive Behavior in Children." At the conference, held at Rockefeller University in New

> "HOW DO KIDS GET THIS way? How are drugs acting to improve their behavior?"

York City, more than thirty biologists, clinicians and social scientists met to discuss the effects of the social and physical environment on childhood aggression. Among the children cited at the conference, Rachel was one of the few whose behavioral problems could be linked to psychiatric illness. What was typical about her case was her treatment, a multi-modal mix of behavioral therapy, psychotherapy and medication that is standard practice. Pressured by shrinking budgets and the deadlines of managed health care, clinicians are faced with the ethical dilemma of turning to the quick fix offered by psychopharmacology. Yet, though available drugs are far from perfect, relatively little research is being con-ducted into how they work or how they might be improved.

"How do kids get this way? How are drugs acting to im-prove their behavior? What effects do such drugs have on an immature nervous system?" No one really knows the answers to such questions, noted Daniel F. Connor, direc-tor of pediatric psychopharmacology at the University of Massachusetts Medical Center in Worcester. Drugs for managing aggression have been tested almost exclusively on adult psychiatric patients; their biological effects on

This article is reprinted with permission of *The Sciences* and is from the March/April 1996 issue, pp. 22–26. Individual subscrip-tions are $21 per year in the U.S. Write to: The Sciences, 2 East 63rd Street, New York, NY 10021.

children are poorly known. The government and the pharmaceutical industry, however, have shied away from developing new treatments to manage violent behavior. As a result, Connor said, children such as Rachel, who might benefit from more-effective medication, remain "research orphans."

Studies by social scientists show that young children identified as impulsive, highly aggressive and disruptive in school track for social failure. They are at risk for future truancy, delinquency, drug abuse, depression, violence and suicide. Abusive parents or other caregivers tend to pass their antisocial behavior on to their children ("violence begets violence"). The dismal cycle is not all-powerful—most classroom troublemakers do not end up in a life of crime and violence, and some children seem mysteriously immune to the effects of childhood victimization—but its grip can be strong. Some children, identified early in life as highly aggressive, show the same antisocial behavior through adolescence.

How early does it start? Some scientists and laypeople believe that such intractable, apparently hereditary behavior must be hard-wired into a person's genes at the moment of conception. Biology, they hope, will solve social problems by showing how to find the defective genes and repair them—or at any rate by revealing which children might pose threats to themselves and to society. In my opinion that hope is premature and, indeed, irresponsible. The evidence of a genetic component to childhood aggression is thin. Almost all of it links the genes not to violent behavior, as such, but to neuropsychiatric illness (most cases of which are non-violent). Elsewhere the contribution of the genes gets lost amid a welter of social factors: prenatal exposure to drugs; parental criminality and unemployment; illiteracy; peer pressure; drug abuse; poverty; neglect; abuse. Such environmental factors have long been known to have powerful effects on a child's personality; now, through studies of laboratory animals, neurobiologists are starting to reveal how those factors alter the biology of the brain. The studies strongly suggest that the most important biological flaws putting children at risk for future violent behavior creep into the brain at certain critical times: developmental windows during which the brain and the nervous system are extremely sensitive to environmental and emotional insults that shape how an organism responds to stress.

> CAN BIOLOGY CURE violence by repairing defective genes? Such a hope is premature—indeed, irresponsible.

O F THE MANY FORMS OF ABUSE AND NEGLECT, perhaps the most damaging to a child is the absence of a mother. A young child or infant lives in a state of constant sensory agitation. To channel that arousal into calm and well-being, the child ordinarily relies on love and physical contact with a mother, father, grandparent, adopted parent or other caregiver. Without such loving physical attention, infants or children may withdraw into themselves, ignoring the outside world and stimulating themselves by repetitive rocking, self-clasping and other stereotypic movements. Later, children de-

prived of a reliable and consistent primary caregiver are at risk of developing problems in controlling their feelings and their behavioral responses to stress. Perhaps as a means of coping with their own anguish, many of them never learn to empathize with the pain and suffering of others. Unable to read the emotions of the people around them, they may stumble into conflicts that emotionally literate children would avoid. By the time they enter school, it may already be too late for them to find the tools they need to build healthy relationships with others.

> OF THE MANY FORMS OF abuse and neglect, perhaps the most damaging to a child is the absence of a mother.

The horrific consequences of maternal deprivation are told in the work of the late psychologist Harry F. Harlow. For more than two decades Harlow and his coworkers at the University of Wisconsin–Madison Primate Laboratory and Regional Primate Research Center bred rhesus monkeys and separated the babies from their mothers at birth. For six months (a period comparable to the first two years in the life of a human child) the young monkeys were given no chance to form bonds with other monkeys. Some were raised in partial isolation, able to see and sometimes touch their human keepers; others neither saw nor interacted with any other living creature.

One result of deprivation is what in human children would be called a learning disability. Monkeys raised in complete isolation can learn to perform many simple tasks as well as other monkeys do, but they lag behind on more complex tasks. For example, they are as good as the control group at concurrent object discrimination—learning to choose "correctly" from a series of paired objects in exchange for rewards. But they have a harder time with oddity discrimination, such as choosing the unusual ball from a group of two blue balls and one red one.

Later on the motherless monkeys develop severe social disturbances. Animals raised in partial isolation show exaggerated oral behaviors, such as thumb and toe sucking. Like emotionally neglected children, they may clutch themselves, rock back and forth for hours on end or repeat a series of stereotypic movements. Many of them mutilate themselves, attacking one of their own arms or legs as if it were a disembodied intruder. Placed in a cage with other young monkeys, they become impulsive, fearful and aggressive. Over time some of them may assimilate into a monkey group and blend in with the crowd, but when confronted with a stressful circumstance (such as the introduction of a strange monkey into the group), they revert to the behaviors that marked their time in isolation: withdrawal, stereotypy and violence.

M ONKEYS RAISED IN TOTAL ISOLATION SUFfer even more devastating, and permanent, changes in psychosocial behavior. It is extraordinarily hard to habituate them into social groups. Most of them remain permanent outsiders, incapable of learning from or communicating with their peers and prone to lashing out indiscriminately at other monkeys—infants and adults alike. Females show no interest in sex.

When artificially impregnated, the mothers at best reject and ignore their babies, and they often attack or even kill the offspring.

Even when once-neglected monkeys join a group and appear normal, the indelible mark of the early deprivation remains on their neurochemistry. At the University of Wisconsin–Madison, the behavioral neurobiologist Gary W. Kraemer and his coworkers raised monkeys in isolation, let them join a group and later treated all the monkeys with low doses of amphetamine. The normal, group-reared monkeys appeared unaffected by the drug. The neglected monkeys, however, went wild, attacking and killing others in the group.

> SIMPLY HANDLING newborn rats can trigger a cascade of molecular events that determine how the rats respond to stress as adults.

The possible parallels to human behavior are frighteningly obvious. Neglected and abused children are at risk for future drug abuse, which begins perhaps as self-medication to alleviate the hostility, depression or suicidal ideas that fill their minds. Kraemer's work raises the possibility that the young people who seek such an escape may be the very ones least likely to withstand it, their nervous systems strung with chemical trip wires for extreme, unpredictable violence.

SIMILAR CONSEQUENCES OF EARLY ABUSE AND neglect appear in studies of laboratory rodents. In a series of elegant experiments, the neurobiologist Michael J. Meaney and his coworkers at McGill University in Montreal, Canada, showed how something as simple as handling newborn rat pups can trigger a cascade of molecular events that determine how the rats respond to stress as adults. In mammals, stress is managed largely by chemical interactions among three kinds of glands: the adrenal glands, resting atop the kidneys, and the hypothalamus and the pituitary gland, both near the base of the brain.

When that system of glands (known as the adrenal-pituitary-hypothalmic axis, or stress axis) is activated, the pituitary gland signals the adrenal glands to release stress hormones called glucocorticoids, which affect a wide array of bodily processes. Normal levels of glucocorticoids are beneficial, indeed, essential to good health, but excessive levels can contribute to nerve damage, heart disease and a crippled immune system. The brain monitors their concentration in the bloodstream and turns down the flow whenever the level creeps into the danger zone. The hormone detectors are receptor cells in the brain. The more receptors there are, the better the brain can control the body's reaction to stress.

Meaney and his colleagues divided newborn rats into two groups. Rat pups in the first group stayed with their mothers, undisturbed; pups in the second group were gently handled for fifteen minutes a day. It turned out that handling rat pups increased the early activity of serotonin, a neurotransmitter that appears to be instrumental in controlling aggressive behavior and in directing the development of the nervous system. As a result, the young rats' brains produced more glucocorticoid receptors in the hippocampus and the frontal cortex, areas of the brain that control the stress axis. Later, compared with the control group, adult rats that had been handled were better able to cope with acute and chronic stress. They also lived longer and had healthier immune systems and fewer nerve-related illnesses. The results provide evidence that there are critical developmental windows during which environmental events can have a lifelong effect on the neural mechanisms that determine how an individual perceives and responds to stress.

THE NEXT CRITICAL DEVELOPMENTAL WINDOW is adolescence. In people adolescence is defined as a period of pronounced physical, cognitive and emotional growth that begins just before puberty and ends in early adulthood with sexual maturity, social awareness and independence. Many other animals go through a similar stage of development. One of them is the golden hamster. When hamsters are between twenty-five and forty-two days of age, they leave their mothers' nests, double their weight and size, reach full sexual maturity and start to breed and establish social relationships.

At the University of Massachusetts Medical Center the behavioral neurobiologists Yvon Delville and Richard H. Melloni Jr. and I have studied the behavioral and biological consequences that ensued when hamsters in our laboratory suffered the equivalent of a troubled adolescence. When the hamsters reached twenty-five days old, we started putting some of them into the home cage of an adult hamster experienced in fighting. Adult hamsters routinely challenge and attack intruders; one hour a day for two weeks, the adolescent intruders were chased, nipped and threatened. Several days after the physical and emotional abuse had ceased, we turned the tables and introduced intruders into the cages of the former victims.

The results were dramatic. Faced with smaller, more timid opponents, the previously abused hamsters attacked fiercely, launching biting attacks both more quickly and more often than normal for a hamster defending its territory. When confronted by intruders of equal weight and size, however, the same animals were abnormally timid—like a playground bully who gleefully pummels a younger child but runs away when the victim's big brother shows up.

Behind such extreme, context-dependent fighting behavior lies stress and the brain's responsiveness to stress hormones. To prove the link, the behavioral neurobiologist Diane M. Hayden-Hixson, then a graduate student in my laboratory, mimicked the behavior by injecting glucocorticoids directly into the hypothalamuses of hamsters. Starting with more than a hundred dominant adult male hamsters, she injected each animal with either a small crystalline pellet of cortisol (a glucocorticoid) or a control pellet of cholesterol, a chemical that does not affect aggression. The next day she put each hamster with a cortisol implant into a neutral arena with a similar-size hamster from the control group, then observed the ensuing confrontations. In every case, the hamster with the cortisol implant fled from its cholesterol-treated opponent. When matched with opponents specially chosen for submissive behavior, however, the hamsters dosed with cortisol promptly attacked.

Apparently the higher cortisol levels in the hypothalamus distorted the way the hamsters perceived and assessed risk, creating a volatile mixture of fearfulness, hypervigilance and the misinterpretation of threats—a recipe for violence. Whatever the exact ingredients might be, the flame under the cooking pot, it appears, is stress. Hamsters that are continually subjugated and lose fights against stronger opponents have a disrupted stress axis. Long after a fight is over, levels of glucocorticoids in their bloodstreams remain abnormally high.

FOR SEVERAL YEARS INVESTIGATORS IN MY LABoratory have examined how two neurotransmitters, serotonin and vasopressin, interact to control aggression. In many species, including humans, aggressive behavior is inversely correlated with the level of serotonin in the brain. Rats, for instance, become much more aggressive when they are given drugs that interfere with the serotonin receptors. When rats are given drugs that increase serotonin levels or stimulate serotonin receptors, the numbers of attacks and bites drop. One drug that increases the level of free serotonin in the brain is fluoxetine, better known as Prozac, which prevents nerve cells from removing the serotonin they produce. Our studies have shown that hamsters injected with fluoxetine do not attack or bite intruders.

Whereas serotonin dampens aggression, vasopressin fuels it. Blocking the vasopressin receptors in the hypothalamus of male hamsters makes the hamsters less aggressive toward intruders; injecting vasopressin directly into the hypothalamus makes them more aggressive. Other investigators have induced similar effects in rats and voles. What is the relation between serotonin and vasopressin? Our hamster studies indicate that serotonin may decrease aggressive behavior, in part, by inhibiting the activity of the vasopressin neurons.

A recent clinical study indicates that the neurotransmitters may be similarly intertwined in people. Emil F. Coccaro, a psychiatrist at the Medical College of Pennsylvania and Hahnemann University in Philadelphia, examined psychiatric patients who had been diagnosed as having personality disorders and most of whom had a history of violence. Coccaro gave the patients fenfluramine, a drug that stimulates nerve endings to release serotonin. Then he tested their blood for a rise in the level of the pituitary hormone prolactin, an indicator of serotonin activity. Coccaro discovered that the more violent the person tested, the more feebly the serotonin system responded to the drug; apparently, aggressive tendencies and a weak serotonin system go hand in hand. The more aggressive subjects also tended to have higher levels of vasopressin in their cerebrospinal fluid. Thus, in people, an inefficient serotonin system may let vasopressin build up in the central nervous system, priming the body for aggressive behavior.

DO EARLY ABUSE AND NEGLECT ALTER THE development of the vasopressin and serotonin systems, thereby predisposing the victims to impulsive and potentially violent behavior? If so, when are children most at risk? When do the developmental windows open; how long do they last; and what biological events lie behind them? What is the most effective way of treating early environmental damage? Why are some children vulnerable and others resilient?

The studies conducted so far have only scratched the surface of such questions. What they do show, unequivocally, is how pointless it is to argue whether childhood violence is, say, 60 percent genetic and 40 percent environmental or the other way around. Such arguments miss the point. Change an organism's behavior, and you change how the organism perceives and interacts with its environment. Change that, and you change the expression of the genes. Change that, and you change behavior. In effect, all behavior is 100 percent hereditary and 100 percent environmental, in an inextricable tangle.

Last July, at the medical center where I work, I heard a thought-provoking talk by Ronald D. G. McKay, a neurobiologist at the National Institutes of Health in Bethesda, Maryland. McKay described how, in a neat piece of experimental neurosurgery, he and his team had implanted cultured cells in the brains of newborn rats. The cultured cells were neuronal stem cells from a rat fetus—small, spherical bodies that, had they been left in place, would have developed into spindly nerve cells in the hippocampus. When McKay put them into the hippocampus of a newborn rat, they did just that. But when he put them into the cerebellum—functionally and biochemically a very different place—the stem cells abandoned their original programming and turned into cerebellar nerve cells. Growth factors and other environmental signals nudged them to forge connections with surrounding neurons, altered their sensitivity to future signals, reprogrammed their responsivity to environmental changes. If a cell failed to connect with the neural network around it, the cell died.

One set of genes, different environments, different destinies, an imperative to fit in or die: I can think of no better metaphor for the development of a child's personality, no sharper warning of the penalty paid by those for whom things go disastrously wrong. ●

> IT IS POINTLESS TO ARGUE about nature versus nurture. Behavior is 100 percent hereditary and 100 percent environmental.

CRAIG F. FERRIS *is a professor of psychiatry and physiology and director of neuropsychiatric sciences in the psychiatry department at the University of Massachusetts Medical Center in Worcester. With his colleague Thomas Grisso, he organized the conference "Understanding Aggressive Behavior in Children," sponsored by the New York Academy of Sciences at Rockefeller University from September 29 until October 2, 1995.*

PRISONERS OF PLEASURE?

People will abuse anything from cream cakes to crack. What can or should a society do about it in the face of escalating addiction? In the first of three articles, **David Concar** asks whether we can ever hope to understand what makes some of us turn to drugs

Illustrations: Andy White

THE year is 2025 and you are the troubled parent of a teenage boy. You suspect his friends have started to do drugs—and not just the occasional line of coke. "SuperA's", synthetic opiates with twice the potency of heroin, are in vogue, and there's a new amphetamine on the streets, "storm", that's said to kick into the brain like crack, only quicker. You've heard talk about some people being inherently vulnerable to drug abuse. Is your child one of them? Didn't your father do coke back in the 1980s? And wasn't your grandfather an alcoholic?

Desperate for reassurance, you book your child into the nearest Dependency Diagnosis Center, where he's subjected to a bewildering range of tests—DNA profiling, neural imaging, psychological questionnaires, life history analysis. A few weeks later comes the diagnosis: "Environmental risk factors for substance dependency, normal; biological risk factors, high." You must do what you can to keep him away from drugs, pay for "aversion" counselling, or put him on a medication designed to kill off any chance of drug-induced euphoria.

At the moment, this scenario is just a bleak flight of fancy. Some would say it could never be otherwise. The causes of substance abuse are too much of a mishmash of biology, social circumstances and life experience to be coldly dissected and quantified in this way.

Or are they? Edythe London, a researcher at the National Institute on Drug Abuse in Baltimore, Maryland, is bringing what shes describes as a "flashlight" to the problem—the brain-imaging technique of positron emission tomography. This year she and her colleagues identified what they believe are telling differences in brain activity between addicts and nonaddicts. Scans of "detoxified" drug abusers revealed evidence of unusually high levels of neural activity in an area of the brain thought to be involved in judgment and reward-seeking behaviours, the orbitofrontal cortex. Could these differences ever be used to identify people at unusually high risk of drug dependency?

London is optimistic: "If we can establish a link between abnormality in the orbitofrontal cortex and vulnerability to addiction, then I think we'll have a case for thinking about intervening with adolescents." That could involve counselling or, in future, offering medications to ward off addictive behaviour, she says.

But none of this is going to happen in a hurry—and not just because some people might object to implementing tests that could absolve addicts of personal responsibility ('I can't help it, it's the way I'm made'), or policy makers of the need to tackle the social causes of drug abuse ('Why throw good money after bad genes and brain chemistry?'). No, there's a more basic obstacle: at the moment, the researchers cannot say whether the brain "abnormalities" exposed by PET imaging are a cause or an effect of drug abuse.

It's a problem that crops up time and again in addiction research. Psychiatrists report a high prevalence of antisocial behaviour, depression and paranoia in cocaine abusers—but again, are these causes or effects of drug abuse? Biochemists report unusually low levels of certain messenger molecules or receptors in the brains of chronic alcoholics: are these part of the reason why some people turn to booze, or are they biological adaptations to heavy alcohol consumption? A sociologist reports a high level of drug abuse in people who have recently lost their jobs: did they turn to drugs because of unemployment, or get fired because they were drug abusers? If you're trying to tease apart the reasons why people get hooked in the first place, it's all hopelessly confusing.

One way of cutting through this cause-and-effect problem is to look for genes linked to addictive behaviour. Taking drugs might alter brain chemistry and personality, but it doesn't affect genetic makeup. Here, however, researchers face other gigantic challenges. First, how to define addictive behaviour. Is the bottle-a-day whisky merchant suffering from the same problem as the twice-weekly binger? And secondly, how to identify links between addictive behaviour and "nature" when the influence of "nurture" is clearly so strong and many different genes are likely to be involved. In effect, researchers are looking for faint genetic signals against a noisy background of life history and social circumstance.

The ongoing debacle of the so-called "alcoholism gene" throws all this into stark relief. At the centre of the controversy is

> **'Is the compulsive shouting of obscenities really on the same biological spectrum as slot-machine mania?'**

Ken Blum, a pharmacologist at the University of Texas at San Antonio. Four years ago, Blum and his colleagues reported, to a fanfare of press coverage, what they claimed to be the first example of a gene linked to alcoholism. Dubbed the "A1 allele", it was one of four naturally occurring forms of a gene encoding a receptor for a brain chemical known as dopamine. By no means a certain passport to Alcoholics Anonymous, the gene just made some people more vulnerable to alcoholism than they might otherwise

From *New Scientist*, 144, pp. 26–31, October 1, 1994. Reprinted by permission of IPC Magazines Ltd.

be. Or so the researchers claimed.

Even so, jaws dropped. How could any one gene play such a dominant role in a complicated behaviour like alcoholism? A frenzied round of attempted replications followed in which other teams drew a conspicuous blank. Blum and his colleagues soon found themselves accused of building a palace on quicksand. Unabashed, however, they continued to look for fresh evidence. Now they are extending their claims. The A1 allele doesn't just predispose people to alcoholism, says Blum, it's a risk factor for a breathtaking range of other "compulsive diseases"—crack and heroin abuse, Tourette's syndrome, compulsive gambling, carbohydrate bingeing. "If you carry the A1 allele," he says, "the chances you will have some kind of addiction at some point in your life are 75 per cent."

Nor does Blum stop there. He likes to call the A1 allele a defective "reward gene" and argues that, at bottom, all the disparate kingdoms of addiction and compulsive disease can be viewed as members of one gigantic medical superstate—"reward deficiency syndrome". It's the single biggest health problem in the world, says Blum, affecting tens of millions of people in the US alone. And to add one final inflammatory twist, the frequency of the A1 allele varies from one ethnic group to another, being highest in American Indians and lowest in Hebrews.

Much of this incites scepticism from other researchers. Is the harried executive who can't get through the day without a couple of lines of coke really suffering from the same basic deficiency as the 16-year-old streetwalker from an underprivileged background who's hooked on crack? Is the compulsive shouting of obscenities really on the same biological spectrum as slot-machine mania? But not everyone is so dismissive of Blum's core

'There are no genes that raise a glass to someone's lips, but it's crazy to say there is no genetic influence on addiction'

claim. This year alone, teams in France, Japan and Finland have reported findings linking the A1 allele to addictive behaviour. Even so, the debate has reached something of an impasse, partly because nobody seems able to agree on what would constitute a good control group of subjects—or indeed on how to set the boundaries of alcoholism. Do you draw the line at the equivalent of one bottle of wine a day, or two or three? Should your control group exclude alcoholics and other substance abusers? Ask geneticists about it and most throw up their hands in despair.

Body sway

Yet most researchers do at least agree that some of our biological reactions to addictive drugs are partly hereditary. "There are no genes that raise a glass to someone's lips, but it's crazy to say there's no genetic influence on addiction," says Hugh Gurling, a geneticist at University College London. There's some evidence, for instance, that the rate we break down alcohol in the blood might be partly inherited. And one study has even examined alcohol-induced body sway, claiming it is markedly lower in healthy men with an alcoholic sibling or parent than in men with no known alcoholic relatives.

It's easy to question the relevance of such findings, but studies of alcoholism in adoptees are harder to dismiss. In the 1980s, researchers found that 62 per cent of a group of male adoptees whose biological parents had been alcoholics had become alcoholics themselves—in some cases even when their adopted parents had been teetotallers. By contrast only 24 per cent of a control group of adoptees were alcoholic.

All well and good, but can we predict who might be at risk? C. Robert Cloninger, a psychiatrist at Washington University in St Louis, Missouri, believes we can, up to a point. He postulates that there are two broad types of alcoholism which match up with distinct personality traits. The evidence comes questionnaire-based tests and interviews. "Type 2"

. . . But can we predict who might be at risk? C. Robert Cloninger, a psychiatrist at Washington University in St. Louis . . . postulates that there are two broad types of alcoholism which match up with distinct personality traits.

alcoholics—the most severe abusers—come out on the high end of a scale for "novelty seeking", and on the low ends of scales for "harm avoidance" and "reward dependence". In other words, they are typically reckless, self-destructive and antisocial. By contrast, "type 1" alcoholics—the "problem drinkers"—tend to be cautious, fearful and constantly seeking social approval. Cloninger says that it is possible to identify these extreme temperaments in individuals as young as 10 years old. More controversially, he also believes such tests could be used to identify children at risk of addiction.

But even if that's the case, researchers are a long way from identifying the neurochemical basis of such traits, let alone the genes and environmental factors that might influence them. In the meantime, many are hoping that clues to the causes of drug dependency will come from very different quarters: neurobiological studies of the way different drugs interact with neurons in the brain.

Few would deny that the way people respond to the rewarding effects of drugs could, in principle, be influenced by their biological make-up. The clearest evidence comes from a classic experiment done in the 1970s. In controlled conditions, researchers offered a group of people with no known history of drug abuse the choice of two unmarked pills, one an amphetamine stimulant, the other a placebo. Some subjects always preferred the placebo, while others switched from placebo to amphetamine when asked to do demanding tasks. But a third subgroup always chose the amphetamine. Were these nature's own speed merchants, people biologically predisposed to getting a kick out of amphetamines? And if they were, what role could that kick conceivably play in addiction?

A couple of decades ago, the answer would have been "a small one". Researchers believed it was fear of physical withdrawal symptoms that mainly kept people hooked—flu-like symptoms in the case of heroin dependency, and convulsions and seizures in the case of severe alcohol dependency. Since cocaine doesn't induce any such symptoms, some even doubted it was truly addictive. Times have changed. The crack epidemic has arrived and it's clear to everyone that avoiding cold turkey is only part of the equation of dependency. Euphoria must also play a part. But what part?

Clues are coming thick and fast from studies of how drugs of abuse interact with the brain's "reward" systems. Cocaine, heroin, nicotine and alcohol all exert different patterns of influence on the brain's systems of neurons and neurotransmitters. Yet over the past decade it has become clear that they share one powerful attribute: the ability to hijack some of the neural pathways in the brain that make eating, having sex and mothering infants seem pleasurable and worth repeating. In cold biological terms, the threat of addiction is the price we must pay for having evolved the capacity to respond to pleasure; or if you like, for not being bored to death by sex and food.

And this is where dopamine enters the picture. The neural pathways in question

Animals seeking oblivion

A HERD of waterbuffalo browses on opium poppies, wild elephants gorge themselves on fermented fruits, and a heroin addict shoots up in a disused railyard. What do they have in common? The pursuit of intoxication is rife in the animal kingdom. But are animals motivated in the same way as human drug addicts? Or is the self-destructive nature of drug addiction a uniquely human trait?

Intoxication satisfies a basic biological need in the same way that food, drink and sex do. Or so says Ronald Siegel, a psychopharmacologist at the University of California, Los Angeles. He believes that intoxication is the fourth primary drive and can never be repressed. "It is biologically inevitable," he says—and not just in humans.

But he adds one puzzling qualification: the need to find oblivion through drugs is acquired, he argues, whereas the other three are innate. Take koalas for example. If reared naturally in the wild, they will feed exclusively on eucalyptus leaves and die without them. Their bodies become literally saturated with the pungent eucalyptus oils until they smell like large furry cough sweets. But what might appear to be an innate addiction is actually a dependence learnt in early infancy, claims Siegel. Once the baby koala becomes habituated to its mother's eucalyptus-flavoured milk, it is hooked and it will refuse all other foods. Yet orphaned koalas which have never been conditioned to eucalyptus can thrive on a diet of cow's milk, bread and honey.

But koalas have very little in common with human drug addicts. Their behaviour is by no means self-destructive, unless you consider it rash to rely exclusively on one food source. They have adapted to their chosen diet in a way that can only increase their chances of survival. As well as providing water, eucalyptus leaves contain aromatic oils which repel parasites from their skin and fur, keep their blood pressure and temperature down and relax their muscles.

So do animals in the wild indulge in self-destructive addiction? Jared Diamond, a zoologist also at the University of California, Los Angeles, thinks not. "Our self-destructive abuse of chemicals diverged from its animal precursors to become truly a human hallmark," he writes in his book *The Third Chimpanzee*.

> Are animals motivated in the same way as human drug addicts? Do animals in the wild indulge in self-destructive addiction?

But Siegel reports plenty of examples to the contrary. Consider the unusual relationship of the yellow ant, *Lasius flavus*, and the *Lomechusa* beetle. The beetles secrete an intoxicating substance from their abdomens which the ants lick until they become disoriented and unsteady on their feet. In return, claims Siegel, they lovingly provide food and care for their beetle guests. So enamoured with those secretions are the ants that they will care for the beetle larvae over their own in times of crisis. Furthermore, "*Lomechusa-mania*" causes the female ant larvae to be damaged so that they grow into infertile mutants rather than reproductive queens. Here is an organism which would sacrifice its own survival to feed its addiction.

More dramatic experiments have been staged in the laboratory. When a group of Canadian researchers allowed rats to inject themselves with cocaine solution by pressing a lever for a continuous period of 30 days, 83 per cent of those rats became heavy users. Some lost a third of their body weight and stopped grooming. A few even had severe convulsive fits before returning to the lever for their next fix. By the end of the experiment, 90 per cent of the animals were dead. "Suicidal lemmings" is how Siegel sees them.

Why do animals seek intoxication with drugs? Perhaps for the same reasons that humans do. In the words of one ex-heroin addict: "The whole world is surrounded in cotton wool, puffy white clouds, and nothing can touch you. You love everybody and everybody loves you." But does a chimpanzee really strive to find puffy white clouds? Why not, says Siegel: "After all, we share the same drive and pursuit for the drug, even similar brain mechanisms."

According to Vincent Dole of the Department of Biology of Addictive Diseases at the Rockefeller University, New York, people are turning to psychotropic drugs to escape from increasing emotional tension in their lives. And self-destructive addiction is at the extreme of the drug use spectrum. If so, the future looks bleak. As the world's population grows, says Dole, competition for food and space will become more intense. So stress is likely to increase, and with it, consumption of addictive substances. "It may be that we are now exposed to substances for which we have no evolutionary preparation."

Laura Spinney

"trade" in a number of neurotransmitters. But of these, it's dopamine that is most closely allied with the brain's response to pleasure. When lab rats eat or become sexually aroused, dopamine levels increase in certain parts of their brain, most notably in a tiny cluster of nerve endings and neurons known as the nucleus accumbens. The same thing happens when rats are allowed to inject themselves with addictive drugs. Some will press a lever or turn a wheel hundreds of times just for the pleasure of a single shot of cocaine.

But it isn't just the chemistry of the dopamine pathway that fascinates addiction researchers. Buried deep inside the brain, the pathway links up structures in the "emotional brain", or limbic system, with areas at the front of the brain's cortex, engine of rational thought and perception (see Diagram). And that suggests it could influence the way moods and emotions impinge on conscious thought. But does it?

Turn down, drop out

Enter PET imaging, again. By scanning the brains of people as they experience drug-induced highs, London and her colleagues at NIDA , as well as researchers elsewhere, have found what they believe is a distinctive pattern. Cocaine, opiates, alcohol, nicotine, barbiturates all reduce metabolic activity in the brain, to the tune of 10 to 15 per cent.

"The message here," says London, "is that it feels good to have your brain turned down." What's more, she adds, "we can correlate the magnitude of the change with the state of euphoria". With their eyes covered, subjects listen to a tape that periodically asks them how much euphoria they're experiencing. The high and the reduction in brain activity go hand in hand. Why, nobody knows, but one tentative idea says that stimulating the dopamine pathway has the knock-on effect of "turning the lights down" in the cortex. This, in turn, could influence the way emotions feed into consciousness, learning and memory.

All in all, it's tempting to cast dopamine in the role of addiction's molecular familiar, a substance that helps to convert the neurochemical spells of drugs into the brain's own language of habit and pleasure. But things may not be quite that simple. In the case of cocaine, dopamine probably is crucial to the development of dependency. Of all drugs of abuse, it acts the most directly and potently on dopamine-producing neurons. In the form of its crack derivative, it is also one of the easiest drugs to get hooked on, delivering a high in a matter of seconds, which, in the words of Steve K., a 26-year-old crack addict from South London, is "like nothing you have experienced before, like a big hormone rush".

But the same may not be true for other drugs. Rats can become hooked on heroin and alcohol, for example, even when parts of their dopamine pathway have been blocked off. With these drugs, effects on other neurotransmitter systems may be just as important.

Take the case of alcohol. In addition to stimulating dopamine release, it indirectly makes neurons more sensitive to a "sedating" neurotransmitter known as GABA. This probably explains why alcohol helps to relieve anxiety and stress; and why overworked executives are prone to boozing at the end of the day. It may also explain why some people develop a strong dependency.

In the end pleasure is a highly subjec-

> **In the end pleasure is a highly subjective experience, and it would be ludicrous to suppose that it could be boiled down to the actions of neurotransmitter pathways.**

> **'In cold biological terms, the threat of addiction is the price we must pay for having evolved the capacity to respond to pleasure'**

tive experience, and it would be ludicrous to suppose that it could boiled down to the actions of neurotransmitter pathways. Other influences clearly come into play. It's usually more rewarding, for example, to administer a stimulant to yourself than have one thrust upon you by someone else. Perhaps the self-centred ritualism of drug abuse, the studied rolling of the joint, the preparation of the fix, serves to heighten the biological rewards. As might expectations and peer behaviour. The lone soul-searcher propping up the bar behaves in one way to alcohol, beery revellers in quite another.

Nobody is being especially dogmatic about the dopamine pathway. "We don't know if it's the essence of addiction," says Alan Leshner, NIDA's director. "We assume it is—but it might not be." Even so, the "dopamine hypothesis" has prompted much speculation about vulnerabilty to drug abuse. Blum's enthusiasm for linking dopamine receptor genes to inherited addictive behaviour is one extreme example. His argument is a reworking of an older theory about addicts being "self-medicators": if you carry defective "reward" genes, you instinctively try to compensate by seeking drugs that boost levels of "rewarding" neurotransmitters.

Another idea points to natural variations in levels of dopamine itself. "Certainly, we're all endowed with different levels of dopamine activity," comments Trevor Robbins, a neuroscientist at the University of Cambridge. "If your dopamine system is already revved up a bit then perhaps you get a bigger kick out of amphetamines."

But it would be a mistake to equate this idea with the simplistic notion that addicts may be "born not made". Life history shapes the neurochemistry we're born with, says Robbins, and may leave neurochemical imprints that make us

Addictive drugs share the ability to hijack a neural pathway in the brain linked to food and sex. Acting at various sites, drugs increase levels of the neurotransmitter dopamine at a cluster of nerve cells, the nucleus accumbens. This could be the trigger for more permanent changes in the brain

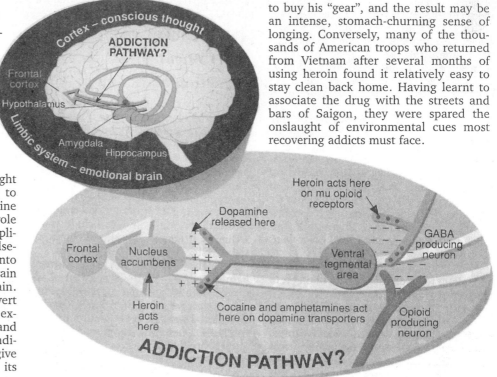

more vulnerable to the rewards of drugs. That may be particularly true of early life traumas. Rats reared in isolation tend to become hyperactive. They also tend to have dopamine pathways that are unusually responsive to drugs and they get hooked on cocaine far more easily than normal, socialised rats. Could traumatic experiences do the same to humans?

Stuff of hedonism

A firm answer could be years away; right now neuroscientists are still trying to work out exactly what the dopamine pathway does in the brain. Its main role may be to respond, like a neural amplifier, to "pleasure signals" generated elsewhere in the brain, converting them into the kind of learned experience the brain would like to relive over and over again. According to Robbins, it may also convert "pain signals" into the kind of learned experience the brain likes to avoid over and again. When a lab rat is being conditioned to avoid a footplate that will give it an electric shock, for example, its dopamine pathway swings into action as it learns the equation "footplate equals pain". Hardly the stuff of hedonism.

All of which highlights a key message now emerging from addiction research: it's not so much the pleasure of the high that causes drug dependency as the brain's response to it. Many researchers believe that drugs such as cocaine, heroin and alcohol can produce long-term, perhaps even permanent changes in neural function that go well beyond those linked to physical withdrawal symptoms. With crack cocaine, the intense pleasure of the first few highs soon diminishes. "It used to make me feel happy," laments Steve K., "but not any more." Yet at the same time the craving for more deepens. "Your stomach starts pulling and that's it, you've got to get some stuff." Where do those sensations come from? Might some people be predisposed to develop drug cravings? Neuroscience is only beginning to scratch the surface. It's clear that people "learn" to crave a drug, and that whatever this learning process involves it is rooted in physical changes in neurons and their biochemistry.

London's team has just completed some preliminary studies using PET imaging to scan the brains of former addicts as they watch video scenes of people buying and taking cocaine. It will be a while before anyone can draw firm conclusions, but London is optimistic: "It looks as if this kind of craving is accompanied by the

selective activation of some regions of the limbic system." This ties in with the little that is known about craving from animal studies, which point to a role for one structure in particular in the limbic system, the amygdala. Surgically remove this structure, and a rat no longer responds to env-ironmental cues associated with drugs.

Elsewhere, researchers are looking for clues to the origins of craving in biochemistry. Working with rats, Eric Nestler and his colleagues at Yale University and researchers elsewhere have identified changes in the cells of the dopamine pathway which could form part of an addict's "memory" for drugs. Taken over long periods, morphine, alcohol and cocaine all produce alterations in levels of proteins, messenger molecules and enzyme activities in the dopamine pathway. Such adaptations may be part of the reason why substance abusers invariably develop tolerance to their drugs and have to up the dose to recover the euphoria of the early days. But it will be years before anyone knows for sure, and in the meantime rival theories about the nature of tolerance and craving will continue to compete.

But whatever their physical basis, it's clear that these drug "memories" can evoke powerful responses. Take a former addict to the street corner where he used

to buy his "gear", and the result may be an intense, stomach-churning sense of longing. Conversely, many of the thousands of American troops who returned from Vietnam after several months of using heroin found it relatively easy to stay clean back home. Having learnt to associate the drug with the streets and bars of Saigon, they were spared the onslaught of environmental cues most recovering addicts must face.

There's a feeling among scientists that the hunt for the "essence of addiction" has only just begun. The rewards of the pursuit may in the end go well beyond the development of better tools for diagnosing and treating addicts, much though they are needed. They may take scientists to the very brink of understanding some of the web of influences—genes, environment, brain chemistry—that govern our behaviour. But along the way, two points must surely be kept in mind.

First, even if the tree of science does eventually yield genetic or other biological markers for addictive behaviour, how many people would want to embrace the fruit given the stigma, and threat of discrimination, that goes with being labelled an addict? Secondly, are scientists (and the rest of us) even looking at the problem the right way round? Given that drugs of abuse feed into neural pathways which evolved to respond to food and sex, and that each and everyone of us relies on those pathways, maybe the question is not "what makes some people vulnerable?" but "why don't we all turn to drugs?" The answer, says NIDA's Chris-Ellyn Johanson, lies not in the brain but in understanding the environmental constraints. What are these constraints, she asks, and how can we strengthen them? □

Additional reporting by **Laura Spinney**

PART IV

Controversial Diagnoses: Gender-Bound and Culture-Bound Syndromes

No topic in abnormal psychology has been more contentious than the distinction between normality and abnormality. How should psychopathology be operationalized and what are its boundaries? In this section of the book, we will examine several controversial psychiatric diagnoses that raise complex questions concerning the definition of mental illness and the differences between adaptive and maladaptive functioning. As we will see, one of these diagnoses, namely multiple personality disorder, has been criticized largely on the basis of inadequate validity evidence. Several others, such as premenstrual dysphoric disorder, have been criticized largely on the basis of possible gender bias. In addition, in this chapter we will explore the intriguing hypothesis that the manifestations of many psychiatric diagnoses are culture-bound. This possibility bears important implications for our current system of psychiatric classification and diagnosis, which according to some critics places relatively little emphasis on the ways in which cultural factors shape the overt expression of pathological conditions.

In the first reading of this section, David Cohen briefly describes the heated controversy regarding the diagnosis of multiple personality disorder (MPD). This diagnosis, which has become extremely popular in the United States in recent years, refers to a condition characterized by the simultaneous coexistence of discrete personalities or personality states within the same individual. Many proponents of the MPD diagnosis, Cohen notes, posit that severe childhood abuse lies at the core of this disorder. Children who are severely abused are thought by these researchers to *dissociate* or "split off" aspects of themselves in order to avoid painful memories of the trauma. Skeptics of MPD, however, argue that this disorder is largely or entirely *iatrogenic* (therapist-induced): by using hypnosis and other suggestive procedures, many clinicians may be encouraging their patients to assume new identities and to "remember" instances of child abuse that never actually took place. Cohen's piece raises an interesting and vexing question: Are the alternate personalities of MPD patients being discovered in psychotherapy or are they being created?

The next article, by Gail Vines, discusses a proposed diagnosis that is just as controversial as MPD, but for different reasons: premenstrual dysphoric disorder (PMDD). The PMDD diagnosis, which is currently languishing in the Appendix of DSM-IV, is closely related to premenstrual syndrome, a condition marked by affective and physical changes that afflicts many women prior to their periods. Proponents of the PMDD diagnosis contend that this condition is characterized by a relatively consistent constellation of symptoms and that it tends to produce marked impairment. Opponents of this diagnosis argue that it stigmatizes females for essentially normal biological processes and that its symptoms are hopelessly heterogeneous. Vines's discussion of this debate underscores the fact that decisions concerning the inclusion or exclusion of controversial diagnoses in the diagnostic nomenclature involve a complex admixture of both scientific and sociopolitical considerations.

In a scathing and often humorous look at the DSM decision-making process, Carol Tavris next addresses the issue of gender bias in the current diagnostic system. She takes aim at a number of personality disorder diagnoses in either current or recent versions of the DSM, particularly self-defeating, histrionic, and dependent personality disorders, which tend to be more commonly applied to women than men. These diagnoses, she contends, correspond to stereotypes of traditional female gender roles. Tavris's central thesis is that the developers of the DSM have implicitly adopted traditional masculinity as their benchmark for mental health. Consequently, women who adopt traditionally feminine gender roles are often stigmatized with personality disorder diagnoses. Tavris concludes with a critique of the criteria used by DSM decision-making committees to decide upon the inclusion or exclusion of diagnoses in the diagnostic manual. Tavris's remarks raise interesting questions concerning the possibility of gender bias in our current diagnostic system, as well as concerning the criteria used by the mental health profession to gauge psychological normality and abnormality.

In a brief update from *Scientific American*, Gary Stix reviews recent developments in the burgeoning discipline of cross-cultural psychiatry. Stix notes that the last several years have witnessed increased attention to the influence of cultural factors on the expression and treatment of psychopathology. For example, a study of the Hopi Indians discussed by Stix revealed several psychiatric conditions that appear to exhibit only partial overlap with extant diagnostic categories. These findings raise the possibility that at least some DSM-IV categories may fail to capture cross-culturally different manifestations of underlying pathological disorders.

The final article in this section is an interesting analysis by Robert Bartholomew of a culture-bound syndrome known as latah, which is found almost exclusively among middle-aged women in Malaysia and Indonesia. According to Bartholomew, when startled or surprised, women exhibiting latah react with wild and outrageous behavior, often shouting obscenities and making sexual gestures while disrobing or dancing uncontrollably. Afterward, these individuals almost always report experiencing amnesia for their latah episodes. Bartholomew contends that latah is a culturally specific expression of fakery and serves the primary function of getting attention and other personal gain. Bartholomew concludes his article with a discussion of latah's relationships to several other culture-bound syndromes.

DISCUSSION QUESTIONS

READING 25. D. Cohen, "Now We Are One, or Two, or Three . . ."

1. Cohen points out that although the diagnosis of MPD is prevalent in the United States, it is extremely rare in England. What factors could account for this disparity? How might you attempt to determine whether this disparity is attributable to differences in diagnostic practices across the two countries, or to differences in the actual rates of MPD?

2. Do you find the hypothesis that child abuse can lead to MPD plausible? Why or why not? How might you attempt to test this hypothesis?

3. As Cohen notes, skeptics of the MPD diagnosis argue that many clinicians are unintentionally creating alter "personalities" in their patients by means of suggestive techniques. Do you agree that practitioners can lead patients to assume different identities, both inside and outside of the therapy session? How might you attempt to test the hypothesis that at least some cases of MPD are iatrogenic (therapist-induced)?

4. Even if proponents of the MPD diagnosis are correct that child abuse is etiologically related to MPD, it is clear that most individuals who are abused do not develop MPD. What personality traits might place certain individuals with a history of child abuse at particular risk for MPD?

READING 26. G. Vines, "Have Periods, Will Seek Therapy"

1. If you were an advisor to DSM-V, what suggestions would you make concerning the inclusion or exclusion of the PMDD diagnosis? Explain your reasons for each suggestion.

2. Some critics of the PMDD diagnosis have pointed out that it is one of the few conditions in DSM-IV that can be applied to only one gender. Does this demonstrate that this diagnosis is gender-biased? Why or why not?

3. According to Vines, some critics have suggested that if the PMDD diagnosis were included in the DSM, this diagnosis could be used against women in child custody battles or be used by attorneys as a defense in criminal trials. Do you believe that the societal implications of a diagnosis should be considered when deciding on its inclusion or exclusion in the diagnostic nomenclature? Or should such decisions be based strictly on scientific considerations? Defend your answer.

READING 27. C. Tavris, "The Illusion of Science in Psychiatry"

1. Tavris points out that notions regarding the etiology of women's maladjustment have changed dramatically from the 1950s to the present. What societal factors might account for these changes?

2. Tavris notes that the research literature supporting the validity of the diagnosis of self-defeating personality disorder is quite weak. What research findings, if any, might provide evidence for the validity of this diagnosis?

3. Do you concur with Tavris that "if a mental disorder reliably and stereotypically fits a narrow category of people, then we should be looking at what is wrong with the conditions of people in that category" (p. 145). Why or why not?

4. Tavris argues that many personality disorder diagnoses, such as self-defeating personality disorder, can be thought of as caricatures of traditional femininity. Do any mental disorders resemble stereotypes of traditional masculinity?

READING 28. G. Stix, "Listening to Culture: Psychiatry Takes a Leaf from Anthropology"

1. If the proponents of cross-cultural psychiatry are correct, should different versions of the DSM be tailored for different cultures? Or can a single DSM accommodate all of the cross-culturally diverse variants of mental disorder? Explain.

2. Stix observes that the NIMH committee on cross-cultural psychiatry recommended that anorexia nervosa (anorexia), which is limited primarily to the United States and Europe, be listed as a culture-specific syndrome. What cultural factors might be responsible for the dramatic cross-cultural differences in anorexia's prevalence?

READING 29. R. E. Bartholomew, "Culture-Bound Syndromes as Fakery"

1. Although latah may represent a cross-culturally specific expression of fakery, most women in Malaysia and Indonesia do not display severe forms of latah. How would you explain

why only certain women exhibit the features of this disorder in its extreme form?

2. Do you agree with Bartholomew that latah necessarily represents intentional fakery? Or is it possible that individuals with latah are engaging in a kind of play acting in which they are so deeply immersed that they are no longer fully conscious of their behavior? Explain.

SUGGESTIONS FOR FURTHER READING

Fahy, T. A. (1988). The diagnosis of multiple personality disorder: A critical review. *British Journal of Psychiatry, 153,* 597–606.

Gallant, S. J., & Hamilton, J. A. (1988). On a premenstrual diagnosis: What's in a name? *Professional Psychology: Research and Practice, 19,* 271–278.

Kleinman, A. (1988). *Rethinking psychiatry: From cultural category to personal experience.* New York: Free Press.

Kluft, R. P. (1987). An update on multiple personality disorder. *Hospital and Community Psychiatry, 38,* 363–373.

Spanos, N. P. (1996). *Multiple identities and false memories.* Washington, DC: American Psychological Association.

Spitzer, R. L., Severino, S. K., Williams, J. B. W., & Parry, B. L. (1989). Late luteal phase disorder and DSM-IV. *American Journal of Psychiatry, 146,* 892–897.

Westermeyer, J. (1985). Psychiatric diagnosis across cultural boundaries. *American Journal of Psychiatry, 142,* 798–805.

Now we are one, or two, or three...

Wacky American fad or serious psychiatric problem? Debate over multiple personality disorder has left therapists accusing each other of being gullible and unscientific

David Cohen

A WOMAN with an apparently promiscuous attitude takes a man on a date. Halfway through the evening she changes into an uptight person who hates sex. She makes her excuses and escapes from her disappointed, would-be lover.

Such scenarios have been described by a number of psychiatrists as typical of the tangles that people get into when they suffer from multiple personality disorder. Believers in MPD say these patients suffer from memory loss, voices in the head and blackouts, and can "switch" between a number of personalities.

But critics of MPD, many of whom are British, ridicule the condition as a wacky American fad. They see psychiatric patients being "moulded" by their therapists to fit the diagnosis. They ask if the woman in the dating scenario simply changed her mind about the man, or wanted to escape a stressful encounter.

The argument over whether or not multiple personality disorder exists came to a head in March when the usually polite *British Journal of Psychiatry* published a vitriolic editorial that condemned the whole notion of MPD. But psychiatrists speaking at an international conference last month in Amsterdam made it clear that even if the disorder is dismissed in Britain, it is gaining acceptance elsewhere in the world.

One of the best-known cases of MPD was Eve White, whose doctors' account of her treatment became a Hollywood film, *The Three Faces of Eve*, starring Joanne Woodward. When the case was reported in 1957, everyone assumed that Eve was a rare case: she was one of only 47 MPD patients recorded between 1914 and 1969. But in the past ten years, thousands of patients have been diagnosed, especially in the US. The same boom has not been seen in Britain. "It's a very rare diagnosis

in this country," says Tom Fahy of the Institute of Psychiatry in London.

American psychiatrists are also finding patients with more personalities than ever before. Eve had just three selves. But James Carlson of Arizona is host to 16 personalities who include a young cop, a lesbian prostitute and an abused 9-year-old boy. In turn, Carlson is restrained compared with a woman described by Colin Ross of the Charter Hospital in Plano, Texas. She claims to have 335 alter egos, including rebellious teenagers and abused children. Fahy, who is a sceptic, points to one case who claims to have 4000 alter egos.

Advocates describe the condition as a form of "disassociative state", a term that covers a wide spectrum of disturbance ranging from feelings of unreality to frank MPD. In a typical case of MPD, the main conscious personality knows nothing of the alter egos, which tend to emerge at times of stress and "take control of the body".

The disorder has its origins in child abuse, say the advocates. The theory is that when children are abused, they deny what is happening to them. They then "split off" new personalities who experience the abuse. These splits become "other selves" or parts of their selves. As the children grow, the traumatic memories are repressed but not destroyed, and resurface as the symptoms of MPD.

In Britain, many psychiatrists believe that the condition is contrived. Fahy sees the explosion of cases in the US as "largely due to what's happening between doctors and patients". Some American psychiatrists, he says, take suggestible patients and "mould the psychopathology to produce multiple personality".

Facing up to the past

Fahy describes a woman who had been treated for MPD for five years in California. She was emotionally disturbed and had profound mood swings, but Fahy insists that she did not have MPD. There were simply parts of her past that she could not face up to. He treated her in part by getting her to relax and talk out her problems. According to critics such as Fahy, diagnosing MPD in such people, who are often attention-seekers, gives them an excuse to be melodramatic without looking

at their problems.

In its editorial, the *British Journal of Psychiatry* (vol 166, p 281), says some therapists encourage patients to produce evidence of past abuse. "If memories do not come quickly, more pressure is exerted," it says. American therapists deny this.

Other criticisms betray a raw rivalry between psychiatrists on either side of the Atlantic. "There is a certain glee in rejecting the diagnosis," says Jim MacKeith of the Institute of Psychiatry. "One colleague of mine told the Americans we had no intention of allowing that kind of nonsense to take hold here."

The *British Journal of Psychiatry* calls the condition "artificial" and "improbable". It argues that critics were right to relate MPD to "insufficient exercise of the critical faculties" by psychiatrists. It accused Ross of going too far in suggesting that the CIA had implanted multiple personalities in patients as part of brainwashing experiments. Ross denies that he ever said this.

The journal also ridiculed a study by Ross in which he concludes that up to 3 per cent of Americans suffer from severe disassociation or MPD. Surveys in the US suggest that about 1 per cent are likely to be "pathological disassociaters", likely to produce alter egos. In Britain this would translate to about 600 000 people.

However the condition is viewed in Britain, it is clear that it is gaining credibility elsewhere. Last month in Amsterdam, the chief psychiatrist of the Dutch health ministry, Rob Smeets, told a meeting of the International Association for the Study of Disassociation that he had been sceptical about MPD initially. "But I now have to admit that there is serious scientific work going on," he said.

The ministry funded a survey by psychologists Suzette Boon and Nel Draijer of the Free University of Amsterdam, which found that nearly 19 per cent of a representative sample of Dutch psychiatric patients had disassociative states or multiple personalities. The Netherlands now has four clinics devoted to disassociative states.

Frank Putnam of the National Institute of Mental Health (NIMH) near Washington DC and a key figure in the controversy, believes that psychiatrists in Britain are simply ignoring the large number of cases

> 'Some therapists encourage patients to produce evidence of past abuse. If memories do not come quickly, more pressure is applied'

and scientific studies of the condition. "British psychiatrists are simply not reading the data on multiple personality and disassociation," he says. "They're just relying on stereotypes." He points out that psychiatrists in Germany, Switzerland, Turkey, South America and Japan have written up hundreds of cases.

Putnam says that many MPD patients have been unsuccessfully treated for schizophrenia, depression and personality disorders. Independent studies by Ross and Putnam have found that patients see psychiatrists for an average of six years before they are "correctly" diagnosed.

MacKeith suggests that British psychiatrists may be rejecting MPD because admitting its existence might force a re-evaluation of traditional diagnoses such as schizophrenia.

The correct diagnosis matters because there are crucial differences between the treatments for MPD and schizophrenia or depression. Multiple personality patients are not usually out of touch with reality to the same extent as some schizophrenia sufferers, and antipsychotic drugs may not help them. The treatment for MPD offered by American psychiatrists centres on discovering how many alter egos a person has, and then talking out with each alter ego the causes of the trauma.

The theory underlying MPD is growing in sophistication, says Putnam. Young children can certainly make up imaginary playmates and even imaginary worlds. Recent work by Peter Wolff of the Children's Hospital in Boston suggests that young children switch moods quickly and easily. They laugh, then they cry. Putnam claims that four-years-olds have not learnt to integrate these different moods and feelings into one self. Abuse interferes with the normal processes of integration.

Catherine Fine, a psychologist from Pennsylvania, told the Amsterdam conference of a woman whose alter egos included an "uncle" figure and a number of scared children. She remembered in therapy being taken as a four-year-old to a lodge by an "uncle", a friend of her father's. There, a number of men abused her. The frightened children were splits of herself aged four.

Such a process is not so bizarre. Research on traumatic memories shows that they are often repressed and cause nightmares, flashbacks and intrusive thoughts. After the First World War, British psychiatrists treated shell shocked soldiers with the barbiturate Sodium Amytal to "disinhibit" their blocked memories of the horrors of the trenches. By remembering what went on they were helped, if not cured.

The connection between MPD and child abuse is another factor that disturbs British psychiatrists. They credibility to alleg which may turn patients often recov forms of abuse wh upon by people arg of satanic abuse. seen keeping that company," says one British psychiatrist.

Absurd models

Research has also shown that recovered memories can be inaccurate ("When memory plays us false", *New Scientist*, 23 July 1994). In the US, parents accused of abuse have set up a foundation that campaigns against the idea of multiple personality. Advocates of MPD claim that many of their critics are frightened of the fuss made by parents angry about being accused of abuse.

Other criticisms of MPD are aimed at out-of-date targets, Putnam says. Patients are no longer hypnotised to make contact with their alter egos, he says. Neither do psychiatrists believe that alter egos are fully decked out personalities. Fahy sees these changes as just tinkering "to reduce the absurdity of their models".

Uncertainty also exists over how successful therapy is for MPD. Initial claims that many patients integrate —that their many selves become fused into one— were too optimistic, according to Boon. Research by Ross claims that about a third of patients integrate, and are free of symptoms two years later.

In the US, MPD appears to be well accepted. A survey of 1200 doctors in hospitals run by the Veterans Administration found that over 70 per cent believed in the diagnosis and had seen at least one case. Only 12 per cent did not believe in the diagnosis.

So how will the two sides be reconciled? John Morton, director of the Medical Research Council's Cognitive Development Unit in London hopes to repeat studies first done in 1972 into the existence of MPD. By using the latest measurement techniques he hopes to shed new light on the diagnosis. But so far, neither side is prepared to give an inch in what has become one of the most heated debates in psychiatry. □

David Cohen *is a writer, and founder of* Psychology News.

e women go mad every month? An influential
up of psychiatrists seems to think they do

Have periods, will seek therapy

Gail Vines

THOUSANDS of women regularly feel severely depressed, angry or irritable a week or so before their periods, only to recover as menstruation begins. This month the American Psychiatric Association voted to categorise them as mentally ill.

The APA estimates that 5 per cent of American women of reproductive age may suffer from the disorder and need to see a psychiatrist. According to its critics, notably Paula Caplan, a psychologist at the University of Toronto, this is a classic example of "bad science" motivated by financial incentives and antifeminist ideology.

The fourth edition of the psychiatrists' bible, the *Diagnostic and Statistical Manual*, will list "premenstrual dysphoric disorder" (PMDD) as an "unspecified" form of depression. But, bowing to widespread criticism even from fellow psychiatrists, the APA—the manual's publishers—has given the disorder an ambiguous status, calling it a "proposed diagnostic category needing further study".

The APA argues that researchers must have a standard definition to evaluate treatments and to investigate its cause. "We believe this will result in better health care for women and reduce the suffering of women with this disorder." Caplan argues that special interests lie behind this decision. Because the manual is used by funding bodies, giving PMDD such recognition will help psychiatrists to win awards for research. But "the disorder does not really exist", Caplan argues, "any more than premenstrual syndrome does".

Premenstrual syndrome (PMS) has proved notoriously difficult to pin down. The term was first invented 40 years ago and, since then, 150 symptoms have been ascribed to PMS and as many as 327 different treatments have been tried. Most PMS researchers would agree with John Richardson of Brunel University, the syndrome is "at best a loose heterogeneous grouping of symptoms rather than a single diagnostic entity," he says. "There is no agreement over any 'core' set of symptoms."

But in the mid-1980s, a working group of psychiatrists at the APA became convinced that they could, "narrow the boundaries of the syndrome to those that would define a disorder".

Changing moods

This would "minimise the clinical inaccurate use of the term 'PMS' and the consequent underdiagnosis, overdiagnosis and misdiagnosis of the syndrome, which have prevented optimal assessment and clinical care," according to Robert Spitzer and his colleagues of the New York State Psychiatric Institute. The diagnostic criteria the psychiatrists drew up focus on mood changes severe enough to lead to "functional impairment", but also include physical symptoms such as bloating (see Box).

But Spitzer's critics claim that a description is no guarantee that a category is "valid"—that it corresponds to what everyone agrees is a single disorder with a definable cause. "PMS is not a valid syndrome, and neither is some arbitrary subset of its symptomatology," says Jane Ussher, a lecturer and clinical psychologist at University College London who has been studying PMS since the early 1980s.

John Bancroft of the Medical Research Council's Reproductive Biology Unit in Edinburgh is also critical of the APA's decision. "The field is in something of a mess," he concludes. The concept of PMS is no longer useful. By defining a "premenstrual dysphoric disorder", the APA has "jumped from the frying pan into the fire", Bancroft contends. "It's no better than the old concept of PMS."

The APA's committee of six women, set up earlier this year to review the literature and decide how to handle premenstrual symptoms in the fourth edition of the manual, failed to reach a consensus. "The full range of opinion and perspective was represented," says Nada Stotland, a psychiatrist on the committee and an associate professor at the University of Chicago. "Opinion ranged from those convinced that PMDD should be a bona fide disorder accorded its own code number, all the way to me," says Stotland; "I wanted PMDD out of the manual altogether."

Because the committee could not reach agreement, the APA asked two other psychiatrists, with no special expertise in the field, to make the decision—a move that Caplan finds astonishing. "If the experts couldn't agree, how do you choose two other people to make the decision?"

Another committee member, Sally Severino of Cornell Medical College in New York City, would have preferred to "leave things as they were" in the previous edition, published in 1987. There, a similar condition, called "late luteal phase dysphoric disorder", or LLPDD, lurked in the limbo of the appendix. "I see no point in changing the name again," says Severino. "There have been 15 names already. It just confuses people." Moreover,

> **"Opinion ranged from those convinced that PMDD should be a bona fide disorder accorded its own code number, all the way to me; I wanted PMDD out of the manual altogether."**

Is PMDD a new mental illness?

To qualify for the diagnosis of premenstrual dysphoric disorder, according to the new edition of the *Diagnostic and Statistical Manual*, to be published next year, a woman has to have symptoms that appear during the last week before bleeding begins, but which disappear within a few days after the period starts, in most menstrual cycles during the past year.

She must also suffer a disturbance that "markedly interferes" with work, education or social relationships and have at least five of the following symptoms premenstrually, including at least one of the first four:
- markedly depressed mood, feelings of hopelessness
- marked anxiety, tension

- "marked affective lability" (such as sudden sadness)
- "persistent and marked" anger or irritability
- decreased interested in work, education, friends, hobbies
- difficulty concentrating
- lethargy
- marked change in appetite
- hypersomnia (excessive sleepiness) or insomnia
- sense of being "overwhelmed or out of control"
- physical symptoms such as tender or swollen breasts, headaches, joint or muscle pain, bloating or weight gain

The disorder must not be merely an "exacerbation" of some other disorder, and the symptoms must be "confirmed" by the patient's own daily ratings through two menstrual cycles.

From *New Scientist*, 139, pp. 12–13, July 31, 1993. Reprinted by permission of IPC Magazines Ltd.

'Women who suffer most premenstrually are more likely to be in upsetting life situations'

Despite the focus on women's hormones, PMS has no established biological cause. . . . No single psychological cause has turned up either. Women's experiences of their menstrual cycles seem to be intimately related to their social, psychological, cultural and even economic circumstances.

clear hormonal abnormalities have also proved elusive. "It can be useful for women who experience distress to blame it on their hormones—then they are taken seriously," says Walker. But they then become labelled as ruled by their biology, at the mercy of their "raging hormones". Caplan adds another twist: "It's as if the APA are bribing women—we're willing to believe you, take you seriously, they say, but you have to say you're mentally ill."

Defending the APA's decision, Spitzer points out that the category is purely descriptive: the manual does not suggest a cause for PMDD. Yet, Ussher argues that "there are very few psychiatrists who don't adopt the medical model of mental illness"—a model which describes mental disorder as having a biological cause, like any other illness.

"Women ought to be able to receive help without having to receive a diagnosis implicitly tied to biology," says Ussher. "PMS may be a vehicle for women to express real unhappiness that is not necessarily caused by the menstrual cycle."

Despite the focus on women's hormones, PMS has no established biological cause. No hormonal or other physical abnormalities can account for the diverse symptoms reported. No single psychological cause has turned up either. Women's experiences of their menstrual cycles seem to be intimately related to their social, psychological, cultural and even economic circumstances.

Men suffer too

Such conclusions often inspire headlines such as: "Cheer up, say scientists, you're only imagining you feel bad" and "PMS—all in the mind". Yet researchers do not deny the reality of women's experiences. "I know some women feel worse before their periods—I believe them," says Caplan. "But good research indicates that women who suffer most premenstrually are more likely to be in upsetting life situations. They are not mentally ill . . . They need help to change their social and physical environment."

Researchers have found that men too suffer cyclical changes in mood. Mary Brown Parlee of City University of New York gave PMS symptom checklists to men,

without saying what they were. It turned out that the men reported more monthly problems than women. And in a preliminary study of heterosexual couples, Walker found that men as well as women felt better at the weekend, and worst midweek. Married men also had mood changes, linked to their wives' menstrual cycle.

People rarely attribute men's depressed or irritable moods to their biology, nor anyone's positive moods, as Richardson has shown. Yet both men and women—including many researchers—tend to attribute negative moods experienced by women around the time of menstruation to the biological process. At other times precisely the same moods are put down to external stresses.

Where do we go from here? Can research settle the debate? For Severino, this is an opportunity to understand how "the interaction of various inputs, from physiology, culture, socioeconomic conditions and life experiences, are all contributing to the symptoms". It is "a fascinating, scientific puzzle," she says. The trouble is, says Stotland, "doctors of medicine have trouble seeing that psycho-social research is valid research".

Spitzer, who has been influential in setting the APA's agenda, was in the vanguard of a movement in American psychiatry that began in the late 1970s. It was to sweep away the "biopsychosocial model" of mental illness which was prevalent at the time. This emphasised the role of social and cultural influences in the development of mental illness. Spitzer and like-minded colleagues favoured the medical model with its apparently more "scientific" diagnostic categories based on a person's "objective" behaviour.

But psychologists such as Walker argue that progress in this field depends on finding ways of doing research that "acknowledge our own subjectivity". And if Severino is right, PMDD is a "biopsychosocial condition par excellence, being railroaded into a narrow medical model"

Medically-based psychiatric diagnoses may be dangerous in practice, Ussher argues. "Women are being given drugs with often serious side effects that are no more effective than placebos," she claims. Doctors increasingly prescribe antidepressants for menstrually related depression. "It seems to be a continuation of the 1960s and 1970s, when women who expressed unhappiness were given antidepressants," Ussher argues. "There was a backlash against this, but it is now seems to be returning through the backdoor with PMS.

"In the long term, antidepressants do not help women to cope or to find out why they are so unhappy in the first place—reasons that are not to do with their bodies. We need to help women in more empowering ways." The race is on. The next edition of the manual is scheduled for 2002. □

she says, "this new classification puts an emphasis on depression, rather than keeping an open mind." Severino supported the initial decision to put a premenstrual disorder in the manual, and is convinced that having LLPDD in print for the past seven years "has stimulated research and encouraged physicians to think about mental functioning. It did all we hoped it would."

She does not believe that including the category has proved socially damaging for women. Fears have been expressed in the US that lawyers might use the diagnosis in court as a weapon against women in child custody battles; as a defence in criminal trials; or that health insurers would refuse cover on the basis of the diagnosis. Stotland says: "Those fears, thank goodness, are not well founded so far." She worries however, that "lay people and even some doctors" will not make the distinction between a vast array of premenstrual symptoms that affect most women to some degree, and the severe "psychiatric" symptoms apparently linked to the menstrual cycles of a few women.

Such diagnoses can be a powerful way of "dismissing women who are assertive in the workplace or unhappy at home—a way of not hearing what women are saying," argues Ussher. Partners or work colleagues can trivialise a woman's feelings by saying, "It's just your hormones, dear."

The APA's critics argue that women are in a double bind. Anne Walker, a psychologist at the University of Dundee, draws parallels with postnatal depression, in which

THE ILLUSION
OF SCIENCE
IN PSYCHIATRY

By Carol Tavris

In the antebellum south a physician named Samuel Cartwright argued that many slaves were suffering from two forms of mental illness. One was *drapetomania*, diagnosed as the uncontrollable urge to escape from slavery. The other was *dysathesia aethiopica*, whose symptoms included destroying property on the plantation, being disobedient, talking back, or refusing to work. So doctors, of course, could assure slave owners it was not the intolerable condition of slavery that caused these "problems," but some disease in the slaves themselves that made them seek freedom.

Drapetomania now sounds as dated as Plato's view that female hysteria is caused by a lonely womb that wanders through the body crying for a baby. Surely, most people would say, the bad old days in psychiatric diagnosis are past, thanks to modern technology and the scientific method. Yet when we peer beneath the surface, we find that the old attitude that transforms normal desires and deeds into pathology is alive and well. What I want to argue today is that *drapetomania lives*.

There is something solid, permanent, and official about a list of symptoms in a scholarly-looking tome like the *Diagnostic and Statistical Manual*

of Mental Disorders. The DSM is the mental equivalent of the *Physicians' Desk Reference*, the medical dictionary upon which all doctors rely. You can look up any of a long list of psychological symptoms in the DSM index (including excessive worrying, indiscriminate socializing, indecisiveness, insomnia, untidy appearance, delusions, and cross-dressing), and there find all possible disorders that the symptom might reflect. "Irritable mood," for instance, is associated with 24 different disorders, including nicotine withdrawal, pathological gambling, insomnia, and Organic Anxiety Syndrome.

The DSM strives to classify varieties of mental disorders and their symptoms with a degree of precision to a hundredth of a decimal point. A depressed person who has Bipolar Disorder (known commonly as manic depression) might get any of this range of diagnostic identification numbers:

296.50 unspecified
296.51 mild
296.52 moderate
296.53 severe, without psychotic features
296.54 with psychotic features
296.55 in partial remission
296.56 in full remission

The last one—depression in full remission—is my favorite. Even if your depression has completely disappeared, you still have a disorder. The purpose of such precise numbers and diagnostic criteria, say the compilers of the DSM, is to enhance agreement in diagnosis among clinicians and investigators.

It is important to understand the claims, intentions, and methods of the DSM because the manual has had an extraordinary impact, both in the United States and worldwide. It has succeeded in standardizing the categories of who is, and who is not, mentally ill. Its categories and terminology have become the common language of most clinicians and researchers. Virtually all major textbooks in psychiatry and psychology base their discussions of mental disorders on the DSM. Insurance companies require clinicians to assign their patients the appropriate code number of the diagnosed disorder. Attorneys and judges often refer to the manual's list of mental disorders, even though the DSM warns that its categories "may not be wholly relevant to legal judgments," such as those of individual responsibility and

Adapted from a presentation to the Skeptics Society Lecture Series at Caltech, Sunday, September 12th, 1993, and from a chapter in *The Mismeasure of Woman*. Published by Simon & Schuster. This article appeared in *Skeptic, 2*(3), pp. 77–85, 1994, and is reprinted with permission by Lescher & Lescher, Ltd.

competency. The current edition of the DSM, in its full or abbreviated version, has been translated into Chinese, Danish, Dutch, Finnish, French, German, Greek, Italian, Japanese, Norwegian, Portuguese, Spanish, and Swedish. The Manual generates a yearly revenue of over one million dollars for its publisher, the American Psychiatric Association.

Now, the DSM is not called the "Diagnostic and Statistical Manual of Mental Disorders and a Whole Bunch of Everyday Problems in Living." A collection of mental disor-

---

"...the DSM is not called the 'Diagnostic and Statistical Manual of Mental Disorders and a Whole Bunch of Everyday Problems in Living.'"

---

ders, one might assume, would include serious, universally recognized problems such as schizophrenia, depression, and paranoia. But the territory of psychiatry and clinical psychology keeps expanding, and as it has, so has the DSM. The 1952 edition of the manual contained 60 categories of mental illness. By 1968, the DSM-II contained 145 categories. By 1980, the DSM-III had ballooned to 230 disorders. In 1987, the DSM-III-R—a revision that added enough changes to warrant a new volume, but not enough to warrant calling it a fourth edition— crossed the 300 mark. And the fourth edition, which will be published in 1994, contains yet more disorders in all their minute variations.

Many of these additional categories are "Everyday Problems," including tobacco dependence, marital conflicts, and sexual difficulties. Of course these matters can be troubling to people and many seek help in dealing with them. But their presence in the DSM raises some nagging questions. What are they doing in a compendium of mental disorders? How did they get there? Where do old diagnoses go when they die, and where do new ones come from? And how, in particular, did something called Self-defeating Personality Disorder make its way onto the latest list of official mental problems?

A woman I'll call Emily, who is 39 years of age, decides to enter psychotherapy for help with a persistent problem: chronically low self-esteem, a vague but persistent unhappiness, and a general uneasiness about her life. She briefly contemplated going back to school to improve her skills, but her husband and mother have persuaded her that this is not a practical idea. Her husband, Mark, believes that there really isn't much point in her returning to the workplace, since any job she did get would barely be enough to cover the costs of day care for their two preschool-age children, ages two and four. Emily agrees. Mark wants to be helpful, but whenever he offers suggestions to her—such as getting involved with a volunteer program, looking for a part-time job, or taking a weekend for herself at a spa— Emily rejects them out of hand.

Mark is becoming irritated with Emily's complaints and bitterness. Her intransigence about not doing anything for herself is becoming annoying to those who love her. She takes no pleasure even from the things she does well. She doesn't seem to want to do anything that's fun anymore, and it annoys Mark that Emily has taken to wearing a mantle of martyrdom. "She'll do anything for everybody," he complains, "whether they want her to or not." Occasionally, after she has refused once again to even listen to any of his offers of help, Mark erupts in an angry outburst, to which she invariably reacts with tears and withdrawal.

What's the matter with Emily?

You can find Emily's symptoms on pages 373 and 374 of the DSM-III-R. According to the DSM, Emily is suffering from Self-defeating Personality Disorder, which is characterized by a "pervasive pattern of self-defeating behavior, beginning by early adulthood and present in a variety of contexts."

In order to be diagnosed as a self-defeating person—as opposed to someone who just occasionally shoots herself in the foot—you must meet at least five of the descriptions on the DSM's checklist:

(1) You choose people and situations that lead to disappointment, failure, or mistreatment.

(2) You reject offers of help.

(3) You respond to good news or successes with depression, guilt, or actions that produce pain.

(4) You provoke others to reject or be angry with you, and then feel hurt, defeated, or humiliated.

(5) You turn down opportunities for pleasure.

(6) You are able to do well but you keep sabotaging your own objectives.

(7) You reject people who treat you well; e.g., you are turned off by considerate sexual partners.

(8) You like to play the martyr, sacrificing your own interests for others who do not solicit or need your help.

It's a portrait of Emily, all right. Of course, it is also a portrait of all of us, some of the time.

Self-defeating Personality Disorder is the latest incarnation of an old American game that we might call "Name What's Wrong With Women." Every few years a wave of best-selling books sweeps over the land, purporting to explain to women the origins of their unhappiness. In many of the self-help versions of these books, the author begins by describing how she herself suffered from the disorder in question, and through persistence, effort, or revelation, found the cure.

Thus, in the 1950s, women's problem was said to be their inherent masochism, an idea that derived from Freud's theory that female psychology includes an unconscious need for, and pleasure in, suffering. Wrong, said Matina Horner in the late 1960s. The problem is women's fear of success; the cure is to understand and then overcome their internal barriers to achievement. Wrong, said Marabel Morgan, Phyllis Schlafly, and other religious conservatives in the 1970s. The problem is that women want success, when they should be spending their energies being obedient to God and husband; the cure is to strive to become

"The Total-Woman," "The Fulfilled Woman," or "The Positive Woman." Wrong, said Colette Dowling in 1981. The problem is that women have a "Cinderella Complex— a hidden fear of independence;" they must struggle against their desires to be rescued by Prince Charming. Wrong, said a spate of writers in the early 1980s. The problem is that women "say yes when they mean no," and "when they say no, they feel guilty;" the cure is assertiveness training. Wrong, said Robin Norwood in 1985. The problem is that women love too much. Wrong, said a flurry of books in rebuttal. It's not that women love too much but that they love the wrong men—men who are immature, angry, abusive, chauvinistic, and cold. Wrong, said Melody Beattie in 1987; the poor guys aren't to blame, because they are sick. Women love too much because they are codependent—addicted to addicts, addicted to bad relationships.

Long ago in The *Feminine Mystique,* Betty Friedan wrote of "the problem that has no name"—the vague emptiness and desolation that plagued many women in the postwar era. But in fact the problem has gone by far too many names. The symptoms that all of these books attempt to treat are invariably the same: low self-esteem, passivity, depression, dependency on others, an exaggerated sense of responsibility to other people, a belief that it is important to be good and to please others, and an apparent inability to break out of bad relationships. I do not doubt that many women are unhappy, and I do not doubt that these descriptions apply to many women—and to a goodly number of men. But it is time to ask why these psychological diagnoses of women's alleged inner flaws, which keep returning like swallows to Capistrano, year after year, fail to deliver on their promises. And it is time to ask why the explanations we make of female problems differ in kind and function from those we make of male problems.

Thus, the problems that are more characteristic of men than women—such as drug abuse, narcissism, rape, and other forms of violence—are

rarely related to an inherent male psychology the way women's behavior is. When men have problems, it's because of their upbringing, personality, or environment; when women have problems, it's because of something in their very psyché. When men have problems, society tends to look outward for explanations; when women have problems, society looks inward.

For example, psychologist Silvia Canetto has compared attitudes toward people who attempt suicide (typically women) with those toward people who abuse drugs (typically men). Both of these actions, says Canetto, are "gambles with death;" both actions can be lethal although the individual may not intend them to be. Suicide attempters and drug abusers share feelings of depression and hopelessness. Yet mental-health experts tend to regard suicide attempts as a sign of a woman's psychological inadequacy, reports Canetto, whereas they regard drug abuse as "caused by circumstances beyond the person's control, such as a biological predisposition."

Likewise, people speculate endlessly about the inner motives that keep battered wives from leaving their husbands. Are these women masochistic? Do they believe they deserve abuse? Are they codependent, unwittingly collaborating in the abuse against them? Whatever the answer, the problem is construed as the battered wives, not the battering husbands. But when experts ponder the reasons that some husbands abuse their wives they rarely ask comparable questions: Are these men sadistic? Do they believe they deserve to abuse others? Rather, their explanations focus on the pressures the men are under, their own abuse as children, or the wife's provocations. Male violence is not considered a problem that is inherent in male psychology; but the female recipients of male violence are responsible because they "provoked" it or "tolerated" it or "enabled it" or are "masochistic"—problems presumed to be inherent in female psychology. A man who gets into a fight with a stranger and hits him may spur an observer to ask: "Why is this guy so aggressive and hostile?" But if

the same man goes home and hits his wife, the same observer is likely to wonder: "Why does she stay with him?"

Of course, almost everyone knows people who are, often or on occasion, self-defeating, sadistic, dependent, martyrish, or who otherwise behave in annoying and exasperating ways. And I do not deny that therapy can be helpful for such individuals. But the question is: Do they have *problems,* or are they sick? Further, as the example of Self-defeating Personality Disorder illustrates, many of the problems associated with women today can be considered signs of mental illness only in comparison to a male standard of what is healthy and normal.

The story of the creation of Self-defeating Personality Disorder has a curious history. In the early 1980s, the American Psychiatric Association decided to commission an official revision of the DSM-III. Work Groups were assembled to discuss each category of mental disorder and decide what, if anything, should be done with it. Each Work Group was given a set of guidelines in studying a proposal for change, starting with the most important: "Was the proposal supported by data from empirical studies?" There were other matters to consider as well, including whether there was "a consensus among experts" that the change would be clinically useful.

In the spring of 1984, the Work Group on Personality Disorders recommended that a new diagnostic label be included in the next DSM, which they called Masochistic Personality Disorder. Although the criteria for this alleged disorder were carefully phrased in "his or her" terms, no one was fooled. Everyone knew it was a term that was far more likely to be applied to women than to men.

The proposal generated an immediate firestorm of protest from the Committees on Women of the American Psychiatric Association and the American Psychological Association. The protesters raised numerous objections: that the proposed new category was biased against women, that it perpetuated Freud's discredited belief that women enjoy suffering, that it blamed the victim of abuse rather than attending to the abuser, and—oh, yes, by the way—that it was utterly without scientific merit.

For the next year, the Work Group listened to an outpouring of objections and read countless research papers from many professionals inside and outside the psychiatric establishment. Its members then decided . . . to keep the new category anyway. But in an effort to placate the opposition, they made what they regarded as three concessions:

1. They changed the name of the proposed new category from Masochistic Personality Disorder to Self-defeating Personality Disorder. This change, the compilers of the DSM-III-R explained, avoids "the historic association of the term *masochistic* with older psychoanalytic views of female sexuality and the implication that a person with the disorder derives unconscious pleasure from suffering."

2. They agreed to include a cautionary note that the disorder would not be diagnosed when a patient is showing normal responses to sexual or physical abuse. That is, clinicians should realize that a woman might stay with an abusive man not because she is "self-defeating" but because she knows her life would be in danger if she left him.

3. To counter the charges that this diagnosis would apply mostly to women, the Work Group added what its members thought would be a parallel problem applying mostly to men: "Sadistic Personality Disorder," characterizing people who gain pleasure from inflicting pain on others.

The Board of Trustees of the APA then made one further compromise. Instead of placing Self-defeating Personality Disorder in the main text of the DSM-III-R, as its advocates wished, they relegated it to an appendix consisting of "diagnostic categories needing further study." Nevertheless, it was given an official code number (301.90) and a set of supposedly characteristic hallmarks, which meant it could be used as a legitimate diagnosis.

You might assume that for Self-defeating Personality Disorder to make its way into the DSM-III-R, leapfrogging over piles of documents protesting its inclusion, it must have been supported by data from empirical studies, as the Work Group was instructed to consider first and foremost. You would be wrong. The editors of the DSM revision admitted: "In attempting to evaluate proposals for revisions in the classification and criteria, or for adding new categories, the greatest weight was given to the presence of empirical support from well-conducted research studies, *though, for most proposals, data from*

> ## "When men have problems, it's because of their upbringing, personality, or environment; when women have problems, it's because of something in their very psyché."

empirical studies were lacking." [My emphasis.]

In the case of this particular proposal, for instance, no one had determined the extent to which self-defeating personality traits were prevalent among normal women and men who were not in treatment. Indeed, some of the defining qualities of the "disorder," such as sacrificing one's own interests and putting other people first, are highly esteemed traits for both sexes in many cultures and are virtually a role requirement for women in our own. Moreover, no one knew whether this new disorder was significantly different from other personality or emotional problems. For example, a self-defeating person might actually be suffering from depression (depressed people also feel chronically pessimistic and "reject opportunities for pleasure") or primarily have the problem of low self-esteem (such individuals also reject offers of help and fail to complete tasks they could easily do).

None of these concerns deterred the Work Group. The reason for the decision to keep the new diagnosis is stated in the preface to the DSM-III-R: " . . . the diagnostic criteria for Self-defeating Personality Disorder were studied by examining the data from an anonymous questionnaire that was distributed to several thousand members of the American Psychiatric Association who had indicated a special interest in Personality Disorders."

A vote! The decision was made, in essence, because a lot of psychiatrists, replying to a survey, said, "Yes, I've seen these women in my practice. It's the damnedest thing. They actually want to play the martyr." One psychiatrist, reviewing a paper that was highly critical of the lack of research evidence for Self-defeating Personality Disorder, noted that this criticism "hardly does justice to those who felt there was a rich clinical tradition that justified this category in the DSM-III-R."

When all the pretensions to science are blown away, the "rich clinical tradition" approach to defining mental illness proves to be the real basis for DSM diagnoses: "We psychiatrists think this disorder belongs here, because we have seen it in our practice." Perhaps they have. Yet psychiatrists have seen many things as a result of their clinical judgment that, over the years, proved to be ephemera of the biases and beliefs of the time—including hysteria, penis envy, masochism, drapetomania and nymphomania. As a college student I was taught in all seriousness that I and every other female person were suffering from penis envy—and would continue to suffer from this until we had small children with penises of their own. Freudians really saw "penis envy" in their clients. This was, of course, before feminist researchers showed conclusively that Freud was right about penis envy, just wrong about which sex suffers from it!

As times change, so do ideas about mental illness. Over the years, some "disorders," such as masturbation and homosexuality, have been voted out. Other problems, such as Inhibited Sexual Desire, have been voted in. In modern America, after all, it cannot be healthy not to want sex, and so clinicians now debate degrees of desire. (In the latest DSM, Inhibited Sexual Desire has been split into "hypoactive sexual desire disorder"—meaning you don't want to do it often enough—and "sexual aversion disorder"—meaning you don't want to do it at all). As recently as 1980, the DSM banished Freud's old standby, neurosis, to what psychiatrist Matthew P. Dumont calls "the limbo of disappeared disorders."

The group vote approach would have something to commend it, however, if enough clinicians actually achieved something like consensus. Unfortunately, all too often clinicians do not agree with each other on what the patient in question is suffering from. The very purpose of the DSM—to improve agreement among clinicians on what, precisely, they are diagnosing—has repeatedly been questioned by research. Two clinicians, independently evaluating a patient's case, should agree that his problem is, say, "agoraphobia with panic attacks." But if one says that patient has an "obsessive compulsive disorder," the DSM considers those two clinicians in basic agreement—because they both think the patient suffers in general from an anxiety disorder. Despite the use of methods that inflate the chances of agreement (in some studies clinicians' agreement with one another was boosted by their being allowed to make several diagnoses instead of just one), the reliability in tests of many of the DSM's categories, particularly of personality disorders, has constantly been poor. In spite of the DSM's own generous standards of what constitutes good clinical agreement, not a single major diagnostic category of personality disorders achieved it.

Even with all these problems, a case could be made for the "rich clinical tradition" approach to a compendium of mental disorders—if the compilers of such a manual acknowledged their professional biases, the social context of the times, and the subjective enterprise of labeling people. But the DSM tries to have it both ways. It repeatedly asserts that it is based on science and empirical validation, while then admitting that little such validation exists.

Some dissenting psychiatrists argue

that the whole enterprise is a foolhardy effort to impose a veneer of science on what is ultimately an art form. Diagnosis of mental disorder rests on human judgment, they say, governed by all the wisdom and prejudice that human judgment involves. "Who can calculate the wasted hours of foolish, futile discussion about how to compartmentalize patients who never seem to fit the numbered cubicles in which we are forced by insurers to place them?" says Matthew Dumont. "[It] is like being forced to choose from some

---

"...feminist researchers showed conclusively that Freud was right about penis envy, just wrong about which sex suffers from it!"

---

endless, infernal Chinese menu . . . . Time and thought are scattered in making differences which make no difference; instead of simple prose to describe our patients, we are forced to use numbers and an esoteric jargon base on bits of yes-no data supposedly adding up to a picture of a mental state."

The goal of all the precise numbers and scientific language is to convey the impression that teams of scientists, rooting around in the mind, have uncovered the "real" disorders of mental life. The DSM wants to sound and look like a medical textbook, a purely descriptive set of problems, as if there were no bias or subjective choice involved. "In fact," says Dumont, "the entire system is an expression of a theoretical bias so rigid and pervasive that it renders alternative ways of thinking about mental disorder not just difficult or even impossible, but inconceivable. It has to do with the attention given to the figure rather than the ground, the case rather than the context, the individual rather than the social setting."

Well, many people say, so what if a diagnosis is based only on clinical judgment of some people in therapy? What about Emily, who is making such a mess of her life and can't be cheered up? If Self-defeating Personality Disorder describes her pattern of behavior, shouldn't she be treated for it? Dumont's observation, in my view, holds the key to the answers, unlocking precisely what is wrong with Emily's diagnosis. The reason becomes clearer if we shift the focus, as he recommends, from case to context, from individual to setting. In a series of experiments, psychologist Hope Landrine found that the various personality disorders listed in the DSM neatly fit the roles and stereotypes of several groups in our society. For example, try to imagine the gender, social class, race, and age of a person who meets this description:

This person is lively and dramatic and is always drawing attention to him/herself. This person is prone to exaggeration and often acts out a role such as the "victim" or the "princess" without being aware of it. This person's behavior is intensely expressed. Minor stimuli give rise to emotional excitability, such as irrational, angry outbursts, or tantrums. This person craves novelty, stimulation, and excitement and quickly becomes bored with normal routines. At first this person is perceived as shallow and lacking genuineness, though superficially charming and appealing . . . . This person is attractive and seductive. This individual tries to control the opposite sex or tries to enter into a dependent relationship. Flights into romantic fantasy are common.

This is the DSM's description of a person with Histrionic (formerly Hysterical) Personality Disorder. The chances are that you, like most psychiatrists and nonprofessionals, will envision this person as a single, middle-class young white woman in her early twenties.

Who fits this description?:
This person passively allows others to assume responsibility for major areas of his/her life because of a lack of self-confidence and an inability to function independently. This person subordinates

his/her own needs to those of others on whom he/she is dependent in order to avoid any possibility of having to be self-reliant. This person leaves major decisions to others. For example, this person will typically assume a passive role and allow the spouse to decide where they should live, what kind of job he/she should have, and with which neighbors they should be friendly.

This is not a rendition of Self-defeating Personality Disorder, by the way, but of what the DSM calls Dependent Personality Disorder; if you noticed some overlap, you are not alone. In spite of all those his/her constructions, almost everyone thinks that this passage describes a slightly older, married, middle-class white woman. Everyone agrees that it describes, in a word, a wife.

Now, who fits this description?:
This person habitually violates the rights of others. In childhood, this person engaged in frequent lying, stealing, fighting, truancy, and resisting authority. In adolescence, this person showed unusually early or aggressive sexual behavior, excessive drinking, and use of illicit drugs . . . . This person is unable to sustain lasting, close, warm, and responsible relationships with family, friends, or sexual partners.

Most people will say that this description of Antisocial Personality Disorder (formerly known as the Sociopathic or Psychopathic Personality) is typical of young working-class males.

Landrine found, in short, that untrained observers can predict which individuals are most likely to receive a particular personality disorder diagnosis, based only on knowledge of their age, race, class, gender, and marital status. Two categories were divided exclusively by gender: Everyone saw the Self-defeating Personality as a woman and the Sadistic Personality as a man.

But what if personality disorders are simply distributed that way in society? Aren't more married women than married men likely to be dependent, aren't more young single women histrionic, aren't more men sadistic, and aren't more working-class males antisocial? The answer is that if a mental disorder reliably and stereotypically fits a narrow category of people, then we should be looking at what is wrong with the conditions of people in that category, not exclusively at their individual pathologies. For example, instead of asking, "What's wrong with women that makes them excessively dependent in marriage?," we could be asking, "What's wrong with marriage that makes so many women excessively dependent?" (or "Why are we always labeling the caring work that women do as evidence of 'dependency'?").

> **"...Landrine found...that untrained observers can predict which individuals are most likely to receive a particular personality disorder diagnosis, based only on knowledge of their age, race, class, gender, and marital status."**

Landrine offers an example of how easily modern roles can masquerade as mental illness. As the number of divorced, displaced women in society increases—many of whom lack the resources to support themselves and their children adequately—a new disorder might be discovered: "This hypothetical future category—the Inadequate-Hostile Personality Disorder—will be characterized by disorientation and perplexity, bitterness and hostility; complaints of helplessness; paranoid ideation regarding lawyers, the ex-husband, and men in general, with a subsequent inability to form close and enduring heterosexual attachments; and failure to provide adequate food and shelter for one's children and thus to function as a responsible parent."

Inadequate-Hostile Personality Disorder will (probably!) not be added to the DSM, because everyone knows that most divorces cause tremendous emotional distress and that a life of hardship, let alone of dealing with the courts, can create paranoia and bitterness.

But the DSM's "rich clinical tradition" does not extend the same understanding to its own personality disorders, at least when it comes to women's roles. Three psychologists did a study very similar to Landrine's, and in an early unpublished version of their paper, they had concluded that "it is particularly disturbing that personality disorder behaviors seen as characteristic of women appear to be . . . . close enough to society's stereotype of women that *normal* women *who adopt traditional roles may be receiving personality disorder diagnoses*" (my emphasis). Yet when the paper was later published in *The American Journal of Psychiatry* this statement was gone, replaced only by a bland call for "further research."

Over the years, the American Psychiatric Association has understood that some mental problems are a normal result of particular experiences, not of individual abnormality. The category of Post-traumatic Stress Disorder recognizes that the traumas of war, torture, rape, and other horrific experiences can have long-term psychological consequences, and it places the origins of the sufferer's unhappiness squarely on the traumatic event.

Further, the APA has acknowledged that some "mental disorders" have a social origin and that they properly do not belong in the DSM. When the APA first dropped homosexuality from its list of official Sexual Disorders, it decided to maintain a category called Ego-Dystonic Homosexuality, referring to homosexuals who were unhappy or conflicted about their sexual orientation. In 1987, the DSM-III-R banished even that variation, as well it should have, when its compilers realized that "In the United States almost all people who are homosexual first go though a phase in which their homosexuality is ego-dystonic." In making this change, the DSM-III-R was acknowledging that it is society's discomfort with and outright hatred toward homosexuals that can create their conflicts, not a mental disorder. (Nevertheless, the DSM-III-R couldn't let the matter go completely. Under a category called Sexual Disorder Not Otherwise Specified, one symptom continues to be "persistent and marked distress about one's sexual orientation.") Yet if a black woman came to therapy with persistent and marked distress about being black in a white world, the origin of her conflict would not, should not, be located within her psyché. There is no mental disorder called "ego-dystonic race identity."

A compelling series of wide-ranging studies now suggests that self-defeating behavior and even "choosing to suffer" are often *normal* reactions of people who are reasonably certain (but not positive) that unpleasant things will happen to them in the future and who have had a history of suffering in the past. It's as if they say: "If I shoot myself in the foot now, maybe I won't lose my leg next week." In laboratory experiments, perfectly normal college students will typically choose a masochistic action, giving themselves moderate electric shock, if they think that will offset more severe shock later on or prevent hostility or injury from others. And, granted that plenty of women have been known to treat men miserably, which sex is, in the real world, more likely to experience hostility and injury from the other?

Yet if a woman goes to a psychiatrist complaining of dissatisfaction, conflict, dependency, pessimism, worries about her future, and passivity, she is still likely to be diagnosed as having a personality disorder, and she will probably be given an antidepressant. (And the content of her complaints is likely to be trivialized. One male psychiatrist told a depressed friend of mine that she should "become more active—cleaning the closets would be a good idea.") Women are considered sick if they play their traditional roles too well; correspondingly, men are considered sick if they don't play their traditional roles at all. Many psychotherapists harshly judge male patients who are unconventional—for example, who deviate from traditional standards of masculinity by staying home with the children while the wife has the paying job. In a recent study by two psychologists, 47 therapists were randomly assigned to view one of two versions of a video tape of a depressed man. When the

depressed man was portrayed as a traditional bread-winning guy, they did not think he had much of a problem. When he was portrayed as being a househusband, they thought he was much more troubled and disturbed.

To illuminate the subjective nature of diagnosis, consider what the DSM would look like if it were written by a panel of African-Americans. Right off the bat there would be a diagnosis of Persistent Racial Superiority Delusion Disorder. Similarly, to see what is wrong with the concept with

---

"Some dissenting psychiatrists argue that the whole enterprise is a foolhardy effort to impose a veneer of science on what is ultimately an art form."

Self-defeating Personality Disorder, consider what would happen if female behavior and female role obligations were taken as the norm, the healthy standard for both women and men: putting other people first, behaving modestly, appraising the limitations in one's life. Which sex would now suffer the pathology of deviance? As a group of women psychiatrists noted in their protest of Masochistic Personality Disorder, no one has proposed a diagnosis for the "Aggressive, Power-driven, Exploiting Personality" that currently causes so much trouble in the world.

Now someone has. In 1988, psychologist Paula Caplan and sociologist Margrit Eichler invented a new category for the DSM, which they called Delusional Dominating Personality Disorder—DDPD for short. Individuals with this disorder, they suggested, have at least several of the following symptoms:

(1) They are unable to establish and maintain close relationships.
(2) They are unable to identify and express their feelings and to know how other people feel.

(3) They are unable to respond appropriately to the feelings and needs of others.
(4) They use power, silence, withdrawal, or avoidance rather than negotiation in coping with conflict.
(5) They believe that women are responsible for the bad things that happen to them, while the good things are due to their own abilities or efforts.
(6) They need to inflate their importance and achievements (or those of males in general), while needing to deflate the importance of women.
(7) They suffer various delusions, such as:

A. the delusion of personal entitlement to the services of any woman with whom they are associated.

B. the delusion that women like to suffer and to be ordered around.

C. the delusion that physical force is the best method of solving problems.

D. the delusion that sexual and aggressive impulses are uncontrollable in all males.

(8) They need to affirm their importance by appearing with females who are submissive, conventionally attractive, younger and shorter, and lower on the socioeconomic scale than they.
(9) They have a distorted approach to sexuality, reflected by a pathological need for flattery about their sexual performance and/or the size of their genitals.
(10) They tend to feel inordinately threatened by women who fail to disguise their intelligence.

The standard reaction of most psychiatrists to Caplan and Eichler's proposal was: "Very amusing, dears, but it is a joke, isn't it?" Delusional Dominating Personality Disorder is funny but only in a system which takes masculinity as the norm and regards femininity as abnormal. DDPD is a description of the exaggerated characteristics of the male role; but that is just what Self-defeating Personality Disorder is of the female role.

Caplan and Eichler did not intend to replace a label that is biased against women with one that is biased against men. Rather, they wanted to show that the extreme consequences of rigid male upbringing can cause as many psychological problems as can the consequences of rigid female upbringing. They wanted to emphasize that if you're going to have the latter disorder in the DSM, you had better have the former as well. They wanted to reveal the inherent bias of explaining stereotyped male behavior as a result of social demands on men, while accounting for stereotyped female behavior as a result of an abnormal personality disorder. They wanted to highlight the tendency to blame the woman for what is wrong in a relationship and ignore the man's contribution: "A woman may find her nonpathological responses to [the behavior of men] pathologized as evidence of her alleged, intrapsychic, individual Self-defeating Personality Disorder; instead, it would be more appropriate to recognize that the problem originates in rigid male socialization and is acted out by the man. Before rushing to give women psychiatric labels, [a clinician should investigate] whether they are living or working with someone who suffers from DDPD."

"Our goal," says Caplan, "is to rethink what is normal and what is healthy." She and Eichler invented Delusional Dominating Personality Disorder as a little consciousness-raising exercise, but soon they began to wonder why it shouldn't be taken seriously. DDPD was invisible, they maintained, "because it characterizes so many of the powerful people in our society." But, after conducting a wide-ranging review of a variety of research studies in many disciplines, they concluded that DDPD affects the mental health and well-being of the many men (and some women) who suffer from it. People afflicted with DDPD—that is, those who adhere to the most extreme standards of the traditional male role—are more likely than others to have health problems, shorter life spans, problems in relationships, and little capacity for intimacy. They often suffer from anxiety, stress, homophobia, self-doubt, insecurity and competitiveness. They have high

rates of drug abuse and violence, including homicide. Surely, said Caplan and Eichler, if any personality pattern is worth labeling a "mental disorder," this one is.

The story is not yet over. On September 19, 1988, psychiatrist Allen Frances, Chair of the Task Force overseeing the fourth edition of the DSM, and Harold Alan Pincus, Director of the Office of Research for the American Psychiatric Association, summarized their thoughts about how the revision should proceed. In a memo to the Work Group

---

Women are considered sick if they play their traditional roles too well: correspondingly, men are considered sick if they don't play their traditional roles at all.

---

on Personality Disorders, they began with a positive flurry of admonitions to be scientific: "Essentially, we are undertaking a scientific assessment project, not unlike the treatment and technology assessment projects undertaken by federal agencies and other medical and scientific societies. It is essential that our efforts proceed in as systematic and scientifically based a manner as possible."

But by the end of the memo, they added that "if the resolution of an issue is not clear . . . then the Work Group will need to resolve the issue based upon the best available data, clinical experience and advice from the field." What were the available data on Self-defeating Personality Disorder? That same year, Frances and a colleague, psychologist Thomas A. Widiger, reviewed the evidence and concluded: "The diagnosis of SDPD [Self-defeating Personality Disorder] lacks conclusive or established empirical support." Of course, they added, this is not a reason to remove it from the DSM: "It should be recognized though that many of the psychiatric diagnoses

lack conclusive empirical support . . . . The inclusion of SDPD was justified with respect to clinical usefulness, education of mental health professionals, suitability, or research."

By the same logic, Paula Caplan and her colleagues reasoned, the DSM should look favorably on the addition of Delusional Dominating Personality Disorder. Surely it, too, would be useful to clinicians, would educate mental health professionals, and be suitable for stimulating research. So they submitted their proposal, with supporting evidence, to the appropriate Work Group. Psychiatrist John Gunderson, the group's Chair, replied: "I think it's highly unlikely that enough support will be available in time for DSM-IV . . . . [DDPD] has neither a widespread clinical tradition nor a significant clinical literature. These facts mean that it will take even more empirical support to introduce a category such as DDPD."

Caplan responded that there was ample empirical evidence, far more, in fact, than for Self-defeating Personality Disorder. In a subsequent letter, Gunderson then replied that, in essence, the research wasn't that important: " . . . the most formidable obstacle to overcome is the fact that [DDPD] isn't generally recognized— even if the empirical evidence can be completed."

"Even if the empirical evidence can be completed"! There you have it—in the competition between "empirical evidence" and "clinical experience," clinical experience wins every time.

One final note: "Self-defeating Personality Disorder" will be removed from the forthcoming revision of the DSM. The Work Group *voted* to remove it—not because it lacks scientific validation, but because it has been misused to "diagnose" and stigmatize a woman who lodged a sex discrimination suit against the National Institutes of Mental Health. (A woman who would stay in a job where she was not wanted, said her psychiatrist, must obviously be "self-defeating.") But fear not; Delusional Dominating Personality Disorder will never poke its head through the door of the "rich clinical tradition" in psychiatry. ∎

Listening to Culture

Psychiatry takes a leaf from anthropology

Last April, a Bangladeshi woman who complained that she was possessed by a ghost arrived at the department of psychiatry at University College London. The woman, who had come to England through an arranged marriage, had at times begun to speak in a man's voice and to threaten and even attack her husband. The family's attempt to exorcise the spirit by means py, Jadhav made a series of subtle suggestions that succeeded in getting him to relent on his strictness. The specter's appearances have now begun to subside.

Jadhav specializes in cultural psychiatry, an approach to clinical practice that takes into account how ethnicity, religion, socioeconomic status, gender and other factors can influence manifestations of mental illness. Cultural do not. Moreover, the variants of an illness—and the courses they take—in different cultural settings may diverge so dramatically that a physician may as well be treating separate diseases.

Both theoretical and empirical work has translated into changes in clinical practice. An understanding of the impact of culture can be seen in Jadhav's approach to therapy. Possession and trance states are viewed in non-Western societies as part of the normal range of experience, a form of self-expression that the patient exhibits during tumultuous life events. So Jadhav did not rush to prescribe antipsychotic or antidepressive medications, with their often deadening side effects; neither did he oppose the intervention of a folk healer.

Practitioners of cultural psychiatry noted that although some diseases, such as schizophrenia, do appear in all cultures, a number of others do not. Moreover, the variants of an illness— and the courses they take—in different cultural settings may diverge so dramatically that a physician may as well be treating separate diseases.

At the same time, he did not hew dogmatically to an approach that emphasized the couple's native culture. His suggestions to the husband, akin to those that might be made during any psychotherapy session, came in recognition of the woman's distinctly untraditional need for self-assertion in her newly adopted country.

The multicultural approach to psychiatry has spread beyond teaching hospitals in major urban centers such as London, New York City and Los Angeles. In 1994 the fourth edition of the American Psychiatric Association's handbook, the *Diagnostic and Statistical Manual of Mental Disorders*, referred to as the *DSM-IV*, emphasized the importance of cultural issues, which are mentioned in various sections throughout the manual. The manual contains a list of culture-specific syndromes, as well as suggestions for assessing a patient's background and illness within a cultural framework.

of a local Muslim imam had no effect.

Through interviews, Sushrut S. Jadhav, a psychiatrist and lecturer at the university, learned that the woman felt constrained by her husband's demands that she retain the traditional role of housebound wife; he even resented her requests to visit her sister, a longtime London resident. The woman's discontent took the form of a ghost, Jadhav speculated, an aggressive man who represented the opposite of the submissive spouse expected by her husband. By bringing the husband into the thera-

psychiatry grows out of a body of theoretical work from the 1970s that crosses anthropology with psychiatry.

At that time, a number of practitioners from both disciplines launched an attack on the still prevailing notion that mental illnesses are universal phenomena stemming from identical underlying biological mechanisms, even though disease symptoms may vary from culture to culture. Practitioners of cultural psychiatry noted that although some diseases, such as schizophrenia, do appear in all cultures, a number of others

For many scholars and practitioners, however, the *DSM-IV* constitutes only a limited first step. Beginning in 1991, the National Institute of Mental Health sponsored a panel of prominent cultural psychiatrists, psychologists and anthropologists that brought together a series of sweeping recommendations for the manual that could have made culture a prominent feature of psychiatric practice. Many of the suggestions of the

From Scientific American, 274, pp. 16–17, January 1996. Reprinted with permission. Copyright © 1996 by Scientific American, Inc. All rights reserved.

Culture and Diagnosis Group, headed by Juan E. Mezzich of Mount Sinai School of Medicine of the City University of New York, were discarded. Moreover, the *DSM-IV*'s list of culture-related syndromes and its patient-evaluation guidelines were relegated to an appendix toward the back of the tome.

"It shows the ambivalence of the American Psychiatric Association [APA] in dumping it in the ninth appendix," says Arthur Kleinman, a psychiatrist and anthropologist who has been a pioneer in the field. The APA's approach of isolating these diagnostic categories "lends them an old-fashioned butterfly-collecting exoticism." A Western bias, Kleinman continues, could also be witnessed in the APA's decision to reject the recommendation of the NIMH committee that chronic fatigue syndrome and the eating disorder called anorexia nervosa, which are largely confined to the U.S. and Europe, be listed in the glossary of culture-specific syndromes. They would have joined maladies such as the Latin American *ataques de nervios,* which sometimes resemble hysteria, and the Japanese *tajin kyofusho,* akin to a social phobia, on the list of culture-related illnesses in the *DSM-IV.*

Eventually, all these syndromes may move from the back of the book as a result of a body of research that has begun to produce precise intercultural descriptions of mental distress. As an example, anthropologist Spero M. Manson and a number of his colleagues at the University of Colorado Health Sciences Center undertook a study of how Hopis perceive depression, one of the most frequently diagnosed psychiatric problems among Native American populations. The team translated and modified the terminology of a standard psychiatric interview to reflect the perspective of Hopi culture.

The investigation revealed five illness categories: *wa wan tu tu ya/wu ni wu* (worry sickness), *ka ha la yi* (unhappiness), *uu nung mo kiw ta* (heartbroken), *ho nak tu tu ya* (drunkenlike craziness with or without alcohol) and *qo vis ti* (disappointment and pouting). A comparison with categories in an earlier *DSM* showed that none of these classifications strictly conformed to the diagnostic criteria of Western depressive disorder, although the Hopi descriptions did overlap with psychiatric ones. From this investigation, Manson and his co-workers developed an interview technique that enables the differences between Hopi categories and the *DSM* to be made in clinical practice. Understanding these distinctions can dramatically alter an approach to treatment. "The goal is to provide a method for people to do research and clinical work without becoming fully trained anthropologists," comments Mitchell G. Weiss of the Swiss Tropical Institute, who developed a technique for ethnographic analysis of illness.

The importance of culture and ethnicity may even extend to something as basic as prescribing psychoactive drugs. Keh-Ming Lin of the Harbor–U.C.L.A. Medical Center has established the Research Center on the Psychobiology of Ethnicity to study the effects of medication on different ethnic groups. One widely discussed finding: whites appear to need higher doses of antipsychotic drugs than Asians do.

The prognosis for cross-cultural psychiatry is clouded by medical economics. The practice has taken hold at places such as San Francisco General Hospital, an affiliate of the University of California at San Francisco, where teams with training in language and culture focus on the needs of Asians and Latinos, among others (*photograph*). Increasingly common, though, is the assembly-line-like approach to care that prevails at some managed-care institutions.

"If a health care practitioner has 11 minutes to ask the patient about a new problem, conduct a physical examination, review lab tests and write prescriptions," Kleinman says, "how much time is left for the kinds of cross-cultural things we're talking about?" In an age when listening to Prozac has become more important than listening to patients, cultural psychiatry may be an endangered discipline.   —*Gary Stix*

FIELD NOTES

Changing Their Image

On a cool October evening, troops of female journalists congregated at the august New York Academy of Sciences in Manhattan to appraise a group of blushing male scientists. The courageous men had modeled for the first-ever "Studmuffins of Science" calendar. "I want to change the image of science," explained "Dr. September," Bob Valentini of Brown University, with the wide-eyed earnestness of a Miss Universe desiring to eradicate world hunger. Karen Hopkin, who co-produces "Science Friday" for National Public Radio and is the calendar's creator, offered a more believable rationale for the enterprise: "It was an elaborate scheme for me to meet guys."

To the disappointment of many in the audience, the studs turned out in modest suits and ties. Even the calendar featured only Dr. January, Brian Scottoline of Stanford University, in bathing trunks. "We wanted them to be wholesome, PG-13," said Nicolas Simon, the calendar's designer. "So we can sell to schoolgirls. It's educational." Dr. October, John Lovell of Anadrill Schlumberger, presented an alternative view of the creative process. He had offered to take off his shirt in the service of science, he declared, but "the photographer took one look at my chest and told me

> "I wish I had a wife" is the oft-heard sigh of female researchers who are not similarly blessed with portable (or culinarily capable) spouses.

to put it back on." Still, three editorial assistants from *Working Mother* were suitably impressed. "All our readers will fall over their faces for these guys," one testified.

The truth is, surveys show that male scientists are not the ones who have trouble attracting mates, especially the kind who willingly follow wherever the scientific career leads. "I wish I had a wife" is the oft-heard sigh of female researchers who are not similarly blessed with portable (or culinarily capable) spouses. Some American women who are scientists even speak of how the decision to study mathematics and science, made in high school, was traumatic because it made them instantly unattractive to boys.

In addition to "Studmuffins," Hopkin's plans for 1997 include "Nobel Studs" (which one wag has redubbed "Octogenarian Pinups"). That should be as much of a hit. But her third venture, "Women in Science," may be the only one with a hope of offering a truly different image of scientists to schoolgirls and schoolboys. —*Madhusree Mukerjee*

Culture-Bound Syndromes as Fakery

ROBERT E. BARTHOLOMEW

*Oh, what a tangled web we weave,
when first we practice to deceive!*

—Sir Walter Scott

. . . nearly all forms of deception are now accepted by the medical profession as a form of illness. Even where deception is recognised, as for instance in the confabulations of the Munchausen syndrome, this is attributed to previous mental trauma, or to some form of cultural disadvantage. The deceiver, always referred to as a patient, is said to be "disturbed"; he is regarded as a victim, not as a rogue (Naish 1979).

A Ph.D. . . . does not confer expertise in detecting trickery. Thus, they are just as vulnerable, if not more so, to the magic tricks of a [Uri] Geller, as are people who lack their scientific training (Hines 1988:92).

For the past one hundred years anthropologists and psychiatrists have debated the origin and nature of a curious behavior confined almost exclusively to the Southeast Asian neighboring cultures of Malaysia and Indonesia: Upon being startled, ordinarily timid, exceedingly polite women sometimes respond with vulgarities, obscenities, and outrageous sexual gestures. In severe cases, the women experience

From *Skeptical Inquirer, 19,* pp. 36–41, November/December 1995. Reprinted by permission of the *Skeptical Inquirer.*

The curious and bizarre behavior known as latah has been classified as an exotic syndrome. But evidence indicates it is more likely to be a culturally based deception.

"automatic obedience," doing whatever they are told. Afterward they claim amnesia and are not held responsible for their actions. Episodes of this type last from a few minutes to several hours. Victims of *latah* are almost always middle-aged women of Malay and Javanese descent. It is rare among women of other nationalities (but such a case will be discussed later), even when they are neighbors of those experiencing latah. Scientists have been divided as to whether latah is a disease (Opler 1967; Rosenthal 1970); a disorder (Simons 1985, 1994; Howard and Ford 1992); or a form of symbolic cultural expression (Kenny 1978; Lee 1981). None of these explanations has been able to account for all of the characteristic features of latah, which is typically classified in medical textbooks as a culture-bound psychiatric syndrome.

Robert E. Bartholomew is sociologist at James Cook University, Townsville, Queensland 4811, Australia.

In January 1990, I married into an extended Malay family in which latah is prevalent, and gained the confidence of family members. While having no intention of studying latah despite it landing literally at my anthropological doorstep—the more I observed, the more a number of contradictions became evident. Of 99 living female and male family members surveyed, 30 were classifiable as having "mild" latah and two as having "severe" latah, according to classic textbook definitions of the condition (Bartholomew 1994).

I first observed a severe case while attending my brother-in-law's wedding in the home of the bride's parents. I was astounded to observe my wife's shy, decrepit aunt, who had considerable difficulty even walking, intentionally startled by her elderly uncle. "S" suddenly leapt to her feet, lost all inhibition, and for the next 10 minutes followed each of her teaser's commands, mimicking his every ges-

ture. During the episode, she was made to cry like a baby, perform *silat* (Malay self-defense), dance vigorously, and partially disrobe, all to the hilarity of the entire wedding party which crowded around her. She would occasionally improvise gestures, such as lifting her sarong in a sexually suggestive manner and utter the most repulsive words and phrases. Throughout the episode, after some outrageous display, she would immediately and profusely apologize for her vulgarity, then launch into another series of behaviors, apologizing more than 30 times during this particular "fit." The next day at a crowded wedding reception at the groom's home, I was able to tease her into a similar, less dramatic episode by suddenly slapping my hands onto the floor next to her. She responded with a 10-minute display, mimicking my every action, from dancing to slapping her face repeatedly. Other family members also joined in the teasing.

A few days later I visited "S" at her residence in the presence of two relatives. I startled her and she responded with a short vulgar phrase. Immediately thereafter, I slapped my hands on the floor next to her, exactly as I had done at the wedding reception, but there was no response. I slapped the floor, then my face, hard, but again there was no response. I was perplexed. Just a few days earlier in the presence of about 60 people, even minor startles would send her into prolonged "fits." At both parties she was sitting on the floor next to me,

swearing in response to fright. The reactions vary according to cultural conditioning. Simons takes subjects' explanations at their face value, assuming their truthfulness in claiming their behavior is involuntary.

I was surprised to learn that "S," who would commonly drop and throw objects while in a state of latah, was frequently allowed to cradle babies in her arms, with a perfect record of holding onto them! Since there are many "severe" cases in Malaysia, one wonders why there are no newspaper headlines: "Another Malay Drops

cues that the subject is tired. In this ritual of deception, family members recognize the latah subject is not ill. But they do believe they have temporary and complete control over the subject's mind, and are careful to keep knives and other sharp objects away from subjects during latah episodes.

A Dubious History

Latah has been an enigmatic "ailment" in that its classification has curiously eluded a number of competent researchers. In fact, in the *American Handbook of Psychiatry* (Arieti and Brody 1974) it is placed under "Rare, Unclassifiable, Collective, and Exotic Psychotic Syndromes." To date, outsiders have been able to catch only glimpses of the mysterious world of latah. They have noted considerable difficulty gathering detailed case histories from informants, as has the late, prominent cross-cultural psychiatrist P. M. Yap (1952), despite his fluency in the Malay language. Kenny (1985) remarked that only a single case of latah has been observed and studied in sufficient context and depth to provide some insights into the processes involved—that reported by Australian anthropologist Clive Kessler (1977). Coincidentally, the woman in this case study possesses a marked histrionic personality.

> ## "I was surprised to learn that 'S,' who would commonly drop and throw objects while in a state of latah, was frequently allowed to cradle babies in her arms, with a perfect record of holding onto them!"

and I executed the same sequence— startling her, slapping the floor, then my face. Family elders later explained emphatically that unless there is a large social gathering, "severes" *never* exhibit anything beyond "mild" symptoms, responding only with an offensive word or phrase. They also report that "teasers" are always close relatives— ensuring that the "victim" does not do anything too outrageous, such as responding to a request to stab someone with a knife.

Over the course of a month, I observed "S" teased into 10-minute "fits" at other weddings where she sat in the main crowded room of the groom's house, despite claiming to dread being teased. If "S" genuinely feared teasing, she simply could have told family members not to tease her, avoided wedding crowds, or visited privately instead of prancing onto center stage. I asked her, "If you suffer amnesia during 'attacks,' how can you apologize if you are unaware of your actions?" She had no explanation.

University of Washington psychiatrist Ronald Simons is the leading proponent of the theory that latah is a universal human disorder to startle in response to fright, akin to Westerners

Baby!" or "Latah Claims Two in Yet Another Car Mishap." While claiming to hate being "teased," the "victim" and onlookers seem to heartily enjoy it. This denial of self-control is necessary for the perpetration of the latah deception since it "sets the stage" for the ensuing performance which allows for the violation of Malay norms. The subject enjoys complete immunity from blame. What "victim" can willingly invite the latah condition since it would be tantamount to admitting that they enjoy violating strict taboos? If her protestations were genuine, mothers, sons and grandchildren would certainly not torment their elder loved ones, who are always treated with the utmost dignity and respect in Malayo-Indonesian culture. From this perspective, the latah startler unwittingly serves as a coach, orchestrating and dictating the subject's responses.

This ritual also allows for the release of individual expressions. While the subject is required to perform the coach's choreography, the foul language and obscene body gestures are improvisations by the latah performer. The performance is almost always terminated by both physical and verbal

Exhibitionism best fits the evidence, explaining why latah is not considered an illness by participants and their families, the reluctance of informants to provide detailed information, observations that most subjects are described as clever (Fitzgerald 1923; Murphy 1973), and the conspicuous absence of any sign of mental abnormality outside of episodes. It explains latah's almost exclusive restriction to lower-class women and servants, and their conspicuous tendency to startle in the presence of higher status peers (Geertz 1968; Murphy 1976; Kessler 1977).

It has been observed that "severe" subjects typically lead solitary and reclusive lives to avoid being teased (Langness 1967:149). Yet, it is equally plausible that these subjects become performers *because* they are lonely and desire attention. Previous observers have presented primarily anecdotal evidence that the onset of severe symptoms coincides with depression, financial dependence, and loneliness following the death of a close family member (Yap 1952; Chiu, Tong and Schmidt 1972; Kenny 1978:210). Some anthropologists even argue that latah symbolizes the plight of such people and is a means of conveying to others that something is amiss (Kenny 1978).

"S" first exhibited severe symptoms at public gatherings within a few months after the death of her daughter, followed in close succession by the death of her husband. She was unemployed, in social isolation, and dependent on her surviving children for support. Researchers have focused their attention on the conditions likely to prompt latah, largely ignoring the question of the conditions under which people are likely to feign or exaggerate latah for attention. It is notable that two other family members were in virtually the exact social circumstances as "S" following the deaths of their husbands. Both of these "mild" subjects experienced latah slightly longer than usual. They explained latah as an unconscious means of relieving emotional stress and perhaps an unconscious means of getting attention. Yet, neither became "severe."

It cannot be overemphasized that "severe" latah behavior is exceedingly rare, even in Malayo-Indonesia.[1] Colson (1971) identified five cases in a Malay village of more than 400 residents; Resner and Hartog (1970) stated that traditional Malay villages usually have but one case, while Chiu et al. (1972) located only 69 cases out of a sample of 13,219 East Malaysians. One reason researchers have chosen to downplay the obvious exhibitionistic nature of "severe" cases are reports that it once affected the majority of the populations of Malaya and parts of Indonesia (Van Brero 1895; Clifford 1898). Scientists reasoned that large num-

bers of inhabitants could not be feigning; therefore it must possess some unconscious ritualistic or symbolic quality. Hence, while Yap (1952:537) was convinced that latah is a mental disease of hysterical dimensions, he remarked, "It is often difficult to separate the genuine cases from those which are basically histrionic and exhibitionist in nature." Malaysian psychiatrist Eng-Seng Tan made a similar observation. Like Yap, Kiev (1972) and Murphy (1976), each assumed that this behavior characterizes hysterical and dissociative aspects of latah, especially since most "victims" are female:

> Although there has not yet been any systematic scientific study of the latah phenomenon from a psychological viewpoint, the hysterical nature of the condition is inescapable to the psychiatric observer. The condition invariably occurs in the presence of an audience, the behavior of the subject has a marked theatrical quality about it, often provoking spasms of laughter among the audience, and the subject pleads amnesia for her buffoonery when she comes out of her altered state of consciousness (Tan 1980:380).

Upon closer scrutiny, the argument dissolves that latah cannot be fraud due to its pervasiveness. "Milds" do not consider themselves to be suffering from a disorder. Upon explaining to family members the common psychiatric definition of "mild," I was told "everyone is a little latah." There is no evidence that "severe" cases were any more common in the previous century than they are today. Its habitual form persists in certain families, although it has no major social significance, except as a prerequisite for performers to emulate and elaborate.

"Mild" latahs simply respond to startle in a manner comparable to Western swearing. There is no exaggeration, mimicking, amnesia, or involuntary expression. Then how is its appearance in women explained? In its "mild" form, latah is an infrequent habit formed almost exclusively by post-pubescent females in certain Malay households with cultural traditions of emulating behavior of elders. Since it is considered a feminine trait, most males do not engage in the habit, but if they do, it is infrequent and typically denied. In a similar vein, smoking cigarettes once was considered a solely masculine trait in Western society, and women who smoked usually denied it. The view of "mild" latah as habit is consistent with Murphy's (1976) observations of enigmatic behavior: The condition was extremely rare in Malayo-Indonesia during the first half of the seventeenth century; reported on every street and common among men by the 1890s; scarce during the 1920s; and diminishing in frequency today and almost exclusive to women.

The status of latah as a medical disorder is reminiscent of social scientists' attaching medical labels to other habits and fashions. Penrose (1952) considered the use of the yo-yo and crossword

> ## "She would immediately and profusely apologize for her vulgarity, then launch into another series of behaviors, apologizing more than 30 times during this particular 'fit.'"

puzzle to cause a mild form of crowd disorder. Child psychiatrist W. Burnham (1924:337-38) made a similar evaluation of the brief "craze" in Worcester, Massachusetts, during the early part of this century, of people tickling each other with feather dusters. American psychiatric pioneer Benjamin Rush (1962 [1812]) classified lying as a disease.

Recently, psychiatrist Jack Jenner (1990, 1991) reportedly discovered seemingly indisputable evidence that latah is an abnormality of the human startle mechanism that varies with cultural conditioning. He treated a 40-year-old Dutch woman in Holland who would swear profusely, become abusive, and act oddly upon being startled. He claimed the subject has no ties to Malayo-Indonesian culture, and yet, it is an amazing coincidence that this sole documented case of severe latah occurred in someone from a culture far away from, but with a significant population of Malaysians and Indonesians,[2] both Asian countries having been Dutch colonial outposts for centuries. In fact, the Dutch only agreed to lift sovereignty over Indonesia in 1949. Jenner's case study notes that his patient startled several times daily for 20 years, yet had not sought help. Her husband became so irritated he sought psychiatric assistance. She was successfully treated with "flooding" therapy, consisting of her husband and son startling her dozens of times daily. Unanswered are such fundamental questions as to whether the woman had Malaysian or

"symptoms" then rapidly disappeared and never returned.

Double Standards

There are numerous historical precedents for malingering for social gain, or institutionalized feigning. Anthropologist Michael Kenny contends that "severe" latah subjects do not enter an altered state of consciousness, but are engaged in latah "performance" and "theater" (Kenny 1978:209). Never are the words "fraud," "fakery," or "deception" used. Yet anthropologists appear guilty of employing double standards. A number of researchers have exposed fakery and deception in group settings: the Salem witch trials of 1692; spiritualism during the early twentieth century; epidemic demonic possession in medieval European nunneries; and channeling associated with the contemporary New Age movement. However, anthropologists and psychiatrists tend to use different language in scrutinizing similar non-Western traditions. When studied, Western faith

of "noble savages" living in unspoiled isolation from the decadence of twentieth-century civilization (Sponsel 1990). The media heavily touted the claim that these *Tasaday* people did not even have a word for war. This was later uncovered by Iten (1986) as a hoax after gaining access to their restricted preserve and finding the so-called lost tribe "living in houses, wearing Western clothing and saying they had faked the whole thing" (Willson 1989:18). The conspiracy was apparently perpetrated by the government of Ferdinand Marcos, then president of the Philippines, in order to deceive the world for political and economic gain (Dumont 1988).

Social scientists do an injustice by using such words as "malingering," "histrionic," "performance," and "symbolic action" in describing attempts to achieve social gain in the absence of an organic illness. Stripped of these euphemisms, all too often the underlying content involves conscious deception for personal gain. The entire notion of the perpetration of fraud in non-Western cultures needs to be reevaluated regardless of whether the perpetrators express a belief in their power to heal. In this regard, culture-bound idioms of deception are couched in legitimate scientific terms.

Anthropologists have an unfortunate tendency to emphasize, idolize, and glorify the exotic, especially in someone else's backyard, while psychiatrists are often overly eager to place a convenient "disorder" or "disease" label on deviant or deceptive behavior, no matter where it is found. This is also true of misperceptions involving people whose perceptual orientations are conditioned by pseudoscientific books and media programs purporting the existence of mysterious · creatures. When a community experiences a spate of Bigfoot or flying saucer sightings, it is typically labeled as a form of "epidemic hysteria," yet this behavior is not infectiously contagious and participants are not clinically hysterical.

Another culture-bound "syndrome" is that of "group spirit possession," which, like latah, almost exclusively

> ## "'Severe' subjects typically lead solitary and reclusive lives to avoid being teased. Yet, it is equally plausible that these subjects become performers because they are lonely and desire attention."

Indonesian companions—an excellent likelihood given their presence in Holland—or if she was previously aware of latah. Jenner (1990) curiously noted that startling was often used by the woman to avoid household chores; get her way in deciding holiday destinations; and serving as "her most effective weapon in marital conflicts." A fraud perspective is equally plausible and best conforms to historical and contemporary evidence. I would argue that upon commencement of the "flooding" therapy, the subject rebelled, intensifying her malingering to demonstrate the ineffectiveness of treatment. Upon realizing the determination of her husband, son, and psychiatrist to continue this strategy,

healers are often viewed as fraudulent. But place an exotic label on essentially the same behavior involving shaman in some African tribe and anthropologists are quick to point out the "symbolic" qualities. Yet, there is also symbolism in fraud, quackery, and channeling. Carlos Casteneda's fictional writings contain a seductive, adventurous quality that was ideal for captivating popular American culture during the sixties and seventies, blending mysticism, psychedelic drug use, and a belief in paranormal and supernatural powers (Hines 1988:277). The discovery in 1971 of a "stone age" tribe in the Philippines captured the imagination of the world due in large part to its ultrapacifist symbolism—a community

affects female Malays. Labeled by scientists as stressed-induced "mass hysteria," episodes of screaming, crying, and claims of possession have plagued Malaysian schools and factories since the resurgence of Islam in Malaysia in the early 1960s. In a country where Malay women do not enjoy equal rights and unions are discouraged, such "outbreaks" allow for the protest of undesirable actions or rules from managers and school principals. Anthropologist Aihwa Ong (1987) shows how "epidemic hysteria" in Malaysian factories is a form of political resistance. Lee and Ackerman (1980:79) also document how Malaysian "hysterical epidemics" are utilized in typically restrictive Malay female religious hostels as a form of negotiation in drawing attention to a particular problem. In summarizing the characteristic presentation of complaints by the females in Malaysian schools, Teoh (1975:302) notes a "monotonously similar" pattern: "One or two of the subjects in an altered state of consciousness acted as the mouth-piece on behalf of the group, ventilating their many frustrations and discontentments. The girls characteristically took hints and cues from each other and afterwards claimed amnesia for the episodes." While a tiny fraction of subjects may enter trance states, the vast majority are clearly playacting in a type of "ritualized rebellion" for political gain.

Fraud and deception take many culture-specific forms—from the attention-seeking poltergeist antics of Western children, to the use of chicken blood and sleight of hand during "psychic surgery" by shaman. Latah is one more example.

Notes

1. Anthropologist Michael Kenny of Simon Fraser University in British Columbia argues persuasively that in the few scantily documented groups where latah behavior is reported to occur, such reactions result from social and not biological influences. While accepting the possibility of a universal startle reflex, he considers it irrelevant to understanding latah. Thus, while all people are born with hands, "only some cultures have exploited the fact in requiring them to be shaken in formal greeting" (Kenny 1985:74).

Since latah behavior is often dramatic and thus likely to elicit comments by both scientists and lay persons, the scarcity of accounts prior to the nineteenth century, when the illness category was first devised by Western medical practitioners, is a conundrum (Murphy 1973:43).

2. According to the *Worldmark Encyclopedia of the Nations* (1984), more than 2 percent of Holland's population is composed of repatriates and immigrants from Indonesia.

References

Arieti, S., and E. B. Brody. 1974. *American Handbook of Psychiatry*. New York: Basic Books.

Bartholomew, R. E. 1994. Disease, disorder, or deception? Latah as habit in a Malay extended family. *Journal of Nervous and Mental Disease*, 182(6):331-338.

Burnham, W.H. 1924. *The Normal Mind*. New York: D. Appleton-Century.

Chiu T., J. Tong, and K. Schmidt. 1972. A clinical survey of latah in Sarawak, Malaysia. *Psychological Medicine*, 1:155-65.

Clifford, H. 1898. *Studies in Brown Humanity*. London: Grant Richards.

Colson, A. C. 1971. "The Perception of Abnormality in a Malay Village." In *Psychological Problems and Treatment in Malaysia*, ed. by N. Wagner and E. S. Tan, Kuala Lumpur, Malaysia: University of Malaya Press.

Dumont, J. 1988. The Tasaday, which and whose? Toward the political economy of an ethnographic sign. *Cultural Anthropology*, 3(3):261-275.

Fitzgerald R. 1923. *Far Eastern Association of Tropical Medicine, Transactions, Fifth Biennial Congress*, Singapore, pp. 148-160.

Geertz, H. 1968. Latah in Java: A theoretical paradox. *Indonesia*, 3:93-104.

Hines, T. 1988. *Pseudoscience and the Paranormal*. Buffalo, New York: Prometheus.

Howard, R. and, R. Ford. 1992. From the jumping Frenchmen of Maine to post-traumatic stress disorder: The startle response in neuropsychiatry, *Psychological Medicine* 22:695-707.

Iten, O. 1986. Die Tasaday: Ein Philippinischer steinzeit schwindel. *Neue Zurcher Zeitung* (Zurich), April 12-13:77-79.

Jenner, J. 1990. Latah as coping: A case study offering a new paradox to solve the old one. *International Journal of Social Psychiatry*, 36:194-199.

Jenner, J. 1991. A successfully treated Dutch case of latah. *Journal of Nervous and Mental Disease*, 179:636-637.

Kenny, M. 1978. Latah: The symbolism of a putative mental disorder. *Culture, Medicine and Psychiatry*, 2:209-231.

Kenny, M. 1985. "Paradox Lost: The Latah Problem Revisited." In *The Culture-Bound Syndromes*, ed. by R. Simons and C. Hughes, pp. 63-76. Dordrecht: D. Reidel.

Kessler, C. 1977. "Conflict and Sovereignty in Kelantanese Malay Spirit Seances." In *Case Studies in Spirit Possession*, ed. by V. Crapanzano and V. Garrison, pp. 295-329. New York: Cambridge University Press.

Kiev, A. 1972. *Transcultural Psychiatry*. New York: The Free Press.

Langness, L. L. 1967. Hysterical psychosis: The cross-cultural evidence. *American Journal of Psychiatry*, 124:143-152.

Lee, R. L. 1981. Structure and anti-structure in the culture-bound syndromes: The Malay case. *Culture, Medicine and Psychiatry*, 5:233-248.

Lee, R. L., and S. E. Ackerman. 1980. The sociocultural dynamics of mass hysteria: A case study of social conflict in West Malaysia. *Psychiatry*, 43:78-88.

Murphy, H. B. M. 1973. "History and the Evolution of Syndromes: The Striking Case of Latah and Amok." In *Psychopathology: Contributions from Social, Behavioral, and Biological Sciences*, ed. by M. Hammer et al., pp. 33-55. New York: John Wiley.

Murphy, H.B.M. 1976. "Notes for a Theory on Latah." In *Culture-Bound Syndromes, Ethnopsychiatry, and Alternate Therapies*, ed. by William P. Lebra, pp. 3-21. Honolulu, Hawaii: East-West Center Press.

Naish, J. M. 1979. Problems of deception in medical practice. *Lancet*, ii:139-142.

Ong, A. 1987. *Spirits of Resistance and Capitalist Discipline: Factory Women in Malaysia*. Albany: State University of New York Press.

Opler, M. K. 1967. *Culture and Psychiatry*. Atherton Press: New York.

Penrose, L. S. 1952. *On the Objective Study of Crowd Behavior*. London: H. K. Lewis.

Resner, G., and J. Hartog. 1970. Concepts and terminology of mental disorder among Malays. *Journal of Cross-Cultural Psychology*, 1:369-381.

Rosenthal, D. 1970. *Genetic Theory and Abnormal Behavior*. New York: McGraw-Hill.

Rush, B. 1962. *Medical Inquiries and Observations Upon the Diseases of the Mind*. Facsimile of the Philadelphia 1812 edition. New York: Hafner.

Simons, R. 1994. Commentary: The interminable debate on the nature of latah. *Journal of Nervous and Mental Disease*, 182(6):339-341.

Simons, R. 1985. "Latah II—Problems with a Purely Symbolic Interpretation." In *The Culture-Bound Syndromes*, ed. by R. Simons and C. Hughes, pp. 77-89. Dordrecht: D. Reidel.

Sponsel, L. E. 1990. Ultraprimitive pacifists: The Tasaday as a symbol of peace. *Anthropology Today*, 6(1):3-5.

Tan, E. S. 1980. "The Culture-Bound Syndromes Among Overseas Chinese." In *Normal and Abnormal Behavior in Chinese Culture*, ed. by A. Kleinman and T. Lin, pp. 371-386. Dordrecht, Holland: D. Reidel.

Teoh, J. 1975. Epidemic hysteria and social change: An outbreak in a lower secondary school in Malaysia. *Singapore Medical Journal*, 16(4):301-306.

Van Brero, P.C. 1895. Uber das sogenannte latah. *Allgemeine Zeitschrift fur Psychiatrie und ihre Grenzgebiete*, 51:537-538.

Willson, M. 1989. Two films about truth and falsehood. *Anthropology Today*, 5(5):17-18.

Yap, P. M. 1952. The latah reaction. Its pathodynamics and nosological position. *Journal of Mental Science*. 98:515-564.

PART V

Psychotherapies: Novel or Controversial Psychological Interventions

The effectiveness of psychotherapy remains one of the most hotly debated topics in all of abnormal psychology. Although recent statistical reviews of the psychotherapy literature have consistently indicated that clients who receive therapy are better off than those who receive no treatment, the precise interpretation of this finding remains controversial. For example, how much of the difference between treated and untreated individuals can be attributed to the *placebo effect*—improvement due to the mere expectation of improvement? Are the differences between treated and untreated individuals large enough to have a discernible impact on their real-world functioning? And why does the psychotherapy outcome literature consistently indicate that therapists' effectiveness is unrelated to their amount of experience as clinicians?

In this section of the book, we will examine two dramatically different views concerning the effectiveness of psychotherapy. In addition, we will explore several new or highly controversial interventions for psychological disorders. Several of these treatments, such as virtual reality therapy for phobias, appear to have considerable promise and a growing research foundation. Others, in contrast, such as facilitated communication for infantile autism, appear to have an extremely weak research base and have been criticized by many researchers as pseudoscientific.

The first reading in this section reports the findings from a landmark *Consumer Reports* survey (for which psychologist Martin Seligman was a consultant) examining individuals' satisfaction with psychotherapy. As part of an annual survey in 1994, *Consumer Reports* readers were asked to answer a detailed series of questions concerning their experiences with mental health professionals over the preceding three years, and were asked about their degree of improvement following both psychological and psychopharmacological (drug) treatment. The survey yielded a number of interesting and provocative findings. For example, a large percentage of readers stated that they improved substantially following therapy, and almost all readers reported at least some degree of improvement. Individuals tended to report approximately equal improvement regardless of whether they saw a psychologist, a psychiatrist, or a social worker, although individuals who saw a marriage counselor tended to report less improvement. In addition, individuals reported more improvement the longer they remained in psychotherapy.

The *Consumer Reports* survey bears a number of intriguing implications for both the science and the practice of psychotherapy. Nevertheless, you should bear in mind that this survey was not a strictly controlled experimental study: subjects were not randomly assigned to different conditions, and the readers who responded may not have been a random sample of all those who received therapy. Moreover, all of the data were based on clients' self-reported satisfaction with treatment. As you read this article, you may want to ask yourself how these limitations might influence your interpretation of the results. In addition, you may want to ask yourself whether the survey methodology used in this study offers any important advantages over traditional experimental studies in psychotherapy research.

A dramatically different perspective on the effectiveness of psychotherapy is offered in the next article by psychotherapy researcher Neil Jacobson. Jacobson contends that the psychotherapy profession has exaggerated both the efficacy of therapy and the effects that therapy has on real-world functioning. Moreover, Jacobson argues, psychotherapists frequently fail to inform clients that their treatments are experimental in nature or that other, better validated alternatives are available. Jacobson draws an important, although often overlooked, distinction between *statistical* and *clinical* significance in psychotherapy research. Statistical significance, which has traditionally been emphasized in the psychotherapy outcome literature, refers to whether a treatment's effects are statistically believable; clinical significance refers to whether a treatment's effects are meaningful from the standpoint of real-world functioning. Although acknowledging that some forms of therapy have been demonstrated to have statistically significant effects, Jacobson maintains that relatively few therapeutic procedures have consistently been shown to have clinically significant effects on major psychological disorders. In the words of Gertrude Stein, "a difference is a difference that makes a difference," and Jacobson's thesis is that most forms of psychotherapy have not convincingly made a difference that makes a difference. Jacobson concludes his article with a number of suggestions concerning the proper conduct of psychotherapy and with a series of conjectures regarding aspects of client satisfaction that may be difficult to capture with existing measures of improvement.

Although many studies have examined the question of the effectiveness of psychotherapy, until fairly recently relatively few researchers have addressed the question of whether psychotherapy can be harmful in certain cases. This disturbing possibility is addressed in the next selection by Elizabeth Loftus, a renowned expert in the psychology of memory, who discusses the exceedingly controversial topic of "recovered memories" of childhood abuse. As Loftus notes, increasing numbers of individuals are reporting that they have suddenly "remembered" histories of severe physical or sexual abuse that they had repressed for decades. Most of these individuals claim to have "recovered" these memories following hypnosis and similar suggestive techniques (such as guided imagery) that are used by a sizable minority of psychotherapists. Although Loftus does not dismiss the possibility that at least some "recovered memories" are genuine, she maintains that many if not most of these memories have been unintentionally implanted by well-meaning, but naive, psychotherapists. As a consequence, families and lives have been torn apart by unwarranted accusations of abuse toward innocent relatives. Loftus likens the recent craze of "recovered memories" to the Salem witch trials of the late 17th century, in which innocent individuals were accused and punished on the basis of others' uncorroborated claims.

The next several articles examine novel and in some cases highly controversial treatments for various psychological disorders. First, Donna Bradley briefly discusses a creative and promising new intervention for acrophobia (fear of heights): virtual reality therapy. Bradley notes that the most effective treatment for acrophobia is in-vivo exposure, in which clients are confronted with a series of real-life stimuli that provoke anxiety (for example, the sight of the ground from the top of a tall building). But in-vivo exposure tends to be impractical in a number of cases. As a consequence, psychologist Barbara Rothbaum and her colleagues have pioneered the use of virtual reality therapy, which employs sophisticated computer graphic technology to simulate real-life stimuli, to treat acrophobia and other phobic conditions. Although virtual reality therapy remains an experimental treatment, it has been found to be effective for acrophobia in several preliminary studies. Rothbaum and her colleagues are now extending this technique to other anxiety disorders, such as posttraumatic stress disorder (see Reading 8).

The next selection, by Jill Neimark, Claire Conway, and Peter Doskoch, examines contemporary approaches to the treatment of alcoholism. Neimark and her coauthors begin by summarizing the history of the disease concept of alcoholism in the United States and discuss how our views of alcohol and alcoholics have changed from the colonial era to the present. They also review research on the effects of alcohol on multiple organ systems and on the brain's biochemistry. Neimark, Conway, and Doskoch dispel a number of frequently held myths about alcoholism, including the beliefs that alcoholics cannot quit drinking on their own, that Alcoholics Anonymous treatment is essential for abstinence, and that alcoholics must avoid exposure to any cues that remind them of drinking. Finally, they discuss a number of new and promising treatment approaches for alcoholism, including medications (such as naltrexone) that block endogenous opiates, harm reduction, brief intervention, and cue exposure. As Neimark, Conway, and Doskoch note, increasing numbers of researchers and practitioners appear to be adopting the once heretical view that total abstinence may not always be a necessary or even ideal goal in the treatment of alcoholism.

Scott Lilienfeld next examines the recent storm of controversy surrounding eye movement desensitization and reprocessing (EMDR), a new treatment for posttraumatic stress disorder (see Reading 8) and other anxiety disorders. EMDR has been proclaimed by many of its proponents to be a unique and dramatically effective treatment for anxiety disorders that can, for example, cure PTSD in a single session. In EMDR, the client is asked to internally visualize traumatic imagery while tracking back-and-forth movements of the therapist's finger. Although EMDR superficially resembles exposure treatments, which involve confrontation with anxiety-provoking stimuli and which have been used to treat anxiety disorders for decades, EMDR's advocates claim that EMDR is not simply a variant of existing exposure methods. Lilienfeld reviews the existing literature on the effectiveness of EMDR and concludes that the evidence for its effectiveness is mixed. Moreover, he argues, there is little evidence that EMDR is more effective than extant exposure treatments or that the eye movements purportedly central to EMDR are necessary for whatever effectiveness this procedure may possess. Lilienfeld concludes with a discussion of the implications of these findings for future clinical and research applications of EMDR.

An article by Gina Green next explores both the scientific and social ramifications of an even more controversial and intensely debated treatment—facilitated communication (FC) for infantile autism. Before the introduction of FC, children with autism were almost universally believed to exhibit profound impairments in verbal communication (see Reading 18). But, as Green notes, the advent of FC in Australia and later in the United States raised unprecedented and extraordinary questions concerning autistic children's linguistic competence. In FC, the autistic child types out words (and in some cases, sentences) on a keyboard with the assistance of an adult facilitator who guides the child's hand movements. The rationale underlying FC is that the core deficit in autism is motor, not linguistic, and that autistic children actually possess far greater linguistic capacity than was previously believed. For several years following the appearance of FC, many therapists predicted a dramatic paradigm shift in the way in which autistic individuals were viewed and treated. But, as Green points out, the FC story is a tale without a happy ending. A large body of controlled evidence has now accumulated on the effectiveness of FC, essentially all of which reveals that the power of FC actually resides in the facilitator, not the autistic child. Remarkably, it now appears that the FC "facilitators" were doing far more than facilitating and were instead unintentionally typing out words in the absence of linguistic input from the child. Green concludes her article by drawing parallels between FC and two other phenomena: the use of the Ouija board and the case of Clever Hans, the incredible "counting horse" who was being unintentionally cued by his owner. In the case of FC, however, the consequences have been far more tragic, as Green poignantly documents.

DISCUSSION QUESTIONS

READING 30. Consumer Reports, "Mental Health: Does Therapy Help?"

1. The methodology of the *Consumer Reports* survey differs substantially from that of traditional experimental studies in the psychotherapy literature, in which subjects are randomly assigned to different treatment conditions. What are the potential advantages and disadvantages of each methodology?

2. How would you explain the finding that consumers reported approximately equal satisfaction from seeing psychologists, psychiatrists, and social workers? What limitations, if any, might there be to this finding?

3. What do you think might have happened had the *Consumer Reports* survey asked respondents how much improvement they had experienced from seeing an astrologer or palm reader? Would the amount of improvement have differed from that obtained by seeing a therapist? Defend your answer.

4. Some critics of psychotherapy have suggested that therapy appears to be effective only because clients need to justify to themselves the time, effort, and money they have invested in treatment. Do any of the findings of the *Consumer Reports* survey call this claim into question? Explain.

READING 31. N. Jacobson, "The Overselling of Therapy"

1. Do you agree with Jacobson's criteria for clinical significance (that is, that clients who enter therapy with psychological problems should score in the normal range by the end of treatment)? Why or why not?

2. Jacobson argues that clients who receive a new or experimental therapy should be explicitly informed at the outset of treatment that this treatment is not yet adequately supported by systematic research. But some critics have argued that providing clients with this information might undermine their expectations for improvement and faith in the procedure, which may be essential ingredients in the effectiveness of psychotherapy. Where do you stand on this issue? Explain your reasoning.

3. At the end of his article, Jacobson remarks that "for many people, the process of treatment itself seems to provide some subtle but significant and meaningful benefits that have so far eclipsed our efforts to measure or even define them" (p. 173). If you were a psychotherapy researcher, how might you attempt to assess the kinds of effects to which Jacobson is referring?

READING 32. E. Loftus, "Remembering Dangerously"

1. Loftus conjectures that many if not most "recovered memories" are a consequence of the use of suggestive procedures (such as hypnosis or guided imagery) on the part of psychotherapists. What research evidence might be relevant to evaluating this hypothesis?

2. Is it possible that at least a subset of "recovered memories" are genuine? If so, how might you attempt to distinguish recovered memories that are real from those that have been unintentionally implanted by psychotherapists?

3. As Loftus points out, there has been an enormous increase in the prevalence of "recovered memories" over the past several years. What factors might account for this dramatic recent trend?

READING 33. D. Bradley, "Back in the High Life: A Controlled Study by Emory and Georgia Tech Researchers Tests Virtual Reality Technology in Treating Acrophobia"

1. Other than those mentioned by Bradley, what might be the advantages of virtual reality therapy relative to standard in-vivo exposure treatments? What might be the disadvantages?

2. The study reported by Bradley compared subjects receiving virtual reality treatment with subjects receiving no treatment. This design leaves open the possibility that the positive findings attributed to virtual reality therapy are due to the placebo effect. How might you attempt to control for the placebo effect in a future study?

3. According to Bradley, Rothbaum and her colleagues intend to extend the use of virtual reality technology to posttraumatic stress disorder (PTSD). What types of difficulties might one be likely to encounter in applying virtual reality technology to PTSD, and how might these difficulties be overcome?

READING 34. J. Neimark, C. Conway, & P. Doskoch, "Back from the Drink"

1. Neimark, Conway, and Doskoch note that there has been persisting disagreement regarding whether alcoholism should be classified as a disease. What data, if any, would be relevant to evaluating whether alcoholism is a disease? Or is the classification of a condition as a disease basically a non-scientific question? Explain.

2. Research on the effectiveness of Alcoholics Anonymous (AA) treatment has often been difficult to evaluate because AA groups tend to have a high drop-out rate. How might this high drop-out rate bias the results of studies on AA's effectiveness? As a researcher, how would you attempt to take drop-out rates into account in evaluating the results of treatment studies?

3. Neimark and her coauthors point out that cue exposure appears to exhibit considerable promise as a treatment for alcoholism. Might this treatment be associated with certain risks if used improperly? If so, what risks might they be?

4. Do you believe that complete abstinence should be the goal of alcoholism treatment? Why or why not? Are there certain alcoholics for whom abstinence is an appropriate goal and others for whom it is not?

READING 35. S. O. Lilienfeld, "EMDR Treatment: Less than Meets the Eye?"

1. Lilienfeld observes that at least some of the improvement reported following EMDR may be attributable to the placebo effect. If you were conducting research on the effectiveness of EMDR, how would you attempt to control for the placebo effect?

2. As Lilienfeld points out, psychiatrist Jerome Frank has suggested that all psychotherapies work by means of certain nonspecific factors that are common to every form of treatment. In addition to the therapeutic rituals discussed by Lilienfeld, what might be some of the other nonspecific factors that account for the effectiveness of psychotherapy?

3. Might there be certain dangers associated with the improper use of EMDR? If so, what might they be?

READING 36. G. Green, "Facilitated Communication: Mental Miracle or Sleight of Hand?"

1. What sociological and psychological factors may have accounted for the rapid adoption and acceptance of FC in the absence of adequate controlled data?

2. Why do you think that so many of the sentences generated by means of FC contained reports of sexual abuse, physical abuse, or both, by parents? What might this phenomenon imply about facilitators' implicit beliefs about the etiology of autism?

3. As Green notes, virtually all researchers now agree that FC facilitators were unintentionally typing out words on the keyboard themselves independent of the autistic child's input. But what psychological processes would allow this to occur? What does this phenomenon imply about the existence of unconscious processing?

4. Are there any psychological or medical conditions for which FC might actually be useful? If so, what might they be and why?

SUGGESTIONS FOR FURTHER READING

Christensen, A., & Jacobson, N. S. (1994). Who (or what) can do psychotherapy: The status and challenge of nonprofessional therapies. *Psychological Science, 5,* 8–13.

Dawes, R. M. (1994). *House of cards: Psychology and psychotherapy built on myth.* New York: Free Press.

Jacobson, J. W., Mulick, J. A., & Schwartz, A. A. (1995). A history of facilitated communication: Science, pseudoscience, and antiscience. *American Psychologist, 50,* 755–765.

Jacobson, N. S., & Christensen, A. (1996). Studying the effectiveness of psychotherapy: How well can clinical trials do the job? *American Psychologist, 51,* 1031–1039.

Loftus, E. F., & Ketcham, K. (1994). *The myth of repressed memory.* New York: St. Martin's Press.

Lohr, J. M., Kleinknecht, R. A., Tolin, D. F., & Barrett, R. H. (1995). The empirical status of the clinical application of eye movement desensitization and reprocessing. *Behavior Therapy and Experimental Psychiatry, 26,* 285–302.

Marlatt, G. A., Baer, J. S., Donovan, D. M., & Kivlahan, D. R. (1988). Addictive behaviors: Etiology and treatment. In M. R. Rosenzweig & L. W. Porter (Eds.), *Annual review of psychology.* Palo Alto, CA: Annual Reviews.

Seligman, M. E. P. (1995a). *What you can change and what you can't.* New York: Ballantine Books.

Seligman, M. E. P. (1995b). The effectiveness of psychotherapy: The *Consumer Reports* study. *American Psychologist, 50,* 965–974.

Singer, M. T., & Lalich, J. (1996). *"Crazy" therapies: What are they? Do they work?* San Francisco, CA: Jossey-Bass.

MENTAL HEALTH
DOES THERAPY HELP?

Our groundbreaking survey shows psychotherapy usually works. This report can help you find the best care.

Coping with a serious physical illness is hard enough. But if you're suffering from emotional or mental distress, it's particularly difficult to know where to get help. You may have some basic doubts about whether therapy will help at all. And even if you do decide to enter therapy, your health insurance may not cover it—or cover it well.

As a result, millions of Americans who might benefit from psychotherapy never even give it a try. More than 50 million American adults suffer from a mental or addictive disorder at any given time. But a recent Government survey showed that fewer than one-third of them get professional help.

That's a shame. The results of a candid, in-depth survey of CONSUMER REPORTS subscribers—the largest survey ever to query people on mental-health care—provide convincing evidence that therapy can make an important difference. Four thousand of our readers who responded had sought help from a mental-health provider or a family doctor for psychological problems, or had joined a self-help group. The majority were highly satisfied with the care they received. Most had made strides toward resolving the problems that led to treatment, and almost all said life had become more manageable. This was true for all the conditions we asked about, even among the people who had felt the worst at the beginning.

Among our findings

■ People were just as satisfied and reported similar progress whether they saw a social worker, psychologist, or psychiatrist. Those who consulted a marriage counselor, however, were somewhat less likely to feel they'd been helped.

■ Readers who sought help from their family doctor tended to do well. But people who saw a mental-health specialist for more than six months did much better.

■ Psychotherapy alone worked as well as psychotherapy combined with medication, like *Prozac* or *Xanax*. Most people who took drugs like those did feel they were helpful, but many people reported side effects.

■ The longer people stayed in therapy, the more they improved. This suggests that limited mental-health insurance coverage, and the new trend in health plans—emphasizing short-term therapy—may be misguided.

■ Most people who went to a self-help group were very satisfied with the experience and said they got better. People were especially grateful to Alcoholics Anonymous, and very loyal to that organization.

Our survey adds an important dimension to existing research in mental health. Most studies have started with people who have very specific, well-defined problems, who have been randomly assigned to a treatment or control group, and who have received carefully scripted therapy. Such studies have shown which techniques can help which problems (see "What Works Best?," page 737), but they aren't a realistic reflection of most patients' experiences.

Our survey, in contrast, is a unique look at what happens in real life, where problems are diverse and less well-defined, and where some therapists try one technique after another until something works. The success of therapy under these real-life conditions has never before been well studied, says Martin Seligman, former director of clinical training in psychology at the University of Pennsylvania and past president of the American Psychological Association's division of clinical psychology.

Seligman, a consultant to our project, believes our readers' experiences send "a message of hope" for other people dealing with emotional problems.

Like other surveys, ours has several built-in limitations. Few of the people responding had a chronic, disabling condition such as schizophrenia or manic depression. We asked readers about their past experiences, which can be less reliable than asking about the present. We may have sampled an unusually large number of people in long-term treatment. Finally, our data comes from the readers' own perceptions, rather than from a clinician's assessment. However, other studies have shown that such self-reports fre-

Copyright 1995 by Consumers Union of U.S., Inc., Yonkers, NY 10703-1057. Reprinted by permission from *Consumer Reports*, November 1995.

quently agree with professionals' clinical judgments.

Who went for help

In our 1994 Annual Questionnaire, we asked readers about their experiences with emotional problems and their encounters with health-care providers and groups during the years 1991 to 1994. Like the average American outpatient client, the 4000 readers who said they had sought professional help were mostly well educated. Their median age was 46, and about half were women. However, they may be more amenable to therapy than most.

Many who went to a mental-health specialist were in considerable pain at the time they entered treatment. Forty-three percent said their emotional state was either very poor ("I barely managed to deal with things") or fairly poor ("Life was usually pretty tough").

Their reasons for seeking therapy included several classic emotional illnesses: depression, anxiety, panic, and phobias. Among the other reasons our readers sought therapy: marital or sexual problems, frequent low moods, problems with children, problems with jobs, grief, stress-related ailments, and alcohol or drug problems.

The results: Therapy works

Our survey showed that therapy for mental-health problems can have a substantial effect. Forty-four percent of people whose emotional state was "very poor" at the start of treatment said they now feel good. Another 43 percent who started out "fairly poor" also improved significantly, though somewhat less. Of course, some people probably would have gotten better without treatment, but the vast majority specifically said that therapy helped.

Most people reported they were helped with the specific problems that brought them to therapy, even when those problems were quite severe. Of those who started out "very poor," 54 percent said treatment "made things a lot better," while another one-third said it helped their problems to some extent. The same pattern of improvement held for just about every condition.

Overall, almost everyone who sought help experienced some relief —improvements that made them less troubled and their lives more pleasant. People who started out feeling the worst reported the most progress. Among people no longer in

MENTAL-HEALTH INSURANCE

WHO PAYS—AND HOW MUCH?

Private insurers have always covered mental disorders and substance abuse more grudgingly than medical illness, either by building in limits or by interposing a case manager between you and your benefit. And very few plans deal well with the lifelong needs of people with chronic, severe mental illness. On the whole, says Kathleen Kelso, executive director of the Mental Health Association of Minnesota, "insurers would just as soon cover us from the neck down."

Almost all traditional fee-for-service plans pay 80 percent or more of the fee when you visit the doctor with a medical problem. But for outpatient therapy, the majority pay just 50 percent, and frequently that's after "capping" bills at well below the therapists' actual fees —which range on average from $80 to $120 according to Psychotherapy Finances, an industry newsletter. Most insurance plans also impose one or more other limits on mental-health coverage, such as the number of outpatient visits and hospital days they will pay for. In addition, many plans have annual or lifetime dollar maximums; for outpatient care, it can be as low as $1000 and $10,000, respectively. In recent years consumer advocates have lobbied for state laws that would equalize coverage for psychiatric and other illnesses. So far, just six states—Maine, Maryland, Minnesota, New Hampshire, Rhode Island, and Texas—have passed so-called "parity" laws. Consumers Union supports such laws, and has actively worked for their passage.

Health maintenance organizations (HMOs) also limit access to psychiatric services, typically providing a maximum of 20 outpatient visits and 30 hospital days a year. Patients usually have to go through their family physician or another gatekeeper to gain access to those benefits, and may get less than the maximum.

In our survey of mental-health care, respondents whose coverage limited the length and frequency of therapy, and the type of therapist, reported poorer outcomes. (However, we found no clear difference in outcome between people with fee-for-service coverage and those in HMOs and preferred provider plans.) Paying for therapy on their own was clearly a hardship for many: Twenty-one percent cited the cost of therapy as a reason for quitting.

To hold down spending, increasing numbers of employers, HMOs, and fee-for-service plans are turning to specialized managed-care companies to run their mental-health benefit. These specialty firms refer patients to a network of clinicians who must adhere to strict treatment guidelines. And they *have* reined in spending, saving some employers as much as 30 percent in the cost of mental-health care.

But many patients—and their therapists—feel they're being shortchanged. Psychiatrists complain about the difficulty of extending a hospital stay for patients considered too sick to leave and the challenge of getting approval for more than brief outpatient care.

Although many plans run by managed-care firms nominally have generous benefits, reality may fall somewhat short. All services must be authorized by a case manager. To get approval for additional sessions, therapists must provide details about a patient's problems and the course of treatment.

With scores of managed-care companies nationwide, there's great variability in how they tend to the needs of their subscribers. Even critics acknowledge that some plans are quite accommodating, and that some overly stringent practices have been curbed. But concern about heavy-handed practices has prompted several states to enact laws regulating managed-care services.

How to choose a plan

If you're picking a health-care plan and are concerned about mental-health coverage, you should ask some pointed questions:

■ **What are the stated benefits?** Pay close attention to the benefit limits, including co-payments, limits on the number of hospital days and outpatient sessions, and annual or lifetime dollar maximums. A typical plan with limits covers 30 days of inpatient care and 50 or fewer outpatient visits. But the cap it sets on covered charges may be low, and the copayments high.

■ **If the benefits cover only "medically necessary" treatment, who makes that termination?** It's best if that decision is left to you and your therapist. But in many managed-care plans it's a case manager who decides whether you need therapy or hospitalization, and how long it should last.

■ **What are your rights of appeal if coverage is denied or cut short?** In many plans the grievance process consists of a single appeal.

■ **In a managed-care plan, how large is the provider panel?** The more therapists in your area, the more likely you'll find one whose personality and expertise are a good match for you.

■ **Will the plan add new providers to its panel?** This can be important if you're already seeing a therapist who's not part of the plan but is willing to join.

■ **Which facilities are approved by the plan?** Be sure there's a hospital that's convenient and that offers a broad spectrum of mental-health and substance-abuse services. Also look for transitional and intermediate-care programs, such as mental-health day centers.

treatment, two-thirds said they'd left because their problems had been resolved or were easier to deal with.

Whom should you see?

In the vast field of mental health, psychiatrists, psychologists, and clinical social workers have long fought for turf. Only psychiatrists, who are medical doctors, can prescribe drugs and have the training to detect medical problems that can affect a person's mental state. Otherwise, each of these professionals is trained to understand human behavior, to recognize problems, and to provide therapy.

Historically, social workers have been the underdogs and have had to fight for state laws requiring insurance companies to cover their services. But many of today's budget-minded insurers *favor* social workers —and psychiatric nurses—because they offer relatively low-cost services.

In our survey, almost three-quarters of those seeking professional help went to a mental-health specialist. Their experiences suggest that any of these therapists can be very helpful. Psychiatrists, psychologists, and social workers received equally high marks and were praised for being supportive, insightful, and easy to confide in. That remained true even when we statistically controlled for the seriousness and type of the problem and the length of treatment.

Those who went to marriage counselors didn't do quite as well, and gave their counselors lower grades for competence. One reason may be that working with a fractured couple is difficult. Also, almost anyone can hang out a shingle as a marriage counselor. In some states the title "marriage and family therapist" is restricted to those with appropriate training. But anyone can use other words to say they *do* marriage therapy, and in most places the title "marriage counselor" is up for grabs.

What about doctors?

Many people are more comfortable taking their problems to their family doctor than to a psychologist or psychiatrist. That may work well for some people, but our data suggest that many would be better off with a psychotherapist.

Readers who exclusively saw their family doctor for emotional problems—about 14 percent of

The worse people felt at the start of therapy, the greater their gains.

those in our survey —had a very different experience from those who consulted a mental-health specialist. Treatment tended to be shorter; more than half of those whose care was complete had been treated for less than two months. People who went to family doctors were much more likely to get psychiatric drugs—83 percent of them did, compared with 20 percent of those who went to mental-health specialists. And almost half the people whose doctors gave them drugs received medication without the benefit of much counseling.

The people who relied on their family doctors for help were less distraught at the outset than those who saw mental-health providers; people with severe emotional problems apparently get themselves to a specialist. Even so, only half were highly satisfied with their family doctor's treatment (compared with 62 percent who were highly satisfied with their mental-health provider). A significant minority felt their doctor had neither the time nor temperament to address emotional issues. In general, family doctors did help people get back on their feet—but longer treatment with a specialist was more effective.

However, if you begin treatment with your family doctor, that's where you're likely to stay. Family doctors referred their patients to a mental-health specialist in only one out of four cases, even when psychotherapy might have made a big difference. Only half of those who were severely distressed were sent on, and 60 percent of patients with panic disorder or phobias were never referred, even though specific therapies are known to work for those problems.

Other research has shown that many family doctors have a poor track record when it comes to mental health. They fail to diagnose some 50 to 80 percent of psychological problems, and sometimes prescribe psychiatric drugs for too short a time or at doses too low to work.

The power of groups

It was 60 years ago that a businessman and a physician, both

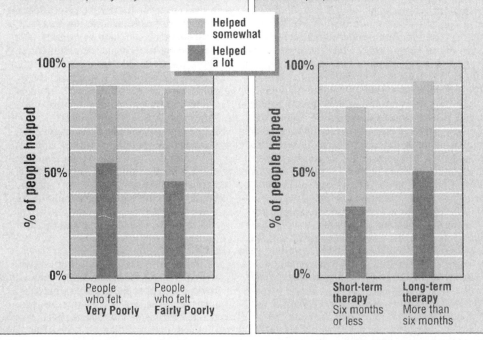

How much can therapy help?

Almost everyone got some relief from the problems that brought them to a therapist, no matter how poorly they felt at the start.

Legend:
- Helped somewhat
- Helped a lot

% of people helped — 100%, 50%, 0%

People who felt **Very Poorly**
People who felt **Fairly Poorly**

Short-term or long-term?

Staying in therapy for more than six months brought greater improvement to more people.

% of people helped — 100%, 50%, 0%

Short-term therapy Six months or less
Long-term therapy More than six months

WHAT WORKS BEST?

THE RIGHT TREATMENTS FOR YOUR TROUBLES

Until a decade or so ago, any evidence that psychotherapy worked came from the testimonials of therapists and their patients. But today, controlled studies have shown that psychotherapy does make a difference: People with a broad range of problems can usually benefit from psychological treatment. More important, for certain conditions researchers have homed in on specific therapies and drugs that can bring swift improvement for the majority of sufferers.

Here is a summary of the top treatment options for four common problems. It was compiled from the scientific literature by psychologist Martin Seligman and reviewed by psychiatrists Stewart Agras of Stanford University and Jesse Schomer of Cornell University, and by social worker Eleanor Bromberg of The Hunter School of Social Work in New York. (For a comprehensive look at treatments that work, see Seligman's book, "What You Can Change & What You Can't," Ballantine Books, New York, 1995.)

Depression

More than the passing blues, depression can sap you of pleasure, hope, and vitality, upend your eating and sleeping habits, and draw a veil of despair that lasts for months or years. In bipolar depression, also called manic-depression, the lows alternate with excessive, frenetic highs. Most of the time, depression can be cut short and considerably relieved.

With cognitive therapy, you learn to recognize and change the negative assumptions and beliefs that color your emotions and shape your world view. If, for example, you react to small setbacks by thinking you can't do anything right, you'll learn to focus on evidence to the contrary—your recent promotion at work, for instance. Cognitive therapy brings considerable relief to about 70 percent of depressed people. It takes about a month to start working, and typically involves a few months of weekly sessions.

Interpersonal therapy is just as effective and runs about as long, but focuses instead on the difficulties of personal relationships. You'll examine current conflicts and disappointments, learn how they sow depression, and work on successful ways of relating to other people.

Drug therapy is about as effective as these psychotherapies. Each of the three major classes of antidepressant drugs works equally well. People who don't respond to one type of drug may respond to another; overall, 60 percent to 80 per-

cent of depressed people get marked relief within three to six weeks. However, the classes differ significantly in their adverse effects: Fluoxetine (*Prozac*) and related drugs tend to be better tolerated, though they frequently produce insomnia, restlessness, and sexual problems. The older, "tricyclic" antidepressants such as amitriptyline (*Elavil*) can cause drowsiness, tremor, weight gain, and heart-rhythm changes. For people with manic-depression, treatment with the drug lithium carbonate (*Escalith, Lithane*) is clearly the best route.

Electroconvulsive therapy is used for severely depressed people who can't take, or don't respond to, antidepressant drugs. Electrodes placed on the head transmit bursts of electricity believed to affect many of the same brain chemicals as antidepressant drugs. The "dosage" has been greatly reduced from the jolts used in the past. Repeated several times over the course of a week, ECT quickly relieves severe depression about 75 percent of the time. The downside is the risk of anesthesia and the side effects—temporary but disturbing—of memory loss and confusion.

Anxiety

Unlike ordinary worrying, clinical anxiety is irrational freezes you into inaction, or dominates your life.

Tranquilizers such as diazepam (*Valium*) and alprazolam (*Xanax*) can provide quick relief, but the benefit ends when the drug is stopped. Extended use may result in tolerance, which diminishes the benefit, and also produces dependency, making it hard to quit.

Everyday anxiety often yields to self-help techniques. Simple forms of **meditation** can be useful. So can various forms of **relaxation**, such as progressive relaxation. Some therapists teach these techniques, or you can check a local YMCA, community hospital, or yoga institute for courses.

If your anxiety is intense and unyielding, it may need professional attention. Cognitive-behavioral therapy is often helpful; you'll learn to counter the irrational thoughts that provoke anxiety and to overcome fears.

Panic

A panic attack isn't easily forgotten. It produces chest pain, sweating, nausea,

dizziness, and a feeling of overwhelming dread. Millions of people suffer such episodes repeatedly and unexpectedly.

Antidepressant drugs and the anti-anxiety drug *Xanax* can dampen or even prevent panic attacks in the majority of people. But side effects include drowsiness and lethargy, and panic rebounds about half the time when therapy is stopped.

Research has shown that many conditions can be helped by more than one kind of therapy.

An alternative approach is cognitive therapy, which provides relief to almost all panic sufferers. Treatment is based on the idea that panic occurs when a person mistakes normal symptoms of anxiety for symptoms of a heart attack, going crazy, or dying. The fear that something is wrong can escalate into a full-fledged panic attack. In cognitive therapy you'll learn to short-circuit that reaction by interpreting anxiety symptoms for what they are.

Phobias

Strong, irrational fears affect more than 10 percent of American adults. Some fear specific objects, such as animals, snakes, or insects; even more can't bear crowded places or open spaces, a condition called agoraphobia. Still others with social phobia recoil from situations involving other people.

Two behavior therapies are now used, with considerable success, to treat phobias. In both, you'll have to confront what you most fear. The more gradual technique is **systematic desensitization**: After learning progressive relaxation, you'll construct a fear hierarchy with the most terror-inducing situation at the top. In the first of a series of steps, you'll go into a relaxed state, then vividly imagine the least fearsome situation—or face it in real life. Gradually you'll move up the hierarchy and face more frightening situations.

During **flooding**, the other therapy, you're thrown in immediately with the thing that scares you; a cat phobic, for instance, will sit in a room full of cats. The goal is to stay for an agreed-upon length of time while the anxiety ebbs.

Behavior therapy is most successful with object and social phobias, producing lasting results in the majority of cases in a matter of weeks or months. In agoraphobia, behavior therapy is best combined with an antidepressant drug to control panic.

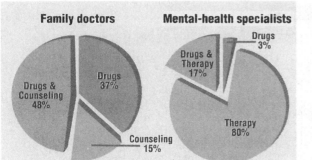

Family doctors   **Mental-health specialists**

Drugs & Counseling 48%
Drugs 37%
Counseling 15%

Drugs 3%
Drugs & Therapy 17%
Therapy 80%

Talk or drugs? Family doctors were much more likely to dispense mostly medication or a mix of drugs and talk. Very few mental-health therapists relied mainly on drugs; the vast majority provided psychotherapy.

struggling with alcoholism, realized they could stay sober by talking to one another. They talked to other alcoholics, too, and eventually worked out the system of long-term recovery known as Alcoholics Anonymous, or AA. Today there are over a million active AA members in the U.S., and attending an AA group is often recommended as part of professional treatment. The AA format has also been adopted by dozens of other self-help groups representing a wide spectrum of dysfunctional behavior, from Gamblers Anonymous to Sex and Love Addicts Anon. Support groups also bring together people who are dealing with medical illness or other trials.

One-third of our survey respondents went to a group, often in addition to individual psychotherapy. Overall, they told us, the groups seemed to help.

Readers who went to AA voiced overwhelming approval. Virtually all endorsed AA's approach to treatment, and most said their struggle with addiction had been largely successful. In keeping with AA's principle that recovery is a lifelong process, three-quarters of our readers had been in the group for more than two years, and most were still attending. Most of those who had dropped out said they'd moved on because their problems had improved.

Certainly, not everyone who goes to AA does as well; our sampling method probably over-represented long-term, and thus successful, AA members. AA's own surveys suggest that about half of those who come to the program are gone within three months. Studies that follow people who have undergone treatment for alcoholism find that AA is no more or less effective than other programs: A year after entering treatment, about half the participants are still in trouble.

Nevertheless, AA has several components that may maximize the chance of success. In general, most alcoholics do well while they are being actively treated. In AA, members are supposed to attend 90 meetings in the first 90 days, followed by three meetings a week for life.

Drugs, pro and con

For decades, drug therapy to treat problems such as depression carried a raft of unpleasant, sometimes dangerous side effects. Then came *Prozac* (fluoxetine), launched in 1988. Safer and easier to take than previous antidepressants, *Prozac* and other drugs in its class—including sertraline (*Zoloft*) and paroxetine (*Paxil*)—have radically changed the treatment of depression. Along the way, people have claimed that *Prozac* seems to relieve a growing list of other complaints—from eating disorders to shyness to, most recently, premenstrual syndrome.

In our survey, 40 percent of readers who sought professional help received psychiatric drugs. And overall, about 60 percent of readers who took drugs said the medication helped a lot.

However, many of our readers did well with psychotherapy alone; in fact, people who received only psychotherapy improved as much as those who got therapy plus drugs.

For many people, having the option of talk therapy is important because every psychiatric drug has potential side effects that some individuals find hard to tolerate. Almost half of all our respondents on medication reported problems with the drug. Drowsiness and a feeling of disorientation were the most common complaints, especially among people taking the older antidepressants such as amitriptyline (*Elavil*).

Although the problems associated with psychiatric drugs are well-known, 20 percent of readers said their provider never discussed them —a disturbing lapse in communication. Equally disturbing was the finding that 40 percent of the people taking antianxiety drugs had done so for more than a year—25 percent for more than two years—even though long-term use results in habituation, requiring larger and larger doses.

Antianxiety medications such as *Xanax* and *Valium* can provide relief if used for a short time during a particularly stressful period, such as the death of a parent. But they haven't been well tested for generalized anxiety—a kind of chronic, excessive worrying combined with physical and emotional symptoms—and therapists have found them only erratically effective.

Xanax is approved by the U.S. Food and Drug Administration for panic disorder, which causes repeated bouts of unbearable anxiety; studies show that it acts quickly to reduce panic attacks. But after two months, *Xanax* apparently performs little better than a placebo. (See CONSUMER REPORTS, January 1993.) The reason many people take antianxiety drugs for so long is that they're extremely hard to kick; if the drug is stopped, symptoms return in full force.

How long will it take?

When a person needs psychotherapy, how much do they need? That has become a critical question—both for clinicians and for the insurers that pay for therapy. And it's a hard one to answer.

Nationally, most people who get therapy go for a relatively short time—an average of four to eight sessions. It's not clear, however, whether people stop going because they have been helped enough, because they don't think the therapy is working, or because they've run out of money. Controlled studies of specific kinds of therapy usually cover only 12 to 20 visits. While brief therapy often helps, there's no way to tell from such studies whether 30 or 40 sessions, or even more, would be even more effective.

For the people in our survey, longer psychotherapy was associated with better outcomes. Among people who entered therapy with

People in therapy more than six months reported the most progress.

similar levels of emotional distress, those who stayed in treatment for more than six months reported greater gains than those who left earlier. Our data suggest that for many people, even a year's worth of therapy with a mental-health specialist may be very worthwhile. People who stayed in treatment for more than two years reported the best outcomes of all. However, these people tended to have started out with more serious problems.

We also found that people got better in three distinct ways, and that all three kinds of improvement increased with additional treatment. First, therapy eased the problems that brought people to treatment. Second, it helped them to function better, improving their ability to relate well to others, to be productive at work, and to cope with everyday stress. And it enhanced what can be called "personal growth." People in therapy had more confidence and self-esteem, understood themselves better, and enjoyed life more.

Despite the potential benefit of long-term therapy, many insurance plans limit mental-health coverage to "medically necessary" services—which typically means short-term treatment aimed at symptom relief. If you want to stay in therapy longer, you may have to pay for it yourself.

Our findings complement recent work by psychologist Kenneth Howard of Northwestern University. By following the progress of 854 psychotherapy patients, Howard and his associates found that recovery followed a "dose-response" curve, with the greatest response occurring early on. On average, 50 percent of people recovered after 11 weekly therapy sessions, and 75 percent got better after about a year.

Recommendations

Emotional distress may not always require professional help. But when problems threaten to become overwhelming or interfere with everyday life, there's no need to feel defeated.

Our survey shows there's real help available from every quarter—family doctors, psychotherapists, and self-help groups. Both talk therapy and medication, when warranted, can bring relief to people with a wide range of problems and deep despair.

With such clear benefits to be had, the strict limits on insurance coverage for mental-health care are cause for concern. As the debate over health care continues, we believe

that improving mental-health coverage is important.

If you want to see a therapist, you should approach therapy as an active consumer. In our survey, the more diligently a person "shopped" for a therapist—consulting with several candidates, checking their experience and qualifications, and speaking to previous clients—the more they ultimately improved. Once in treatment, those who formed a real partnership with their therapist—by being open, even with painful subjects, and by working on issues between sessions—were more likely to progress.

When you look for a therapist, competence and personal chemistry should be your priorities. You'll be sharing your most intimate thoughts and feelings, so it's important to choose someone who puts you at ease.

Many people first consult their family doctor, who has already won their confidence and trust. If you decide to stay with your physician for treatment, bear in mind that the approach will probably be medically based and relatively short.

If you would prefer to work with a therapist, ask your doctor for a referral. Other good referral sources are national professional associations or their local or state chapters. For information or referrals you can call the American Psychiatric Association, at 202 682-6220; the American Psychological Association, 202 336-5800; the National Association of Social Workers, 800 638-8799, ext. 291; the American Association for Marriage and Family Therapy, 800 374-2638; and the American Psychiatric Nurses Association, 202 857-1133. Also contact local universities, hospitals, and psychotherapy and psychoanalytic training institutes. For general information on mental illness, call the National Alliance for the Mentally Ill, 800 950-6264.

Family and friends may also know of reputable therapists; try to get several names to consider. Our readers who located therapists through personal or professional references felt better served than those who relied on ads, their managed care company's roster, or local clinics. ∎

THE TYPES OF THERAPIES AND THERAPISTS

If you're considering mental-health treatment, you're facing a wide choice of therapies and practitioners. Many therapists favor a particular theoretical approach, though often they use a combination.

In **psychoanalysis**, Freud's classical technique employing a couch and free association, patients explore and confront troubling childhood experiences. In **psychodynamic therapy**, the emphasis is on discovering unconscious conflicts and defense mechanisms that hinder adult behavior. The goal of **interpersonal therapy** is to enhance relationships and communication skills. **Cognitive therapy** is aimed at helping people recognize and change distorted ways of thinking. **Behavioral therapy** seeks to replace harmful behaviors with useful ones.

As for choosing a therapist, be careful. Anyone can legally be called a psychotherapist, whether or not he or she has received the training and supervision needed to competently practice. Look for someone licensed or certified in one of the following fields:

∎ **Psychiatrists** are physicians who have completed three years of residency training in psychiatry following four years of medical school and a one-year internship. All are trained in psychiatric diagnosis and pharmacotherapy, but only some residency

programs provide extensive experience in outpatient psychotherapy.

∎ **Psychoanalysts** have a professional degree in psychiatry, psychology, or social work, plus at least two years of extensive supervised training at a psychoanalytic institute.

∎ **Psychologists** with the credential Ph.D., Psy.D., or Ed.D. are licensed professionals with doctoral-level training, typically including a year of clinical internship in a mental-health facility and a year of supervised post-doctoral experience.

∎ **Social workers** typically train in a two-year master's degree program that involves fieldwork in a wide range of human services, including mental health settings. Those who seek state certification or licensing as a clinical social worker need two years of supervised post-grad experience and must pass a statewide exam.

∎ **Marriage and family therapists** may have a master's or doctoral degree from an accredited graduate training program in the field, or may have another professional degree with supervised experience in the specialty.

∎ **Psychiatric nurses** are registered nurses who work in mental-health settings, often as part of a therapeutic team. Advanced practice nurses have a master's degree and can provide psychotherapy.

THE OVERSELLING OF THERAPY

Like it or not, it's time to listen to what clinical researchers are telling us

WHEN MONIQUE, A FIRST-YEAR LAW STUDENT, BEGAN PSYCHO-analysis with a prominent analyst in 1982, she complained of pervasive sadness, hopelessness, fatigue, difficulty concentrating and loss of appetite. She regularly woke up in the middle of the night, unable to go back to sleep. She had been plagued by these problems for most of her adult life and met the diagnostic criteria for "major depression." During the entire eight years that Monique was in psychoanalysis, she remained depressed. Despite her lack of improvement, Monique's psychoanalyst never changed treatments, never suggested alternative approaches and never consulted with colleagues about her case.

While shopping at a pharmacy one day, Monique noticed a self-help book about cognitive therapy. After reading it and doing some investigating, she discovered that there were a number of brief psychotherapies that had some success in helping people with depression.

BY NEIL JACOBSON

This article first appeared in the March/April 1995 *Family Therapy Networker, 19,* pp. 41–47, and is copied here with permission.

Monique also learned of several anti-depressant medications that were often effective. Needless to say, she was disturbed that her analyst had never told her about these options, let alone offered them to her. For all Monique knew when she began treatment, psychoanalysis was the treatment of choice, indeed the only viable treatment, for major depression.

Monique found a cognitive therapist, started taking an antidepressant and recovered from her depression within six weeks of terminating her analysis. By now a practicing attorney, she considered it unconscionable that her analyst had allowed her to suffer for eight years while continuing unsuccessfully with psychoanalysis. Drawing an analogy to physicians who are expected to provide clients with all available treatment options and to outline their costs and benefits, she was astonished to find that it was not common practice among psychotherapists to do the same. Monique believed that her analyst was guilty of malpractice, but, in the end, she was so delighted to be feeling better that she didn't pursue litigation.

There are aspects of this case that are all too familiar to most mental health professionals. It is not uncommon for therapists to keep clients in therapy long after it is obvious that little or no progress is being made. Nor is it unusual to encounter therapists who are either unaware of or do not present their clients with a range of treatment options or discuss the existing scientific knowledge of their relative efficacy. Indeed, numerous surveys of mental health professionals indicate that even those trained in research do not keep up with the research literature, which itself seems to have little influence on clinical practice. Instead, the practice of psychotherapy seems to be influenced primarily by tradition, current fads and fashions and the persuasiveness of charismatic workshop leaders and book writers.

As a clinical scientist, a psychotherapy researcher and the former director of a doctoral program in clinical psychology, I have been training therapists and practicing psychotherapy since 1972. It is clear to me that, as an instrument of human change, psychotherapists have been overselling their product since the days of Freud. If the media and even some of our social science colleagues are beginning to criticize psychotherapy, it may be in part because the culture is beginning to come to this same realization. How bad is the problem? Is there anything that can be done?

WHILE LOBBYING HARD FOR A piece of the health care reform pie, advocates for the mental health professions have presented psychotherapies (and pharmacotherapy) as proven treatments for a variety of mental health problems, citing positive research findings, whenever possible, to support their claims. Where research findings don't exist, they cite opinions, which often amount to nothing more than an endorsement of long-established, unsubstantiated clinical traditions. For example, one common unsubstantiated assumption is that brief therapy may be sufficient for relatively circumscribed problems, such as phobias or panic attacks, but long-term psychotherapy is necessary for lifelong, serious problems, such as personality disorders. This position is not based on any evidence of efficacy, but simply on the *belief* that brief therapies do not work with certain problems. Some proposals by state psychological associations have actually requested insurance reimbursement for up to 150 therapy sessions per year for serious problems, even though there is no empirical basis that would justify such coverage.

Of course, advocates for psychotherapy are no different from advocates for other health care providers, who also practice many unproven techniques with impunity and receive reimbursement for them from insurance companies. In some respects, health care reimbursement has been based on the professional qualifications of the *provider* rather than on the efficacy of their chosen *treatment*. Physicians are prone to practicing unsubstantiated techniques and requesting that the government pay for them, as are mental health lobbyists. For example, until recently, ulcers were treated as psychophysiological disorders, without any empirical basis for this assumption. It has since been discovered that ulcers are infectious diseases that have little or nothing to do with stress, and can be treated quite effectively with antibiotics if discovered early enough. Still, at least some medical treatments offered by physicians make a clinically significant difference in the quality of life of the patients even if they do not "cure" the condition. Can the same be said of psychotherapy?

There is substantial research apparently demonstrating that psychotherapy actually does work. The increasing sophistication of research methodology has made it possible to pool together large numbers of therapy outcome studies and, through a statistical technique called meta-analysis, come to general conclusions about therapy's efficacy. *The Benefits of Psychotherapy*, by Mary Lee Smith, Gene V. Glass and Thomas I. Miller, perhaps the most extensive meta-analysis of therapy research, has been widely cited as providing incontrovertible evidence that psychotherapy helps people. Indeed, the authors conclude, "Psychotherapy is beneficial, consistently so and in many different ways. Its benefits are on a par with other expensive and ambitious interventions such as schooling and medicine . . . The evidence overwhelmingly supports the efficacy of psychotherapy. . . . Indeed, its efficacy has been established with monotonous regularity."

In the widely used textbook on psychotherapy research, *Handbook of Psychotherapy and Behavior Change*, edited by Sol Garfield and Allen Bergin, the chapters are filled with explicit and implicit conclusions that the outcome question has been resolved. Even Robyn W. Dawes, in his muckraking critique of professional psychology, *House of Cards: Psychology and Psychotherapy Built on Myth*, concludes that "Psychotherapy works overall in reducing psychologically painful and often debilitating symptoms . . . . In fact, it is partly because psychotherapy in its multitude of forms is generally effective that I am writing this book."

Unfortunately, these conclusions are premature. For one thing, critics point out that such generalized assertions about psychotherapy's efficacy are meaningless, because they provide no information about what treatments provided by which therapists work for what problems. In other words, just because psychotherapy in general has a positive effect, we cannot infer that a particular treatment will work for a particular type of client treated by a particular therapist. For example, is psychotherapy of any value in the treatment of depression and, if so, what types of treatments are likely to work? Are certain types of therapists more likely than others to be effective with depressives? This sort of question tends not to be addressed in reviews that examine hundreds of studies with diverse client populations, diverse modalities of treatment and diverse types of therapists.

There is, however, a more fundamental problem with any conclusions about psychotherapy efficacy based on statistical comparisons between treatment groups. Suppose you are comparing an experimental treatment for obesity with a control treatment. If the average weight loss in the experimental treatment is 10

False prophets are easy to recognize. They expect you to trust their clinical judgment, while showing no signs of humility or doubts about the wisdom of what they are proselytizing.

▼▼▼▼▼▼▼▼▼▼▼▼▼▼▼▼▼▼▼

pounds and the average weight loss in the control treatment is zero, the size of the statistical effect could be immense. Yet, if the clients entered treatment weighing 300 pounds, an average weight loss of 10 pounds would not make a clinically significant difference in their lives. In other words, the size of a statistical effect tells you little or nothing about its clinical significance.

Statistical comparisons bear no necessary relationship to the clinical significance of the treatment under consideration. Clinical significance refers to the extent to which clients feel that therapy has given them something approximating what they came for or has made a meaningful difference in their lives. But what does this mean in terms that can somehow be measured? Although the concept of clinical significance has taken on increased importance among psychotherapy researchers, there is little consensus as to how it should be defined. My colleagues Dirk Revenstorf, William C. Follette and I have developed a set of statistical techniques that provide a definition of clinical significance in terms

of recovery. We reasoned that if clients make clinically significant changes during the course of therapy, by the end of therapy they should resemble their "functional" counterparts more than their "dysfunctional" cohorts on whatever problem they entered therapy to solve.

For example, if clients enter therapy complaining of depression, by the end of therapy they should score within the normal range on measures of depression in order for their improvement to be clinically significant. Thus, a client who leaves therapy less depressed than when he or she entered, but who still has significant depressive symptoms, would be considered to be improved but not recovered. We have developed statistical techniques to determine whether the magnitude of change is substantial enough to place the client within the normal range by the end of therapy. Generally, consumers of therapy expect that the problem they came in with will be resolved. It is of considerable interest to know how often clients get what they came for, and it is important to recognize that clients enter therapy with little

regard for statistically significant improvement—they simply want to feel better, which they believe will happen as soon as therapy eliminates the problem as they define it, whether or not the therapist deems that belief realistic.

Using these statistical techniques, we have discovered that when psychotherapy outcome is examined under the microscope of clinical significance, its effects appear to be quite modest, even for disorders that are thought to be easily treated and even when so called "established" techniques are used. For example, it is often said that there are many effective treatments for major depression. Biological psychiatrists consider it proven that various forms of antidepressant medication work. A number of brief psychotherapies—most notably Aaron T. Beck's cognitive therapy and Gerald Klerman and Myrna Weissman's interpersonal psychotherapy—have ostensibly received considerable empirical support.

Yet, when the actual outcomes of these treatments are examined in terms of their clinical significance, the results are disturbing. Consider the federally funded, multisite investigation conducted in the 1980s known as the Treatment of Depression Collaborative Research Program (TDCRP), designed to compare the effectiveness of psychotherapies versus antidepressant medication. It is difficult to study depression because it tends to be episodic; that is, most depressives recover within a year even without therapy, and most who recover eventually have another episode of depression. Thus, it is relatively easy to attribute to therapy what may have transpired even without therapy. The TDCRP is widely considered to have achieved the highest degree of methodological rigor of any large-scale outcome study yet conducted, and thus has produced results that are more believable than those from many other trials of dubious design quality.

From the standpoint of clinical significance, the question is, "What percentage of clients stay in treatment, recover from their depressive episode and stay recovered for a reasonable period of time following termination?" In this particular study, where expert therapists were used and millions of dollars were spent to ensure quality control, the proportion of clients who completed the 12-week, 20-session treatment, recovered from their depressive episode, and stayed nondepressed for 18 months ranged from 19 to 32 percent across the three active treatments (imipramine, cognitive therapy and interpersonal psychotherapy). Thus, only a minority of patients recovered and stayed recovered for more than a year. Even the placebo treatment did as well (20 percent). Neither pharmacotherapy nor psychotherapy led to lasting recovery for the great majority of cases.

These findings are not atypical, either for major depression or for other mental health problems. In a series of studies of clinical significance, our research group has examined conduct disorders in adolescents, couples seeking therapy for marital distress and people with anxiety disorders. We have found the recovered patient (the one who shows few or no signs or symptoms of the initial complaint and believes him- or herself to be "cured") to be the exception rather than the rule for every type of disorder examined and for every type of therapy that we have looked at—psychodynamic, behavioral, cognitive and family therapy. When one considers even more intractable problems, such as addictive behaviors, schizophrenia and personality disorders, the clinical significance data are even more bleak. The only exception we have found thus far to these modest recovery rates is the cognitive behavioral treatment of panic disorder, developed by David Clark at Oxford University and David Barlow at the State University of New York in Albany.

This is not to say that psychotherapy never produces recovery or that some therapies are not more effective at inducing recovery rates than others. Rather, it simply attests to the relatively modest average recovery rates shown by psychotherapy when examined under the microscope of clinical significance.

IT IS IMPORTANT TO NOTE THAT there are numerous psychotherapy researchers who dispute my gloomy interpretation of the psychotherapy research literature, arguing that "statistical significance" is a sufficient criterion for determining that a form of psychotherapy is effective. If a treatment works better than nothing, exceeds the outcome of a placebo, or adds to the effectiveness of alternative treatments, they argue, then the effect is worth talking about, however modest it might be. These critics point out that even small changes can enhance the quality of a client's life. They may be right. However, I do think it is important to maintain the distinction between statistical and clinical significance to make sure clients are not misled into expecting the latter when, in all likelihood, they must settle for the former.

Other critics argue that the measures outcome researchers use are too crude to adequately evaluate the changes occurring in psychotherapy. For example, measures of depressive symptoms may not reflect the full impact of therapy on a client's overall sense of well-being, self-confidence and the like. It is hard to know how to answer these critics. If a depressed person *still* feels depressed after therapy, what is the significance to him or her of being able to sleep through the night? What is the meaning of "overall well-being"? At the very least, we know that by currently available measures, the average outcomes of most psychotherapies are modest. Whether outcomes will look better with improved measures remains to be seen. I actually believe that there are a variety of excellent measures of psychotherapy outcome. Asking someone how they feel, which is essentially the basis of most self-report measures of change, is about as direct as one can get. If anything, clients are prone to exaggerate how much better they feel rather than to minimize their improvement, since the desire to please the therapist is a well-established psychological phenomenon.

There are other researchers who criticize randomized clinical trials because they inevitably involve samples of clients who are unrepresentative of those seen in clinical practice. Nobody in their right mind would volunteer for a randomized clinical trial, these critics assert, where they may end up in a control group, especially when they could see a therapist who will focus on their individual needs rather than on the requirements of an experimental design. Yet, there is good reason to believe that the effects of psychotherapy found in randomized clinical trials *overestimate* the positive effects found in the world of clinical

▲▲▲▲▲▲▲▲▲▲▲▲▲▲▲▲▲▲▲▲▲

Psychotherapy has relatively modest average recovery rates when examined under the microscope of clinical significance.

Much as we would like to believe that we are better therapists now than we were before we started our training, the research literature tells us that, on the average, we aren't.

▼▼▼▼▼▼▼▼▼▼▼▼▼▼▼▼▼

practice, because patients who are selected typically have discrete, encapsulated problems, and complicated cases involving, for example, dual diagnoses, are typically excluded. Also, therapists are scrutinized much more carefully during a clinical trial than they are when left to their own devices in private practice: the sessions are taped, rated and regular supervision meetings are held. In fact, there is actually some empirical support for the notion that the psychotherapy works better in efficacy studies than it does in clinical practice. In a landmark study published in the *American Psychologist*, John Weisz reported that child psychotherapy shows a statistical advantage over no treatment only when conducted in research settings. In naturalistic practice settings, child psychotherapies appear to be ineffective, not just from the standpoint of clinical significance, but of statistical significance as well. They apparently are *not* better than no therapy at all!

But perhaps the toughest challenge for those who believe that research underestimates the effectiveness of psychotherapy is the overwhelming evidence that, on the average, psychotherapy outcome is not improved by either years of clinical experience or by professional training. In a famous 1979 study, in which Hans Strupp and his colleagues compared psychodynamic therapists with an average of 25 years of experience to college professors with no therapy training, experience or supervision in the treatment of anxious and depressed college students, the professors did as well as the experienced therapists. The question of whether experience or training enhances outcome has been studied extensively, reviewed exhaustively and meta-analyzed to death. Skeptics have looked at the data in all sorts of ways, trying to find a way to challenge the devastating conclusions of these hundreds of studies. No matter

how determined the advocate, no matter how the data are analyzed, no one has been able to find that either the amount of clinical experience or the degree of professional training enhances outcome. In one of my studies, I found that novice clinical psychology graduate students with no prior experience outperformed licensed psychologists in doing marital therapy.

Much as we would like to believe that we are better therapists now than we were before we started our training, the research literature tells us that, on the average, we aren't. The only advantage that experienced therapists have over inexperienced ones is that they have a lower drop-out rate, an accomplishment that may be of dubious value given the modest effects of psychotherapy, showing that clients valiantly hang in there even when it's not doing them any reasonable good. A substantial body of research tells us that sometimes people recover during the course of therapy, but, more often they do not. Neither the level of experience nor the degree of training influences the likelihood of change.

To make matters even more troubling, it is not even clear that contact with a live therapist is necessary for a positive outcome. Although the research on self-administered treatments (self-help books, inspirational tapes, meditation, adult education courses) and peer support groups is not definitive, the studies completed so far show no advantage for clinical work with a therapist over a self-administered treatment. Moreover, when peer support groups have been examined rigorously (for example, in the treatment of obesity), they appear to perform as well as psychotherapy conducted by a professional.

THERE IS NO PARTICULAR SCHOOL or modality that is uniquely subject to the criticism that therapy has a limited

impact. Cognitive and behavior therapies, as well as specific forms of psychotropic medication, have received more attention in clinical trials than other approaches, and thus can claim at least some support, whereas the same cannot be said of the vast majority of approaches to psychotherapy. However, with few exceptions, the therapies examined all seem to be wanting in terms of clinical significance. Therefore, "empirical validation" too often means only that a form of treatment has been studied in a controlled setting, and has been shown to have some positive effects, however weak they may be.

While family therapy has been shown to do about as well as individual psychotherapy, it is not demonstrably superior to individual psychotherapy for any clinical problem (with the possible exception of schizophrenia). My own research shows that, on the average, when marital discord coexists with major depression, couples therapy does as well as—but no better than—individual psychotherapy. Moreover, this research investigated behavioral marital therapy, not exactly a popular theoretical approach within a field dominated by general systems theory.

Family therapy began with, and continues to be fertilized by, an exceptionally creative group of clinicians who have generated a great many viable and still untested hypotheses about family functioning and how it can be harnessed to generate change. Much of what family therapists write about constitutes an important phase—perhaps the most important phase—of the research process: the generation of hypotheses. The field is ripe with ideas waiting to be validated, confirmed, replicated or disconfirmed. Thus, it is all the more disappointing that family therapy is so guilty of making unsubstantiated claims of success. "This works, trust me!" has become the standard of proof on the family therapy workshop circuit, and the popularity of various approaches becomes a question of who is most persuasive, whose teaching tapes are most pristine, or even whose name is best known. The claims of astoundingly high success in an astoundingly few number of sessions made by some solution-focused therapists are particularly disturbing. Despite the assertion that these success rates are substantiated by research findings, nothing cited in the literature could conceivably be thought of as empirically valid clinical research.

False prophets are easy to recognize and need to be exposed. They expect you to trust their clinical judgment, while showing no signs of humility or doubts about the wisdom of what they are proselytizing. They show an indifference to independent tests of their ideas and sidestep the issue of research evidence. We have to ask our plenary speakers, theorists and workshop leaders questions such as, "How do you know this works?" We have to pin down 90-percent success claims with questions like, "How did you measure success?" "Was the *measurement* process independent of the *therapy* process, to ensure that it was not contaminated by the client's desire to make the therapist feel good?" Family therapists must face the challenge of building a knowledge base if we are to respond effectively to the criticism leveled at other forms of psychotherapy.

TODAY OUR FIELD FACES THE CHALlenge of making sure that therapy promises nothing it can't deliver and delivers the best, most honestly presented care of which clinicians are capable. Therapists can no longer afford to ignore the scientific foundations of their profession for, as Jay Efran and Mitchell Greene

recently pointed out in the *Networker*, in the long run, science is all "that presumably distinguishes [therapists] from the expanding cadre of self-proclaimed psychics, new-age healers, religious gurus, talk-show hosts and self-help book authors." From a therapy researcher's viewpoint, there are a number of changes that need to be made in how our field operates.

First, therapists must treat only clients who have given truly informed consent, and must stop treatment when it is apparent that it is not working. Psychotherapists are obligated to be familiar with the research literature on whatever disorders they are treating, to present to their clients the full range of treatment options along with their costs and benefits—based on currently available information—and to refrain from overselling the brand they happen to be providing. In most cases, therapists should openly acknowledge that their treatments are "experimental," since the success rates of most commonly practiced models for most disorders are unknown. Where outcome evidence is available, it should be presented. Clients should be given the information they need to make informed choices before being asked to consent to treatment.

Therapy should never be interminable, as Freud once referred to psychoanalysis. Progress should be expected to occur in a timely manner, or alternatives should be discussed. Criteria for determining progress should be part of a dialogue initiated by the therapist and regularly assessed by both therapist and client. When therapy isn't working, the therapist has an ethical obligation to try something else—another form of therapy, a referral to another therapist, a psychotropic drug, a self-help book, meditation, yoga, garden-

ing, exercise or something else. A disgruntled ex-client once said to me, "In retrospect, after spending $5,000 on unsuccessful psychotherapy, with no suggestion from the therapist that there was any alternative, it occurred to me that it would have been much more therapeutic to use that money to hire babysitters, a maid service, even a butler." Alternatives to psychotherapy may often be the best solution when timely progress is not evident.

Researchers themselves have been negligent in not focusing on the questions of most interest to psychotherapists. One of the primary reasons that psychotherapists so often operate in an empirical vacuum is that there is no alternative. Until recently, for example, there was no basic research on childhood sexual abuse, and there is still very little on repressed memories. Thus, when faced with these issues, psychotherapists have little scientific support in formulating their treatment approaches. Responding to this need for information, many organizations and interest groups have already developed "clinical digests" that summarize and disseminate research findings for practicing therapists, and these efforts should be applauded and expanded. Until research training receives more attention in all clinical training programs, psychotherapists cannot be expected to rely on primary sources for their information. Meanwhile, agencies that fund clinical research have to become more flexible in their definition of good science. Setting the rigors of randomized clinical trials as the gold standard for research discourages many investigators from exploring the questions most relevant to clinicians.

Managed care services are frequently criticized by psychotherapy advocates for denying coverage for adequate treatment. In fact, managed care providers are placing the burden of proof where it belongs: in the hands of psychotherapists. It is frustrating that we cannot justify long-term treatment, nor can we justify the choice of hiring an M.D. or a Ph.D. to provide services when masters- and bachelor's-level providers would, on the average, perform just as well. We may resent having to talk to case managers, request additional treatment sessions, and lower our fees, but the demands made by managed care bureaucrats follow from the psychotherapy research literature with a great deal more logic than do the criticisms directed at them by psychotherapy lobbyists.

THIS ARTICLE HAS HIGHLIGHTED research findings that should make

ANNOTATED BIBLIOGRAPHY

■ Christensen, A. & Jacobson, N.S. (1994). Who (or what) can do psychotherapy: The status and challenge of nonprofessional therapies. *Psychological Science.*Vol. 5, pp. 8-13. *A review of the studies comparing professional with paraprofessional therapists, experienced versus inexperienced therapists, and therapist-delivered versus self-administered treatments.*

■ Jacobson, N.S. & Traux, P. (1991). Clinical significance: A statistical approach to defining meaningful change in psychotherapy research. *Journal of Consulting and Clinical Psychology 59*, 12-19. *A discussion of the statistics developed by Jacobson, Follette and Revenstorf for assessing the clinical significance of psychotherapy effects.*

■ Shea, M.T., et al. Course of depressive symptoms over follow-up: Findings from the National Institute of Mental Health Treatment of Depression Collaborative Research Program. *Archives of General Psychiatry 49*, 782-787. *A report of the follow-up results from the NIMH Treatment of Depression Collaborative Research Program.*

■ Smith, M.L., Glass, G.V. and Miller, T.I. (1990). *The Benefits of Psychotherapy.* Baltimore: Johns Hopkins. *A widely cited meta-analysis of the psychotherapy literature.*

■ Weisz, J.R., Weiss, B. & Donenberg, G.R. (1992). The lab versus the clinic: Effects of child and adolescent psychotherapy. *American Psychologist 47*, 1578-1585. *A review of studies evaluating child psychotherapy both in clinical trials and in professional settings.*

When therapy isn't working, the therapist has an ethical obligation to try something else—another form of therapy, a referral to another therapist, a psychotropic drug, a self-help book, meditation, yoga or gardening.

▼▼▼▼▼▼▼▼▼▼▼▼▼▼▼▼▼▼

clinicians squirm. Carried away with our popular acceptance, we have promised far more than we can deliver. We need to take a close look at our excesses and our often tenuous relationship to scientific principles. But while research can tell us a lot about the impact of therapy, conclusions about its ultimate merits and its role in the culture cannot be made solely from outcome data. While the existing empirical evidence raises serious questions about the transformative power of the therapy experience, people clearly get *something* from it or they would not keep coming back for more. Consumer satisfaction measures are virtually always higher than outcomes based on measures of psychiatric symptoms. How are we to understand this?

It may be that for many people, the process of being in therapy is the whole point. The collaboration between therapist and client creates an experience of hope and optimistic possibility that many clients prize whether or not their specific presenting problems disappear. Not only does the process of being in

such a relationship feel good to many clients, it may also have outcome benefits that have thus far eluded easy measurement. Even when the outcomes are not clinically significant, many clients are satisfied, and feel they have derived great benefit from the experience. They may not resolve their problem with one therapist, enter therapy with another, still not resolve the original issue, but nonetheless feel satisfied with both experiences of therapy! For many people, the process of treatment itself seems to provide some subtle but significant and meaningful benefits that have so far eclipsed our efforts to measure or even define them. The power of the therapeutic alliance and the availability of a person who, at the very least, is present and caring should never be underestimated.

For all our society's much-vaunted attention to the pursuit of happiness, the mass shuffle of a society dominated by vast, impersonal forces of consolidated power and privilege makes it harder and harder for many people to experience that happiness. In large part, that accounts for

the mushrooming popularity of psychotherapy over the last 25 years. Where else, in an age that has seen the decline of family, church, school and community, and the widespread, creeping anxiety fueled by social violence and economic insecurity, can people find an authentic and personal experience of human connection and compassionate challenge to their own best possibilities? What other professional field has devoted so much intelligence, systematic study and toilsome labor to doing humane work in an inhumane world, trying to instill in people a vision of optimistic realism about their own lives that avoids false sentimentality on the one hand and deadening cynicism on the other? With all its flaws, for all its bumblings and stumblings, psychotherapy keeps some vital spirit alive in a culture that would be much the poorer and more desperate without it. ∎

Neil Jacobson, Ph.D., is on the faculty of the psychology department of the University of Washington. Address: University of Washington, Department of Psychology, Center for Clinical Research, JD-11, Seattle, WA 98195.

Remembering Dangerously

ELIZABETH LOFTUS

We live in a strange and precarious time that resembles at its heart the hysteria and superstitious fervor of the witch trials of the sixteenth and seventeenth centuries. Men and women are being accused, tried, and convicted with no proof or evidence of guilt other than the word of the accuser. Even when the accusations involve numerous perpetrators, inflicting grievous wounds over many years, even decades, the accuser's pointing finger of blame is enough to make believers of judges and juries. Individuals are being imprisoned on the "evidence" provided by memories that come back in dreams and flashbacks—memories that did not exist until a person wandered into therapy and was asked point-blank, "Were you ever sexually abused as a child?" And then begins the process of excavating the "repressed" memories through invasive therapeutic techniques, such

From *Skeptical Inquirer, 19*, pp. 20–29, March/April 1995. Reprinted by permission of the *Skeptical Inquirer*.

as age regression, guided visualization, trance writing, dream work, body work, and hypnosis.

One case that seems to fit the mold led to highly bizarre satanic-abuse memories. An account of the case is described in detail by one of the expert witnesses (Rogers 1992) and is briefly reviewed by Loftus and Ketcham (1994).

A woman in her mid-seventies and her recently deceased husband were accused by their two adult daughters of rape, sodomy, forced oral sex, torture by electric shock, and the ritualistic murder of babies. The older daughter, 48 years old at the time of the lawsuit, testified that she was abused from infancy until age 25. The younger daughter alleged abuse from infancy to age 15. A granddaughter also claimed that she was abused by her grandmother from infancy to age 8.

The memories were recovered when the adult daughters went into therapy in 1987 and 1988. After the breakup of her third marriage, the older daughter started psychotherapy, eventually diagnosing herself as a victim of multiple-personality disorder and satanic ritual abuse. She convinced her sister and her niece to begin therapy and joined in their therapy sessions for the first year. The two sisters also attended group therapy with other multiple-personality-disorder patients who claimed to be victims of satanic ritual abuse.

In therapy the older sister recalled a horrifying incident that occurred when she was four or five years old. Her mother caught a rabbit, chopped off one of its ears, smeared the blood over her body, and then handed the knife to her, expecting her to kill the animal. When she refused, her mother poured scalding water over her arms. When she was 13 and her sister was still in diapers, a group of Satanists demanded that the sisters disembowel a dog with a knife. She remembered being forced to watch

Elizabeth F. Loftus is in the Department of Psychology, University of Washington, Seattle, WA 98195. This article is based on a paper given at the 1994 CSICOP Conference.

Like the witch-hunt trials of old,

people today are being accused

and even imprisoned on

'evidence' provided by

memories from dreams and

flashbacks—memories that

didn't exist before therapy.

What is going on here?

as a man who threatened to divulge the secrets of the cult was burned with a torch. Other members of the cult were subjected to electric shocks in rituals that took place in a cave. The cult even made her murder her own newborn baby. When asked for more details about these horrific events, she testified in court that her memory was impaired because she was frequently drugged by the cult members.

The younger sister remembered being molested on a piano bench by her father while his friends watched. She recalled being impregnated by members of the cult at ages 14 and 16, and both pregnancies were ritually aborted. She remembered one incident in the library where she had to eat a jar of pus and another jar of scabs. Her daughter remembered seeing her grandmother in a black robe carrying a candle and being drugged on two occasions and forced to ride in a limousine with several prostitutes.

The jury found the accused woman guilty of neglect. It did not find any intent to harm and thus refused to award monetary damages. Attempts to appeal the decision have failed.

"The infancy memories are almost certainly false memories given the scientific literature on childhood amnesia."

Are the women's memories authentic? The "infancy" memories are almost certainly false memories given the scientific literature on childhood amnesia. Moreover, no evidence in the form of bones or dead bodies was ever produced that might have corroborated the human-sacrifice memories. If these memories are indeed false, as they appear to be, where would they come from? George Ganaway, a clinical assistant professor of psychiatry at the Emory University School of Medicine, has proposed that unwitting suggestions from therapy play an important role in the development of false satanic memories.

What Goes on in Therapy?

Since therapy is done in private, it is not particularly easy to find out what really goes on behind that closed door. But there are clues that can be derived from various sources. Therapists' accounts, patients' accounts, and sworn statements from litigation have revealed that highly suggestive techniques go on in some therapists' offices (Lindsay and Read 1994; Loftus 1993; Yapko 1994).

Other evidence of misguided if not reckless beliefs and practices comes from several cases in which private investigators, posing as patients, have gone undercover into therapists' offices. In one case, the pseudopatient visited the therapist complaining about nightmares and trouble sleeping. On the third visit to the therapist, the investigator was told that she was an incest survivor (Loftus 1993). In another case, Cable News Network

(CNN 1993) sent an employee undercover to the offices of an Ohio psychotherapist (who was supervised by a psychologist) wired with a hidden video camera. The pseudopatient complained of feeling depressed and having recent relationship problems with her husband. In the first session, the therapist diagnosed "incest survivor," telling the pseudopatient she was a "classic case." When the pseudopatient returned for her second session, puzzled about her lack of memory, the therapist told her that her reaction was typical and that she had repressed the memory because the trauma was so awful. A third case, based on surreptitious recordings of a therapist from the Southwestern region of the United States, was inspired by the previous efforts.

Inside a Southwestern Therapist's Office

In the summer of 1993, a woman (call her "Willa") had a serious problem. Her older sister, a struggling artist, had a dream that she reported to her therapist. The dream got interpreted as evidence of a history of sexual abuse. Ultimately the sister confronted the parents in a videotaped session at the therapist's office. The parents were mortified; the family was wrenched irreparably apart.

Willa tried desperately to find out more about the sister's therapy. On her own initiative, Willa hired a private investigator to pose as a patient and seek therapy from the sister's therapist. The private investigator called herself Ruth. She twice visited the therapist, an M.A. in counseling and guidance who was supervised by a Ph.D., and secretly tape-recorded both of the sessions.

In the first session, Ruth told the therapist that she had been rear-ended

in an auto accident a few months earlier and was having trouble getting over it. Ruth said that she would just sit for weeks and cry for no apparent reason. The therapist seemed totally disinterested in getting any history regarding the accident, but instead wanted to talk about Ruth's childhood. While discussing her early life, Ruth volunteered a recurring dream that she had had in childhood and said the dream had now returned. In the dream she is 4 or 5 years old and there is a massive white bull after her that catches her and gores her somewhere in the upper thigh area, leaving her covered with blood.

The therapist decided that the stress and sadness that Ruth was currently experiencing was tied to her childhood, since she'd had the same dream as a child. She decided the "night terrors" (as she called them) were evidence that Ruth was suffering from post-traumatic-stress disorder (PTSD). They would use guided imagery to find the source of the childhood trauma. Before actually launching this approach, the therapist informed her patient that she, the therapist, was an incest survivor: "I was incested by my grandfather."

During the guided imagery, Ruth was asked to imagine herself as a little child. She then talked about the trauma of her parents' divorce and of her father's remarriage to a younger woman who resembled Ruth herself. The therapist wanted to know if Ruth's father had had affairs, and she told Ruth that hers had, and that this was a "generational" thing that came from the grandfathers. The therapist led Ruth through confusing/suggestive/manipulative imagery involving a man holding down a little girl somewhere in a bedroom. The therapist decided that Ruth was suffering from a "major grief issue" and told her it was sexual: "I don't think, with the imagery and his marrying someone who looks like you, that it could be anything else."

The second session, two days later, began:

Pseudopatient: You think I am quite

possibly a victim of sexual abuse?

Therapist: Um-huh. Quite possibly. It's how I would put it. You know, you don't have the real definitive data that says that, but, um, the first thing that made me think about that was the blood on your thighs. You know, I just wonder, like where would that come from in a child's reality. And, um, the fact that in the imagery the child took you or the child showed you the bedroom and your father holding you down in the bedroom . . . it would be really hard for me to think otherwise. . . . Something would have to come up in your work to really prove that it really wasn't about sexual abuse.

Ruth said she had no memory of such abuse but that didn't dissuade the therapist for a minute.

Pseudopatient: . . . I can remember a lot of anger and fear associated with him, but I can't recall physical sexual abuse. Do people always remember?

Therapist: No. . . . Hardly ever. . . . It happened to you a long time ago and your body holds on to the memory and that's why being in something like a car accident might trigger memories. . . .

The therapist shared her own experiences of abuse, now by her father, which supposedly led to anorexia, bulimia, overspending, excessive drinking, and other destructive behaviors from which the therapist had presumably now recovered. For long sections of the tape it was hard to tell who was the patient and who was the therapist.

Later the therapist offered these bits of wisdom:

I don't know how many people I think are really in psychiatric hospitals who are really just incest survivors or, um, have repressed memories.

It will be a grief issue that your father was—sexualized you—and was not an appropriate father.

You need to take that image of yourself as an infant, with the hand over, somebody's trying to stifle your crying, and feeling pain somewhere as a memory.

The therapist encouraged Ruth to read two books: *The Courage To Heal,* which she called the "bible of healing from childhood sexual abuse," and the workbook that goes with it. She made a special point of talking about the section on confrontation with the perpetrator. Confrontation, she said, wasn't necessarily for everyone. Some don't want to do it if it will jeopardize their inheritance, in which case, the therapist said, you can do it after the person is dead—you can do eulogies. But confrontation is empowering, she told Ruth.

Then to Ruth's surprise, the therapist described the recent confrontation she had done with Willa's sister (providing sufficient detail about the unnamed patient that there could be little doubt about who it was).

Therapist: I just worked with someone who did do it with her parents. Called both of her parents in and we did it in here. . . . Its empowering because you're stepping out on your own. She said she felt like she was 21, and going out on her own for the first time, you know, that's what she felt like. . . .

Pseudopatient: And, did her parents deny or—

Therapist: Oh, they certainly did—

Pseudopatient: Did she remember, that she—she wasn't groping like me?

Therapist: She groped a lot in the beginning. But it sort of, you know, just like pieces of a puzzle, you know, you start to get them and then eventually you can make a picture with it. And she was able to do that. And memory is a funny thing. It's not always really accurate in terms of ages, and times and places and that kind of thing. Like you may have any variable superimposed on another. Like I have a friend who had an ongoing sexual abuse and she would have a memory of, say, being on this couch when she was seven and being abused there, but they didn't have that couch when she was seven, they had it when she was five. . . . It doesn't discount the memory, it just means that it probably went on more than once and so those memories overlap. . . .

Pseudopatient: This woman who did the confrontation, is she free now? Does she feel freed over it?

Therapist: Well, she doesn't feel free from her history . . . but she does feel like she owns it now and it doesn't own her . . . and she has gotten another memory since the confrontation. . . .

The therapist told Ruth all about the "new memory" of her other patient, Willa's sister:

Therapist: [It was in] the early-morning hours and she was just

"We live in a culture of accusations. When it comes to molestation, the accused is almost always considered guilty as charged."

lying awake, and she started just having this feeling of, it was like her hands became uncontrollable and it was like she was masturbating someone. She was like going faster than she could have, even in real life, so that she knew, it was familiar enough to her as it will be to you, that she knew what it was, and it really did not freak her out at all. . . . She knew there was a memory there she was sitting on.

Before Ruth's second therapy session had ended, Ruth's mother was brought into the picture—guilty, at least, of betrayal by neglect:

Therapist: Well, you don't have to have rational reasons, either, to feel betrayed. The only thing that a child needs to feel is that there was probably a part of you that was just yearning for your mother and that she wasn't there.

"Why at this time in our society is there so much interest in 'repression' and the uncovering of repressed memories?"

And whether she wasn't there because she didn't know and was off doing something else, or whether she was there and she knew and she didn't do anything about it. It doesn't matter. All the child knew was that Mom wasn't there. And, in that way she was betrayed, you know, whether it was through imperfection on your mother's part or not, and you have to give yourself permission to feel that way without justification, or without rationalization because you were.

Ruth tried again to broach the subject of imagination versus memory:

Pseudopatient: How do we know, when the memories come, what are symbols, that it's not our imagination or something?
Therapist: Why would you image this, of all things. If it were your imagination, you'd be imaging how warm and loving he was. . . . I have a therapist friend who says that the only proof she needs to know that something happened is if you think it might have.

At the doorway as Ruth was leaving, her therapist asked if she could hug her, then did so while telling Ruth how

brave she was. A few weeks later, Ruth got a bill. She was charged $65 for each session.

Rabinowitz (1993) put it well: "The beauty of the repressed incest explanation is that, to enjoy its victim benefits, and the distinction of being associated with a survivor group, it isn't even necessary to have any recollection that such abuse took place." Actually, being a victim of abuse without any memories does not sit well, especially when group therapy comes into play and women without memories interact with those who do have memories. The pressure to find memories can be very great.

Chu (1992:7) pointed out one of the dangers of pursuing a fruitless search (for memories): it masks the real issues from therapeutic exploration. Sometimes patients produce "ever more grotesque and increasingly unbelievable stories in an effort to discredit the material and break the cycle. Unfortunately, some therapists can't take the hint!"

The Southwestern therapist who treated Ruth diagnosed sexual trauma in the first session. She pursued her sex-abuse agenda in the questions she asked, in the answers she interpreted, in the way she discussed dreams, in the books she recommended. An important question remains as to how common these activities might be. Some clinicians would like to believe that the problem of overzealous psychotherapists is on a "very small" scale (Cronin 1994: 31). A recent survey of doctoral-level psychologists indicates that as many as a quarter may harbor beliefs and engage in practices that are questionable (Poole and Lindsay 1994). That these kinds of activities can and do sometimes lead to false memories seems now to be beyond dispute (Goldstein and Farmer 1993). That these kinds of activities can create false victims, as well as hurt true ones, also seems now to be beyond dispute.

The Place of Repressed Memories in Modern Society

Why at this time in our society is there such an interest in "repression" and the uncovering of repressed memories? Why is it that almost everyone you talk to either knows someone with a "repressed memory" or knows someone who's being accused, or is just plain interested in the issue? Why do so many individuals believe these stories, even the more bizarre, outlandish, and outrageous ones? Why is the cry of "witch hunt" now so loud (Baker 1992: 48; Gardner 1991)? *Witch hunt* is, of course, a term that gets used by lots of people who have been faced by a pack of accusers (Watson 1992).

"Witch hunt" stems from an analogy between the current allegations and the witch-craze of the sixteenth and seventeenth centuries, an analogy that several analysts have drawn (McHugh 1992; Trott 1991; Victor 1991). As the preeminent British historian Hugh Trevor-Roper (1967) has noted, the European witch-craze was a perplexing phenomenon. By some estimates, a half-million people were convicted of witchcraft and burned to death in Europe alone between the fifteenth and seventeenth centuries (Harris 1974: 207-258). How did this happen?

It is a dazzling experience to step back in time, as Trevor-Roper guides his readers, first to the eighth century, when the belief in witches was thought to be "unchristian" and in some places the death penalty was decreed for anyone who burnt supposed witches. In the ninth century, almost no one believed that witches could make bad weather, and almost everyone believed that night-flying was a hallucination. But by the beginning of the sixteenth century, there was a complete reversal of these views. "The monks of the late Middle Ages sowed: the lawyers of the sixteenth century reaped; and what a harvest of witches they gathered in!" (Trevor-Roper 1967: 93). Countries that had never known witches were now found to be swarming with them. Thousands of old women (and some young ones) began confessing to being witches who had made secret pacts with the Devil. At night, they said, they anointed themselves with "devil's grease" (made from the fat of murdered infants), and thus lubricated they slipped up chimneys, mounted broomsticks, and flew off on long journeys to a rendezvous called the witches' sabbat. Once they reached the sabbat, they saw their friends and neighbors all worshipping the Devil himself. The Devil sometimes appeared as a big, black, bearded man, sometimes as a stinking goat, and sometimes as a great toad. However he looked, the witches threw themselves into promiscuous sexual orgies with him. While the story might vary from witch to witch, at the core was the Devil, and the witches were thought to be his earth agents in the struggle for control of the spiritual world.

Throughout the sixteenth century, people believed in the general theory, even if they did not accept all of the esoteric details. For two centuries, the clergy preached against the witches. Lawyers sentenced them. Books and sermons warned of their danger. Torture was used to extract confessions. The agents of Satan were soon found to be everywhere. Skeptics, whether in universities, in judges' seats, or on the royal throne, were denounced as witches themselves, and joined the old women at the burning stake. In the absence of physical evidence (such as a pot full of human limbs, or a written pact with the Devil), circumstantial evidence was sufficient. Such evidence did not need to be very cogent (a wart, an insensitive spot that did not bleed when pricked, a capacity to float when thrown

in water, an incapacity to shed tears, a tendency to look down when accused). Any of these "indicia" might justify the use of torture to produce a confession (which was proof) or the refusal to confess (which was also proof) and justified even more ferocious tortures and ultimately death.

When did it end? In the middle of the seventeenth century the basis of the craze began to dissolve. As Trevor-Roper (1967: 97) put it, "The rubbish of the human mind, which for two centuries, by some process of intellectual alchemy and social pressure, had become fused together in a coherent, explosive system, has disintegrated. It is rubbish again."

Various interpretations of this period in social history can be found. Trevor-Roper argued that during periods of intolerance any society looks for scapegoats. For the Catholic church of that period, and in particular their most active members, the Dominicans, the witches were perfect as scapegoats; and so, with relentless propaganda, they created a hatred of witches. The first individuals to be so labeled were the innocently nonconforming social groups. Sometimes they were induced to confess by torture too terrible to bear (e.g., the "leg screw" squeezed the calf and broke the shinbone in pieces; the "lift" hoisted the arms fiercely behind and back; the "ram" or "witch-chair" provided a heated seat of spikes for the witch to sit on). But sometimes confessions came about spontaneously, making their truth even more convincing to others. Gradually laws changed to meet the growth of witches—including laws permitting judicial torture.

There were skeptics, but many of them did not survive. Generally they tried to question the plausibility of the confessions, or the efficacy of torture, or the identification of particular witches. They had little impact, Trevor-Roper claims, because they danced around the edges rather than tackling the core: the concept of Satan. With the mythology intact, it creates its own evidence that is very difficult to disprove. So how did the mythology that had lasted for two centuries lose its force? Finally, challenges against the whole idea of Satan's kingdom were launched. The stereotype of the witch would soon be gone, but not before tens of thousands of witches had been burned or hanged, or both (Watson 1992).

Trevor-Roper saw the witch-craze as a social movement, but with individual extensions. Witch accusations could be used to destroy powerful enemies or dangerous persons. When a "great fear" grips a society, that society looks to the stereotype of the enemy in its midst and points the finger of accusation. In times of panic, he argued, the perse-

"The rubbish of the human mind, which for two centuries, by some process of intellectual alchemy and social pressure, had become fused together in a coherent, explosive system, has disintegrated. It is rubbish again."

cution extends from the weak (the old women who were ordinarily the victims of village hatred) to the strong (the educated judges and clergy who resisted the craze). One indicia of "great fear" is when the elite of society are accused of being in league with the enemies.

Is it fair to compare the modern cases of "de-repressed memory" of child sexual trauma to the witch-crazes

feuded, should be labeled in this same way.

Trevor-Roper persuasively argued that the skeptics during the witch-craze did not make much of a dent in the frequency of bonfires and burnings until they challenged the core belief in Satan. What is the analogy to that core today? It may be some of the widely cherished beliefs of psychotherapists,

The Case of Jennifer H.

Some writers have offered individual cases as proof that a stream of traumas can be massively repressed. Readers must beware that these case "proofs" may leave out critical information. Consider the supposedly ironclad case of Jennifer H. offered by Kandel and Kandel (1994) to readers of *Discover* magazine as an example of a corroborated de-repressed memory. According to the *Discover* account, Jennifer was a 23-year-old musician who recovered memories in therapy of her father raping her from the time she was 4 until she was 17. As her memories resurfaced, her panic attacks and other symptoms receded. Her father, a mechanical-engineering professor, denied any abuse. According to the *Discover* account, Jennifer sued her father, and at trial "corroboration" was produced: Jennifer's mother testified that she had seen the father lying on top of Jennifer's 14-year-old sister and that he had once fondled a baby-sitter in her early teens. The defendant's sister recalled his making passes at young girls. Before this case becomes urban legend and is used as proof of something that it might not be proof of, readers are entitled to know more.

Jennifer's case against her father went to trial in June 1993 in the U.S. District Court for the District of Massachusetts (*Hoult* v. *Hoult*, 1993). The case received considerable media attention (e.g., Kessler 1993). From the trial transcript, we learn that Jennifer, the oldest of four children, began therapy in the fall of 1984 with an unlicensed New York psychotherapist for problems with her boyfriend and divided loyalties surrounding her parents' divorce. Over the next year or so she experienced recurring nightmares with violent themes, and waking terrors. Her therapist practiced a "Gestalt" method of therapy; Jennifer describes one session: "I started the same thing of shutting my eyes and just trying to feel the feelings and not let them go away really fast. And [my therapist] just said 'Can you see anything?' . . . I couldn't see anything . . .

"Responsible skepticism is skepticism about some claims of recovered memory. It is not a blanket rejection of all claims."

of several centuries ago? There are some parallels, but the differences are just as striking. In terms of similarities, some of the modern stories actually resemble the stories of earlier times (e.g., witches flying into bedrooms). Sometimes the stories encompass past-life memories (Stevenson 1994) or take on an even more bizarre, alien twist (Mack 1994).[1] In terms of differences, take a look at the accused and the accusers. In the most infamous witch hunt in North America, 300 years ago in Salem, Massachusetts, three-fourths of the accused were women (Watson 1992). Today, they are predominantly (but not all) men. Witches in New England were mostly poor women over 40 who were misfits, although later the set of witches included men (often the witches' husbands or sons), and still later the set expanded to include clergy, prominent merchants, or anyone who had dared to make an enemy. Today, the accused are often men of power and success. The witch accusations of past times were more often leveled by men, but today the accusations are predominantly leveled by women. Today's phenomenon is more than anything a movement of the weak against the strong. There is today a "great fear" that grips our society, and that is fear of child abuse. Rightfully we wish to ferret out these genuine "enemies" and point every finger of accusation at them. But this does not mean, of course, that every perceived enemy, every person with whom we may have

such as the belief in the repressed-memory folklore. The repression theory is well articulated by Steele (1994: 41). It is the theory "that we forget events because they are too horrible to contemplate; that we cannot remember these forgotten events by any normal process of casting our minds back but can reliably retrieve them by special techniques; that these forgotten events, banished from consciousness, strive to enter it in disguised forms; that forgotten events have the power to cause apparently unrelated problems in our lives, which can be cured by excavating and reliving the forgotten event."

Is it time to admit that the repression folklore is simply a fairy tale? The tale may be appealing, but what of its relationship to science? Unfortunately, it is partly refuted, partly untested, and partly untestable. This is not to say that all recovered memories are thus false. Responsible skepticism is skepticism about some claims of recovered memory. It is not blanket rejection of all claims. People sometimes remember what was once forgotten; such forgetting and remembering does not mean repression and de-repression, but it does mean that some recently remembered events might reflect authentic memories. Each case must be examined on its merits to explore the credibility, the timing, the motives, the potential for suggestion, the corroboration, and other features to make an intelligent assessment of what any mental product means.

and then all of a sudden I saw this carved bedpost from my room when I was a child. . . . And then I saw my father, and I could feel him sitting on the bed next to me, and he was pushing me down, and I was saying, 'No.' And he started pushing up my nightgown and . . . was touching me with his hands on my breast, and then between my legs, and then he was touching me with his mouth . . . and then it just all like went away. It was like . . . on TV if there is all static. . . . It was, all of a sudden it was plussssh, all stopped. And then I slowly opened my eyes in the session and I said, 'I never knew that happened to me'" (pp. 58-59).

Later Jennifer would have flashbacks that were so vivid that she could feel the lumpy blankets in her childhood bed. She remembered her father choking her and raping her in her parents' bedroom when she was about 12 or 13 (p. 91). She remembered her father threatening to rape her with a fishing pole in the den when she was about 6 or 7. She remembers her father raping her in the basement when she was in high school. The rape stopped just as her mother called down for them to come to dinner. She remembered her father raping her at her grandparents' home when she was in high school, while the large family were cooking and kids were playing. She remembered her father threatening to cut her with a letter opener, holding a kitchen knife to her throat (p. 113). She remembered him chasing her through the house with knives, trying to kill her, when she was about 13 years old (p. 283).

Jennifer also remembered a couple of incidents involving her mother. She remembered one time when she was raped in the bathroom and went to her mother wrapped in a towel with blood dripping. She remembered another incident, in which her father was raping her in her parents' bedroom and her mother came to the door and said, "David." The father then stopped raping her and went out to talk to the mother. Jennifer's mother said she had no recollection of these events, or of

any sexual abuse. An expert witness testifying for Jennifer said it is common in cases of incest that mothers ignore the signs of abuse.

During the course of her memory development, Jennifer joined numerous sexual-abuse survivor groups. She read books about sexual abuse. She wrote columns. She contacted legislators. Jennifer was involved in years of therapy. She wrote letters about her abuse. In one letter, written to the President of Barnard College on February 7, 1987, she said "I am a victim of incestuous abuse by my father and physical abuse by my mother" (p. 175). In another letter to her friend Jane, written in January 1988, she talked about her therapy: "Well, my memories came out . . . when I would sit and focus on my feelings which I believe I call visualization exercises because I would try to visualize what I was feeling or be able to bring into my eyes what I could see" (pp. 247-248). She told Jane about her Gestalt therapy: "In Gestalt therapy, the sub-personalities are allowed to take over and converse with one another and hopefully resolve their conflicts. Each personality gets a different chair, and when one new one starts to speak, the individual changes into that personality's seat. It sounds weird, and it is. But

going on, and probably Dad abusing my siblings as well" (pp. 244-245). In a letter written on April 24, 1989, to *Mother Jones* magazine she said that she had survived hundreds of rapes by her father (p. 231).

Before October 1985, Jennifer testified, she didn't "know" that her father had ever put his penis in her vagina, or that he had put his penis in her mouth, or that he put his mouth on her vagina (p. 290). She paid her therapist $19,329.59 (p. 155) to acquire that knowledge.

In sum, Jennifer reported that she had been molested by her father from the ages of 4 to 17 (p. 239); that she was molested hundreds if not thousands of times, even if she could not remember all of the incidents; that this sometimes happened with many family members nearby, and with her mother's "involvement" in some instances; and that she buried these memories until she was 24, at which time they purportedly began to return to her. No one saw.

These are a few of the facts that the Kandels left out of their article. Jennifer was on the stand for nearly three days. She had "experts" to say they believed her memories were real. These experts were apparently unaware of, or unwilling to heed, Yapko's (1994) warnings about the impossibil-

"Uncritical acceptance of every single claim of a recovered memory of sexual abuse . . . is not good for anyone."

is is also an amazing journey into one's self. I've come to recognize untold universes within myself. It feels often very much like a cosmic battle when they are all warring with one another" (pp. 287-288; see also page 249).

In one letter, written on January 11, 1989, to another rape survivor, she said that her father had raped her approximately 3,000 times. In another letter, dated January 30, 1989, she wrote: "Underneath all the tinsel and glitter was my father raping me every two days. My mother smiling and pretending not to know what the hell was

ity, without independent corroboration, of distinguishing reality from invention and his urgings that symptoms by themselves cannot establish the existence of past abuse. At trial, Jennifer's father testified for about a half-hour (Kessler 1993b). How long does it take to say, "I didn't do it"? Oddly, his attorneys put on no character witnesses or expert testimony of their own, apparently believing—wrongly—that the implausibility of the "memories" would be enough. A Massachusetts jury awarded Jennifer $500,000.

Good and Bad Advice

Many of us would have serious reservations about the kinds of therapy activities engaged in by Jennifer H. and the kind of therapy practiced by the Southwestern therapist who treated pseudopatient Ruth. Even recovered-memory supporters like Briere (1992) might agree. He did, after all, say quite clearly: "Unfortunately, a number of clients and therapists appear driven to expose and confront every possible traumatic memory" (p. 136). Briere notes that extended and intense effort to make a client uncover all traumatic material is not a good idea since this is often to the detriment of other therapeutic tasks, such as support, consolidation, desensitization, and emotional insight.

alternative hypotheses. Andreasen (1988), for example, urges practitioners to be open to the hypothesis of metabolic or neurochemical abnormalities as cause of a wide range of mental disorders. Even pharmacologically sophisticated psychiatrists sometimes refer their patients to neurologists, endocrinologists, and urologists. For less serious mental problems we may find, as physicians did before the advent of powerful antibiotics, that they are like many infections—self-limiting, running their course and then ending on their own (Adler 1994).

When it comes to serious diseases, a question that many people ask of their physicians is "How long have I got?" As Buckman and Sabbagh (1993) have aptly pointed out, this is a difficult

ment of functioning rather than uncovering buried memories. If it is necessary to recover memories, do not contaminate the process with suggestions. Guard against personal biases. Be cautious about the use of hypnosis in the recovery of memories. Bibliotherapeutic and group therapy should not be encouraged until the patient has reasonable certainty that the sex abuse really happened. Development and evaluation of other behavioral and pharmacological therapies that minimize the possibility of false memories and false diagnoses should be encouraged.

Instead of dwelling on the misery of childhood and digging for childhood sexual trauma as its cause, why not spend some time doing something completely different. Borrowing from John Gottman's (1994) excellent advice on how to make your marriage succeed, patients might be reminded that negative events in their lives do not completely cancel out all the positives (p. 182). Encourage the patient to think about the positive aspects of life—even to look through picture albums from vacations and birthdays. Think of patients as the architects of their thoughts, and guide them to build a few happy rooms. The glass that's half empty is also half full. Gottman recognized the need for some real basis for positive thoughts, but in many families, as in many marriages, the basis does exist. Campbell (1994) offers similar advice. Therapists, he believes, should encourage their clients to recall some positive things about their families. A competent therapist will help others support and assist the client, and help the client direct feelings of gratitude toward those significant others.

"Bad therapy based on bad theory is like a too-heavy oil that, instead of lubricating, can gum up the works—slowing everything down and heating everything up."

Some will argue that the vigorous exploration of buried sex-abuse memories is acceptable because it has been going on for a long time. In fact, to think it is fine to do things the way they've always been done is to have a mind that is as closed and dangerous as a malfunctioning parachute. It is time to recognize that the dangers of false-memory creation are endemic to psychotherapy (Lynn and Nash 1994). Campbell (1994) makes reference to Thomas Kuhn as he argues that the existing paradigm (the theories, methods, procedures) of psychotherapy may no longer be viable. When this happens in other professions, a crisis prevails and the profession must undertake a paradigm shift.

It may be time for that paradigm shift and for an exploration of new techniques. At the very least, therapists should not let sexual trauma overshadow all other important events in a patient's life (Campbell 1994). Perhaps there are other explanations for the patient's current symptoms and problems. Good therapists remain open to

question to answer. Patients who get a "statistical" answer often feel angry and frustrated. Yet an uncertain answer is often the truthful answer. When a psychotherapy patient asks, "Why am I depressed?" the therapist who refrains from giving an erroneous answer, however frustrating silence might be, is probably operating closer to the patient's best interests. Likewise, non-conventional "healers" who, relative to conventional physicians, give their patients unwarranted certainty and excess attention, may make the patients temporarily feel better, but in the end may not be helping them at all.

Bad therapy based on bad theory is like a too-heavy oil that, instead of lubricating, can gum up the works—slowing everything down and heating everything up. When the mental works are slowed down and heated up, stray particles of false memory can, unfortunately, get stuck in it.

To avoid mucking up the works, constructive advice has been offered by Byrd (1994) and by Gold, Hughes, and Hohnecker (1994): Focus on enhance-

Final Remarks

We live in a culture of accusation. When it comes to molestation, the accused is almost always considered guilty as charged. Some claims of sexual abuse are as believable as any other reports based on memory, but others may not be. However, not all claims are true. As Reich (1994) has argued:

"When we uncritically embrace reports of recovered memories of sexual abuse, and when we nonchalantly assume that they must be as good as our ordinary memories, we debase the coinage of memory altogether" (p. 38). Uncritical acceptance of every single claim of a recovered memory of sexual abuse, no matter how bizarre, is not good for anyone—not the client, not the family, not the mental-health profession, not the precious human faculty of memory. And let us not forget one final tragic consequence of overenthusiastic embracing of every supposedly de-repressed memory; these activities are sure to trivialize the genuine memories of abuse and increase the suffering of real victims who wish and deserve, more than anything else, just to be believed.

We need to find ways of educating people who presume to know the truth. We particularly need to reach those individuals who, for some reason, feel better after they have led their clients—probably unwittingly—to falsely believe that family members have committed some terrible evil. If "truth" is our goal, then the search for evil must go beyond "feeling good" to include standards of fairness, burdens of proof, and presumptions of innocence. When we loosen our hold on these ideals, we risk a return to those times when good and moral human beings convinced themselves that a belief in the Devil meant proof of his existence. Instead, we should be marshaling all the science we can find to stop the modern-day Reverend Hale (from *The Crucible*), who, if he lived today would still be telling anyone who would listen that he had seen "frightful proofs" that the Devil was alive. He would still be urging that we follow wherever "the accusing finger points"!

Note

1. John Mack details the kidnappings of 13 individuals by aliens, some of whom were experimented upon sexually. Mack believes their stories, and has impressed some journalists with his sincerity and depth of concern for the abductors (Neimark 1994). Carl Sagan's (1993:7) comment on UFO memories:

"There is genuine scientific paydirt in UFO's and alien abductions—but it is, I think, of distinctly terrestrial origin."

References

Adler, J. 1994. The age before miracles. *Newsweek,* March 28, p. 44.

Andreasen, N. C. 1988. Brain imaging: Applications in psychiatry. *Science,* 239: 1381-1388.

Baker, R. A. 1992. *Hidden Memories.* Buffalo, N.Y.: Prometheus Books.

Briere, John N. 1992. *Child Abuse Trauma.* Newbury Park, Calif.: Sage Publications.

Buckman, R., and K. Sabbagh, 1993. *Magic or Medicine? An Investigation into Healing.* London: Macmillan.

Byrd, K. R. 1994. The narrative reconstructions of incest survivors. *American Psychologist,* 49:439-440.

Campbell, T. W. 1994. *Beware the Talking Cure.* Boca Raton, Fla.: Social Issues Resources Service (SirS).

Chu, J. A. 1992. The critical issues task force report: The role of hypnosis and amytal interviews in the recovery of traumatic memories. *International Society for the Study of Multiple Personality and Dissociation News* June, pp. 6-9.

CNN. 1993. "Guilt by Memory." Broadcast on May 3.

Cronin, J. 1994. False memory. *Z Magazine.* April, pp. 31-37.

Gardner, R. A. 1991. *Sex Abuse Hysteria.* Creskill, N.J.: Creative Therapeutics.

Gold, Hughes, and Hohnecker. 1994. Degrees of repression of sexual-abuse memories. *American Psychologist,* 49:441-442.

Goldstein, E., and K. Farmer, eds. 1994. *True Stories of False Memories.* Boca Raton, Fla.: Social Issues Resources Service (SirS).

Gottman, J. 1994. *Why Marriages Succeed or Fail.* New York: Simon & Schuster.

Harris, M. 1974. *Cows, Pigs, Wars, and Witches: The Riddles of Culture.* New York: Vintage Books.

Hoult v. *Hoult.* 1993. Trial testimony. U.S. District Court for District of Massachusetts. Civil Action No 88-1738.

Kandel, M., and E. Kandel. 1994. Flights of Memory. *Discover,* 15 (May): 32-37.

Kessler, G. 1993a. Memories of abuse. *Newsday,* November 28, pp. 1, 5, 54-55.

———. 1993b. Personal communication,

Newsday, letter to EL dated December 13, 1993.

Lindsay, D. S., and J. D. Read. 1994. Psychotherapy and memories of childhood sexual abuse: A cognitive perspective. *Applied Cognitive Psychology,* 8:281-338.

Loftus, E. F. 1993. The reality of repressed memories. *American Psychologist,* 48: 518-537.

Loftus, E. F., and K. Ketcham. 1994. *The Myth of Repressed Memory.* New York: St. Martin's Press.

Lynn, S. J., and M. R. Nash. 1994. Truth in memory. *American Journal of Clinical Hypnosis,* 36: 194-208.

Mack, J. 1994. *Abduction.* New York: Scribner's.

McHugh, P. R. 1992. Psychiatric misadventures. *American Scholar,* 61: 497-510.

Neimark, J. 1994. The Harvard professor and the UFO's. *Psychology Today,* March-April, pp. 44-48, 74-90.

Poole, D., and D. S. Lindsay. 1994. "Psychotherapy and the Recovery of Memories of Childhood Sexual Abuse." Unpublished manuscript, Central Michigan University.

Rabinowitz, Dorothy. 1993. Deception: In the movies, on the news. *Wall Street Journal,* February 22. Review of television show "Not in My Family."

Reich, W. 1994. The monster in the mists. *New York Times Book Review,* May 15, pp. 1, 33-38.

Rogers, M. L. 1992. "A Case of Alleged Satanic Ritualistic Abuse." Paper presented at the American Psychology-Law Society meeting, San Diego, March.

Sagan, C. 1993. What's really going on? *Parade Magazine,* March 7, pp. 4-7.

Stevenson, I. 1994. A case of the psychotherapist's fallacy: Hypnotic regression to "previous lives." *American Journal of Clinical Hypnosis,* 36: 188-193.

Steele, D. R. 1994. Partial recall. *Liberty,* March, pp. 37-47.

Trevor-Roper, H. R. 1967. *Religion, the Reformation, and Social Change.* London: Macmillan.

Trott, J. 1991. Satanic panic. *Cornerstone,* 20: 9-12.

Victor, J. S. 1991. Satanic cult "survivor" stories. SKEPTICAL INQUIRER, 15: 274-280.

Watson, B. 1992. Salem's dark hour: Did the devil make them do it? *Smithsonian,* 23: 117-131.

Yapko, M. 1994. *Suggestions of Abuse.* New York: Simon & Schuster.   □

Back

in the

High Life

**A controlled study by
Emory and Georgia Tech
researchers tests virtual
reality technology in
treating acrophobia**

by Donna Bradley

Acrophobia is classified in the DSM-IV as a specific phobia. It is also a relatively common one. About 0.4 percent of people report some amount of anxiety when life's adventures take them off the ground. Approximately 2 percent of that group seek treatment. The degree of anxiety varies according to the individual and the situation. Those with a mild fear of

From *Dialogue*, 9(1), pp. 8–13. Copyright ©1996 The Emory Clinic.

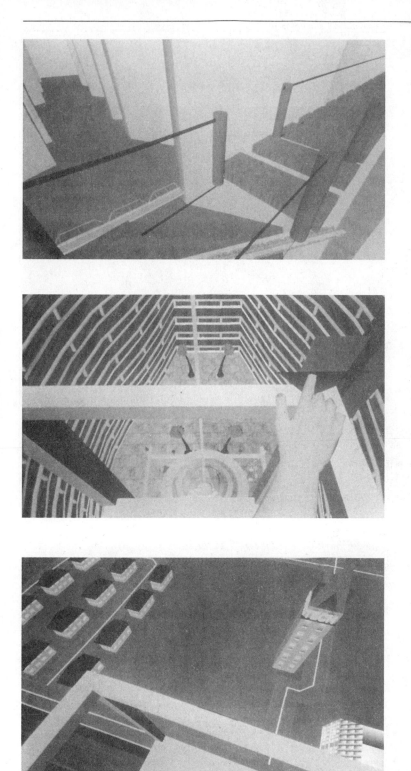

Top to bottom: The "Indiana Jones" bridge spanning a river canyon, a forty-nine story hotel, and a balcony on the Georgia Tech campus comprised the study's virtual environments. While basic in design, the computer-generated venues gave participants the same feelings and anxieties that real life exposure to heights did.

Virtual reality technology gives participants the perception of real presence in an artificially created setting.

typically be considered less than frightening circumstances.

"Some people avoid the upper levels of parking decks, and if the only parking space is on the top level or close to the edge, they will circle until a spot on a lower level opens up," says Barbara O. Rothbaum, PhD, an assistant professor in the Department of Psychiatry and Behavioral Sciences at the Emory University School of Medicine. "In hotels, they can stay only on the lower floors. And some will not work on the upper floors of a high-rise building."

Last year Rothbaum and Larry F. Hodges, PhD, associate director of the Graphics, Vizualization, and Usability Center at the Georgia Institute of Technology, completed what is thought to be the first controlled study using virtual reality to treat acrophobia. Their initial results are encouraging and may lead to a better way of treating a number of specific phobias.

Rothbaum and Hodges demonstrated that a successful treatment for acrophobia can be effected using computer-generated virtual environments. Virtual reality technology gives participants the perception of being present in an artificially created setting.

Once a patient wears a virtual reality helmet, the sensation of height felt in real life is recreated without leaving the ground. Because of this, a therapist can chart patient responses and progress as accurately as in traditional therapies.

Traditional therapies expensive, time-consuming

Historically, there have been two types of treatment for acrophobia. Imaginal treat-

heights can lead normal lives simply by avoiding extreme situations.

True acrophobia, however, is characterized by severe anxiety when exposed to heights and avoidance of heights to the extent that day-to-day functioning is impaired. People who suffer from acrophobia will go out of their way to keep both feet on the ground in what would

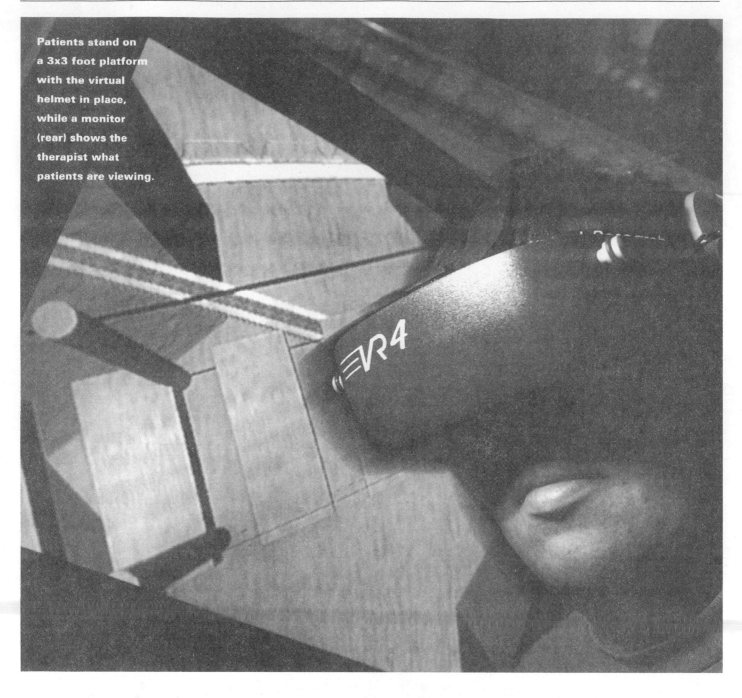

Patients stand on a 3x3 foot platform with the virtual helmet in place, while a monitor (rear) shows the therapist what patients are viewing.

Virtual Environments: The Patient Perspective

Writer Donna Bradley took her own tour of the virtual environment to find out what participants were experiencing. She chose to "ride" the elevator.

At ground level I was in the vast atrium of a Marriott Marquis hotel clone. Looking up, I saw the hotel ceiling. Turning my head from left to right changed the view exactly the way it does in real life.

Controlling my upward journey by pushing a button on the hand-held control (you can do it one floor at a time if you want, or opt for the express), I ascended to the top, leaving the marble-floored lobby far below.

After several minutes of riding up and down, the computer-created environment became my reality. The real challenge was holding on to the handrails and leaning over the "edge." When I finally took off the head-mounted display and left the platform, it took me a couple of minutes to adjust to terra firma. The sensation was similar to what you might feel after a long roller coaster ride.

ment allows patients to use their imaginations to recreate an anxiety-producing situation. Imaginal exposure is usually combined with relaxation techniques, and gradual desensitization is eventually achieved.

For acrophobes, in vivo treatment usually proves more successful than imaginal treatment. It requires that the therapist and patient undertake a series of excursions to parking decks, balconies, glass-walled elevators or other high places

Noted among the participants' physical anxiety symptoms were sweating, butterflies, light-headedness, nervousness, and loss of balance.

where, one level at a time, they view what lies below. After multiple exposures and appropriate guidance from the therapist, anxiety attenuates and the patient's fear should become controllable. This method typically proves to be expensive and time-consuming.

In their pilot study for virtual reality therapy, Rothbaum and Hodges administered a screening questionnaire to 478 college students in introductory psychology and computer classes. Forty-six students were identified as possible acrophobes. Twenty were entered into the study and randomly assigned to a virtual reality treatment group (N=12) or a no treatment control group (N=8).

Students who also suffered from agoraphobia, panic disorder, or claustrophobia were not admitted because of a possible intolerance for the virtual reality helmet. Pretreatment assessment was conducted by administering the acrophobia questionnaire, the rating of fear questionnaire, and an attitudes toward heights questionnaire

to both the treatment and control groups.

For those randomized to the treatment group, graded exposure to heights using virtual reality was conducted individually in seven weekly thirty-five to forty-five minute sessions.

Virtual scenarios, real anxieties

Prior to treatment, the twelve participants attended an orientation session to get acquainted with the hardware — a virtual reality helmet with an electromagnetic sensor that tracks the user's movements and a hand-held control unit that allows interaction with the virtual environment. The virtual reality site at Georgia Tech is a three-feet square platform only a few inches off the floor with handrails on all four sides. The handrails correspond to those in the virtual environment, thus reinforcing the sense of reality.

Three virtual scenarios were used: an open elevator inside a forty-nine story hotel modeled after Atlanta's Marriott Marquis, a building with a series of four outside balconies ranging in height from ground level to 60 meters, and three bridges spanning a river canyon.

The lower two bridges, at 7 and 50 meters respectively, were solidly constructed. The uppermost bridge at 80 meters, dubbed the Indiana Jones bridge by one of the study participants, was a rope-secured suspension type with wooden slats. Not only was the river below visible between the slats, but one of the slats was missing. To add to the illusion of height, each bridge was visible from the one above.

In all three scenarios, participants were in control of how far off the ground they wanted to be, starting at the lowest level of anxiety and progressing upward as they became habituated to the environment. A video monitor allowed the therapist to see exactly what the subject was seeing.

The therapist asked participants every five minutes to rate their levels of anxiety using a subjective unit of discomfort scale ranging from 0 (no anxiety) to 100 (panic-level). Among the physical anxiety symptoms were sweating, abdominal discomfort (butterflies), light-headedness,

Some study group members ventured to high places to see if their phobia was truly diminishing.

nervousness, and loss of balance.

Initial responses included, "I feel weak in the knees," "I feel like I'm on the edge," and "If I don't see the rail, I feel like I'm going to fall." Over time, however, the responses became more positive. "I feel more secure this week," said one participant, "It's not as scary as it was."

After the seven weeks, the assessment questionnaires were again administered to both groups. The treatment group showed a definite decrease in anxiety levels. Their subjective unit of discomfort ratings collectively decreased from session to session over the treatment period. In fact, during treatment seven of the participants ventured to high places such as the Peachtree Plaza elevator or various parking decks, just to see if their phobia was truly diminishing.

Rothbaum and Hodges are encouraged by their positive results and expansive about the possibilities of this technology in treating simple phobias. "We would like to explore treating fear of flying, for instance, or post-traumatic stress disorder among Vietnam veterans eventually," says Rothbaum. Right now, the high cost of virtual reality equipment makes routine treatment prohibitive.

Rothbaum hopes that recreational popularity of virtual reality technology will eventually reduce costs. "There are possibilities for treating almost any anxiety phobia this way," she says. "All we have to do is design effective programs." ■

For more information about virtual reality therapy or to speak with Dr. Barbara Rothbaum, physicians should call the Emory HealthConnection at 404/778-7777 or 800/22-EMORY.

Back From The
DRINK

**by Jill Neimark,
Claire Conway,
and Peter Doskoch**

"His [Dionysus'] blood, the blood of the grape, lightens the burden of our mortal misery. When, after their daily toils, men drink their fill, sleep comes to them, bringing relief from all their troubles. There is no other cure for sorrow."
Euripides

"Boys should abstain from all use of wine until their eighteenth year, for it is wrong to add fire to fire."
Plato

"A man hath no better thing under the sun, than to eat, and to drink, and to be merry."
Ecclesiastes 8:15

Each year it kills 40,000 Americans. It can damage and destroy every organ in the body, scarring and pocking the liver until it looks like a lump of drying lava, laying waste to the heart, pancreas, arteries, throat, and stomach, snuffing out receptors in the brain. Every year alcoholism costs our country over $80 billion, is implicated in 30 percent of suicides and 46 percent of teen suicides, and is a factor in one of four hospital admissions. No wonder it has long been decried as not far removed from original sin.

Yet like the music of Greek sirens, alcohol has also been the hymn song of poets, monks, philosophers, and soldiers. It is a ritual substance in most religions, intimately linked to God and altered consciousness. It is the supreme seductress: "For not even the gates of heaven, opening wide to receive me," wrote author Malcolm Lowry of a bar in Mexico, "could fill me with such celestial complicated and hopeless joy as the iron screen that rolls up with a crash. All mystery, all hope, all disappointment, yes, all disaster, is here." Or, as Rabelais put it: "I drink for the thirst to come. I drink eternally. ...The soul can't live in the dry."

What other substance has so mesmerized and polarized us as alcohol? It has a long and illustrious role in our culture, from social lubricant to lethal intoxicant. There are those who contend that culture itself owes its existence to alcohol—that the first primitive, agricultural societies sprang up around the farming and ferment of hops. Even now, as this issue goes to press, there is convening a worldwide conference on wine where health experts from Harvard and the World Health Organization advocate a glass or two of wine daily, citing wine's healthful antioxidants and significant potential to reduce heart disease. Yet the same organization has a formal policy calling for an astounding 25 percent reduction in alcohol consumption by the year 2000. Sound confusing? Not surprising. Alcohol is one of the most potent pharmacologic agents around, one whose effects seem as protean as human nature itself.

From *Psychology Today*, 27, pp. 46–53, September/October 1994. Reprinted with permission from Psychology Today Magazine, Copyright ©1994 (Sussex Publishers, Inc.).

For that reason, perhaps, it has taken the maturation of neuroscience and psychology to give us a realistic glimpse into alcohol use and abuse—and the picture is no longer black or white. Researchers are now beginning to ferret out the causes of alcohol addiction, of liquor's fiery path across the cells of the brain, its social underpinnings and cultural power—as well as new, innovative, and flexible treatments for this condition. "There's tremendous excitement, a watershed feeling, as if something is just beginning to happen," notes Henry Kranzler, M.D., a psychiatrist at the University of Connecticut who has pioneered new pharmacologic approaches to alcoholism. "This field now is at the same place that the treatment of depression was 30 or 40 years ago. We're really beginning to understand this condition, to develop promising medications and psychosocial interventions."

THE SHIFTS ARE PROFOUND. Perhaps most important, according to Dennis Donovan, M.D., a psychiatrist and director of the Alcohol and Drug Abuse Institute at the University of Washington, is the willingness to look at the goal of treatment for alcoholism as far more than abstinence or the lack of it. "Abstinence is no longer the gold standard, it's simply one standard."

There is a growing understanding among mental health experts that alcohol abuse occurs on a continuum and must be treated thusly. According to Steven Liljegren, Ph.D., clinical director of Child and Adolescent Services at Brookside Hospital in Nashua, New Hampshire, traditional alcohol treatment programs work for less than half of drinkers. An unprecedented multisite study called Project MATCH, involving over 80 therapists, is now underway to match patient characteristics with different kinds of therapy. Researchers are discovering that, while some former alcoholics require unequivocal abstinence, others can drink in moderation.

As the field moves away from an absolutist, all-or-nothing view, the definition of treatment success, too, is widening. Some of the new findings sweeping the field include:

• Alcohol is not, as was long believed, simply a chemical sledgehammer. It seems to act specifically on neurotransmitters and receptors, primarily GABA, the prime inhibitory neurotransmitter in the brain, and one that accounts for much of alcohol's effects. This discovery may lead to new medications for helping drinkers overcome the condition.

• Most alcoholics do not have preexisting psychiatric conditions. However, about 20 percent are suffering from psychiatric disorders that they may be attempting to medicate with alcohol, and which are beginning to be treated with the latest psychotropic drugs.

• Social support—whether from friends, family, therapists, or self-help groups—is crucial to recovery. In fact, peer and family support may be the "missing link" that allows some alcoholics to quit on their own, without any formal treatment, according to Donovan. Social support can be provided by contact with recovering people, access to self-help groups, and a family that helps the drinker to readjust to life without substances. Social support does not mean that the family should keep on protecting the alcoholic when he or she is in trouble; it means creating enthusiasm in both the drinker and the family that a life without alcohol is possible.

• In the arena of alcoholism, motivation to quit reigns supreme. The latest research shows that brief, motivationally based interventions, where counselors work with patients for one to four sessions—to both establish and to reinforce reasons for quitting—can be as effective as far more intensive therapy.

• The motivation to quit drinking varies considerably among alcoholics. For one, losing job and family isn't enough; for another, an embarrassing moment at a corporate party may change a man's life. It's always subjective.

• One of the key genetic factors in alcoholism is an ability to metabolize liquor too well, because of the presence of the liver enzyme alcohol dehydrogenase. Indeed, a common trait among alcoholics is the early ability to "drink others under the table."

• Twenty percent of all alcoholics can and do quit successfully on their own. Researchers are just beginning to explore what is "special" about them and how to apply it to all alcoholics.

• In sum, no matter where and how an alcoholic recovers, this powerfully complex condition imposes three requirements for recovery: high, sustained motivation for quitting; readjustment to—and building—a life without liquor that includes family and peer support; and relapse prevention based on specific, well-rehearsed strategies of "cue" avoidance. These factors are being incorporated into treatment programs around the country.

As the tectonic plates of alcohol treatment shift, with new, flexible views sending a shudder through the mental health field, the person who may finally benefit is the alcoholic. New insights into alcoholism are yielding exciting treatment approaches, creative uses of medication, and innovative psychological interventions.

No one can ascertain exactly when man discovered that carbohydrates could be fermented into alcohol, although we know that in 6000 B.C., beer was made from barley in ancient Sumeria. What is clear is that societies have long venerated and feared alcohol. Ancient Egypt and Mesopotamia allowed liquor into temple rites but regulated its general use; the Greeks linked their entire intellectual flowering to grape and olive growing; medieval monks brewed beer.

CAN YOU PICK HIM OUT OF A LINEUP?

Most alcoholics, explains Mark Schuckit, are not out on the street; they are individuals as unique and at the same time ordinary as you and me. That's one more reason not to apply a uniform treatment. "Alcoholics have jobs and close relationships, rarely (if ever) develop severe problems with the law, and many go unrecognized as alcoholics by their physicians. While most areas of these people's lives will eventually be impaired by their substance use, it is amazing how resilient people are." Other myths about the alcohol abuser:

• Drunks stay drunk. Actually, says Schuckit, most people drink more heavily on weekends, and start out each day alcohol-free.

• Drinkers can't quit. The truth is, substance abusers have little or no trouble quitting, and often do. Temporary drying out is easy and common. The problem is that sooner or later they begin drinking again.

• Alcoholics can't control their drinking. Actually, most alcohol abusers can and do control their drinking—for a short time, and often after a period of abstinence.

• Alcoholics have a preexisting psychiatric disorder, such as anxiety or depression, which they are attempting to medicate with alcohol. The truth: Only about 20 percent of alcoholics suffer from a psychiatric disorder. And though many claim they drink to combat depression or sleeplessness, those problems are often caused by drinking and disappear when drinking stops.

• Alcoholism is genetically determined. In fact, only about 20 percent of sons of alcoholics become alcoholics themselves; the number of women is even less. And though the risk of alcoholism is higher for identical than fraternal twins, most children of alcoholics do not become heavy drinkers themselves. As Schuckit emphasizes, "Predisposition does not mean predestination."

• Alcoholics drink because their friends do. Although it's true that we drink more often when our peers drink, the fact is that once a person begins to drink heavily, light-drinking or nondrinking friends are likely to fall away, leaving a peer group that consists mostly of other alcoholics.

• Once an addict, always an addict: therefore alcoholics should not take any psychotropic drugs, even prescribed medications. A growing body of research indicates that for some alcoholics, pharmacotherapy can provide a specifically targeted therapy that helps maintain recovery and abstinence. The AA model is traditionally distrustful of any medication.

TIPS FOR QUITTERS

Alcoholics can quit or control their drinking—in fact they do it all the time. The real issue is, how to sustain recovery? Relapse is the bugaboo of alcoholism treatment. Whether the goal is total abstinence or controlled, moderate alcohol consumption, there are effective ways to minimize the dangers of a relapse.

✓ Avoiding situations like parties or bars, where you might feel pressured to drink, minimizes the need for self-discipline. "If you need to be strong, you haven't been smart," says one expert.

✓ Rehearse in advance what you will do or say when you are confronted with a high-risk situation. You'll be better equipped to resist.

✓ Keep in mind that for most alcoholics, the urge to drink lessens over time. The first 90 days are the hardest.

✓ Motivation for abstinence is bound to waver. Renew that motivation by frequently reminding yourself why you quit in the first place.

✓ Realize that relapses will occur. Don't use a minor slipup as an excuse to resume heavy drinking. Don't get fixated on recording consecutive days of abstinence. A relapse does not wipe out all that you've accomplished.

✓ Join a self-help group. AA is but one, Rational Recovery another. Recognize that they don't work for everyone, but since they're free, there's no risk in trying one.

In the U.S., in turn, alcohol has a history marked by ambivalence that has shaped treatment so powerfully that a singular model has prevailed for nearly a century.

DURING COLONIAL days, alcohol consumption was extremely prevalent—and there was no concept of the "alcoholic." The dawn of the 19th century brought with it a temperance movement that, according to Harry Levine, Ph.D., professor of sociology at Queens College in New York City, viewed alcohol as an addictive substance as dangerous as today's heroin or crack. Abstinence was the only solution.

Prohibition flowered directly out of the rich soils of the temperance movement, and yet it only set the stage for a very dismal failure: Consumption of hard liquor (which was easier to smuggle) rose, while overall drinking fell. A typical "temperance" culture, the U.S. gave birth to Alcoholics Anonymous, which has flourished in other temperance cultures, such as England, Canada, and Scandinavia. Notes Levine, "AA is really a religious movement that has tremendous continuity with the 19th century temperance movement. And AA's understanding of alcoholism is the central understanding of addiction in American culture overall."

Alcohol consumption, especially hard liquor, has seen a steady decline to a mere 74 percent of its mid-1970s record high. Still, 13 million Americans are alcoholics. As researchers increasingly realize, a society's attitudes about alcohol strongly impact how individuals handle drinking. In Mediterranean, nontemperance cultures, wine is as common as bread, and individuals drink every day without becoming "problem" drinkers. The per capita rate of

---

MYTHOLOGY OR METHODOLOGY?

Bill Wilson, the founder of Alcoholics Anonymous, based his groundbreaking 12-step program on what worked for him. Half a century later there are 2 million AA members worldwide, half of them in this country, and many clinicians prescribe attendance. There's no doubt that AA has helped or even saved the lives of many. Yet the fundamental tenets of the AA-style self-help movement will always remain unverified—simply because the program is anonymous and cannot be formally studied.

According to Emil J. Chiauzzi, Ph.D., and Steven Liljegren, Ph.D., there is no rigorous scientific evidence to support some widespread AA teachings. Some of the disputed myths include:

• The most essential step in treatment is admitting alcoholism. Acceptance of the label "alcoholic" is considered half the battle in traditional treatment. "Hi, my name is John and I'm an alcoholic," is the typical opener at AA meetings. Yet researchers find that some individuals feel demoralized and depressed by labeling themselves the victims of an incurable, lifelong disease.

• Addicts cannot quit on their own. In fact, say Chiauzzi and Liljegren, 95 percent of smokers stop without the help of peers or professionals, even though addicted people themselves consider nicotine more addicting than alcohol. Although only about 20 percent of alcoholics recover solo, many may not be tapping their ability to do so.

• AA is crucial for maintaining abstinence. The number of alcoholics far outnumbers AA members (13 million versus 1 million), indicating that AA is not for everyone. Any increased propensity for AA members to stay on the wagon may reflect the fact that alcoholics who are already committed to recovery are also more likely to join AA.

• Recovering patients must avoid cues associated with drinking. Researchers find that systematically exposing the patient to long-standing cues can dramatically reduce the relapse danger those cues pose. Using slides, videotapes, and other paraphernalia, researchers found decreased reactivity among those addicted to heroin, cocaine, and alcohol. Cue exposure and coping skills may offer alcoholics a helpful tool in recovery.

---

alcohol consumption is high; cirrhosis is common; but behavioral problems from alcohol are rare, and society does not lay the blame for its ills at alcohol's door.

In sharp and astonishing contrast, a temperance culture is highly ambivalent about "demon" alcohol, which is seen as a significant cause of our society's problems. In America, for instance, addiction is considered a root cause of violence. "In temperance cultures, people drink to get drunk. They tend to drink in short bursts of explosive, binge drinking. Wine cultures rarely get fall-down drunk," says Levine.

Levine cites the typical European view: "Papa comes in with liver disease, and the doctor calls in the family and says, 'Look, he's got to make life-style changes, stop drinking for a while, eat less fatty food, exercise, and minimize stress, and the whole family needs to work together to help him because these changes are hard.' Apparently this works. Tell these European practitioners that what they really need to do is send their patient to 90 meetings in 90 days and turn themselves over to a higher power and they'll say, 'I've got somebody with health and dietary problems and you've got a religious solution?'"

In a temperance culture where alcoholism is widely—if incorrectly—regarded as a disease, the cure until now has been relentless abstinence. Levine calls this model a "useful fiction" that works for some, but by no means all, alcoholics.

For any person, the first step in reducing alcohol intake is to understand alcohol itself. Advances in neuroscience have given us new insight into the actual impact of alcohol on the body—and the mind.

ROM AN $800 BOTTLE OF DE LA Romance-Conti, vintage 1978, to the crudest, rudest moonshine, alcohol impairs far more than our judgment and coordination. While we absorb the active ingredient of many psychoactive drugs in minuscule quantities—an ant can carry a few hits of LSD comfortably on its back—a drinker literally floods the body with alcohol. "Alcohol is problematic in part because it's so impotent," points out John Morgan, M.D., pharmacologist at City University Medical School in New York. "Other mood-altering substances are active in the bloodstream at literally thousands of magnitudes below what is required for alcohol."

As a result, alcohol—particularly in alcoholics, who can tolerate large amounts of liquor—exerts its toxic effect on virtually every organ system in the body, says Anthony Verga, M.D., medical director of Long Island's Seafield Center. The repercussions range from W.C. Fields's perpetually red nose to a torqued and failing liver common in alcoholics.

The liver, in fact, is the body's main line of defense against intoxication. But the fight is hardly fair. The organ's supply of alcohol dehydrogenase—the enzyme that helps break alcohol down into harmless water and carbon dioxide—can only handle about one drink's worth of alcohol an hour. Worse, the process produces acetaldehyde, a highly toxic chemical that attacks nearby tissues. The result is a variety of disorders. One of the gravest, cirrhosis, kills 26,000 Americans each year. But the liver is by no means the only casualty of alcoholism.

• After a few years of heavy drinking, some alcoholics develop pancreatitis, a painful inflammation of the pancreas.

• The heart wastes away, a condition called alcoholic cardiomyopathy.

• Drinking impairs blood flow. Heavy drinking can increase risk of stroke.

• A pregnant woman who drinks heavily can give birth to a baby with Fetal Alcohol syndrome (FAS), one of the leading causes of mental retardation. FAS occurs in up to 29 out of every 1,000 live births among known alcoholic mothers. Babies suffer lifelong neurological,

anatomical, and behavioral problems. Some of them never learn to speak. Recent research indicates the casualty rate may be higher than once thought: Even babies appearing normal in infancy often grow up to manifest FAS disabilities.

• Alcohol takes its greatest toll on the brain. A small percentage of alcoholics may, after years, develop such severe brain damage that they remain permanently confused or become psychotic, suffering from auditory hallucinations. At least 45 percent of alcoholics entering treatment display some difficulty with problem solving, abstract thinking, psychomotor performance, and difficult memory tasks. About one in 10 suffers severe disorders like dementia.

Why can't a drunk brain think? Is there any way to correct the misfiring that chronic alcohol use induces? Alcohol appears to stimulate GABA in the brain: "What GABA does is slow down the firing of the cell on which the receptor is located," says Kranzler. This neuronal inhibition may contribute to the telltale signs of intoxication, from slurred speech to nodding off in mid-sentence. And, while Valium and barbiturates are distinctly different drugs than alcohol, they also target the GABA(A) receptor, suggesting a kinship.

Alcohol cuts a far wider swath than GABA; it alters other receptors in the human brain:

• Drinking inhibits two of the three receptors for glutamate, the primary brain fuel and GABA's chemical opposite.

• Alcohol increases levels of a chemical messenger known as cyclic AMP, crucial for the healthy functioning of brain cells. To compensate, the brain reduces cyclic AMP levels, and over the long term, cells require alcohol to achieve normal levels.

• Levels of dopamine and serotonin, which contribute to behavioral reinforcement, also rise with alcohol consumption. Their increase may explain how alcohol tightens its grip on a drinker's habit.

• Alcohol increases levels of the brain's natural opiates, endorphins and enkephalins. This may be the key to the eternal, if politically incorrect, question: Why is drinking so much fun?

Alcohol addiction is real, and withdrawal from alcohol can require a period of unpleasant detoxification. During that period, a former drinker can suffer acute anxiety, irritability, insomnia, increased blood pressure and body temperature, and severe, though temporary, confusion. Acute symptoms may fade after a week, but subtler symptoms of unease and insomnia may persist for months, making it difficult to remain alcohol-free.

Until recently, it has been an axiom of alcoholism treatment that withdrawal requires a (usually) month-long intensive inpatient treatment regimen, and then often a modified regimen where former drinkers live in halfway houses for up to six months. During the intensive phase, the alcoholic can detoxify from the drug while immersed in 24-hour support with other recovering alcoholics and counselors (often former alcoholics themselves). Group therapy is a feature of these programs, designed to break through the alcoholics' wall of denial and help set them on the straight and narrow path to a substance-free life. These programs can cost $16,000 or more per month.

The good news is that the very physiological nature of alcohol's seductive hold can lead us to new treatments for the condition. Pharmacologists are investigating drugs that may aid in nearly every aspect of alcohol abuse, reducing the craving of newly detoxified drinkers and even alleviating cognitive impairment.

NALTREXONE, FOR EXAMPLE—A DRUG originally developed to combat heroin addiction—may prevent binges when alcoholics relapse. Naltrexone blocks the opiates that the brain releases when someone drinks, so that an imbiber literally gets no kick from champagne. The drug may be most useful in the months after detoxification, when alcohol craving is strongest. Joseph

"Traditional treatment says it's heresy to expose the drinker to cues, it will just increase his craving. In fact, the opposite seems true."

R. Volpicelli, M.D., a University of Pennsylvania psychiatrist, and his colleagues found that only 23 percent of naltrexone patients relapsed within 12 weeks of treatment, versus 54 percent on placebo.

Volpicelli thinks that naltrexone may prove far more valuable than disulfiram, a 40-year-old drug well known as Antabuse. Disulfiram interferes with alcohol metabolism, so that takers suffer nausea, cramps, headaches, and vomiting when they drink. In practice, though, the drinker stops taking it, because the physiological effects often build to such a crescendo—including violent heartbeats and hot flushes—that impending death is feared.

Buspirone (BuSpar), an antianxiety agent, may help alcoholics by minimizing the effects of withdrawal. Many doctors traditionally give benzodiazepine drugs, such as Valium, to dampen withdrawal symptoms—but those drugs can be addictive and may further blunt the memory of heavy drinkers. Buspirone may be a safer alternative. Other drugs that have shown promise include cipramine, which helps alcoholics who are also suffering from major

depression, and deispramine, another antidepressant that seems to reduce drinking.

The new view of alcoholism is of a complex condition arising from the intricate and unpredictable interplay of social, biological, and psychological factors. "Alcoholism is not a disorder caused uniquely by genes," explains Mark Schuckit, M.D., of the Veteran's Administration Medical Center in La Jolla, California. "Some persons become alcoholic solely through environmental exposure; others have biological and psychological predispositions. There are many different paths to alcoholism. Once a person drinks regularly, however, the body's reaction to and tolerance of alcohol changes, so that the person needs more alcohol. Patients need to be educated about the many factors that contribute to the disorder, so they can understand that the situation is not hopeless."

Studies show that the type of therapy an alcoholic receives isn't as important as the fact that he or she gets some treatment.

"There are very few harmful or useless treatment programs for substance use disorders," says Schuckit. "If you are highly motivated, then you are likely to do well in almost any program you choose."

The programs most alcoholics choose are based on the Minnesota Model, which views alcoholism as an incurable disease. It involves group counseling to confront a "denying" drunk, education about alcohol's consequences, and confessional self-help organizations like the AA.

There are already cracks in the Minnesota Model's clinical monopoly. Although the personal experiences of thousands of alcoholics attest to the model's value, its failure rate—about 50 percent—reveals the futility of assembly-line treatment. Indeed, aversion therapy, stress-management, and family therapy are proving effective for many alcoholics.

Take the fact that an alcoholic's memory

may be impaired—leading to treatment problems that have little to do with the so-called ubiquitous "denial" syndrome. "Ten years ago, if an alcoholic didn't seem to be catching on to treatment, it was assumed that he or she was 'in denial,' " says Tim Sheehan, R.N., Ph.D., of Minnesota's Hazelden Foundation, arguably the archetypal inpatient treatment center. "Now we're recognizing that there may be lingering cognitive deficits." During treatment, these patients are exposed to fewer concepts, which are reinforced often.

THREE NEW APPROACHES—ALL OF them "heretical" by the traditional abstinence model—eschew ideology and spiritual baggage in favor of simple pragmatism. Some alcoholics do quite well with them. They are:

• Harm reduction, which recognizes that moderate drinking is preferable to lost weekends. Any decrease in alcohol intake is grounds for a (alcohol-free) toast.

• Brief intervention. In as little as half an hour, an intervention attempts to show the subject how drinking may be impairing everything from his liver to his livelihood; helps him rate himself on a series of questions about his life and drinking; and then places him on a continuum with his drinking peers so that he has a sense of the nature of his problem. In addition, brief sessions help the person focus on motivations for reducing drinking. Brief intervention, lasting four sessions at most, can be as effective as more intensive treatments for many individuals, says Donovan.

• Cue exposure, or systematically exposing and desensitizing the alcoholic to cues that might trigger drinking. According to Liljegren, "traditional treatment says it's heresy to expose the drinker, it will just increase his craving. In fact, the opposite seems true; the data suggest cue exposure is the very thing we should be doing."

By exposing the drinker to cues for drinking that might normally stimulate intense craving, and by refusing to reinforce those cues with the "pleasure" of drink, alcoholics become less responsive to those cues over time. The drinkers' sense of self-confidence and efficacy rise, proving that they can restrain from drinking in the presence of cues. And it provides the opportunity for drinkers to learn how to cope with their problem in the outside world.

Typical drinking cues, notes Liljegren, include money, payday, peers, parties, bars and other drinking settings, and emotions—particularly anger, sadness, and fear. "I had a young woman here," recalls Liljegren, "who was very upset about her ex-boyfriend, who himself was a drinker. I asked her mother to bring in a picture of him. When she saw the picture she was very upset." Liljegren and the patient were able to explore the patient's feelings until she was confident that she would not drink when she actually bumped into the young man out in the world.

One of the biggest shifts in alcohol treatment is from inpatient to outpatient therapy. "Research has found that less costly outpatient programs may be as effective as inpatient programs," points out Donovan. Outpatient treatment allows patients whose prognosis is more favorable to adjust to life without booze in a real-world environment. And it's a lot cheaper.

In contrast, alcoholics with preexisting medical or psychiatric illnesses—and whose insurance company or bank account can cover bills—should consider inpatient treatment. So should those who have failed outpatient therapy, or whose family environment is chaotic.

It's during the months and years that follow initial treatment, says Schuckit, that the real work of recovery takes place. "Counselors work with the patient and family. Giving up alcoholism is a loss of a way of life—and the alcoholic needs to grieve. Magical thinking needs to be corrected: many patients and families have the idea that all problems will fade as they become sober. Families need a way to deal with the spouse anger that inevitably comes out as the patient becomes sober, and to maintain enthusiasm.

"Contact with recovering people is important, as is access to self-help. The former drinker needs to set up plans about what to do with free time that used to be spent drinking. A whole life needs to be rebuilt without alcohol. Relapse prevention is important. A former alcoholic needs to identify the triggers to drink and rehearse strategies to help him handle those triggers. Perpetual alertness is required."

Ironically, the months following intensive treatment can put more strain on a family than years of chronic alcohol abuse. About 25 percent of marriages break up within a year of one partner's joining AA, says Barbara McCrady, Ph.D., clinical director of the Rutgers Center for Alcohol Studies. She cites three reasons:

• Traditional AA protocol calls for meetings—lots of them. "Spouses often say, 'First I lost him to alcohol, now I've lost him to AA,' " says McCrady. The alcoholic's reliance on fellow program members, rather than family, can foster considerable resentment.

• Some families have for years blamed all of their difficulties on the alcoholic's addiction. Only when the drinker is no longer drinking do they realize that long-established alcohol problems do not just vanish overnight.

• Families that remain intact despite a member's drinking have worked out their own ways to remain a family unit. "They've reallocated responsibilities, roles, and chores, and the family functions pretty well," McCrady says. "Now there's this person who is sober and wants to reestablish a position in the family." But the family may be hesitant if the alcoholic has tried—and failed—to stay sober in the past.

Perhaps one of the most interesting new paths of research is the study of alcoholics who quit on their own. "We are beginning to explore in depth the characteristics of these people—the ones who can just walk away from their addiction in the absence of any formal treatment," explains Donovan. Perhaps they simply have in greater measure the same hope and courage of the ordinary alcoholic, who frequently quits for a day or a week or a month, and then returns to the bottle. As researchers are beginning to realize, if they can emphasize the innate capacity present in most drinkers to improve, a great deal may be gained. A shift in viewpoint can help lift the burden of an all-or-nothing view where "one drink, one drunk" means that a glass of champagne on one's wedding day is an unequivocal failure. ■

EMDR Treatment:
Less Than Meets the Eye?

Eye movement desensitization and reprocessing has been hailed by many as a major breakthrough in the treatment of post-traumatic anxiety. It rests on a surprisingly weak foundation of research evidence.

SCOTT O. LILIENFELD

"Quick fixes" for emotional maladies have struck a responsive chord in the general public, as biopsychologist B. L. Beyerstein (1990) has noted. Because these interventions often hold out the hope of alleviating long-standing and previously intractable problems with a minimum of time and effort, they are understandably appealing to both victims of psychological disorders and their would-be healers.

More often than not, however, the initial enthusiasm generated by such treatments has fizzled as soon as their proponents claims have been subjected to intensive scrutiny. In the case of certain highly touted techniques such as neurolinguistic programming (Druckman and Swets 1988), subliminal self-help tapes (Moore 1992; Pratkanis 1992), and facilitated communication for autism (Mulick, Jacobson, and Kobe 1993), controlled studies overwhelmingly indicate that

From *Skeptical Inquirer, 20,* pp. 25–31, January/February 1996. Reprinted by permission of the *Skeptical Inquirer.*

"In the past few years, a novel and highly controversial treatment known as 'eye movement desensitization and reprocessing' (EMDR) has burst onto the psychotherapy scene. EMDR has been proclaimed by its advocates as an extremely effective and efficient treatment for Post-Traumatic Stress Disorder (PTSD) and related anxiety disorders."

gories: (1) psychological reexperiencing of the traumatic event (e.g., recurrent and disturbing flashbacks and dreams of the event); (2) avoidance of stimuli (e.g., television programs, conversations) that remind the individual of the event; and (3) heightened arousal (e.g., sleep disturbances, increased startle responses).

Although PTSD is difficult to treat, there is accumulating evidence that "exposure treatments," which involve confronting clients with memories and images of the traumatic event, are effective for many cases of PTSD (Frueh, Turner, and Beidel 1995). One of the best known of such interventions is "flooding," in which clients are exposed to trauma-related stimuli for prolonged time periods

early reports of their effectiveness were illusory. In other cases, such as biofeedback for psychosomatic disorders, there is some limited evidence for efficacy, but scant evidence that this efficacy exceeds that of less expensive and less technologically sophisticated treatments (Druckman and Swets 1988). The benefits of biofeedback, for example, are not demonstrably greater than those of relaxation training (Silver and Blanchard 1978).

In the past few years, a novel and highly controversial treatment known as "eye movement desensitization and reprocessing" (EMDR) has burst onto the psychotherapy scene. EMDR has been proclaimed by its advocates as an extremely effective and efficient treatment for Post-Traumatic Stress Disorder (PTSD) and related anxiety disorders. These assertions warrant close examination because PTSD is a chronic and debilitating condition that tends to respond poorly to most interventions.

Although PTSD was not formally recognized as a mental disorder until 1980, descriptions of "shell shock," "battle fatigue," and similar reactions to wartime trauma date back at least to the late nineteenth century (Barlow 1988). PTSD is defined by the American Psychiatric Association (1994, p. 427) as an anxiety disorder resulting from exposure to "an event...that involved actual or threatened death or serious injury, or a threat to the physical integrity of self or others." Among the most frequent precipitants of PTSD are military combat, rape, physical assault, motor vehicle accidents, natural disasters, and the witnessing of a murder or accidental death. The primary symptoms of PTSD fall into three cate-

(often two hours or more) until their anxiety subsides. Flooding can be performed using either real-life stimuli or visual imagery, although the inability to recreate the actual details of the traumatic scene typically means that the treatment must be conducted imaginally. The mechanisms underlying the success of exposure techniques are still a subject of debate, but many psychologists believe that the effective ingredient in such treatments is "extinction"—the process by which a response dissipates when the stimulus triggering this response is presented without the original emotional concomitants.

Despite their advantages, exposure treatments for PTSD tend to provoke extreme anxiety and consume much time. Often 20 sessions are required for maximal efficacy (Frueh et al. 1995). As a result, many clients with PTSD are reluctant to undergo such treatments, leading some practitioners to search for less stressful and more time-efficient interventions. Enter EMDR.

EMDR: Method, Rationale, and Claims

Francine Shapiro, the psychologist who originated EMDR, recalls having fortuitously "discovered" this technique when she found that rapid back-and-forth eye movements reduced her own anxiety (Shapiro 1989b). Shapiro thereafter applied this procedure to her own clients with anxiety disorders and claims to have met with remarkable success. Since the initial published report of its use in 1989, EMDR has skyrocketed in popularity among practitioners. As of mid-1995, approximately 14,000 therapists were licensed to perform EMDR in the United States and other countries (Bower 1995), and this number is growing. EMDR is also attracting international

Scott O. Lilienfeld is an assistant professor in the Department of Psychology at Emory University, 532 Kilgo Circle, Atlanta, GA 30322. His research interests include the assessment and etiology of anxiety and anxiety disorders.

attention. For example, a team of American psychologists recently trained 40 European therapists to administer EMDR to victims of war trauma in Bosnia (Cavaliere 1995).

Although EMDR is alleged to be a complicated technique that requires extensive training (Shapiro 1992), the treatment's key elements can be summarized briefly. Clients are first asked to visualize the traumatic event as vividly as possible. While retaining this image in mind, they are told to supply a statement that epitomizes their reaction to it (e.g., "I am about to die"). Clients are then asked to rate their anxiety on a Subjective Units of Distress (SUDs) scale, which ranges from 0 to 10, with 0 being no anxiety and 10 being extreme terror. In addition, they are told to provide a competing positive statement that epitomizes their *desired* reaction to the image (e.g., "I can make it"), and to rate their degree of belief in this statement on a 0 to 8 Validity of Cognition scale.

Following these initial steps, clients are asked to visually track the therapist's finger as it sweeps rhythmically from right to left in sets of 12 to 24 strokes, alternated at a speed of two strokes per second. The finger motion is carried out 12 to 14 inches in front of the client's eyes. Following each set of 12 to 24 strokes, clients are asked to "blank out" the visual image and inhale deeply, and are then asked for a revised SUDs rating. This process is repeated until clients' SUDs ratings fall to 2 or lower and their Validity of Cognition ratings rise to 6 or higher.

Although EMDR technically requires the use of eye movements, Shapiro (1994a) claimed that she has successfully used the technique with blind clients by substituting auditory tones for movements of the therapist's finger. Recently I attended a presentation on EMDR given by a clinician who reported that, when working with children, he uses alternating hand-taps on the knees in lieu of back-and-forth finger movements.

Since its development, EMDR has been extended to many problems other than PTSD, including phobias, generalized anxiety, paranoid schizophrenia, learning disabilities, eating disorders, substance abuse, and even pathological jealousy (Beere 1992; Marquis 1991; Shapiro 1989b). Moreover, Shapiro (1991, p. 135) asserted that "EMDR treatment is equally effective with a variety of 'dysfunctional' emotions such as excessive grief, rage, guilt, etc." The theoretical rationale for EMDR has not been clearly explicated by either Shapiro or others. Indeed, a recent attempt by Shapiro (1994b, p. 153) to elaborate on EMDR's mechanism of action may mystify even those familiar with the technique: "The system may become unbalanced due to a trauma or through stress engendered during a developmental window, but once appropriately catalyzed and maintained in a dynamic state by EMDR, it transmutes information to a state of therapeutically appropriate resolution." Shapiro has further conjectured that the eye movements of EMDR are similar to those of rapid eye movement (REM) sleep. Because there is evidence from animal studies that REM sleep is associated with the processing

of memories (Winson 1990), Shapiro has suggested that the eye movements of EMDR may similarly facilitate the processing of partially "blocked" memories. Because there is no evidence that EMDR produces brain changes resembling those occurring during REM sleep, however, the analogy between the eye movements of EMDR and those of REM sleep may be more superficial than real.

EMDR has been hailed by its advocates as a novel treatment that produces much faster and more dramatic improvements than alternative treatments. Shapiro (1989b), for example, asserted that EMDR can successfully treat many or most cases of PTSD in a single 50-minute session, although especially severe cases may require several sessions. Moreover, claims for EMDR's efficacy have not been limited to Shapiro. Psychologist Roger Solomon (1991, cited in Herbert and Mueser 1992) described EMDR as "a powerful tool that

> ## "Does not the spirit of open scientific inquiry demand that the proponents of a novel technique remain agnostic regarding its efficacy pending appropriate data?"

rapidly and effectively reduces the emotional impact of traumatic or anxiety evoking situations." Beere (1992, p. 180) reported "spectacular" results after using EMDR on a client with multiple personality disorder.

Similar reports of EMDR's sensational effectiveness have appeared in the media. On July 29, 1994, ABC's "20/20" newsmagazine show aired a segment on EMDR. Host Hugh Downs introduced EMDR as "an exciting breakthrough . . . a way for people to free themselves from destructive memories, and it seems to work even in cases where years of conventional therapy have failed." Downs stated, "No one understands exactly why this method succeeds, only that it does." The program featured an excerpt from an interview with Stephen Silver, a psychologist who averred, "It (EMDR) leads immediately to a decrease in nightmares, intrusive memories, and flashback phenomena. It is one of most powerful tools I've encountered for treating posttraumatic stress" (ABC News 1994).

Although based largely on unsystematic and anecdotal observations, such glowing testimonials merit careful consideration. Are the widespread claims for EMDR's efficacy substantiated by research?

Uncontrolled Case Reports

Many uncontrolled case reports appear to attest to the efficacy of EMDR (e.g., Forbes, Creamer, and Rycroft 1994; Lipke and Botkin 1992; Marquis 1991; Oswalt, Anderson, Hagstrom, and Berkowitz 1993; Pellicer 1993; Puk 1991; Spates and Burnette, 1995; Wolpe and Abrams, 1991). All of these case reports utilize a "pre-post design" in which clients are treated with EMDR and subsequently reassessed for indications of improvement. These case reports, although seem-

Similarities of EMDR to Other Treatments

Although EMDR is of recent origin, the seeds of many of its therapeutic components can be found in much earlier treatment methods. At least some of EMDR's intuitive appeal might derive from its superficial similarity to another technique that has long captured the fascination of the general public: hypnosis (Gastright 1995). James Braid, the nineteenth-century eye doctor and surgeon who is generally credited with coining the term *hypnosis*, also introduced the technique of optical fixation (sometimes referred to as the "Braid effect") to induce the hypnotic state. In one familiar variation, the hypnotist rhythmically swings a watch on a chain or other pendulous object in front of the patient, who is asked to visually track its movement.

Interestingly, Braid discovered that moving this object was not needed to induce hypnosis; a stationary fixation point worked equally well. EMDR, like Braid's induction technique, involves the use of alternating eye movements. The eye movements associated with EMDR, like those in hypnotic induction, may well be superfluous (Renfrey and Spates 1994). Braid, like many advocates of EMDR, perceived deep-seated commonalities between the processes occurring during therapy and the phenomenon of sleep. Indeed, Braid believed that the eye movements associated with hypnotic induction produce a sleeplike state, which he termed hypnosis ("hypno" is Greek for "sleep") (Rowley 1986).

EMDR also bears certain similarities to neurolinguistic pro-

ingly supportive of EMDR, are for several reasons seriously flawed as persuasive evidence for its effectiveness.

First, case reports, probably even more than large controlled investigations, are susceptible to the "file drawer problem" (Rosenthal 1979)—the selective tendency for negative findings to remain unpublished. It is impossible to determine the extent to which the published cases of EMDR treatment, which are almost all successful, are representative of all cases treated with this procedure.

Second, in virtually all of the published case reports, EMDR was combined with other interventions, such as relaxation training and real life exposure (Acierno, Hersen, Van Hasselt, Tremont, and Meuser 1994). As a result, one cannot determine whether the apparent improvement reported in such cases is attributable to EMDR, the ancillary treatments, or both.

Third, and most important, these case reports cannot provide information regarding cause-and-effect relations because they lack a control group of individuals who did not receive EMDR. The ostensible improvement resulting from EMDR in these reports may be due to numerous variables other than EMDR itself (Gastright 1995), such as placebo effects (improvement resulting from the expectation of improvement), spontaneous remission (natural improvement occurring in the absence of treatment), and regression to the mean (the statistical tendency of extreme scores at an initial testing to become less extreme upon retesting). Consumers of uncontrolled case reports thus must be chary of falling prey to the logical fallacy of *post hoc, ergo propter hoc* (after this, therefore because of this): Only in adequately controlled studies can improvement following EMDR treatment be unequivocally attributed to the treatment itself.

Controlled Studies

Despite abundant claims for EMDR's efficacy, few controlled outcome studies on EMDR have been conducted. They are of two major types: (1) between-subject designs, in which subjects are randomly assigned to either a treatment or a control group; and (2) within-subject designs, in which subjects serve as their own control.

Between-Subject Designs

In the first controlled investigation of EMDR, Shapiro (1989a) randomly assigned 22 individuals who had experienced a traumatic event to either an EMDR treatment group or an exposure control group. In the latter condition, subjects were provided with imaginal exposure to the trauma, but without the eye movements involved in EMDR. Shapiro reported that after only one session, EMDR subjects exhibited significantly lower SUDs levels and significantly higher Validity of Cognition ratings than subjects in the control group. The control group subjects showed essentially no improvement on either measure.

Superficially, these findings seem to provide impressive support for the effectiveness of EMDR. Even a casual inspection of the study's methodology, however, reveals serious deficiencies in experimental design (Acierno et al. 1994; Herbert and Mueser 1992). First, Shapiro herself conducted both treatments and elicited the SUDs and Validity of Cognition ratings from subjects in both groups. Because Shapiro knew the subjects' treatment condition, her findings are potentially attributable to the well-documented experimenter expectancy effect (Rosenthal 1967)—the tendency for researchers to unintentionally bias the results of their investigations in accord with their hypotheses. Specifically, Shapiro might have unwittingly delivered treatment more effectively or convincingly to the EMDR group, or subtly influenced subjects in this group to report greater improvement. Second, the cessation of traumatic imagery was contingent on low SUDs ratings in the EMDR group, but not in the imaginal exposure group (Lohr, Kleinknecht, Conly, Cerro, Schmidt, and Sonntag 1992). It is therefore possible that subjects in the EMDR group reported low SUDs ratings in order to terminate this aversive imagery. Moreover, the total amount of exposure in the two groups may have differed (Lohr et al. 1992). These methodological shortcomings render the results of Shapiro's study (Shapiro 1989a) virtually uninterpretable.

Since this initial report, a number of investigators have attempted to replicate Shapiro's methodology of comparing EMDR with an imaginal exposure control condition for clients with PTSD or other anxiety disorders. Several of these researchers used a "dismantling" design in which EMDR was compared with an otherwise identical procedure minus the eye movements; in this design certain components of the treatment that are purported to be effective (in this case, eye movements) are removed from the full treatment package to determine if their omission decreases therapeutic effectiveness. Renfrey and Spates (1994), for example, compared EMDR with an imaginal exposure condition in which subjects stared at a stationary object.

In virtually all of these investigations, EMDR was not consistently more effective than the exposure control condition, although both conditions appeared to produce improvements on some measures. In one study (Boudewyns et al. 1993), EMDR was found to be more effective than the control condition, but only when within-session SUDs ratings were used. In this investigation, however, as in Shapiro's study (1989a), cessation of the traumatic scene was contingent on low SUDs ratings in the EMDR condition only, so this finding may again reflect the subjects' desire to terminate exposure to unpleasant imagery. Interestingly, SUDs ratings obtained outside of sessions in response to audiotaped depictions of clients' traumatic experiences indicated no differences between conditions. Moreover, physiological reactions (e.g., heart rate increases) to these depictions showed no improvement in either condition.

Sanderson and Carpenter (1992), who administered EMDR and imaginal exposure in counterbalanced order, found that EMDR and imaginal exposure yielded equivalent improvements (using SUDs ratings taken outside of treatment sessions) but that EMDR was effective only when preceded by imaginal exposure. Renfrey and Spates (1994, p. 238) reported that EMDR was no more effective than a control procedure involving fixed visual attention, leading them to conclude that "eye movements are not an essential component of the intervention."

Only one published study has directly compared EMDR with a no-treatment control group. Jensen (1994) randomly assigned Vietnam veterans with PTSD to either an EMDR group or a control group that was promised delayed treatment. EMDR produced lower within-session SUDs ratings compared with the control condition, but did not differ from the control condition in its effect on PTSD symptoms. In fact, the level of interviewer-rated PTSD symptoms *increased* in the EMDR group following treatment.

Within-Subject Designs

Three teams of investigators have used within-subject designs to examine the efficacy of EMDR. Acierno, Tremont, Last, and Montgomery (1994) treated a client with phobias of dead bodies and the dark using both EMDR and "Eye-Focus Desensitization," the latter identical to EMDR except that the therapist's finger remained stationary. In the case of the client's fear of dead bodies, EMDR was administered first; in the case of the client's fear of the dark, Eye-Focus Desensitization was administered first. EMDR showed little or no advantage over the control procedure on self-report, physiological, or behavioral measures, the last of which involved assessments of the client's willingness to approach feared stimuli.

In contrast, Montgomery and Ayllon (1994a) reported that EMDR yielded significant decreases in SUDs levels and client reports of PTSD symptoms, whereas a control procedure consisting of EMDR minus eye movements did not. These two procedures were not, however, administered in counterbalanced order; the control procedure was always presented first. Consequently, the improvements following EMDR may have been due to a delayed effect of the control procedure. Alternatively, they might have resulted from the cumulative effect of the exposure provided by both procedures, regression to the mean effects, or to other factors unrelated to EMDR. EMDR did not produce improvements on physiological indices (heart rate and systolic blood pressure).

Finally, Montgomery and Ayllon (1994b) treated a client with PTSD who had experienced two distinct traumatic events (a car accident and an assault at knifepoint). EMDR was applied separately to the memories of each event. EMDR appeared to show beneficial effects on sub-

gramming (Bandler and Grinder 1975), in which the client's eye movements and visual imagery both play a pivotal role. The developers of neurolinguistic programming claimed that their procedure could cure anxiety disorders (e.g., phobias) in as little time as 20 minutes. Like the claim that EMDR can alleviate most PTSD symptoms in a single session, credible evidence for this neurolinguistic programming assertion has yet to be presented (Druckman and Swets 1988).

In his classic book *Persuasion and Healing: A Comparative Analysis of Psychotherapy*, Jerome Frank (1973) posited that all psychotherapies share certain nonspecific ingredients that account for their effectiveness in combatting distress. These common ingredients, although often denigrated as "placebo" factors, are posited by Frank to be essential to therapeutic efficacy. Among these factors are what Frank termed therapeutic procedures or rituals: highly specialized techniques that, although not in and of themselves necessarily effective, help to inspire the confidence of both client and therapist and provide a rationale for treatment. Frank contended that these procedures, of which the free association method of the psychoanalyst and the induction procedure of the hypnotist are exemplars, are akin to the ceremonial rites of faith healers in that they cultivate the impression that deeply mysterious and significant changes are occurring. In many respects, the eye movements and other accoutrements of EMDR can similarly be viewed as therapeutic rituals that, although perhaps not directly relevant to therapeutic success, may foster clients' and therapists' faith in their chosen method of healing. ☐

jective distress, although the degree of improvement was much less than that reported by Shapiro (1989a). Because EMDR was not compared with a control procedure involving imaginal exposure, its unique effects cannot be ascertained.

The Verdict

Because of the paucity of adequately controlled studies on EMDR, it would be premature to proffer any definitive conclusions regarding its effectiveness. Nevertheless, the following assertions are warranted on the basis of the evidence.

1. Although a multitude of uncontrolled case reports seemingly demonstrate that EMDR produces high success rates, these reports are open to numerous alternative explanations and thus do not provide compelling evidence for EMDR's effectiveness.

2. Controlled studies provide mixed support for the efficacy of EMDR. Most of the evidence for EMDR's effectiveness derives from clients' within-session ratings (which in some cases may be influenced by the desire to terminate exposure), but not from more objective measures of improvement. There is no evidence that EMDR eliminates many or most of the symptoms of PTSD in one session.

3. There is no convincing evidence that EMDR is more effective for post-traumatic anxiety than standard exposure treatments. If EMDR works at all, it may be because it contains an exposure component (Steketee and Goldstein 1994). The proponents of EMDR have yet to demonstrate that EMDR represents a new advance in the treatment of anxiety disorders, or that the eye movements purportedly critical to this technique constitute anything more than pseudoscientific window dressing.

> "Assertions about the utility and validity of psychological techniques . . . must answer to a commonsense demand: 'Show me.' EMDR has thus far failed to convincingly pass the 'Show me' test."

Thus, the most justified conclusion concerning EMDR's effectiveness is: Not proven. Nonetheless, many proponents of EMDR remain convinced that the treatment utility of EMDR will ultimately be demonstrated. Shapiro (1992, p. 114), for example, opined, "When the efficacy of EMDR is fully established, I would like to see it taught in the universities. When that happens, three-hour workshops on specialized applications of EMDR will undoubtedly be offered. . . ." These statements, which were made after approximately 1,200 licensed therapists had already received formal training in EMDR (Shapiro 1992), raise troubling questions. Should not the efficacy of a therapeutic technique be established *before* it is taught to clinicians for the express purpose of administering it to their clients? Moreover, does not the spirit of open scientific inquiry demand that the proponents of a novel technique remain agnostic regarding its efficacy pending appropriate data, and that the two sentences quoted above should therefore begin with "if" rather than "when?"

Concluding Comments

Dawes (1994) has argued that assertions about the utility and validity of psychological techniques, like assertions in all areas of science, must answer to a commonsense demand: "Show me." EMDR has thus far failed to convincingly pass the "Show me" test. Claims for its efficacy have greatly outstripped its empirical support. Although Shapiro has suggested that "there is more to EMDR than meets the eye" (1994b, p. 155), a skeptical consumer of the literature might well be tempted to draw the opposite conclusion.

Moreover, because EMDR has not been clearly shown to be beneficial for the condition for which it was originally developed, namely PTSD, its extension as a treatment for schizophrenia, eating disorders, and other conditions is even more premature and ethically problematic. Furthermore, both scientific and logical considerations dictate that the developers of a treatment should specify the boundary conditions under which this technique is and is not effective. Because EMDR purportedly facilitates the processing of traumatic memories, one would not expect it to be useful for conditions (e.g., schizophrenia) in which severe emotional trauma has not been found to play a major causal role. Indeed, claims that EMDR is helpful for such conditions (Marquis 1991) actually call into question the presumed mechanisms underlying EMDR's mode of action. So far, however, the proponents of EMDR have made little or no effort to delineate the boundary conditions of their method's effectiveness. Moreover, the assertion that EMDR works equally well with auditory tones and hand-taps as with eye movements (Shapiro 1994a) runs counter to Shapiro's theoretical conjectures regarding EMDR's commonalities with REM sleep.

Although further research on EMDR is warranted, such research will likely be impeded by the prohibitions placed on the open distribution of EMDR training materials (Acierno et al. 1994). For example, participants in EMDR workshops must agree not to audiotape any portion of the workshop, train others in the technique without formal approval, or disseminate EMDR training information to colleagues (Rosen 1993). It seems difficult to quarrel with Herbert and Meuser's (1992, p. 173) contention that although "this procedure is justified to maintain 'quality control,' such a restriction of information runs counter to the principle of open and free exchange of ideas among scientists and professionals."

Because of the limited number of controlled studies on EMDR, both practitioners and scientists should remain open to the possibility of its effectiveness. Nevertheless, the standard of proof required to use a new procedure clinically should be considerably higher than the standard of proof required to conduct research on its efficacy. This is particularly true in the case of such conditions as PTSD, for which existing treatments have already been shown to be effective. The continued widespread use of EMDR for therapeutic purposes in the absence of adequate evidence can be seen as only another example of the human mind's willingness to sacrifice critical thinking for wishful thinking.

Note

1. I thank Lori Marino and Irwin Waldman for their helpful comments on an earlier draft of this manuscript and Cherilyn Rowland for assistance in library research.

References

ABC News. 1994. *When All Else Fails.* "20/20" transcript, July 29.

Acierno, R., M. Hersen, V. B. Van Hasselt, G. Tremont, and K. T. Meuser. 1994. Review of the validation and dissemination of eye-movement desensitization and reprocessing: A scientific and ethical dilemma. *Clinical Psychology Review,* 14: 287-299.

Acierno, R., G. Tremont, C. Last, and D. Montgomery. 1994. Tripartite assessment of the efficacy of eye-movement desensitization in a multiphobic patient. *Journal of Anxiety Disorders,* 8: 259-276.

American Psychiatric Association. 1994. *Diagnostic and Statistical Manual of Mental Disorders.* 4th ed. Washington D.C.: American Psychiatric Association.

Bandler, R., and Grinder, J. 1975. *The Structure of Magic.* Palo Alto, Calif.: Science and Behavior Books.

Barlow, D. H. 1988. *Anxiety and its Disorders.* New York: Guilford Press.

Beere, D.B. 1992. More on EMDR. *Behavior Therapist,* 15: 179-180.

Beyerstein, B. L. 1990. Brainscams: Neuromythologies of the New Age. *International Journal of Mental Health,* 19: 27-36.

Boudewyns, P. A., L. A. Stwertka, J. W. Hyer, X. Albrecht, and E. G. Sperr. 1993. Eye movement desensitization for PTSD of combat: A treatment outcome pilot study. *Behavior Therapist,* 16: 29-33.

Bower, B. 1995. Promise and dissent. *Science News,* 148: 270-271.

Cavaliere, F. 1995. Team works to quell stress in Bosnia. *American Psychological Association Monitor,* 26(8):8.

Dawes, R. M. 1994. *House of Cards: Psychology and Psychotherapy Built on Myth.* New York: Free Press.

Druckman, D. and J. A. Swets. Eds. 1988. *Enhancing Human Performance: Issues, Theories, and Techniques.* Washington, D.C.: National Academy Press.

Forbes, D., M. Creamer., and P. Rycroft. 1994. Eye movement desensitization and reprocessing in post-traumatic stress disorder: A pilot study using assessment measures. *Journal of Behavior Therapy and Experimental Psychiatry,* 25: 113-120.

Frank, J. D. 1973. Persuasion and Healing: A Comparative Analysis of Psychotherapy. Baltimore: John Hopkins University Press.

Freuh, B. C., S. M. Turner, and D.C. Beidel. 1995. *Exposure therapy for PTSD: A critical review.* Unpublished manuscript.

Gastright, J. 1995. EMDR works! Is that enough? *Cincinnati Skeptic,* 4(3):1-3.

Herbert, J. D., and K. T. Meuser. 1992. Eye movement desensitization: A critique of the evidence. *Journal of Behavior Therapy and Experimental Psychiatry,* 23: 169-174.

Jensen, J. A. 1994. An investigation of eye movement desensitization and reprocessing (EMD/R) as a treatment for post-traumatic stress disorder (PTSD) symptoms of Vietnam combat veterans. *Behavior Therapy,* 25: 311-325.

Lipke, H. J., and A. L. Botkin. 1992. Case studies of eye movement desensitization and reprocessing (EMDR) with chronic posttraumatic stress disorder. *Psychotherapy,* 29: 591-595.

Lohr, J. M., R. A. Kleinknecht, A. T. Conley, S. D. Cerro, J. Schmidt, and M. E. Sonntag. 1992. A methodological critique of the current status of eye movement desensitization (EMDR). *Journal of Behavior Therapy and*
Experimental Psychiatry, 23: 159-167.

Marquis, J. N. 1991. A report on seventy-eight cases treated by eye movement desensitization. *Journal of Behavior Therapy and Experimental Psychiatry,* 22: 187-192.

Montgomery, R.W., and T. Ayllon. 1994a. Eye movement desensitization across images: A single case design. *Journal of Behavior Therapy and Experimental Psychiatry,* 25: 23-28.

———. 1994b. Eye movement desensitization across subjects: Subjective and physiological measures of treatment efficacy. *Journal of Behavior Therapy and Experimental Psychiatry,* 25: 217-230.

Moore, T. E. 1992. Subliminal perception: Facts and fallacies. SKEPTICAL INQUIRER, 16: 273-281.

Mulick, J. A., J. W. Jacobson, and F. H. Kobe. 1993. Anguished silence and helping hands: Autism and facilitated communication. SKEPTICAL INQUIRER, 17(3) (Spring): 270-280.

Oswalt, R., M. Anderson, K. Hagstrom, and B. Berkowitz. 1993. Evaluation of the one-session eye-movement desensitization reprocessing procedure for eliminating traumatic memories. *Psychological Reports,* 27: 99.

Pellicer, X. 1993. Eye movement desensitization of a child's nightmares: A case report. *Journal of Behavior Therapy and Experimental Psychiatry,* 24: 73-75.

Pratkanis, A. R. 1992. The cargo-cult science of subliminal persuasion. SKEPTICAL INQUIRER, (3) 16 (Spring): 260-272.

Puk, G. 1991. Treating traumatic memories: A case report on the eye movement desensitization procedure. *Journal of Behavior Therapy and Experimental Psychiatry,* 22: 149-151.

Renfrey, G., and C. R. Spates, 1994. Eye movement desensitization: A partial dismantling study. *Journal of Behavior Therapy and Experimental Psychiatry,* 25: 231-239.

Rosen, G. M. 1993. A note to EMDR critics: What you didn't see is only part of what you don't get. *Behavior Therapist,* 16: 216.

Rosenthal, R. 1967. Covert communication in the psychological experiment. *Psychological Bulletin,* 67: 356-367.

———. 1979. The "file drawer problem" and tolerance for null results. *Psychological Bulletin,* 86: 638-641.

Rowley, D. T. 1986. *Hypnosis and hypnotherapy.* London: Croom Helm.

Sanderson, A., and R. Carpenter 1992. Eye movement desensitization versus image confrontation: A single session crossover study of 58 phobic subjects. *Journal of Behavior Therapy and Experimental Psychiatry,* 23: 269-275.

Shapiro, F. 1989a. Eye movement desensitization: A new treatment for post-traumatic stress disorder. *Journal of Behavior Therapy and Experimental Psychiatry,* 20: 211-217.

———. 1989b. Efficacy of the eye movement desensitization procedure in the treatment of traumatic memories. *Journal of Traumatic Stress,* 2: 199-223.

———. 1991. Eye movement desensitization and reprocessing procedure: From EMD to EMD/R—a new treatment model for anxiety and related traumata. *Behavior Therapist,* 14: 133-135.

———. 1992. Dr. Francine Shapiro responds. *Behavior Therapist,* 15: 111-114.

———. 1994a. Alternative stimuli in the use of EMD(R). *Journal of Behaviour Therapy and Experimental Psychiatry,* 25: 89-91.

———. 1994b. EMDR: In the eye of a paradigm shift. *Behavior Therapist,* 17: 153-156.

Silver, B. V. and E. B. Blanchard. 1978. Biofeedback and relaxation training in the treatment of psychophysiological disorders: Or are the machines really necessary? *Journal of Behavioral Medicine,* 1: 217-238.

Spates, C. R. and M. M. Burnette. 1995. Eye movement desensitization: Three unusual cases. *Journal of Behavior Therapy and Experimental Psychiatry,* 26: 51-55.

Steketee, G., and A. J. Goldstein. 1994. Reflections on Shapiro's reflections: Testing EMDR within a theoretical context. *Behavior Therapist,* 17: 156-157.

Winson, J. 1990. The meaning of dreams. *Scientific American,* 263: 86-96.

Wolpe, J., and J. Abrams. 1991. Post-traumatic stress disorder overcome by eye-movement desensitization: A case report. *Journal of Behavior Therapy and Experimental Psychiatry,* 22: 39-43.   □

Facilitated Communication:

By Gina Green

The cliché that "there is nothing new under the sun" applies more than ever to the mental health profession today. We seem to be experiencing a myriad of new techniques to treat the developmentally disabled, Facilitated Communication being one of the most popular, yet in reality their underlying characteristics have been seen before. These components make up the structure of what might be considered a social movement:

—Assertions that a new technique produces remarkable effects are made in the absence of solid objective evidence, or what little evidence there is becomes highly overblown.

—Excitement about a possible breakthrough sweeps rapidly through the communities of parents, teachers, service providers, and others concerned with the welfare of individuals with disabilities.

—Eager, even desperate for something that might help, many invest considerable financial and emotional resources in the new technique.

—In the process, effective or potentially effective techniques are ignored.

—Few question the basis for the claims about the new treatment or the qualifications of the individuals making them.

—Anecdotal reports that seem to confirm the initial claims proliferate rapidly.

—Careful scientific evaluation to determine the real effects of the technique are not completed for some time, and can be made more difficult than usual by the well-known and powerful effects of expectancies.

—Some of these techniques have small specific positive effects, or at least do minimal harm.

—Eventually they fall out of favor, sometimes because they are discredited by sound research, sometimes simply because experience reveals their lack of efficacy, but probably most often because another fad treatment has come on the scene. Each retains some adherents, however, and some go relatively dormant for a while only to emerge again.

Parallel phenomena occur in other areas, such as treatments for AIDS, cancer, and various psychological problems. At present the field of developmental disabilities (especially autism) seems to be experiencing an epidemic of novel techniques, or "interventions," as they are called. Despite its parallels with other techniques, Facilitated Communication (FC) has probably had a greater impact than any other novel intervention in the history of treatment for persons with disabilities.

How FC Works

How does FC work? If you have never seen it in action it is quite a phenomenon to observe. Individuals with "severe communication impairments" (e.g., severe mental retardation, autism) are assisted in spelling words by "facilitators" (teachers or parents) who provide physical support, most often (at least initially) by holding their hand, wrist, or forearm while they point to letters on a keyboard or printed letter display. Right before your eyes, a mentally disabled person that just previously had virtually no communication skills, suddenly begins to spell out words, sentences, and whole paragraphs. Stories are told. Answers to questions are given. A child that did not appear to know the difference between a dog and an elephant can now be shown a series of pictures, correctly identifying them one by one, as his or her hand glides deftly over the keyboard, pecking out the correct letters. The assumption, of course, is that most of the words spelled in this fashion actually originate with the disabled partner and not the facilitator.

On its face, FC can seem simple and benign, and sometimes looks quite convincing. Its main proponents sometimes characterize FC simply as a strategy for teaching individuals to point in order to access systems like synthetic speech devices and keyboards to augment their

Mental Miracle or Sleight of Hand?

communication. At the same time, however, they claim that it is a revolutionary means of unlocking highly developed literacy, numeracy, and communication repertoires in large numbers of individuals previously thought to have severe learning difficulties. For all the world it looks like a mental miracle, the kind of stuff they make movies about, as in "Awakenings."

The theory is that many such individuals do not have cognitive deficits at all, but instead have a presumed neuromotor impairment that prevents them from initiating and controlling vocal expression. Their average or even above average intelligence is locked away, awaiting release. The neuromotor disorder is also presumed to manifest itself in "hand function impairments" that make it necessary for someone else to stabilize the individual's hand and arm for pointing, and to pull the pointing hand back between selections to minimize impulsive or poorly planned responding. Candidates for FC are also presumed to lack confidence in their abilities, and so require the special touch and emotional support of a facilitator to communicate, (i.e., a strap or device to hold the person's arm steady will not work).

FC thus has an almost irresistible appeal for parents, teachers, and other caring persons who struggle mightily to understand and communicate with individuals who often do not respond or communicated in return. But the very features that make FC so seductive, in combination with some other potent factors, have made it a topic of heated debate between believers and skeptics since its "discovery" in Australia nearly two decades ago.

Beginnings Down Under

It all began in the 1970s with Rosemary Crossley, a teacher in an institution in Melbourne in the Australian state of Victoria. She suspected that some of her young charges with severe cerebral palsy had far more ability than their physical impairments allowed them to demonstrate. When she gave them hand or arm support to help them point to pictures, letters, and other stimuli, Crossley became convinced that several of the children revealed literacy and math skills that they had somehow developed with little or no instruction, despite having lived most of their lives in an impoverished institutional environment.

Right away there was controversy about the technique that Crossley called Facilitated Communication Training. Two people were involved in creating the messages, and simple observation could not reveal how much each was contributing. Plus, many of the messages Crossley attributed to these institutionalized individuals defied plausibility. "Facilitated" accusations of abuse and expressions of wishes for major life changes (like leaving the institution) made it imperative to determine whether communications actually originated with the disabled individual or the facilitator. Matters were complicated by Crossley's emerging status as a heroine to many in the deinstitutionalization movement. Eventually, after a series of legal proceedings, a young woman with cerebral palsy with whom Crossley had developed a special relationship through FC was released from the institution to reside with Crossley. The institution was closed, and in 1986 Crossley started (with government financial support) the DEAL Centre (Dignity through Education and Language) to promote alternative communication approaches—principally FC—for individuals with severe communication impairments. Use of the method spread to programs in Victoria serving persons with various disabilities, accompanied by controversies about communications attributed to FC users on the basis of subjective reports.

Sufficiently serious issues arose to

provoke formal statements of concern from professionals and parents in 1988, and a government-sponsored investigation in 1989. Despite Crossley's resistance to objective testing (on the basis that FC users refused to cooperate when their competence was questioned), some small-scale controlled evaluations were conducted in the course of that investigation. When the facilitator's knowledge about expected messages was well-controlled (more on this later), and the accuracy of messages was evaluated objectively, the effect disappeared. The disabled individuals were unable to communicate beyond their normal expectation. Instead, it appeared that the facilitators were authoring most FC messages, apparently without their awareness. These early studies suggested that FC was susceptible to a somewhat unusual kind of abuse: Allowing others to impose their own wishes, fears, hopes, and agendas on nonspeaking individuals.

A Social Movement is Born

At about that time Douglas Biklen, a special education professor from Syracuse University, conducted a four week observational study of 21 DEAL clients said to be autistic, who were reported to engage in high-level discourse with the help of facilitators. Professor Biklen was already established as a leader in the "total inclusion movement," which seeks the full-time placement of all students with disabilities, regardless of their competencies and needs, in regular classrooms. The report describing his first qualitative study of FC, which Biklen said was begun "in an attempt not to *test* hypotheses but rather to generate them," appeared in the *Harvard Educational Review* in 1990. He reported that the communication of the individuals he observed (some of whom were being "facilitated" for the first time) was sophisticated in content, conceptualization, and vocabulary, and contained frequent references to feelings, wishes to be treated normally and to attend regular schools, and society's treatment of individuals

Can people can learn, without being deliberately taught, to respond to subtle, subconscious, involuntary cues if an animal can? In the early 1900's, a horse, Clever Hans, astonished Germany by its self-learned ability to interpret visual cues and answer simple questions by tapping its hoof.

with disabilities.

This was in sharp contrast with the well-documented difficulties in social, play, cognitive, and communication skills that constitute current diagnostic criteria for autism (not to mention that the diagnosis is difficult to make and is applied to individuals with a wide range of competencies and deficits in all those domains). In his seminal article, Biklen mentioned the controversy over the Australian findings, but asserted that informal "indicators that communication was the person's own were strong enough, in my view, to justify the continuing *assumption of its validity*" [italics added].

Some of the indicators he reported observing were disabled individuals typing independently or with minimal physical contact with the facilitator; content (spelling errors, unexpected word usage, etc.) that appeared to be unique to each individual; and facial expressions or other signs that the individual understood the communication. He also noted that facilitators often could not tell who was doing the spelling and that they could be influencing the FC in subtle ways without their awareness, and that this could be a problem. Finally, on the basis of his uncontrolled observations and the reports of Crossley and other facilitators, Biklen decided that autism had to be redefined as a problem not of cognition or affect, but of voluntary motor control. He returned from Australia to establish the Facilitated Communication Institute (FCI) at Syracuse University, and the North Ameri-

can FC movement was underway.

The Movement Takes Off

Word of FC spread quickly with the help of several media reports of FC "miracles." The rate of information exchange increased geometrically, feeding the system and driving it forward. FC newsletters, conferences, and support networks contributed to the spread of astonishing success stories, along with examples of prose and poetry attributed to FC authors. The Syracuse FCI began training new facilitators in earnest, in workshops that lasted from a few hours to two or three days. At least two New England universities became satellite programs of the Syracuse FC Institute, as did numerous other private and public agencies that provided training and support for facilitators. Initiates (parents, paraprofessionals, and professionals in several disciplines) were often told that the technique was simple and required no special training. They were urged to train others, and to go out and try FC with disabled individuals. Thousands did. Soon FC was being heralded as a means of "empowering" individuals with severe disabilities to make their own decisions and participate fully in society. FC was rapidly becoming the politically correct treatment of choice.

Soon after publication of Biklen's article, special education personnel and parents around Syracuse, then throughout the U.S. and Canada, adopted FC enthusiastically. Scores of children were placed in regular classrooms doing grade-level academic work with "facilitation." Decisions about the lives of adults with severe disabilities—living arrangements, medical and other treatments, use of hearing aids, and so on—were based on "facilitated" messages without any attempt to verify authorship objectively. In many cases FC supplanted other communication modes, including vocal speech and augmentative communication systems, that do not require another person for message creation. Some psychologists, speech pathologists, and others began giving I.Q. and other standardized tests with "facilitation," changing diagnoses and program recommendations in accordance with the "facilitated" results. Suddenly "retarded" individuals were proclaimed to have average or above-average intelligence. "Facilitated" counseling and psychotherapy were promoted to help FC users deal with personal problems. Colleges and universities offered courses on FC. Millions of tax dollars were invested in promoting its widespread adoption, with little objective evaluation of its validity or efficacy.

Enter Psi, Exit Science

Not surprisingly, the experience of accomplishing a breakthrough and being part of a movement was a heady experience for many facilitators. Some, however, reported wondering all along whether the words being produced through FC were really coming from their disabled partners. Others who had serious doubts about the method from the outset found themselves under considerable pressure from parents, peers, and employers to adopt the method wholesale and without question. Reports that facilitators' private thoughts were being expressed through FC led some to conclude that individuals with autism must have telepathy—a view espoused by a professor of special education at the University of Wisconsin, among others.

Facilitators were also imbued, explicitly and implicitly, with a

> **"FC ...has an almost irresistible appeal for parents, teachers, and other caring persons who struggle mightily to understand and communicate with individuals who often do not respond or communicate in return."**

strong ideology that presents dilemmas for many who want to know who is really communicating in FC. Some components of the ideology include:

—Assume competence.

—Don't test.

—Prevent errors.

—Expect remarkable revelations in the form of hidden skills as well as sensitive personal information.

—Use circumstantial, subjective data to validate authorship.

—Avoid objective scrutiny.

—Emphasize "facilitated" over spoken or other communications.

Contradictory evidence from the controlled evaluations that had been conducted in Australia and those that emerged later in the U.S. were mentioned rarely, if at all, in FC training materials and newsletters. When that evidence was mentioned it was to criticize the evaluation methods and the people who employed them, and to explain away the results by saying essentially that FC could not be tested. In short, FC's

validity was to be accepted largely on faith. With this, science was abandoned.

Concurrently Biklen, Crossley, and their colleagues published further reports of qualitative studies suggesting that FC was highly effective in eliciting unexpected literacy skills from large proportions of individuals with severe autism, mental retardation, and other disorders. Many of these individuals had received little instruction in reading and spelling, or if instruction had been attempted many had not appeared to learn very much. How, then, had they developed age-level or even precocious literacy skills? According to Biklen they acquired these skills from watching television, seeing their siblings do homework, and simply being exposed to words pervading the environment. Or perhaps some had actually been learning from instruction all along, but because their speech was limited they could not demonstrate what they learned.

How did they verify their claims? Biklen and his colleagues used participant observation and other methods employed by anthropologists, sociologists, and educators in field studies of cultures and social systems. The research was strictly descriptive, not experimental, and employed no objective measurement or procedures to minimize observer bias. Despite their acknowledgement of the real possibility of facilitator influence in FC, these studies did not control that critical variable.

Late in 1991 a few parents of stu-

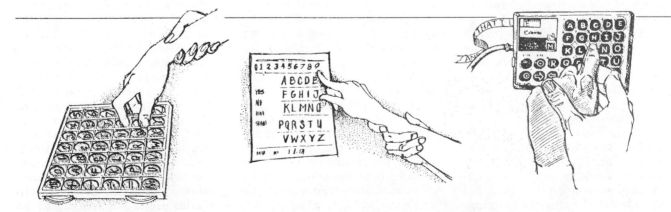

Facilitated Communication requires the "facilitating" hand of the therapist and an alphabet board. The board can be a simple sheet of paper taped to a wall, or it can be a shophisticated electronic keyboard that produces a taped record of the responses.

dents at the New England Center for Autism, where I serve as Director of Research, began pressing our program to adopt FC. They asked us to make rather drastic changes in their childrens' lives on the assumption that messages produced with FC represented the childrens' true wishes and competencies. Some were angry when we decided instead to use it only under conditions of a small-scale experimental study employing the kind of objective evaluation methods that we try to apply to all techniques. At that time we could find nothing about FC in the research literature, so we consulted respected colleagues around the country. Some (in California, surprisingly enough) had not heard of it yet. Others invoked a Ouija board analogy or Clever Hans effect, and suggested that FC would be a short-lived fad. None knew of any objective evidence about FC. To our chagrin, we also encountered individuals with scientific training who were promoting the use of FC without considering the fundamental question about authorship.

The Sexual Abuse Component

The real possibility that "facilitated" words were those of the facilitators was not a cause for much concern as long as the process seemed benevolent. Few wished to throw a wet blanket on the euphoria created by reports of a breakthrough. But almost from the beginning, strange things began to happen: Some FC messages said—or were interpreted by facilitators to say—that disabled FC users had been abused by family members or caregivers. Often the abuse alleged was sexual, and many allegations contained extensive, explicit, pornographic details.

So many social movements have a sexual component in them, and FC is not different. Production of sex abuse allegations usually set in motion an inexorable chain of events. Beliefs about FC, the complexities inherent in the method, and the fact that the alleged victim may be seen as particularly vulnerable because he or she is disabled, now

> "These early studies suggested that FC was susceptible to a somewhat unusual kind of abuse: Allowing others to impose their own wishes, fears, hopes, and agendas on nonspeaking individuals."

began to interact with the zealous pursuit that seems to typify investigations of sex abuse allegations. School or program administrators were notified, who in turn called in representatives of social services and law enforcement agencies. If the accused was a family member with whom the FC user resided, that person was either required to leave the home or the FC user was placed in foster care. If a parent was accused, both parents often faced criminal charges, one for perpetrating the alleged abuse, the other for knowing about it and failing to act. Often actions were initiated by social service workers to terminate parental custody or guardianship. If the accused was a school or program employee, they may have been suspended from their job or even fired. A long and trying ordeal was virtually guaranteed for all involved. An investigation began. Police interrogated the accused, and questioned the alleged victim through their facilitator. Other evidence was sought in the results of medical and psychological examinations of the alleged victim, and interviews with others who may have had information about the alleged events. A presumably independent facilitator was sometimes called in to try to corroborate the allegation, introducing another complexity: There appear to be no established safeguards or objective criteria for ensuring that independent facilitators in fact have no access to information about cases, nor for deciding what constitutes corroborating "facilitated" content.

False allegations have devastating emotional and financial effects on

the accused and their families, but leaving individuals in situations in which they may be abused jeopardizes their physical and emotional welfare. It would seem that extreme caution and stringent rules of evidence should apply. A number of cases have arisen in which the only evidence was a "facilitated" allegation, although there have also been reports of cases in which corroborating evidence or confessions were obtained. When an allegation is made through FC, two separate but related questions must be addressed: Who made the allegation, and did the alleged events actually occur? Some courts and investigative bodies in Australia, the U.S., and Canada have decided that the first question must be answered by controlled testing of FC under conditions where independent observers can verify when the facilitator does and does not have information necessary to produce communications. If the FC user does not convey information accurately and reliably under those conditions, and there is no other solid evidence, the legal action is usually terminated. That has been the outcome of testing in every case of which I am aware, but by the time that determination has been made the accused have been traumatized for the better part of a year and have spent tens of thousands of dollars defending themselves. Solid corroborating evidence would certainly answer the second question—whether abuse occurred—but it does not follow logically that it answers the question about who authored the "facilitated" allegation.

Unfortunately, it wasn't until a number of false "facilitated" allegations of sexual abuse came to light that FC began to be scrutinized closely. As issues about the validity and reliability of FC were addressed in courtrooms all over the U.S., critical and questioning stories appeared in the print and electronic media. Concurrently (though somewhat slowly), results from a rapidly growing number of controlled evaluations began to be disseminated, and a few more skeptical voices were raised.

How To Test FC

The rationale for conducting controlled observations to determine authorship in FC is straightforward: If the disabled FC user is actually the source of the messages, then accurate and appropriate messages should be produced on virtually every opportunity when the facilitator has no knowledge of the expected message. Some controlled evaluations of FC have been mandated by legal questions like those just described, but a number were carried out by clinicians, researchers, and program administrators who simply wanted an objective empirical basis for making decisions about FC. Even James "The Amazing" Randi was consulted in the early stages of testing, some calling him in to make sure fraud and trickery was not involved, others because they genuinely wondered if psychic power was the cause. Randi's skepticism of the phenomenon was not welcomed by FC supporters. The first major American study was conducted by psychologist Douglas Wheeler and colleagues at the O.D. Heck Developmental Center in Schenectady, NY, who wanted objective evidence to convince skeptics that FC was valid.

How do you do a controlled study of FC? Recently I analyzed reports of 17 evaluations of FC that have appeared or have been accepted for publication in peer-reviewed professional journals, and eight presented at scientific conferences. The common and critical ingredients were:

1. Consent for participation.

2. Objective measures, i.e., use of independent, nonparticipating observers or judges, "blind" to the conditions in effect, who recorded data and/or evaluated the accuracy of FC output.

3. Maintenance of physical and emotional support by the facilitator.

4. With only a few exceptions, facilitator/FC user dyads who had been working together with apparent success for a considerable period before formal evaluations were conducted.

5. Familiar, common communication contexts (e.g., typical academic and language-development activities, discussing everyday events, naming or describing familiar pictures or objects).

6. Establishment of apparently successful FC in the evaluation context.

7. Control of information available to the facilitator.

The necessary control was established in a number of ways. In some studies, facilitators were simply asked to look at their partner and not the letter display, or were actually screened from the letter display. These kinds of tests were suggested by the observation that many facilitators focus intently on the letters while their partners look at the letters infrequently, if at all. Others presented visual stimuli like pictures, objects, or printed materials only to the FC user while the facilitator was screened from seeing them. Alternatively, spoken questions were presented only to the FC user while their facilitator wore earplugs or headphones playing masking noise. Several evaluations used a procedure described as "message passing:" FC users were engaged in some familiar activities in the absence of facilitators, who then used FC to solicit descriptions of the activities. A couple of evaluations involved independent facilitators, unfamiliar with the FC user, who solicited information that was presumably unknown to the facilitator (e.g., the FC user's favorite food, a recent event in their life, names of family members, etc.).

The Results

The most telling evaluations used double-blind procedures, in which facilitators and their partners saw or heard different items on some trials, and the same item on other trials. Neither could tell what information their partner was receiving. Responses that corresponded to information presented to the facilitator and not to their partner provided direct evidence that facilitators were controlling those FC productions. Multiple tasks and control procedures were used by several investigators. Facilitators in all evaluations had been trained by leading proponents of FC, or by others who had had such training. They seemed representative of the general population of facilitators, including parents, paraprofessionals, teachers, speech pathologists, and other human service workers. The sample of FC users in these evaluations also appeared representative, comprising a total of 194 children and adults with autism, mental retardation, cerebral palsy, and related disorders.

None of these controlled evaluations produced compelling evidence that FC enabled individuals with disabilities to demonstrate unexpected literacy and communication skills, free of the facilitator's influence. Many messages were produced over numerous trials and sessions, but the vast majority were accurate and appropriate to context only when the facilitator knew what was to be produced. The strong inference is that facilitators authored most messages, although most reported that they were unaware of doing so. Sixteen evaluations found no evidence whatsoever of valid productions. A total of 23 individuals with various disabilities in nine different evaluations made accurate responses on some occasions when their facilitators did not know the answers, but most of those productions were commensurate with or less advanced than the individuals' documented skills *without* FC. That is, they were primarily single words and an occasional short phrase, produced on some trials by individuals whose vocal or signed communication exceeded that level, some of whom had documented reading skills before they were introduced to FC.

> "Reports that facilitators' private thoughts were being expressed through FC led some to conclude that individuals with autism must have telepathy."

For most of these individuals, there was clear evidence that on many other trials their facilitators controlled the productions. The controlled evaluations also demonstrated that most facilitators simply could not tell when and how much they were cueing their partners, emphasizing the importance of systematic, controlled observations for identifying the source of "facilitated" messages. The legal, ethical, and practical implications of these findings are obvious and serious. Together with the legal cases and critical media reports, they have made it a little more acceptable to voice skepticism about FC.

The Proponents Respond: Parallels With Psychics

Proponents of FC have criticized the controlled evaluations on several counts. The parallels of their responses to those received by James Randi when he tests psychics are startling. FC supporters, for example, argue that incorrect answers were due to lack of confidence, anxiety, or resistance on the part of FC users, who "freeze up" or become offended when challenged to prove their competence. Likewise, psychics claim they cannot perform in front of video cameras or in the presence of skeptics who make them anxious. In the case of FC, if this were true—if testing *per se* destroyed the FC process—participants in the controlled evaluations would not have responded at all, or would have produced inaccurate responses throughout, not just when their facilitators did not know the answers. Instead, many accurate words, descriptions, and other responses were produced, but for the most part only when facilitators knew what they were supposed to be.

Additionally, many evaluations took place in familiar surroundings in which individuals had engaged in FC for numerous sessions, with their regular facilitators and letter displays. Sessions typically were not conducted or were terminated if there were any signs of distress or unwillingness to continue. Few

> "In other words, when the data contradict their claims, experiments are not valid; when the data support their claims, experiments are useful."

refusals were reported. Participants in most evaluations completed numerous trials and sessions over extended periods of time. Most appeared cooperative, even enthusiastic, throughout. Several evaluations were conducted in the context of typical FC sessions, using the same types of materials and questions to which participants had appeared to respond successfully. Questions were no more confrontational or intrusive (perhaps less so) than those often asked in regular FC sessions; in fact, many tasks were identical to those recommended for FC training, except that conditions were arranged so that facilitators could not know all the expected responses. Finally, if FC users simply become too anxious to communicate when challenged, one has to wonder how they are managing to perform in regular academic classrooms, on I.Q. and other tests, in front of TV cameras, and before large audiences at FC meetings. And how can they give "facilitated" testimony, under questioning by judges and attorneys (which is anxiety producing for anyone), as prosecutors in some sexual abuse allegation cases are now arguing is their right?

Another criticism of the controlled evaluations is that the facilitators were not familiar with their partners, were inadequately trained, or did not provide appropriate "facilitation." That is simply not true. As indicated in the summary above, the FC users' preferred facilitators participated with them in most evaluations. The only exceptions were two studies that assessed initial responsiveness to FC with facilitators and FC users who were "beginners" when the evalua-

tion started, and a couple of legal cases in which unfamiliar facilitators were involved (who nonetheless "facilitated" successfully with the FC users before controlled testing began). Many facilitators were trained by leading proponents of FC. Most were encouraged to provide whatever physical and emotional support they wished during the evaluation. If they were not "facilitating" properly, few understandable communications would have been produced. Quite the opposite was true. There is a peculiar irony in this criticism, however, since proponents offer no specific guidelines or standards as to what constitutes sufficient training and experience for facilitators. Some facilitators have started using the method after reading an article, watching a videotape, or attending a brief workshop. When we began to take a look at FC at the New England Center for Autism, for example, our three speech-language pathologists were trained by Biklen in a two-day workshop. That appeared to be the norm at that time (late 1991). A further contradiction is that there are reports throughout the descriptive literature on FC that facilitators who were complete strangers had some individuals with severe disabilities "facilitating" sentences (more, in some cases) in their very first session.

Implausibilities and Inconsistencies

An oft-cited criticism of the controlled evaluations is that they required FC users to perform confrontational naming tasks, which proponents consider inappropriate because individuals with autism have global "word-finding" problems. This argument is implausible for several reasons. First, many evaluations did not require FC users to spell specific names; descriptions, copying, multiple-choice options, yes/no responses, and answers to open-ended questions were just some of the other kinds of responses solicited. Second, there is no solid evidence that such problems are exhibited by individuals with autism. It can be difficult to distinguish words that an individual presumably knows but cannot produce from words that they simply do not know, even with individuals who at one time had well-developed language (e.g., neurologic patients). This would seem to be even more difficult with individuals with autism. Even if this rationalization applied to individuals with autism, what accounts for the results with the many FC users who did not have autism? Additionally, at least three studies documented spontaneous oral naming responses by FC users with autism that were more accurate than their "facilitated" responses. That certainly goes against the "word-finding" hypothesis for those individuals.

Some FC proponents attribute negative findings to the supposition that most FC users are not experienced with the kinds of tasks presented to them in the controlled tests. This criticism is especially puzzling. By law, the skills of individuals with special needs must be evaluated on a regular basis, so most FC users have probably had a great deal of test experience. The tasks used in most controlled evaluations were like those used to teach and test academic and language skills in classrooms and training programs everywhere. In fact, many were precisely the kinds of activities that are recommended for FC training, on which the FC users in the controlled evaluations had been reported to perform very well. Again, if inexperience with the tasks were a plausible explanation, FC users should perform equally poorly when their facilitators did and did not know the expected answers. That was not the case in the controlled evaluations.

Finally, FC proponents are inconsistent in claiming that controlled testing undermines the FC user's confidence, while in the next breath they are quick to tout reports that some attempts at controlled evaluations have produced evidence of FC's validity. In other words, when the data contradict their claims, experiments are not valid; when the data support their claims, experiments are useful. A report from Australia (referred to as the IDRP report) said

Are there parallels between the ideomotor responses that direct dowsing sticks and the Ouija board and the response of the autistic subjects to the touch of their facilitators?

that three individuals with disabilities succeeded in "facilitating" the name of a gift they were given in the absence of their facilitators, but one was said to type his responses independently, without FC. The report provided no background information about the individuals, no details about the procedures, and described only one controlled trial completed by each individual. Another exercise described in a letter to the editor of a speech disorders journal claimed that four of five students thought to have severe language delays performed remarkably better with FC than without on a test of matching pictures to spoken words. The facilitator wore headphones but was not screened visually from the nearby examiner who was speaking the words, and no expressive communication was required of the FC users. At best, these exercises must be considered inconclusive, but they have been cited widely by proponents as scientific validations of FC. The contradiction inherent in arguing that controlled testing interferes with FC while endorsing exercises like these seems lost on them. The clear implication is that tests that appear to produce evidence supporting beliefs about FC are good, and tests that fail to do so are bad.

Silent Skeptics

If FC is so obviously not the mental miracle supporters claim it is, why does the movement continue to grow? Why hasn't the scientific community made a significant public statement against FC? A number of variables probably account for the

initial and continuing reluctance of many skeptics to speak up. First, scientists in general are cautious about drawing conclusions without data. When FC first hit the disability community in North America, there were no objective data to be had. A rejoinder to Biklen's first report by Australian psychologists Robert Cummins and Margot Prior was submitted to the *Harvard Educational Review* early in 1991. Their paper summarized the results of controlled tests of the validity of FC and the legal and ethical problems it had engendered in Australia. It was not published until late summer 1992, and by that time the FC movement already had considerable momentum. Even then, many skeptics withheld judgment on the basis that the Australian data were limited. This was essentially our reasoning at the New England Center for Autism—that some individuals with autism might write or type better than they could speak (we knew a few), and that if there were some merit to the claims about FC, it would be revealed through careful research using objective methodology.

At the same time, however, we sensed something ominous in the rapidity and zeal with which FC was being applied, the resistance to critical scrutiny, and the antiscience stance of many adherents. Even as the dark side of the FC story began to unfold, relatively few in developmental disabilities who knew how to test the claims about FC experimentally wanted to get involved, perhaps thinking that the best response was to continue to do sound research in their own areas. Others did not to want to be seen as naysayers or debunkers.

Cummins and Prior, both with long histories of involvement in treatment and research in developmental disabilities, were among the first in Victoria to go public with their concerns about FC. Their expressions of skepticism and calls for caution were met with hostility and personal attacks from FC proponents in Australia, a scenario that has repeated itself in the U.S. That suggests another variable, in my opinion one of the most potent: It was (is) not Politically Correct in many circles to suggest that FC might not be all it appears, or even to call for objective evaluation to determine if it is. Those who do are likely to be labelled heretics, oppressors of the disabled, inhumane, negative, jealous of others' discoveries, "dinosaurs" who cannot accept new ideas, and out for financial gain.

The FC Future

Needless to say, considerable attention and acclaim have accrued to the leaders of the FC movement, but as the data and the harms have mounted, so has the criticism. Recent months have seen a marked shift in media coverage from the glowing reports of miracles that made almost no mention of objective evidence (e.g., *PrimeTime Live*) to stories about families for whom FC has been anything but a miracle. A documentary on the PBS investigative news program, *Frontline,* honed in on the implausibility and lack of empirical support for Biklen's initial claims, along with the emerging evidence from experimental evaluations

showing overwhelmingly that most FC is *facilitator* communication.

The public position of Syracuse University officials appears to be that Professor Biklen's notions are simply provoking the furor and resistance that all radical new ideas encounter. Perhaps that is the case; time and objective data will tell. Time will most certainly be required for the legal system to do its part in determining the future of the FC movement. A number of cases involving "facilitated" sexual abuse allegations are in process at this writing. To my knowledge, there has been one conviction so far. Several individuals and families who have been cleared of false allegations have filed damage countersuits against the facilitators, school and program administrators, and social service agencies involved. On January 10, 1994 a civil suit was filed in federal District Court for the northern district of New York seeking $10 million in damages on behalf of a family who were among the first victims of FC allegations in the U.S. Among the ten defendants are Douglas Biklen and Syracuse University.

Finally, if FC is not a mental miracle, is it sleight of hand? By this I do

not mean there is intentional deceit on the part of the facilitators. Far from it. Most are genuine, honest, caring individuals who wish the best for their charges. Herein lies an explanation. The power of a belief system to direct thought and action is overwhelming. A full and complete explanation for the FC phenomenon is still forthcoming, but clearly there are parallels with the ideomotor responses that direct dowsing sticks and the Ouija board. As the facilitator gently directs the hand to begin typing, letters are formed into words and words into sentences. Just as with the Ouija board where elaborate thoughts seem to be generated out of thin air while both parties consciously try not to move the piece across the board, the facilitators do not appear to be conscious that it is them generating the communication. Even with the autistic child looking elsewhere, or not looking at all (eyes closed), the hand is still rapidly pecking out letters as if it were a miracle. Unfortunately there are no miracles in mental health. All of us wish FC were true, but the facts simply do not allow scientists and critical thinkers to replace knowledge with wish. ∎

Bibliography

Biklen, D. (1990) Communication unbound: Autism and praxis. *Harvard Educational Review, 60,* 291-315.

Biklen, D. (1992). Autism orthodoxy versus free speech: A reply to Cummins and Prior. *Harvard Educational Review, 62,* 242-256.

Biklen, D. (1993).*Communication unbound: How facilitated communication is challenging traditional views of autism and ability/disability.* New York: Teachers College Press.

Crossley, R. (1992a). Lending a hand: A personal account of the development of Facilitated Communication Training. *American Journal of Speech and Language Pathology,* May, 15 18.

Crossley, R. (1992b). Getting the words out: Case studies in facilitated communication training. *Topics in Language Disorders, 12,* 46-59.

Cummins, R.A., & Prior, M.P. (1992). Autism and assisted communication: A response to Biklen. *Harvard Educational Review, 62,* 228-241.

Dillon, K.M. (1993). Facilitated Communication, autism, and ouija. *Skeptical Inquirer, 17,* 281-287.

Green, G. (forthcoming). The quality of the evidence. In H.C. Shane (Ed.), *The clinical and social phenomenon of Facilitated Communication.* San Diego: Singular Press.

Green, G. (1993). Response to "What is the balance of proof for or against Facilitated Communication? *AAMR News & Notes, 6 (3),* 5.

Green, G., & Shane, H.C. (1993). Facilitated Communication: The claims vs. the evidence. *Harvard Mental Health Letter, 10,* 4-5.

Hudson, A. (in press). *Disability and*

facilitated communication: A critique. In T.H. Ollendick & R.J. Prinz (Eds.), *Advances in Clinical Child Psychology* (Vol. 17), New York: Plenum Press.

Jacobson, J.W., Eberlin, M., Mulick, J.A., Schwartz, A.A., Szempruch, J., & Wheeler, D.L. (in press). Autism and Facilitated Communication: Future directions. In J.L. Matson (Ed.,), *Autism: Etiology, diagnosis, and treatment.* DeKalb, IL: Sycamore Press.

Jacobson, J.W., & Mulick, J.A. (1992). Speak for yourself, or...I can't quite put my finger on it! *Psychology in Mental Retardation and Developmental disabilities, 17,* 3-7.

Mulick, J.A., Jacobson, J.W., & Kobe, R.H. (1993). Anguished silence and helping hands:
Miracles in autism with Facilitated Communication. *Skeptical Inquirer, 17,* 270-280.

PART VI

In this sixth and final section of the book, we will examine a number of somatic therapies—interventions, such as drug or electroshock treatments, that involve direct manipulation of the body. As we will see, many of these treatments have engendered considerable controversy among both clinicians and researchers. This controversy has centered around several issues. First, there are lingering questions regarding the effectiveness of a number of somatic therapies. For example, some researchers, such as Fisher and Greenberg (see Reading 38), maintain that the effectiveness of drug therapies for depression and other psychological disorders has been greatly overestimated. Second, some researchers argue that certain somatic therapies, such as electroconvulsive therapy, have lasting negative side effects. Third and most recently, a number of researchers and social critics contend that some medications designed to treat psychological disorders are being misused to treat ordinary, everyday distress and maladjustment. The use of medications for such purposes raises fascinating, and in some cases troubling, ethical and scientific questions.

The first reading in this section, by David Concar, addresses precisely this third point. Concar reviews the budding controversy regarding the rapidly growing field of "cosmetic psychopharmacology," which uses psychotropic medications, such as Prozac, for personality transformation and amelioration of "normal-range" maladies. This field, which was introduced to much of the general public by psychiatrist Peter Kramer in his book *Listening to Prozac,* has been made possible by the introduction of "smart" drugs, drugs that are highly specific in terms of their pharmacological effects. Prozac and several other medications, for example, are extremely selective in terms of their effects on the brain's serotonin systems. But as Concar notes, the use of Prozac and similar medications to treat mild disturbances in mood has met with far from unanimous approval from psychologists and psychiatrists. For one thing, such a practice may blur the distinction between abnormality and normality, and could lead to a "medicalizing" of mild and transient problems in living. In addition, others question whether our understanding of the underlying neurochemical basis of personality is sufficiently well developed to fore-

see the implications of this practice for longstanding personality change.

A quite different perspective on psychopharmacological treatments is offered in the next article, by Seymour Fisher and Roger P. Greenberg. Fisher and Greenberg, who are long-time skeptics of many somatic therapies for abnormal behavior, question whether Prozac and related mood-altering medications (for example, Paxil and Zoloft) are as effective as most researchers have claimed. Specifically, Fisher and Greenberg contend that researchers who have investigated the effectiveness of these drugs have greatly underestimated the power of the placebo effect. Most placebos, they note, produce no noticeable side effects. As a consequence, participants in controlled drug trials often can tell whether they are on the placebo or on the active drug and are therefore not "blind" to their experimental condition. According to Fisher and Greenberg, studies using active placebos (such as atropine), which simulate the side effects of active drugs, tend to yield much lower success rates for these drugs than traditional placebo studies. In addition, they review evidence consistent with the hypothesis that researcher motivation can bias the results of drug outcome studies. Fisher and Greenberg contend that the distinction between biological and psychological treatments is artificial, and that individuals' responses to medication are influenced by a host of psychological and social factors, including expectation effects and the sense of control over one's environment.

Rosie Mestel and David Concar next summarize recent developments in the biological treatment of drug addiction. As they note, approximately 80 percent of addicts have been reported to relapse within the first year of treatment, making the search for effective interventions for addictions an extremely high research priority. Concar and Mestel begin by focusing on methadone, which has been widely used as a treatment for heroin addiction. Despite methadone's documented effectiveness, its use remains a topic of heated debate. For example, critics charge that using methadone to treat heroin addiction is tantamount to using one drug of abuse to treat another, and that methadone is far more hazardous than heroin. Concar and Mestel go on to review other promising interventions for addiction, including naltrexone (see Reading 34), slow-acting drugs that mimic the effects of cocaine, and nicotine replacement therapies. In addition, they discuss the results of studies using a potentially effective psychological treatment—voucher therapy—and comment on its practical limitations.

In the book's final selection, Renee Twombly provides a helpful overview of perhaps the most controversial of all currently used somatic therapies—electroconvulsive therapy (ECT). This treatment, which in the United States is generally used as a last resort intervention for severe depression, involves triggering a seizure by administering electric current to one (unilateral ECT) or both (bilateral ECT) sides of the patient's head. Twombly notes that although the use of ECT declined in the 1960s and 1970s due to bad publicity and potentially dangerous side effects, it now appears to be making a major comeback. ECT as practiced today, which involves careful physiological monitoring and the administration of anesthesia and muscle relaxants, is considerably safer than it was 20 or 30 years ago. Nevertheless, the use of ECT remains a topic of active and often acrimonious debate. Critics contend that ECT produces long-term, if not permanent, memory loss, and that ECT "works" only because it produces brain damage that allows patients to forget about their current life circumstances. Twombly concludes by discussing some of the socioeconomic, racial, and cultural factors that are associated with the use of ECT.

DISCUSSION QUESTIONS

READING 37. D. Concar, "Design Your Own Personality"

1. Do you agree that individuals should be able to use Prozac and other medications to alleviate mild and ordinary maladies? Why or why not? Are there cases in which such a practice could be harmful or countertherapeutic? If so, what are they?

2. Is the distinction between normal personality and personality disorders one of kind or of degree? What research findings might help to shed light on this question?

3. Some might argue that just as individuals can seek counseling for a mild or transient disturbance in mood, individuals should be able to take a pill to alleviate such a disturbance. Do you agree, and why? Are there fundamental differences between "cosmetic psychotherapy" and "cosmetic psychopharmacology"?

READING 38. S. Fisher & R. P. Greenberg, "Prescriptions for Happiness?"

1. Fisher and Greenberg argue that the absence of active placebos biases the outcome of psychopharmacological studies of depression. But how might their arguments apply to psychotherapeutic studies of depression? Is it possible to have an "active placebo" in psychotherapy research? Explain.

2. As Fisher and Greenberg note, placebos can often have powerful physiological effects. How might researchers attempt to ascertain placebos' underlying biological mechanism of action?

3. Fisher and Greenberg contend that certain unpleasant mood states, such as depression, often have adaptive functions. What might some of these functions be? At what point does depression become maladaptive?

READING 39. R. Mestel & D. Concar, "How to Heal the Body's Craving"

1. Do you agree with Dr. Alan Leshner, who asserts that "addiction is not a failure of will or morality, but a chronic brain disease" (p. 224)? Why or why not?

2. What are some of the ethical concerns involved with the use of methadone and similar treatments, which involve replacing one addictive drug with another, somewhat less addictive drug? In what cases, if any, is this practice ethical and in what cases is it unethical?

3. Mestel and Concar discuss some of the practical obstacles involved in implementing voucher therapies. Can you think of other potential limitations to the use of this procedure?

4. Mestel and Concar note that in the U.S., as compared with Europe, drug addiction has generally been viewed as an intolerable evil. What factors might account for this cross-cultural difference in attitudes toward drug addiction?

READING 40. R. Twombly, "Shock Therapy Returns"

1. Before reading this article, what preconceptions did you have regarding the use of ECT, and from what sources (for example, films, magazine articles) did you derive these preconceptions? Have any of your beliefs regarding ECT changed after reading this article, and why?

2. As Twombly points out, some critics, such as Lee Coleman, have charged that ECT "works" only by producing brain damage. Such damage, Coleman contends, leads patients to forget about their current life circumstances. How could Coleman's claim be tested?

3. Twombly notes that in England, as opposed to the United States, ECT is often used as a treatment of first choice, rather than a treatment of last resort. Do you agree with this practice? Should ECT only be used after all other treatments (such as antidepressant medication and psychotherapy) have failed? Explain your reasoning.

SUGGESTIONS FOR FURTHER READING

Breggin, P. R. (1991). *Toxic psychiatry.* New York: St. Martin's Press.

Fisher, S., & Greenberg, R. P. (Eds.). (1989). *The limits of biological treatments for psychological distress: Comparisons with therapy and placebo.* Hillsdale, NJ: Lawrence Erlbaum.

Kramer, P. (1993). *Listening to Prozac.* New York: Viking.

Sackheim, H. A. (1989). The efficacy of electroconvulsive therapy in the treatment of major depressive disorder. In S. Fisher & R. P. Greenberg (Eds.), *The limits of biological treatments for psychological distress: Comparisons with therapy and placebo* (pp. 275–307). Hillsdale, NJ: Lawrence Erlbaum.

Weiner, R. D. (1984). Does electroconvulsive therapy cause brain damage? *Behavioral and Brain Sciences, 7,* 1–22.

Wender, P. H., & Klein, D. F. (1984). *Mind, mood, and medicine: A guide to the new biopsychiatry.* New York: Meridian.

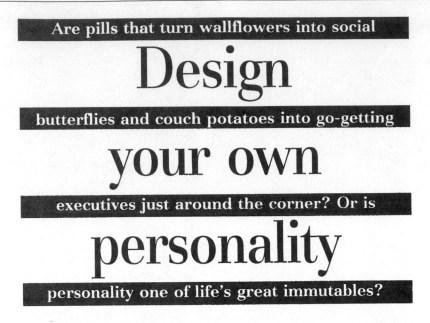

Are pills that turn wallflowers into social

Design

butterflies and couch potatoes into go-getting

your own

executives just around the corner? Or is

personality

personality one of life's great immutables?

David Concar

IT'S winter 2030. Work is going badly, your love life is in tatters. Feeling irritable and melancholic, you reach for your computer and call up Normopsych, an on-line drugs service specialising in personality restructuring. After downloading your life history and personality profile data and completing virtual reality tests of rejection sensitivity and mood, you sit back in your chair. A few seconds later the screen fills with a rotating, three-dimensional image of the brain. A handful of neurotransmitter pathways are flashing ominously. The diagnosis reads: "Serotonin levels 15 per cent below par in limbic system. Boost with 100 milligrams per day of MoodStim and AntiGrief."

Before you dismiss this scenario as a cheap and pointless parody of something from *Brave New World*, consider the following views on the future of neuroscience. From Richard Restak, a neuropsychiatrist attached to various universities in Washington DC: "Researchers are on the verge of chemical attempts to modify character . . . Most of the new drugs will be aimed not so much at patients as at people who are already functioning on a high level . . . altering for the good their internal moods." From Malcolm Lader, a psychiatrist at the Institute of Psychiatry in London: "I don't see any fundamental technical obstacle to altering personality with drugs. After all, the traits that make up personality are rooted in neurochemicals." And from Jerome Kagan of Harvard University, who studies the biological basis of shyness: "Fifty years from now we may have drugs that can alter personality profiles. Things are moving very fast".

Hardly a week goes by without a magazine or newspaper telling us, with the mandatory mixture of horror and fascination, about the pharmacopia of the 21st century, replete with pills which can turn wallflowers into social butterflies and couch potatoes into go-getting executives. Indeed, for a minority of psychiatrists, the era of the personality pill has already arrived. The controversial antidepressant Prozac, which has had the media in a tailspin for the past two years, offers a powerful taste of things to come, argues American psychiatrist Peter Kramer in his book *Listening to Prozac*. The drug can not only restore depressed people to their premorbid states, he writes, but it can also transform personalities. It can make people "feel better than well".

For a minority of psychiatrists, the era of the personality pill has already arrived.

The glamorous mnemonic Kramer coined for this effect of Prozac—cosmetic psychopharmacology—has turned him into the high priest of personality as malleable neurochemistry. And his compelling, if contentious and speculative, account of how Prozac seemingly transformed the lives of a half dozen or so healthy people suffering from mild personality disorders—obsession with housework, shyness, and so on—has long since reached the dinner tables of the chattering classes.

But amid all the chatter and acres of newsprint, few people seem to have noticed that Prozac is only the tip of a pharmacological iceberg. Other high-tech psychoactive drugs, distinguished like Prozac by the precision of their biochemical action, are beginning to reach the marketplace. And the pharmaceuticals companies plan many more. If you talk to psychiatrists about the prospects for cosmetic psychopharmacology, you quickly realise that the controversy about the efficacy and social desirability of Prozac is only the trailer for a much bigger debate.

> **Prozac is only the tip of the pharmacological iceberg.**

At issue will be questions that strike at the heart of modern psychiatry. Can drugs developed as therapies for serious mental illnesses, such as depression, obsessive-compulsive disorder and anxiety attacks, also benefit people with minor personality disorders—people who have never suffered from depression, say, but have a gloomy outlook, people who have never suffered from anxiety attacks but who are uptight and anxiety prone? If so, where do you draw the line between therapy and enhancement, between medicine and personality engineering?

Smart bombs for simple minds?

There is a simple reason why these questions must now be asked: the ability of neuroscience to produce biochemically specific drugs which affect the brain has outstripped our understanding of how the brain works. Neuroscientists have spent the past two decades identifying new neurotransmitters and the receptors that respond to them. As their knowledge has accumulated, they have steadily refined their techniques for selecting compounds that can influence the workings of specific neurotransmitter pathways.

Now they are enjoying the payoff: the birth of a new generation of psychoactive drugs which are being hailed as the pharmacological equivalents of "smart" bombs. While older psychoactive drugs, LSD, amphetamines and tricyclic antidepressants (such as imipramine) tend to lash out indiscriminately at different neurotransmitter pathways, these new drugs seem to strike their neurochemical targets much more cleanly, producing fewer serious side effects.

Prozac is the example par excellence. The billion-dollar-a-year celebrity drug took 15 years to develop. And evidence so far suggests that Prozac interferes only with those neural circuits whose functioning depends on the neurotransmitter serotonin, blocking molecules on the surfaces of neurons which normally act to absorb serotonin (see figure 1). As a result, Prozac's action is mainly confined to boosting the amount of serotonin circulating in the brain. Or so everyone assumes. Older antidepressants such as the tricyclics act in a similar way, boosting levels of the neurotransmitter norepinephrine. But they also interfere with the dopamine neurotransmitter system, and this partly explains why people get hooked on them. Prozac has plenty of listed side-effects—nausea and loss of libido for instance— but nothing to compare with the sedative and addictive effects of the older antidepressants.

Already chemists' shelves are filling up fast with Prozac wannabes, compounds with brand names like Zoloft and Paxil which, like Prozac, act selectively on serotonin. And this is only the beginning. Information processing in the brain depends on upwards of two dozen neurotransmitters interacting with scores if not hundreds of molecular receptors, many of which could end up as targets for Prozac-style drugs. Hardly a month passes without neuroscientists reporting a new type or subtype of brain receptor, its gene or chemical structure.

But having a firm grasp of the brain's molecular alphabet does not necessarily mean you understand its language—or can rationally go about

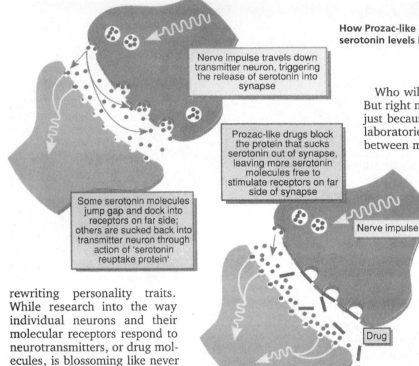

How Prozac-like drugs boost serotonin levels in the brain

Nerve impulse travels down transmitter neuron, triggering the release of serotonin into synapse

Prozac-like drugs block the protein that sucks serotonin out of synapse, leaving more serotonin molecules free to stimulate receptors on far side of synapse

Some serotonin molecules jump gap and dock into receptors on far side; others are sucked back into transmitter neuron through action of 'serotonin reuptake protein'

Nerve impulse

Drug

rewriting personality traits. While research into the way individual neurons and their molecular receptors respond to neurotransmitters, or drug molecules, is blossoming like never before, neuroscience remains almost totally ignorant about how neurotransmitters and networks of neurons act together in the brain to produce complex mental states such as depression or anxiety. This knowledge gap leaves the field wide open for debate about personality-altering drugs.

Quirks of temperament

On one side stand Kramer and other committed believers in the coming of cosmetic psychopharmacology. At the level of neurochemistry, they say, personality traits such as persistent melancholia and introversion are merely quieter expressions of the kinds of brain chemistry that lead to clinical conditions like depression. As such, these mood disorders (or deep-seated quirks of temperament, if you prefer) can be modfied with the same kinds of drugs. The reason Prozac can rewrite someone's whole personality is that mental illness and temperament are both written in the same kind of neurochemical ink.

Or so Kramer and like-minded psychiatrists contend. But to psychiatrists of a more traditional bent this is at best wild-eyed speculation. Mental illnesses and serious disorders, they say, are more likely to stem from tangible biological deficits, such as defective neurotransmitter receptors, which lie well outside the realms of normal neurochemistry. Just because you can compensate for such deficits with drugs, doesn't mean you can reshape personality? Take depression, say traditionalists. According to one theory, it may be caused not so much by a surfeit or deficit of any one neurotransmitter as by the brain being, in effect, trapped in a gloomy neurochemical state. Prozac-like drugs may act like chemical switches helping depressed brains to regain their equilibrium. To a healthy brain, however, such help may be redundant. As Larry Siever, a psychiatrist at Mount Sinai Medical school, puts it: "You can try to heat up a thermostat by putting your hands around it, but if it's a bright sunny day nothing much happens."

Who will be vindicated in this debate it is impossible to say. But right now the traditionalists are on the defensive—and not just because of the the runaway public response to Prozac. In laboratories and clinics everywhere the traditional divisions between mental illness and the extremes of everyday personality, between the science of the abnormal mind and that of the normal mind, are beginning to unravel.

Increasingly, researchers looking for the biological and social roots of traits such as shyness and aggression are focusing on neurochemicals that have long been implicated in mental illness—particularly, serotonin, norepinephrine and dopamine. Increasingly, too, researchers are applying the brain imaging techniques of PET and MRI to studying how the building blocks of normal behaviour might be encoded in the structures of the brain. We all recognise a shy or outgoing person when we meet one. But do these familiar labels tie into particular patterns of neural activity, into particular forms of neurochemistry and structures of neuroanatomy? Are these patterns the same in all shy or outgoing people? Only now are researchers beginning to tackle such questions in earnest.

Over the past few years, researchers have used PET to identify a variety of neural centres that flicker into action as people perform specific mental tasks—reading, looking at different kinds of visual images, listening to Mozart, even playing musical instruments. It is easy to imagine the same kind of approach being applied to moods and personality traits: "Think of something sad while I image your cerebral cortex . . . now think of something that makes you happy . . . anxious . . . threatened."

Here's a foretaste of the possibilities. A team in the US has used PET to trace an abnormal pattern of brain activity in people with obsessive-compulsive disorder, an illness that often leads to fanaticism about cleanliness and housework. The problem may stem from the way certain patterns of brain activity get stuck in a loop. Touch a normal person with a dirty rag for instance, and the brain responds by passing a signal through three main structures—the prefrontal cortex, the basal ganglia and the thalamus. But do the same with an obsessive-compulsive person and the signal cycles through these structures endlessly. The signal itself is part of the normal repertoire of brain responses. What seems to be missing is the ability to turn it off. A drug that could correct that problem might prevent the symptoms. Could it also help people with very mild symptoms of obsessive-compulsive disorder—"normal" people who endlessly line up their pencils?

Many people see dangers in this approach. If mental illness and quirks of temperament are on the same continuum, won't the ups and downs of ordinary life be seen as medical problems? Others question science's ability to make sense of the vagaries and complexities of personality, let alone its ability to leap the huge distances from molecules to behaviour

We all recognise a shy or outgoing person when we meet one. But do these familiar labels tie into particular patterns of neural activity?

and from brain images to neuro-chemistry. But that is not deterring psychobiologists from looking for—and even claiming to find—basic building blocks of temperament and character from which they believe all personalities are constructed.

Personality maps

More important, psychobiologists believe it may eventually be possible to relate these "maps" of personality directly to levels of different neuro-transmitters in different parts of the brain. That wouldn't necessarily open the door to altering rationally the composition of a healthy individual's personality. But it would certainly have an enormous impact on the way we see ourselves and, perhaps, the way doctors diagnose illnesses.

Some of the most influential findings are coming from Jerome Kagan, a child psychologist at Harvard University who is trying to trace the biological roots of the "inhibited" behaviours typically seen in shy people. Everyone accepts that inhibition, like any other behaviour pattern, is the result of a cocktail of social learning—or character—and genetic predisposition—or temperament. Kagan believes it is possible to identify the genetic component by studying the behaviour of infants and then monitoring them as they grow older. Based on close observations of 300 individuals, he believes that about 15 per cent of babies are born predisposed to developing into timid, and fearful infants.

More revealingly, Kagan has found that they tend to have higher-than-average heart rates and produce unusually high levels of the hormone cortisol and norepinephrine—both well known markers for stress and fear. As they grow up, these children are more likely to have intense fears of going to bed alone or of violence. They are also the children most likely to remain shy until the age of at least seven. These children, speculates Kagan, may be born with an unusually low biological threshold for fear. And that trait, in turn, could stem from having an overly sensitive amygdala, a tiny brain structure that when activated signals the heart to race, palms to sweat and norepineprine to swirl around the brain.

This line of research has bolstered some controversial ideas about norepinephrine and personality. Hypersensitivity in general—to some small rejection by a lover, to slights from work colleagues and so on—may be liked to an excess of norepinephrine, say some researchers, while a deficit of norepinephrine may lead to poor concentration and an inability to work out what is important. The logic here is that our fight-or-flight response to danger evolved in part as a mechanism for focusing the mind of threatening things in our environment. The lions and tigers are, for most of us, long gone.

The lions and tigers are, for most of us, long gone. What remains is the threat of unmet deadlines, social rejection and anxiety about missing the last train home.

What remains is the threat of unmet deadlines, social rejection and anxiety about missing the last train home. Does this mean that drugs which rein in norepinephrine could be used to treat inhibition in otherwise normal people?

It's far too early to know, says Kagan. Shyness in general may turn out to have nothing to do with norepinephrine. Everyone investigating the biological basis of personality has been obsessed with amines (dopamine, norepinephrine and serotonin), but inhibition could just as easily be governed by a hormone, says Kagan. "We know the amygdala is loaded with receptors for corticotrophin releasing hormone. The inference about amines is just a guess." So too is the assumption that inhibition is caused by any one brain state. "We can't yet point to particular neural circuits and say they're involved in inhibition," says Kagan.

What is clear is that character can overwhelm temperament. In Kagan's study, up to 90 per cent of shy-born infants eventually lost their inhibitions as a result of experience, underlining the fact that the personalities of adults are a complex tangle of genetics and life experience. Can they be teased apart? Robert Cloninger, a psychiatrist and geneticist at Washington University in St Louis, believes they can, and with this aim in mind he has recently developed a complicated questionnaire-based system. Right now he is reaping the first fruits of his labour.

In December last year, Cloninger and his colleagues reported striking results from studies of different groups of people, some healthy, some suffering from illnesses such as depression. Based on these, Cloninger is convinced temperament consists of four basic, heritable components: reward dependence, harm avoidance, novelty seeking and persistence. And layered on top of these, he argues, are three, learned components of character: self-direction, cooperation and self-transcendence.

The details are complex, but each component can be thought of as a sliding scale. Someone who sits high on the reward dependence scale, for example, "is highly dependent on emotional supports and intimacy with others, highly sensitive to social cues . . . extremely sensitive to rejection from even minor slights," writes Cloninger. At the opposite end of the scale are socially detached people who never share intimate feelings with others and are unmotivated by an ambition to please. Other psychiatrists have come up with broadly similar theories. In some, reward dependence approximates to rejection sensitivity and novelty-seeking to impulsiveness. Science, says Cloninger, is gradually producing a "gold standard" measure of personality.

Ambitious words, but what will it tell us about the

Tangled roots of personality

Serotonin pathway—depression, aggression, reward dependence, impulsiveness?

Norepinephrine pathway—depression, shyness, fight-or-flight response?

Dopamine pathway—schizophrenia, suspicion, novelty seeking, introversion?

Speculation is rife about the links between neuro-transmitters and personality

neurochemistry of personality and its susceptibility to modification by drugs? Can clear links be forged between the model and neurochemistry? Cloninger believes so and is try to make his model clinically predictive.

In one study, Cloninger and his colleagues asked if they could use the four-dimension model of temperament to spot patients with depression who would respond most effectively to a Prozac-like antidepressant, rather than to imipramine. "In the case of the women," says Cloninger, "we found exactly what Kramer speculates in his book—individuals who are very high in harm avoidance and reward dependence tend to respond best to antidepressants like Prozac".

If Cloninger and his colleagues are right, in the clinics of the 21st century, traditional concepts like depression and anxiety may end up being usurped by terms such as reward dependence and novelty seeking as doctors seek diagnostic measures that more accurately reflect brain chemistry. Up until now there has been little pressure for this to happen as the available drugs have been relatively crude. Smart bomb pharmacology, whatever else it may achieve, will surely change that.

Mood brighteners

It may also hasten the breakdown of traditional divisions between acute mental illnesses that run in cycles, like depression and schizophrenia, and milder personality disorders such as impulsiveness and introversion. "People have been asking questions about the origins of temperament since the time of Socrates," says Siever. "Now we have the tools to work out the vocabulary of temperamental states that underpin personality disorders." More and more doctors are acknowledging that there is a spectrum of behavioural symptoms, and possibly a corresponding spectrum of neurochemistry, he says.

Since the early 1980s Siever has been studying people who have what he describes as a schizotypal personality: introverted people who are extremely aloof and eccentric. They don't think the CIA is watching their every movement but show milder signs of paranoia. The underlying psychological problem, says Siever, seems to be an inability to respond to social cues and rhythms, a trait that leaves the patients feeling disconnected from their environment and suspicious. At the level of brain chemistry, he argues, these people may be victims of milder expressions of the kinds of imbalances in dopamine implicated in schizophrenia.

Biochemical tests and brain imaging studies, for example, show that some of the patients have too much dopamine circulating around their frontal cortex, while others have too little dopamine in the limbic system. Most important of all, the patients seem to improve on drugs which act on dopamine receptors and are usually prescibed for schizophrenia.

Another fashionable theory says that a shortage of serotonin in the frontal lobes and in the limbic system may encourage impulsive behaviours like aggression. Evidence from animal research and biochemical studies in humans suggest serotonin may be part of the mechanism by which the brain connects behaviours like shoplifting or thumping a policeman with the inevitable consequences, argues Siever. But turning fascinating conjecture of this kind into evidence of concrete causative links between neurotransmitter systems and specific kinds of behaviour is no easy task.

Sceptics will point out that there is hardly a personality trait or mental illness left which hasn't at some time been linked to dopamine or serotonin. Even seemingly clear-cut studies with drugs can be misleading. For example, a compound that acts on dopamine receptors may make someone less suspicious, but that doesn't make it safe to assume dopamine causes suspicion; the drug may simply act to paper over the real neurochemical cracks. "Think of aspirin," says Steven Rose, an expert on memory at the Open University. "It solves the problem of toothache but it would be silly to argue that tooth ache is cause by a lack of aspirin."

As for Prozac: far from nailing down the biological causes of depression, it has thrown everything into confusion. Until this pharmacological superstar arrived, animal research and cellular studies suggested that clinical depression might be caused by a deficit of receptors for norepinephrine. Now researchers are being forced to add serotonin to the equation as they accept that personality traits are sure to governed by the combined actions of several neurotransmitter systems. Cloninger is already working with theoretical physicists to help sort out the possible interactions that underlie the building blocks of personality he is studying.

Will accepting complexity in the ways in which temperament is related to patterns of neurotransmitter activity do anything to affect the public debate about cosmetic psychopharmacology? Probably not. It will certainly not hinder the flow of new psychoactive drugs into clinics, for pharmacologists have all the necessary tools to develop candidate compounds. Nor will it stop some people from taking drugs as personality uppers or mood brighteners. Consumers are likely simply to ask whether a drug helps them and whether it has side effects. And sometimes not even that. Already hard-pressed executives in the US have begun seeking extra-helpings of concentration from Ritalin, a potentially addictive stimulant that boosts norepinephrine levels and is normally prescribed for children diagnosed with attention-deficit disorder. Can anyone say how many of the 10 million people who have been prescribed Prozac suffer from clinical depression rather than ennui? Or perhaps ennui is simply on its way to becoming a recognised disorder. If history is any guide, the next two decades will see a gradual expansion of psychiatric categories into the realms of normality as psychiatrists and pharmaceuticals companies indulge their habit of defining as abnormal anything that responds to drug treatments. Once you start prescribing drugs for people who are impulsive but don't have a severe gambling problem or who are eccentric and aloof but not psychotic aren't you on the slippery slope towards the "improvement" of personality rather than the treatment of disorder?

Not necessarily, argues Siever. The problem, he insists, is in principle no different from the situation with rising blood pressure or the hardening of coronary arteries. Both take place progressively, yet doctors have no difficulty agreeing on where to start treatments. But what if people looking for a quick, if temporary and biologically costly, mood change disagree? Couldn't they accuse doctors of pharmacological Calvinism, of denying people their inalienable right to a happier life? Apparently not: "There are plenty of substances out there which such people can take," says Siever. "Nicotine and alcohol for a start."   □

Perhaps ennui is simply on its way to becoming a recognised disorder.

Prescriptions for Happiness?

by Seymour Fisher, Ph.D., and Roger P. Greenberg, Ph.D.

The air is filled with declarations and advertisements of the power of biological psychiatry to relieve people of their psychological distress. Some biological psychiatrists are so convinced of the superiority of their position that they are recommending young psychiatrists no longer be taught the essentials of doing psychotherapy. Feature stories in such magazines as *Newsweek* and *Time* have portrayed drugs like Prozac as possessing almost a mystical potency. The best-selling book *Listening to Prozac* by psychiatrist Peter Kramer, M.D., projects the idyllic possibility that psychotropic drugs may eventually be capable of correcting a spectrum of personality quirks and lacks.

As longtime faculty members of a number of psychiatry departments, we have personally witnessed the gradual but steadily accelerated dedication to the idea that "mental illness" can be mastered with biologically based substances. Yet a careful sifting of the pertinent literature indicates that modesty and skepticism would be more appropriate responses to the research accumulated thus far. In 1989, we first raised radical questions about such biological claims in a book, *The Limits of Biological Treatments for Psychological Distress: Comparisons with Psychotherapy and Placebo* (Lawrence Erlbaum). Our approach has been to filter the studies that presumably anchor them through a series of logical and quantitative (meta-analytic) appraisals.

HOW EFFECTIVE ARE ANTIDEPRESSANT DRUGS?

Antidepressants, one of the major weapons in the biological therapeutic arsenal, illustrate well the largely unacknowledged uncertainty that exists in the biological approach to psychopathology. We suggest that, at present, no one actually knows how effective antidepressants are. Confident declarations about their potency go well beyond the existing evidence.

To get an understanding of the scientific status of antidepressants, we analyzed how much more effective the antidepressants are than inert pills called "placebos." That is, if antidepressants are given to one depressed group and a placebo to another group, how much greater is the recovery of those taking the active drug as compared to those taking the inactive placebo? Generous claims that antidepressants usually produce improvement in about 60 to 70 percent of patients are not infrequent, whereas placebos are said to benefit 25 to 30 percent. If antidepressants were, indeed, so superior to placebos, this would be a persuasive advertisement for the biological approach.

We found 15 major reviews of the antidepressant literature. Surprisingly, even the most positive reviews indicate that 30 to 40 percent of studies show no significant difference in response to drug versus placebo! The reviews indicate overall that one-third of patients do not improve with antidepressant treatment, one-third improve with placebos, and an additional third show a response to medication they would not have attained with placebos. In the most optimistic view of such findings, two-thirds of the cases (placebo responders and those who do not respond to anything) do as well with placebo as with active medication.

We also found two large-scale quantitative evaluations (meta-analyses) integrating the outcomes of multiple studies of antidepressants. They clearly indicated, on the average, quite modest therapeutic power.

We were particularly impressed by the large variation in outcomes of studies conducted at multiple clinical sites or centers. Consider a study that compared the effectiveness of an antidepressant among patients at five different research centers. Although the pooled results demonstrate that the drug was generally more effective than placebo, the results from individual centers reveal much variation. After six weeks of treatment, every one of the six measures of effectiveness showed the antidepressant (imipramine) to be merely equivalent to placebo in two or more of the centers. In two of the settings, a difference favoring the medication was detected on only one of 12 outcome comparisons.

In other words, the pooled, apparently favorable, outcome data conceal that dramatically different results could be obtained as a function of who conducted the study and the specific conditions at each locale. We can only conclude that a good deal of fragility characterized the apparent superiority of drug over placebo. The scientific literature is replete with analogous examples.

Incidentally, we also looked at whether modern studies, which are presumably better protected against bias, use higher doses, and often involve longer treatment periods, show a greater superiority of the antidepressant than did earlier studies. The literature frequently asserts that failures to demonstrate antidepressant superiority are due to such methodological failures as not using high enough doses, and so forth.

We examined this issue in a pool of 16 studies assembled by psychiatrists John Kane and Jeffrey Lieberman in 1984. These studies all compare a standard drug, such as imipramine or amitriptyline, to a newer drug and a placebo. They use clearer diagnostic definitions of depression than did the older studies and also adopt currently accepted standards for dosage levels and treatment duration. When we examined the data, we discovered that the advantage of drug over placebo was modest. Twenty-one percent more of the patients receiving a drug improved as compared to those on placebo. Actually, most of the studies

From *Psychology Today, 28*, pp. 32–37, September/October 1995. Reprinted by permission of R. Greenberg.

showed no difference in the percentage of patients significantly improved by drugs. There was no indication that these studies, using more careful methodology, achieved better outcomes than older studies.

Finally, it is crucial to recognize that several studies have established that there is a high rate of relapse among those who have responded positively to an antidepressant but then are taken off treatment. The relapse rate may be 60 percent or more during the first year after treatment cessation. Many studies also show that any benefits of antidepressants wane in a few months, even while the drugs are still being taken. This highlights the complexity of evaluating antidepressants. They may be effective initially, but lose all value over a longer period.

ARE DRUG TRIALS BIASED?

As we burrowed deeper into the antidepressant literature, we learned that there are also crucial problems in the methodology used to evaluate psychotropic drugs. Most central is the question of whether this methodology properly shields drug trials from bias. Studies have shown that the more open to bias a drug trial is, the greater the apparent superiority of the drug over placebo. So questions about the trustworthiness of a given drug-testing procedure invite skepticism about the results.

The question of potential bias first came to our attention in studies comparing inactive placebos to active drugs. In the classic double-blind design, neither patient nor researcher knows who is receiving drug or placebo. We were struck by the fact that the presumed protection provided by the double-blind design was undermined by the use of placebos that simply do not arouse as many body sensations as do active drugs. Research shows that patients learn to discriminate between drug and placebo largely from body sensations and symptoms.

A substance like imipramine, one of the most frequently studied antidepressants, usually causes clearly defined sensations, such as dry mouth, tremor, sweating, constipation. Inactive placebos used in studies of antidepressants also apparently initiate some body sensations, but they are fewer, more inconsistent, and less intense as indicated by the fact that they are less often cited by patients as a source of discomfort causing them to drop out of treatment.

Vivid differences between the body sensations of drug and placebo groups could

Vivid differences between the body sensations of drug and placebo could signal to patients whether they are receiving an active or inactive agent.

signal to patients as to whether they are receiving an active or inactive agent. Further, they could supply discriminating cues to those responsible for the patients's day-to-day treatment. Nurses, for example, might adopt different attitudes toward patients they identify as being "on" versus "off" active treatment—and consequently communicate contrasting expectations.

THE BODY OF EVIDENCE

This is more than theoretical. Researchers have reported that in a double-blind study of imipramine, it was possible by means of side effects to identify a significant number of the patients taking the active drug. Those patients receiving a placebo have fewer signals (from self and others) indicating they are being actively treated and should be improving. By the same token, patients taking an active drug receive multiple signals that may well amplify potential placebo effects linked to the therapeutic context. Indeed, a doctor's strong belief in the power of the active drug enhances the apparent therapeutic power of the drug or placebo.

Is it possible that a large proportion of the difference in effectiveness often reported between antidepressants and placebos can be explained as a function of body sensation discrepancies? It is conceivable, and fortunately there are research findings that shed light on the matter.

Consider an analysis by New Zealand psychologist Richard Thomson. He reviewed double-blind, placebo-controlled studies of antidepressants completed between 1958 and 1972. Sixty-eight had employed an inert placebo and seven an active one (atropine) that produced a variety of body sensations. The antidepressant had a superior therapeutic effect in 59 percent of the studies using inert placebo—but in only one study (14 percent) using the active placebo. The active placebo eliminated any therapeutic advantage for the antidepressants, apparently because it convinced patients they were getting real medication.

HOW BLIND IS DOUBLE-BLIND?

Our concerns about the effects of inactive placebos on the double-blind design led us to ask just how blind the double-blind really is. By the 1950s reports were already surfacing that for psychoactive drugs, the double-blind design is not as scientifically objective as originally assumed. In 1993 we searched the world literature and found 31 reports in which patients and researchers involved in studies were asked to guess who was receiving the active psychotropic drug and who the placebo. In 28 instances the guesses were significantly better than chance—and at times they were surprisingly accurate. In one double-blind study that called for administering either imipramine, phenelzine, or placebo to depressed patients, 78 percent of patients and 87 percent of psychiatrists correctly distinguished drug from placebo.

One particularly systematic report in the literature involved the administration of alprazolam, imipramine, and placebo over an eight-week period to groups of patients who experienced panic attacks. Halfway through the treatment and also at the end, the physicians and the patients were asked to judge independently whether each patient was receiving an active drug or a placebo. If they thought an active drug was being administered, they had to decide whether it was alprazolam or imipramine. Both physicians (with an 88 percent success rate) and patients (83 percent) substantially exceeded chance in the correctness of their judgments. Furthermore, the physicians could distinguish alprazolam from imipramine significantly better than chance. The researchers concluded that "double-blind studies of these pharmacological treatments for panic disorder are not really 'blind.'"

Yet the vast majority of psychiatric drug efficacy studies have simply *assumed* that the double-blind design is effective; they did not test the blindness by determining whether patients and researchers were able to differentiate drug from placebo.

We take the somewhat radical view that this means most past studies of the efficacy of psychotropic drugs are, to unknown degrees, scientifically untrustworthy. At the least, we can no longer speak with confidence about the true differences in therapeutic power between active psychotropic drugs and placebos. We must suspend judgment until future studies are completed with more adequate controls for the defects of the double-blind paradigm.

Other bothersome questions arose as we scanned the cascade of studies focused on antidepressants. Of particular concern is how unrepresentative the patients are who end up in the clinical trials. There are the usual sampling problems having to do with which persons seek treatment for their discomfort, and, in addition, volunteer as subjects for a study. But there are others. Most prominent is the relatively high proportion of patients who "drop out" before the completion of their treatment programs.

Numerous dropouts occur in response to unpleasant side effects. In many published studies, 35 percent or more of patients fail to complete the research protocol. Various procedures have been developed to deal fairly with the question of how to classify the therapeutic outcomes of dropouts, but none can vitiate the simple fact that the final sample of fully treated patients has often been drastically reduced.

There are still other filters that increase sample selectivity. For example, studies often lose sizable segments of their samples by not including patients who are too depressed to speak, much less participate in a research protocol, or who are too disorganized to participate in formal psychological testing. We also found decisions not to permit particular racial or age groups to be represented in samples or to avoid using persons below a certain educational level. Additionally, researchers typically recruit patients whose depression is not accompanied by any other type of physical or mental disorder, a situation that does not hold for the depressed in the general population.

So we end up wondering about the final survivors in the average drug trial. To what degree do they typify the average individual in real life who seeks treatment? How much can be generalized from a sample made up of the "leftovers" from multiple depleting processes? Are we left with a relatively narrow band of those most willing to conform to the rather rigid demands of the research establishment? Are the survivors those most accepting of a dependent role?

The truth is that there are probably multiple kinds of survivors, depending upon the specific local conditions prevailing where the study was carried out. We would guess that some of the striking differences in results that appear in multicenter drug studies could be traced to specific forms of sampling bias. We do not know how psychologically unique the persons are who get recruited into, and stick with, drug research enterprises. We are not the first to raise this question, but we are relatively more alarmed about the potential implications.

RESEARCHER MOTIVATION AND OUTCOME

We recently conducted an analysis that further demonstrates how drug effectiveness diminishes as the opportunity for bias in research design wanes. This analysis seized on studies in which a newer antidepressant is compared (under double-blind conditions) with an older, standard antidepressant and a placebo. In such a context the efficacy of the newer drug (which the drug company hopes to introduce) is of central interest to the researcher, and the effectiveness of the older drug of peripheral import. Therefore, if the double-blind is breached (as is likely), there would presumably be less bias to enhance the efficacy of the older drug than occurred in the original trials of that drug.

We predicted that the old drug would appear significantly less powerful in the newer studies than it had in earlier designs, where it was of central interest of the researcher. To test this hypothesis, we located 22 double-blind studies in which newer antidepressants were compared with an older antidepressant drug (usually imipramine) and a placebo. Our meta-analysis revealed, as predicted,

A patient's attitude toward the therapist is just as biological in nature as a patient's response to an antidepressant drug.

Administering a therapeutic drug is not simply a medical, biological act. It is also a complex social act, its effectiveness mediated by the patient's expectations.

that the efficacy rates, based on clinicians's judgments of outcome, were quite modest for the older antidepressants. In fact, they were approximately one-half to one-quarter the average size of the effects reported in earlier studies when the older drug was the only agent appraised.

Let us be very clear as to what this signifies: When researchers were evaluating the antidepressant in a context where they were no longer interested in proving its therapeutic power, there was a dramatic decrease in that apparent power, as compared to an earlier context when they were enthusiastically interested in demonstrating the drug's potency. A change in researcher motivation was enough to change outcome. Obviously this means too that the present double-blind design for testing drug efficacy is exquisitely vulnerable to bias.

Another matter of pertinence to the presumed biological rationale for the efficacy of antidepressants is that no consistent links have been demonstrated between the concentration of drug in blood and its efficacy. Studies have found significant correlations for some drugs, but of low magnitude. Efforts to link plasma levels to therapeutic outcome have been disappointing.

Similarly, few data show a relationship between antidepressant dosage levels and their therapeutic efficacy. That is, large doses of the drug do not necessarily have greater effects than low doses. These inconsistencies are a bit jarring against the context of a biological explanatory framework.

We have led you through a detailed critique of the difficulties and problems that prevail in the body of research testing the power of the antidepressants. We conclude that it would be wise to be relatively modest in claims about their efficacy. Uncertainty and doubt are inescapable.

While we have chosen the research on the antidepressants to illustrate the uncertainties attached to biological treatments of psychological distress, reviews of other classes of psychotropic drugs yield similar findings. After a survey of anti-anxiety drugs, psychologist Ronald Lipman concluded there is little consistent evidence that they help patients with anxiety disorders: "Although it seems natural to assume that

the anxiolytic medications would be the most effective psychotropic medications for the treatment of anxiety disorders, the evidence does not support this assumption."

BIOLOGICAL VERSUS PSYCHOLOGICAL?

The faith in the biological approach has been fueled by a great burst of research. Thousands of papers have appeared probing the efficacy of psychotropic drugs. A good deal of basic research has attacked fundamental issues related to the nature of brain functioning in those who display psychopathology. Researchers in these areas are dedicated and often do excellent work. However, in their zeal, in their commitment to the so-called biological, they are at times overcome by their expectations. Their hopes become rigidifying boundaries. Their vocabulary too easily becomes a jargon that camouflages over-simplified assumptions.

A good example of such oversimplification is the way in which the term "biological" is conceptualized. It is too often viewed as a realm distinctly different from the psychological. Those invested in the biological approach all too often practice the ancient Cartesian distinction between somatic-stuff and soul-stuff. In so doing they depreciate the scientific significance of the phenomena they ascribe to the soul-stuff category.

But paradoxically, they put a lot of interesting phenomena out of bounds to their prime methodology and restrict themselves to a narrowed domain. For example, if talk therapy is labeled as a "psychological" thing—not biological—this implies that biological research can only hover at the periphery of what psychotherapists do. A sizable block of behavior becomes off limits to the biologically dedicated.

In fact, if we adopt the view that the biological and psychological are equivalent (biological monism), there is no convincing real-versus-unreal differentiation between the so-called psychological and biological. It *all* occurs in tissue and one is not more "real" than the other. A patient's attitude toward the therapist is just as biological in nature as a patient's response to an antidepressant. A response to a placebo is just as biological as a response to an antipsychotic drug. This may be an obvious

point, but it has not yet been incorporated into the world views of either the biologically or psychologically oriented.

Take a look at a few examples in the research literature that highlight the overlap or identity of what is so often split apart. In 1992, psychiatrist Lewis Baxter and colleagues showed that successful psychotherapy of obsessive-compulsive patients results in brain imagery changes equivalent to those produced by successful drug treatment. The brain apparently responds in equivalent ways to both the talk and drug approaches. Even more dramatic is a finding that instilling in the elderly the illusion of being in control of one's surroundings (by putting them in charge of some plants) significantly increased their life span compared to a control group. What could be a clearer demonstration of the biological nature of what is labeled as a psychological expectation than the postponement of death?

Why are we focusing on this historic Cartesian confusion? Because so many who pursue the so-called biological approach are by virtue of their tunnel vision motivated to overlook the psychosocial variables that mediate the administration of such agents as psychotropic drugs and electroconvulsive therapy. They do not permit themselves to seriously grasp that psychosocial variables are just as biological as a capsule containing an antidepressant. It is the failure to understand this that results in treating placebo effects as if they were extraneous or less of a biological reality than a chemical agent.

PLACEBO EFFECTS

Indeed, placebos have been shown to initiate certain effects usually thought to be reserved for active drugs. For example, placebos clearly show dose-level effects. A larger dose of a placebo will have a greater impact than a lower dose. Placebos can also create addictions. Patients will poignantly declare that they cannot stop taking a particular placebo substance (which they assume is an active drug) because to do so causes them too much distress and discomfort.

Placebos can produce toxic effects such as rashes, apparent memory loss, fever, headaches, and more. These "toxic" effects may be painful and even overwhelming in their intensity. The placebo literature is clear: Placebos are powerful body-altering substances, especially considering the wide range of body systems they can influence.

Actually, the power of the placebo complicates all efforts to test the therapeutic efficacy of psychotropic drugs. When placebos alone can produce positive curative effects in the 40 to 50 percent range (occasionally even up to 70–80 percent), the active drug being tested is hard-pressed to demonstrate its superiority. Even if the active drug exceeds the placebo in potency, the question remains whether the advantage is at least partially due to the superior potential of the active drug itself to mobilize placebo effects because it is an active substance that stirs vivid body sensations. Because it is almost always an inactive substance (sugar pill) that arouses fewer genuine body sensations, the placebo is less convincingly perceived as having therapeutic prowess.

Drug researchers have tried, in vain, to rid themselves of placebo effects, but these effects are forever present and frustrate efforts to demonstrate that psychoactive drugs have an independent "pure" biological impact. This state of affairs dramatically testifies that the labels "psychological" and "biological" refer largely to different perspectives on events that all occur in tissue. At present, it is somewhat illusory to separate the so-called biological and psychological effects of drugs used to treat emotional distress.

The literature is surprisingly full of instances of how social and attitudinal factors modify the effects of active drugs. Antipsychotic medications are more effective if the patient likes rather than dislikes the physician administering them. An antipsychotic drug is less effective if patients are led to believe they are only taking an inactive placebo. Perhaps even more impressive, if a stimulant drug is administered with the deceptive instruction that it is a sedative, it can initiate a pattern of physiological response, such as decreased heart rate, that is sedative rather than arousing in nature. Such findings reaffirm how fine the line is between social and somatic domains.

What are the practical implications for distressed individuals and their physicians? Administering a drug is not simply a medical (biological) act. It is, in addition, a complex social act whose effectiveness will be mediated by such factors as the patient's expectations of the drug and reactions to the body sensations created by that drug, and the physician's friendliness and degree of personal confidence in the drug's power. Practitioners who dispense psychotropic medications should become thoroughly acquainted with the psychological variables modifying the therapeutic impact of such drugs and tailor their own behavior accordingly. By the same token, distressed people seeking drug treatment should keep in mind that their probability of benefiting may depend in part on whether they choose a practitioner they truly like and respect. And remember this: You are the ultimate arbiter of a drug's efficacy.

How to go about mastering unhappiness, which ranges from "feeling blue" to despairing depression, puzzles everyone. Such popular quick fixes as alcohol, conversion to a new faith, and other splendid distractions have proven only partially helpful. When antidepressant drugs hit the shelves with their seeming scientific aura, they were easily seized upon. Apparently serious unhappiness (depression) could now be chemically neutralized in the way one banishes a toothache.

But the more we learn about the various states of unhappiness, the more we recognize that they are not simply "symptoms" awaiting removal. Depressed feelings have complex origins and functions. In numerous contexts—for example, chronic conflict with a spouse—depression may indicate a realistic appraisal of a troubling problem and motivate a serious effort to devise a solution.

While it is true that deep despair may interfere with sensible problem-solving, the fact is that, more and more, individuals are being instructed to take antidepressants at the earliest signs of depressive distress and this could interfere with the potentially constructive signaling value of such distress. Emotions are feelings full of information. Unhappiness is an emotion, and despite its negativity, should not be classified single-mindedly as a thing to tune out. This in no way implies that one should submit passively to the discomfort of feeling unhappy. Actually, we all learn to experiment with a variety of strategies for making ourselves feel better, but the ultimate aim is long-term effective action rather than a depersonalized "I feel fine." ∎

> **If a stimulant drug is administered with the deceptive instruction that it is a sedative, it can initiate a physiological response characteristic of a sedative, such as decreased heart rate.**

How to Heal the Body's Craving

No one knows whether drug addicts ever find permanent relief. **Rosie Mestel** and **David Concar** investigate the latest methods for treating addiction

IT SOUNDS almost too good to be true. Imagine you are a heroin addict, your life an endless seesaw of highs and lows, your health in constant danger from overdose, dirty drugs, or HIV picked up from someone else's needle. And then you take a hit of a strange, hallucinogenic powder, derived from the roots of a West African shrub. You come down from your high, and you are cured. You don't want heroin any more.

The drug is known as ibogaine, and people in the Netherlands are taking it to kick their drug addiction. There are glowing testimonies to its success from former drug abusers, but there are no scientific studies to show that it works. And there are some disturbing tales circulating. Two addicts died after taking it, and worrying studies show that rats fed ibogaine suffer a loss of cells in certain parts of the brain.

Ibogaine will soon get its day in the court of science. Small-scale trials to test its effect are now under way in the US. For ethical reasons, only volunteers who have already used the drug have been enrolled. But until the reports roll in, most doctors will remain sceptical.

Ibogaine is just one of the many drugs and therapies that addiction researchers, community workers and addicts themselves are exploring and fine-tuning to alleviate the effects of coming off drugs, and to lessen the hazards of drug taking for addicts who cannot or will not go clean. But this is only the start. Also needed are better ways of tackling another gigantic problem: how to stay weaned from a drug, be it nicotine, heroin, cocaine or alcohol, instead of relapsing weeks, months or even years after kicking the habit.

Therapeutic options already exist of course. For the heroin addict, there's the synthetic opiate methadone or the drug-free therapeutic community; for the chronic smoker, nicotine replacement therapy in the form of nicotine gum and patches. Some alcoholics turn to the drug Antabuse, which makes drinking a nauseating experience by disabling an enzyme essential for breaking down alcohol in the liver. Other options include counselling, a stretch in specialised clinics, or step-by-step "self-help" programmes.

Still, these approaches by no means help everybody. Up to 80 per cent of addicts who seek treatment relapse within a year, and for some addictions—notably cocaine—there are few avenues of help available. One of the key problems is that addicts are a hotchpotch of personalities, physiologies and life histories. "We shouldn't be giving everybody the same treatment," says Charles O'Brien, professor of psychiatry at the University of Pennsylvania. "One of the biggest defects in the US is clinics trying to get the patient to fit their mould instead of moulding the treatment to fit each patient."

Unrealistic expectations are another problem. While the public hopes for "cures" and Saul-to-Paul transformations, neuroscientists insist that the best we can hope for are therapies that produce remissions. "Addiction is not a failure of will or morality, but a chronic brain disease that should be ranked alongside schizophrenia and Tourette's syndrome," argues Alan Leshner, director of the National Institute on Drug Abuse (NIDA) in Bethesda, Maryland, the biggest research centre of its kind in the world.

In many research projects, the aim is not even to produce remission from addiction, but simply to limit the harm it causes by helping addicts switch from street drugs to less dangerous substitutes. Methadone is the familiar example here. You replace heroin which has to be bought from street pushers and injected up to three times a day with methadone that can be taken orally once a day and is available in a pure form from clinics. The result (in theory) is that fewer addicts overdose and fewer contract HIV or hepatitis, and yet craving is satisfied. In practice, however, complications abound (see Box: Methadone: crime cure or therapy?).

Street value

For one thing, methadone stimulates the same opiate receptors in the brain that heroin does, even if it doesn't produce the same kind of high. As a result, it has now acquired its own street value. The fact that the drug is metabolised so quickly doesn't help here. With a single dose lasting barely 24 hours, addicts have to visit the clinic every day, or be entrusted with a quantity of methadone that can all too easily be traded for heroin. "Some people will walk out of a clinic on Friday with a weekend dose of methadone and immediately try to sell it," says David Nutt, a pharmacologist at the University of Bristol.

That's why clinics are pinning their hopes on newer and longer-lasting heroin mimics. One of these is a compound called LAAM, which lasts up to 72 hours, enabling addicts to visit the clinic less often. As long ago as 1979 it was clear that LAAM ought to replace methadone for routine use, says Stanford University's

Neuroscientists insist that the best we can hope for are therapies that produce remissions.

Avram Goldstein, a pharmacologist and neurobiologist who has worked on heroin addiction for 25 years. But drugs companies couldn't see any money in it, so it languished in limbo until last year when approval was finally secured by NIDA. It will be some time yet before it is widely adopted by clinics.

Another heroin substitute waiting in the wings is buprenorphine, a poorly understood chemical that relieves withdrawal symptoms. Some researchers hope buprenorphine's unusual pharmacology will pay extra dividends. On the one hand, it seems to stimulate opiate receptors less vigorously than heroin, which could make it less addictive. On the other, it sticks to those receptors tightly enough to fend off the advances of any heroin molecules. And that could make it doubly effective. If addicts taking buprenorphine were to try to top up with heroin, they might not experience a high.

Damage limitation is all very well, but shouldn't we be trying to wean addicts off drugs altogether? Not necessarily, argues Goldstein. Chronic use of a drug may irrevocably alter a person's brain chemistry, he says. Moreover, some people may turn to drugs because they have some kind of chemical imbalance to begin with. Either way, they may simply be incapable of becoming drug-free.

Society has little problem with long-term medication for chronic illnesses like diabetes, so why not for a chronic condition like drug dependence? "There's a big stigma about being on methadone," says Goldstein, "and so the patients themselves try to get off it. They usually fail."

Methadone worries people because it is just as addictive as heroin. Less contentious are substances that prevent street drugs from kicking in. The best known of these "killjoy" compounds is naltrexone, which shields opiate receptors from heroin without stimulating them itself. "If you take naltrexone, shooting up heroin gives you nothing," says Nutt. "When addicts realise this, they stop buying."

Well, in theory they do. In fact, most addicts soon stop taking naltrexone instead, making it useful only for the most determined of opiate addicts, such as a nurse or doctor in danger of losing his or her licence. Partly for this reason, the search for more appealing heroin blockers, or "antagonists", continues apace in laboratories.

For example, Nutt and his team are studying a series of recently discovered compounds which offer the equivalent of a spoonful of sugar to help the medicine go down. Animal research suggests that these molecules initially behave like heroin mimics, stimulating the same receptors to produce a rush. Gradually, however, over a few hours, they are broken down to produce a substance that has the opposite effect—locking opiate receptors for weeks on end.

Pleasurable stimuli

It could be years before anyone knows whether such compounds would work in humans. In the meantime, researchers must grapple with the ethical problems posed by such compounds. Is it right to give someone a drug that can lock up brain receptors for weeks on end? The natural, everyday job of opiate receptors is to control pain and the body's responses to food, water and temperature changes. Blocking these receptors can produce symptoms of depression. With drug-dependent patients, it may also precipitate withdrawal symptoms. And according to one unconfirmed study, naltrexone may even reduce a person's ability to experience other pleasurable stimuli, such as music.

But for people desperate to quit, such drawbacks may be a small price to pay, particularly as the latest research indicates that opiate antagonists may be useful in treating other addictions. In a finding published in 1992, O'Brien's group at Pennsylvania and another team at Yale University discovered that alcoholics given naltrexone abstained from drinking longer, reported less craving, and were less likely to have a full-blown relapse after sneaking a drink—effects that are completely different from the "thwarted high" experienced by heroin addicts who take naltrexone. O'Brien, for one, hopes that naltrexone will soon be approved for alcoholics in the US. "It's the most exciting thing that's come along for a while," he says.

Naltrexone may also hold out some promise for those addicted to nicotine. But help with cocaine addiction seems less likely, since heroin addicts on naltrexone merrily continue to take cocaine during treatment. And more's the pity, since the medications' cupboard for cocaine addiction is sadly bare. There is no equivalent of methadone for cocaine. Nor are there any drugs that beneficially block its effects on brain receptors. Consequently, many addicts feel there is little point in visiting a clinic.

But that could change as neurobiologists learn more about how cocaine casts its addictive spell on the brain. It's clear that the drug interferes with nerve cells deep in the brain that specialise in releasing dopamine—a neurotransmitter implicated in the neural mechanisms that produce reward signals inside the brain. More specifically, cocaine snarls up a "transporter" protein that would otherwise "suck" dopamine back into nerve cell bodies. The resulting excess of dopamine overstimulates receptors, setting off a chain of biochemical events.

The details are far from fully understood, but one outcome seems to be that the user's taste for the drug is reinforced. And speed of delivery seems to be crucial: most cocaine addicts end up freebasing (smoking) the drug or its derivative, crack, to maximise the hit—and by implication, the biological reward.

Some researchers are trying to develop slower-acting cocaine mimics—substances that mimic cocaine's effect on the transporter molecule, satisfying addicts' craving and weaning them off street drugs. Michael Kuhar, a pharmacologist at the NIDA, and his colleagues have screened 300 cocaine-like chemicals, and have found ten or so likely candidates, all of which last longer than the paltry 30 minutes cocaine survives in the body. Clinical trials, though, are far away.

Other researchers at NIDA are testing substances that act in various ways on the dopamine pathway, and might also help in treating cocaine dependency. In some cases, the aim is to find an "anticocaine" compound, something that could block the rewarding effects of the drug and render it less addictive. One approach focuses on compounds that could shield the transporter from cocaine. Another looks at substances that could shield receptors from cocaine-induced bursts of dopamine.

So far, however, success has been in short supply. Moreover, some researchers believe that even if an "anticocaine" drug aimed at dopamine receptors could be developed, people taking it might find themselves unable to respond normally to other rewarding stimuli—notably, food and sex.

Pharmacology, thankfully, is not the only option. Behavioural tools are also a crucial part of any addiction treatment. While Twelve Step programmes are as popular as ever, their dogmatic philosophy jars on some—one reason why researchers are looking at alternatives. Most are aimed at cocaine addiction, because of the dearth of chemical treatments. But these new approaches could easily be adapted for treating other drug addictions—or, for that matter, addictions to gambling and to sex, as well as eating disorders.

Methadone: crime cure or therapy?

IN CLINICS, it's usually doled out in small plastic bottles of orange-flavoured water. You'd never guess it could excite so much controversy.

But it does. Depending on who you talk to, methadone is either one of our best hopes of severing the connection between crime and drugs and rehabilitating addicts, or an unsafe recipe for state-approved addiction and stupefaction. And opinions have been that polarised since the earliest days of methadone maintenance in the 1960s.

Right now, though, it's the proponents who are firmly in the ascendancy. In Britain, the number of people registering as methadone addicts each year has increased fivefold since 1989 to almost 10 000, reflecting the spread of government-approved programmes. In the US, too, policy makers faced with the rising tide of drug related crime are implementing more and more methadone programmes.

It's not hard to see why. In 1984, a follow-up study of former drugs offenders in California reported that those who enrolled onto a methadone maintenance programme in 1971 almost halved the time they spent committing crimes, while slashing the amount of time they wanted taking drugs each day (see figure below). And similar benefits have been reported time and again.

The latest pat on the back for methadone came in August from a report by the California Department of Alcohol and Drug Programs in Sacramento. The study, a $2 million exercise billed as offering the most comprehensive analysis to date of the costs and benefits of different treatments for drug addiction in the US, concluded that for every $1 spent on methadone maintenance, the government recoups nearly $5 in the long run from lower crime and health costs.

Of course, the notion of clinics meting out addictive substances to wean people off illicit street drugs still goes down like a barrel of lead with antidrugs crusaders of a more puritanical bent, especially in the US. And winning the hearts and minds of addicts is easier said than done.

Steve K., a South London addict going through detoxification for both heroin and crack, dreads the effects of methadone: "You don't get a high like on heroin, but it stops you from being sick—it holds you. Coming off the methadone is the worst because it gets your bones, it settles on your joints."

The belief that methadone "rots" bones is not the only reason some addicts are wary. For every person who switches from heroin to methadone, there are many more who choose not to—either because they are afraid to register their addiction, or because they see methadone maintenance as just another addiction.

Jo, a housewife and mother in her late thirties, refused to use methadone when she finally kicked her heroin habit 10 years ago: "I went the hard way. I think that's really the only way to do it."

Moreover, a vociferous minority of researchers and doctors continue to point to hidden health costs—and not just the fact that addicts seem to find methadone harder to give up than heroin. Equally problematic is the drug's incapacity to give a real high, says Russell Newcombe, who studies drug abuse trends in Britain for local governments.

To recapture a high, says Newcombe, many registered addicts mix and match their oral dose of methadone with alcohol, speed, over-the-counter travel sickness pills, and anything else they think will produce a buzz. Or they resort to injecting methadone, exposing themselves once again to the threat of HIV. Some go further still. Newcombe knows of addicts who have injected ground-up gel capsules of methadone straight into their veins. The whole point of the capsules was to prevent injections.

The critics also believe that methadone's toxicity has been grossly understated. In April, John Marks, a longtime campaigner against methadone who runs an addiction treatment clinic in Widnes, Cheshire, published a letter in *The Lancet* claiming that methadone is 19 times more toxic than heroin. The claim is based on overdose deaths reported to the British Home Office. Between 1982 and 1991, says Marks, deaths related to heroin in Britain numbered 243 to methadone's 349, despite there being up to ten times as many users of heroin in the population.

"Given the dangers of methadone," says Marks in *The Lancet,* "perhaps the current vogue for methadone in the management of addiction should be reviewed." Newcombe is a mite more strident: "To call methadone a good treatment is as absurd as saying 'the operation was a success; the patient died'."

All of which is fiercely disputed by those who run and advocate methadone maintenance programmes. Overdose cases are not the whole story, they say. Methadone reduces a whole range of hazards, not least the spread of infectious diseases and the risk of incarceration for criminal activities.

Certainly, defenders of methadone are not hard to find. Avram Goldstein, a pharmacologist in California with 25 years' experience of studying heroin treatments, is one. "As long as addicts stay on methadone and have adequate doses, they seem to feel OK," he says. "Many hold down jobs and don't use heroin, and often as a consequence put other drugs behind them."

People like Goldstein say they are tired of fending off attacks based on what they see as selective samplings of medical data and ideological objections. But these are unlikely to vanish into the night. For in the end, methadone's greatest selling point, its ability to reduce drug-related crime, is also its greatest weakness. It makes the drug a soft target for anyone who feels inclined to caricature it as a soma-like substance, something an authoritarian state might want to dole out to potential troublemakers.

With reporting by **Laura Spinney**

> "You don't get a high like on heroin, but it stops you from being sick—it holds you."

> The study, a $2 million exercise billed as offering the most comprehensive analysis to date of the costs and benefits of different treatments for drug addiction in the US, concluded that for every $1 spent on methadone maintenance, the government recoups nearly $5 in the long run from lower crime and health costs.

One method seems almost ridiculously simple: paying someone not to take drugs. It's also remarkably successful, and is backed up by a stack of data from experiments with rats and monkeys. Hook a rat on cocaine, then give it a "distracter" along with the cocaine—some particularly tasty food, perhaps—and the rat will take less of the cocaine as a result. What better distracter for human beings than money?

Stephen Higgins, a behavioural pharmacologist at the University of Vermont, conducted a study in which cocaine addicts had their urine tested for presence of the drug several times a week, and earned vouchers every time their sample tested drug-free. The payments started at $2·50, and went up by $1·50 for each consecutive time the urine was clean. Long spells without cocaine were clearly the best way to cash in. One positive urine test, though, and the amount of payment crashed back to the baseline.

No actual money left the clinic. Instead, therapists and clients discussed the way in which the vouchers would be spent, plumping for something that was pleasurable to the client but also in keeping with the changes in lifestyle that the programme's intensive counselling was intended to foster. To help heal family rifts, an addict might splurge on a fancy dinner out with them; to take up neglected hobbies and sports, he or she might buy basketball shoes or time on the courts.

Flying colours

The voucher-therapy results were excellent. Eighty-five per cent of the patients stayed in the programme for 12 weeks, while 65 to 75 per cent stayed for 6 months—and this for an addiction where a 70 per cent drop-out rate at 6 weeks is the norm for treatment programmes. Not only that, but most of the patients "passed" their urine tests with flying colours for several months at a time. The voucher system was recently retested by Kenzie Preston at the NIDA with a hard-core, inner-city group of cocaine addicts, worlds apart from Higgins's study, which involved mainly white addicts in Vermont. Again, the results were glowing.

Despite the programme's promise, it does have some creases that need ironing out before a voucher system could be put into practice. In the US, healthcare isn't free. Is the client or his insurance company to pay the clinic a little bit extra so that the clinic can offer the client a cash incentive?

Perhaps the biggest stumbling

One method seems almost ridiculously simple: paying someone not to take drugs. It's also remarkably successful.

What better distracter for human beings than money?

block will be the scheme's political palatability. Even if it is the best treatment going, the notion that drug users will be paid for simply obeying the law and keeping off drugs will go down like a ton of bricks in some quarters. The notable exception, perhaps, is addicts who are pregnant. Here, after all, there is the baby's life to consider as well.

Ronith Elk, psychologist at the University of Texas at Houston, is heading one of several efforts to test the voucher method with a group of pregnant addicts. She hopes to get positive results: not only drug-free urine, but—because one of the urine samples must be taken on the day of antenatal classes—women who will take better care of themselves during pregnancy.

Relapse cycle

But weaning someone off drugs is only the beginning; they must also be able to maintain their drug-free state. Whatever the addiction, clients may come to treatment time and time again, only to fall back into using the drug weeks, months or even years after they quit successfully. How can they break the relapse cycle?

The voucher incentive scheme is not the only one to be backed by animal experiments; schemes on ways to combat relapse are given added credibility from old-fashioned classical conditioning studies. For addicts, cues that mean "drugs" and trigger their cravings are everywhere. They can be people they've used cocaine with, locations where they've purchased cocaine, even raids on the evening news.

These cues are very powerful—videos of drug paraphernalia cause changes in brain chemistry and skin temperature in addicts. And they are also very hard to avoid. In arming the addicts who are participating in their study with tools to fight those urges, O'Brien and colleagues first ask the individual to remember a time of intense craving, and then practise dealing with it, using seven different coping tools. In the spirit of individualised treatment, clients then opt to use the two tools that work best for them—deep relaxation, perhaps, along with carefully writing down all the negative consequences of giving in to their urges. Results, which are not yet published, show more samples of cocaine-free urine in the group taught the coping skills

than in a control group who were not.

For addicts trying to manage on methadone and nicotine replacements, one way to nip a relapse in the bud is to give the addict the right dose of drug at the start. But this isn't always done, perhaps because many people including physicians feel ambivalent about replacing one drug with another. But the dose may make all the difference. Studies have shown that the success rates of various methadone clinics in the US are clearly related to the dosage dispensed.

And the same appears true for nicotine replacement therapy. Last year, David Sachs, director of the Smoking Cessation Research Institute in Palo Alto, published a study showing that most people receive too little nicotine when they use nicotine gum or an arm patch. By contrast, when people are supplied with enough nicotine to boost blood levels to at least 50 per cent of that experienced during smoking, 86 per cent of them didn't smoke for six weeks compared with 40 to 50 per cent for standard nicotine patch therapy. Dosage, says Sachs, should be tailored to each and every person, by monitoring the nicotine levels in their blood.

Still, research psychologist Nina Schneider argues that the patch alone is just too passive. Smoking is an activity, after all, and smokers who give up can find the sensation of having nothing to do with their hands maddening. Schneider, of the University of California Los Angeles School of Medicine, favours gum as well as the patch and a new, nicotine nasal spray that ex-smokers could carry around and spray up their noses when they get the urge.

Some people worry about some of these aids becoming addictive in their own right. Shouldn't one aim for total abstinence rather than damage limita-

tion? We need to do both, stresses Alan Marlatt, addiction researcher at the University of Washington in Seattle. "We've got to get together on this issue so that we can get both messages across," he says.

For political and cultural reasons, that has always been easier to achieve in Europe than in the US, where in the past drug abuse has often been seen as an intolerable evil. But now things are changing. In American towns and cities, needle-replacement programmes are springing up. New York activists are encouraging crack users

Even if it is the best treatment going, the notion that drug users will be paid for simply obeying the law and keeping off drugs will go down like a ton of bricks in some quarters.

to switch to marijuana. Therapies where people are asked to "come explore their drinking, or their cocaine use"—instead of "come end their cocaine use"—are also on the rise, attracting more addicts. A new support group, Moderation Management, offers an alternative to Alcoholics Anonymous, for people who want help but are not ready to stop drinking.

Is there a new and more realistic view of addiction gradually spreading beyond the frontiers of clinics and labs? If there is, it is borne of the realisation that there are no magic bullet cures for addiction just around the corner, that the brain is a complex, mysterious organ, and that for too many, drug addiction is rooted in a lifetime of poverty and deprivation—things that pills will not put right.   □

As more and more Americans demand electroconvulsive therapy
to treat their severe depression, researchers try to find out why
ECT works and critics warn of its long-term side effects.

Shock therapy returns

Renee Twombly

THE fifty-something woman was ready for her treatment. In a room at Duke University Medical Center, North Carolina, she bantered with five nurses, a psychiatrist and an anaesthetist, joking that her shock of white hair made it hard to place the electrodes. Then, oxygen mask on, an intravenous tube to pump fast-acting barbiturates and muscle relaxants into a vein in her hand, she was out. Her right toes began a jerky dance as if they were keeping time with the erratic tracings of the heart and brain monitors nearby.

Thirty-four seconds later her brain seizure stopped and her second toe stayed coiled around the big one, like crossed fingers hoping she would stay well. Several months earlier, a course of 10 shock treatments over a three-week period had stopped her severe depression in its tracks; she was now in for a "maintenance" session to prevent a relapse.

Buying time

Like tens of thousands of people in the US, she took a chance that a burst of electricity lasting only a few seconds, at less than half the power it takes to burn a 40-watt light bulb, would stave off deep depression, buying her time from thoughts of suicide. Electroconvulsive therapy (ECT) is casting off its past image to become the treatment of choice for many severely depressed Americans. To so-called "shock doctors" at private US hospitals, and to most of their patients, ECT in its new and improved form is a neat and clean medical procedure, with few complications apart from some initial memory loss and confusion in the hours following the treatment.

With the American Psychiatric Association saying that ECT can work for more

Like tens of thousands of people in the US, she took a chance that a burst of electricity lasting only a few seconds, at less than half the power it takes to burn a 40-watt light bulb, would stave off deep depression.

than 80 per cent of severely depressed patients, the treatment is increasingly being accepted as the most effective treatment available when all other therapies have failed. In 1986, the last year for which national data for psychiatric treatment are available, some 36 500 people received ECT, more than a 15 per cent increase over 1980. Researchers estimate that figure to be much higher now.

"There's no question that ECT is making a comeback, despite its terrible image," says Richard Weiner, the psychiatrist at Duke who treated the depressed woman, and an international leader in

ECT research. "For the first time, people have come to me specifically asking for ECT, when before it was always the doctors who convinced the patients they needed it."

Deborah Norris, a 38-year-old missionary nurse, didn't take long to decide to use ECT when her doctor recommended it. Suffering from severe depression brought on by post-traumatic stress disorder from her years at the Gaza Strip, she tried a variety of antidepressants that left her sleeping for 22 hours a day. "I tried ECT because I couldn't live like that. I was nervous, but after the first treatment there was nothing to it," she says. Twelve treatments later, Norris says "I am just about back to my old self. If I had a depression again, I'd go right back to ECT."

Seizure crucial

It is the seizure, not the shock, that is the "healing" agent in ECT. The origins of the treatment date back to the early part of the century, when the erroneous belief that epilepsy and schizophrenia could not exist in the same patient led doctors to induce seizures as a cure for schizophrenia.

In 1938, the first "electroshock" was administered, and it quickly became the main medical treatment for the mentally ill; there was little else available. But its efficacy in treating depressive diseases led the to excessive, sometimes abusive, use of ECT in a wide range of mental illnesses for which it was ineffective.

When the first generation of antidepressant drugs came on the market in the 1960s, ECT fell out of favour and was restricted to the disorders it treats best— severe depression and catatonic and affective schizophrenia disorders. But during the lull of the 1960s and 1970s, researchers found ways to mitigate many

From *New Scientist*, 141, pp. 21–23, March 5, 1994. Reprinted by permission of IPC Magazines Ltd.

of the worst side effects of the therapy, such as broken bones in patients and severe loss of memory. Now psychiatrists tell patients that there may be some temporary memory impairment; rarely is there severe, persistent memory loss.

Today's treatment little resembles the whammy delivered to conscious patients by Big Nurse in Ken Kesey's book *One Flew Over The Cuckoo's Nest*. Modern ECT therapy uses anaesthetists to deliver intravenous fast-acting barbiturates to put the patient to sleep, muscle relaxants to stop muscle spasms and broken bones, and masks to make sure the patient gets enough oxygen. The procedure has moved from the bedside to a more elaborate treatment room, using heart and brain monitors. In all, the treatment takes about 15 minutes from the time patients lie down on the treatment table to when they start to wake up.

Less juice

Physicians also calibrate the electrical dose to suit each patient: they deliver low doses initially and gradually build up to just the current that will produce a seizure. There is enormous variation in the seizure threshold between patients because there are big differences in the geometry of skulls and scalps, the relative thickness of the subdural spaces between the skull and brain, and the excitability of the underlying nerve cells. The typical seizure threshold varies between 30 and 100 milliampere seconds; the previous generation of machines delivered at least twice as much juice.

The way the current is delivered to the patients has also changed. Doctors now prefer to mimic the spiky, rhythmic activity of the nerve cells by sending short pulses of electricity between 00 and 100 in a second. The original method of sending the current in a continuous sine wave produced too big a seizure for too long, and this probably also affected memory.

Psychiatrists are still debating the best position for the electrodes to produce maximum benefit with minimum side effects. Some favour placing one electrode on the temple of the nondominant side of the brain and the other on the top of the head. This produces a bilateral seizure, but the seizure will be less intense on the dominant side and, therefore, less likely to affect memory. Others believe the traditional method of placing electrodes on both temples is more effective.

A study published in the *New England Journal of Medicine* in March 1993 found that the position of the electrodes and the amount of electricity delivered strongly

A study published in the *New England Journal of Medicine* in March 1993 found that the position of the electrodes and the amount of electricity delivered strongly influences clinical outcome: a low current to one side of the brain has little effect in reducing depression, whereas current applied bilaterally, at any dose, is effective but results in greater memory loss.

influences clinical outcome: a low current to one side of the brain has little effect in reducing depression, whereas current applied bilaterally, at any dose, is effective but results in greater memory loss.

In pace with clinical advances, researchers are still trying to find out why ECT works. One theory—for which there is some evidence—is that ECT alters the volume of neurotransmitting signals that pass between nerve cells. Although they cannot pinpoint which neurotransmitters are affected—options include gamma aminobutric acid, noradrenaline and serotonin—scientists think that brain chemistry is "reset" following an ECT seizure, correcting abnormal production of signals that control affective behaviour.

While such clinical refinements and

laboratory investigations steadily improved the practice of ECT, the ineffectiveness as well as the side effects of some drugs to treat depression have become clearer. Some patients using Thorazine, for example, developed tardive dyskinesia—twitches in the mouth and tongue—due to brain damage.

Firm support

In 1978, the American Psychiatric Association published the report of its task force on ECT, which came down firmly in support of ECT to treat depression. That same year, six teams of British researchers started conducting a landmark series of experiments to compare two groups of patients: one group were given ECT, and the other believed they had ECT, but did

ECT produces the kind of acute brain injury that you would expect when you put electricity into your brain. It's like what happens from a blow to the head—confusion, loss of memory, inability to retain new information.

not actually receive a shock. All real ECT treatments demonstrated a clinical advantage. Then in 1985, the US National Institutes of Health in Maryland concluded that the treatment was "demonstrably effective for a narrow range of severe psychiatric disorders, including depression, mania and schizophrenia".

ECT is certainly enjoying a new acceptance in the US, aided by testimonies from entertainers such as Dick Cavett—one of the more erudite of the talk show hosts—that ECT saved his life. At the same time, the treatment is still a topic of controversy.

Linda Andre is one of many worried about the increasing use of the therapy. She says that ECT "wiped out five years of memory and brought my IQ down 40 points". Andre, who had ECT in 1984, sued the manufacturer of the ECT machine and New York Hospital three years after her treatment. She has now set up the Committee for Truth in Psychiatry, which has 500 members. The group is lobbying for ECT machines to be investigated for safety and for stronger warnings in patient consent forms about the possibility of memory loss.

A second grass-roots organisation, the 182-member World Association of Electroshock Survivors, has also hit the headlines. Its founder, Dianna Loper, claimed on the Oprah Winfrey Show last December that ECT, used to treat her depression without her consent, had "fried" her brain, bringing on recurrent bouts of epilepsy.

Lee Coleman, a psychiatrist practising in Berkeley, California, describes ECT as producing "the kind of acute brain injury that you would expect when you put electricity in your brain. It's like what happens from a blow on the head—confusion, loss of memory, inability to retain new information."

Coleman maintains that ECT's side effect is the treatment itself: "Patients can't remember what was upsetting

them. It's interesting that when you use less treatment, such as with unilateral electrode placement, you get less memory loss. That's exactly what you would suspect if the treatment works by brain injury." Psychiatrists, patients and their families who allow the use of ECT are copping out, he says. "It's a quick fix. Everyone is avoiding the real cause why people are depressed, and that is because life is not going in such a good way."

Shocks for the rich

Although statistics are hard to come by, ECT appears to be more widely used in some other parts of the world than in the US. In Britain, for example, patients are three times more likely to receive ECT (see Box). According to Allen Scott, a consultant psychiatrist at the Royal Edinburgh Hospital, this is partly because ECT is used differently in Britain. First, it is often the first treatment given to severely depressed, suicidal patients rather than a last-ditch solution as in the US. Secondly, Scott says that the people who receive ECT in Britain are "representative of people who get depressed, rather than people who can afford it".

According to Scott, the debate that is not being heard in the US, and that should be, is that ECT is mostly used on patients who can pay for treatments, which can cost up to $1000 a treatment or $12 000 for a full series over two weeks. While ECT may have become the treatment of choice, it is only within reach of depressed Americans with private medical insurance. It is not available to everyone who gets depressed, he says, only those who can afford it.

"This criticism is, unfortunately, true," says Harold Sackheim, chief of biological psychiatry at New York State Psychiatric Institute. "In the 1980s, there wasn't a single nonwhite to receive ECT in a state facility in America." According to James Thompson, a psychiatrist and epidemiologist at the University of Maryland, 71 per cent of ECT recipients in 1986 were women, mostly elderly and medically insured. Whites were also eleven times more likely to receive ECT than blacks.

Government funding for ECT treat-

Britain's shock story

AMERICA'S love-hate relationship with electroconvulsive therapy has not played itself out with quite such emotion in Britain. Allen Scott, a consultant psychiatrist at Royal Edinburgh Hospital and a member of the Royal College of Psychiatry's committee on ECT, says it never fell from favour in Britain, although its use did decline with the arrival of anti-depressant drugs.

John Pippard, a senior researcher at the Royal College of Psychiatry and a leading British authority on the use of the therapy, maintains that the use, per capita, is up to three times higher in Britain as in the US, with up to 20 000 people in England and Wales receiving treatment in 1991.

ECT is also used differently in Britain in that it is generally more low-technology: there is less monitoring, and fewer nurses in attendance. It is also available in public and private hospitals, and tends to be the first rather than last therapy offered to deeply depressed individuals, especially those who are suicidal.

But that does not mean that problems do not exist in administering ECT in Britain. In a survey of health regions in 1992, Pippard found that physicians giving ECT had no hands-on training and the treatment was unregulated. "It means that perhaps 20 per cent of those patients were not getting adequate treatments," he says. Additionally, half of ECT machines being used may be inadequately powered to trigger a full seizure, says Pippard.

New guidelines expected this spring by the Royal College of Psychiatry will specify that clinics should upgrade to newer, more efficient machines that deliver the electricity in brief bursts and that psychiatrists receive more intensive hands-on training in administering the treatment.

ments in public hospitals plummeted when ECT's image took a nose dive, and has never recovered. But, according to Sackheim, ECT was still accepted in private or teaching hospitals. Recently, however, several public hospitals in New York City, including the Bronx Lebanon and the Harlem, have begun to reverse that trend by starting ECT programmes.

"The public has a visceral reaction to ECT and that's why it has always been controversial and will probably remain so," says Sackheim. "No one would ever rationally think that inducing a seizure by applying electricity would be a therapy. It can be seen as a grotesque drama."   □

Renee Twombly *is a freelance health and science reporter based in Durham, North Carolina.*

Index

TO THE OWNER OF THIS BOOK:

I hope that you have found *Looking into Abnormal Psychology: Contemporary Readings* useful. So that this book can be improved in a future edition, would you take the time to complete this sheet and return it? Thank you.

School and address: _____

Department: _____

Instructor's name: _____

1. What I like most about this book is: _____

_____

_____

2. What I like least about this book is: _____

_____

_____

3. My general reaction to this book is: _____

_____

4. The name of the course in which I used this book is: _____

_____

5. Were all of the chapters of the book assigned for you to read? _____

   If not, which ones weren't? _____

 6. In the space below, or on a separate sheet of paper, please write specific suggestions for improving this book and anything else you'd care to share about your experience in using the book.

_____

_____

_____

_____

_____

_____

Optional:

Your name: _____ Date: _____

May Brooks/Cole quote you, either in promotion for *Looking into Abnormal Psychology: Contemporary Readings* or in future publishing ventures?

Yes: _____ No: _____

Sincerely,

Scott O. Lilienfeld

FOLD HERE

NO POSTAGE
NECESSARY
IF MAILED
IN THE
UNITED STATES

BUSINESS REPLY MAIL
FIRST CLASS   PERMIT NO. 358   PACIFIC GROVE, CA

POSTAGE WILL BE PAID BY ADDRESSEE

ATT: *Scott O. Lilienfeld* _____

Brooks/Cole Publishing Company
511 Forest Lodge Road
Pacific Grove, California 93950-9968

FOLD HERE